INFANTS and CHILDREN

INFANTS and CHILDREN

Their Development and Learning

MILDRED C. ROBECK

University of Oregon

McGraw-Hill Book Company

New York   St. Louis   San Francisco   Auckland   Bogotá   Düsseldorf
Johannesburg   London   Madrid   Mexico   Montreal   New Delhi   Panama
Paris   São Paulo   Singapore   Sydney   Tokyo   Toronto

INFANTS AND CHILDREN

Their Development and Learning

1234567890 FGRFGR 78321098

This book was set in Helvetica by Black Dot, Inc.
The editors were Jean Smith and David Dunham;
the designer was Elliot Epstein;
the production supervisor was Dennis J. Conroy.
The drawings were done by J & R Services, Inc.
Fairfield Graphics was printer and binder

Library of Congress Cataloging in Publication Data

Robeck, Mildred Coen.
    Infants and children.

    Includes bibliographical references and index.
    1. Child psychology. 2. Infant psychology.
3. Learning, Psychology of. I. Title.
BF721.R613   155.4'13   77-25844
ISBN 0-07-053108-0

To Martin Jay, Donna Jayne, and Bruce Wayne
whose becoming gave me the courage to write this book

Contents

Preface

This book is for adults who are or expect to become professionally involved with infants and young children. Child development, as an area of specialization, began with the interdisciplinary search for knowledge that would make childrearing more scientific and less dominated by folkways. This book rushes in where angels fear to fly in proposing (1) to return to basic research for cues about the present needs of children and (2) to make a conceptual leap from there to the real world of teaching and parenting. This decision to take a cross-disciplinary approach imposes a heavy task on the reader, who cannot possibly have background in all relevant subjects, and on the writer, who must try to make technical information less complex than it really is.

Basic knowledge in the behavioral sciences has become so complicated as to defy easy application. Laboratory research may seem far removed from the child's environment, and field research cannot always be fitted to a different educational ecology. Despite these limitations I have always trusted students to make a sensitive application of principles rather than use techniques in an unquestioning way. There are practices in early childhood which persist decade after decade without improvement because knowledge that is available has not been brought to bear on the problems.

This text has been prepared for upper-division college students and graduate students who are beginning their studies about children. I have tried to come to grips with the new biology, the new genetics (which has real-life photographs of the structures that were mere theories when I was a student at Wisconsin), and the new psychology. Some references to neurobiology have been included because this is an area of research that will resolve many of the issues about learning, some of them in the near future. I have even tried to explain the neopsychologist's view to the student uninitiated in learning theory, with the hope that some will choose to go beyond this brief discussion by pursuing the references. The concept load is heavy, especially in the first three chapters, because some messages do not come through without using the scientific terms of the people who spawned the ideas. I have cited a limited number of references because the total literature is beyond the scope of this book. Nevertheless, the guideposts to further study are there for readers who are eager, as well as for those who doubt the summations. Many of the statements in this book are contrary to conventional beliefs about young children and their early education. It is hoped that the reader will search the original sources and make his or her own judgments about the issues.

PREVIEW OF THE BOOK

This book is organized into four parts. Part One, Human Origins, cues the reader on the focus to be expected throughout the book. The first chapter presents major principles of growth and learning, and the second builds a basic understanding of human growth and reproduction.

Part Two, Growth Patterns, is organized chronologically, beginning with prenatal learning and development. In Chapter 3 the focus is on the influence of the intrauterine environment and the evidence of adaptive behavior before birth. The chapter on infancy emphasizes the sensory capabilities of the neonate and the intellectual development of the prespeech infant. Three additional periods, distinguished by the child's increasing mobility and physical independence, are treated in separate chapters: toddlerhood (extending to age 2½ or 3), preschool age (children approximately 3 to 5 years old), and early childhood (incorporating the primary school years from kindergarten through second or third grade). This organization of chapters reflects the challenges children face as they expand their control over their own experience.

Part Three, Experience and Learning, includes four topics of special interest to parents and teachers: cognitive development, play, language, and affective development. Each of these discussions overlaps the developmental periods from birth through early childhood. Theories of learning are summarized in Chapter 8, with particular focus on the developmental psychology of Jean Piaget. A learning-motivation model is proposed which shows the relationship between the neobehaviorist and cognitive views of development. The purpose of this eclectic approach is to help professionals use theory selectively. The relationships of motivation to learning and achievement are presented in Chapter 11.

Part Four, Responsibility of Care-Givers, is written from the point of view that adults have a role in childrearing which is different from and in many ways superior to that of peers and siblings. The implications of the first three parts of the book are synthesized in a developmental approach to early education that is individualized. Chapter 12 outlines the kinds of programs the society provides for all its children. Chapter 13 presents the gifted child as the forgotten child in most school programs, even though many children in all ethnic groups have potential talents and special abilities. The physical handicaps and emotional problems that emerge in early childhood differ in their severity and persistence, the most frequent being those which fall within a range of normalcy. Chapter 14 focuses on developmental problems, as a way of helping parents and teachers decide when the help of a specialist is needed. The final word is for significant adults: parents, teachers, sitters, older siblings, extended family members, and all care-givers who inevitably are modeled and trusted by infants and little children.

Throughout the writing of this book I have been indebted to Mary Armes for giving the manuscript priority in her busy life. I am grateful also to Rhona Robbin of McGraw-Hill for organizing so efficiently the many contributions that make up this book. A special thanks is reserved, also, for my students who critiqued the manuscript, researched special topics, shared their own expertise, and stimulated me to give my best.

Mildred C. Robeck

Part One

HUMAN ORIGINS

This part, the first of four, introduces the reader to basic questions and characteristics of human development. It focuses on the human young, describing their origins as members of the human community and as individuals, in order that they may be better understood by those who nurture them.

Chapter 1, "Significance of the Early Years," is intended to point up the unique status of the human young. Their biological dependence requires the kind of nurturance that eventually allows them the freedom to choose or remake their own environment. Each human generation inherits an extended cultural history from which the newborn builds its individual future. Childhood, for all its openness, flexibility, potential, and playfulness is a journey of no return that defines and delimits what the larger segment of life, adulthood, will be like. This first chapter sets down eight principles that describe, in part, how infants attain personhood among Homo sapiens.

Chapter 2, "Genetic Origins and Reproduction," contains basic knowledge designed to help the reader decide what information to accept and how to temper judgments when attempting to move from theories of child development to interaction with children on a daily basis. The functioning of cells, described only briefly in this chapter, is basic to the processes of conception, growth, and memory. By understanding the laws of genetics, the major questions of heredity and environment become less simple, but more significant. If there is a bias in this book, it is a bias toward the concept of interaction—the interaction of phylogeny (the history of the species) and ontogeny (the life-span of the individual)—as having tremendous potential for guiding adults in their caregiving. This first part contains the concepts and terminology to take the student far beyond this book to the sources from which it was derived.

I
Significance of the Early Years

I Significance of the Early Years

Recent knowledge of child development is changing what adults do for their young children. Discoveries about early learning are stimulating the expansion of opportunities for children through the upgrading of nursery schools, primary schools, and "home start" programs. Each society has its own biases about childrearing, but these folkways tend to alter when family patterns change, when the economic situation imposes new pressures, or when research findings become public knowledge. Most laboratory research which is significant as new knowledge merely implies that changes should be made, but the important test of research findings is at the practice level where people interact with youngsters and observe them. Present knowledge, of itself, will not settle all the issues of feeding, discipline, peer relationships, the timing of beginning reading, or the need of a particular child for speech therapy. But knowledge disseminated does give adults new alternatives in their decisions about what is best for their infants and young children.

All issues about early education have deep roots in the culture. Whenever the results of studies are conflicting or complex, biases prevail and little change occurs. Some examples of value-based issues in early education are the following: group versus individual needs, discipline versus permissiveness, adult versus child priority for scarce commodities, and affective versus cognitive goals. The current trend in some schools, orphanages, and rehabilitation centers toward grouping children of various ages together is one example of change based on cultural values, rather than on research. This kind of organization, called family grouping, is favored on the assumption that concerns for the individual member will determine the program. This system is the reverse of that used in most schools and day-care centers, which is based on age separation. Either plan for organizing (or not organizing) the child's day is based in cultural bias, and neither plan is supported by research on the quality of the experience for a particular child. This book attempts to make a conceptual leap from present issues in early childhood education to basic research in the disciplines: genetics, biology, neurology, psychology, and cultural anthropology. These are the academic areas from which child development principles were drawn traditionally.

One trend which currently affects the roles of professionals and parents alike is the widespread coverage by mass media of relatively technical research. This mass dissemination brings new evidence to laypeople almost as soon, and sometimes sooner, than professionals read the same studies in their journals. A case in point is the issue of marijuana smoking and its effect on human health. NBC television reported the work of Dr. Robert Heath of Tulane University, showing pictures of his marijuana-smoking rhesus monkeys. Shortly thereafter, HEW announced a review of their previous stand on marijuana smoking. This report, again on NBC television, was followed by various statements of experts who differed in their opinion and gave conflicting testimony to the agency and to the public. They discussed several health issues, including sterility and birth defects tied to marijuana smoking. A professor of a great university, while not recommending the use of marijuana, said there was no evidence that tissue damage resulted from its use. He cited alcohol and other drugs as similar or worse in their effect on health. The professor appeared not to have done his homework.

Having visited Dr. Heath in his laboratory, having observed his primates both during and after marijuana treatment, and having plowed through several of the publications based on this research, I took particular note of the NBC special reports. The media tend to present two sides of an issue. To the nonspecialist, the pros and cons may seem equally valid, or equally confusing. The weight of the evidence indicates that serious and long-term brain damage can result from marijuana smoking, but to accept this conclusion one must do some heavy reading of neurological evidence. As early as 1972, precise accounts were published of studies on the comparative effects of marijuana and other drugs on a human subject that were made by studying encephalogram (EEG) readings from deep within the brain. The readings were obtained by implanting electrodes surgically into the septal and other deep areas of the brain and comparing them with EEGs from the surface (cortical) areas. As in much of the brain research, the subject was conscious and could talk about feelings. Heath found that unusual deep brain activity accompanied the euphoria of marijuana smoking. This reaction was not characteristic of EEG responses to alcohol, tobacco, or amphetamines. Heath cited many studies, and his own research with human subjects and primates, which suggest (1) that cells of the septal area of the brain are affected by marijuana, (2) that lesions in the septal area result in reduced awareness, reduced motivation, and deficient pleasure feelings, and (3) that prolonged smoking of marijuana by some rhesus subjects resulted in severe emotional disturbance which remained long after the smoking was discontinued (Heath, 1972). Although this research does not prove that similarly harmful effects would occur with all individuals, other researchers are finding chromosome changes and prenatal damage to offspring which they attribute to marijuana smoking.

The issue of marijuana is only one of countless instances in which the need for knowledge is obvious for prospective parents and voting citizens. Professionals who work with children need to go beyond the news media presentations to more technical reports in order to evaluate the practical meanings of research. The student is entitled to be confused by lack of agreement on some issues involving early childhood development and learning. However, great bodies of literature have become available in recent years which strongly suggest, if not conclusively prove, that one side of some issues is correct.

The purpose of this book is to review and synthesize research findings about infants and children, suggesting wherever possible some implications of recent findings in childrearing practices. Each author's conceptualization of the relevance or significance of any particular study is inevitable. However, the format of this book provides a clear separation between the basic information gleaned from various disciplines and the implications of this research for early education. The parents and teachers who live with and care for the children make the final decisions and the applications.

This chapter presents nine conceptual themes that appear and reappear through the pages of this book. These strands constitute some principles of human development which are widely discussed in the literature. A few studies, some widely known and classic and some recent but significant, are cited. A deeper treatment of these topics is reserved for relevant sections in the chapters to follow.

UNIVERSAL ORDER OF DEVELOPMENT

Children around the world learn and grow by a series of accomplishments that are common to Homo sapiens. Apparent (but insignificant) differences in color or in culture may obscure the basic commonalities among all people. This universality of human development can be observed in the behavior of children of all countries, whether in the parks, the shops, or the schools.

In a Leningrad park two children played in a sandbox. The toddler dipped her hands full of sand, rotated her firm little torso to the edge of the box, and dumped the sand on the grass. A four-year-old, who played beside her but not with her, was intent on building a castle.

Near a children's hospital in Helsinki a young father escorted his twin sons, about five years old, toward the speech pathology entrance to the hospital. One of the twins ran ahead, exploring gate locks, parked cars, and garden stakes. The other twin held his father's hand, or the trouser leg when the hand was not within reach. Even a casual observer could guess which was the dominant and which the nondominant twin. Observation and background suggested that both twins were receiving therapy to overcome "twin jargon" and to learn Finnish—the language of their family.

In Khatmandu an eight-month-old boy, his eyes beautifully lined with antimony mascara, stared at the American visitor. He whimpered when she approached, but paid no attention to two dark-skinned visitors who also were strangers.

The Soviet youngsters were showing play patterns typical of children everywhere. The Finnish twins, who were living out their roles of dominance and nondominance, had invented a common speech for communicating with each other, a behavior pattern typical of twins. The Nepalese infant was showing a fear of different-looking strangers at the age when this behavior is anticipated across cultures.

In any country, differences can be observed in how infants are cared for, and how older, acculturated children respond to strangers. However, the differences in the quality of child care indicate the social and economic status of a family much more than they reflect the country in which it lives.

In Srinagar a young "man of commerce" carried his daughter proudly and introduced her to visitors. Although it was midsummer she wore a pink coat, long white stockings, and Western shoes. This child was tall for her age, smiled easily, looked well fed, and was obviously valued by her family. Outside on the street, little girls were seldom seen, although little boys roamed and played everywhere. On the rare occasion when the female toddler of a poor family was seen on the street, she wore a short dress without pants. This is the typical dress for poor children of both sexes, prior to toilet training, in many countries.

Whether young children are well cared for, physically, depends more on the socioeconomic position of the parents than on climate, culture, or country. Whether children are valued greatly or not depends very often on how many there are for a family, or a country, to care for.

One obvious difference between peoples, which tends to obscure their likenesses and to create ethnic barriers, is language. However, research on language development has shown a universal sequence in the language learning of young children. Slobin (1972) analyzed the speech acquisition, within families, of children from eighteen different countries. He concluded that all normal children master their native language by the same principles and in a similar order.

In Slobin's many studies, children around the world began speech with one word, usually the name of an object or a person. At approximately age 2, they spoke two-word sentences, using appropriate stress and intonation. Later, three-word sentences were constructed showing an understanding of the relationship between noun phrases and verbs. Still later, two sentences were compressed, and finally children learned to imbed a second sentence within the main sentence, thus producing the complexity of mature speech. In all cultures, language syntax was learned by approximately age 4. The differences were minor. In English, for example, a young child may overgeneralize "breaked" for the irregular past tense "broke," or "mouses" for the irregular plural "mice." Some of these overgeneralizations persist into later childhood, and correct forms must be learned by association in a meaningful context.

Roger Brown (1973) analyzed five developmental stages in sentence construction and sentence understanding in the child's acquisition of syntax. Allowing for differences in detail, his design of stages appears to apply to all languages. Brown noted that the child's imitation of adult language, and the adult's imitation of child language, interact in shaping the child's speech. His studies suggest, however, that imitation is only one phase in language acquisition. The model he proposed takes into account Chomsky's theory of deep structure (meaning), which the child is mentally equipped to grasp innately (Chapter 9).

The development of speech is detailed in Chapter 9, Acquisition of Language. The important point here is that language differences between peoples may obscure basic commonalities in the ways youngsters learn and grow. Similarly, socioeconomic differences may create patterns of rearing and caring for children that are greater across class levels than across national boundaries. The study of child development in a variety of cultural settings is helpful when trying to identify the elements that are common to happy, healthy childhood. When working with culturally different families, it is important to help them improve the environment in critical areas while leaving the culture basically intact.

PHYLOGENIC AND ONTOGENIC INFLUENCES

The relative importance of genetic versus environmental influences is a matter for continuing debate in the study of child development. Parents like to know whether the extreme persistence they see in their Lisa is a hereditary trait shared with Uncle Henry, or whether their own patterns of interaction are reinforcing her refusal to leave a play activity for essential family routines. Administrators, legislators, and parent boards like to know where to allocate a community's economic resources in order to make the greatest impact on the future of its children. The issue of heredity versus environment, or nature versus nurture, has repeatedly emerged as a topic in program development. People in childhood education believe that the child's environment makes a difference in what the child becomes, or they likely would be doing other work. However, the distinction social scientists make between phylogeny and ontogeny in human development needs to be understood if the environment that adults design is to provide maximum opportunity for the child's natural abilities to develop.

Phylogeny Defined

Phylogeny is the evolutionary development of the species; in this instance, human beings, or Homo sapiens. Controlled studies of human generations to determine whether a persisting behavior is characteristic of the species or has been taught by the culture are not feasible. Researchers have placed young mammals in new environments, without a parent model to learn from, and observed whether innate behaviors persisted. By using laboratory mice, for example, the environment can be controlled and its effect over many generations can be observed in a single project of a few years' duration. Even cultural influences on behavior, far more complex than factors such as diet or climate, have been investigated by focusing on behavior differences within a species.

Calhoun (1956) was curious whether the characteristic home-building behaviors of different strains of mice were genetically determined or whether the young learned their practices within the social organization. He selected two strains of mice, one a nomadic strain that burrowed and lived under the ground and the other an "apartment dwelling" strain that built layers of homes above the ground by using plant materials and dirt. The nomads moved on and dug new burrows when their quarters were soiled, while the apartment dwellers had a penthouse arrangement by which dominant mice lived at the top and waste was pushed down, level by level, to be removed by the dwellers on the ground floor. To control the nature-nurture relationship, Calhoun took newborn mice from one strain and gave them to be fostered by mothers of the other strain. At weaning time, new and separate colonies were established, one for the apartment-dwelling mice that had been fostered by nomad mothers and another for nomadic mice that had been fostered by apartment-dwelling mothers. For two generations Calhoun noticed little or no difference in the building behavior of the different colonies; however, a tendency was observed for the offspring of apartment-dwellers to cluster their diggings in contrast to the nomadic mice, who continued to scatter their diggings. The observable differences between strains emerged first in the socializing patterns of the youngsters. After two or three generations, the young of the apartment-dwelling strain were building knolls from which certain mice dominated the play of their peers. In fifteen generations the architectural and social behaviors of one strain had been reestablished, while the nomads, fostered by apartment dwellers, continued the pattern of burrowing and moving.

One of the most significant observations to come from this research concerns the manner by which social intelligence reemerged through the spontaneous play of the youngsters. Calhoun's results suggest the importance of providing an early environment in which positive social behavior can be experienced and learned. The importance of environment was apparent in that fifteen generations were required to reestablish a pattern of behavior that the mice would have followed without exception had the nurture been consistent with the inherited pattern for home building.

The social inheritance of the species Homo sapiens is fragile at best. History and anthropology demonstrate that culture can be eradicated in one generation. Even the simplistic patterns of home building in field mice required fifteen generations for restoration, a period comparable to 500 years of cultural development in humans.

Although animal studies provide evidence that behavior patterns can be inherited, it should be remembered that Homo sapiens are infinitely more complex and their potential for change during one life-span is infinitely greater. It is generally accepted that the phylogenically old parts of the central nervous system have significant influence over autonomic, reflexive, and arousal responses of human beings. These primitive mechanisms are the basis for early attention and later motivation in humans. The distinction between autonomic and directed behavior is important in observing early motor development. The phylogenic development of the human brain reflects the complex functions human beings have gradually brought under control.

Ontogeny Defined

Just as phylogeny sets Homo sapiens apart from other creatures, ontogeny establishes the uniqueness of each person. *Ontogeny* refers to the growth and development of the individual from conception to death. This life-cycle is a constant interaction of the individual's *genotype*, or specific genetic constitution, and the environment into which the individual is conceived and grows. The studies of twins are the major source of nature-nurture knowledge in human beings because their genotype can be precisely determined as . . . nonidentical or identical. Nonidentical, or *familial*, twins are different in the same way that siblings differ. Identical, or *monozygotic*, twins share a common genotype because they grow from a single fertilized ovum that has duplicated, thus providing both twins with identical chains of chromosomes. When reared separately, monozygotic twins can be compared on the basis of different environments. When reared together, monozygotic twins can be compared with nonidentical, or *dizygotic*, twins. Dizygotic twins are derived from two separate fertilized ova and are no more alike in genotype than siblings of the same mating.

In a typical family setting, the environment varies for children reared together. Studies involving order of birth and number of siblings have shown that educational advantages accrue to the firstborn. Boys and girls are treated differently, even as newborns. The dominant member of twins has different learning experiences than the nondominant. Careful examination of many studies is needed to understand the subtle interaction of genetic and environmental influences.

Studies of physical characteristics in monozygotic twins have shown that they are remarkably similar given adequate conditions for growth. When monozygotic twins are reared apart, their heights at maturity are similar, although they vary much more in weight. Tanner (1970) reported research on physical development of twins which showed the influence of heredity in growth patterns including age of skeletal maturity, growth curves, time of tooth eruption, and menstrual age in girls (pp. 134–135).

Research has not yet been designed which appropriately compares the intelligence of different socioeconomic groups, because the factors of intelligence selected for comparison have not been controlled to reflect learning opportunity. However, the nature-nurture question becomes very important if the different kinds of intellectual functions that respond to teaching can be separated from more general abilities. Vandenberg (1966) compared the intellectual patterns of dizygotic and monozygotic twin pairs by analyzing their variability in six mental abilities subtests. He reported significant hereditary influence for four factors of intelligence: verbal, spatial, number, and word fluency. Evidence was lacking for hereditary influence in memory or reasoning abilities. It should be noted that human subjects are not exposed to extreme deprivation or to markedly superior environments when being studied, so the potential of the environment, if matched to individual strength, is not known. The lack of evidence for strong genetic influence on factors affecting memory and reasoning has important implications for child learning and teaching.

The interaction of nature and nurture is even more difficult to assess in personality development than in measures involving physical traits or intellectual functioning. One technique for determining whether mental illness is inherited has been to identify the twins among patients in institutions for schizophrenia and then to locate the twin. McClearn (1970) showed that 86 percent of the monozygotic twins but only 14 percent of the dizygotic twins had or had had the condition. When monozygotics with severe schizophrenia were separated out, the incidence of symptoms of schizophrenia in both twins was even higher. Other personality traits that have shown a hereditary relationship are depression, social introversion, and activity level. For those interested in the development of a healthy personality in their young children, an encouraging study was reported by Thomas, Chess, and Birch (1968), which suggests that early temperamental characteristics of infants and children are highly responsive to environmental influences of the home and the school.

The interaction of phylogenic and ontogenic influences is implicit at every state of child development. Some characteristics of growth await a timetable, coded in the genes, for the release of appropriate enzymes to set off a particular growth process. To summarize, genetic influence on physical traits is strongest, and becomes decreasingly important as a determinant of intellectual functioning and personality characteristics as the child develops.

Some recent scholars have discussed the impact of genetics and environment on human development in the broader context of the ecosystem. An ecosystem defines the interaction of biological makeup (genotype), the physical environment, and the cultural milieu of people (Stein & Rowe, 1974). Group differences in intelligence scores are suspect whenever the measures used are foreign to the ecological surround of the subject (Bronfenbrenner, 1976). The separation of genetic, environmental, and cultural influences in research is especially difficult in human beings because of the prolonged nurturance of the young and the attention given to acculturation. One conspicuous example of cultural indoctrination, clouded by biological factors, is the different treatment and behavior of the sexes.

REALITY OF SEX DIFFERENCES

Another conceptual thread that weaves through this book is the concern in early childhood with sex differences. Comparisons of boys and girls of the same age have not been conclusive on the nature of sex differences, partly because the environments of the two sexes cannot be fully accounted for or controlled in studies of human families. One approach to the problem of controlling the social environment has been to study primates, but even macaque mothers are known to treat their male offspring differently than their female young. Most studies of sex differences in boys and girls have been a spinoff from other research where the investigator found it easy to sort the data into two categories and allow the computer to locate any sex differences that showed.

More recently, Kagan designed a study specifically to observe sex differences in the cognitive development of 8-, 13-, and 27-month-old human infants at an age when social behaviors were being formed. He found that the two sexes were very similar on means, or averages, of cognitive development at the ages observed; but he found significant differences between boys and girls in the organization and patterning of their responses. He hypothesized that these differences are biologically based initially, and become further extended by cultural emphases on sex differences. Girl infants showed a link between vocalization and exciting visual or auditory experiences. This link was not characteristic of boys, although they vocalized as frequently. Kagan also found that responses such as visual fixation, attention, and vocalization were more stable from early infancy to early childhood in girls than in boys (Kagan, 1971, pp. 182–187).

Boys, as a group, were awake longer and fretted more frequently than girls. Kagan observed sex differences in the patterns of mothering which were associated with infant behavior. He also found that behavior toward sexes varied with social class. Middle-class mothers tended to value and recognize language ability in their daughters and to support gross motor ability and independence in their sons. Girls, as a group, increased their responsiveness to parent education over the period of the experiment, while boys did not. Upper-middle-class mothers tended to believe that the quality of their interaction, such as talking with their babies, would make a difference in the child's "brightness," while lower-class mothers tended to think of cognitive ability as inborn and enduring. These attitudes toward cognitive development were reflected in the changes in vocalization and attentiveness of upper- over lower-middle-class daughters over the period from 8 to 27 months. Nevertheless, daughters at both social levels showed greater response to mothers' training patterns in cognitive abilities than did sons.

Kagan's analysis suggests that boys, by showing greater variability in their responsiveness and higher activity levels, may have conditioned the mothers' nurturance patterns. By showing less responsiveness, the mothers of boys received less reinforcement for their effort. This suggestion is consistent with previous observations that mothers tended boy infants more frequently in response to fretting, but reversed this pattern and began to attend girl infants more frequently at about 4 months (Lipsitt, 1967).

Another important Kagan (1971) finding was that well-educated mothers were three times more likely to expect high standards of performance from daughters than were mothers with less than average schooling. More highly educated women criticized their daughters' omissions and mistakes, but they also were more tolerant of divergent behavior from them than mothers having less than average education. Mothers from different social classes were very similar in their expectations and criticism of sons. Further, their sons did not show the differences in vocabulary understanding, attention, and responsiveness that was found in girls. As infants, boys showed greater variability in temperament, which probably contributed to their being less amenable to parent education than girls. It should be remembered, however, that Kagan's findings refer to group tendencies.

Certain biological realities contribute to sex differences in the development of infants. The hereditary makeup of girls includes two X chromosomes, while boys inherit one X and one Y chromosome, which is relatively smaller in size and gene complement. Females have a greater selection of sex-linked genes than males, who show greater variance on sex-linked traits (Chapter 2). Further, an inherent difference exists in the prenatal environment of the sexes in that the male fetus must compensate in hormone balance for the essentially female estrogen-progesterone hormone balance of the mother (Chapter 3). These are among the factors that help to explain why male infants are more vulnerable than female infants to certain diseases and handicaps, as well as why they exhibit wider variability in some behaviors.

The earlier maturation of girls accounts for some of the differences between the sexes. This difference has many implications for childrearing. Girls have an earlier understanding of adult speech, earlier differentiation of visual and auditory cues, earlier establishment of speech areas in the dominant hemisphere of the brain, and earlier interpretation of affective cues in the social environment. Research shows that girl infants also display earlier fear and anxiety when placed in unfamiliar situations. Social experiences seem to influence the attention patterns of girls, while "congenital" temperament has been more predictive of the responses of boys (Moss & Robson, 1970).

Boys and girls of kindergarten age differed in learning success when they were grouped as high, medium, or low in orienting response. Farley and Manske (1969) used heart rate as a measure of the level of orienting and paired-associate scores as a measure of learning. They found that males in either the high or the low groups learned more efficiently, while females who were medium-level orienters learned most effectively (Figure 1-1). Similar differences were found when concept learning was tested, but the differences were not significant.

SPECIES-SPECIFIC BEHAVIOR

According to the concept of *species-specific* behavior, an individual develops through an interaction of biological structures inherited by all members of a species and environmental stimulation. Species-specific behaviors are fixed action patterns that evolve at a predictable stage in the growth of an individual. The notion of species-specific behavior focuses on genetic influences but also emphasizes the differences between Homo sapiens and other species. Species differences are apparent in the number of chromosomes a normal individual carries in each cell: 46 for Homo sapiens, 48 for chimpanzees, 23 for pigeons, 8 for fruit flies,

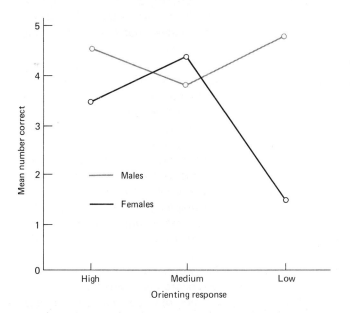

FIGURE 1-1   Sex differences in learning a paired-associates task. Boys classified as high or low were more successful than those at medium levels of orienting response, while the opposite was true for girls.

Source: Frank H. Farley and Mary E. Manske, *The Relationship of Individual Differences in the Orienting Response to Complete Learning in Kindergarteners*, Wisconsin Research and Development Center, 1970.

Smiling and laughing are species-specific behaviors. (Doug Magee/ Editorial Photocolor Archives)

and 2 for amoebas. Inherited physical characteristics are easy to observe and therefore easier to understand than species-specific behaviors, which may appear as late as adulthood. Some examples of species-typical behavior in humans are smiling as social interaction (Freedman, 1974), mating patterns (Lorenz, 1969), and using propositional language (Krech, 1969).

Smiling behavior in infants has been studied extensively to learn whether fixed behavior patterns are transmitted in the genetic code and how smiling emerges as important behavior in socialization. The process by which an inherited genetic code evolves as a species-typical behavior has been suggested by Hess (1970). The first requirement is the availability of an *inherited potential* for the neurological organization of the action. Smiling behavior can be seen in newborn and prematurely born infants, especially when the infant is drowsy or in light sleep. It is known that a neural structure which organizes the schema for smiling is developed prenatally, hence before social conditioning is possible (Chapter 4).

A second precondition for species-typical behavior is the *spontaneous activation* of the action pattern. Blind babies smile at birth under environmental conditions similar to those in which normal, sighted infants smile. Hess suggests that activation of a species-specific behavior is generated by action-specific energy— an extremely important concept in understanding the spontaneous activity of children. Action-specific energy builds up in the appropriate mechanism, where a pattern of release and rest can be observed. The smiling reflex in newborn full-term infants occurs at intervals of five minutes or longer, during the drowse states between deep sleep and alertness.

The third requirement for species-typical behavior is a *response* from the environment that has survival value for the infant. Mothers are more attentive to smiling infants than to unresponsive ones. Adults respond to infant characteristics, including smiling, by tending and nurturing them. Through this interaction infants become socialized to their own species. Probably all social species have fixed actions patterns which are activated early to assure attachment to one's kind. Blind babies, who do not take in these visual responses, lose the fixed-action smile, but they can and should be conditioned to smile in response to cutaneous stimulation as social reinforcement.

The fourth step in species-typical behavior is the *selection and discrimination of stimuli* which release the behavior. By the end of the first month, the infant smiles more readily for the human face than for masks, more for views of eye than for views of mouth, and more for moving objects than still ones. By the beginning of the second month, smiling is already related to mood. At this stage, smiling is dispelled when a stimulus is used repeatedly, but reappears when the stimulus is changed. This smiling behavior pattern differs from the automatic and reflexive smile of the newborn.

The fifth characteristic of species-typical action patterns is their limited period of *peak sensitivity* to adaptation. The peak of sensitivity for smiling responses to human faces appears to terminate at about the time the infant becomes fearful of strange faces, usually at 8 to 12 months, depending on the sex of the child and the social context in which the infant is observed. Smiling in infants is but one example of the interaction by which a species-specific pattern of behavior gradually comes under social control.

Some developmental psychologists believe that certain behavior patterns are programmed as specifically in the DNA of the chromosomes as are physical characteristics such as eye color or hair texture. This book takes the position, however, that inherited and available neural structures must be activated by appropriate stimulation from the environment for fixed action patterns to become operative. The uterine environment in which numerous action patterns evolve is controlled by the mother's hormone system and by the nurturance she provides through her own life-style.

TIMETABLES FOR OPTIMUM DEVELOPMENT

A consistent and predictable timetable for growth was discovered in the human fetus long before modern techniques for observing intrauterine life were invented. Physicians charted and diagrammed the prenatal periods by observing aborted pregnancies and premature births. Much later environmental damages to the fetus were related to health factors, such as the mother having rubella during early pregnancy. Physicians pooled their experience on birth defects caused by rubella, and discovered that the part of the anatomy that had growth priority at the time of the disease often became the part that developed abnormally. Rubella usually causes heart defects, sensory impairment, and/or mental retardation when contracted during the early weeks of pregnancy. Variations occur, but the relationship between the time of the insult and organ(s) damaged has been clearly demonstrated (Chapter 3). Eight weeks after conception, when most systems are intact, different kinds of development become critical. The drug thalidomide dramatically deformed the limbs of babies because the treatment for nausea corresponded in many pregnant women with the growth of limbs in the babies. The nature of the deformity and the timing of the drug usage were important factors in establishing that the cause of these limb deformities was environmental and not genetic. Much attention is now being given to the quality of the prenatal environment, so that these and many other defects can be prevented.

Critical periods are those stages of development when an individual is susceptible to particular forms of stimulation from the environment according to an inherited timetable. Priorities in growth and behavior normally have positive effects in that they relate the growth potential of the organism to survival needs. Early in fetal life particular organs, tissues, or neural systems have priority for growth. Early childhood behavior and learning are believed to involve similar critical periods.

The critical periods in physical development, now widely recognized in prenatal growth, have parallel implications for the intellectual development of the child. Environmental stimulation which enhances the development of the central nervous system, including the brain, almost certainly affects the child's learning potential. Bower (1976) has shown that environmental exercise of infant reflexes results in earlier learning of actions such as reaching and grasping than when the action pattern is allowed to disappear without environmental responsiveness at the reflex stage. Behaviors such as reaching and grasping, visual following, and attending to speech are examples of learning that is basic to cognitive (intellectual) development. Each is responsive to stimulation of the kind that some parents provide for their infants.

The negative aspect of this principle of critical periods is that the organs or systems that are developing most rapidly are particularly vulnerable at that time to insults or deprivations from the environment. Any damage to a particular sensory system, such as vision or hearing, changes the nature of intellectual experience by altering the information an individual receives. The different sense modalities must function together for cognitive experiences to be integrated. Although the evidence is less direct in psychological than in physical development, many clinicians believe that critical periods occur in learning that correspond to critical periods in the development of the brain and the nervous system.

Critical periods in the learning of a native language have been suggested. Wepman (1972) explained that discrimination of phonemes, the sound units that make up a spoken language, cannot be acquired without auditory acuity. Although speech and reading come later in the sequence of language development, the critical periods for learning to listen to and discriminate speech sounds are infancy and early childhood. Delay of auditory perception at that point results in a delay in conceptual thought and language production. Wepman observed in his own research that the ability to learn auditory perception of speech units and to sequence them correctly tapered off rapidly after the age of 8 years. He considered the critical period for learning the auditory perception skills that are basic to speech and reading to be 2 to 8 years of age.

Critical periods in cognitive development were implied by Hofstaetter (1954). He used the intelligence data from Nancy Bayley's longitudinal growth studies at Berkeley to analyze the trends in intellectual functioning from birth to age 17 (Figure 1-2). His analysis of different factor clusters showed that factor I, sensori-motor alertness, peaked at 9 months. This functioning was distinct from factors II and III, which Bayley called "more truly adaptive." Factor II, which showed a negative loading before birth, peaked between the ages of 2 and 4, and stabilized at the age of 9 or 10. Hofstaetter described factor II behavior as positive "persistence" toward the cognitive activity at hand together with a lack of the sensory alertness infants showed. Factor III, which appeared to govern the ability to do abstract thinking, developed consistently until the ages of 8 or 9, and then leveled off to remain the most significant factor in intelligence tests in later childhood. No factor was found to correspond to Piaget's description of formal operations, which he says begins at age 11 or 12. However, Hofstaetter noted a scarcity of test items that

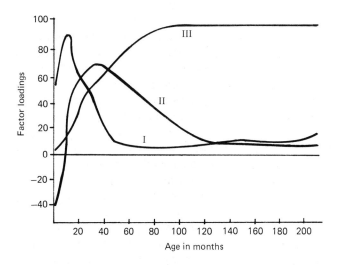

FIGURE 1-2 Critical periods in intellectual development. Factor analysis of intelligence test items shows peaking at about 9 months, 3 years, and 8 years. Factor I has been identified as sensory motor alertness, factor II as adaptive persistence, and factor III as reasoning. (After Peter H. Hofstaetter, in *Journal of Genetic Psychology*, 1954, 85, 161. By permission of *The Journal Press* and the author.)

would allow children to show logical thought. If Piaget is even partially correct in describing sensorimotor structures as the basis for later perception and cognition, the critical first two years of sensorimotor learning should be taken seriously in childrearing (Chapter 8).

Some characteristics that are generally considered acquired and not innate, such as morality, may be more amenable to education at some periods in development than at others. Studies using classroom-based programs on morality and socialization found that children in the preadolescent period from 9 to 12 years were highly responsive to the training, whereas similar studies using children 6 to 9 years old did not show significant results (Kohlberg, LaCross, & Ricks, 1972). On the basis of their research on critical periods in ego development, the researchers recommended mental health intervention for 6- to 9-year-olds that focuses on cognitive development and takes into account interests, intellectual style, and attention abilities. They recommended intervention for older elementary children in areas of character development, peer relations, and interaction with adults. Some schools tend to reverse this order by giving devoted attention to social adjustment in kindergarten and focusing on cognitive development in the middle grades. Perhaps these teachers and parents should consider the need to develop cognitive competence at 6 to 8 years of age as basic to ego strength and healthy peer relationships in the preadolescent period (Chapter 7).

AFFECTIVE AND COGNITIVE INTERACTION IN LEARNING

Growth results from the complex interaction of many forces, factors, influences, tendencies, and determinants. Any manageable study of infants and children requires that cognitive and affective factors be identified and considered separately, even though neither functions in isolation. The human child is an *organism*, meaning that its living systems function interdependently. This organismic wholeness is implied in the interaction of phylogeny and ontogeny, of nature and nurture, and of physical and social maturation in behavior change.

Every human experience has elements of knowing and feeling. The *affective* side of the learning interaction is concerned with affection, motivation, drive, incentive, esthetics, and other generalized feelings. The pleasure, punishment, fear, and longing that are part of each experience determine whether it will be repeated or avoided at a later time. The *cognitive* side of learning has to do with intellectual content, both the sensory information received from the environment and the individual's organization of the impulses. Past experience when stored and retrieved combines with present information from the senses to make up the content of thought. Most of this sensory and conceptual content is considered cognitive by psychologists.

To understand the difference between affective and cognitive learning, as well as the interaction between them, we must examine the mechanisms of the brain. The centers for reward and punishment are located primarily in the limbic system, deep in the core of the brain (Magoun, 1969). The neural action in this system is closely related to primitive needs for survival; hence it is very old in the phylogenic order of

Affective interaction precedes cognitive interaction. (Erika/Peter Arnold)

brain development. Pribram (1971) called this the motivation mechanism which actuates the four activities basic to survival: feeding, fleeing, fighting, and sex. The several parts of the limbic system are interconnected (by neurons) and the system itself is connected with the sensory and cortical areas of the brain.

The cerebral cortex has long been considered the location of cognitive functions because of the extensive folds of the surface layers in humans. The cognitive information from past experience, which is stored in the cortex, is associated by neural interconnections to the feeling, or emotional, experience that occurred at the same time. Fortunately, other brain mechanisms, primarily in the forebrain, enable people to anticipate the results of an action and to redirect their behavior to avoid unpleasant experiences or unsafe environments. Some evidence of how people initiate and create new approaches to living is available in the neural connections.

Behavior is a complex expression of the cognitive and affective psychomotor functioning of an individual. Motor skills, thought processes, and motivations all are learned behaviors which emerge as a condition of growing. The deprivation of fear, pain, and hunger in the overprotected child has been considered as a potentially negative factor in later motivation (Lorenz, 1972). The effects of sensory deprivation, such as the dull and unstimulating environment some poor children endure, will be considered in Part Four, Responsibilities of Care-Givers.

ADVANTAGES OF PROLONGED DEPENDENCE

Human parents have approximately two decades in which to nurture independence, self-direction, and social responsibility in their children. The ultimate choices a child or an adolescent makes are based in early experience when the options for selection are under the control of others. Although the infant unconsciously and inherently makes species-typical choices, such as mildly sweet foods over those that taste bitter, the selecting process includes only those possibilities that are there within an environment provided and controlled by others. Parents and teachers who want their children to become self-directed, self-motivated persons need to remember that the ability to make the choices that enhance productivity and well-being are learned gradually.

Dependence, which is almost total in human neonates, involves the basic necessities of survival: food that can be assimilated, protection from temperature changes, removal from danger, and personal cleanliness. In each of the physical contacts of caring for an infant, the care-giver creates a relationship that assures a significant someone to turn to for imitation and reinforcement. Food, the pleasure of hunger satisfied, oral stimulation, the handler's touch, the object that contains the food are associated but undifferentiated in the neonate. These are the bits and pieces of experience from which later trust of self and others is built. Some adults neglect to control the child's behavior at times when the wrong decisions by the child can have permanent and destructive consequences. In contrast, others retain too much control for too long because they need the dependence of children for their own psychological gratification. Insecure adults cannot free the children to take over their own lives as they mature. Preparing a child for independence means (1) creating an environment in which growth-producing experiences are available, (2) being sensitive to the child's own efforts to become independent, and (3) encouraging and extending the child's self-control to those areas where previous learning allows a reasonable choice. The physical needs of children and the physical environment which provides those needs are relatively easy to know and to manage in a prosperous society or family. However, the psychological environment by which a child attains emotional independence is complex, and demands awareness, specialized knowledge, and intervention on the part of adults; far more is required than attention to simple physical needs.

Infants and children are dependent on the social environment into which they are born for the development of ego strength, a healthy self-concept, communication skills, and intellectual power. Human babies usually get the attention they need, in part because of their helplessness, their early smile, their responsiveness to physical gratification, and their unthreatening overtures to whomever is near. If full gratification, uninterrupted attending, and complete protection were possible, the choices some parents make about childrearing might reinforce the egocentrism of childhood too long. Fortunately for most children, the needs of other persons—spouse, siblings, self, and neighbors—make full attention to one individual baby impossible.

The attention span of young daughters is related to the mother's attitude about the learning abilities of her daughter and her own role in developing these abilities (Kagan, 1971). Sons who are attended closely tend to stay closer to their mothers, to use less time in play exploration, and to return to their mothers more frequently than do sons who spend more time by themselves or with persons other than mother.

Neonates show a prebirth adaptation to the life-style of the mother's home environment with reference to the timing and regularities of activity and resting. Toddlers whose eating patterns are regular adapt to toilet use more easily than do children who eat irregularly. The gradual transition from near-total nurturance within the intrauterine environment to the final adaptation of the child's need to the mutual needs of family members is necessary in all socially interdependent species. Probably the necessity to be with other persons, who have different and individualized needs, is healthy for the social development of the child. A qualified permissiveness which expects the child to grow into the family organization gradually may stimulate social responsibility at an early age.

The prolonged period of dependence gives human beings a longer and potentially more significant influence over the ontogeny, or individual life experience, than any other species. As a society, humans have a decade or two in which to transmit cultural experience and values. In most cultures the period of dependency is extended in affluent families to the mid-twenties and is decreased markedly in economically poor families, often to the early teens. The important point is that adults always inherit this responsibility and knowing how to use it is important to the psychological maturity of the young. To become a healthy person, a child must be free to interact with other people, have a secure self-concept, and be able to arrange his or her activities in ways that complement the body systems.

EGOCENTRISM OF CHILDHOOD

Humans are born without knowing that a separation exists between themselves as an organism and the surrounding environment. Infants learn gradually to separate the self from persons and objects in the surround. During early childhood they learn that one's cognitive perspective depends on where one stands when looking. Egocentrism in affective areas means the assumption that others feel the same about people and events. Clinical studies of emotional illness suggest that emotional egocentrism is more persistent and less age-related than cognitive development.

Jean Piaget observed and described the approximate ages at which children arrive at different levels of egocentrism in cognitive development. In one experiment he constructed three mountains on a miniature plane (Figure 1-3). He seated his young subjects in one location and asked them to select one of four pictures to

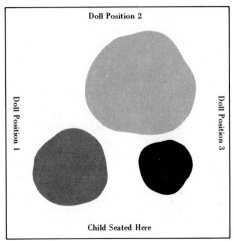

Doll Position 2

Doll Position 1

Doll Position 3

Child Seated Here

Mountains are arranged on a square board in this relationship, shown from above.

FIGURE 1-3   Model of three mountains, designed by Piaget to observe egocentrism in children.

Source: John A. R. Wilson, Mildred C. Robeck, and William B. Michael, *Psychological Foundations of Learning and Teaching*, page 353. Copyright, 1974, McGraw-Hill Book Company.

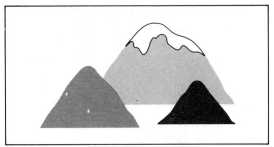

Interviewer asks child to sit at table where model of mountains is seen in relationship shown here. Child is asked to select one of eight drawings of mountains as he sees them.

Note test pictures are also shown from corners.

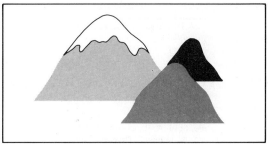

Mountains as seen from doll position 1.

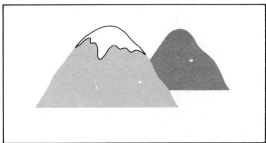

Mountains as seen from doll position 2.

Mountains as seen from doll position 3.

show what they saw. Then he walked a doll around the mountains and asked the child to choose a picture that showed what the doll saw. Until age 6 or 7, most children continued to choose the picture that represented what they were seeing. Children of 8 or 9 usually showed an awareness that the doll's perspective might be different, and tried to guess the right picture. By age 10 or 11 most children could readily, and without error, select the view the doll was "seeing." Piaget considered the younger children's responses egocentric rather than incorrect. He accepted the children's answers as cues to the cognitive stages of all children (Chapter 8).

Erik Erikson, a psychiatrist, considered it important for the affective egocentrism of childhood to culminate in a mature personality at adulthood. He described the

Piagetian studies of egocentrism reveal the child's way of seeing things. Here the child's conception of space is tested by rotating the miniature landscape. (George Roos/Peter Arnold)

stages of emotional development by which egocentrism is outgrown. His goals for a mature personality include a generous and generative outlook which will promote healthy ego development in offspring. Anna Freud, Erikson's teacher and colleague, was concerned that teachers and parents understand the child's way of perceiving social relationships in order to guide children in their expanding awareness of sex roles and sexual identity (Chapter 11).

Each person is egocentric in some ways and at some times. Individuality, when recognized and valued for children, as well as for adults, encourages growth in knowing oneself. Unfortunately some individuals reach adulthood without ever conceptualizing that each person's world is private and unique.

GENERALIZATIONS

Some conceptions that are central to infant and child development, and are significant in rearing children, have been presented in this chapter. These conceptualizations are the themes of the book as a whole; they have determined the selection of topics within chapters and the supporting documentation.

Children develop by a universal timetable which is similar for all human beings. Differences between individual children in their cognitive awareness and their social skills are greater between groups within a country than between countries. The development of language is one well-documented example of a behavior that all human beings learn according to the same timetable.

Phylogeny and ontogeny are forces that interact in the adaptation of living things and cannot be isolated completely in research on children. The terms "nature" and "nurture" refer, respectively, to inherited and environmental influences on how children develop. The ecosystem of a society includes biological, individual, and cultural factors.

Sex differences are real, but nurtured differently in different cultures. Research on child development has recently identified some of the differences which have implications for the personality growth of both sexes.

Species-specific characteristics of Homo sapiens include the use of language to project, predict, and plan alternatives. The genetic inheritance is a blueprint for physical structures that are sensitive to particular stimuli. Infants respond to spoken language at very early ages and learn to understand the language of the culture. Propositional language enables human offspring to acquire the cultural heritage very quickly.

An innate timetable of development reveals peaks, when the organism selects particular tissues or organs for optimum growth. Normal development requires the protection from insults that affect growth selectively. Optimum development requires a superior environment appropriate for particularized growth during the critical periods.

Learning differs in kind, as well as in complexity. *Behavior is a complex expression of different levels of cognitive and affective functioning of an individual.* Skills, thought processes, and motivations all are learned behavior. Animal studies define human learning only to the extent that similar brain structures for intellectu-al functioning exist.

The prolonged period of dependency of infants and children provides time for the gradual development of self-direction in them. Adults have a responsibility to make the decisions for children too young to be responsible, but to transfer decision making gradually to their older children.

Egocentricity is characteristic of childhood; that is, the individual perceives objects and relationships from his or her own perspective, and assumes that others see things the same way. Personality development includes the gradual differentia-tion between the private world of self and the private worlds of other persons.

2
Genetic Origins and Reproduction

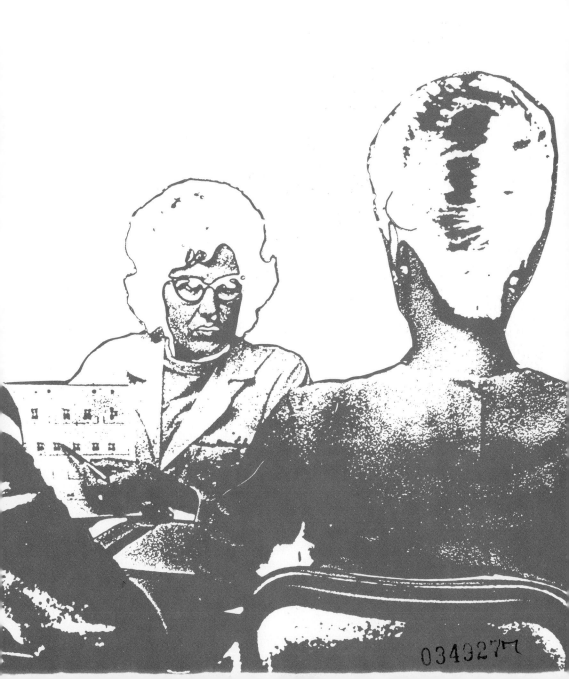

2 Genetic Origins and Reproduction

Physiology reveals the body structures that make human behavior possible. Genetics reveals the laws by which a species, or a family line, continues. In order to know which human traits are determined genetically and which are altered by the environment, a knowledge of the physiology of human reproduction is needed. The process by which two single germ cells unite and develop into a complex human individual is a variation of the process by which all living cells reproduce. How do cells multiply? How do cells reproduce and grow differently, so that various body structures develop? Questions about heredity are both personal and practical. Will the baby have her mother's brown eyes, or hazel eyes like her father? Can this child inherit an uncle's epilepsy? A grandmother's cancer? The chromosomes within each human cell contain both the blueprint and the timetable for growth.

Although human reproduction went on for 50,000 years without our knowing anything about cells or their functions (Lenski & Lenski, 1974), science has been expanding the control humans have over the biological segment of their lives. Many infants and children who once would have died of inherited defects are being saved through the intervention of science. Many people live productive lives because some inherited vulnerability toward a disease (such as diabetes) was predicted and preventive measures were taken early. Many types of medical intervention are now possible because research has revealed the processes by which the cell carries and transmits the genetic code. Genetic counseling is not yet routine, but it is possible.

Human beings seem compelled to discover as much about themselves as time and affluence allow and to put this knowledge to use in making life better. One result is that many children who would have died in earlier and grimmer times (or put out to die) now grow to adulthood, reproduce, and pass defective genes on to their offspring. When overpopulation threatens, and vital supplies and services become scarce, genetic knowledge can help solve some of the problems through family planning.

Knowledge of genetics gives individuals a great deal of control over their own reproduction. A couple who plan to have only two children, for example, may consider the sex of the children important. The mates can juggle the odds for having one boy and one girl. If a child is born mentally retarded, the chances for a later child to be normal can be estimated and the options for having another child or adopting one can be considered. Although many people are afraid of genetic control and its implications, genetic counseling has become a common step for couples to take when potentially defective genes are suspected in either family line, or the age of one parent is less than optimal. About 1600 diseases are known to have an hereditary component (Stein & Rowe, 1974, p. 60). Many of these diseases develop from an interaction of the environment with a genetic vulnerability and thus can be prevented and/or treated. The environment is similarly important in the development of inherited abilities and strengths. This chapter is concerned with the genetic bases of human reproduction and how our knowledge in that area can help decision making.

The functioning of cells is basic to all issues of heredity and environmental intervention. An important difference exists between the division of cells in normal growth (mitosis) and the reproduction cycle that produces cells for union in conception (meiosis). The early sections of this chapter explain the organization and functions of cells, chromosomes, and genes; cell functions in learning; and the hereditary basis of individual uniqueness, the genotype. The middle section deals with the genetic advantages to mammals from innate differences between males and females in reproduction and selection. The final section discusses some abnormalities that are transmitted through the genetic code, and explains how some forms of genetic control, including genetic counseling, can be used to help prospective parents.

PHYSICAL BASES FOR REPRODUCTION

The genetic code is filed in the molecules that make up the genes. Genes are the significant proteins in the physical structure of the chromosomes. The full complement and the precise arrangement of chromosomes that characterize a species is present in every normal cell. In human beings, each cell (whether muscle, bone, nerve, or blood) contains 46 chromosomes (Figure 2-1). Minute sample cells of any of these parts can be cultured in a laboratory, photographed, and arranged to show an individual's chromosome array, or *karyotype*. Any deviation from a normal chromosome complex results in an abnormality of some degree, or in the death of the organism.

Cells: The Units of Life

The cell is the basic unit of all life. In humans, as in all living things, cells are the smallest units which organize their own functions to sustain life. Cells use energy, excrete waste, repair themselves, adapt to environmental change, and reproduce. Although the cells of various parts of the body appear different under a microscope, all cells share a common anatomy (Figure 2-2).

STRUCTURE OF CELLS

The most significant function of a cell is its own reproduction. Each cell is made up of three main structures. The *cell wall* is a membrane that surrounds and contains the nucleus and the cytoplasm. The cell wall controls the environment within the cell by changing the permeability of its membranes to select the nutrients and enzymes that may enter at any given time in its life-cycle. Cell duplication is programmed by enzyme messages that coordinate the growth phases of the organism. The cell wall also controls the release of the biochemical materials by which a cell communicates with other cells. Hormones have a role in intracellular communication.

The *nucleus* encloses the chromosomes, together with various protein units that produce growth, throughout the life-cycle of the cell. During the phases when genes are being replicated, the chromosomes are loosely organized (literally,

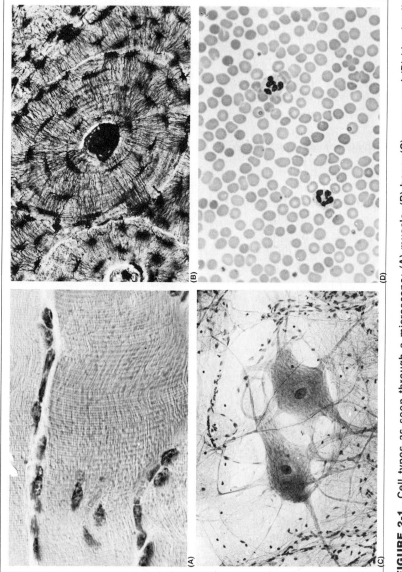

FIGURE 2-1 Cell types as seen through a microscope: (A) muscle, (B) bone, (C) nerve, and (D) blood cells. (Courtesy of Carolina Biological Supply Company.)

strung out) and their containment within the nucleus is critical. By a process not fully understood, information is released through the nuclear membrane for activating the support systems in the cytoplasm. The timing of the changes in the structure of cells during duplication is communicated through the nuclear membrane. One significant event that occurs inside the nucleus is the transcribing of appropriate parts of the genetic code along the chromosome chains.

The *cytoplasm* is a highly flexible structure between the nucleus and the outer wall of the cell. Proteins and carbohydrates are synthesized there, and other life-support activities for different phases of cell division are carried out. The cytoplasm contains and arranges the *organelles*, clusters of molecules that each have specialized functions in the life and growth of cells. Cytoplasmic material changes in texture from fibrous to fluid according to the activity of the organelles and the life phase of the cell. Cell activities are believed to be controlled by

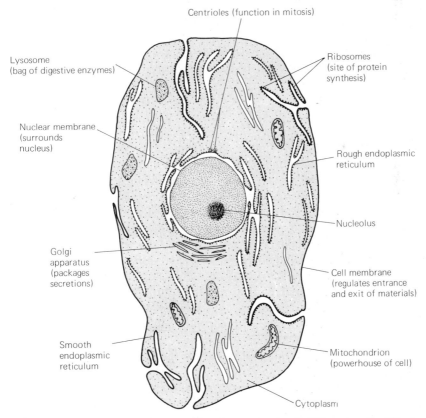

Centrioles (function in mitosis)

Lysosome
(bag of digestive enzymes)

Ribosomes
(site of protein
synthesis)

Nuclear membrane
(surrounds
nucleus)

Rough endoplasmic
reticulum

Nucleolus

Golgi
apparatus
(packages
secretions)

Cell membrane
(regulates entrance
and exit of materials)

Smooth
endoplasmic
reticulum

Mitochondrion
(powerhouse of cell)

Cytoplasm

FIGURE 2-2 **Cross section of a generalized animal cell. Although cells differ in size and appearance, they have a common anatomy of cell body, a cell wall that surrounds it, and a nucleus that contains a full set of chromosomes.**

Source: P. William Davis and Eldra Pearl Solomon, *The World of Biology*, McGraw-Hill Book Company, 1974, page 45. By permission of the publisher.

hormones and other substances acting directly on the genes. The chemical element magnesium has been reported to have an important function in cell growth (Rubin, 1975).

The interworkings within cells and the communication between them are basic to all growth, including learning. The structure of cells generally is characteristic of the neural cell bodies that make up the brain, the spinal cord, and the peripheral nervous system. The connections between neural cell bodies form a specialized network for communication. The fine dendrites deliver electrochemical impulses into the cell body, and the axons transmit selected messages to the next neuron in the relay. The same primary genetic material that directs physical growth generally also directs the growth of the brain and the central nervous system. Intellectual functions, which require memory storage, are theoretically possible through the coding and encoding of the various forms of RNA chains of protein material (Wallace, 1975).

Life begins and is sustained through two basic forms of cell division, mitosis and meiosis. *Mitosis* is the cycle of cell duplication by which the body grows and worn-out cells are replaced. *Meiosis* requires an additional division to produce the sex cells, reduced to half the chromosome complement, in preparation for the union of conception. The first division of meiosis is similar to the phases of mitosis, which will be explained first.

PHASES OF MITOSIS

Each cell division requires a complete duplication of the chromosomes in the nucleus, a perfect separation of the chromosome sets with each gene in its proper location, and an adequate sharing of the support systems in the cytoplasm. Although the stages of cell division are continuous, rather than discrete, biologists usually begin their description at *interphase*, when the new cell has just completed separation from its sister cell (Figure 2-3A). During interphase the main structures of the cell appear stable under a light microscope, but the slow process of chromosome duplication is going on inside the nucleus. Chromosome duplication requires the precise synthesis of matching strands of DNA (the genetic code) from protein units and other materials in the cytoplasm. During the duplication of the genes, the DNA chains are extended so that space for intermingling with protein units is available. At interphase, the chromosomes appear invisible under a light microscope. The molecules of the single centriole which lies just outside the cell nucleus also duplicate. These will separate to form the two poles for orienting the two sets of chromosomes.

The *prophase* of cell duplication is one of active reorganization throughout the cell. The nuclear membrane disintegrates, allowing free intermingling of attenuated genes with the nutrients in the cytoplasm. During prophase the long threads of genetic material (chromatid threads) condense until they can be seen under the light microscope as double chains (sister chromatids), attached, like Siamese twins, at some point along the chain. The point of attachment, the centromere, is significant in organizing and aligning the genes in identical chains so that perfect separation is possible.

An intermediate stage, *prometaphase*, has been identified recently as the transition from prophase to metaphase (Figure 2-3B). This phase has become critical in preparing karyotypes. At prometaphase the chromatids are coiled into rodlike structures and are still attached in pairs to the centromere, but have not yet massed at the equator of the cell. The chromosomes are amenable to staining and microscopic observation, thus making the difficult laboratory procedure possible. Karyotyping has become widely used to study the chromosomal makeup of individuals for purposes of diagnosis, treatment, and genetic counseling. Fans of the 1976 Olympic games may remember the sex tests required of female athletes. Karyotypes were prepared from cells obtained by smears inside the cheek, and the presence of two X chromosomes confirmed that the individual being tested was female.

By late prometaphase each chromatid gravitates toward the center of the cell. During this coiling and gravitation, the two centrioles (poles) take positions at opposite sides of the cell and begin to form two separate spindles by attracting and attaching to themselves one end of many translucent fibers, newly formed from protein materials in the cytoplasm. The centrioles and their fibers temporarily organize the chromatids at the equator of the cell and away from the poles.

By *metaphase* the chromosomes become aligned on an equatorial plane, and each attaches itself to a separate fiber of the miotic spindle. During this period the centromeres, which hold the pairs of chromatids together, duplicate.

Early in *anaphase* the threads of the miotic spindle contract, pulling the duplicated centromeres apart and drawing the separated chromatids toward opposite ends of the poles (centrioles). Upon separation chromatids become technically known as chromosomes. One complete set of chromosomes gravitates toward one side of the cell and the other, identical, set gravitates to the opposite pole (Davis & Solomon, 1974). One theory is that chromatids appear to repel each other in anaphase because of changes in the electrical potential of centromere atoms.

During the last stage of mitosis, *telophase*, the chromosomes move to their respective poles and the fibers of the miotic spindle disintegrate (Figure 2-3C). A constriction occurs around the equator of the cell until it cleaves, separating the two daughter cells. Each contains an identical complement of chromosomes and each retains a like portion of the cytoplasmic material. Following cell division, the nucleus membrane reforms around the chromosomes, which begin again to attenuate and duplicate.

The control over the timetable of cell reproduction, especially the triggering of a cycle, is outside the cell itself and is coordinated with cell growth in other parts of the body. Cell reproduction is probably stimulated by enzymes, which penetrate the cell wall, bearing their instructions to the genes within the nucleolus, a body within the cell nucleus (Handler, 1970). Some cancers are caused when cell duplication goes out of control at some point in mitosis, presumably just after cell

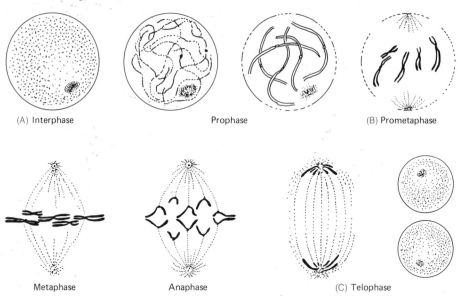

(A) Interphase   Prophase   (B) Prometaphase

Metaphase   Anaphase   (C) Telophase

FIGURE 2-3 Phases of mitosis. Stages in the continuous reproduction of a 5-chromosome cell. Human cells contain 46 chromosomes. **A.** During *interphase*, the chromosomes double in number by duplication. During *prophase*, the threads of duplicated chromosomes condense. Centromeres are seen here as five black dots. This phase ends as threads coil into identical sister chromatids and become visible. Note (1) the gradual disintegration of the nuclear cell wall and (2) the bits of biochemical material that will self-duplicate to form centrioles (poles).

B. During *prometaphase*, the two centrioles separate and organize fibers of the cytoplasm into two spindles at opposite ends of the cell. During *metaphase* the sister chromatids position themselves along the equator of the cell and the self-duplication of the centromeres begins. During *anaphase* the spindle fibers attach randomly to the nearest centromere of each pair of chromosomes and attract them toward opposite centriole poles.

C. During *telophase*, chromosome pairs move to their respective poles, forming two clusters of chromosomes that are exactly alike. Note cleavage at the equator of the cell. (Drawings by Donna Thompson.)

differentiation. The mitosis cycle requires ten to fifteen hours for the reproduction of most mammalian cells.

Chromosomes: The Units of Reproduction

Chromosomes are the rods, or chains, of genetic information that is confined in the nucleus of each cell. Each chromosome (in meiosis) or chromosome pair (in mitosis) carries specified portions of the hereditary blueprint. The genetic code is spelled out in the sequence and arrangement of DNA molecules along the chromosome chains. In mitosis the chromosomes duplicate, exactly, the arrangement of DNA molecules to form sister chromatids, so that when divided each cell maintains a full complement of 46 chromosomes. In the second division of meiosis a reduction of chromosomes to 23 results in different genetic materials being assigned (by chance) to different cells.

PROCESS OF MEIOSIS

Meiosis is the process of cell growth and reduction which produces the specialized cells for sexual reproduction. During mammal conception, two sets of genetic information are combined in the fertilized ovum, one set of chromosomes from the sperm cell and one set from the egg cell. Meiosis occurs in the genital tissues of both sexes (Stein & Rowe, 1974). It would be a biological disaster if the germ cells were to carry 46 chromosomes each; the resulting union would total 92 chromosomes. Such duplication would mean conflicting genetic instructions for an otherwise orderly transcription of DNA specifications for growth. These 23 chromosomes, when combined with a similar complement of 23 chromosomes in mating, restore the cell count to 46 chromosomes and preserve the essential arrangement of matching pairs of genes. Two divisions occur in meiosis, each with its phases of duplication and separation (Figure 2-4). Gamete production in the female (oogenesis) requires that most of the cytoplasm be retained by the fertilized cell when the three polar bodies are excluded from the union. Meiotic division in the male (spermatogenesis) results in four gametes of like anatomy but carrying different genetic traits.

The *first division* in meiosis results in the separation of pairs of *homologous chromosomes*, by the same phases that sister chromatids separated in mitosis (Figure 2-5A). The sequences are identified by I or II to distinguish the first and second divisions. During prophase I, the strings of molecules duplicate and organize themselves like siamese twins joined at the centromere. During metaphase I, two homologous pairs (tetrads) align at the equatorial plane of the cell (Figure 2-5B). The first division, at telophase I, separates homologous pairs; one diploid (fused nucleus of the chromosomes) goes to one cell and the other to the other cell. At this point there are 46 chromosomes in each cell (Figure 2-5C).

During the *second division* in meiosis, there is no duplication of genes, and cell reduction proceeds immediately (Figure 2-5D and E). At metaphase II the sister chromatids separate, with one set of chromosomes being drawn by one spindle to one pole and the other to the opposite pole. Note that the sets of chromosomes number 23, but represent different genetic makeups. Oogenesis produces one gamete and three polar bodies; two will disintegrate. Spermatogenesis produces four gametes, each with equal potential for fertilizing the ovum.

DETERMINATION OF SEX

It has been noted that in meiosis, the second cell division reduces the chromosomes to 23 in each normal cell body. The ovum, or germ cell from the female, always carries an X sex chromosome, shown in the karyotype as the 23d pair (Figure 2-5). The sperm cell, also reduced to 23 chromosomes, carries only one sex chromosome, which will determine whether the offspring is a boy or a girl.

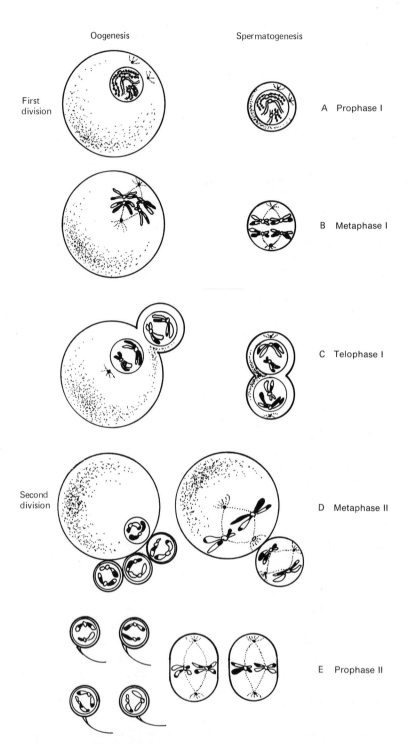

Oogenesis   Spermatogenesis

First
division

Second
division

A   Prophase I

B   Metaphase I

C   Telophase I

D   Metaphase II

E   Prophase II

FIGURE 2-4 Phases of meiosis.

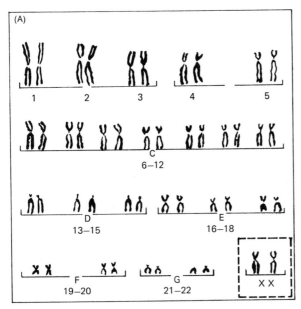

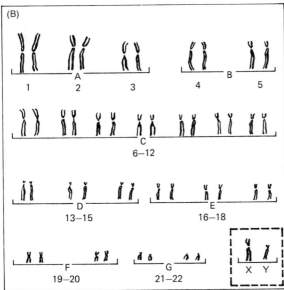

FIGURE 2-5 Human chromosome pairs. Drawing from photographs of full complement of chromosome pairs. Normal human beings have 23 pairs, or 46 chromosomes. (Drawing by Donna Thompson.)

A. Female chromosomes. Note sex chromosomes XX at position 23, separated by broken lines.

B. Male chromosomes. Note sex chromosomes XY at position 23, separated by broken lines.

Efforts to choose the sex of one's infant are based on knowledge of slight differences in the vulnerability of X- and Y-bearing sperm cells at the time of mating. Some evidence suggests that Y-bearing spermatids thrive in an alkaline environment and are destroyed in an acidic environment. A change from an acidic to an alkaline environment usually occurs in the cervical mucus at the time of ovulation. Couples who want to produce a boy are advised to have intercourse at the time of ovulation, or shortly thereafter. Couples who want a girl should time their mating a day or two prior to ovulation when the environment of the vagina is acidic and an X-bearing spermatid is more likely to survive the race to the ovum. Some research is underway to develop a chemical product the female would insert in the vagina which would be destructive of one type of spermatid and not of the other (Davis & Solomon, 1974, p. 285).

Genes: The Units of Heredity

The biological units that explain heredity and growth were discovered over a period of time in reverse order to their size. This was because the necessary improvement in laboratory techniques came very gradually. The new technology included microphotography and biochemical analysis so sophisticated that the working of cells could be observed. Cells, although described in theory for several decades, were confirmed when a microscope was developed to observe them during mitosis. The chromosomes within the cells were first seen after a light microscope was invented and complex procedures were devised for culturing and staining cell tissue. The structure of genes and their arrangement along the chromosome chain is now observable in a very limited way by x-ray photography through an electron microscope (Figure 2-6).

To discover how the genetic code is transmitted required a theory, a laboratory procedure, and advanced hardware for isolating the molecules and photographing them. The search for the gene is one of the most fascinating stories of molecular biology and requires an entire book for even a partial telling (Roller, 1974). This section presents only basic information that concerns the beginning of human life directly. This knowledge is essential for making private and public decisions about human reproduction, genetic selection, abortion laws, and preventive medicine.

Master Plan for Growth: DNA

The master plan of human development is coded, literally, in the structure of the chromosomes within the nucleus of each cell. This genetic code is made up of biochemical units that maintain a particular organization. The 23 pairs of human chromosomes are made up of chains of genes, sometimes extended into invisible threads and sometimes tightly coiled and visible. Each gene is a unique protein and each of about one million genes is assigned to a particular location along a particular chromosome strand.

The *gene* is a unit of hereditary material which transmits a set of traits from either parent to the offspring. A gene is sometimes defined as the point of activation in

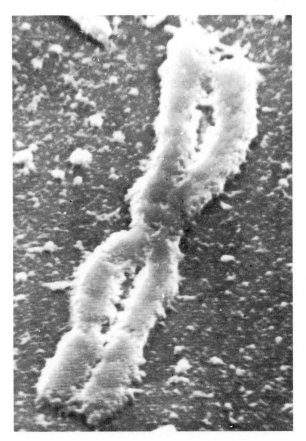

FIGURE 2-6 Electron micrograph of a metaphase chromosome. Two sister chromatids are joined at the region where a spindle fiber attaches and pulls them apart. (W. Scheid and H. Traut, *Mutation Research*, 11:254 [1971]. Courtesy of the authors.)

the prophase of cell division. The concept of genes was first conceived when geneticists observed that some traits, or sets of traits, were passed on intact to the next generation.

Further support for the reality of genes was discovered when certain traits became linked to the sex chromosomes. The relatively large X chromosome of the mother was observed to carry genetic material not matched in the relatively small Y chromosome that determined maleness. Hemophilia in boys and certain patterns of baldness in men are traits that consistently appeared to come from the mother's family line and showed in male offspring but not in daughters. Hemophilia was called the royal disease because it appeared in the family line of Queen Victoria and afflicted her sons and the sons of her daughters. This dramatic and historical event probably advanced the science of genetics throughout the Western world. The discovery of DNA (deoxyribonucleic acid) as both the carrier of the genetic code and the master plan of reproduction supported the early theory of genes. The concept of genes as unique proteins is very recent.

Little is known about the ordering of genes within the 46 chromosomes of each human cell. However, molecular biologists now regard the DNA double-helix coil as one chromatid of the chromosome pair. Biologists also consider the basic unit of growth to be a segment of the helix ladder which contains a particular unit of the genetic code (Figure 2-7). The double-helix chromosome model has become the common visual aid of museums and textbooks on biological science. The DNA components are the distinguishing features of a chromosome, but the smaller molecules (RNA, enzymes, and nutrients) enable the DNA to duplicate and to communicate with other cells throughout the body.

DNA, largest of the organic molecules, contains nearly all the hereditary material needed for the growth of a person. DNA molecules are slender (about 10 atoms across) and thousands of times greater in length, depending upon which of the DNA molecules is involved and which phase of duplication it is in. DNA molecules weigh hundreds of millions times as much as hydrogen molecules, the chemist's unit of comparison. Duplication of a chromosome is initiated by an enzyme message to one or more of the genes that lie along the DNA chain, probably at many points in close succession. One or more forms of RNA (ribonucleic acid) are believed to be the message content of the enzymes that stimulate growth.

Chemically speaking, DNA molecules consist of a complex arrangement of subunits called *nucleotides*. Bonded together they make up the intricate ladders of the double helix. Each nucleotide contains three chemical units: a sugar unit (deosyribose), a phosphate unit, and one of four base units (Roller, 1974). The sugar unit is constructed of five carbon atoms plus oxygen and hydrogen (Figure 2-8, left). The phosphate unit consists of a stable arrangement of phosphate and oxygen atoms. Together the sugar and phosphate units form the backbone of the DNA chain (Figure 2-8, middle). The third unit of the nucleotide, a weak base, may be any one of four organic molecules, commonly labeled and remembered by the capitalized first letter of the base name: adenine (A), cytosine (C), guanine (G), and thymine (T) (Figure 2-8, right). Note that each base contains nitrogen atoms, an element also found in all proteins. The four basic units attract in chemically compatible pairs to form rungs of the ladder, A with T and C with G.

The double edge of the DNA chain is formed from two strings of stable phosphates and sugars, bonded together by the hydrogen atoms of the base molecules in various arrangements of A-T, C-G, G-C, and T-A. A segment of a DNA arrangement along the chromosome chain is shown in Figure 2-9. Note that the double rings of A and G attach to the single rings of T and C, thus keeping the distance consistent between the two strands of the DNA chain and forming the horizontal hydrogen bars. In prometaphase, the double DNA chains twist and thicken to form the double-helix pattern familiar in atomic models of DNA. The stable skeleton of sugar and phosphates helps to maintain the proper sequence of the nucleotides during duplication.

The duplication of DNA, which is called *replication*, occurs within the cell nucleus prior to cell division and results in two identical strands, earlier described

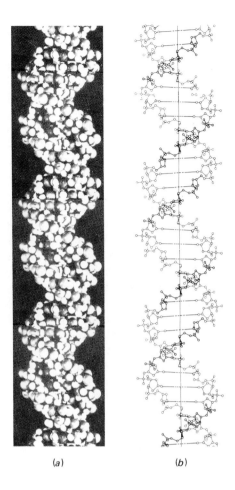

(a)   (b)

FIGURE 2-7 Model of a double helix. Photograph shows how the sugar-phosphate backbones twist around each other, with the base pairs lying between them. (Courtesy of M. H. F. Wilkins.)

as sister chromatids. When perfect duplication occurs, as is typical in mitosis, the process is called semiconservative replication (Figure 2-10A). Replication within a cell nucleus explains how sister cells are formed which carry identical genetic codes, but replication does not explain how the code for growth is transmitted to other cells as a blueprint for red blood cells or brown eye tissue. An intermediary holding pattern is needed. The templates which hold and communicate the genetic code to other cells are made up of RNA.

Specifications for Growth: RNA

RNA takes at least three different forms in performing three different functions of carrying segments of the genetic code from the DNA inside the nucleus through its walls to other cells. Messenger RNA (mRNA) is a segment of genetic information

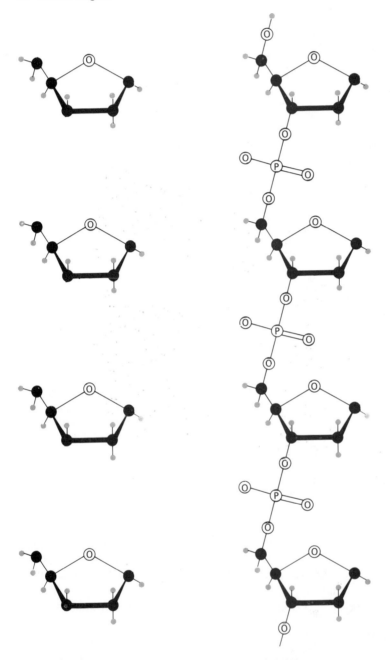

FIGURE 2-8 Structure of a DNA chain. Left: Sugar molecules with 5-carbon rings. Atoms are carbon, oxygen, and hydrogen. Middle: Alternating molecules of sugar and phosphate make up the backbone of DNA. Right: Four bases, T C A G, attach to the sugar-phosphate backbone to form one strand of the double helix DNA. Nitrogen atoms N are part of all nuclei bases.

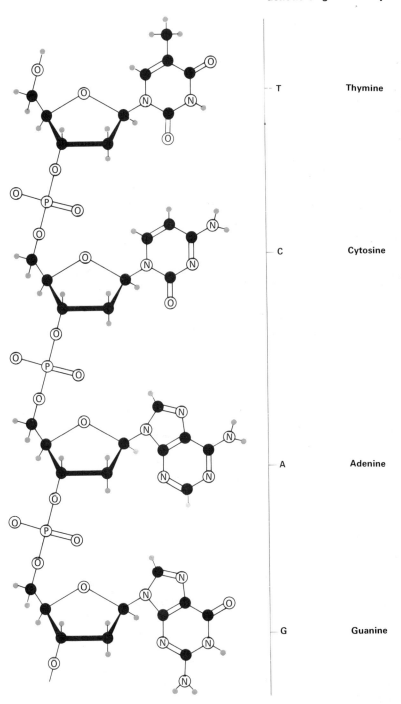

T   Thymine

C   Cytosine

A   Adenine

G   Guanine

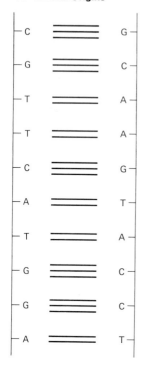

FIGURE 2-9 Arrangement of base units in a segment of DNA. Bonds form between C (cytosine) and G (guanine); between A (adenine) and T (thymine).

which is assembled inside the nucleus of the cell as a complementary pattern of one strand of DNA. This process is called *transcription*. A strand of mRNA is thought to be the length of a structural gene, therefore a relatively short strand. Being single, it can slip through the perforated nuclear wall while the larger chromosomes remain contained. Each unit (nucleotide) consists of a sugar (ribose in RNA), a phosphate, and one of four bases U, A, C, G. Note that U (uracil) replaces T and combines with A in making up a mirror image of the genetic material (Figure 2-10B).

Outside the cell nucleus, but still within the cell wall, the mRNA is recoded to transfer RNA (tRNA) and then to amino acid chains by a process called *translation* (Figure 2-10C). Note that the translation to tRNA returns the code sequence to the original arrangement in the DNA. There is one important difference—the substitution of uracil (U) for the original base thymine (T).

The process by which tRNA codes the assembly of amino acids that make up proteins is both intricate and fascinating. Tiny assembly factories called *ribosomes* line up along the mRNA strand and process the nucleotides in information-bearing groups of three. These three-base mRNA units, called *codons*, accept and attach a three-base unit of tRNA which carries the complementary triplet of the base code the *anticodon*, and an amino acid of like base combination (Figure 2-11). The

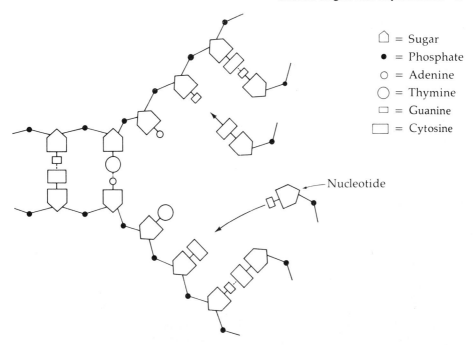

= Sugar
= Phosphate
= Adenine
= Thymine
= Guanine
= Cytosine

Nucleotide

FIGURE 2-10A Diagram of the replication of the DNA molecule during cell division. The double strand uncoils and opens, exposing the base units to growth material in the nucleus. Outer strands attract complementary base pairs (A-T and C-G) to form two new strings that are identical chromatids to the original pair.

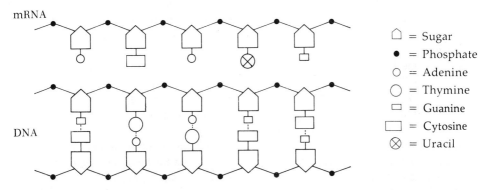

mRNA

DNA

= Sugar
= Phosphate
= Adenine
= Thymine
= Guanine
= Cytosine
= Uracil

FIGURE 2 10B Diagram of the transcription of a small segment of DNA, the genetic code to messenger RNA, a single-stranded complement of DNA. Note the replacement of uracil for thymine.

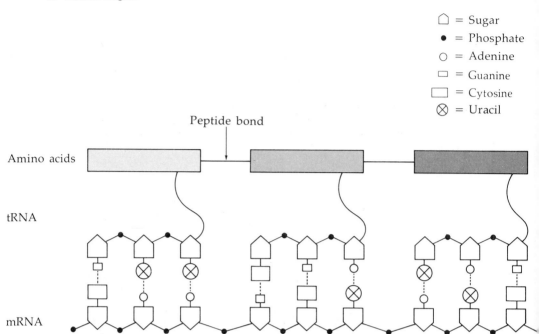

FIGURE 2-10C Diagram of the translation of messenger RNA to transfer RNA (tRNA) and to amino acid chains. The organization of amino acids on the peptide chain is determined in the genes.

Source: Philip L. Stein and Bruce M. Rowe, *Physical Anthropology*, pages 80, 82-83. Copyright 1974, McGraw-Hill Book Company. By permission of the publisher.

amino acids are bonded into peptide chains, according to the genetic instructions from the chromosomes, and the tRNA is released to assemble another (identical) amino acid.

Ribosomal RNA (rRNA) is associated with protein, but its functions are the least understood of the ribonucleic acids. It is stored in the nucleolus of the nucleus during prophase and probably has a role in producing and having available the proteins needed for chromosome duplication.

Amino Acids: The Units of Growth

Scientists discovered the triplet (three-base) message of the codon with the help of nutrition research which had already identified twenty different amino acids that combine to make up protein (Pai, 1974). This was a greater number than a double-base message (2X2X2) could account for. The code has now been deciphered as meaningful combinations of three of the four bases in the RNA molecules: uracil, adenine, guanine, and cytosine. Each codon represents an

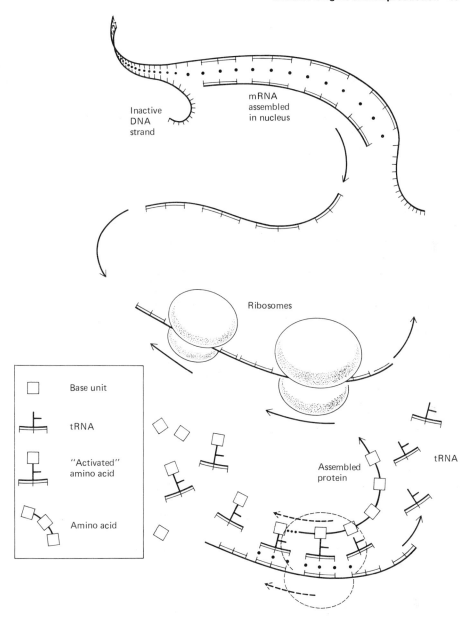

FIGURE 2-11 Detail of protein synthesis. The active strand of DNA is the template for mRNA, which is assembled in the nucleus. Ribosomes serve as assembly plants, which move along the chain, transcribing the complementary sequence (mRNA) to tRNA to triplets of bases that code for particular amino acids. (Drawings by Donna Thompson.)

amino acid, and each of the twenty amino acids is made up of a specific arrangement of the possible 64 triplet combinations (4X4X4) (Table 2-1). Several different combinations of bases (codons) may make up an amino acid, but the first two, and their order, are always the same. The replication of the DNA chain also occurs in meaningful segments of RNA that transcribe in meaningful triplets.

If the twenty amino acids are thought of as an alphabet and the four identifying bases are thought of as a Morse code (dot, dash, pause), the potential in the genetic code for communicating a complex blueprint can be understood. The million or so proteins that comprise a complement of chromosomes, if spelled out in maps of amino acids, would require ten volumes the size of this book! The complexity of the master plan for the growth of each human being is within the mathematical limits of this code, although scientists still have much to learn about the functions of individual genes. In humans, only a few of the genes have been located on particular chromosomes, usually through the absence of a functioning gene and the traits that are consistently associated with it.

One further step in protein synthesis is the structuring of body materials from the peptide chains (meaningful arrangements of amino acids). Proteins are exceedingly varied, not only because of the coded arrangement of the amino acids, but also because of the nature of the final bonding that produces such varied structures as blood, bone, and tissue. As shown in Figure 2-12, polypeptide chains are the primary structure of proteins formed when they bond chemically, end to end. The secondary structure is formed when the polypeptides arrange themselves in a pattern by coiling, as in the double helix. Other bonds are involved at a third level of

Table 2-1
ABREVIATIONS FOR THE AMINO ACIDS

UUU UUC	phen	UCU UCC	ser	UAU UAC	tyr	UGU UGC	cyst
UUA UUG	leu	UCA UCG		UAA UAG	nonsense	UGA UGG	nonsense try
CUU CUC CUA CUG	leu	CCU CCC CCA CCG	prol	CAU CAC / CAA CAG	his / gin	CGU CGC CGA CGG	arg
AUU AUC AUA	ileu	ACU ACC ACA	thr	AAU AAC / AAA AAG	asn / lys	AGU AGC / AGA AGG	ser / arg
AUG	met	ACG					
GUU GUC GUA GUG	val	GCU GCC GCA GCG	ala	GAU GAC / GAA GAG	asp / glu	GGU GGC GGA GGG	gly

Source: Anna C. Pai, *Foundations of Genetics*, page 138. Copyright 1974, McGraw-Hill Book Company.

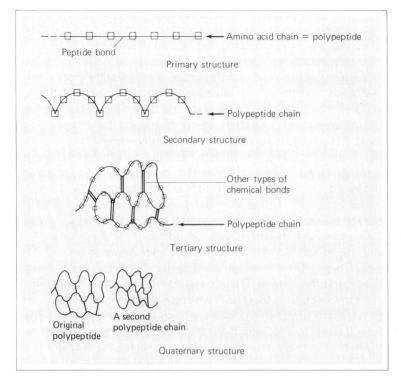

Primary structure

Secondary structure

Tertiary structure

Quaternary structure

FIGURE 2-12   Diagram of the structure of proteins. Polypeptide chains form increasingly complex structures which, in the final structure, form different body materials such as nerves, blood, bone, and tissue.

Source: Anna C. Pai, *Foundations of Genetics*, page 111. Copyright 1974, McGraw-Hill Book Company.

organization when several like chains of polypeptides bond. At the fourth level, which is identifiable in body structures, similar structures are bonded together to form a tissue or organ.

LEARNING AS GROWTH

The remarkable consistency in the way living cells function implies that the processes for genetic memory and memory storage are related. The growth of neural cells during the embryonic period, when the brain and nerve systems are formed, is controlled and patterned by RNA carriers of DNA codes. A similar process, involving tRNA and mRNA, transcribes experience into a memory code which the neural system stores for later use by the person. Scientists from many disciplines have been at work to create a biology of learning (Pribram, 1972). Their hypotheses differ in detail but each concerns the functioning of the large molecules (*macromolecules*) such as nucleic acids (RNA and DNA) and proteins. Protein synthesis is known to occur in the brain when learning is taking place (Wallace, 1975). These are difficult concepts, but central to the issues of heredity versus environment as they affect human development.

By looking at the life-cycle, how cells divide and how polypeptide chains bond into patterns, the growth of living tissues can be understood. The reproduction of chromosomes explains how the genetic plan is carried from parents to offspring. The translation of gene messages to the proteins of life and growth has been presented. The next step in understanding the nature of humans is to learn how cells differentiate in early development to form the different cell structures seen in the photographs in Figure 2-1. Growth is organized so that the human organism functions as an integrated whole from the moment of conception.

The concept of growth as learning is new to many people. At least three questions concern the relationship of brain and somatic (body) cells. First, how do some protein structures evolve as neural cells (for thinking), while other protein structures become the bones and muscles for doing what the brain orders? The answer, in part, is in biological differentiation. Second, how does the common anatomy of cells adapt to the special functions of memory and communication? The answer involves the existence of an electrochemical code and the ma ny forms of RNA. Third, how do the physical processes of growth and the psychological process of learning interact? Interdisciplinary studies suggest that although the separation of growth and learning may be convenient for scholars, in reality they are part of one interdependent process, at least in the early stages of life.

Differentiation in Biology

The process of *differentiation* begins with early cell division, moments after 23 chromosomes from each parent unite to recreate a 46-chromosome cell, or *zygote*. Differentiation in biology means the formation during development of different organic structures to perform different life functions. Early differentiation in the zygote results from the growth of three layers of cells. The outer layer of cells and tissues becomes the brain and nervous system (Chapter 3). The neural system, throughout the body, is comprised of neural cells that duplicate from this initial outer layer, the *ectoderm*.

Neural cells are unique in that nearly all of them (11 billion) are present, at least in rudimentary form, at birth. Rakic (1974) studied neural cell formation in the visual cortex layers of rhesus monkey infants. By injecting a dye into the fetuses of twelve female monkeys at different stages of pregnancy, he was able to identify the "birthday" of neural cells as the time DNA is replicated and to chart the development of the cortex. He learned that neural cells divide along the inner area of the ectoderm, near the blood supply to the brain. From there they gravitate to their appropriate location in the layers of the cerebral cortex. Layers V and VI, the innermost (deep) layers are formed first, near the end of the first trimester of fetal life. The cell bodies of layers IV to I are formed during the second trimester. Within three to seven days after a cell's birthday it has gravitated to its proper location.

Although the timetable proceeds more slowly for human embryos, they develop by a comparable sequence which gives growth priority to the brain. Most neural cell bodies are in place by the end of the second trimester. The axons and dendrites, which interconnect the cells, begin to grow early in fetal life and continue to grow through most of adult life. Experience is coded by sense receptors, and these impulses are communicated along appropriate pathways of the nervous system (Figure 2-13). The stimulation to neurons from the environment within the uterus is believed necessary to the growth of the nervous system.

Anatomy of Neural Cells

The neuron is the basic unit of the central nervous system. Figure 2-14 shows a prototype of the structure of a neuron from a human cortex. Like other cell bodies brain cells include a nucleus, a cell body, and a surrounding wall which controls the environment of the cytoplasm (nutrients, enzymes, nucleic acids, protein structures). Each brain cell nucleus contains a full complement of chromosomes, hence a complete genetic code for the proteins involved in the coding of sensory

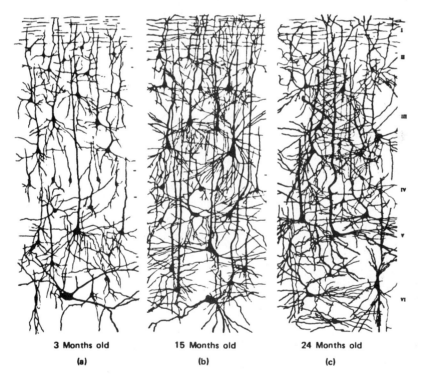

3 Months old	15 Months old	24 Months old
(a)	(b)	(c)

FIGURE 2-13   Drawings of stained sections from the cerebral cortical areas of infants. Note the increased elaboration of the dendrite system.

Source: J. L. R. Conel, The postnatal development of the cerebral cortex. © (a) 1947, (b) 1955, (c) 1959 by the Harvard University Press. By permission of the publisher.

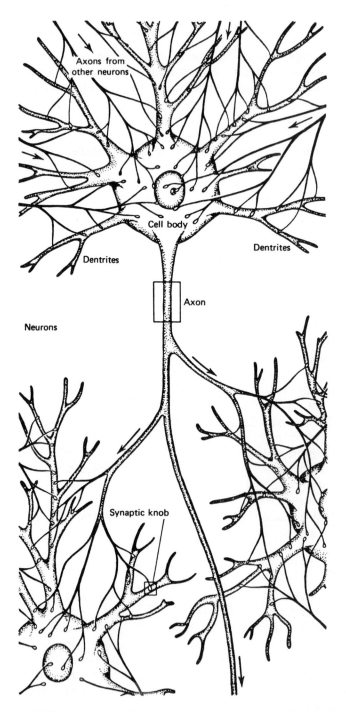

FIGURE 2-14 Drawings of a prototype of a cortical cell. Dentrites transmit impulses to the cell body. The axon carries cell activation information to other neurons.

Source: Mildred C. Robeck and John A. R. Wilson, *Psychology of Reading*, page 52. Copyright, Wiley and Sons, 1974. By permission.

experience and memory storage. Neurons are classified according to their function: *receptors*, which detect and code sensory experience; *connectors*, which communicate messages within the system; and *effectors*, whose axons terminate in muscles and glands. Physical appearance of the neurons varies according to these functions, but the organization and communication within a cell body is basic to all.

The effect heredity has on intelligence resides in at least several different genes, which is one reason their location on particular chromosomes is difficult. Since they do not continue to duplicate, the chromosomes of brain cells remain locked within the wall of the nucleus throughout the life of an individual. These genes are the DNA transcribers of RNA, some forms of which can pass through outer cell walls and communicate with other cells. It is known that the nucleolus of a brain cell is heavily weighted with rRNA, or some macromolecule with similar proportions of uracil (Hyden, 1969).

Growth and learning occur together as the extension of the neural system increases the capability of the central nervous system to communicate. In development axons are sent out from one cell body to genetically determined locations throughout the nervous system. Neural cells are rich in RNA compared with other cells. One function of mRNA and tRNA is the transcription and translation of the genetic plan to particular proteins needed for growth.

Learning involves both the coding of sensations picked up by the neural receptors and the storing of coded information for future use. Learning is considered an ontogenic process which is possible through exercise of genetic structures. Pribram (1971) suggested that memory is encoded initially in the protein structure of the cytoplasm of cells. Complex brain functioning, such as thought, requires many patterns of activation across the dendrite structures. This neural activity is not fully understood, but it is known that increased protein synthesis occurs during new experiences that result in learning. At least some neuropsychologists believe that exercise of the system (through sensory stimulation) promotes the growth of neural structures, which are the control mechanisms for growth of the organism as a whole.

Inheritance of Behavior

In development there is no clear separation between growth and learning. All growth is learning in the sense that neural structures are required for actions and reactions, whether the activity is internal (thought) or external and can be observed by others. These neural structures develop and change as a function of the interaction between the child and the environment. Very little growth (in a physical sense) is possible without learning (behavior change in sensorimotor structures). The neural cells that receive and code sensory information are developed from the same layer of ectoderm as the effectors of muscle action.

The same forms of RNA that carry growth messages are found to be associated with learning in laboratory animals. Hyden (1969) created a laboratory environment in which right-pawed mice learned to reach deep into a test tube to retrieve food pellets. Some mice were sacrificed in order to analyze the RNA content of the cells of the motor control areas of the brain. It was found that RNA weights increased significantly in the motor areas of the left hemisphere where right-pawed action is controlled. Litter mates of these mice were forced to relearn the task after the right paw was bound. The mice with changed handedness, also sacrificed, showed increased RNA content in the motor control areas of the right hemisphere. Even more surprising was a decrease in the C (cytosine) and G (guanine) content in the formerly dominant left hemisphere, suggesting a possible transfer of RNA material.

A different question, equally significant and more obscure, involves the extent to which behavior is inherited through the genetic code. Granted that Johnnie's lack of interest in books reflects his model (father) who avoids reading, the possibility of a gene-based factor must be considered. Are behaviors such as cognitive style, mixed hand-eye dominance, or slowness in processing symbolic information inherited? Hicks and Kinsbourne (1976) reported that 90 percent of humans in several cultures studied used the right hand for skilled activities. By adulthood their writing hand correlated significantly with handedness in natural parents but not with stepparents.

Teachers wonder whether special aptitudes for learning, such as motor talent or verbal abilities, are inherited. In the biological sciences, questions such as these emerge in the discussions of species-specific behaviors. Pribram is one of many psychologists to be concerned with inherited mechanisms in language and learning.

I have always been puzzled by the category "species-specific." In man, for example, the most characteristic species-specific behavior is the making of propositional utterances. . . . For me, the important problem is to discern the mechanism that allows us to make propositional utterances when this appears precluded in the apes. We inherit something that *structures* our communication and that other creatures do not share. Yet the *content* of our language is obviously learned: some of us discourse in English, others in Arabic, still others in Chinese. For me . . . the question is to define the innate structure or structures of this species-specific behavior. . . . (Pribram, 1969, p. 2)

As Pribram implies, the symbols of communication reflect the particular learning environment of the child, but the neural structures that are used to assimilate and organize linguistic units are part of human inheritance. The same biochemical processes that explain growth are probably involved. Increases in cell weight have been associated with the organism's increased control over body structures. Sometimes this control is automatic and primarily innate; sometimes control is voluntary and is monitored consciously by the human individual.

As the functions of RNA and protein synthesis in learning are understood, the interaction of innate and learned behavior can be used to help enhance learning opportunities for children. It is critical that the adults who control the learning environments of the future also evolve a standard of ethics which gives the child as much control as possible over his or her own learning.

The discussion to this point has focused on the anatomy and functions of cells as the basis for reproduction and growth in all humans. The next section considers how these principles affect the endless variations in behavior and appearance that we observe in human individuals.

PHYSICAL BASES FOR INDIVIDUAL UNIQUENESS

Biologists define a species by describing the physical characteristics that are common to all its members. To state this idea more scientifically, species are morphologically similar and they can mate to produce offspring. To this point, Chapter 2 has focused on the processes of heredity and reproduction that are characteristic of and common to the species Homo sapiens. All scientists are aware, of the *variability*, or range of individual differences, within a species. The human species is the most complex species on earth, and shows the greatest range of uniqueness among its members. There are phylogenic advantages to the species and ontogenic advantages to the individual because of this variability.

Advantages in Variability

Because of variation among members, Homo sapiens was able to survive 200,000 years of climatic change and ecological competition. The species was enhanced in the process (Stein & Rowe, 1974, p. 353). Variability within the species allowed some members to survive these challenges and to reproduce, passing on to their offspring the characteristics that were associated with survival. The uniqueness of human potential has enhanced the group's ability to organize and to cooperate in the competition with other species for food and space. Complex societies evolve as individuals find and develop their specialized abilities.

Society generally is strengthened and enriched by members who can contribute different kinds of service and unusual talents. From prehistoric times, human groups have selected the hunters, the artists, the healers, and the cooks for specific kinds of work that were needed and appreciated by others. In some societies these roles have been "inherited" by tradition; but in other cultures the interests and abilities of the youngster have been more important than following the parent's role in the group. Historically, roles have generally divided along sex lines to the disadvantage of the women, although some societies live by a matriarchial organization in which unusual control over family, economics, and culture has been exercised by women.

When a society undergoes great change, as American Indian people did when Europeans arrived with their superior weaponry, some flexibility in role and ability is advantageous. Indian tribes who rigidly defined the role of males as hunters have found adaptation to modern living very difficult. Individuals who were allowed to practice (or allowed themselves to practice) the crafts or the service skills were better able to survive by doing work that was seen as important. Individuals within a society, especially the children, increase their potential for later adaptation by learning many skills at the participation level and also becoming good at something the culture values. Many of the physical traits that make individuals unique can be explained by the laws of genetics.

Genetic Principles of Mendel

Gregor Mendel is recognized as the founder of modern genetics. Although his work preceded the present knowledge of DNA or chromosomes, he discovered the laws of heredity and stated them so precisely that, with few modifications, they have come to be called laws, rather than the theories he presented. Mendel bred pure strains of sweet peas according to traits such as red-white color, short-tall stems, green-yellow pods. His experiment was a model of the scientific method. His choice of seven particular characteristics, which later were found to be expressed by seven different genes, was more than a happy accident because he observed and selected traits that were clearly expressed from generation to generation.

Mendel's now famous experiments with sweet peas shattered the belief, common in the nineteenth century, that mating resulted in a "blending" of parental traits. His work required (1) breeding pure strains of sweet peas, (2) controlling their pollination so that the heredity (genotype) would be known, (3) carefully counting characteristics of phenotypes, and (4) analyzing the results mathematically. Mendel hypothesized the existence of the genetic unit now called the gene, and discovered the principle of dominant-recessive characteristics. The same genetic principles Mendel discovered in plants now apply to human inheritance but they have been restated in the context of present knowledge (Davis & Solomon, 1974, p. 359).

LAW OF DISCRETE UNITS

Mendel's first principle states that hereditary traits are transmitted intact, in units (called genes) which exist in pairs. Genes do not mix, but emerge as distinct characteristics (phenotypes) in offspring. Each gene has its location (locus) on a chromosome. Gene pairs, called *alleles*, each carry the genetic code for a particular trait (Figure 2-15a). For example, a pair of alleles might code for hair texture. The phenotype of an individual is the observable characteristic(s). The genotype is the genetic makeup of an individual, which includes the genes not expressed of the gene pairs.

LAW OF SEGREGATION

During meiosis, when the cell divides to 23 chromosome gametes, each receives one gene of each allelic pair. When alleles are mixed (genetically impure), the pair is called *heterozygous*. Upon separation, one gene goes to one gamete, and the other (unlike) gene goes to a different gamete. The genes both carry the blueprint for the same traits, but the specifications are different; one gene becomes half the genotype of the new organism and one gene is lost to that individual (Figure 2-15b). To follow the example of hair texture, one gene might code for straight hair while the other allele might code for curly hair.

LAW OF DOMINANCE

According to the third law, when two alternative forms of the same gene are present in the genotype of an individual, only one is expressed in the phenotype.

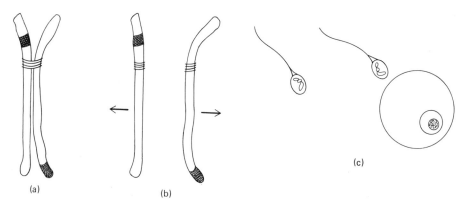

FIGURE 2-15 Drawing of the location and separation of allelic genes. (a) Each gene has a location (locus) on the chromosome which is identical for gene pairs (alleles). (b) During meiosis allelic genes separate. (c) Allelic genes go to different gametes, only one of which reproduces. (Drawing by Donna Thompson.)

When two gametes unite in conception to form a zygote, the chromosome number is restored to 46, meaning that two genes are again available as genetic material. The gene which is expressed as a trait is called *dominant*. When a gene trait is inherited but does not appear as a phenotype of the individual, the gene is said to be *recessive*. Table 2-2 shows traits that tend to be dominant when alleles from the two parents include one dominant and one recessive gene. Gene expression is influenced by the environment, and gene effects are varied. A person may have one attached ear and one free earlobe, or, rarely, one brown and one blue eye.

LAW OF INDEPENDENT ASSORTMENT

If two or more independent characteristics are involved in a cross, each characteristic is inherited without relation to other traits. All possible combinations will appear in the gametes. When Mendel crossed two different (but pure) strains such as long stems/short stems, the first generation usually looked alike. (The phenotype was determined by Mendel's law of dominance.) The second generation, however, showed predictable ratios of three tall- to one short-stemmed plant (Figure 2-16). When neither trait is dominant, and one masks the other, the offspring of the first generation will be look alikes, but will be different from either parent. The second generation will show a predictable 1:2:1 ratio, two being like the parents, one reverting to one genotype, and the other reverting to the other genotype.

Mendel's law of independent assortment is shown in Figure 2-16, where all possible combinations of curly hair (C), straight hair (s), brunette (B), and red head (r) are shown. In real life these predicted combinations hold true for large numbers of people over several generations. The probability of particular gene combinations showing in the children of a couple is a problem for experts.

Table 2-2
SOME DOMINANT AND RECESSIVE HUMAN TRAITS

Trait	Dominant	Recessive
Eye characteristics	Brown, hazel, or green	Blue or gray
	Astigmatism and far-sightedness	Normal
	Normal	Nearsightedness (a less common form is dominant)
	Normal	Red-green color blindness (sex-linked)
	Long lashes	Short lashes
	Tendency to cataracts	Normal
Nose	High convex bridge	Straight or concave bridge
	Narrow bridge	Broad bridge
	Straight tip	Upturned tip
	Flaring nostrils	Narrow nostrils
Ears	Free earlobe	Attached earlobe
Other facial traits	Full lips	Thin lips
	Normal	Recessive chin
	Dimpled chin	Undimpled chin
	Dimpled cheeks	Undimpled cheeks
	High cheekbones	Normal
	Freckled	Nonfreckled
Hair	Dark	Blond
	Nonred	Red
	Kinky	Curly
	Curly	Straight

The genes for skin color are expressed in the phenotype very much as some flower colors are. Mendel crossed red and white sweet peas, which appeared as all pink in the first generation. In human beings, skin color is influenced by at least three different genes, so the combinations are more complex than any of the illustrations shown here. A black/white skin cross would likely result in neither extremely black nor very white offspring. The subsequent result of such hybrid crosses would result in large numbers of individuals with medium pigmented skin and some who were very dark or very light.

Process of Crossing Over

The intriguing question that remains is how heredity achieves a mix in the chromosomes from the two parents. It will be recalled that gametes, the 23 chromosome cells of conception, are produced through meiosis. At prophase I, each chain of a chromosome pair replicates, forming a tetrad, or four chains of comparable genetic material (Figure 2-17). According to one theory, breaks occur

Table 2-2 (Continued)
SOME DOMINANT AND RECESSIVE HUMAN TRAITS

Trait	Dominant	Recessive
	Baldness (males)	Normal
	Normal	Baldness (females)
	White forelock	Normal
	Premature grayness	Normal
	Abundant hair on body	Sparse
	Heavy, bushy eyebrows	Normal
Hands, fingers toes	Index finger longer than ring finger (in males)	Index finger longer than ring finger (in females)
	Second toe longer than big toe	Second toe shorter than big toe
	Hypermobility of thumb	Normal
	Right-handedness	Left-handedness
Other	Dark skin color	Light skin color
	A, B, AB blood groups	Group O
	Tendency to varicose veins	Normal
	Normal	Phenylketonuria
	Normal	Tendency to schizophrenia
	Normal	Congenital deafness
	Normal	Tendency to diabetes mellitus
	Normal	Hemophilia (sex-linked)
	Normal	Albinism

Source: Ann Roller, *Discovering the Basis of Life*, page 32. Copyright 1974, McGraw-Hill Book Company.

in the chain and segments of the chain containing groups of comparable gene units are interchanged. The genetic instructions remain complete because of the organization of comparable genes (alleles) away from the centromere. Upon the first division of the cell, these chromosome crossovers, carrying new combinations of genes, will separate. Upon the second division, each chain will be assigned to only one of four gametes, and, in normal births, only one gamete will provide the genetic inheritance at conception.

Crossing over has enabled geneticists to map the location of certain genes on the chromosome chain. Genes that appear on the same chromosome are said to be linked. When linked genes are seen in "impossible" combinations, in terms of genetic prediction, they are identified as having crossed over. Because the likelihood of crossing over increases with the distance between gene locuses, the ordering of many alleles has been calculated. About 10 percent of the characteristics of an individual cannot be attributed to Mendel's laws and are thought to indicate crossing over (Davis & Solomon, 1974, p. 368).

To summarize, genetic uniqueness occurs in several ways. First, variation in

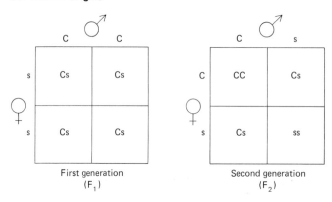

First generation
(F₁)

Second generation
(F₂)

FIGURE 2-16A A. Possible combinations of pure genotypes.
Mendel's law of dominance states that one gene expresses a
characteristic, while the other does not. Dominant traits are
usually shown in capital letters (C for curly hair) and recessive
traits in lowercase letters (s for straight hair). The father carries
2 alleles for curly hair and all the children potentially have curly
hair, the prototype.

B. Possible combinations of second generation having crossed
or mixed genotype. Both parents carry curly hair/straight hair
genes. Their offspring may be curly haired CC, Cs, Cs; or
straight haired ss, by a ratio of 3:1.

individuals is assured by the potential combinations of twenty amino acids and
four bases of the DNA molecules that make up the master plan. Roller (1974, p. 159)
estimates that diagrams of the molecular structure of the million genes arranged
along the chromosomes would fill ten volumes the size of this book. Stein and
Rowe (1974, p. 74) point out that the possible recombinations of 23 pairs of
chromosomes number 8,324,608.

Another source of variability is recombination of the genes through the joint
heredity of two parents according to the laws discovered by Mendel. It is important
to understand that either gene of a pair (of alleles) is expressed in the phenotype
and that characteristics do not appear on a 50:50 ratio from each parent. Heredity
is further complicated by the existence of suppressor genes which modify the
expression of other genes (pleiotropism). Multiple alleles (such as those which
code three blood types, A, B, O) are known to exist in more than two forms
although they occupy only one locus (Figure 2-18). Genetic knowledge of multiple
alleles is critical in blood transfusion where mixing blood types can cause fatal
action of the antibodies in the plasma on the foreign antigens of incompatible
blood.

A third source of variability is crossing over: genetic material is not inherited
exactly as it existed in the parent. Variation among gametes assures variation
among living individuals, the biological basis of selection. There will never be
another person genetically like yourself unless you are an identical twin.

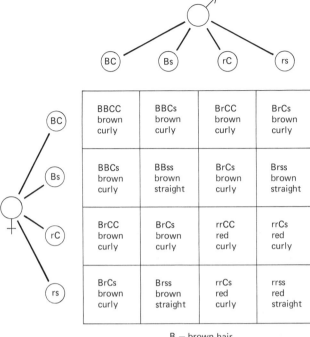

B — brown hair
C — curly hair
r — red hair
s — straight hair

FIGURE 2-16B Independent assortment of inherited traits. When one considers that approximately 1 million genes make up the chromosome chains, the complexity of human genetics is apparent. In the example, two individuals mate who have brown curly hair (phenotype). Because of recessive genes in the genotype, these many characteristics are possible in their offspring.

Finally, *mutation* is an abrupt change in genetic makeup which is not due to crossing over, but to change in quality or arrangement of genes. Mutation changes the ordering of bases; hence, the coding of amino acids and the transcription of proteins are changed in the individual and in future generations.

GENETIC SELECTION IN HUMANS

The survival of a species is made more likely by a wide range of variability in its individual members. Differences allow some members to adapt to change and to continue to reproduce while others do not mature and reproduce. Modern changes which will affect the future of the race include both changes in climate and human-created hazards that threaten the ecosystem. The long-term effects of

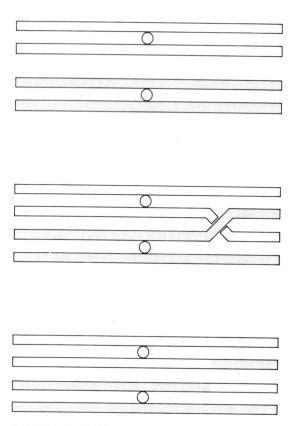

FIGURE 2-17 Diagram of the recombination of genes by crossing over during meiosis.

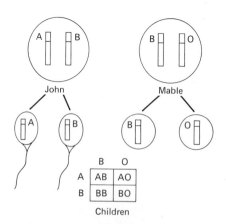

FIGURE 2-18 Diagram of multiple alleles. More than two forms exist, as in blood types. In this cross, each parent provides only two kinds of gametes, but their combination results in four possible genotypes.

changes in the physical environment are beyond the scope of this book. Concerns for our children, present and future, are relevant here.

Knowing the effects of natural selection over time helps to identify genetically based anomalies and to provide a compensating environment. Genetic selection that accrues from differences between males and females in mammals is important in parenting. Some cultures dictate who marries whom and thus exert control over transmission of genes to new generations.

Natural Selection over Time

In a species as varied as humans, the pressures of life are certain to be selective in their impact. An epidemic, for example, would have its differential impact on a family according to standards of cleanliness, general fitness, and adaptiveness in crises. For example, childrearing in a sterile environment would deny the child antibodies, and leave him or her vulnerable to an epidemic. In contrast, certain blood types can favor recovery and build immunity, such as type ABO in smallpox epidemics (Stein & Rowe, 1974, pp. 120–124). When large numbers of a population fail to survive and reproduce, the gene pool of that population changes to increase the incidence of the characteristics in those who survive.

Dominant traits that are fatal to children, such as cancer of the retina, are very rare because the patient dies before the age of reproduction and the allele that is responsible is lost. Hemophilia, which is a recessive trait, tends to be more durable in a population because it is carried in the genotype, without showing up in the phenotype where natural selection would tend to eliminate the alleles from the gene pool (only homozygous recessive individuals are eliminated). Up to 25 percent of hemophilias have no family history of the "bleeding" disease (Marx, 1975). Mutations continue to recreate the amino acid irregularities which then continue to be carried in the gene.

Bisexual Selection in Mammals

Many accidents of meiosis are eliminated at conception because alleles are not properly matched and the zygote does not develop or attach. Genetic selection also occurs from having two alleles available for a single hereditary unit. All mammals have the hereditary advantages that result from different and sex-related selection processes at conception.

Competition of Spermatozoa

Selectivity in the male's contribution of genes results from the numerous gametes in coitus and the competition between sperm cells in the race to reach and penetrate the ovum. Of the 200 to 500 million sperm cells ejaculated in human copulation, only one fertilizes the ovum. Some selection factors are strength and rate of motility, orientation toward the chemical messages of a mature ovum, and survival in the chemical environment of the female vagina. The spermatozoan is one of the smallest cells in the human body (Nilsson, 1974). The bombardment of the wall of the ovum by many spermatozoa is thought to allow one to penetrate (Langman, 1975).

Production of sperm cells is stimulated at puberty by two hormones, testosterone and androsterone (in addition to the estrogens). This production continues into later years in reduced numbers. Sexual fitness in a male also includes production of the secretions that provide chemical protection for spermatozoa and enhance their motility. There is some evidence in lower mammals that the number of penetrations and the duration of the stimulation during copulation contribute to the pregnancy rate. If this factor holds in humans, the nature of the intercourse could be an additional selective factor in heredity.

Nurturance of the Ovum

While competition and proliferation are selective factors among fathers, maternal selectivity is focused on nurturance and timely preparation of the ovum. Only about 1000 egg cells mature during the lifetime of a woman. In meiosis only one of four gametes receives a major portion of the cytoblast, the gamete that is fertilized. Cytoblast carries both nutrients and hereditary coding for early growth and cell differentiation. The ovum is the largest of human cells. From puberty to menopause the female's biological cycle is hormonally tuned to production and release of one egg cell per month and the readiness of uterus walls for nurturance of a potential zygote. The focus of the menstrual cycle is the readiness for one offspring and is accomplished through the interaction of five hormones (Langman, 1975). Probably the genetic material of the relatively large X chromosome is responsible for the coding of these hormones and some other sex-linked characteristics. It is probable, also, that the cytoblast of the ovum is responsible for the environmental conditions within the cell that initiate the differential growth in the early stages of the zygote.

In coitus, female responsiveness increases the blood supply within the pelvis area and engorges the erectile tissues in the clitoris and vagina (Sherfey, 1972). Sex activities in mating which assure an increased blood supply to the wall of the uterus are likely to contribute to pregnancy. Considering the high proportion of couples who want but do not conceive children this factor of sexuality, or mutual participation in the sex act, is likely to affect the gene pool in the long run.

Social and Cultural Influences on Mating

The physical characteristics which come to be value in a culture influence the mating choices of couples. Only the extremes of pulchritude or ugliness are likely to be agreed on from one culture to another. Cultural groups which place great emphasis on physical beauty find ways, such as using makeup, wearing fancy dress, or undergoing plastic surgery, to compensate for or correct undesired characteristics. Families who can afford orthodontics may increase the chances that their daughter will marry well, but she may expect to go through the same expensive process of having the teeth of her children straightened.

Families who require that their children marry within a selective (minority) class may have so little choice of mates that inbreeding results. When this happens recessive genes are likely to match, and undesirable phenotypes are likely to emerge. Hemophiliacs among the royal families of Europe in the eighteenth and nineteenth centuries have been cited as one example. Some inbred groups, such as the royalty of native Hawaiians, practiced infanticide to eliminate defective heirs and improve the gene pool. Advanced societies usually opt to care for defective offspring, often well enough so that they mate and rear children.

GENETIC DEFECTS AND DISEASES

Only a few years ago, inherited birth defects were estimated to occur approximately once in 100 live births. Recently there has been an increase from 1 to approximately 3 percent, and heredity is thought to be a significant factor in an additional 5 percent. Birth defects are a national health problem. Davis and Solomon (1974, p. 384) report that approximately 25 percent of all pregnancies abort spontaneously because of fatal defects in the chromosomes. Langman (1975) reports that natural abortions may be as high as 47 percent. Each person typically carries an estimated eight defective genes, but these are usually recessive and are masked by a healthy gene which determines the phenotype, or observable characteristics.

Abnormal Chromosome Separation

During meiosis, the chromosome pairs are disjoined (separated) and incorporated into different gametes. If the separation is imperfect, one cell will receive additional (duplicated) chromosome portions while the other gamete will be missing genetic material. Sometimes an entire chromosome is displaced. The most common abnormal chromosome disjunctions occur in the sex chromosomes. Table 2-3 shows combinations of sex chromosomes which exist in individuals. XX and XY are normal; XO indicates an individual with 45 chromosomes. Multiple sex chromo-

Table 2-3
COMBINATIONS OF SEX CHROMOSOMES WHICH EXIST IN INDIVIDUALS

	Sex phenotype	Fertility	Number of barr bodies	Sex-chromosome constitutions
Normal male	Male	+	0	XY
Normal female	Female	+	1	XX
Turner's syndrome	Female	−	0	XO
Klinefelter's syndrome	Male	−	1	XXY
XYY syndrome	Male	+	0	XYY
Triple X syndrome	Female	±	2	XXX
Triple XY syndrome	Male	−	2	XXXY
Tetra X syndrome	Female	?	3	XXXX
Tetra XY syndrome	Male	−	3	XXXXY
Penta X syndrome	Female	?	4	XXXXX

Source: Anna C. Pai, *Foundations of Genetics*, page 226. Copyright 1974, McGraw-Hill Book Company.

somes increase the normal complement beyond 46 chromosomes. Mosaicking occurs when the cells of different body parts or locations differ in their chromosome constitution.

Sex Chromosome Disjunction

Turner's syndrome is an abnormality in females which is caused by the lack of one X chromosome (XO), presumably because the unfertilized gamete received three sex chromosomes rather than two. The individual shows lack of development of the breasts, and, because of undeveloped ovaries, is sterile. Some depression of intelligence is often reported, and webbing at the sides of the neck is typical. The Turner's-syndrome individual has a total chromosome count in the karyotype of 45, rather than the normal complement of 46.

An interesting but unanswered question about Turner's syndrome arises because the second X chromosome has been observed to be present within the cell nucleus but to remain inactive during development. Evidence is accumulating that one chromsome may be inactive in some cells while both are active in other cells. This observation raises the possibility that chemical treatment could be found to stimulate the inactive chromosome. The incidence at birth of Turner's syndrome is 1 in 2500 (Hurst, 1972).

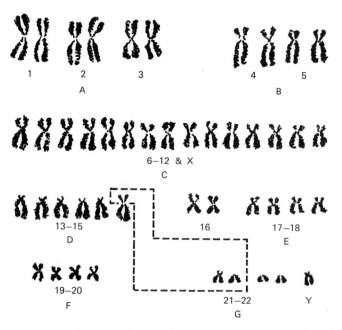

FIGURE 2-19 Translocation of chromosomes in Down's syndrome. The arm of chromosome 21 is attached to a D group chromosome. Translocation can occur in either sex. (Drawing by Donna Thompson.)

Klinefelter's syndrome is a male abnormality in which two female chromosomes, plus the male chromosome, XXY, are contained in each cell. This individual, who has a total of 47 chromosomes, is male, taller than average, has underdeveloped genitals and some breast development, and is sterile. Klinefelter's syndrome may be caused when a spermatozoan from a nondisjunction XY cell fertilizes a normal X cell, or when a nondisjunction ovum XX is fertilized by a normal Y cell. Klinefelter's syndrome is present in 1 of 400 male births (Hurst, 1972).

Another syndrome, XYY, is created by nondisjunction of the Y chromatids prior to the second division of meiosis. There have been reports that aggressive and hostile behavior accompanies this condition (Jacobs, 1965). A significantly high percentage of XYY has been found in male state hospital patients who are considered dangerous. Recent attempts to research the XYY syndrome for personality related traits, by taking chromosome counts of a large population of infants and following their later development, have been thwarted by pressure groups who object to the study on the ground that childrearing practices might be altered by previous knowledge of chromosome irregularity. Hook (1973) has suggested that broad studies of genotypes XXY, YYX, and XXYY be made.

There is a tendency for mental retardation to be associated with an abnormal number of sex chromosomes. Davis and Solomon (1974) have pointed out that approximately 12 percent of all genes are involved in brain development. The expectation that additional chromosomes produced a "supersex," either male or female, appears not to be true. Part of the price humans pay for the advantages of brain specialization is the possible effect on intelligence of a wide range of genetic irregularities.

Mosaicism is the coexistence in an individual of somatic (body) cells of genetically different types. Mosaicking is caused by gene mutations, especially nondisjunction, after fertilization or by fusion of embryos. For example, when a condition such as Down's is present in A cells but not in B cells, there may be little evidence of the disease. Some females have one X chromosome active in some cells and the other sex chromosome active in other cells. Apparently the Barr body (still present in female cells) was not inactivated early in development. Females having two active X chromosomes are helping scientists study cell growth in heart disease and cancer (Benditt, 1977). Sex chromosomes are distinguished from *autosomes*, which are all chromosomes other than the sex chromosomes.

Down's Syndrome

Down's syndrome, commonly but improperly called mongolism, is the most common of the autosomal abnormalities. It is a condition in which more than the normal complement of chromosome material is contained in the cell. There are three different chromosomal rearrangements which cause the symptoms: trisomy, translocation, and mosaicking. Trisomy, the most frequent cause of Down's syndrome, shows three, rather than two, number 21 chromosomes. Translocation usually shows a karyotype in which one chromosome has an abnormally long arm, meaning additional genes. Often the genes attach to chromosome 19 in the example (Figure 2-19). Translocation usually occurs during the prophase of meiosis.

The infant who inherits Down's syndrome shows lack of muscle tone, mental retardation, and certain physical characteristics which identify the condition to the trained professional even before a karyotype is ordered. The physical traits are folds in the eyelids, small ears, wispy hair, transparent skin, and unusual hand creases. Many Down's individuals have loops rather than whorls in the fingerprints and a short little finger, often with one less joint. Programs which begin in infancy, designed to teach body control and language skills, are producing amazing results in Down's-syndrome children (Chapter 14).

Enzyme Malfunctions

Some inherited diseases are caused by the lack or malfunction of an enzyme. Enzymes, like other proteins, are coded in the DNA. Phenylketonuria (PKU) is a common disease in infants which is caused by a malfunction in metabolism. The enzyme which breaks down the amino acid phenylalanine to the essential amino acid tyrosine is lacking. As a consequence the unmetabolized amino acid builds up in the blood and damages neural tissue and cells. The disease can be treated by control of proteins in the diet from birth to adolescence. Urine tests for PKU are routinely given neonates born in hospitals. The responsible gene is recessive; therefore both parents must have carried it unless a new mutation has occurred.

Sickle-cell anemia is a disease caused by the substitution of one amino acid for another in the hemoglobin cells. This inherited form of anemia gets its name from the elongation of red blood cells, which are normally saucer shaped. These distorted cells are low in the ability to transport oxygen to other cells. It is common in black people of African origin from areas where malaria is prevalent. Anemia has persisted among them because of an incompatibility of sickle cells and malaria, providing survival value in those areas where malaria takes a heavy toll (Chapter 14). The disease persists with a low incidence in the United States because it is recessive, but it is fatal to many black Americans during childhood and adolescence.

Albinism is a condition in which an enzyme which is essential for the metabolism of the pigment melanin is nonfunctional. Albino individuals have white skin, white hair, and pale eyes. The condition is not serious, except that the person requires unusual protection from sun and wind. One of my students, a Chinese albino, is exceptionally intelligent, competent, and personable, and he thrives in the Oregon mist.

Inherited Tendencies

When a disease seems to "run in the family" a genetic counselor can prepare a pedigree chart which predicts the chance that the anomaly might appear in offspring (Pai, 1974). A family history of heart disease, diabetes, cancer, and other ailments can be compiled.

CHILDHOOD SCHIZOPHRENIA

Schizophrenia is the most common of psychoses which appear to have a genetic base. In a comprehensive review of the evidence, Hurst (1972) concluded that the genetic factor is significant. Kallman and Roth (1956) found an increasing likelihood of schizophrenia in children and adults with increasing blood relationship to a schizophrenic. The following rates of incidence were reported: general population, 1.9 percent; siblings, 12.1 percent; dizygotic twins, 17.1 percent; monozygotic twins, 70.6 percent; and parents, 12.5 percent. Burch (1964) designed mathematical procedures to show that a single recessive gene is responsible for a *predisposing mechanism* toward schizophrenia which interacts with another single recessive gene that is responsible for a resistance or *modifying* mechanism. When an individual inherits recessive alleles which code for schizophrenia, the allele for a resistance mechanism may carry one dominant gene, which would tend to obscure the predisposing mechanism. Some children have high constitutional resistance to schizophrenia; others can be helped if compensating activity to control stress is provided (Hurst, p. 91). Researchers are encouraged when single genes are responsible for malfunctions because a single enzyme is indicated and treatment is likely to be simplified. Childhood schizophrenia is much more common in boys than girls, but it is autosomal (not sex-linked), meaning that both parents contribute equally.

COMMUNICATION HANDICAPS

Genetic anomalies which lower the child's ability to hear, speak, read, or write are considered communication handicaps because they make social interaction more difficult. When such conditions exist, it is important to identify the condition and provide environmental support and special instruction at critical times in development. Infantile congenital deafness is a recessive trait which sometimes accompanies schizophrenia. It is believed that deafness increases the stress for the child, lowers the ability to cope, and increases the tendency to withdraw (Rainer, Altshuler, & Kallman, 1963).

According to Waardenburg, Franceschetti, and Klein (1961, 1963) there is no part of the eye that is not subject to genetic diseases, some of them resulting in total blindness. Cancer of the retina in children has been mentioned. Most color blindness is a malfunction of the cones and is sex-linked. Glaucoma is a recessive trait. Early detection is always advantageous in treating a disease, and early education to compensate for visual defects is similarly important.

There is a three to four times greater tendency to stutter in children who have a first-degree relative who stutters than in children in the normal population. Andrews and Harris (1964) found the highest risk occurs among male relatives of female stutterers and the lowest risk to female relatives of male stutterers. Apparently a dominant gene is part of the explanation, with other genetic and environmental factors playing a role.

Even more controversial is the possibility of congenital influences on reading disability. Hallgren (1950) studied the families of clinic children with severe reading problems (dyslexia) and did a follow-up on their siblings. He estimated that 10 percent of the general population is affected and offered an explanation that a dominant autosomal gene was responsible. Since it is a matter of record that a percentage of children in various cultures have difficulty in learning to read, by whatever method used to teach them, this clinical evidence should not be rejected without further study. Some of the money given for research on reading methodology might be directed toward research on hereditary questions. Potential help for these children and their families is urgently needed.

DEVELOPMENTAL MALFORMATIONS

Although many malformations that appear at birth are caused by environmental insults during pregnancy (Chapter 3), some are genetically caused. Some examples are congenital dislocation of the hip, which is five times as common in girls as in boys; harelip and cleft palate; clubfoot; congenital heart disease; and central nervous system syndrome (Hurst, 1972). The genetic base is usually established by preparing a pedigree of the afflicted child's family and comparing the incidence of the trait with the normal population. Twin studies also provide evidence. Parents of afflicted children can determine through genetic counseling the likelihood of their having another afflicted child.

SPLICING AND RECOMBINING THE GENES

Genetic researchers have recently made a spectacular advance in technology: the genes of a virus and those of certain bacteria can be split into segments and recombined to form an organism with a new genetic makeup. The technique allows a particular segment of the viral chromosome to enter the cells of the bacteria and replace a segment of the host chromosome. The mutations are then separated out to form a collection of the new organism. The bacteria used is a strain of *Escherichia coli* which is different from the bacteria by the same name which inhabits the human gut.

Scientists hope to use this discovery to do further research on the treatment of genetic diseases. Congress is holding hearings to decide whether the law should limit the research to this particular strain of *E. coli* and confine it to certain laboratories. The National Institute of Health has written guidelines which are similar to those used in other parts of the scientific world that ensure that laboratory workers and the public at large will be safe from infection (Wade, 1977).

GENETIC COUNSELING

Some couples worry needlessly, or at least more than reality justifies, when genetic counseling could lessen their fear and give them a more factual basis for family planning. Genetic medicine is an increasingly important specialization in all developed countries.

Forms of Genetic Control

Euphenics is the treatment of genetic diseases by control of the symptoms. Diseases such as PKU are treated by eliminating from the diet certain protein foods that cannot be metabolized. Treatment from birth, before neural damage and mental retardation have occurred, is critical. Since many DNA-based diseases involve a nonfunctional enzyme, a more direct treatment would be to supply the missing enzyme. This approach presents difficulties because antibodies have already been built up during fetal life. Some new techniques in immunology are being researched which may solve this problem. Another possibility is treatment of the fetus in early stages of pregnancy, before antibodies have been produced in large amounts.

Anemias which result from low hemoglobin production might be treated by suppressing the synthesis of abnormal cells, as in sickle-cell anemia, or stimulating hemoglobin synthesis, as in thalassemia (Pai, 1974, pp. 331–332). As euphenic science becomes more successful, more individuals who have defective genes will survive, and there will be an even greater need for health services which provide genetic counseling.

Genetic counseling reassures prospective parents, prevents birth defects. (March of Dimes)

Eugenics attempts to improve the human species by selective reproduction or restraint of reproduction. Some scientists are fearful of this kind of control because it tends to narrow the range of individual differences in ways that may eliminate some phenotypes from the population. Knowledge is not available to suggest which humans will be most adaptable to future threats such as pollution. Some minority groups, for example, native American Indians, resist attempts to control their population because they claim past discriminations have already dissipated their numbers.

Voluntary negative eugenics leaves the couple free to seek genetic counseling and to arrive at their own decisions. It should be recalled, however, that laws which prevent the marriage of relatives and laws which punish incest are ancient attempts by societies to improve the gene pool. Nations which are overcrowded and lack the means to feed their growing numbers tend to try social pressure and legal rewards to limit family size.

Euthenics is the science that attempts to improve the future of Homo sapiens by improving the environment. The invention of tools changed the nature of the phenotype that survived and reproduced. In pioneer America, physical strength and endurance were important in turning a homestead into a home. This became a selective factor in mating in a society where women were scarce. Technology has decreased the importance of strength and increased the survival value of symbolic intelligence. Reading disability, an insignificant disadvantage in pioneer America, has become the primary eliminator in the competition for employment. Enlightened educational practices could conceivably create a school environment in which every child learns to read. This has not been accomplished for a broad population.

Genetic Engineering

The immediate and available help for couples who want some control over their familial future is through family planning. The present risk for having a genetically handicapped child is only about 1 in 40 live births. If high-risk diseases exist in a couple's pedigree, they should seek professional counseling in one of the genetic medicine centers available in most major cities in the United States and Canada. The genetic diseases for which counseling is advised include diabetes, psychotic illness, and a previous afflicted child. In certain populations, counseling should be more generalized because of the presence of unusually high-risk conditions such as sickle-cell anemia, inbred hemophilia, and diseases of the infant nervous system. A recent technique which makes possible the early detection of many genetic diseases is called *amniocentesis* (Cohn, 1975). By this procedure amniotic fluid is tapped from the sac that surrounds the fetus. Cells that are sloughed off can be captured, reproduced in culture, and analyzed. Biochemical analyses reveal other diseases. With this information, couples may be emotionally relieved during the continuation of the pregnancy or decide to have a seriously defective fetus aborted.

With most congenital diseases, the risk of a second child having the same anomaly as the sibling is not much greater than in the general population because most defects are recessive. However, if the risk is 25 percent (when both parents are carriers) the couple may decide on adoption. When one parent's genotype carries a dominant gene for a serious handicap, but the couple strongly desires direct progeny, artificial insemination is a possibility.

Private and Public Responsibility

Fear of misuse of genetic controls has hampered the use of genetic medicine in treating hereditary diseases. Similar fears have kept some persons from seeking the help that has become available. The decisions that must be made in the near future regarding population control, development of energy sources, and the polluting effects of industry require the kinds of information that some citizens resist.

Davis and Solomon (1974) suggested that the same mathematics that show the harmful spread of genetic diseases also show that the increase is very slow. Many genetic traits that now seem undesirable may be invaluable in future societies. Mild schizophrenia, for example, may be part of the highly creative personality. Deviantly high intelligence, which may not enhance social adaptivity, is another example of a phenotype that a future society may understand and nurture.

SUMMARY

Growth and learning depend upon the reproduction and continuous functioning of cells. Each cell contains chromosomes and DNA molecules, which together make up the cell's genetic material. Each gene is a specific protein. Each protein is made up of its particular pattern of amino acids.

Neural cells have the same basic structure as other cells: a cell body, a cell membrane that surrounds it, cytoplasmic material that contains the minute supporting organelles, and a nucleus. The nucleus of each cell is the site where strands of RNA, the messengers of growth and learning, are patterned from DNA. Neural cells send out axons and dendrites which interconnect with other cells to form the central and periferal nervous systems.

Mendel studied heredity by controlled experimentation with sweet peas. He discovered genetic principles which have come to be accepted in all reproduction: law of discrete units, law of segregation, law of dominance, and law of independent assortment. Genetic selection in humans changes the gene pool over time through cultural preference that encourages some matings over others, through strengths of the kind that ensure survival, and through mutations that help individuals avoid disease. All mammals benefit from selection in the fertilization process: proliferation and competition of the spermatozoa and nurturance and conservation of the ovum.

Genetic defects can be caused by the disjunction of sex chromosomes, where some individuals have only one, or three or more, instead of the normal two. Enzyme malfunctions occur when a gene that codes for a particular enzyme is defective. Some individuals inherit a tendency, or vulnerability, for a disease. New techniques of splicing and recombining genes, although controversial, offer some far distant hope for treating inherited diseases. Genetic counseling enables a couple to examine their karyotypes and pedigrees so that they can estimate the probability of good health in their offspring.

Part Two
GROWTH
PATTERNS

This part, Growth Patterns, is the core of the book. The themes outlined in Chapter 1 that appear most often are the universal timetables of development, the critical periods for growth and learning, the advantages of prolonged dependence, and the interaction of cognitive and affective factors.

The discussions begin with life before birth, because behavior and learning begin then. Children's handicaps, most of them preventable, are usually caused during intrauterine life or conception. Dividing a continuous topic into parts is difficult and can never conform to the expectations of all readers. The division of chapters in Part Two is based on the developmental stages in the life of a child. The five chapters that follow are concerned with five stages of early childhood: prenatal life, infancy, toddlerhood, preschool life, and the primary years.

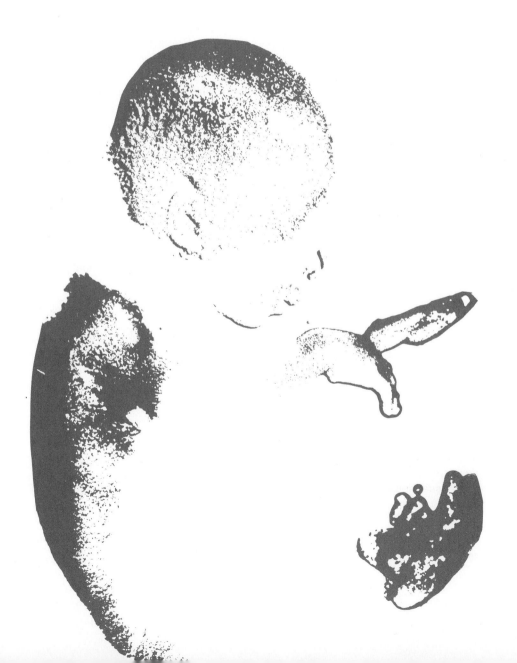

3
Prenatal Growth and Behavior

3 Prenatal Growth and Behavior

Life before birth has fascinated people since primitive times. Prior to recorded history, even before the cause of pregnancy was known, artists depicted the enlarged torsos of women and the emergence of male children. Many scholars whose names are familiar to students of child development were concerned with embryology at some point in their professional careers: Arnold Gessel, Jean Piaget, and Sigmund Freud.

Most research on prenatal life has one of three focuses: (1) the inherited mechanisms that control growth; (2) critical periods in the nature-nurture interaction that may be the source of birth defects; and (3) the prevention or prenatal treatment of birth defects. This chapter presents current knowledge of prenatal life, both to enhance excitement about being human and to provide a basis for intelligent choices on behalf of unborn children.

Prenatal life is seen by some scholars as the playing out of the evolution of all animal life. For example, the *grasping reflex* which is exhibited by newborns is thought to be a vestige of the behavior of prehuman mammals whose infants had to cling to their mothers for protection and survival. No fewer than twenty-seven behavior responses, no longer functional for humans, have been observed in prenatal development. Although our babies are highly dependent at birth, they are specifically human in social responsiveness, and their cognitive processing is superior to the more active and independent newborn of other species. The riddles of such complex behaviors as thought and language may be answered by learning how the tiny brain of the embryo develops and directs its own growth.

Roger Sperry, a behavioral scientist, explained his interest in embryonic development as the basis for the new insight into the neural circuitry that makes complex behavior a possibility.

The new outlook holds that the cells of the brain are labeled early in development with individual identification tags, chemical in nature, whereby the billions of brain cells can thereafter be recognized and distinguished, one from another. These chemical differentials are extended into the fibers of the maturing brain cells as these begin to grow outward, in some cases over rather long distances, to lay down the complicated central communication lines. It appears from our latest evidence that the growing fibers select and follow specific prescribed pathways, all well marked by chemical guideposts that direct the fiber tips to their proper connection sites. (Sperry, 1964, p. 5)

His own research was on the pathways interconnecting the eye with visual centers in the brain in lower vertebrates. Through surgery he rotated eye tissue during development so that the leads to the brain were crossed. The animals behaved as if their visual fields were reversed, indicating brain communication according to an inherited plan rather than the development of space perception by experiencing the real world.

Although Sperry was impressed by the genetic influence on prenatal brain development, he suggested that stimulation from the environment is necessary for neural pathways to function. In another experiment he deprived kittens of light stimulation by sewing their eyes shut at birth for controlled periods of time. He concluded that atrophy and degeneration result from prolonged deprivation at critical times (1964, p. 9).

A different approach to the study of embryology is taken in preventive medicine, which focuses on the intrauterine environment. The health and well-being of infants is enhanced by providing health care for prospective mothers. For example, whereas specialists only a few years ago advised prospective mothers against gaining much weight during pregnancy, informed opinion now warns that poor nutrition can cause low birth weight in the newborn (Winick, 1976). The notion that growth retardation during the prenatal period will be overcome during infancy and early childhood is no longer accepted by many experts (Gruenwald, 1968). Another notion that is being revised is that the maternal placenta is a barrier to disease and infection (Dancis, 1968). Although the blood is not exchanged, a modern concept based on research holds that mother and infant interact via the placenta, which is seen as a bridge for the transport of hormones and other small molecules.

These and other findings support the concept of *critical periods* when the environment is important in specific ways for normal development. This chapter continues a theme for this book that knowledge helps care-givers provide an environment for optimal growth of inherited structures. Certain limitations imposed by the genes may be overcome by intervention or treatment at critical times in development. The prenatal growth period has been divided into three stages, usually referred to as the *trimesters* of pregnancy.

FIRST TRIMESTER: PERIOD OF DIFFERENTIATION

The first trimester of prenatal development is characterized by differentiation: first of cells which initially are identical; then of tissue layers, which make up the human body; and finally of sex organs, which are initially female. Growth begins with the division of the fertilized cell (zygote) to increasingly smaller cells of like structure, until they number thirty-two. *Differentiation* occurs when increasing numbers of cells separate into a cluster that will become the embryo and a surrounding ring of cells that will become the support structures.

A second significant differentiation divides the growing embryo into three layers. The outer *ectoderm* forms the brain and nervous system. The inner *endoderm* forms the digestive and respiratory systems. The middle layer, the *mesoderm*, forms the circulatory, skeletal, and muscular systems.

The third important differentiation is sexual, which includes sex organs and the complicated hormone production that affects many aspects of development. Sex differentiation begins about the seventh week after conception and continues into the third month. By the end of the first trimester the brain and organs are performing their initial functions and the major skeletal and muscular structures are in place. The organism has grown through zygote and *embryo* stages to become a *fetus* and has taken on humanlike characteristics. It is no longer vulnerable to minor insults from drugs or viral disease.

An Organism Adrift: The First Week

At conception the genetic content (23 chromosomes) of one ovum unites with the genetic content (23 chromosomes) of one spermatozoan to form a single cell, which contains the full complement of 46 chromosomes (Chapter 2). The particular gene combination within the ovum represents only one of approximately 400 different genetic combinations the human female carries in her ova. The genetic inheritance contributed by the male spermatozoan represents only one combination of genes from a potential 300 to 400 million spermatozoa released during a single ejaculation. At conception about 2000 spermatozoa have survived the chemistry of the uterus and the mazes of female anatomy to be in location of the mature ovum (oocyte) and in a position to penetrate its outer membranes. At the moment the first spermatozoan pierces the surface of the oocyte, its permeability changes and, normally, all other sperm cells are rejected. Although only one spermatozoan fertilizes the ovum, apparently large numbers are necessary to create the chemical conditions for mobility and penetration (Davis & Solomon, 1974, p. 283).

ZYGOTE

The single cell of the fertilized ovum is technically known as a zygote. The first cleavage, or division, of the zygote takes place by the process of *mitosis*, in which sister cells, identical in chromosome content, are produced. Prior to division, during interphase, the DNA content of the cell is doubled. Although the sperm and egg cells contribute equal numbers of chromosomes, the bulk of the zygote cytoplasm comes from the ovum (Davis & Solomon, 1974, p. 302).

At this stage of development, which requires about thirty-six hours, each sister cell is independent in makeup; that is, it contains a complete blueprint for an individual. Although these cells seem to be attracted and cling together, they do separate on rare occasions and produce separate and complete human beings, or identical twins. Cleavages are thought to explain multiple human births, as well as identical littermates in some mammals. In normal development, cells are believed to be identical until they have increased to sixteen cells. Cell division increases rapidly at this stage and within three to four days after conception the cells have increased to about 64 and are interdependent. The organism remains about the same overall size; even though the number of cells has increased, the amount of cytoplasm within each cell is reduced.

The cells of the zygote have the growth potential for a complete human with some 200 different cell types that make up the organs and tissues. The process by which cells become specialized is called cellular differentiation. Growth occurs through mitosis and morphogenesis. Morphogenesis is the formation of many different patterns in the growth of tissues and organs. Chapter 2 explained how different fiber structures bind the chains of amino acids to build different proteins.

MORULA

The *morula* is a cluster of integrated cells developed from the zygote and encased in a membrane. At this stage, if one cell were separated from the others it would not be able to develop into a complete individual. The morula appears under the microscope like a mulberry with its many cells of similar size and concentration of fluid at the core. The downward migration of the morula through the fallopian tube is propelled by cilia and pelvic contractions. Rapid cell division occurs in preparation for the differentiation of body layers at the next stage (Rugh & Shettles, 1971, pp. 23–24)

BLASTOCYST

The stage of the *blastocyst* begins with the differentiation of cells that will become the embryo and the cells that will develop into supporting organs. These support systems are the chorion (a protective covering), the placenta (the organ of exchange between the baby and the mother), the amnion (a membrane filled with fluid in which the developing organism floats), and the yolk sac. Between the fourth and the sixth days, the cells of the blastocyst form an *embryo germ disk*, specialized cells surrounding the embryo germ disk, and a layer of flattened cells that form a sphere (Langman, 1975). By the end of the first week, the blastocyst will have entered the uterus where it may drift for a day or two while cell division continues (Figure 3-1).

Implantation: The Second Week

Implantation of the blastocyst into the wall of the uterus begins as early as the fifth or sixth day and is complete by the twelfth or thirteenth day (Langman, 1975). Invasion of cells to begin this attachment is possible because hormone changes that correspond with the menses of the female have thickened the uterine wall and made it vulnerable. The thicker side of the blastocyst attaches at the place on the sphere where the embryo germ disk is located.

At about the eight day the embryo germ disk, called the *embryoblast*, divides into two distinct layers. The outer and thicker layer, the *ectoderm*, will become the brain, spinal cord, sensory systems and skin of the fetus. The inner layer, the *endoderm* germ layer, will become the digestive system, including the esophagus, stomach, liver, intestines, and anus. Considerable differences have been found in human growth rates, even at this early stage (Langman, 1975).

The blastocyst bores into the wall of the uterus, rupturing blood vessels that provide nutrients needed for rapid growth. The uterus first reacts with swelling at that site, which has the effect of further embedding the embryo and enhancing its

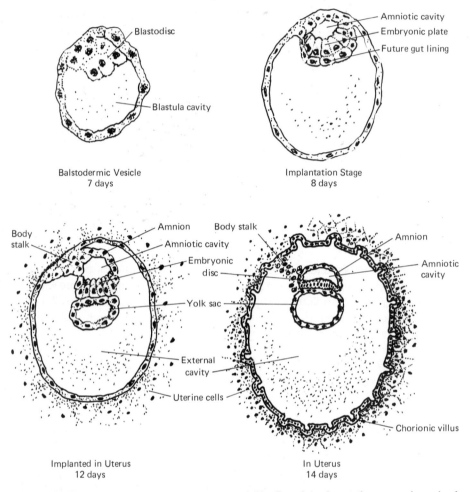

FIGURE 3-1 **Differentiation in early neonatal life. Drawing shows the second week of development, in which blastocyst becomes implanted in the wall of the uterus.** (Drawing by Donna Thompson.)

implantation. White corpuscles are released which serve to absorb the debris caused by implantation. At the time of implantation, the organism is one-hundredth of an inch in diameter. The hormones which suspend menstruation are being released. Approximately 25 percent of all pregnancies are terminated spontaneously at this stage due to genetic defects that cause failure to implant (Davis & Solomon, 1974, p. 385). The mother may experience heavier than normal menstruation but may not know she is experiencing an abortion.

The differentiation which began with the specialization of cells proceeds rapidly as fluid nutrients and blood become available. The amniotic membrane and fluid surround the fetus. Opposite the fetus the yolk sac develops. The chorion forms an outer encasement, part of which attaches to the uterine wall to form the placenta. The genetic plan for development of the support systems for the embryo is believed to be contained in the cytoplasm of the ovum. By the end of the second week the organism is firmly implanted.

Development of the Embryo: Third to Eighth Weeks

Embryology is the study of life before birth, beginning with conception and ending with *parturition*, the separation of the organism from its protective membranes. In humans parturition corresponds to birth. The reader will think of many levels of dependence at birth within the animal kingdom, from the marsupials to the grazers. Scientists have noted the similarity of appearance of all animals during the embryonic stages of development.

The embryonic stage is usually defined as the stage in prenatal life that begins when implantation into the uterine wall of the mother is complete and ends when the bone structures begin calcification. These structures are formed originally of tissue, then of cartilage, and finally hardened by deposits of calcium.

Although the beginning of the stage of the fetus is considered by some writers to be that time when the unborn child appears human (Rugh & Shettles, 1971), other writers have pointed out that baboon fetuses are indistinguishable from humans beyond the embryonic period and into the fifth month postconception (Axelrod, 1967). In humans the stage of the embryo lasts to the end of the eighth week, approximately.

PLACENTA: ORGAN OF EXCHANGE

The placenta is a temporary organ, unique to pregnancy, in which the maternal and fetal circulations are brought into close proximity. In appearance the placenta is a disk-shaped mass of tissues. The maternal placenta covers 20 percent of the uterus at three weeks after conception; at this time the fetal placenta and the fetal circulation are relatively well developed (Dancis, 1968). Not until approximately seven weeks into gestation is the maternal placenta sufficiently well developed to serve as an effective barrier to fetal insult from certain viruses and drugs. The placenta continues to grow for seven months and to increase its coverage of the uterine wall. During the eighth month the placenta begins to regress in size. It is discharged immediately following the birth of the baby. Overterm babies may be deprived by regression in the functioning of the placenta. The relationship of the embryo to the placenta is shown in Figure 3-2.

After much research, embryologists have come to conceptualize the placenta as a bridge, rather than a barrier, over which are transferred numerous nutrients, hormones, liquids, amino acids, proteins, viruses (and germs), antibodies, and other solubles and gases. The fetal and maternal circulation systems are separated by membranes, so their blood does not mix.

Dancis (1968) listed the known processes by which placental transfer can occur. *Diffusion* transfers gases, water, and numerous small molecules through the

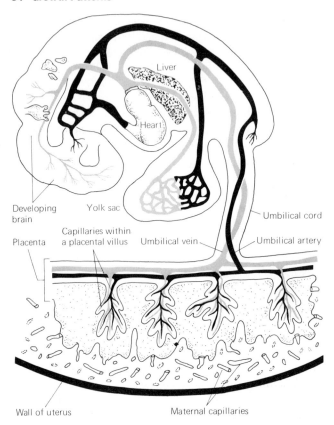

Developing brain

Yolk sac

Placenta

Capillaries within a placental villus

Umbilical vein

Umbilical cord

Umbilical artery

Liver

Heart

Wall of uterus

Maternal capillaries

FIGURE 3-2 Relationship of an embryo to its placenta. Maternal and fetal blood both circulate through the placenta where an exchange of materials occurs.

Source: The World of Biology, P. William Davis and EIdra Pearl Solomon, page 305. Copyright, 1974 by McGraw-Hill, Inc.

tissues in the direction of the least concentration. This is the familiar process by which digested nutrients and oxygen from the mother's blood are exchanged for waste from the developing embryo (or fetus). *Active transfer* is the mechanism for transfer of water-soluble carbohydrates, amino acids, and vitamins. Liquid-soluble materials may transfer directly via the placenta from one organism to the other. Certain proteins transfer from mother to fetus across a specialized part of the placenta. Leaks can occur through torn vessels, particularly at birth, and bodies as large as blood cells can then pass through the placenta. *Placental infection* may occur when the infectious agent of a disease carried by the mother transfers to the circulatory system of the fetus.

Attempts to study the function of the placenta are limited by restrictions to research on human subjects. Considerable differences exist between people and laboratory animals in the nature and timing of transplacenta processes. Baboons have been used as models for laboratory investigations of placenta exchange. They have a relatively long gestation period (six months) during which placental functions can be observed. In baboons the time of conception can be controlled precisely, and they can be infected with certain human diseases that affect embryos. The link between thalidomide and birth defects was proved by using baboon subjects. The sensitive period for forelimb defects was established at 23 to 26 days postconception and hindlimb malformation at 26 to 28 days by giving thalidomide to baboons and observing the effect on their offspring (Axelrod, 1968, p. 93).

Test-tube babies will not become a reality of the brave new world until the intricate functions of the human placenta are understood. Scientific knowledge is still very primitive on this aspect of child development.

GROWTH PRIORITIES: BRAIN, HEART, GUT

Immediately following implantation and the ready availability of nutrients, the embryo differentiates very rapidly. About day 15, the outer ectoderm germ layer (which will form the brain, nervous system, and skin) and the inner endoderm germ layer (which will form the stomach and digestive systems) separate to allow new cells to migrate between them. This middle layer, the mesoderm germ layer, will become the skeletal, muscle, and reproductive systems. This differentiation into three anatomical layers is common to all higher animals (Table 3-1).

Growth priority is on the nervous system because its prompt functioning is essential to initiate the development of other systems (Rugh & Shettles, 1971). Neural development is thought to be induced by RNA, directly or indirectly, at the time the first cell specialization occurs at the fourth or fifth day. The ectoderm germ layer is responsive to stimulation from RNA, which interacts with genetic

Table 3-1

SYSTEMS WHICH DEVELOP FROM THREE LAYERS OF THE BLASTOCYST

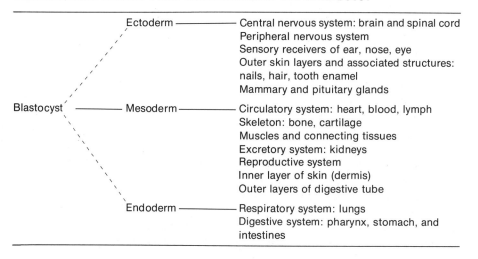

	Ectoderm	Central nervous system: brain and spinal cord Peripheral nervous system Sensory receivers of ear, nose, eye Outer skin layers and associated structures: nails, hair, tooth enamel Mammary and pituitary glands
Blastocyst	Mesoderm	Circulatory system: heart, blood, lymph Skeleton: bone, cartilage Muscles and connecting tissues Excretory system: kidneys Reproductive system Inner layer of skin (dermis) Outer layers of digestive tube
	Endoderm	Respiratory system: lungs Digestive system: pharynx, stomach, and intestines

material in the responding cells (Lasher, 1972). Stated more simply, particular genes, containing the codes for development of brain and spinal column, respond to RNA messages. Research has demonstrated that the ectoderm and mesoderm germ cell layers when separated in the laboratory and given the same environment respond differently at this time. Endoderm cells show a readiness to increase in numbers.

The visible formation of the nervous system begins at about 18 days with the formation of a fold in the ectoderm called the *primitive streak*. Within days this fold becomes the *neural tube*, a primitive spinal cord. The formation of the neural tube, the inner structure of the visible streak, is interesting because it is a prototype of the growth of new organs.

The process begins with the thickening of the midline of the ectoderm of the embryo by layers of new cells called the neural plate (Figure 3-3). This skeletal axis is common to all vertebrates and organizes head-to-toe (cephalocaudal) development of the organism. Cell movement to the edges of the plate results in a thickening and folding until a *neural groove* is formed, and then the *neural tube*. The anterior (front) of the tube differentiates to form the brain, and the posterior (back) part of the tube forms the spinal column. The crest of cells at either side of the tube form the major cranial and spinal nerves. By the end of the third week (day 20), the foundations of the child's brain, spinal cord, and entire nervous system have been laid down.

The brain develops from the forepart of the neural tube. Bulges appear to form the forebrain, midbrain, and hindbrain parts (Figure 3-4). The neural tube develops rapidly in the third week to a primitive brain. Photographs of the embryo show rudimentary eyes, which are an extension of the cortex. The neurons at this time are primitive (called neuroblasts) and lack direct connection to other neurons. The head develops faster than lower parts and appears to dominate the anatomy throughtout embryonic life.

Later in the third week the organism's growth priority shifts to the heart, which is central to the circulatory system. This system develops from the mesoderm. The embryo forms its own blood and distributes the nutrients and oxygen it needs for growth. The heart initially forms as an S-shaped tube and as such it functions with a regular beat (60 per minute) by day 28 after conception (Figure 3-2).

The digestive and respiratory systems form from a tube in the endoderm. This layer of cells gives rise to the respiratory system, the stomach and digestive glands, the thyroid gland, and the intestinal system and bladder (Figure 3-5). At approximately 4 weeks postconception, the embryo appears to have gill arches in the region of the pharynx. Although these look like the gills of fish and amphibians, in humans a temporary tissue cuts off circulation of fluid through these structures. Called *branchial grooves*, they later develop into the ear canal, the eardrum, and the eustachian tube.

A great deal of scientific interest focuses on certain temporary structures of the human embryo that make it appear at certain stages like animals more primitive than humans (Figure 3-6). One of the most prominent of these phylogenic vestiges is the embryonic tail. At 4 weeks this tail is prominent, but it regresses and is absorbed in most individuals by the end of the first trimester. However, about

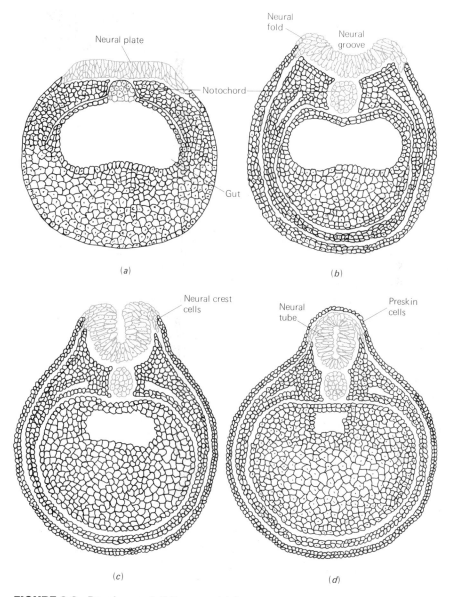

FIGURE 3-3 Development of the neural tube.

A. Thickening of the ectoderm creates the neural plate. The notochord is a flexible cable of mesoderm which stabilizes the embryonic growth during proliferation and migration of neural cells and provides an inhibiting environment at the location of the neural groove. The undignified term *gut* describes a developmental channel through which nutrients, amino acids, and endocrine materials are available for growth.

B. The neural groove appears as an indentation along the length of the tube.

C. The neural crest is formed by migrating cells at the sides of the groove.

D. The neural tube is formed and rudimentary skin tissue encloses it.

Source: William Davis and Eldra Pearl Solomon, *The World of Biology*, page 309. Copyright 1974, McGraw-Hill, Inc.

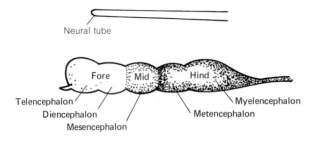

Neural tube

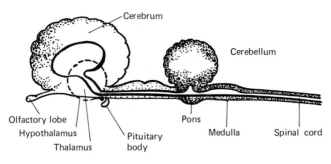

Fore   Mid   Hind

Telencephalon
Diencephalon
Mesencephalon
Metencephalon
Myelencephalon

Cerebrum

Cerebellum

Olfactory lobe
Hypothalamus
Thalamus
Pituitary body
Pons
Medulla
Spinal cord

**FIGURE 3-4   Early differentiation of the central nervous system.
The neural tube forms early in the third week. The first bulge in
the tube becomes the forebrain, which later differentiates to
cerebral hemispheres, thalamus, and hypothalamus. The midbrain remains a stocklike conduit. By the end of the first trimester,
the hindbrain becomes pons, cerebellum, and medulla.** (Drawing
by Donna Thompson.)

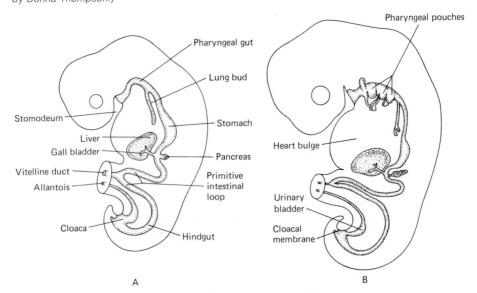

Pharyngeal gut
Lung bud
Stomodeum
Stomach
Liver
Gall bladder
Pancreas
Vitelline duct
Allantois
Primitive intestinal loop
Cloaca
Hindgut

Pharyngeal pouches
Heart bulge
Urinary bladder
Cloacal membrane

A   B

**FIGURE 3-5   Embryo development of the endodermal germ layer. Two stages
in the development of respiratory, digestive, and elimination systems.**

Source: Jan Langman, *Medical Embryology,* page 74. Copyright © 1975, The Williams and Wilkins
Company, Baitimore.

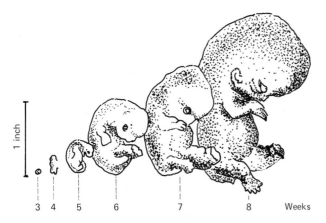

1 inch

3 4   5   6   7   8   Weeks

FIGURE 3-6 Human embryos showing growth and body
form from 3 to 8 weeks. Note the gill-like formations at 5
weeks and the gradual regression of the fetal tail. (Drawing
by Donna Thompson.)

one-sixth of all human neonates still have remnants of the embryonic tail which is
easily removed surgically. During the fourth to eighth weeks, all major organs and
systems are formed (Langman, 1975).

Beginnings of Fetal Life: The Third Month

The human fetus is defined by embryologists as "the developing body *in utero* from
the beginning of the ninth week after fertilization through the fortieth week," or
until birth (Lapedes, 1974). Variations on this definition are numerous. One
definition, which allows for variations in individual development, cites the beginning of calcification in cartilege structures as the beginning of fetal life. This
criterion is difficult to confirm in a growing fetus without x-rays, a procedure which
is usually avoided. Rugh and Shettles (1971) cite the emergence of a human
appearance as "the criterion for having outgrown the embryonic stage" to become
a fetus. *Medical and Health Encyclopedia* defines fetus as the prenatal stage
beginning with the fourth month of pregnancy (1970, p. 1093), implying that the
first trimester of human life is embryonic. Although the reader must be prepared to
cope with these variations in the literature, this book considers fetal life as
beginning with the third month after conception, when the basic forms of organs
common to both sexes have been laid down and calcification of the skeletal
structures has begun.

CEREBRAL DIFFERENTIATION

Biologists use the word *differentiation* to mean the modification of tissues and
organs in structure and function during development. Differentiation of a cell
involves the attainment of the structure, chemistry, and behavioral characteristics

of the adult state (Lasher, 1972). Basic differences between the cells of some human body structures were discussed in Chapter 2 (Figure 2-1).

The brain and the spinal column develop rapidly during the third month (Figure 3-8). The cerebral hemispheres expand outward from the fore part of the embryonic brain. Cortical layers develop around the brain to become the sensory storage and motor control areas. Neural cell bodies proliferate in the inner layer of the cortical tissues and then migrate to predetermined layers of the cortex. Layers of cell bodies in the cortex are laid down generally from the inside out toward the scalp. When cell bodies have gravitated to their proper location, some of them send out long axons to form the major interconnections (the primary circuitry) of the brain. How the genetic plan manages to direct these axons over long distances to their appropriate target areas in another part of the brain or the sensory system is a current and fascinating question (Berry, 1974).

The third month in human prenatal life is considered a vulnerable period in brain development of the fetus and a critical period for adequate protein intake on the part of the mother. During a period when proliferation of neural cells is the growth pattern, malnutrition curtails cell division. When cell enlargement is the growth characteristic, the effect of malnutrition can be measured in weight of the cortical layers, DNA count, and myelination (Winick, 1976, p. 91).

Laboratory research in which adequately nourished rat mothers were given additional growth hormone (GH) at a critical period in gestation showed a selective effect on the brain development of the fetuses. Compared with controls, the fetuses of GH-injected mothers had significantly increased brain weight and significantly higher cerebral neuron content. The voluntary intake of food was not different for control and experimental mothers, nor was the weight of their fetuses different. The researchers believe that this selective effect on brain growth is due to a secondary messenger, responsive to the hormonal messenger, which originates in the placenta and influences fetal brain growth directly (Sara, Lazarus, Stuart, & King, 1974).

Primitive nerve cells called neuroblasts proliferate during the first trimester until the primitive structures of the brain and spinal cord are laid down (Figure 3-7). The spinal neuroblasts are formed from cells in the ectoderm and migrate upward to form the ascending (input) neurons, or downward to form the descending (motor

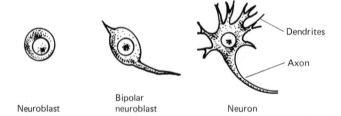

Neuroblast   Bipolar neuroblast   Neuron   Dendrites   Axon

FIGURE 3-7 **Development of neurons from primitive cells, called neuroblasts. Once formed, neuroblasts lose their ability to divide. They elaborate to form neurons.** (Drawing by Donna Thompson.)

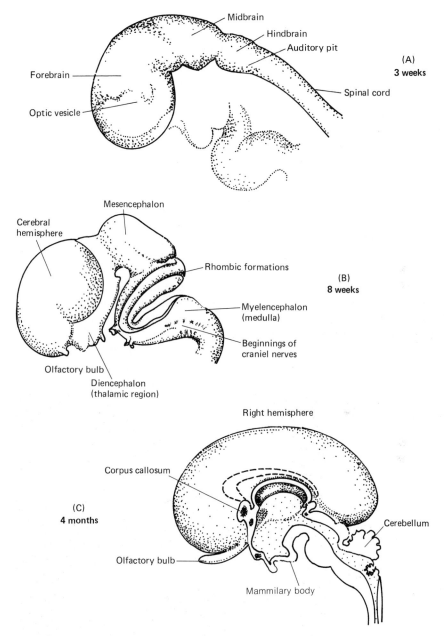

FIGURE 3-8 Development of the major areas of the brain.

A. At 3 weeks the embryo shows optic vesicle, forebrain, midbrain, hindbrain, auditory pit, and spinal cord.

B. At 8 weeks the fetus shows the beginnings of cranial nerves which will relay sensory information in the myelencephalon. The rhombic formations will become the cerebellum and will coordinate posture and movement.

C. View of the middle surface of the right hemisphere. Dotted lines show the future expansion of the corpus callosum, the major connecting structure. (Drawings by Donna Thompson.)

output) neurons. Neuroblasts are round in shape, and once they are formed, they lose their ability to divide (Langman, 1975, p. 327). Early in development they become bioplar in appearance but lack the elaboration of adult structures. By the end of the third month a healthy human fetus will show reflexive movement when touched (Langman, 1975).

HEART FUNCTIONING AND RESPIRATION

The heart is formed from two tubes that are in place by the end of the third week. By the end of the fourth week separate embryonic artery and vein systems have been formed. The primitive heart forms the connection between these two systems. As mentioned earlier, it appears as an S-shaped formation. The large bulge in front of the embryo will become the systems that will supply and carry nutrients from the digestive system.

By the third month the fetal heart is functioning to circulate blood through its own body systems and the fetal placenta. The distribution of nutrients and the removing of waste are controlled by the fetal heart, through the artery and veins in the umbilical cord. The circulation of hormones within the organism's own system is important in the differential development of sex organs.

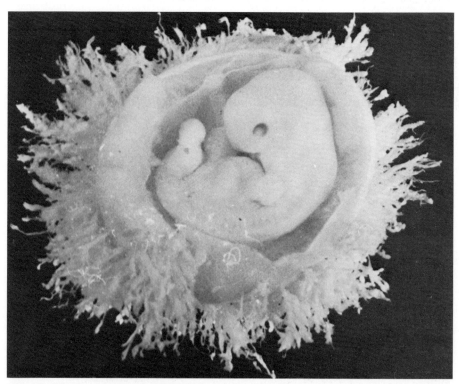

Major body parts are being formed in the 6-week fetus. (Courtesy of Landrum B. Shettles, M.D.)

Early elimination of fetal wastes is accomplished through the respiratory system. The fetus performs breathing movements, pumping amniotic fluid in and out of the lungs. By the end of the first trimester the circulation and respiration systems are supplying oxygen and will continue to supply it until birth, when breathing begins.

SKELETAL DIFFERENTIATION

The beginning of the third month has been defined as the beginning of the fetal stage, the final growth stage in neonatal life. During the third month, skeletal and muscular systems differentiate. Certain bone structures accept calcium deposits and are recognized as primitive bone structures. Although skeletal and muscular growth is most visible, this growth must be preceded by brain systems which direct it and blood systems which supply it. During the third month, the fetus doubles in length and takes on humanlike characteristics.

Skeleton and muscles develop together from the middle layer of embryonic cells. In some complicated way the tension of growing muscle tissues stimulates the firming of skeletal tissues. Neural endings are visible at the edges of muscle growth which indicates the overall direction of growth from the central nervous system outward. The instructions for growth priorities or growth inhibition are contained in the circulating hormones. The relative balances that are maintained among hormones create the environment that activates the cells of a particular body part.

In early differentiation muscular tissues are visibly different from skeletal tissues. Skeletal tissues become cartilage, partially as a result of the different ways proteins become structured from the amino acid chains (Chapter 2). Cartilage is firmed into bone by the depositing of calcium molecules among the cells already differentiated as cartilage. The location of the structures to calcify is predetermined by the genes. Although growth proceeds in a cephalocaudal-proximodistal order (Chapter 1), the calcification begins in the large bones, and at both ends simultaneously (Nilssen, 1973).

SEX DIFFERENTIATION

External genitalia are the same for males and females until the beginning of the fetal period when the gonads of the fetus begin to produce their own sex hormones (Figure 3-9). Prior to that time the sex of the embryo can be determined by either of two laboratory tests. A karyotype analysis of sex chromosomes reveals the YX chromosome pair (one larger, one smaller) as male). The Barr test is a procedure for staining and counting the inactive Barr bodies within a cell which identifies it as a female.

All mammals begin life as a female organism, and unless a redirection of development is induced by male hormones, an individual will be female (Sherfey, 1972). All fish and reptiles, unless differentiated, develop into males. Mammalian evolution, which gives mammals a prolonged period of gestation, appears to require that the embryo be female in order to ensure its compatibility with the mother's own hormones during early differentiation. Later in development biological protection against feminizing the male fetus must be accomplished. By the

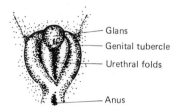

— Glans

— Genital tubercle

— Urethral folds

— Anus

FIGURE 3-9 External genitalia of the embryo at 7 weeks old. The undifferentiated sex organs are female. Male structures appear after the release of the organism's own androgens into the bloodstream at 7 to 8 weeks following gestation. (Drawing by Donna Thompson.)

third month the placenta has grown into a mutually compatible organ which is maternally accepting of a fetus of either sex. The advantages to mammals of *in utero* development and nurturance are widely recognized.

The yolk sac, which is the main source of nutrients in birds and reptiles, has evolved unique functions in mammals. The yolk sac produces germ cells which gravitate to the fetus and stimualte sex differentiation (Rugh & Shettles, 1971). In genetic males, the germ cells arise in the endoderm of the yolk sac and migrate to the gonadal medullae, which will become testes. Upon arrival in the gonads, germ cells stimulate the growth of gonadal medullae and the production of fetal androgen, a male sex hormone. Androgen suppresses the growth of oviducts, which arise from the first kidney ducts, and the gonadal cortex, which becomes the ovaries. Fetal androgens induce the growth of internal and external genitals into the male pattern. These become increasingly visible from the seventh to the twelfth weeks. After the twelfth week, the critical period of sex differentiation is passed and reversals in the transformation of male structures due to hormone medication of the mother are no longer a potential hazard (Sherfey, 1972, p. 39). Vas ducts for discharge of spermatozoa in the adult male arise from the second of three kidney duct systems.

If the genetic sex is female, the (primordial) germ cells arrive at the gonadal cortex and stimulate the production of fetal estrogens (female sex hormones). If the gonads are surgically removed at this point, feminine structures continue to develop. However, genetic females without estrogens do not develop fallopian tubes; and the production of primitive ova, which normally occurs at the fetal stage, does not take place. The interacting role of maternal and fetal estrogens is not fully clear. It is known that lactation-producing hormones in the mother affect both male and female neonates, who are equally likely to have breast milk at birth. It is generally accepted that male fetuses must produce counteracting androgens to suppress the structures that are specifically feminine and to elaborate the structures of male reproduction.

Pathology of the First Trimester

Most pregnancy failures occur very early, either before or during implantation. Severe defects of the chromosomes result in spontaneous abortion during the first twenty days. By the time the first menstruation is missed, only 42 percent of the eggs exposed to spermatozoa have survived (Hertig, 1967). Even when conditions are optimal, 15 percent of oocytes are not fertilized, and 10 to 15 percent start cleavage but fail to implant. Of those that implant only 58 percent survive to the second week, and of them 16 percent are abnormal. At this stage the mother who aborts spontaneously usually is not aware she has been pregnant. Genetic causes of malformation and disease were outlined in Chapter 2.

Environmental causes of fetal damage in the first trimester, sometimes called *extrinsic* factors, are of three origins: *physical agents*, such as radiation; *chemical agents*, such as the drug thalidomide, well known as a cause of birth defects; and *biological agents*, such as rubella, a viral disease that can affect the embryo when contracted by the mother (Dugeon, 1973). In general, the younger the organism, the more vulnerable it is to severe damage from environmental insults, although certain pathologies are more common to the second or third trimesters. The part of the organism that is growing most rapidly at the time is most vulnerable to a destructive agent. Timing is very important, therefore, in determining the extent and nature of damage.

IONIZING RADIATION

Ionizing radiation can come from natural sources, from x-rays, or from other radiation-producing processes and appliances. Gentry, Parkhurst, and Bulin (1959) studied the relationship of congenital malformations and residence in areas of high versus low natural radiation in New York State. In a sample of over 1 million live births they found 1.69 percent malformations in newborns whose mothers drank water from radioactive areas compared with 1.24 percent in low-radiation townships. Concerns over the location of radiation-producing industries appears to be justified (Ferreira, 1969). Consumer groups and government agencies are actively engaged in testing radiation from appliances, such as microwave ovens and color television, and attempting to determine the prenatal and postnatal effect on youngsters.

MEDICATIONS AND DRUGS

Maternal medications and drugs are a major problem in early pregnancy because pills in common use are taken at a time when the mother does not suspect pregnancy. Thalidomide was considered an innocent tranquilizer and was widely prescribed to pregnant women to alleviate symptoms of nausea, a common complaint in the second month of pregnancy. The link between deformed limbs of infants (as well as heart defects, mental retardation, and vision or hearing deficiencies) was difficult to prove to drug manufacturers because many fetuses of mothers who took thalidomide were not affected, at least not in obvious ways. Eventually researchers were able to prove a causal relationship in the laboratory by controlling the time of conception in baboon mothers, administering thalidomide according to a predesigned schedule, and predicting which limbs would be malformed (Axelrod, 1968). Although thalidomide has not been used for pregnant women since the early 1960s, the children known to have been crippled by the drug number more than 8000 (*Newsweek*, 1975). Medication such as sleeping pills, tranquilizers, thyroid regulators, and common pain-killing chemicals may cause malformations in the embryo (Rugh & Shettles, 1971).

VIRAL INFECTIONS

At least ten viruses that strike female adults are known to cross the placenta and infect the embryo (or fetus). These include rubella, poliomyelitis, tuberculosis, and Coxsackie virus, a disease resulting from innoculation with live pox virus (Benirschke, 1968). Viral infections can also invade the uterus through the cervix, but this is less common during early pregnancy.

A breakdown in maternal protection to the fetus may occur in several ways (Dugeon, 1973). Infections are apt to damage the unborn when the mother herself has not established immunity to a disease, when infection attacks the placenta itself, and when the fetus (or embryo) is not able to react to the infection by building its own antibodies. Vulnerability is greatest in the first trimester when basic structures are forming rapidly and when the maternal placenta is not yet fully developed.

Infections differ in their effect on the fetus according to the virulence of the strain and the developmental characteristics at the time of insult. Infections such as measles, smallpox, poliomyelitis, and mumps are associated with a high incidence of fetal death. Rubella, cytomegaloviruses, and Coxsackie viruses are more likely to damage than to kill the fetus. Cytomegalovirus (CMV) is a mild virus disease which affects the salivary gland and is very common in adults (50 percent). Its attack may not be noticed in the mother, but the virus crosses the maternal placenta with ease. The fetus is afflicted with low birth weight, which is sometimes mistaken for prematurity (Dugeon, 1973).

Damage from viruses probably causes many marginal symptoms, such as reduced intelligence, which are not counted in the statistics on birth defects. Also worth noting is that profound and multiple defects, while having only marginal impact on public health statistics, take a heavy toll of human joy and societal resources.

The most important actions in preventing birth defects are to know when conception has occurred and then to avoid radiation, undue medication, and risk of infection, especially during the early critical periods. Table 3-2 summarizes the stages of prenatal life and the major growth events during each stage.

SECOND TRIMESTER: PERIOD OF ACTIVITY

The fourth through the sixth months of prenatal life is a time for practice of breathing, and development of circulatory, digestive, and elimination systems. The

Table 3-2
SUMMARY OF PRENATAL GROWTH

Name and length of stage	Major growth event
ZYGOTE*	
0 hours	Fertilization—union of sperm and oocyte
30 hours	Cleavage—2-cell stage†
30–40 hours	4-cell stage
MORULA	
40–72 hours	12–16 cells—cell cluster reaches uterus
4 days	16–64 cells—embryonic cells mass
BLASTOCYST	
4–4½ days	Separation‡ 58–107 cells—outer cells flatten to form sphere
5½–6 days	Implantation—beginning of attachment
8 days	Separation of embryo germ layers
EMBRYO	
12–13 days	Implantation complete
15–16 days	Formation of mesoderm germ layer
15–20 days	Formation of primitive brain and spinal cord
16 days	Formation of primitive streak in ectoderm layer
18 days	Formation of cephalic end broadened; caudal end elongated
21 days	Formation of two tubes of primitive heart
28 days	Beginning of heartbeat
3–5 weeks	Appearance of somite segments of skeletomuscular system
4–8 weeks	Formation of digestive organs from mesodermal gut
5–6 weeks	Sex differentiation
FETUS	
8–13 weeks	Functioning of fetal organs
14–27 weeks	Practice and elaboration of somatic (body) systems
28–40 weeks	Elaboration and exercise of neural systems; myelination.

*Organism is called zygote until time of implantation.

†Time estimates are from Langman (1975).

‡Evidence comes from two clinical observations.

neural relays that make integrated body movements possible are laid down. The fetus is about 5 centimeters (2 inches) long at the beginning of the second trimester and weighs about 45 grams (1⅓ ounces). It grows rapidly to about 6 inches long and about a pound in weight by the end of the sixth month. The most important distinction between this and the third trimester is that the fetus is dependent on maternal functions for life and growth and cannot survive on its own outside the uterus.

Neural Development and Behavior

The fetus arrives at the second trimester with the cerebral hemispheres already differentiated and rudimentary olfactory, auditory, and optic systems already laid down. The diencephalon, initially differentiated from the forebrain, has divided into an upper thalamus and a lower hypothalamus (Lasher, 1972). It may be assumed

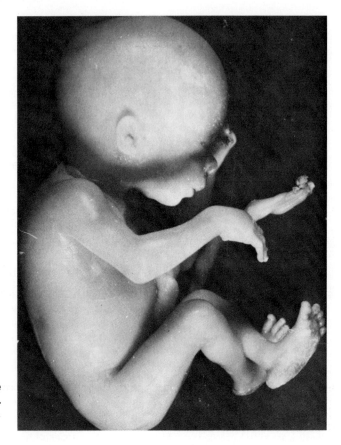

Body systems are active in the 18-week fetus.
(Courtesy of Landrum B. Shettles, M.D.)

that separation of functions occurs with the differentiation of brain areas. Major thalamus axons shoot out to connect to associative areas of the cortex, and the hypothalamus cells develop into clusters that differentiate pleasure and punishment sensations. Figure 3-8 shows brain formations at 3 weeks, 8 weeks, and 4 months.

Elaboration of the Central Nervous System

The neural development of the second trimester includes the appearance of true reflexive behavior, which implies the growth of long axonal connections from neural cells in the brain through spinal column neurons to the limbs. While the midbrain remains relatively small and serves as a conduit for interconnecting axons, the growth priorities shift to the hindbrain. There, differentiation of the medulla, the pons, and the cerebellum take place (Figure 3-8). During the fourth month the brain evolves from a tube to a compact structure.

The development of compartments in the fetal brain is basic to later brain functions. Nearly all human behavior involves the interaction of different areas of the brain. Knowledge of the terms for these compartments will provide some basis for exploring more detailed accounts of brain development. At some point in the second trimester, maturation of motor-sensory relays from spine to brainstem has growth priority. Some sources, such as Langman (1975), explain brain development from the lower (caudal) areas to the cephalic (higher) brain areas as shown in Table 3-3.

The *myelencephalon*, low in the brain stem, relays sense messages from all parts of the body to sense analyzers in the brain. Major cranial nerves, each representing a different sensory system, are visible on the surface.

The sensory systems for balance, hearing, and smell develop very early and precede the maturation of taste sensations and vision. Each of these systems is in place in rudimentary form by the beginning of the second trimester and growth of neural connections with higher brain areas is stimulated by the environment at the time.

The *metencephalon* compartment of the brain is formed from a rhombic area, just above the medulla. Two structures form there, the pons and the cerebellum. The pons becomes a relay center, interconnecting the spinal cord, the cortex layers of cerebral hemispheres, and the cerebellum.

In the taking-of-turns that characterizes early development, the cerebellum becomes the central organizer of reflexive activity in the same way the forebrain emerged as director of growth priorities and processes. The cerebellum sends input fibers to the motor cortex, preceded slightly by the growth of output fibers from the cortex back to the cerebellum. Crosslinkages form to and from the pons and the medulla. These fibers are essential before organized motor responses can

Table 3-3
MAJOR BRAIN COMPARTMENTS IN FETUS

MYELINCEPHALON

   Medulla: contains motor and sensory relay neurons; site of cranial nerve beginnings

METENCEPHALON

   Cerebellum: coordinator for posture and movement
   Pons: pathway for nerve fibers between spinal cord and cerebral/cerebellar cortexes

MESENCEPHALON

   Primitive structure; eye reflex, visceral activity, sphincter control

DIENCEPHALON

   Hypothalamus: regulates sleep, digestion, body temperature, and emotional behavior
   Thalamus: integrates sensory reception and responses

TELENCEPHALON

   Cerebral hemispheres
   Corpus collosum

be made. Some experts suggest that neural growth of the motor areas of the cortex is stimulated by the body movements of the fetus as it drifts in the amniotic fluid (Windle, 1971).

The *mesencephalon* is formed early, but remains a primitive structure. Reflexive eye responses, visceral activity, and sphincter control are centered in this compartment. The *diencephalon* differentiated earlier into lower *hypothalamic* and higher *thalamic* areas. The hypothalamus regulates hormone production, both directly and by stimulation of the pituitary body. Emotional behavior and the related body responses are centered in the hypothalamus. The *telencephalon* compartment divides to form two interconnected hemispheres. The major area for cross-linkage of the hemisphere is the corpus collosum, clearly visible by the tenth week.

Somewhere near the fourth month after conception, truly reflexive behavior appears, meaning that the fetus responds to a stimulus by a coordinated movement. Such tests are made by touching the fetus by pressing on the amniotic wall. As already reported, the 8-week fetus moves away from such stimulation, but only shows a lateral (one-side) response. Early in the second trimester, however, the movements are left-right coordinated, indicating the growth of crossed axonal connections within the spinal column and connecting with the appropriate hemispheres of the brain.

BEGINNING OF AFFECTIVE BEHAVIOR

Affective behavior may be inferred from the appearance of feeding behavior. Although avoidance reflexes are seen earlier, for example, when the fetus turns from a touch on the cheek, the fetus learns to move *toward* stimuli during the second trimester. This seeking movement is followed by fetal sucking movements (Windle, 1971, pp. 66–67). Swallowing increases if saccharin is injected into the amniotic fluid (p. 96).

This modification of behavior (learning) and the appearance of true reflexive action suggest that synaptic junctions are transmitting neural messages from one neuron to another. The earliest synaptic functioning is associated with excitation. The high activity levels of the fetus during the second trimester suggest that the synapses which inhibit neural activity are not yet functioning (Windle, 1971). Although the chemistry of synaptic transmission is beyond this discussion, the alternative behaviors of the fetus between avoidance action and approach can be logically related to the affective areas of the brain. Readers who are interested in the growth of synaptic functions might consult the classic resource Eccles (1965).

This sketch of the relation of the central nervous system to the behavior of the fetus is exceedingly simple; the actual development of many interacting systems in the prenatal human is far more complex. The purposes here are to document these early capabilities of the human fetus and to impress the reader with the precision of the genetic plan. Research on fetal learning continues to suggest earlier, rather than later, appearance of particular functions and their structures. Embryologists continue to seek evidence of the earliest neural development in human beings and try to confirm the relationship between neural mechanisms and the behavior that is observed.

FORMATION OF THE PERIPHERAL NERVOUS SYSTEM

Like other parts of the anatomy, the peripheral system functions only in coordination with the organism as a whole, and the central nervous system in particular. The distinction becomes important in knowing whether learning is internally or externally directed.

The cells of the peripheral nervous system proliferate later than those which form the central nervous system, but they also migrate from the neural tube or the neural crest. *Macroneurons* make up the major connecting pathways. They are highly specialized and specific in the timing and direction of their growth (Lasher, 1972). The *microneurons* form the integrating, or interconnecting, pathways between major neurons. Microneurons are unspecified until they begin to function in behavior. This distinction allows for plasticity in development because major pathways are laid down by a highly determined plan, but later connections are tied to experience. According to Lasher, activity in the fetus results in the imprinting of neural circuits. *Neuroglia* are supportive cells that surround neurons. These and similar but smaller cells provide much of the chemical environment which makes impulse transmission possible.

The spinal cord is the lower (caudal) portion of the neural tube. The location of a cell within the layers of the neural tube and its location in the third dimension, or length of the tube, determine where it will migrate and how it will function. The cells in the neural tube are radial in their arrangement. The timing of the proliferation and the migration of these cells, as well as their bonds to each other, determine when and where the major axons are sent out to the periphery. During the fourth month, a preskin forms around the fetus which incorporates motor end plates, muscle spindles, and sensory endings (Windle, 1971).

Practice of Autonomic Systems

Respiration is practiced by taking in and "exhaling" amniotic fluid. The structures for breathing are laid down early, are relatively solid in texture, and contain pulmonary fluid. Practice of the system is probably initiated by a gasping reflex (appearing at about 8 weeks) which starts the rhythmic movements of breathing (Windle, 1971).

The digestive organs (stomach, intestines, and liver) are in place by the eighth week; but it is during the third trimester that fetal swallowing becomes important. The amount of amniotic fluid swallowed increases gradually to 500 milliliters daily (Windle, 1971). It is now feasible to give medication to a fetus by injection through the uterine wall and into the amniotic fluid. At 11 weeks, peristalsis, the rhythmic contraction of muscles, appears in the intestines. At 4 months, gastric secretions are available; and at 5 months, liver secretions begin. Kidneys produce a dilute urine, and the bladder functions throughout the latter half of the second trimester.

The practice of these systems over so long a time before birth is needed to stimulate and coordinate the nervous and endodermic systems. These rhythms of living are gradually extended to endocrine systems and to circulation. The organization of autonomic functions is centered in the diencephalon, which develops rapidly during this period and continues its monitoring of life processes without conscious direction. During the second trimester the fetus becomes less vulnerable to environmental insult and more self-sufficient. Although dependent on maternal body for nourishment, respiration, and elimination the fetus assumes control over its own endocrine environment and produces its own growth hormones (Ferreira, 1969, p. 37).

Pathology of the Second Trimester

Influenza is one of the major hazards at this stage of pregnancy and is accompanied by a high incidence of abortion, considering the mildness of the infection for the mother. Reinfection of both mother and fetus is a danger because there are too many related viruses to immunize against all of them and because natural immunization is of short duration. The development of its own antibodies by the fetus is possible, but this is more likely to be successful later in the pregnancy (Dugeon, 1973). Why the fetus is particularly vulnerable to flu viruses at this stage of development is not fully understood. Metabolic and emotional factors are less likely to harm the fetus at this stage than later in neonatal life.

THIRD TRIMESTER: COMING OF AGE

From the seventh to the ninth months, the fetus becomes increasingly able to survive outside the mother's body. During this time the body weight doubles and the risk of premature labor increases also.

Premature infants are those weighing at least 2500 grams (5¹/₂ pounds) but are born prior to full term of 266 days after fertilization. When the exact time of fertilization is not known, birth expectancy is calculated from the previous menses as 10 lunar months. A minimum period of 28 weeks gestation is considered necessary for survival. The full-term but low-weight newborn is known as a small-for-date infant.

The longer premature infants remain *in utero* the more likely they are to live. The younger they are at birth, the greater the need for a specialized hospital environment, such as the new intensive care units, to keep them alive and nurture them to maturity. Figure 3-10 shows the relative growth in size during each of the trimesters. The growth accomplishments of the third trimester improve viability by the week, if not by the day.

Changes in Body Size

The most obvious growth of the third trimester is body weight and size. Table 3-4 shows the relatively rapid increase in weight and crown-to-rump length of the fetus

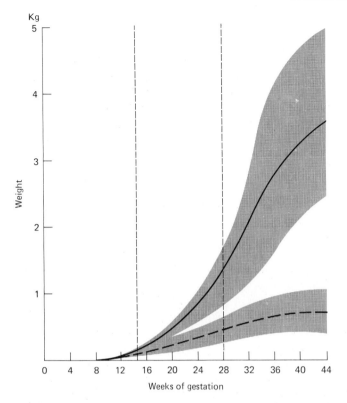

FIGURE 3-10 Body weights of the human fetus in kilograms. Solid line shows mean body weight; shading around it shows the range of body weights. Dotted line shows the mean weight of the placenta. Some scientific sources count prenatal age from the last maternal menses—ten to fourteen days before conception. Vertical dotted lines show approximate trimester periods. (Redrawn from Ramsey Greenhill, *Obstetrics*, 13th ed. Philadelphia: Saunders, 1965.)

from the sixth through eighth months, with some leveling off in weight gain during the ninth month of normal gestation. During the third trimester the fetus grows from 6 to 19 or 20 inches in length. At the birth of an unusually small infant, the physician tries to determine whether the neonate is genetically small, malnourished, or premature. Low birth weight is also a symptom of diseases such as hypoxia and pregnancy toxemia which are discussed in the section on pathology.

PREMATURITY AND LOW BIRTH WEIGHT

Numerous longitudinal studies have been made of children with low birth weights. Drillien (1973) followed 110 Edinburgh children who weighed less than 3 pounds at birth to the ages of 4 or 5 years. Ninety percent of them survived to the end of the

Table 3-4
GROWTH IN LENGTH AND WEIGHT DURING THE FETAL PERIOD

Age		Crown-rump length		Weight	
Weeks	Lunar months*	cm	in	gm	lb
9–12	3	5–8	1¼–2	10–45	0.1
13–16	4	9–14	2¼–3½	60–200	0.13–0.44
17–20	5	15–19	3¾–4¾	250–450	0.6 –0.9
21–24	6	20–23	5 –5¾	500–820	1.1 –1.8
25–28	7	24–27	6 –6¾	900–1300	1.98–2.9
29–32	8	28–30	7 –7½	1400–2100	3.1 –4.6
33–36	9	31–34	7¾–8½	2200–2900	4.8 –6.4
37–40	10	35–36	8¾–9	3000–3400	6.6 –7.5

*Lunar months are 4-week periods from the previous onset of menses 14 days ±1 day prior to conception (Langman, 1975).

study. A high percentage of them remained small. One-fourth of the group ranked below the fifth percentile in both weight and height when compared with population norms. Only 9 percent scored 100 or over on intelligence tests. By the end of the study period, one-third were enrolled in classes for the ineducable and one-third were retarded in their normal classes. Seventy percent showed behavior disturbances; the most common abnormalities cited were hyperactivity or restlessness. Drillien found that the smaller member of twins usually was the less capable. When siblings were available for comparison, 76 percent were less capable than their larger-born siblings.

DeHirsch, Langford, and Jansky (1965) compared fifty-four children born prematurely at an American hospital with a control group of fifty-three children born at term and matched for characteristics other than birth weight. They studied both groups in the kindergarten, using a series of tests that covered a broad range of cognitive development. At the end of second grade, school learning was evaluated with additional tests in reading, spelling, and mathematics. An "almost uniformly poor showing of the prematures" was reported for thirty-five of thirty-six tests. Clinically the prematures seemed to show more primitive central nervous system patterning, a relatively lower level of neurological integration and more diffuse ego organization" (p. 358). The neurological development of the third trimester seems to proceed more normally *in utero* than in a neonatal environment.

Braine, Heimer, Wortis, and Freedman (1973) compared 351 low-birth-weight (2100 grams) black infants with a reference group of 50 full-term infants born in the same hospital to mothers of similarly low socioeconomic status (SES). Five different examination sessions from age 4 days to 13 ½ months were conducted. These included strength of grasp, Moro reflex, gross motor development, visual following, and a mental scale. The analysis of the data showed how different complications correlated differently in long-term effects on the premature infants. Hypoxia (oxygen deficiency) and neonatal weight loss combined to show significant retardation of gross motor and cognitive functions, even though no comparable overall loss in IQ or visual following abilities was found. However, pregnancy toxemia (of mother's blood) was correlated with overall impairment, which persisted at least beyond the first year.

Improvements in the care of premature infants of the 1970s may improve the opportunities for premature infants of the future. However, the lack of a biologically determined environment to full maturity is considered generally handicapping. Perhaps prematurity substantially reduces the potential for superior capabilities in some low-birth-weight children who appear to be within normal ranges in size, intelligence, and behavior.

SEX DIFFERENCES

Sex differences were also analyzed by Braine et al. (1973). Very little difference between males and females was found on weight at birth, the types of damage, or numbers of infants having complications. The more severe and widespread damage they found in males was interpreted as "indicating greater vulnerability to insult (rather than exposure to higher levels of insult)" (p. 225). One reason that birth weight varied so little between the sexes was that weight differences appear in the late stages of pregnancy, showing up most significantly in full-term babies. The later sex differentiation of males may account for their greater vulnerability. Complications to the mother from carrying a male child did not appear to be increased.

Neurological Development

The monumental event of the third trimester, less obvious than size increase, is the elaboration of neural systems during the prenatal experience. Evidence of learning before birth is seen in the motor response patterns of the full-term newborn, their selective response to human speech, and their rhythms of sleeping and waking. The cues to neurological development and behavior in the unborn come from observations of the myelination of particular nerve fibers. Myelination is a growth stage that shows commitment of a neuron to a particular function, and the location of this maturation in the nervous system indicates the behavior that has been learned.

MYELINATION OF NEURAL FIBERS

Myelination is the growth of protective and insulating cells around neural fibers. The growth of myelin around an axon is myelogenesis (Figure 3-11). The illustration shows the creation of the sheath around a motor neuron in the output, or effector, system through growth of a Schwann cell (Katz, 1961). Other cells, including Golgi cells, create myelin in the central nervous systems. In myelogenesis these specialized cells move close to neural fibers, surround them, and

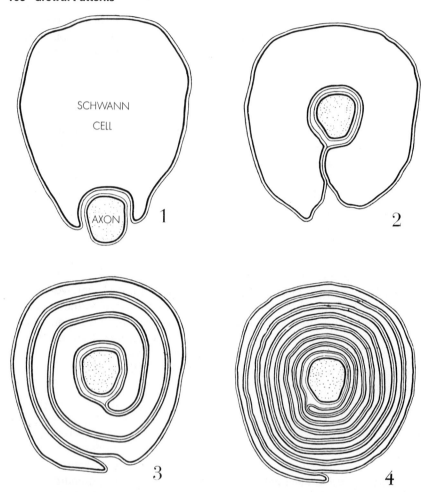

FIGURE 3-11 Myelin growth around an axon. A sheath is created when a Schwann cell migrates to an axon and folds around it. The growth of a myelin sheath suggests both the activity in the neural cell body and the differentiation of the neural unit in its message-bearing function.

Source: Bernhard Katz, "How Cells Communicate," Copyright © 1961, *Scientific American*, Inc. All rights reserved.

gradually thicken to form sausagelike structures at regularized locations along the axons. This thickening may take days, or years, but the length of the cycle of myelination is exceedingly important in revealing the behavioral competence of the child. The location and timing of the myelination indicate which systems are maturing and when.

Yakovlev and Lecours (1967) studied the myelination of nerve fibers from the fourth month of fetal life through the first year of infancy and compared them with the typical states of 28-year-old adult males. (Samples from 200 victims of accidental death were stained by special procedures that revealed the extent of myelin sheathing in each layer of central nervous system tissue.) They found that very little myelination occurs until the seventh month when Golgi cells begin to surround the motor fibers of the spinal cord. This timing of development is consistent with the findings of another researcher who reported a shift in developmental priority from the frontal brain to hindbrain and spinal cord midway in the fetal period (Windle, 1971).

Yakovlev and Lecours (1967) also suggest that the cycle of myelination is species-specific in its ordering and biologically initiated by the needs of the organism (p. 67). For example, animals who must be mobile at birth to survive show early prenatal maturation of vestibular systems. Visual development is delayed in kittens who are born blind and "nested" during early infancy. These differences explain why human studies of brain myelination are important. The order of myelination of sensory analyzers, before and after birth, is particularly significant in the pre- and postnatal care of the human young.

Regions of myelination identify the growth priority of the sensorimotor systems. Motor neurons myelinate early, beginning just prior to birth and reaching near adult density of sheathing at 1 month following birth. The acoustic-vestibular system myelinates next, perhaps because of biological demands on the fetus for righting itself *in utero* and in response to the auditory stimulation that penetrates the fetal environment. These systems are vulnerable to damage from anoxia at birth, perhaps because their development is rapid at that time.

DEVELOPMENT IN SENSORY SYSTEMS

Visual analyzers and tactile analyzers begin myelination near birth, but develop their mature states very rapidly, by the fourth or fifth month after birth. Yakovlev and Lecours (1967) noted the differences between the cycles of myelination of visual and auditory analyzers. "The body wall is opaque to light, whereas the fluid internal medium is a good sound conductor" (p. 63). The fetus is bombarded with acoustic stimulation, and the auditory fibers, including radiations to the temporal lobe of the cortex, myelinate before birth. Visual analyzers, including the optic nerve and sense endings, show little myelin sheathing until birth, but then develop very rapidly and are relatively complete by the fourth month after birth. Myelination of the cortical areas where speech is understood and produced begins at birth, but progresses more slowly than visual systems, and proceeds strongly to the fourth year of age. The authors suggest that myelination of speech reception systems may begin *in utero* as response to *stimuli signals* (spoken words as physical agents) and during early childhood as responses to *stimuli symbols*, or language (p. 64).

Uterine Environment and Fetal Responses

The uterine environment varies with the life-style of the mother, especially from one part of the day to another. Mothers who keep regular schedules of rest, activity, and eating are likely to bear infants who are already conditioned to the day and night cycles of the family living. During the third trimester of pregnancy the growing size of the fetus forces it into closer and closer contact with the body movements and functions of the mother as it crowds into the limited dimensions of the pelvis. The increased size of the fetus imposes increasing demands on the supply of nutrients and oxygen and the potential for elimination of the maternal body. Hence the third-trimester fetus is increasingly vulnerable to nutritional deprivation, drug addiction, emotional factors, and anoxia.

DRUGS

Ferreira (1969) assumes that "everything ingested by, or injected into, the pregnant woman reaches the fetus" (p. 68). The consequences of certain drugs may not become apparent for a long period of time because some affect only a small percentage of the unborn or may affect many individuals only slightly. The interaction of the age and genetic characteristics of the fetus, the frequency and amounts of dosage, and the interaction of fetal and maternal genotypes are some of the factors that cause difficulty in establishing the effect of drugs.

The potentially damaging effects of cigarette smoking by mothers was suspected as early as the 1930s because of significant changes in heart rate in the older fetus (8 months) following the mother's smoking (Sontag et al., 1935). It was not until the 1960s that systematic research was undertaken to correlate maternal smoking with neonatal pathologies. Low birth weight, spontaneous abortion, and premature birth all occur with significantly greater frequency in smoking than in nonsmoking mothers.

Two Johns Hopkins physicians, Barry Burns and Gail Gurtner, reason that the carbon monoxide present in cigarette smoke replaces the oxygen molecules in the oxygen-binding enzymes that carry maternal oxygen to the fetus. As the fetus grows larger, the increased oxygen needed for the growth of cells is not supplied and lowered birth weights or premature delivery result (*Newsweek*, Sept. 29, 1975, p. 93). Drugs such as morphine and certain tranquilizers may act similarly to reduce the available oxygen in fetal blood.

Infants born to addicted mothers are also likely to be addicted to the same drug. Once severed from the maternal supply, they suffer withdrawal symptoms and must be treated over a period of time to overcome the habit. For a more complete account of drug effects on the fetus consult Baker (1960).

The sedative drugs administered during labor in most obstetric hospitals are known to cross the placenta within minutes and to achieve equilibrium between fetal and maternal blood systems. Stechler (1964) compared the visual attention of neonates born without medication being administered to the mother during the last $1\frac{1}{2}$ hours of labor with those who had had one of four major drugs commonly administered. The important findings were (1) significant differences in visual attention favoring neonates who received no depressants immediately before birth, (2) the effects of the drugs persisted to at least $4\frac{1}{2}$ days (when the observations terminated), and (3) the amount of medication correlated negatively with neonate visual attending.

Newborn sucking behavior is also influenced by drugs administered during labor. Routine doses of barbiturate or meperidine act upon the central nervous system to depress the sucking rate, and presumably the intake of milk, for at least the first 4 days of life. Since feeding behavior is closely related to birth weight loss, this factor is important. The effect of the drugs presumably linger longer in infants postpartum than in mothers because the infants lack comparable systems of elimination (Kron, Stein, & Goddard, 1966). Full-term normal infants usually leave the hospital when they are 4 days old; therefore the duration of sedation effects has not been adequately researched to date.

MALNUTRITION

The small-for-date infants have been divided into two groups: those with errors in the genetic makeup of the fetus (intrinsic growth failure) and those where environmental factors are causes of the abnormality (extrinsic growth failure). The environmental failures are of two types: those which affect the various organs of the fetus differently and those which result in organs of reduced size. When the mother has a vascular disease, the brain is likely to be of normal size, but the liver disproportionately small. Winick (1976) reported that the placentas from poorly nourished mothers were reduced in weight and had fewer cells than placentas from well-nourished mothers. Because of the reduced birth weights of their newborn, he assumed that the vascular supply was insufficient for fetal growth (p. 115). Maternal undernutrition was also related to reduced brain cell count in the infant. Amino acids are needed to form the proteins for growth. At least eight of these (lysine, threonine, tryphophane, methionine, phenylalanine, lucine, valine, and isoleucine) are required for growth and nitrogen balance in all mammals. Lack of any of these, or disproportionate amounts in the protein intake of the mother, will alter metabolism and lead to metabolic difficulties (p. 55). The amino acid requirement of the developing nervous system in the fetus is not known, but severe malnutrition was related to lowered intelligence in early childhood (p. 145)

Fortunately the maternal body functions normally in most pregnancies to supply the growing fetus with all the nutrients that are needed. Some critical minerals, vitamins, and proteins are not always present in adequate amounts in the typical adult diet to supply the third trimester fetus. Vitamin A, riboflavin, and thiamine deficiencies in late pregnancy have been tied to lowered learning performance in rats (Thompson & Sontag, 1956). A causal relationship between specific deprivation and learning is difficult to establish in human infants because strict dietary controls are rarely possible. When clinical experience with infants confirms laboratory research with mammals, however, responsible observers tend to listen (Joffe, 1969).

Proteinuria is the presence of protein in the urine (Lapedes, 1974). In effect, proteinuria during pregnancy is incomplete protein metabolism which deprives the fetus of sufficient protein for growth. Rosenbaum, Churchill, Shalcheshiri, and Moody (1969) studied fifty-three offspring of proteinuric mothers, identified by routine testing in the last half of pregnancy, each of whom lacked other complications. A comparison group of fifty-one infants was matched for sex, race, SES, and hospital of birth.

Although the groups were found to be similar in birth weight and gestation age, they differed on several neuropsychological measures. Proteinuric infants were significantly lower at 8 months on Bayley mental scores, at 12 months on posture and mobility scores, and at 4 years on Binet IQ scores. The researchers were not able to find evidence in the medical histories of the mothers of diseases other than proteinuria which might explain the results.

Second-generation impairment of brain development has been demonstrated in a protein-restricted diet for pregnant rats (Zaminhof, Marthens, & Gravel, 1971). The investigators reduced the protein intake of female rats (from the usual 20 percent to 8 percent of the diet). Treatment began 1 month before mating and continued to the time of delivery. At that point part of the experimental group was sacrificed for brain analysis. Animals from protein-restricted mothers had significantly lower cerebral brain weight and a lower DNA count than controls. Remaining animals were allowed to mature and then were subdivided into three groups for second-generation studies. Group A was protein-restricted during pregnancy and nursing; group B was restricted during pregnancy but changed to normal (20 percent) protein diets during nursing; and group C was fostered by control mothers on normal protein throughout. Two control groups were established: group D, protein-adequate newborns fostered by experimental protein-restricted mothers, and group E, changed to low protein (8 percent) during nursing. All five groups received normal protein from weaning to maturity. In all groups, protein restriction during prenatal development resulted in a significant reduction in brain weight and lowered DNA content in the second generation of offspring. This finding did not appear in groups in which only the lactation period was protein-restricted. When protein-deprived males were mated to normal females, the offspring were normal, suggesting that protein deprivation was environmental and not genetic in its effect. Deprivation of protein in fetal stages apparently produced inadequate mothers who affected the second generation offspring significantly.

EMOTIONAL FACTORS

Superstition has produced a collection of folklore which ties any unusual experience of a pregnant woman to birthmarks, physical defects, and personality characteristics of the child. Prenatal influences of the dramatic, single experience have been discredited. However, persisting tensions in the life of the mother have been shown to influence the activity level of the fetus and the later emotional states of infants. Emotional states of the mother are likely to affect the fetus because biological responses are involved. Endocrine balances, respiration, heart rate, and metabolism all respond to affective experience.

To test the potential detriment of noxious sound on the fetus, Thompson and Sontag (1956) subjected pregnant rats to high-frequency noise for a short time daily, beginning after the period of vulnerability to abortion was ended. Their offspring were not significantly different in litter size, birth weight, and general activity measures from the offspring of controls. In water-maze learning, however, the youngsters subjected to prenatal noise took significantly longer to learn the mazes and made significantly greater numbers of errors in performance.

Sontag (1966) summarized his own and other research on the effect of maternal stress during pregnancy on the behavior of the offspring. Severe emotional stress in human mothers caused a change in the activity levels of their fetuses. In clinical cases when fetal responses to maternal stress were prolonged, the offspring showed no congenital defects but tended to be hyperactive, irritable, and had frequent bowel movements. Any aspect of the prenatal environment that produces prolonged emotional stress on the mother should be viewed as risky.

Perception and Learning

Long before birth, the sensory systems develop to the extent that they take in information from the uterine environment and respond with appropriate activity. Carmichael (1970) considered the influence of sensory experience before birth on prenatal behavior and mental development. The movement of the organism and the chemical composition of the amniotic fluid are thought to stimulate the development of the different sensory systems in species-determined ways. All sense systems transmit messages by the same electrochemical code.

By the third trimester, specialized receptors in the skin have developed to the point that, when appropriately stimulated, the fetus moves in precise patterns that are related to the point stimulated. Proprioceptors in the muscles and joints develop early enough to develop organized control over behavioral responses to a single field of stimulation. There is evidence of feedback systems, such as prenatal eye movements, in coordination with vestibular activation through change in body position. The fetus startles to loud sounds, adapts to sleeping and waking patterns, and practices eye movements (Carmichael, 1970). It also sucks its thumb, hiccoughs, cries, and stretches (Nilssen, 1974).

Providing a Healthy Prenatal Environment

The notion that an unborn child is protected and safe from environmental hazards is no longer supported by the evidence. Prenatal life can be safeguarded and enriched by knowing and doing those things which enhance the growth and learning of the conceptus. Most environmental insults are preventable. The best defense against damaging viruses is the presence of antibodies in the mother. Since live virus immunizations are not usually recommended to pregnant women, girls should be protected from common diseases such as rubella prior to the childbearing age (Silverstein, 1968).

The present state of knowledge permits women to know, through temperature taking and observing the cyclic reactions of their own bodies, when ovulation occurs. The advantage of family planning is that the embryo can be protected from the insults of ordinary living during the early stages when it is most vulnerable. When an unplanned pregnancy occurs, an immediate check with a physician or clinic can help a young mother establish a protective environment. Rugh and Shettles (1971) recommend that no medication of any kind be taken by prospective mothers without specific instructions from the physician.

Pregnancy is usually not the time in life to lose weight. A balanced diet plus additional amounts of protein, calcium and other minerals, and the required known vitamins can be determined by a physician for each trimester of the pregnancy. Despite contrary advice from some sources, Winick (1976) recommended a 25-pound weight increase for mothers during a pregnancy.

Moderate exercise on a regular schedule provides vestibular stimulation for the unborn child. Exercise keeps the maternal muscles toned for giving birth and for the exertion of caring for a newborn. Some restriction of active sports or work may be necessary in the third trimester when body balance and freedom of movement are restricted. The pregnancy goes faster psychologically when a schedule of activities preoccupies the mind. Music, conversation, and the sounds of normal living penetrate the uterus and activate the developing auditory systems of the fetus. The sounds which call up pleasure feelings in a pregnant woman are extended, through their interacting endocrine systems, to the unborn child.

Ninety-five percent of all full-term infants are born normal (Milunsky, 1973). Emotional health and freedom from unusual stress are a parent's great gift to an unborn child. If either parent is concerned about the intrauterine environment or the possibility of the fetus being abnormal, expert advice should be sought. Presently it is possible to photograph a fetus in the uterus when severe malformations are suspected. Prenatal diagnosis of many viral and hereditary disorders is possible through tests of the mother's urine and blood or by sampling the amniotic fluid in which the fetus lives. Milunsky recommended prenatal diagnosis and counseling whenever the risk of having defective children is high (p. 150).

FETAL EXPERIENCE DURING THE BIRTH PROCESS

Laymen and pediatricians each have their private views of when a newly conceived individual becomes a person: at conception, at implantation, at the end of the first trimester when human characteristics distinguish the fetus, or at the end of the second trimester when there is a chance (albeit a slim one) of survival. The birth of an infant is accepted by almost everyone as the primordial event, the natal day, the beginning of life. To the neonate, life functions are continuous from one protective environment (*in utero*) to another protective environment (postpartum). When considered ontogenically, birth is a transition point; it is neither a beginning nor an end. The individual who emerges crying from the womb is an integrated person equipped by genetics and prenatal learning to interact in unique ways with people and objects. The process of being born is a hazardous experience, not without discomfort and frustration. Society (including parents) cannot spare the perinatal individual the pangs of growth; but much can be done to reduce the trauma and the risks of being born. The neonate is fortunate who has had the normal period of 266 days to develop and to practice the biological systems for living and learning.

Fetal Influence on the Onset of Labor

The human infant is thrust into a relatively cool world by the contractions of the pelvic muscles of the mother, or taken by surgery through the abdomen. It is believed that the interaction between the fetus, the mother, and the placenta is responsible for the onset of labor. One explanation is that the endocrine productions of the fetus respond to its own increasing need for sustenance while the potential of the placenta to supply these needs decreases. In any case appropriate maternal hormonal secretions are required to induce labor.

Normal labor requires about twelve hours, although this varies by six hours either way in deliveries that are considered normal. During this time the ingestion and elimination processes of the fetus continue to be supported via the umbilical cord. Two dramatic changes must occur simultaneously with the severance of the cord: a shift to self-contained circulation of blood that formerly flowed through the placenta and the expansion of the lungs to process air rather than fluid. The timing of these changes is vital in order that oxygen be continuously supplied to the blood of the neonate and that this oxygen be circulated continuously to the brain.

Perinatal Hazards

At delivery the umbilical cord is immediately clamped and cut. The neonate breathes within a few seconds and cries within half a minute. The shock of emerging into a relatively cold world, and sometimes then being slapped on the buttocks by the physician, is accompanied by a gasp reflex on the part of the perinatal infant. This gasp takes in air and expands the lungs. The muscles that had brought fluid into the lungs and expelled it are capable of inhaling and expelling oxygen-bearing air. The continuous supply of oxygen to all cells is essential for the separate survival of the neonate.

Important changes occur at birth in the pattern of circulation of blood through the heart. During fetal life the limited blood flow needed by the lungs is routed from the pulmonary artery through a special blood vessel, called the *ductus arteriosus*, into the aorta. At birth the wall of the ductus arteriosus contracts, constricting the flow of blood through it and rerouting the necessary amounts of blood to the lungs. Following birth new tissue grows into the collapsed vessel, permanently closing it. Before birth the wall between the right and left atria is incomplete and blood entering the two sides of the heart mixes. When the infant begins to breathe, a flap of tissue is pressed into place, closing the opening between the two chambers. Later the flap grows into place and normal circulation patterns are assured (Rugh & Shettles, 1971). This intricate process is sometimes incomplete and heart surgery during infancy is necessary.

Anoxia

Even a short interruption between the severing of the umbilical cord and the rhythmic breathing of the neonate can result in brain damage. The condition in which an organism is deprived of oxygen is called *anoxia*. Brain cells are most vulnerable of all the cells to oxygen deprivation. Severe damage often occurs to the brainstem, or bulbar cells, causing a *palsy*, a disease in which muscular control is inadequate and coordinated movements required for walking and talking are affected (Chapter 12). Epilepsy and mental retardation are also associated with severe or prolonged anoxia.

Mild anoxia during birth is much more common. The most frequently documented syndrome is *minimal brain dysfunction*, which is the most common cause of referral in clinics that treat behavioral disorders or learning difficulties in children (Wender, 1971). Children with minimal brain dysfunction are seen as unorganized, hyperactive, and unresponsive to the typical social reinforcement of family life and school experience (Pasamanick & Knoblock, 1960). Although their general intelligence is normal or above, they frequently experience difficulty in learning to read (Robeck, 1971). Anoxia is associated with both prolonged and very brief labor.

Joffe (1969) suggested that fetal anoxia may cause premature birth. Anoxia may result from maternal high blood pressure, which reduces the blood supply to the fetus, or from maternal anemia, which reduces the oxygen-transporting molecules in the blood. Anoxia cannot be considered apart from fetal responses that induce premature labor and from other birth complications which are related. Anoxia in the neonate is accompanied by lower weight gains shortly after birth, less responsive feeding behavior (Brazelton, 1971), and greater vulnerability to infection.

Other Birth Complications

Hyperanxious mothers are more likely than confident mothers to experience complications in delivery. Anxious mothers are also more likely to bear infants who experience difficulty in establishing their own respiration than less anxious mothers (Pasamanick, Rogers, & Lilienfeld, 1956). It has been suggested that an unhealthy fetus may have a causal influence on the mother's negative reaction to pregnancy (Moss, 1970). Although males are conceived at a ratio of 3:2 compared with females, that ratio is evened to 1:1 by the end of the first year of life (Serr & Ismajovich, 1963). The interaction between the mental health of the mother and the physical stresses on the fetus at birth remains complex.

Socioeconomic status is related to birth complications. In a comparison of white and nonwhite Americans, lower SES classes of both groups were more likely to have had unfortunate perinatal experiences. Mothers from low-income groups were more likely to have had substandard prenatal care, more birth complications, and greater instances of prematurity. Upper-income classes in both white and nonwhite groups resembed each other in having fewer postnatal complications and infant deaths (Hendricks, 1967).

Contributions of the Newborn to Medicine

The vein from the umbilical cord of newborn infants is being used experimentally to provide replacement veins for adults. The vein is used because it is of greater diameter than either of the two arteries. The umbilical vein is easy to suture into place, it is available in long segments, it is less likely to be rejected than other tissues, and it tends not to develop clots in the receiving patient as frequently as blood-vessel grafts made from synthetic fabrics do (*Newsweek*, Sept. 29, 1975, p. 93).

SUMMARY

The first trimester of prenatal life is a period of differentiation. The fertilized ovum differentiates within the first two weeks to three cell layers. The ectoderm, or outer layer, is the beginning of the brain and other parts of the nervous system. The inner layer, the endoderm, becomes the respiratory and digestive systems. The mesoderm, which forms between the other layers, is the beginning of the heart, skeleton, muscles, and reproductive systems. By the end of the second week the organism has implanted itself in the wall of the mother's uterus and the placenta has begun to grow. The placenta is now understood to be an organ of exchange of enzymes, hormones, and antibodies, as well as the mechanism for supplying nutrients and removing waste from the unborn. The placental membranes selectively transfer molecules without mixing the blood of the fetus and the mother.

During the life of the embryo all the important systems are laid down. The brain forms from a neural tube and apparently directs much of the growth in other systems. The heart begins to function during the third week, and circulates its own blood from that time on. The respiratory and elimination systems form in the embryo, using amniotic fluid to function. By the end of the eighth week the cartilage which forms the fetal skeleton begins to accept deposits of calcium to form bones. This is the medical distinction which marks the end of embryonic life and the beginning of the fetal stage.

Sex differentiation also occurs in the first trimester. Although sex is determined in the genes, all mammals are typed as female in embryonic life. The differentiation of male genitalia begins when the organism begins to produce its own androgens (male sex hormone) which suppress the further development of female genitalia and stimulate the growth of male structures.

The second trimester is a period of activity in which the various systems, laid down in the embryonic stage, are elaborated and practiced. The fetus begins many new behaviors such as coordinated movement of the limbs, hiccoughing, and thumb-sucking. These behaviors can be thought of as primitive learning during which actions become patterns. Stimulation of systems through activity may be reinforcing to the organism in much the same way that newborns are stimulated to practice their biological systems and adapt.

The third trimester is characterized by rapid growth in body size. All biological systems reach the maturity that enables the neonate to survive on its own. The nervous systems mature and elaborate. Dendrites interconnect the neural cell bodies that were laid down earlier in development. Many of the axons which transmit messages from one part of the system to another grow a myelin sheath which insulates the cell from interfering messages, commits the cell to a particular function, and speeds the transmission of neural impulses. The motor systems develop reflexive patterns of response to touch. The auditory and vestibular systems, which receive considerable stimulation before birth, mature markedly during the third trimester. The intrauterine environment is believed to interact in biologically determined ways to prepare the human fetus for its particular social existence.

4
The Competence of Infants

4 The Competence of Infants

From the first day of life the human infant is a responsive, perceiving, learning individual. The processing of sensory information, which began in fetal life, is intensified at birth by increased stimulation from an environment suddenly less protective than the womb. Because the neural systems have been functioning throughout the third trimester, neonate behavior adapts quickly to new sources of nurturing. The baby is not only prepared developmentally to respond to the demands of a changed environment but is prepared biologically to influence this environment through appeals and demands toward other persons.

The title for this chapter was inspired by a large and impressive book called *The Competent Infant*. Stone, Smith, and Murphy (1973) selected and republished 200 articles written primarily by researchers who had observed and been impressed by the psychological functioning of human infants. The collective views of these writers differed greatly from more traditional scientific sources. To make their point the editors quote from many experts who mistakenly present neonates and young infants as nonsocial organisms whose perceptual world is undifferentiated (pp. 3–4).

Unfortunately many adults treat newborn humans as if they were as unintelligent as they are helpless. Therefore some care-givers fail to initiate the interactions a newborn human needs to develop physically, socially, and intellectually. Some researchers have considered the possibility of intelligent behavior on the part of human neonates and have developed new techniques to observe their perceptual processes and responsiveness. Since babies cannot talk, some investigations have been limited because the researchers assumed the infants' inability to perceive and the appropriate questions were not asked. It is no accident that infants failed to smile for Spitz until the third to fifth month (1965, p. 20), whereas many of them smiled for Brazelton on the second day after birth (1969). These two good doctors both loved children, but they approached them with very different assumptions about the competence of neonates and infants.

As early as 1959, Peter Wolff published observations in which the infant smile was observed repeatedly. He described the smile and interpreted it as a beginning of affective expression.

Spontaneous *smiling* (defined as a slow, gentle, sideward and upward pull of the mouth, without rhythmical mouthing movements or contraction of other facial muscles) was observed after the first 24 hours in all 4 infants during irregular sleep, drowsiness, and alert inactivity, but never during regular sleep, alert activity, or between bursts of crying. (1973, p. 264)

Wolff reported wide individual differences in the instances of smiling in neonates.

The purpose of this chapter is to describe the nature and individuality of human infants, so that adult care-givers can interact with their infants in ways that nurture and teach long before the baby learns to speak. The focus is on the social and sensorimotor capabilities of human infants from birth to approximately 1 year, when mobility increases their control over their own environment and radically changes the nature of their experience. The sources included here were selected primarily from research that probes beyond the obvious dependence of human infants. An effort has been made to include sources that help parents and teachers know what the baby is discriminating and how to respond intelligently.

ACCOMPLISHMENTS OF THE FIRST YEAR

The developmental achievements of the first year of life are unmatched during any of the later years. The physical growth rate of the infant is exceeded only by the weight and height increases of fetal life. Emotionally the infant's well-being requires an early smile, an early attachment toward another person, and the skills for affective communication with people generally. Intellectually the infant learns to understand human speech, to visualize objects or persons not present, and to direct body movements with intention. The young of the human species is biologically equipped to do these things. Motor skills such as turning over, sitting, crawling, and standing are self-taught.

Biological Survival

The first major task of the newborn is to breathe. Mammals share the advantages of a life prolonged *in utero*. Lung breathing allows mammals to reach a relatively complex development within the protection of the maternal body, but also involves the necessity of switching from using fluid-bound oxygen to breathing air. Practice of autonomic life-support systems before birth is necessary to prepare the fetus for the trauma of birth.

The necessity of regulating the respiratory system in order to get oxygen from the air evolved late in the phylogenic sequence. This shift in the way oxygen is received, and the necessity for the newborn to integrate circulation, respiration, digestion, and elimination, may account for the late development of the mammal cerebellum at the base of the brain. The cerebellum is the only part of the brain where massive duplication and migration of cell layers occur after, rather than before, birth (Figure 4-1). Although these functions are programmed in the genetic code of the species, they arise from within the infant, who takes in sensory cues from a radically changed environment.

A second necessity for survival is to establish an emotional relationship with other humans. The major affective accomplishment of infancy is learning to separate *self* (the organism) from the *surround* (the environment of objects and persons) (Spitz, 1965). Social psychologists and psychoanalysts have given much attention to this aspect of human development. Infants are said to be egocentric in their emotional interaction. In the psychoanalytic sense, *egocentrism* means that the infant does not know the boundaries of his or her own body as distinct from all else—the handler, the mother's breast, the bottle, or the blanket. Even after learning to discriminate moods and emotions the infant still does not know there is another way of feeling (the other person's). Responsible parenting requires that an infant have opportunities for exploring the social surround, while being protected from destructive elements in the environment.

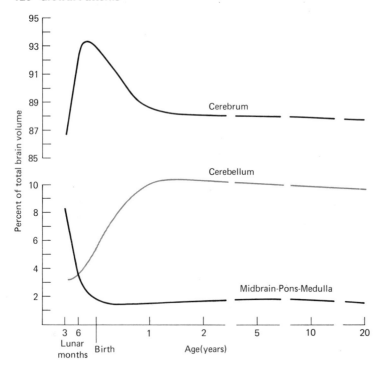

FIGURE 4-1 Percentage of total brain volume contributed by cerebrum, cerebellum, and midbrain before and after birth. Note the relatively late increase in structures of the cerebellum. (Data from Dunn, 1921; White House Conference, 1933.)

Source: J. M. Tanner, *Education and Physical Growth.* Copyright © University of London Press, 1970. By permission of Hodder & Stoughton, Ltd.

Very young infants explore the emotional behavior of their handlers by attending to their facial expressions and associating changes with voice and body language. Freedman (1974) showed that human neonates follow a human face significantly more than a shiny object and follow a combination of face and voice the most. The human visual system is equipped at birth to select survival-significant cues (Figure 4-2). The vision of newborns accommodates best to near-point stimuli, which is the typical distance of the handler. Infant interpretation of mood as revealed in facial expression develops very early; parents need to be aware of the infant's early ability to read their emotions.

A third major accomplishment of infancy is what cognitive psychologists call *object constancy* (Piaget, 1952). To have learned object constancy means to have conceptualized that concrete things exist, even though not seen at the moment, that things in the physical environment are real. The infant learns this gradually and through many sensorimotor experiences. Actions on an object create mental structures of the object in the form of sight, touch, and sound images. Seeing an object from many perspectives and exploring it through tactile and kinesthetic senses, including grasping and mouthing, is conducive to the child's learning. The

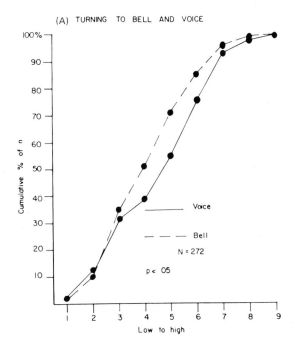

(A) TURNING TO BELL AND VOICE

Voice

——— Bell

N = 272

p < 05

Cumulative % of n

Low to high

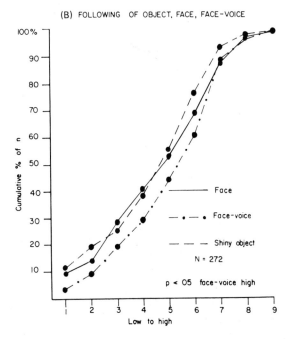

(B) FOLLOWING OF OBJECT, FACE, FACE-VOICE

Face

— · — Face-voice

— — — Shiny object

N = 272

p < 05 face-voice high

Cumulative % of n

Low to high

FIGURE 4-2 Neonates respond more to human stimuli than to objects. **A.** Preference of voice over bell, shown by turning. **B.** Preference of face with voice over silent face or object, as shown by visual following.

Source: Daniel G. Freedman, *Human Infancy: An Evolutionary Perspective.* Hillsdale, N.J.: Lawrence Erlbaum Associates, 1974, page 25.

adult-infant game of hiding and uncovering objects can be helpful in the discovery of object constancy.

Piaget (1952) played the game of hiding and uncovering objects with his own infants. He believed that the sensory representations of objects experienced by infants are the concrete images of symbol representations and the foundations of human intelligence. Piaget noted that the reflex systems of the neonate were the observable, behavioral counterpart of the internal (neurological) structures that make the behavior possible. This assumption of inner structures that change with experience is an important concept in child development.

Freedman (1974) studied child development from an evolutionary perspective. He described the uniqueness of the human infant among species as involving:

. . . its relative immaturity at birth, its slow motor development, its complex, extended vocal and visual interaction with the caretaker (including smiling and babbling), its excellent eye-hand coordination and manipulative abilities (at about seven months) and, at about 1 year, its ability to walk erect, to use language, and its developing sense of self or "me." . . . (p. 50)

He pointed out the uniqueness of caretaking within the human family unit. He also suggested that human adults (like macaques) are completely nurturant of very young infants but are able to provide flexible guidance when the youngster becomes mobile and assertive.

Physical Growth

Growth patterns are determined genetically and are regulated by the hormone production of the organism itself. Tanner (1970) described the cycles of physical development in childhood (Figure 4-3). The reader will recall that brain and nervous system develop from the ectoderm. These structures increase more rapidly during infancy than physical growth in general.

By averaging the weight and height of many infants, researchers have determined the norms for growth in the early years. The newborn's weight of $7\frac{1}{2}$ pounds nearly triples during the first year to about 20 pounds (Bayley, 1956). Height, measured when lying stretched on the table, increases by about one-third—from 20 ± 1 inches to a range of 26 to 28 inches. Individual children, if nourished adequately, will vary around those averages according to their individual genetic makeup.

Body proportions change as legs increase more rapidly than the trunk and the head becomes smaller in relation to the rest of the body. The bones continue to harden from the calcium deposits that invade already formed cartilage structures. The calcification of bones is revealed by x-rays which sometimes are used as a measure of organismic age. The skeletons of girls tend to ossify faster than those of boys and broad-framed children mature faster than slimly built children (Bayley, 1956). The muscle structure is laid down before birth, but growth is achieved through the lengthening and thickening of fibers.

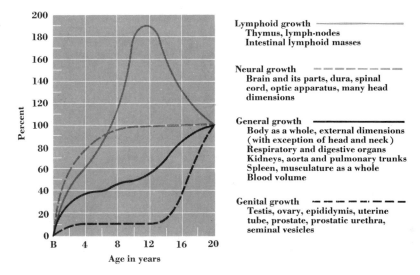

FIGURE 4-3 Growth patterns from birth to maturity.

Source: R. E. Scammon, *The Measurement of Man*, 1930. By permission of the University of Minnesota Press.

Motor Development

Some important events of neuromotor development are rolling over and gaining a sitting position alone. McGraw (1945) identified four positions that lead to rolling from a supine (face up) to a prone (face down) position (Figure 4-4). She found individual differences in age but overall consistency in the behaviors which evolved. She considered rolling to face an extension of the righting behavior of the fetal period.

Sitting alone enables the child to manipulate with both hands and to explore space on a horizontal plane. McGraw used motion-picture sequences of many infants to identify five phases of rising activity that strengthen the back and limbs for sitting alone (Figure 4-5). The infants she photographed were able to achieve and maintain a sitting position during the tenth month. She described creeping as the forerunner of climbing. Standing, the precursor to walking and running, is described as a single sequence in the present book in Chapter 5 on toddlerhood.

This section previewed the major affective and cognitive accomplishments for survival during the first year as background for more detailed discussion of the following topics: (a) the inherited mechanisms which make coping possible for the newborn, (b) the effectiveness of sensory systems in early infancy, (c) vision as the organizer of human experience, (d) hearing and understanding, (3) scales of infant development, and (f) implications of research for the infant environment.

FIGURE 4-4 Four positions involved in rolling from a supine to a prone position.

Source: Myrtle B. McGraw, *The Neuromuscular Maturation of the Human Infant*, page 45. Copyright Columbia University Press, 1945.

COPING BEHAVIORS OF NEONATES

The neonate is born with many survival mechanisms including the neonate's own innate drives, some well-developed reflex systems, at least eight functioning sensory analyzers, and the potential for adaptation (learning). The neural system of the newborn regulates the sleep states. Such regulation, which continues throughout life, is important because essential stimuli are received while asleep but unessential responses are repressed. Thus the newborn and other persons are allowed regular periods for rest and recovery.

By medical criteria the period of the neonate begins with the cutting of the umbilical cord at parturition and ends with the shedding of the cord when the navel is healed, when the infant is about 2 weeks old. During this time the infant will adapt to independent life by stabilizing the life-sustaining functions of breathing, feeding, and eliminating. Normally, the adjustments of metabolism to temperature change have been stabilized, and the weight lost while feeding patterns were established has been regained. The shedding of the umbilical cord is one of many landmarks in growing up.

Innate Drives

Brazelton (1969) described the infant as biologically prepared for tuning in parts of the environment that catch attention and also for reaching out to establish contact

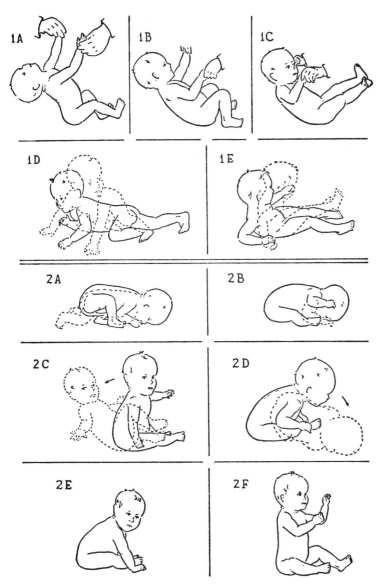

FIGURE 4-5 Five phases of rising and six phases of achieving a sitting position. Drawn from motion pictures frames.

Source: Myrtle B. McGraw, *The Neuromuscular Maturation of the Human Infant*, page 64. Copyright, 1945, Columbia University Press.

with people and things. He discussed the inner forces which the behavior of the newborn reflects: (1) the drive to survive independently in a complex world, (2) a drive toward mastery, together with an excitement that accompanies it, and (3) the drive to fit into and identify with other people, to please, and to become part of the environment. The drive toward sociability and identification must be nurtured, according to Brazelton, to maintain its impact as a reinforcer in the child's learning. According to this theory the caring behaviors of adults condition the infant to particular affects that accompany need gratification. The infant becomes responsive to social rewards which in turn become the reinforcers for a wide variety of cognitive and social learning.

Reflexive Behavior

A *reflex* is defined by physiologists as an automatic response mediated by the nervous system (Lapedes, 1974). Reflexive behavior is a sequence of responses to particular external stimuli or internal conditions; hence, reflexive behavior may be observed in the absence of external environmental change. These automatic responses enable newborn infants to practice movement patterns that they will control voluntarily at a later period. The reflexes of neonates are observed and evaluated as evidence of their neurological maturation and integration. Brazelton (1969) used the early reflexes as part of his neonatal behavior assessment scales to observe individual viability in infants. Although many reflex responses are functioning at birth, only a few of them have been studied extensively.

Knowing how an infant will respond to particular stimulations can be reassuring to young parents. One important sequence of behavior patterns which have immediate survival values is *rooting, sucking,* and *swallowing.* Rooting is the mouth searching and head turning that is set off by a soft touch to the cheek or the chin. The rooting reflex has survival value initially because it helps the newborn to find the breast. Within a few days, rooting behavior may be initiated by the infant and may cue the parent when an infant is hungry. The sucking reflex follows rooting behavior, but it is also seen during sleep. Sucking is stimulated (in order of effectiveness) by touches to the soft palate, to the mouth interior or lips, and to the cheek or the chin. The swallowing reflex follows sucking movements, even when the infant is not feeding. Within a few days after birth, the alert infant has learned to associate this chain of responses to feeding; but the vestiges of the sucking reflex can be observed years later in adult tooth grinding during sleep.

The *hand-to-mouth* cycle is established long before birth and stimulates fetal development when the sucking of thumb or fingers results in the swallowing of amniotic fluid. After birth, this reflex has survival value in helping the neonate swallow to rid itself of mucus. During this gagging and spitting effort, the neonate sometimes stops breathing momentarily and then gasps to regain the breathing rhythm. Gagging is essential to life and is reinforced by the infant's own efforts to clear its respiratory tracts. By lowering the neonate's head slightly when held and by raising the foot of the crib when putting the neonate down to sleep, care-givers can make spitting and clearing easier for the infant (Brazelton, 1969). The *gasping*

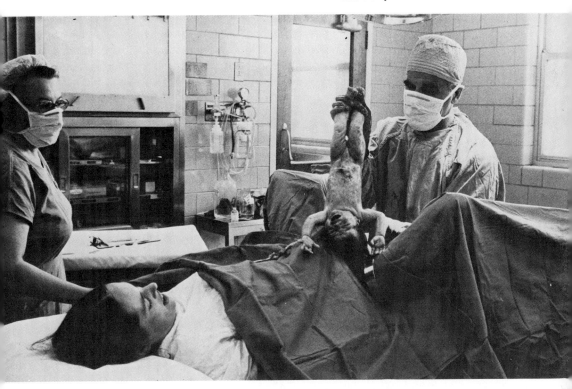

Newborn humans come equipped with reflex patterns that help them survive. (Bob Combs/Photo Researchers, Inc.)

reflex is one of the strongest at birth, even in premature infants who often lack other strong reflexive responses.

The *Moro reflex* is a startle response to a sudden change in sensation, such as a loud noise or a marked shift in position. The infant's head drops back, arms are thrown out, and neck (and often legs) is extended. Then the infant cries and brings the arms together in a clasping motion, sometimes flexing the thumb in a grasping motion. The Moro reflex is considered a remnant of primate behavior, exhibited when the newborn had to clasp and cling to the mother to stay with the troop. The infant is startled because the flow of sensations to which she or he has habituated are disrupted. Swaddling usually helps to settle a startled infant and many cultures use the procedure for all newborns. The Moro reflex disappears in three months or less, indicating that a stage in the normal development of the nervous system has passed.

The *Babinski reflex*, the fanning of toes when the bottom of the foot is touched, is similarly considered a vestige of primitive behavior. One function of this fanning is the activation of neural relays to and from the motor cortex at a time when the lower limbs of humans have little necessity for functioning.

The *stepping reflex* is the walking motion of infants when held upright with feet touching a level surface. Part of the reaction is a stiffening of the legs, called *pushing off*, upon contact with the soles of the feet. Like the grasping reflex, which is strong in the newborn, these reflexive behaviors often convince the parents of the firstborn that theirs is a precocious child who is already eager to hold things and to walk. The *righting reflex* is seen in the infant's efforts to keep the head upright even though turned in different positions. These responses disappear, sometimes just before a proud father tries to show them to visitors, and must be acquired gradually as a directed behavior. Nevertheless, the neural structures for standing and walking have been laid down and practiced early.

The *tonic neck reflex*, referred to as TNR in the literature, is a complex sequence of actions. When the head is turned to one side, the body arches away from the face side, and the arm on the side faced extends while the opposing arm flexes. The leg on the face side flexes while the opposing leg extends. The reader may recall (Chapter 3) that fetal motor responses first involve the use of one side of the body or the other side; this type of response occurs prior to the bilateral integration that is shown in the TNR. The TNR is important in diagnosing neurological deficiencies at birth and in testing the effects of various drugs used during labor. At 4 weeks normal infants assume the TNR reflex spontaneously; however, by 20 weeks they maintain the head in midposition, assuming a symmetric pattern of body position rather than the previous asymmetric pattern.

The dominant face direction of the TNR is predictive of later handedness in most infants (Gesell and Ames, 1937). Parents may be assured that normal patterns of TNR are indicative of normal motor development. When the reflex pattern does not occur and disappear at the approximate scheduled time, intervention may be needed in the form of physical therapy to enhance motor development (Rider, 1972).

Care-givers are often intrigued by the *propel reflex*, an amphibianlike movement during bathing, which happens also to be integrated with inhibited breathing. Island babies, Polynesians for example, can swim before they can walk because the movements are learned easily and the water supports most of the body weight.

The *Babkin reflex*, only recently discovered, is elicited by pressing the neonate's palms. The response is a wide opening of the mouth and a turning of the head toward midline from the TNR. Kaye (1965) was able to demonstrate conditioning in the newborn by pairing this reflex to an armsweep stimulation while eliminating the palm stimulation, thus demonstrating learning in human newborns.

The *stretch reflex* is a prewalking action. Neurologically, the stretch provides a bombardment of conflicting impulses which must be processed. These relay systems will later call forth the sustained muscle control needed for standing erect, for walking, and for turning (Woodburne, 1967, p. 113). Another suggestion by Peiper (1963) is that reflexive behaviors appear because the neural circuits are completed while the appropriate inhibiting mechanisms are not. Part of the development necessary before deliberate walking can occur is the growth of inhibiting mechanisms. Learning to run occurs before learning to stop suddenly (Chapter 6).

Defecation and urination require more complex response sequences than *knee-jerk* or fetal *withdrawal* reflexes. In infants elimination functions involve a global effort which is partially retained in the squatting posture of older children and adults when defecating.

Many other reflexes assist the neonate in coping with life. The *conjugate movements* of two eyes in following, *pupillary contraction*, and *distance accommodation* all function at birth. Adaptation to light is very efficient, but accommodation is limited to near points (Woodburne, 1967). The *doll's-eye reflex* is the tendency for the eyes to open when the infant is pulled to a sitting position. It is a phenomenon often noted by adoring parents without any cues from experts. The *blink reflex* protects the infant from foreign material getting into the eyes. Researchers observe this reflex to find out when the eye is responding to an approaching object (White, 1968).

Neonatal reflexes are species-determined; they are relatively simple behaviors, and all are responsive in predetermined ways to environmental forces (Woodburne, 1967, p. 4). From birth the reflexes adapt rapidly, become more and more flexible, and come increasingly under the control of the infant. Some reflexes, such as blinking, remain under the subcortical control; but others, such as eye movements in reading and breathing during speech, are controlled from the cerebral cortex. Knowing the prominent infant reflexes assures a parent or caretaker that inner mechanisms are functioning normally.

Adaptive Potential

Despite this portrait of the neonate as an integrated, adaptive individual the appearance of the newborn is in sharp contrast to the cute dimpled baby pictured in the diaper ads. The newborn is covered with *vernix caseosa*, a cheesy, slick coating which has the dual functions of protecting the fetal skin from irritants in the amniotic fluid and of smoothing the birth passage. Admitting the father to the delivery room may have advantages for later parenting, but he should be prepared for the arrival of a messy-looking offspring and for the hospital procedures which follow. To initiate breathing within half a minute after the umbilical cord is clamped, the neoate is sometimes held with its feet up and slapped sharply. A more gentle delivery has been developed in France during which the newborn is placed in warm water and comforted by stroking, and generally spared the birth trauma. The possible need for a lusty birth cry has not been researched.

The parents of firstborn children, whether witnesses to the birth or not, are likely to be shocked by a drowsy, unresponsive neonate or by one who wails with rage and refuses to be quieted. Often the newborn's head is misshapen from the birth channel. Sometimes there are facial indentations left by a forceps, and perhaps there are red splotches around the eyes from silver nitrate. The baby is so unlike the alert dimpled beauty on the birth announcements that the naive father may feel loathe to mail them. (An army officer, whose 5-year-old daughter tested at about 150 IQ on the Binet scales, confessed he had worried for months following her birth that she was mentally retarded.) An infant from birth needs messages of caring, along with holding, changing, feeding, and greeting. Subtle and unconscious rejection, even though temporary, may have long-term consequences for a youngster. On the positive side, a human newborn usually quiets from a rage when lifted from the crib, cradled on a shoulder, and is spoken to face to face in gentle tones. Freedman (1974) proposes that this behavior is innate to the species since it occurs within the first 24 hours, prior to any feeding or other reinforcement.

States of Sleep and Alertness

Among the most important tasks in interpreting the behavior of an infant is observing and understanding its state of sleep (Table 4-1). The researcher, particularly, must know the baby's level of alertness before useful observations can be made. The parent will find it exciting to be able to detect the rapid eye movements (REM) and to know the brain is very active at that moment during sleeping.

SLEEP BEHAVIORS

Peter Wolff (1959) initially classified the neonate states of sleep and waking by making the most detailed observations recorded at that time. With the help of an assistant, he observed neonates, almost around the clock, to cover the full sequence of tending and feeding. Although his sample included only four infants, the perceptiveness of the observations and the precision of the recording became the basis for classification of infant alertness states for many years (Wolff, 1966). In *regular sleep* the infant is at full rest, showing low muscle tonus, little or no motor activity, closed lids with no spontaneous eye movements, no grimaces, and an even respiration. More recent classifications refer to this state as deep sleep (Eisenberg, 1976, pp. 268–269). In *irregular sleep* some muscle tonus is apparent; limb and general movements occur; grimaces are frequent and varied; eyelids, though closed, show rapid eye movements (both vertical and horizontal); gross mouthing movements occur; and respiration is irregular. In *periodic sleep* the behavior patterns alternate between regular and irregular sleep, as shown by periodic shifts in the respiration rhythms.

Rapid eye movements.   Current research on sleeping and dreaming relies on the presence or absence of rapid eye movements. Laboratory measures of brain waves (EEG), heart rate, respiration, and body movement have made it possible for researchers to know the sleep and alertness states precisely. Eisenberg (1976) used these measures to refine "eyeballing" techniques for observing infant behavior to the point where observers could record data in natural settings without the use of special equipment.

Rapid eye movements have come to mean the beginning of light sleep or the ending of deep sleep. In adults, REMs identify the dream state. Roffwarg, Muzio, and Dement (1966) studied dreaming in the newborn using both visual and EEG indicators. They found that almost half of the sleeping time of neonates up to less than 5 days old is accompanied by REMs. As in adults they found infant brain

Table 4-1
STATES OF SLEEP AND ALERTNESS IN YOUNG INFANTS

State	Motor activity	Visual activity	Other observations	Electrophysical indicators
Deep sleep	Full rest; little or no movement; spontaneous startles (2-3 minutes)	Closed lids; no eye movements	Low muscle tonus; even respiration	Slow heart rate
Irregular sleep	Some body writhing; twitching of extremities; occasional limb movement; few startles	Closed lids; bursts of REM (vertical and horizontal	Some muscle tonus; mouthing and sucking movements; irregular grimaces; smiling; shifts in breathing to shallow and rapid	Increase waves in EEG; irregular pattern
Doze	Stretching and writhing when awakening (not when falling asleep); considerable limb movement	Eyes open and close; glassy in appearance; eyelid flutter; blinking	Vocalizations, sucking and grimacing; regular respiration	Sporadic EEG
Awake: inactive	Nominal motor activity; mostly head and extremities	Eyes open and fairly bright	Face relaxed; respiration regular but more rapid than deep sleep	EEG rhythmic at central cortex
Awake: alert	Little motor activity	Eyes open and bright; visual scanning, tracking, or focusing	Occasional breath holding; state for testing visual-auditory tracking	Flat EEG during focus of attention
Awake: active	Much body movement; gross arm movements	Eyes open and shiny	Irregular respiration	Motor overlay in EEG
Crying	Gross motor activity	Not focused; eyes close when mouth opens	Flushed skin; intensified breathing	Rapid heart rate; EEG pattern obliterated by motor activity

activity vigorous during REM sleep. Since the dream in adults is a sequence of visual-auditory imagery, and since neonates lack the stored experience to conjure an adult-type dream, investigators have been curious about the function of REM sleep in infants.

Premature infants show a greater percentage of REM sleep than do full-term babies. Corresponding negatively to the age from conception the most premature survivors show nearly 100 percent REM sleep, while eighth-month babies show 80 percent REM sleep (Parmelee, Akiyama, & Wenner, 1964). During early childhood the proportion of REM activity during sleep falls off, as does the amount of total sleep. By late childhood the REM is present in only about 20 percent or less of the sleeping hours.

Neural activity in dreaming.   According to neurological evidence, the REM control mechanism is located in the *pons*, which is located in the primitive brainstem. The reader will recall that the pons and the cerebellum differentiated near the end of the first trimester. The pons contains interconnecting axons between the two parts of the cerebellum (which integrate automatic movements) and higher formations, especially the hypothalamus. Interesting to note is that the area which controls consciousness is located higher in the brainstem, in a newer, more recently evolved region. Multiple relays of impulses fan out from this higher region (of the hypothalamus and the thalamus) to locations on the cerebral cortex that store sense data and control motor activity (Penfield, 1975).

One possible function of REM before birth is to stimulate the maturation of the central nervous system at a time when external sensory stimulation is minimal (Roffwarg, Muzio, & Dement, 1966, p. 280). The REM responds to growth needs that arise from within the organism. Following birth, REMs continue to occur through one-third of the daily life of the full-term neonate. In older children REMs and dreams, prior to awakening, are thought to tone the nervous system for taking in and responding to experience upon awakening. Even in adulthood, REMs synchronize the eyes for the complex task of bilateral perception.

WAKING STATES

Wolff (1966) was definitive about states of the neonate when awake. In *drowsiness* the infant is more active than in regular sleep, but less active than in irregular sleep. The eyes open and close. Stretching or writhing is noted when awakening, but not when falling asleep. During *alert inactivity* the face is relaxed, the eyes are open and bright, motor activity is nominal, and respiration is regular but more rapid than in drowsiness. Brazelton (1969) later found the alert inactive state to be essential when testing the sensorimotor abilities of the newborn.

During *waking activity* the infant shows spurts of widespread body movement; the eyes are open but do not "shine" as in alert inactivity (Wolff, 1966). The infant may make the cry grimace or whimper but does not cry. The respiration is grossly irregular but the patterns are in concert with the varied motor activity. *Crying* is accompanied by gross motor activity, flushed skin, and intensified breathing. Wolff did not classify the crying states, but he did observe differentiation in crying during the first 5 days of life and recommended further study.

Wolff's classification of waking states enabled him to study the visual and auditory abilities when the neonate was in an optimum state of responsiveness, the awake-alert state. This distinction suggested why various observers disagreed on whether the newborn was capable of *auditory pursuit*, as shown by turning toward a tuning fork, or *visual pursuit*, as shown by following a moving object with the eyes. Wolff also observed that during the alert inactive state he could elicit a spontaneous smile by gentle tactile stimulation. Citing the difficulty in distinguishing "affect expressive" movements of infants, he launched a behavioral study of affective states by comparing the activities of neonates before and after meals. Before feeding the infants cried with a synchronized kicking action, there was intensive mouthing, hand-to-mouth contact, and finger sucking. When the infants were hungry, crying was preceded by the cry grimace and the infants self-soothed by finger sucking. After feeding, the infants' cries were less rhythmical and were not alleviated by finding a finger to suck or even by being offered the observer's own finger. Infants did not smile during bursts of crying, but some of them smiled just before urination (1973, p. 264), a finding that should interest psychoanalysts. Erection in male neonates has been affiliated with smiling (Freedman, 1974). The neonate smile, the differentiated cry, the auditory-visual pursuit and the function of dreams are all subjects of controversy in the literature in part because many investigators have not controlled for the infant's state of alertness when collecting data.

Functions of Habituation

Because neonates need to sleep through the noises of family living, rapid adjustment to novel and startling sensations has survival value. They must also learn to continue nursing through sensory interruptions and to tolerate the unaccustomed rigors of handling. *Habituation*, in a psychological context, means a decrease in the response to a repeated stimuli. An example is the extinction of the Moro reflex when the infant is lowered quickly into the crib. Brazelton (1969) observed the habituation of newborns to a sharp sound or a bright light by counting the number of startles until repeated stimuli no longer produced visible response. The lower the count (the more rapid the habituation) the better the neural integration of the individual baby was assumed to be. This ability to habituate on the part of neonates is regarded as evidence of their adaptive, or learning, ability.

The abilities of infants to make sensory discrimination can be studied by habituating them to one stimulus, such as a bell tone, and changing it to a different frequency or intensity. If the infant alerts and responds, discrimination is indicated; while a continuation of the habituation patterns suggests lack of discrimination. Lipsitt (1971) used a polygraph record of neonate body movements, heart rate, and breathing to study neonatal response to bad odors. The control trial consisted of the presentation of nonodorous cotton-tipped stick in the same way test odors were presented. Lipsitt reported that neonates (1) showed response decrement to offensive odors followed by recovery of the response after a time interval and (2) showed discrimination of odors by responding selectively to chemically unlike and chemically similar compounds.

Interactions with Care-Givers

The influence of mothers on the adaptive behavior of young infants has been well documented. Bell (1968) suggested, however, that research has been biased toward environmental effects on the behavior of infants with little attention being given to the conditioning of adult behavior by the infant. Evidence is obscure concerning the effects of adopted mothers, other primary care-givers, and fathers because most studies have involved only natural mothers. More recently Lewis and Rosenblum (1973) compiled research which focused on the effect of the infant on its care-giver. Chapter 15 discusses the role of adults in care-giving; the focus here is on how the helpless neonate establishes contact and adapts within an interdependent (social) species.

Although incomplete, the research clearly supports learning by neonates in their interaction with significant adults. Some of the evidence of conditioning by adult handlers comes from experiments in which an infant behavior pattern is reinforced and response changes are monitored mechanically. The reinforcers are selected to reflect the innate needs of the infant and not to take maternal adaptations into account. This section cites important literature on behavioral change in neonates when conditioned by need fulfillment, on animal studies of social conditioning, and on the social smile as an infant-affiliation overture.

CONDITIONING BY NEED GRATIFICATION

Unconditioned newborns turn more frequently to the dominant side when rooting or seeking to suck. Turkewitz, Gordon, and Birch (1965) demonstrated that neonates learn to discriminate, and also that they tend to select reinforcers that have survival value for them. When left-side turning is rewarded by a bottle containing sweetened water and right-side turning is followed by presentation of a bottle containing plain water, human neonates learn to turn their heads to the left side in response to cheek stimulation (Siqueland & Lipsitt, 1966).

Learning to obtain nutrients through sucking is critical in early life; hence sucking behavior has received considerable attention from researchers. Newborns sucked more on a "natural-shaped" nipple than on a tube of similar size and flexibility (Lipsitt, 1971). Also important, nipple sucking continued at an increased rate (*perseveration*) while tube sucking decreased significantly. In another experiment sweetened water was supplied to an experimental group through a tube that could be sucked. The group's sucking behavior increased significantly (Figure

4-6). A control group was given the same sweetened solution by syringe and their sucking did not increase. When the sweetener was removed as a conditioner, the sucking behavior in the experimental group eventually extinguished. The sucking response can be increased for nonoptimum nipples by pairing the reinforcer, such as a sweetener, with a tone or other stimuli.

During the lying-in period at the hospital, infants adapt to a new environment both through habituation and in response to care-giving routines. Multiple cues from the environment, such as voice and body position of the handler, help breast-fed babies discriminate feeding from nonfeeding contacts very quickly. These studies suggest to parents who are trying to help a neonate adapt to a nursing bottle to: (1) assume the holding position that is natural for sucking, (2) present the nipple initially to the favored side for the individual baby, and (3) repeat the conditions, such as music, that prevailed when feeding was most successful. If feeding is a problem, care-givers might try palm stimulation to get the infant to open its mouth (Babkin reflex) and then insert drops of formula.

Different techniques for quieting an infant have also been researched. Girl neonates were tested by using one of three modes of adult intervention for crying: (1) lifting to left shoulder, (2) lifting to right shoulder, and (3) clasping hands and

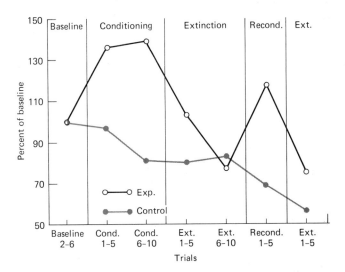

FIGURE 4-6 Model of a conditioning experiment with neonates. Baseline data show the rate of sucking before the treatment began. Conditioning with sweetened fluid increased the sucking rate, while control-group infants declined in sucking behavior. Extinction (the return to preconditioning behavior) occurred when the sweetener was withdrawn.

Source: L. P. Lipsitt, H. Kaye & T. N. Bosack, Enhancement of neonatal sucking through reinforcement. *J. exp. child psychology*, 1966, 4, 163–168. By permission of the authors.

raising to sitting position. These responses to distress were compared with (4) nonintervention, that is, allowing the infant to cry (Korner & Grobstein, 1966). The results showed that subjects brought to either shoulder position were soothed, and each infant opened her eyes and scanned the environment. Analysis of the data for variance showed that mere handling and upright positioning, mode 3, did not result in significant eye opening and scanning. The infants who were shouldered and soothed received a more stimulating learning environment than either those who were raised to sitting in the crib or those left alone to acquire self-soothing patterns, such as finger sucking. The fact that boy infants were not included in the study, because they had recently been circumcised and experienced pain during shouldering, raises a question of early differential handling of the sexes. Soothing interaction patterns may be acquired very early by both infant and handler, as both will tend to repeat the behavior that succeeded.

Boys and girls 203 days old were studied for responsiveness to various soothing techniques that are used widely: (1) sound intervention in the form of a continuous tone emitted from a speaker near the baby's head, (2) a sweetened pacifier, (3) gentle rocking of the bassinette, and (4) immersing the baby's foot in warm water. A like time period, without stimulation, was used for the experimental control group (Birns, Blank, & Bridger, 1966). No one soothing agent was found more effective than another; however, individual neonates responded differently to soothing techniques. The preferences persisted in follow-up trials of all the subjects. This individuality in early response to soothing seems likely to shape the caretaker's behavior toward a child, as the care-giver will select those patterns that prove effective. This cycle of mutual reinforcement might result in the use of a pacifier as the favored technique by one parent, whereas rocking, warming-cuddling, or auditory intervention might become a dominant pattern of a parent or care-giver toward another child.

Individual differences in coping style and temperament of infants have been studied rather carefully for their influence on maternal behavior. Moss (1970) reported that very young infants differed markedly in irritability and fussiness, and that the total amount of body contact an infant received was related (positively correlated) to these negative behaviors. In addition, the maternal responsiveness to infant distress was significantly related to an inventory of attitudes that the investigators obtained during her pregnancy. Positive attitudes of "acceptance of the maternal role" and "the degree that babies are seen in a positive sense" (p. 20) were followed by attentiveness toward the baby. Individual infants were found to differ in their need for sucking, clinging, and crying.

Infants show individual differences in their responses to physical contact with adults. Schaffer and Emerson (1964) compared cuddlers and noncuddlers, distinguished by the amount of active struggle, protest, and effort they made to break free when restrained. Based on monthly interviews with their mothers, over the course of more than a year, the investigators reported that cuddlers made greater use of "security objects," showed more autoerotic behavior (sexual response), and were less active than noncuddlers. As they developed, noncuddlers were more advanced in motor skills, resisted being dressed or put to bed, slept less, and showed higher scores on the Cattell Infant Scale. Although cuddlers were more intense in their attachment behaviors through the first year, this need leveled off by the age of 18 months. The investigators concluded that congenital factors seemed more important to the infant's receptiveness to being cuddled than the mother's preferred mode of interaction.

Behavior modification strategies for extinguishing crying and increasing smiling were demonstrated in two youngsters (Etzel & Gewirtz, 1967). A 6-week-old infant, who cried excessively, had been reinforced by the caretaker's attention to its crying. The investigators established a schedule for reinforcement of smiling behavior by attentiveness and nonreinforcement to crying by nonattention. The infant's crying decreased and the smiling behavior increased. The same reinforcement strategy resulted in extinction of "crying for attention" in an older infant of 20 weeks. Ainsworth, who observed infants in their natural setting, reported that children who are soothed when they cry early in life cry less at age one than others (Ainsworth, Salter, Bell, & Stayworth, 1971).

ANIMAL STUDIES OF SOCIAL CONDITIONING

Scholars interested in the phylogenic basis of social behavior have studied lower primates for cues to infant-adult interaction. Harlow (1960) found that infant monkeys clung to a soft, terry-covered mechanical mother in preference to a wire-covered mother, even when the feeding bottle was consistently held by the wire-covered mother. Freedman (1974) noted the decreasing numbers of offspring in primates, compared with other mammals, was associated with their increasing interest in parenting, and the prolonged dependence of their infants.

Birds have been interesting to students of childrearing because they use auditory signals and because some of their young form attachments by imprinting. The distance of the caretaker from a duckling influenced the number of cries or distress calls in baby ducks (Hoffman, Schiff, Adams, & Searle, 1966). Their calls were also related to the way the mother substitute responded to distress. Ducklings were imprinted to follow a moving white plastic bottle attached to a toy train engine. When the mother substitute was removed, the ducklings emitted a high rate of distress calls, which decreased significantly when the mother object was returned to their view. The imprinted ducklings were then paired (yoked to each other to assure a like spatial environment) and assigned randomly to two groups. The experimental duckling of each pair was reinforced for emitting distress calls by bringing the substitute mother closer. The result was that reinforced ducklings increased their calls significantly when compared with controls who were reinforced only by accident. When the experimenters reversed their strategy by reinforcing the control ducklings consistently, the distress calls of the controls increased. The species-specific behaviors of human infants are not fully understood, but many researchers are convinced that the reinforcing behaviors of mothers are important, as well as their attitudes of caring.

AFFILIATION THROUGH SOCIAL SMILING

The *reflexive smile*, which Wolff (1959) and Brazelton (1969) interpreted as socially significant, has stimulated a flurry of research on early social behavior. Traditionally the *social smile*, which appears at about 2 months, was defined as the beginning of smiling behavior (Spitz, 1965). Emde and Koenig (1969) reported that neonate smiling occurred almost exclusively when REMs were present, which in turn were noted during drowsiness, sucking, and sleep. Careful analysis has shown a relationship between neonatal smiling and later smiling behavior in childhood (Lewis, Kagan, & Kalafat, 1966).

The cessation of smiling for several weeks following the neonatal period has also stimulated scholarly study. Freedman (1974) observed that infant smiling, whether in the first week of life or when smiling reappears in the third month, is elicited most readily when the eyes of the infant and the adult meet, so both are called social smiles (p. 34). The human voice also elicits smiles. He reports that blind, deaf, or blind and deaf infants show a reflexive smile and smile again at 4 months, although their cues for smiling are from the affective senses. All infants will respond to tactile cues for smiling and laughing. Normal babies, even as neonates, vary in the frequency of their smiling. As might be expected, smiling babies were reported to be the darlings of the nursery, while unsmiling babies inhabited a rather different social environment.

Freedman (1974) also speculated on the disappearance of the neonate smile. He noted that mothers often remark about the beginning of social smiling as the time they first thought of the baby as a "real person." Freedman thinks that perhaps the lack of affiliation between infant and parent during the first 2 months of life helped adults endure the psychological pain of the frequent loss of young infants due to high mortality at that age in primitive peoples. The ugliness of the newborn was conducive to infanticide in certain cultures, where deformed and sometimes female infants were destroyed.

On a happier note, cooing and smiling, which appear at about the same time, help the infant establish contact with adults and assures their continuous caregiving. Infant girls smile more quickly than boys. Although the sexes are similar in most behaviors, the ways they differ in affective responsiveness have received the attention of researchers (Chapter 11).

SEX DIFFERENCES IN ATTACHMENT

The temperament of a young infant determines to some extent the amount and nature of attention given by parents or caretakers. Fretful infants elicit different reactions than do smiling infants. Moss (1970) reported that male infants 3 to 12 weeks old were more irritable (as a group) and slept less than did female infants. Careful observation in the homes also showed that mothers spent more time attending and comforting boy infants during early weeks. Before the end of the second month, however, mothers showed a tendency to ignore boys when awake and quiet; but mothers of girl babies spent more time with them, thus reversing the sex-linked time difference. The female babies, who also tended to be more responsive, were stimulated more by face-to-face talking, by imitating utterances, and by handling when awake (Figure 4-7). Infants of either sex who reward an adult's efforts to nurture are likely to get more attention at times when they are awake, alert, and ready to take in the environment. The face-to-face social interaction is probably very important in forming social attachments (Moss & Robson, 1968).

EFFECTIVENESS OF THE SENSORY SYSTEMS

The *sensory analyzers* are the source of all information available to the human organism. Each sensory system receives, encodes, transmits, and interprets stimuli. In order to understand what an infant is experiencing it is helpful to know

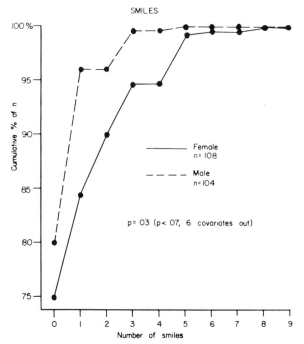

FIGURE 4-7 Sex differences in the smiling behavior of neonates. Newborn females gave indications of a more affiliative orientation than males. For one thing, they exhibited more frequent eyes-closed ("reflexive") smiling.

Source: Daniel G. Freedman, *Human Infancy: An Evolutionary Perspective,* page 65. Copyright, 1974, by Lawrence Erlbaum Associates, Hillsdale, N.J.

the effectiveness of vision, hearing, and other analyzers at different ages. Tactile systems receive information about the comfort or discomfort of the environment. Knowing the infant's visual and auditory competence enables a care-giver to provide appropriate stimulation for the growth of intelligence without overstimulating or threatening the ego. What does the neonate see? Does a caring adult select toys for color, or pattern? Does the infant "feel" a wet diaper? When does the infant learn to discriminate a mother's voice? Recognize a stranger? Know whether it is hunger or thirst that is felt?

The sensory competence of infants has been studied intensively since the 1960s. Generally, the research has revised downward the ages at which the separate systems become as acute as those of adults. Evidence from laboratory animals should be read with caution because it does not answer questions of sensory discrimination in children. Human infants are phylogenically more complex and have evolved survival systems which are unique to the species.

Two approaches by which the nature of sense reception is studied in infants have been included in this section. First, the physical maturation of the neural receptor systems has revealed a timetable for growth which is similar in all full-term babies. Human newborns are genetically and developmentally prepared to select and respond to certain stimuli in the environment. For example, the human infant "tunes in" human speech from birth and "searches" for small objects to grasp. Second, the behavior changes of infants, under experimentally controlled stimulation, reveal their ability to make specific sensory discriminations. Another technique for studying the maturation of the sensory systems is to establish the time of initial myelination of the axons that relay a particular sensation. This is done by analyzing the brain development of healthy youngsters killed in accidents.

Myelin Growth as an Indicator of Sensorimotor Organization

The growth of the myelin sheath around an axon is necessary for effective transmission of a sensory impulse to the receiving areas in the brain. This insulating cover, formed by special cells, speeds the electrochemical relay and prevents dissipation of the impulse. The onset of the growth of the myelin sheath is considered an indicator of the beginning of effective message relay by the nerve and a commitment of the nerve to particular stimuli. Myelination of the neural system is continuous from the prenatal period into adulthood.

The developmental timetable of the nerve tissues of healthy individuals who died accidentally has been charted by laboratory examination. Techniques for staining the myelin in the neural tissues have enabled neuropathologists to describe what they call the cycles of myelogeneses in human development (Yakovlev & Lecours, 1967). The age of the subject, and the density of the stained fibers and the intensity of their coloration, provide an approximation of when development in a particular neural system begins and how long it continues. The gradations of coloring from light gray (as in fetal development) to blue-black (as in heavily myelinated adult fibers) identify the extent of the maturation in various regions of the brain. During infant development the major nerves of different sensory pathways appear to take turns for priority.

The initial appearance of myelin cells indicates prenatal development of motor roots in the spinal column (Figure 4-8). The sensory roots in the motor structures myelinate later, indicating earlier growth of the nerves that control reflexive body movements than of the ascending (input) nerves to the motor control areas in the brain. The cerebellum myelinates relatively late and over an extended period of time. As indicated earlier the automatic control of complex body movements, such as walking, running, and skipping, are centered there. The integration of breathing and respiration is controlled through neural communication involving pons, cerebellum, and hypothalamus. The growth and stratification of cells in the cortex of the cerebellum is delayed until after birth, whereas the cells in the cortex of the cerebral hemispheres are generally in place before birth (Chapter 1).

Of special interest to care-givers is the maturation of hearing mechanisms. The lower (reflexive) neurons of the acoustic systems complete their myelination before birth (3, Figure 4-8), in contrast to the acoustic analyzer areas for interpreting sound reception which continue myelin growth into the second year of life (4). The myelination of auditory radiation fibers in the cortex corresponds to the reception and interpretation of language, which continues to the fourth year and perhaps beyond (10). Yakovlev and Lecours (1967) suggest that speech in humans

FIGURE 4-8 Myelination of the neural pathways. Arrows show established growth patterns; vertical lines show projected growth; question marks show indefinite growth during adult life. (Redrawn from Yakovlev & Lecours, 1967. Courtesy Blackwell Scientific Publications.)

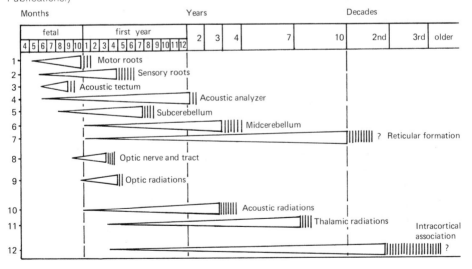

is a species-specific function, and that speech acquisition is reflected in the myelination cycles during development. Prenatal acoustic mechanisms and reflexive pathways myelinate quickly. They probably respond to the visceral sounds that penetrate the amniotic fluid. The complex sounds of language demand a more complex phonic analysis. The sounds of speech, available after birth, stimulate the human organism in ways that are species-specific and are the beginning of the development of symbolic language. Yaklovlev and Lecours concluded:

> . . . In the case of man . . . external sounds have a highly species-specific significance in the development of language. So, while the reflex patterns of motor responses to sound are organized early at the tegmental level and are provided long before term with the space committed (i.e., myelinated) to the paths of conduction, the cortical analyzer . . . maintains long after birth its quasi embryonal plasticity, and has a late and protracted cycle of myelination. . . .
>
> A fibre system, before it has become myelinated, may serve as a path of conduction for many different kinds of stimuli; however, once it has become myelinated, it becomes exclusively a path only for the conduction of stimuli with specified characteristics. . . . (pp. 67–68)

The myelination cycle, then, both reflects and serves the species-specific language function of humans. Language reception and language interpretation precede the infant's own speech.

Visual stimuli are processed according to a different timetable. The optic nerve (8) and the optic radiations from the thalamus to visual analyzer areas in the cortex (9) begin to myelinate near birth and are committed during the first 4 months of life. A growth priority in the visual mechanism, which is different from audition, is indicated. These species-specific cycles are important indicators of the kinds of sensory experience that infants are sensitive toward. Other evidence, presented in a later section, indicates that visual acuity at an adult level is attained between the fourth and the sixth months.

The lack of complete myelination, which preserves flexibility in a neural system, is retained beyond infancy in many complex structures. For example, the integration of sensory information and the initiation of voluntary action are not completed in the first year. The reticular formation (7) myelinates early in some of the long fibers that course through it, but the feltlike dendritic structure that makes up most of this receiving center myelinates very slowly and remains largely undifferentiated through the childhood years and at least to 28 years old. The nonspecific thalamic (11) radiations (to the cortex) myelinate over an extended period from early infancy (3 months) to age 7 or 8 at which time the cerebral hemispheres have attained close to their adult weight. The neural connections from one sensory association area to another and across hemispheres continue their development well into adulthood. Consistent with the concept of critical periods in learning, it is important to remember that neural analyzer systems are laid down in infancy and that specific neurons become committed very early in the responsiveness to particular stimuli. These critical periods of maturation in the nervous system are considered common to the human species.

Behavior Indicators of Discrimination

Direct observation of infant behavior has been the historical method for judging the sensory responsiveness of infants. Piaget (1952) brought the art of direct observation to a peak of professional skill by using scheduled observations, by making systematic changes in the infant's environment, and by recording what he saw in detail. Afterward he was able to abstract some principles of cognitive development by generalizing from the three infants he observed so meticulously.

Piaget's description of the sensorimotor development during infancy remains a major framework for interpreting infant behavior. Piaget noted the tactile sensitivity in the lip-cheek areas, the infant's almost daily adaptation to the breast, and the contrast in response toward an object depending on whether the infant was hungry or nursed. He observed that at approximately 1 month old the infant began to suck its fingers in a self-comforting act, and concluded that such inner-directed behaviors were evidence that sensory pleasure was derived from the exercise of sensory systems. This internal response is the organism's own primitive intrinsic reward; Piaget's belief in such internal rewards separates him from psychologists who see rewards as external, or environmental.

Piaget (1971) assumed that organized external actions had a counterpart in the inner (neurological) organization. The earliest behavior patterns were assumed to be reflexive. Changes in behavior patterns (adaptation) meant structural changes in the neural system. He used the word *schema* to describe the coordinated action of the whole child (organism). His observations of how the infant utilized the sound of a toy against the sides of its wicker bassinette allowed him to describe the beginnings of the infant's control of his or her own auditory environment.

While two generations of psychologists from Watson to Skinner were locked into research based on controlled (external) stimulation and measured behavioral responses, Piaget persisted in interpreting the behavior of infants and children in terms of the organism's own developmental priorities and its human-specific readiness to assimilate particular experiences at particular times. From his early observations of his own infants, published in French in the late twenties, Piaget has continued to reject purely stimulus-response (S-R) explanations for human development. He has spent fifty years researching children's learning by observing children's interaction with the environment and interpreting the thinking processes behind the behavior. Piaget's infantile states of sensorimotor intelligence are explained in detail in Chapter 11, Cognitive Development.

The early behaviorist movement created pressures on American psychologists to attain scientific respectability by conducting strict "objective" research. This meant a controlled environment (stimulus), quantified reports of the behavior (response), and no speculation about the process the child was going through. Throughout the middle half of this century, S-R experiments on infant sensation avoided the question of the infant's own role in learning. So that the experimenter could know the sources of the child's stimulation and could limit the input to those variables under investigation, increasing controls were needed. Studies of sensory stimulation or deprivation became untenable for human infants because of the possible long-term effects; thus laboratory animals were substituted for most experimental research. This shift produced new insight into learning behavior; but some psychologists became increasingly dubious about applying the research to humans. Studies in biology and physiology revealed important differences in the sensory analyzing systems of different species, and research with children again appeared necessary.

In the sixties, researchers began to use S-R learning theory to condition infants to particular visual, auditory, or tactile stimuli and to determine when and what stimuli were being discriminated. In some pioneer studies Fantz (1966) discovered that infants perceived visual patterns, colors, and grays. The timing of visual fixation was interpreted as selective for a variety of targets including regular versus scrambled human faces (Chapter 1). By analyzing infants' body movements, Condon and Sander (1974) demonstrated that human infants responded selectively to human speech. Bower (1966) created a literature on young infants' perception of objects in space, sometimes by conditioning them to head turning and sometimes by following their eye movements.

During the seventies, investigators of infant sensory competence have attended increasingly to the role of the subject in the selection and perception of the environment. The stimulus-response paradigm has been replaced by neobehaviorists as a S → O → R model, meaning stimulus → organism → response (Figure 4-9). This effort has been assisted by new technology which provides quantitative measures of the inner activity of the infant during experience and learning.

Technology helped to open the "black box," the unseen interior of the organism, by making neurological information available for study. Biological correlates of behavior include heart rate, respiration, and galvanic skin response. Electroencephalographs locate the activities of the central nervous system and provide information on the nature of the learning. This technology has enabled researchers to correlate inner functioning with outer manifestations and thus to become more reliable observers of infant behavior (Eisenberg, 1976).

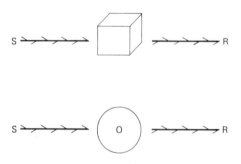

FIGURE 4-9 Research models. Top line shows the stimulus (S) which is manipulated by the experimentor, the "black box" which is closed to objective interpretation and the response (R) which must be measured. The bottom line shows a neobehaviorist approach in which the organism (O) is an active force in the interpretation of the results.

Classification of Sensory Systems

Many possible classifications of the different senses (sensory analyzers) have been proposed (Robeck & Wilson, 1974). When studying child development, the basic concern is to make appropriate estimates about the competence of sensory systems and the timing of their integration. Adults need to know how to interact with youngsters in ways that are meaningful to the child and conducive to early learning. A classification of major sensory analyzers which focuses on development as well as on function has been proposed in Table 4-2.

All the sensory systems are integrated in complex activity. The afferent neural pathways converge in the central receiving centers in the brain stem, where all sensory information is evaluated. This is the center for arousal, orientation, and attention. Neural radiations fan out from this brain stem to receiving areas to genetically specified areas of the cortex. Needless to say, the individual's focus of attention is based on past learning. Interpretation of present experience from previous experience stored in the various cortical areas begins before birth. The present experience is selected by attention and irrelevant data are repressed. Pleasure-punishment associations, activated by the limbic areas around the brain stem, influence the selection of some stimuli and the repression of others. Chapter 11, "Affective Development," presents further detail on the function of affects in the child's own construction of experience.

In a very general way, the sensors organize themselves into systems that relate to the cell layer differentiation that followed conception (Chapter 3). The ectoderm layer includes the neural cell bodies but the dendrites of these cells differ markedly in their length and in the location of their receptors in other body tissues. *Distance sensors* detect environmental or external stimuli: light, sound, and odors. The reception and analysis of these data occur all within the head, and response actions are initiated within the brain itself. The sense of smell is classified as a distance sensor because, in many mammals, smell remains the primary organizer of experience. Although this classification is arbitrary, the system which has priority as an arousal mechanism is a prime organizer of experience. In humans, vision and hearing are more important in checking out the environment for possible danger.

The *surface sensors* which produce tactile and taste sensations are located in the ectoderm, but they rely on direct contact with the stimulus object. These systems are widespread and are intimately related to the mesoderm structures. The skin includes both temperature (heat-cold) detectors and pressure-contact analyzers. In contact sensors, reflexive responses can occur via a neural arc to and from the spinal column, with information of the stimuli going to the brain after an action has already occurred. Touch and taste sensations are interconnected with pleasure centers in the midbrain and contribute to early reinforcement. They have an important function in the infant's responding to and seeking out physical comforts such as warm milk, adult caresses, or a security blanket.

Table 4-2
CLASSIFICATION OF SENSORY ANALYZERS

	Source of stimulation/ site of receptors	CNS organization*	Function in survival	Function in learning	First-year accomplishments
DISTANCE SENSORS					
Vision	Light impulses on rods and cones in retina of eye	Optic nerve (2d cranial nerve → RAS → visual association areas at back of head (occipital lobe)	Discrimination of form, color, size, movement, and distance of objects	Exploration of facial cues, objects in space, size relations, sensory organization	Visual recognition of other persons, object permanency, depth and distance perception, fine line and color discrimination
Audition (hearing ability)	Sound waves/ receptors in cochlea of inner ear	Auditory nerve (8th cranial nerve) → RAS → cortical association areas in temporal lobe	Alerting to noises from enemy, mating calls, distress calls from young	Location of caretaker, speech reception, prespeech meanings, language modeling, affective associations	Auditory-visual integration for naming objects, voice recognition, understanding of language in context, e.g. bottle, rattle, mama
Olfaction (sense of smell)	Volatile molecules/ chemical detectors in membrane of nose	Olfactory nerve (1st cranial nerve) → olfactory bulb† located deep in each anterior lobe of brain → RAS → lower cortical surfaces	Alerting to presence of enemy or mate; location of food and water; rejection of dangerous food and water	Pleasure associations; detection of dangerous chemicals in food and surround	Primitive olfactory sense diminishes in function during development
SURFACE SENSORS					
Cutaneous sensations (pressure, temperature, touch)	Cutaneous sensors of pain, pressure, warmth, cold, touch/skin receptors	Long dendrites lead from body surface to cell bodies near spine and to brain, largest of sense systems	Seeking a growth supporting environment, avoiding pain and injury, responding to handlers	Source of affective associations, reward and punishment	System functional at birth, helps establish trust relationship

Gustatory sensations (taste)	Soluble molecules/chemical detectors on tongue, lips, mouth, esophagus‡	Multiple pathways in RAS, closely associated with other sensory analyzers in temporal lobe	Selection of food when on own, avoidance of dangerous food	Enculturation to food, effective reinforcers in early childhood	Sensitive at birth species inclined toward sweetness, disinclined toward strong flavors
DEEP SENSORS: PROPRIOCEPTION					
Vestibular sensation (balance)	Semicircular canals near inner ear	Vestibular nerve (sensory branch of auditory nerve → RAS → scattered cortical areas	Righting reflex, early mobility, sound orientation, postural changes	Perceptual-motor skills, body (somatic) expression, rhythmic expression	Strong stimulation produces nausea
Kinesthetic sensation (position and movement)	Detectors in skeletal muscles, heart, genitals; Detectors in tendons, joints	Input-output relays at three levels: spinal column (reflex arc), motor cortex (automatic response schema), major brain mechanisms (intentional behavior)	Coordination of body movements in walking, fleeing, fighting, hunting	Action upon objects; sensorimotor integration in speaking, reading and writing	Head turning toward sights and sounds, grasping, sitting, crawling, walking around furniture, sometimes toddling
DEEP SENSORS: ORGANIC					
(body state)	Interceptors in visceral organs of body cavity; membranes of heart, lungs	Coordinated in hypothalamus	Control of vital life systems: breathing, circulation, digestion; control of body fluid, hunger satisfaction, thirst	Association of well-being in need satisfaction	Regulated during neonate period

*The central nervous system organization is complex. For greater detail on relay pathways see Robeck and Wilson (1974).

†The olfactory bulb is a prominent structure in lower mammals, but is greatly reduced in humans, suggesting different arousal and attention priorities in development.

‡Infant taste receptors are widespread; they recede during development.

The *deep senses* give an organism information and feedback on its own internal functioning. Proprioception includes information on body orientation, position, and movement. The sense of vertical and horizontal orientation in space is detected by the *vestibular system*, three canals adjacent to (or part of) the inner ear. These structures contain hairs that detect change orientation. They enable the human embryo to right itself and thus prepare an infant to "know" its relationship to space. A sloped position with head elevated about 60° is the most conducive position for neonate attention. During the first few months the optimal attention-alert position shifts to upright. After that time a reclining posture may be resisted by an alert infant who may struggle to maintain a fully vertical position.

Body position is known by kinesthetic messages from muscles and joints. Body movement is coded through a complex system of receptors which signal the stretching and relaxing of muscle fibers. These neurons function in on-off volleys, described as neural firing (Chapter 1). Other cells send continuous signals to tell the brain, more specifically the cerebellum, that a muscle is at rest. New action patterns are directed by the motor control areas of the cerebral cortex. When they become automatic, control shifts to the cerebellum. Although the different analyzers have their genetic priorities, the integration of the several sense modalities is the principal characteristic of growth during the first year of life. Piaget noted this by calling the infancy period *sensorimotor integration* at a time the hard evidence of neural functioning was not yet available.

VISION AND THE ORGANIZATION OF EXPERIENCE

Most humans learn more through the visual modality than through all other senses combined. Rock (1966) did some experiments by having adult subjects explore three-dimensional objects inside a curtained box with their hands. Without their knowing it, the experimenter replaced the objects with others that were similar but required a reinterpretation. To alter visual images, laboratory glasses were used to distort vision in ways unknown to the subject. When given discrepant information through kinesthetic or visual analyzers, approximately 85 percent of the subjects accepted the visual information and adapted to it, while rejecting tactile-kinesthetic information even when correct. It is important to note that 15 percent of the adults responded to somatic rather than visual cues, even when the visual information was correct. In experiments such as this, adults adapt their motor responses very quickly when guided visually even though the visual image may be distorted.

Although many studies have been made to determine how infants organize sensory input, researchers do not agree on a dominant modality during infant development. Piaget seems to believe that motor activities are primary and that they are exercised initially because of inherited predispositions. The month-old infant explores objects with the mouth when grasped accidentally, and explores visually, without sucking, when older (Piaget, 1952). Fantz (1965), on the other hand, believes that infants first explore the world of objects and space through the visual modality. They are enticed by what they see and are therefore stimulated to motor explorations such as reaching and then grasping, crawling and then walking. It seems reasonable that optimum growth requires the interaction of both the somatic and visual sensors, according to a genetically determined sequence of development. The best guidelines for providing an optimum environment for sensorimotor and visual activity is probably one which anticipates the infant's next adaptive accomplishment.

Competence of the Visual Analyzer

Vision in infants is usually studied by observing the coordination of the two eyes, by testing the reflexive response of pupils to light, by enticing the subject to pursue objects visually, and by reading the neural activity on an electrogram. *Visual acuity* refers to the ability to see the details of an object. *Visual coordination* requires the muscular direction of both eyes on the same object. *Convergence* means the focusing of both eyes to produce a single image, which is necessary for effective binocular vision. *Visual accommodation* is the adjustment of the lens curvature to

Infants discover their hands, later use their vision to guide their reaching. (Erika/Peter Arnold)

focus the light rays on the retina. Some observers are misled about what the infant sees because they do not know the distance at which infants of various ages accommodate visually. Inappropriate distances restrict the infant's attempts to fixate on the stimulus object.

At birth visual accommodation is most effective at 19 centimeters (8 to 9 inches) from the eyes (Haynes, White, & Held, 1965). This near-point vision assures a visual environment which supports the human infant's own visual seeking for the human face by its proximity to the handler. Affective associations are formed which include the adult's facial expression during feeding, changing, and other personal ministrations.

Research which shows the visual ability of young infants is extensive. The pupillary reflexes are functional at birth, although adaptation is difficult for neonates if brightness is increased rapidly (Mann, 1964). Neural activity in the retina, as recorded by an electroretinogram (ERG) is similar to adult patterns (Barnet, Lodge, & Armington, 1965). Young infants orient their heads and eyes to a light or a slowly moving object, but their visual pursuit is jerky. By 3 to 4 weeks, they can sustain coordinated pursuit. Their general activity changes with different brightness values, even when asleep. By 4 months old flexibility of accommodation, size and depth perception, and fine acuity are comparable to the vision of adults (Kessen, Haith, & Salapatek, 1970).

Attentional Preferences

When presented with two stimulus objects, infants show a preference by looking at one significantly longer than the other. This selective attention shows that a visual discrimination is being made and cues the researcher as to the development of perception. Fantz and Nevus (1967) demonstrated that infants from 1 week old prefer patterned disks (checkered, bull's-eye, newsprint) over plain disks, either gray or colored. Fantz (1965) reported that infants a few days old spent more time looking at stripes less than $1/8$ inch wide than at gray disks. By 12 weeks old they preferred, and therefore discriminated, pinstripes that were only $1/64$ inch wide.

Increasing *complexity* in checkerboard designs was preferred by infants as their age increased (Brennan, Ames, & Moore, 1966). Groups of infants were studied at ages 3, 8, and 14 weeks. A simple checkerboard with only four squares appealed most to the youngest group, 64 squares appealed most to the middle-aged group, and the most complex board, having 576 squares, appealed most to the oldest group. Other studies, in which sets of shapes were presented, showed that the older babies attended more to those cards which pictured a variety of shapes.

Infants show a preference for *novelty* in some studies and for *familiarity* in others, suggesting caution in how the research is controlled and interpreted. Fantz (1966) reported that infants looked longer at a pattern when it was presented with a variety of comparison patterns. His infants showed a preference for facelike disks over disks with scrambled features until about 5 months of age when scrambled features (novel) were attended to longer and regular features (familiar) were apparently less attracting. Fantz suggested that when infants become bored they seek novelty; care-givers have noted that when tired or fearful infants seek familiarity.

Clearly, infants 4 months old find meaning in their visual environment, and by 6 months old (or earlier), people and objects are recognized (Kessen et al., 1970). Infants 8 months old anticipate the direction of a moving object. When a car was sent down a slope toward a toy, Kagan's infant subjects would look where the crash was about to take place, and they looked to the opposite side of a barrier when a moving toy disappeared behind it (1972). In a different study, Bower and Patterson (1973) projected a target moving in a constant arc. Their infants, 6 weeks old and unpracticed, followed the target after it disappeared behind a screen so that their eyes met the target when it reappeared at the other side of the screen. Increased heart rate accompanies the anticipation of exciting sights, according to polygraph records.

Attention to persons or representations of persons has some implication for the social tendencies of human young. McCall and Kagen (1967) found that infants from 2 to 9 months old preferred a human face to a mask when both were presented simultaneously. From 9 to 36 months, these subjects reversed the typical reaction and attended more to masks (Kagen, 1972). This result seems to indicate that by 9 months of age the normal infant attends to masks because of their novelty. Haaf and Bell (1967) suggested that the species-specific meaning of the human face may be more important in infant visual preferences than the complexity of facial features over other patterns used as stimuli. When infants look at scrambled features they may be responding to a discrepancy between the face schema which they assimilate and the novel face which they must accommodate to. The Piagetian explanation was supported by McCall and Kagen (1967) who found that slight discrepancies attracted the infant gaze for longer time intervals than did the more gross distortions.

Perceptional Competence

The infant's ability to perceive depth is observed in several ways. If a flat target object and a three-dimensional object are presented, researchers assume that an infant sees depth when one subject is given more attention than the other. Fantz (1965) reported that infants attended to depth of a sphere and preferred the sphere over a flat disk by 10 weeks of age. When shown patterned or plain disks at different distances (5, 10, or 20 inches) infants from 1 week to 4 months old showed no preferred distance for viewing, but consistently spent more time studying the patterned than the plain disk (Fantz, Ordy & Udelf, 1962). Infants smiled more for three-dimensional masks than two-dimensional pictures. Apparently the accommodation necessary to produce effective binocular and far-point vision expands rapidly during the early weeks of life.

APPROACHING OBJECTS

Infants blink their eyes, although with irregular and jerky movements, to a fast-approaching object by 3 weeks old (White, 1968). By 14 weeks old, the blink response has become firm and regular. There is evidence that regular blink responses to approaching objects can be accelerated by environmental stimulation. When the infant was provided attractive patterns over the crib beginning at 5 weeks old, the blink response was effected approximately three weeks earlier than normal (Greenberg, Uzgiris, & Hunt, 1968).

COLOR VISION

Although young infants have shown preference for patterned disks over color disks, they also attended more to some colors than others. Early research on color discrimination has been questioned because of the difficulty in preparing samples of different colors that were equal in intensity. Experiments have been conducted recently which project white and red lights on a screen. Female infants 2 months old discriminated reds of varied intensity (Peeples & Teller, 1975).

SIZE CONSTANCY

A different test of depth perception uses objects, such as cubes, presented in different sizes and at different distances so that they cast retinal images of identical size. Infants develop *size constancy*, the ability to interpret the real size of objects, as distinct from the size of the retinal image when only a few weeks old. Bower (1964) trained infants to turn toward a 12-inch cube, presented at 3 feet (just out of reach). They showed real depth perception by responding to the larger cube, even when seen at a distance. This ability broke down, however, when the objects were projected on a screen (Bower, 1965).

Bower (1972) used an optical illusion created by mirrors to study size-depth perception in infants. He created two balls that varied in size and distance but produced retinal images of the same size. At 1 to 2 weeks, infants reached for the illusion of a small ball nearby but did not arm wave toward the large ball projected at a distance. Using a similar technique Bower demonstrated shape constancy and slant perception.

CLIFF AVOIDANCE

When infants are able to crawl, their depth perception can be tested by placing them on a glass-topped table which is divided between a deep side and a flat side. Usually a checkerboard design is used at both tabletop and deep levels. The infant is placed on a crawl-strip and successively coaxed by the mother to cross the two sides. The willingness of the infant to cross is interpreted as a lack of fear because the depth is not perceived.

A visual cliff tests the child's ability to perceive depth. (Lawrence Roth-blat)

Crawling infants have shown a strong tendency to remain on the center board rather than to cross the glass on the deep side of the table, but they crossed the shallow side readily (Walk, 1966). By varying the conditions such as raising the floor to lesser depths, providing experience, or changing the size of the checks, nearly all infants could be persuaded to cross the deep side. Age factors were important in that older infants tended to cross a higher percentage of the time. Sex differences were nonsignificant, although a trend toward less cliff avoidance appeared in male infants more than 10 months old.

An interesting finding was that fear of depth appeared rare in infants who are crawling by the early age of 7 months (Kessen et al., 1970). This raises the question of which aspects of the behavior are innate and which are the result of experience. Walk and Gibson (1961) reported species-specific differences in the marked aversion of chicks and young lambs to depth, as contrasted with turtles, which showed no fear. Human infants have developed visual perception of depth prior to the typical age for crawling.

A practical concern is why infants fall from high places if they can perceive depth. Attempts to correlate the age of crawling with cliff avoidance have been unsuccessful because of the lack of precision mothers share in knowing when an infant started to crawl. It seems reasonable that parents of all crawlers should protect them from cliffs until they experience smaller falls and bumps. Many a young mother has been petrified when an infant 3 or 4 months old has managed to fall off the side of a dressing table or an unguarded bed by rolling or creeping in her absence. Infants see depths, but perhaps they cannot deal with the problem of depth and the problem of crawling simultaneously.

Hand Watching and the Development of Prehension

Prehension is the grasping of an object by a single hand. Humans are able to use a *power grip* (as are primates) by wrapping their fingers around an object and reinforcing them with the thumb. By approximately 6 months of age, human infants learn to make a *precision grip* by which the thumb is fully opposed to the fingertips, an accomplishment unique to humans (Stein & Rowe, 1974). Infant macaque monkeys are delayed in development of prehension if an apron is put around their necks to prevent hand watching, even if given the same objects to grasp as normally reared monkeys have (Held & Bauer, 1967). When a limb is exposed from beneath the apron, the macaque infant spends a great deal of time hand watching in ways that are characteristic of an earlier age. It is clear that eye-hand coordination is practiced very early and that species use their environmental opportunities in unique ways.

Piaget (1952) described five stages during which the infant acquires the ability to see and grasp an object through "deliberate action," meaning the ability to coordinate hand and eye actions to some purpose (p. 88). He observed that the grasping reflex of neonates was different from other reflexes such as sneezing or yawning. When the palm was touched and the grasping reflex followed, the infant's attention was captured in some way so that she stopped, or paused, in other movements. Stage 1, reflexive grasping, also included waving the arms, opening and closing the fingers, or catching the hands in the field of vision. These actions, according to Piaget, followed from a biological necessity to exercise the systems. Over time the reflexive grasping of the blanket was prolonged by the infant and the blanket was held.

At stage 2 (1 to 4 months) the impulsive movements of the first stage, together with accidental contact, lead to prolonged grasping for the sake of grasping. Systematic fingering of objects indicated to Piaget an attempt to accommodate the hand to the object. Tactile-kinesthetic experience was seen in finger searching and finger sucking; objects were "recognized" by touch. At this stage Piaget's infants held objects, but did not bring them to the mouth for coordinated hand-mouth exploration. Piaget noted the beginning of hand watching during the second stage. (p. 95). Other observers have interpreted this period differently, believing that infants grasp objects that attract them visually first (Fantz, 1965). Probably both somatic and visual stimulation capture the infant's attention and encourage reaching and grasping.

During the third stage the infant grasped and carried objects to her mouth to be sucked, and by a reciprocal action took hold of things being sucked. Piaget noted that when the hand opened to an object, the mouth opened also. This coordination between prehension and sucking occurred at different ages in his own children, but Piaget believed the delay in one of his daughters was caused by her being born in midwinter. Rearing practice at the time in Switzerland called for her being bundled tightly and given fresh air during much of her waking hours.

From observations such as this Piaget built his theory of sensorimotor experience as the basis for cognitive development. He described how a child begins to interest himself or herself in the objects which the hand has touched:

So . . . after having practiced in space various hand movements and having grasped for the sake of grasping, after having used his prehension with respect to all the solid objects he encounters and having thus acquired an increasingly precise accommodation to objects . . . after having even developed a sort of tactile-motor recognition of things, the child finally becomes interested in the objects he grasps, inasmuch as prehension, which has thus become systematic, is coordinated with an already completed schema, such as that of sucking. (p. 101)

During the fourth stage of prehension, acquired between the fourth and sixth months, the child grasped objects seen and not only those she touched or sucked. Piaget's daughter had earlier watched her hand without seeming to know it

Object constancy means knowing that things exist even when not seen. (Zimbel/ Monkmeyer)

belonged to her. There were two worlds for her—one visual and the other kinesthetic. From the act of seeing her own grasping, she became able to grasp under the guidance of the glance. But as yet the infant was dependent on simultaneous sight of hand and object.

During the fifth stage of prehension, usually the sixth to the eighth month, the child systematically grasped objects seen whether or not the hand was also visible at the time of reaching. Piaget noted the physical development when fingers and thumb began to oppose each other in organized grasping. Infants, by this stage, accommodated differently to different shapes and textures when grasping (p. 121).

Bower (1976) analyzed the relationship of the early reflexive grasp and later coordination of tactile and visual exploration. He noted that infants reach out and touch visible objects during the first month of life and even grasp them occasionally. This level of eye-hand coordination disappears at about 4 weeks, and does not reappear until about 20 weeks. This lack of continuity is not understood, but it reappears, is significant. Piaget was also a pioneer in the study of object constancy in infants.

Object Constancy and Search

Object permanence, or *object constancy*, means knowing that persons and things continue to exist even when not seen. This is a concept which infants acquire, through experience, as they acquire the concept of self as separate from other persons and things. Infants learn people permanence before they learn object permanence (Bell, 1970). Perhaps this is because of their attachment to a care-giver whose coming and going is followed attentively. Piaget tested for object constancy by getting the child to focus attention on a toy and then placing it under a blanket while the child watched. Infants under 4 months did not usually search for objects not seen. Between 4 and 8 months old they began to search by trying to remove the blanket or screen (Piaget, 1954). By 1 year old, typical infants will search in a cupboard or in a toybox for familiar objects they have not seen for several hours, or even for a day or two. Bower (1976) speeded up the acquisition of object constancy by giving infants the opportunity to observe a cube (on a string) pass through a tube.

HEARING AND UNDERSTANDING

The state of sleep or wakefulness is probably more important in the infant's responsiveness to sound than is the frequency or the intensity of the sound as long as they fall within the normal ranges of human audition. Neonate response to sound has been studied by changes in the heart rate, by head turning, by ceasing to suck, or by other measures. Eisenberg (1976) reported that human infants were tuned toward the frequencies of human speech, 500 to 900 cycles per second. Some investigators have observed that neonates quiet to the recorded heartbeat of the human female, supposedly imprinted before birth (Salk, 1962). This response, however, disappears rather early and aroused infants quiet to a variety of rhythmic sounds (Brackbill, Adams, Crowell, & Gray, 1966).

Responsiveness to Symbolic Language

There is growing evidence that infants respond differently to sounds presented to the left and right ears. This organization of the hemispheres of the brain is to a large extent inherited. Language is differentially received in the right ear and processed in the left hemisphere by about 90 percent of the human population (Geschwind, 1971). Complex sounds that are nonverbal, such as musical notes, are normally processed in similar areas of the opposite (right hemisphere). Crosslinkages are numerous and more complex than indicated here. Chapter 9 presents an account of how the brain functions in speech and language development.

Organization of Time and Space

The association of visual and auditory messages that are received together is one of the most important sensorimotor integrations to be accomplished during the first year of life. It is now believed that intricate timing of auditory messages is resonsible for the *temporal organization* of human experience (Paivio, 1975). The proper sequencing of sound signals is important in interpreting events in the environment, including speech sequences. Receiving, storing, remembering, and understanding speech are processes which must consistently be ordered for communication to take place. Phonemes, the elements of words, have a particular order, and the ability to perceive sequence extends to the more advanced communication skills (reading and spelling).

The visual signals indicate *spatial arrangement* of people and things in the environment. The association of spatial and temporal information helps the infant learn cause-and-effect realities such as that an object hitting the floor will make a noise, shaking a rattle produces a sound, and familiar sounds in the kitchen mean the presence of a care-giver. The orientation of the neonate toward the sound of a tuning fork has been clearly demonstrated (Kessen et al., 1970). Given the known competence of infants to take in the sounds and sights of ordinary family living, and given the known neural mechanisms for putting temporal and spatial information together, the potential for learning to understand language is clear.

Integration of Visual Objects and Word Meanings

Infants learn the contextual meanings of spoken language in their day-to-day participation in family living. When adults talk with them about the objects and actions they are involved in, infants learn the labels for familiar objects long before they begin to say the words that are intelligible to others. The social orientation of human infants to other humans renders them sensitive to the going and coming of caretakers. The gratification of a variety of biological needs reinforces infant attention to important objects such as blanket, juice, or bottle. By the end of the first year of life, the infant has learned to identify significant persons by voice or sight and has acquired a repertoire of words understood when used in a familiar setting.

SCALES OF INFANT NORMALCY

The traditional function of tests for infants has been to assure adults that normal development was taking place, or to identify retarded development early so that appropriate treatment might be given. Often early in life adopting parents have wanted to know that the child they were receiving was normal in intelligence and other growth attributes. Medical specialists such as Gesell learned through experience that early intervention in cases of retarded development improved the prognosis for the infants to catch up and to live a normal life. Sometimes research has called for repeated measures of development over time, such as studies of the effect of premature birth on later growth. Infant tests of intelligence have also been used to research questions on the nature-nurture controversy. A few scales for evaluating the growth progress of infants are described below. Some of them have been in use a long time, but still are considered useful in medical, clinical, or child-care situations.

Brazelton's Scale of Psychophysiologic Reactions in Neonates

This scale rates the organization potential of newborns and infants to the age of 1 month (Brazelton & Freedman, 1971). The influence of medication given to mothers during the birth process has been studied by repeating the observations over several days. This scale measures the reaction of the infant to the handler, thus giving a measure of the infant's early social awareness when cuddled, soothed by the voice, or approached face to face. It samples the neonate's repertoire of behaviors, including habituation to particular auditory and visual stimulation; his or her ability to self-quiet after aversive stimulation; visual tracking (of red ball); and auditory tracking (of bell). Brazelton scores all behaviors when the infant is at its peak of attentiveness, the alert, quiet state. He also measures temperature adaptation and reflexive responses as further indicators of neurological organization.

Bayley's California First-Year Mental Scale

Bayley (1933) organized detailed observations of 1400 babies up to 15 months of age to create the California First-Year Mental Scale and various other scales of child development. The Bayley scales for infants include 163 tasks which have been ordered according to the normal age at which they occur, that is, the age at which 50 percent of the infants tested achieved the task. Most of the observations are based on sensorimotor responses to objects presented by the examiner. For example, the infant 6 months old reaches persistently for a cube placed just out of reach. At 11.5 to 12 months old the child imitates an adult in hitting a doll, speaking single words, or rattling a spoon in a cup. Although Bayley later found only slight correlations between the infant scales and intelligence scores of children 6 or 7 years old, the scales have been useful to identify normalcy and retardation at an early age (Bayley, 1943). It should be noted that intelligence scales for older children measure rather different abilities, such as abstract thinking and language development.

Gesell and Armatruda's Developmental Diagnosis

Among a series of scales developed at Yale's Clinic of Child Development, Gesell and Armatruda's assessment focused on the spontaneous actions of infants of particular ages, called "key ages" for observation. Their norm at 28 weeks included a series of accomplishments, such as: sits erect momentarily, holds two cubes more than momentarily, brings feet to mouth, and vocalizes m-m-m and extended vowel sounds. At 52 weeks old the typical Gesell baby walked with one hand held, tried to build a block tower, cooperated in dressing, and said two words besides "mama" and "dada" (1941). This diagnosis has the advantage of using a natural setting and typical behaviors as the basis for assessment.

Cattell's Intelligence Test for Infants

Cattell (1940) also used the key ages of 6 months and 12 months as points for assessment of normal progress. Many of the tasks have been included in other scales, but his clear description of the conditions under which a behavior was observed set new standards for observation of infant behavior. His tests enabled parents or child-care teachers to assure themselves that an infant was developing normally. An example of a 6-month accomplishment is: "reaches unilaterally." Child sits with shoulders square to front and both hands an equal distance from examiner. A 2- to 3-inch door key or peg is presented in perpendicular position. A 12-month achievement is: "beats two spoons together." Two spoons are taken, one in each hand, and beaten gently together while child watches, then they are presented to child, one in each hand. Cattell's precise description of his items makes this an instrument which can be learned easily and implemented with equipment at hand.

Griffiths's Abilities of Babies

Ruth Griffiths (1954) refined the Cattell tests, added new items, and organized them into a more complete inventory. Five categories (locomotor, personal-social, hearing and speech, eye and hand, and performance) were arranged to assess mental development at 1-month intervals to the end of the second year. Because of the continued use of the scales at the toddler age they are discussed in Chapter 5.

Uses of Testing Measures

One exciting possibility is the use of developmental scales to prepare criteria for child-development programs (Chapter 14). Infant scales have been used to evaluate the effects of special programs for mentally retarded or handicapped children for some time. Intervention programs designed to stimulate the sensori-motor development of poor or disadvantaged children usually require measures of the growth as one form of program evaluation. In cognitive research two or more scales can be used as covariants, that is, independent measures that vary in the same direction.

IMPLICATIONS OF INFANT RESEARCH

Research on the competence of infants encourages adults to interact with their babies in ways that stimulate development. The immobile infant is dependent on the caretaker to provide the changing environment which infants like and seek. Some early childhood specialists have tried to break the poverty cycle by teaching parents how to provide a stimulating environment for their babies (Gordon, 1971).

A physically active life for infants helps them to develop strong respiratory, circulatory, and muscular systems. A Czechoslovakian study at Prague's Research Institute for the Care of Mother and Child encouraged vigorous exercise to provide motor stimulation for infants before they could walk (Kupferberg, 1972). Three-month-old infants were trained to grasp rings, roll on large balls, and climb ladders. The purpose was to encourage physical activities that were not normally acquired by infants in a typical protected environment. The experimental programs produced infants who laughed and cooed during physical exercise, who ate and slept well, and who gained weight without the typical amount of fat. Most infants crawled at 6 months. By 1 year old the typical youngster walked well alone and had a vocabulary of fifty words. Their development ranged 1 to 2 months ahead of group norms for the age. The observations are continuing to the age of 6 years, but the most surprising results have been the favorable affective and cognitive responses of the infants to stimulation programs.

Care-givers need to be aware of the range of reinforcers they use in the daily care of infants. Social reinforcement can be used very early in the training of an infant. Self-feeding, for example, comes easily if pleasure responses from the caretaker accompany the infant's attempts at self-feeding. Some parents need consciously to give infants attention and sweet words for behaviors they like, such as smiling, and to avoid attending the infant (if possible) when whining.

Rapid neural growth requires a protein-rich diet including six or more amino acids which must be injected directly to produce twenty to twenty-three amino acids in protein structures. Appropriate weight gain does not assure the DNA and brain weight increases that accompany adequate nutrition (Winick, 1976). A visually stimulating environment is provided by frequent changes of scene from room to room or even by trips away from the house. A young mother who was also a university student discovered she could prepare dinner and feed an older child without having the baby become anxious if she placed the baby in the carrier on her back. The infant was so fascinated by the changing environment, by watching the preparation of the food and the setting of the table, that she was quiet until the mother could manage to feed her.

Some adults feel embarrassed to talk to babies, to explain what is happening, to name objects used. Infants attend to mouth movements during speech when given a chance to have face-to-face conversation. I travel a great deal, and often take the vacant seat next to a mother holding a small infant. Too many times infants wail in airplanes and the efforts to pacify them fail. Holding a frightened baby so one's face can be seen and talking happy nonsense soothes the baby and stops the wailing.

The games people play with babies provide important learning. Hide-and-seek is passed down from one generation to the next as one way to quiet and distract an unhappy infant. "This little pig . . .," played with toes, helps the infant to discover his or her toes and so to initiate development of the back muscle tone that is important at that stage of growth. Pat-a-cake and block building are examples of the kind of activities that can be modeled by caretakers and imitated by babies.

SUMMARY

Biological survival has equipped the human newborn with characteristics that appeal to adults and with innate behaviors for establishing social contact. Refined techniques for studying the competence of the human infant have changed the views of some experts about the environment an infant needs. Negative research results about infant capabilities do not necessarily disprove the positive results of other studies; sometimes techniques are used that fail to consider the infant's state of alertness or do not read the infant's internal action. At the present state of the science, positive findings are a surer guide for childrearing.

Genetically evolved behavior enables the newborn to exhibit numerous reflex patterns practiced before birth. Some reflexes are extended and refined to become deliberate actions, while others disappear in early infancy. Many reflexes are vestiges of primitive needs for survival. Some reflexes, such as grasping, disappear in the first weeks of life to reappear later as controlled action.

Although the infant's life appears to be dominated by body needs for nourishment, body comfort, and sleep, learning through activation of the sensory systems is also a biological necessity for growth. Of the varied states of sleep and wakefulness that have been described, the alert-quiet state is most conducive to skills such as tracking a sound or a light. Sensory stimulation has value for need gratification, but it is secondary to food as a reinforcer when the infant is hungry.

Sensorimotor integration has growth priority during the period of early infant development. Studies of the myelination of neural pathways in the brain show that transmission in the different sensory systems takes place at this time. The organization of body movements and their automatic coordination with breathing and other life processes take place during this period as the cerebellum matures. Cross-cortical connections from one sensory area to another (such as the integration of visual images with their auditory labels) also occur at a high rate.

Vision is the predominant source of information from outside the human organism. Vision is functional for light and dark as soon as neonates open their eyes. They follow (visually track) human face features selectively and within several hours of birth. Twenty/twenty vision is normally present by 4 to 6 months of age.

The hearing mechanisms are functional as soon as medication, given to the mother, is eliminated and the amniotic fluid is drained from the ears of the neonate. Audition is close to adult efficiency for the range of the human voice. Infants respond selectively to the human voice and to human speech.

Space perception is primarily a visual function; time is organized by the auditory sequence of sounds perceived; time and space are integrated through human experience. Neonates are able to take in separate messages, but they must learn the space-time relations of symbolic language, object manipulation, and body movement.

Normal development of intelligence may be confirmed by one or more of several infant scales which tie emerging behaviors to an age norm. Norms are usually the age in months when 50 percent of tested infants show a particular accomplishment. The most important reason for knowing when to expect an infant to show new stages in development is that growth can be anticipated and stimulated. Many environments are so protective as to be drab and monotonous. Overstimulation and unusual expectation can both be avoided by adapting norms to the individual growth patterns and temperament of a baby.

5
Toddlerhood: Age of Locomotion and Identity

5 Toddlerhood: Age of Locomotion and Identity

Toddlerhood has been slow to attain recognition as an entity in the span of human development. Considering that childhood, as distinct from infancy and adulthood, has been recognized for only about 200 years, it is not surprising that toddlers as a group are only recently finding a separate identity in the textbooks, the market-place, and the culture generally.

By definition the toddler is "a child who has learned to walk but not yet perfectly" (Morris, 1973). Toddlers are treated as a separate age group in this chapter because of the tremendous change in the environment of the child that is brought about by mobility. The environments of an 11-month-old child and an 18-month-old child who are both learning to walk have much in common, while the 18-month-old child who is not mobile is still an infant. The effort and concentration of youngsters when learning to stand and walk is marvelous to see.

In an early study of the stages in the achievement of *erect locomotion*, McGraw (1940) distinguished between infants, toddlers, and runabouts. Infants hold their feet in juxtaposition and their arms flexed tight to the body. Toddlers walk independently but with feet excessively wide apart and arms spread in antigravitational position. Runabouts use their legs as a normal base and move contralaterally with rhythmic synchronized steps.

This chapter is about youngsters who are learning to get around on their own two feet, but are not yet able to run, jump, and skip. For purposes of continuity, all the stages of mobility, including the infant stages that precede walking, are described. The different sections focus on the changes in autonomy that accompany the increased mobility of the toddler.

The monumental accomplishments of the toddler period are spatial independence through locomotion, sphincter control, and communication through verbal language. The attachment patterns of infant and care-giver during the first year of life are important causal factors in how the toddler will handle the freedom which walking brings. The individual variation in the timing of mobility and the nature of the coping patterns the toddler learns are significant elements in personality development.

Locomotion enables the child to explore the environment(s) made available by adults. The quality of this environment determines to some extent the child's early learning opportunities. The motor control that is necessary for walking usually coincides with the sphincter control that is necessary for voluntary use of the bathroom. Wetting or nonwetting, at least during the daytime, is the young child's most potent evidence of autonomy and the most available means of asserting power over adults. By using consistent reinforcement approaches in toilet training, adults can build positive associations with toileting and prevent its becoming a power play.

Communication, although limited usually in toddlers to two- and three-word sentences, called telegraphic speech, is increasingly verbal. Affective communication decreases in toddlers, although they still tune in constantly to the affective signals from adults when the adults talk together above the child's level of verbal understanding. The importance of speech in attaining autonomy is that the toddler learns to ask for what is wanted and to say "no" emphatically to anything not wanted.

Toddlerhood, the time normal babies can take a few steps unassisted, begins as early as 9 months old and as late as 18 months old. As early as the third birthday some children are coordinated, heel-toe, arm-swinging walkers and are no longer toddlers. For others, toddlerhood ends around the fourth birthday or even later. During this brief 1- to 3-year period the child comes to know that she or he is a person and becomes aware of the status she or he has in social groups, whether family, extended family, or day-care center peers.

STAGES OF LOCOMOTION

Locomotion is the act of moving from one place to another. A child is said to be mobile when capable of locomotion. The ability to achieve erect, bipedal locomotion enables people to use the hands to produce food, to manipulate the environment, and to examine objects. Some child development specialists believe that the infant in its ontogenic stages of proneness to erect locomotion goes through the phylogenic stages which preceded Homo sapiens.

The most definitive descriptions of the progression from infant crawling to mature walking were initiated or published in the 1930s. Shirley (1931) described the behavior involved in locomotion by recording the sequence of movements that lead to walking for 24 infants. She averaged the ages in months at which each new accomplishment evolved. Gesell (1946) reported a series of studies conducted by himself and his colleagues which provide detailed descriptions of criterion behaviors at different ages in the development of young children, and which are still used as guides today. McGraw (1940) was unique in combining observed behaviors with laboratory observations of neurological development to explain the periods of neuromuscular development. These three researchers all noted the coordinated reflexive behavior patterns of neonates, the gradual disappearance of those action patterns, and the slow attainment of controlled and erect walking. They clearly show that learning to walk, for the human child, involves a series of definable stages of less than perfect walking, covered by the imprecise term of toddlerhood. Usually from 1 to 3 years after a child takes the first independent steps, he or she can stride with heel-toe progression (Gutteridge, 1939). *Bipedal locomotion* requires maintaining control of body weight on alternate feet and swinging the arms in synchronized motion. The child who has accomplished *erect* bipedal locomotion is no longer a toddler, and has demonstrated yet another of the unique attributes of humans.

Orders of Locomotion: Shirley

Shirley (1931) specified the conditions and described criterion behavior so precisely that her procedures became a model for later research. She identified five *orders of locomotion* which, according to her interpretation, followed the principle of cephalocaudal development. The *first order* (birth to 20 weeks old) terminated in postural control of the head, upper trunk, and arms. From a prone position, the infant by the end of this stage can raise head and chest with self-support from the arms while extending the legs to knee-straight position. Shirley considered this accomplishment an important postural control for future walking.

The *second order* (25 to 31 weeks old) involves postural control of the entire trunk, which is required for rolling over and standing with support. The *third order* of development involves active efforts at locomotion, although the limbs still do not yet support body weight; therefore, abdomen contract with the supporting surface is maintained. Crawling and worming provide some spatial movement for the infant and enhance the development of power and coordination of the limbs. The *fourth order* (40 to 50 weeks old) establishes postural control with simultaneous limb coordination. At this stage the infant uses creeping as an effective means of locomotion, with body weight supported by arms and legs.

Shirley's *fifth order* (52 weeks or older) of prewalking skills describes an infant who coordinates trunk, arms, and legs. This accomplishment allows the infant to pull to a standing position and to walk with support around furniture. The time gaps between the orderly advances noted by Shirley were observed also by Gesell and Ames (1940). Table 5-1 summarizes and compares the stages of skill development in locomotion that lead to walking.

Cycles of Prone Behavior: Gesell and Ames

Gesell (1946) believed that the early patterns of mobility in human infants corresponded to the survival behaviors of phylogenically older species. He pointed to the long period of infancy and early childhood when the patterns of racial inheritance are practiced and modified to achieve the more complex behavior of humans. As an embryologist he noted that growth patterns were organized before birth. Development followed three directional principles: (1) cephalocaudal, from the head downward; (2) proximodistal, from the midline outward to the periphery; and (3) control states, from fundamental to accessory functions. To Gesell the neuromuscular organization and the functional activity were of the same order in developmental priority and both followed the three directional principles.

In their study of locomotion, Gesell and Ames (1940) were interested in the reciprocal contraction and relaxation of opposing muscles in body movement and how the central nervous system directed muscle groups to effect the flexion and extension of joints. *Flexion* is the act of bending, and the flexor is the muscle that acts to bend a joint. In anatomy, *extension* is the act of straightening or extending a limb.

Since neonatal responses indicated a highly coordinated neuromuscular system, Gesell and Ames were interested in how movement patterns occurred without the conscious direction of the infant. Lacking modern techniques of monitoring the internal behavior, they carefully observed the movements made by their subjects and used anatomy to describe the behavior of infants in terms of flexion-extension of limbs and bilateral coordination. (The reader will recall that the embryo makes one-sided movements of the limbs before making coordinated bilateral movements.) The increasingly controlled behaviors of infants were grouped by Gesell and Ames into major cycles of locomotion.

Table 5-1
THREE STUDIES OF MOTOR BEHAVIORS THAT LEAD TO WALKING

Weeks	Shirley (1931) orders of locomotion: cephalocaudal development	Gesell and Ames (1940) cycles of prone behavior: innate development	McGraw (1945)* periods of motor control: neuromuscular responses	
3–4	INITIAL ORDER	CYCLE 1	PERIOD 1	
5–8	Postural control of head, upper trunk, arms	Ten stages from bilateral flexion of limbs to unilateral flexion and extension, body contact with supporting surface	Reduction in rhythmic activity and subcortical control, increase in cortical control of motor responses	
9–12				
13–16			PERIOD 2	
17–20			Voluntary movements of superior spinal regions and arms, reduction in undirected activity of pelvis and legs	
21–24				
25–28	SECOND ORDER			
29–32	Postural control of trunk; knee pushing, rolling over, standing with help			
33–36	THIRD ORDER	CYCLE 2	PERIOD 3	
37–40	Attempted locomotion; moves on stomach	Nine stages of crawling, rocking, and creeping with alternate extension-flexion	Voluntary control extended to lower spinal region and extremities	
41–44	FOURTH ORDER			
45–48	Limited locomotion: creeping, weight sustained by arms, legs			
49–52				
53–56	FIFTH ORDER	CYCLE 3	CYCLE 4	
57–60	Coordination of trunk, limbs; pull to standing, walking with help	Plantigrade progression	Full trunk extension, upright posture	
61–64				PERIOD 4
65–68				Rapid development of association areas of cortex. Coordination of locomotion, orientation,
69–72				and purpose

*McGraw's data, presented in days and emphasizing individual differences, have been extrapolated.

Gesell used the term *cycle* to mean a continuum of closely related stages; each cycle terminated in more mature patterns of movement. The first cycle (birth to 29 weeks old) covers ten stages during which a dominant pattern of bilaterial flexion of arms and legs gradually gives way to a unilateral flexion and extension of the limbs. (Recall the fetal position with both arms and legs flexed; recall the Moro reflex when extension occurs bilaterally.) Although the limbs produce some locomotion when the infant is in a prone position, the trunk remains in contact with the floor or table.

The second cycle (30 to 42 weeks old) includes nine stages which begin with the infant's reverting temporarily to bilateral flexion of the arms while new patterns of behavior are being organized. New achievements in locomotion are the backward crawl, the low creep, and the high creep (with abdomen suspended off the surface). The final stage of the cycle is reached when the infant creeps with coordinated movements in which opposite sides alternate, including the extension of arms and the alternate flexion of legs. (If this progression is difficult to follow, try walking in stride and analyze your own bilateral coordination of flexion-extension of limbs.)

The third cycle (49 to 56 weeks old) is the stage of the *plantigrade stance*, which means creeping with the soles of the feet flat on the floor. The infant reverts temporarily from bilateral coordination while plantigrade movement is practiced, after which right arm–left leg movements occur together. The importance of the plantigrade position of the feet for later balance and control in bipedal movement is obvious.

Children who have grown up with animals in the wild have been reported to move in a plantigrade position most of the time, with occasional strides on two feet (Brown, 1958). An advanced level of locomotion has been observed in chimpanzees reared with humans in that much of the chimp's walking is bipedal, accomplished on two feet.

During the fourth cycle (50 through 60 weeks old) the infant develops the capability to fully extend the trunk and to maintain an upright posture. The abilities to walk with arms and legs extended bilaterally and move the limbs left–right and right–left alternately evolve later, but the pattern has already been established in creeping.

I recently observed a handicapped child learning to walk with the help of arm crutches. The child persisted in using a bilateral (left arm and right foot) advance while the volunteer attempted to teach her to advance the left foot and arm together. A knowledge of Gesell's cycles of locomotion would have solved the problem for the teacher.

Periods in Neuromuscular Control: McGraw

McGraw (1945) combined her observations of motor development and the knowledge of neuromuscular development available at that time to trace coincidences between them and thus interpret infant behavior at a new level of sophistication. Hers was the best explanation at the time of the disappearance of neonate reflexive movements and their later reappearance in voluntary locomotion.

The first period (birth to 4 months old) marked the gradual decline of infant reflexive responses and the beginning of voluntary control. Reflexive, rhythmic activity was assumed to be under control of subcortical (primitive) areas of the brain; voluntary movement of neck and arms became possible when the appropriate motor control areas of the cerebral cortex had matured.

The Moro reflex is a startle response in which complex bilateral and contralateral coordination movement is involuntary (Figure 5-1). McGraw's data indicate that infants show an average peaking of about 48 seconds duration of the Moro reflex at just under 1 month old (1966, p. 26). A second peaking of about 29 seconds duration occurs at about 3 months old, after which this reflexive response declines rapidly to about 4 seconds duration. According to McGraw, this decline represents a decline in the neuromuscular energy expressed as the startle is brought under control of the higher cortical areas. The motor control area suppresses the unproductive Moro reflex, which no longer has the primitive survival function of initiating flight. The movements in the Moro reflex are interesting in this context because they show some bilateral coordination of both limbs in flexion and extension, which an infant later practices for months to bring under control. McGraw details a similar shift from reflexive to voluntary grasping.

McGraw (1941) made nearly 2000 observations of eighty-two infants to delineate nine phases in the development of prone progression. The infant's prone posture is flexion, the flexor-extensor movements are rhythmic, and bilateral and alternate

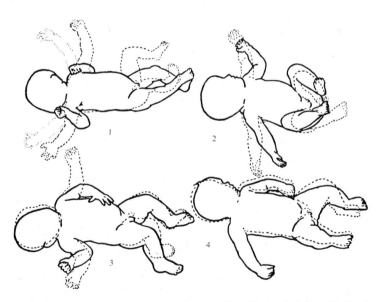

FIGURE 5-1 Movements in the Moro reflex. Phase 1 shows bilateral extension-flexion of arms and flexion-extension of legs. Phase 2 shows head turning to left and upward extension of left arm. Phase 3 shows the alternate lateral movement. Phase 4 shows a return to relaxed, supine position. Redrawn from film frames.

Source: Myrtle B. McGraw, *Growth: A Study of Johnny and Jimmy.* Copyright © 1935, Appleton-Century Co. By permission.

movements are observed. The highest percentage of phase A movement is seen at about 2 months old, although a few infants retain the flexion position and phase A movements up to 6 months old (Figure 5-2).

Phase B in prone progression, seen most frequently at 30 months old, appeared as an extension of the upper spine and neck muscles and a brief sustaining of the head. Some cortical control of arms was seen, although the fingers usually remained flexed. The movement of legs became random, rather than rhythmic, and knee bending was frequent. Ages of phase B infants ranged from 2 weeks to 7 months.

In the second period of neuromuscular control (2 to 9 months old) the infants showed voluntary movements of the superior (upper) spinal regions, including the arms, and a reduction in the undirected activity of pelvis and legs. Phases C and D of the prone progression sequence fall roughly into this period. Phase C, seen most frequently in infants 4 to 6 months old, shows further spinal extension of controlled movement. Head and chest are supported on palms or elbows, and random activity is seen as kicking and waving action. The infant may reach for objects but does not make an effort at body propulsion. This movement pattern is seen as early as 6 weeks and as late as 11 months old.

Phase D, during which the infants made an effort at propulsion, was the characteristic crawling behavior of the 6-month-old infant in McGraw's study; the total age range was approximately 2 to 13 months old. Typically the infant strained arm and shoulder muscles to move the body, sometimes pulling at the bed, to move the body forward. The superior control of upper extremities, showing cephalocaudal development, was indicated. Some infants pivoted at this phase and some moved backward. Backward crawling, noted also by other observers, was interpreted by McGraw as an imbalance in the relative strength of arms over lower extremities.

The third period (6 to 13 months old) extends voluntary control to the lower spinal region and the extremities. Phase E of the creeping sequence is seen in most infants most frequently at 7 months old. McGraw's filmed observations showed frequent leg pushing, with toes flexed. Sometimes movements of the pelvic region and the legs seemed to be emphasized more than movements of the upper trunk and arms. Awareness of body position and awareness of location in the environment were indicated. Some infants showed extension of voluntary control to the lower extremities as early as 2 months, while in others the phase E pattern continued to the thirteenth month.

Phase F, the creeping posture, dominated the prone progression at 8 months old, with a range of 4 to 13 months old during which there was a pause in the propulsion urge. The infants focused instead on coordination of shoulder and pelvic areas and learned to support the abdomen. Many infants rocked in position.

The fourth period of neuromuscular control begins at 9 to 18 months old. It marks the rapid development of association areas of the cortex. Behavior shows the coordination of locomotion, orientation, and intention. The phases of prone progression from G through I show the deliberate propulsion of the body to serve the interests and intentions of the infants.

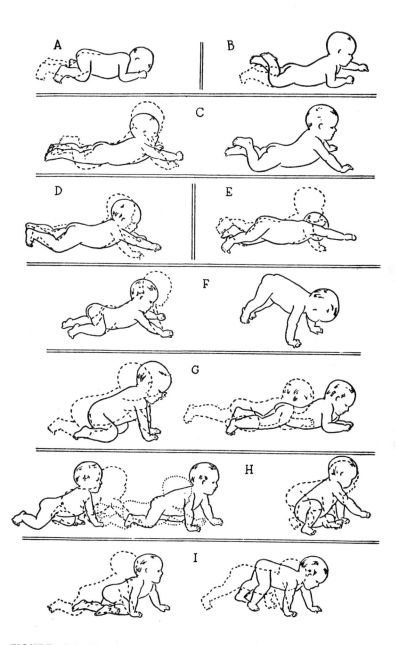

FIGURE 5-2 Development of prone progression. Nine phases of creeping-crawling behavior are redrawn from film frames of the same infants over a period of time. Phase A—flexion posture of newborn; phase B—extension of upper spine and neck; phase C—extension of lower spine; phase D—efforts at propulsion; phase E—propulsion in lower extremities; phase F—creeping posture; phase G—deliberate, unorganized progression; phase H—organized progression; phase I—integrated progression.

Source: Myrtle B. McGraw, *The Neuromuscular Maturation of the Human Infant.* Copyright © 1945, Columbia University Press. By permission.

Phase G, deliberate but unorganized progression, appears with high frequency from 9 to 18 months old. Both arms and legs are used to get somewhere and the infant covers appreciable distances. Some abdominal creeping, some tripedal, and some quadripedal propulsion are seen, but the infant typically has not settled on the best pattern of mobility.

Phase H, organized progression, is seen most frequently from 1 to 2 years old, although a wider range was reported. The infant creeps by repeated patterns of movement, typically with palm-knee contact, using contralateral (right arm–left leg) movements. During this phase the infant propels the body in his or her own adopted system, which may be combined with sitting.

Phase I. integrated progression, spans the same age period as phase H, but may continue as floor play behavior long after the infant can walk. It is distinguished from previous phases of creeping by the smooth performance and the synchronized contralateral movements. Although integrated progression is adept, some infants persist in their individual patterns of scooting or tripedal locomotion. Most however, go through a phase of palm-knee or plantigrade creeping before walking erectly.

McGraw's (1941) interpretation of initial control of neuromuscular functions in the subcortical nuclei of the brain, with subsequent suppression and control by the cerebral cortex as it matured, has been modified somewhat. In a recent publication of McGraw's early studies, she continued to explain the shift from reflexive to voluntary movements in neurological terms, but she came to emphasize growth and development as a complex transaction between old (phylic) and new (human) structures (McGraw, 1966, p. xvi).

Bower (1976) noted that infants a few days old will march along a flat surface with remarkable motor coordination if properly supported, yet walking is not seen again for several months. It is difficult to prove a relationship between reflexive and later walking because the same infant cannot be practiced and yet unpracticed during the first phase. Although conclusive evidence is not available, Bower is moderately certain that practice of early reflexive walking is followed by earlier walking when it reappears. He interprets this observation to mean that the reflexive walking has a function in later locomotion. Early reflexes may disappear, according to this view, because they are not practiced.

The physical accomplishments that lead to walking have been reported with remarkable consistency by Shirley (1931) and Gesell and Ames (1940). As developmentalists they found it difficult to explain how accomplishments or behaviors of one period could be superseded at an earlier period. Ainsworth (1967) reported earlier walking among Ugandan infants than the norms indicate for Western Caucasian youngsters. The relation between the environment and locomotion is far from clear.

Achievement of Erect Locomotion

By maintaining an erect posture and learning erect locomotion the human infant assumes many advantages over subhuman species. This ontogenic development overlaps the phylogeny by which it evolved. Erect locomotion leaves the hands free to carry and use tools, and to manipulate and to examine objects. To walk independently, the young child must maintain balance on the skeletal and muscular structure of alternate legs while propeling the body forward.

McGraw (1940) compiled nearly 3400 observations of the same eighty-two infants who made up the prone-progression studies to identify seven phases of locomotion (Figure 5-3). Phase A, reflexive stepping, is characterized by rhythmic movements of the lower limbs when the infant is held upright with feet touching the surface. During this phase the infants maintains marked flexion of both arms and legs with little space between the feet. At times the legs cross. Typically the stepping reflex increases from birth to the third week, when diminution sets in. Some individual babies did not show reflexive stepping, but they did show the flexion posture.

Phase B, inhibition of reflex stepping, was observed across the group from 1 to approximately 7 months old. During this phase the infants increase their equilibratory control of the head, show a diminution of flexion of limbs, and rapidly advance in their efforts to achieve an upright posture.

Phase C, transition to an antigravity position, is the characteristic mode of infants, who stand in position when helped and make stamping movements. Stepping is diminished, but when it occurs the body is extended in a way that is different from reflexive stepping. The age range of the transition was 3 to 8 months old.

Phase D, deliberate stepping, differs in quality from neonate stepping in that the shoulder and pelvic girdle are held in line. This behavior peaks at about 7 months, but individual babies show deliberate stepping as the mode of erect locomotion from about 6 to 13 months old. Typically they do more rapid stepping when held by the hand than when held under the arms. The amount of foot watching babies did suggested to McGraw that the stepping was deliberate. Although help was needed throughout this phase, the extent of support needed gradually declined.

Phase E, independent stepping, is the characteristic early walking of the toddler and was the predominant mode of the majority of McGraw's subjects from as early as 9 months to as late as 13 months old. At this stage the toddler walks alone with exaggerated movements. Arms are held out for balance and are there to help catch a fall. The feet are wide apart in whole-sole contact. The knees and hips are flexed in high-stepping, staccato movements. Toes grip the surface, usually in plantigrade position. Coordination gradually improves, the length of stride increases, flexion diminishes in the lower limbs, and the incidence of falling decreases.

In phase F. heel-toe progression, the child shows better coordination than in the independent-stepping phase, but is still short of mature walking. The heel of the forward foot touches the surface while the back foot rises on the toes. There is flexion in the ankles and the arms, and fingers are relaxed. The range of age differences among children is great: from approximately 1 to 4 years old.

Phase G, mature erect locomotion, marks the end of the toddler period. About one-half of McGraw's subjects reached this phase at about 2½ years old. Although

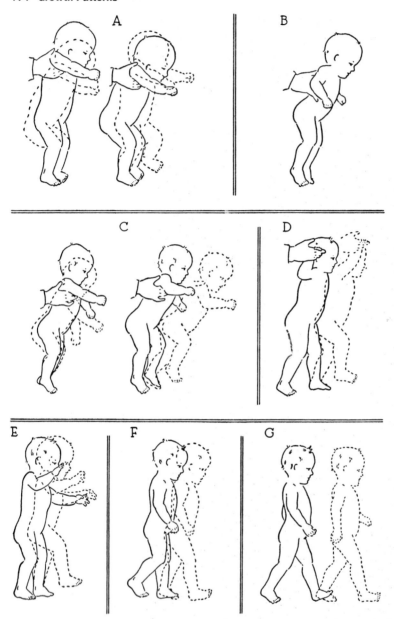

FIGURE 5-3 Seven phases of erect locomotion, drawn from film frames. Phase A—reflexive stepping; phase B—inhibition of reflexive stepping; phase C—transition to antigravity position; phase D—deliberate stepping; phase E—independent stepping; phase F—Heel-toe progression; phase G—mature erect locomotion.

Source: Myrtle B. McGraw, *The Neuromuscular Maturation of the Human Infant.* Copyright © Columbia University Press, 1945. Reproduced by permission.

As a father helps the toddler to walk, one foot advances while contralateral arm extends. (Erika/Peter Arnold)

changes in gait and improvement in coordination will continue with age, the walking style by this phase is integrated. The child's arms and legs move in synchronous and contralateral action, and the arms swing from the shoulders. Most important, the child is liberated from attending to balance and progression so that concentration can be given to the purpose of locomotion.

Group Variation in Age of Walking

Scholars have been interested for some time in the average age at which children learn to creep and to walk. Ethnic differences, race differences, and sex differences have been reported. Usually the researcher interprets these findings in environmental or in genetic terms.

Urban children in five European countries showed important differences in the average age at which the child began to take a few steps independently (Hindley, Filliozat, Klackenberg, Nicolet-Meister, & Sand, 1966). Stockholm children walked the earliest, at an average of 12.5 months, and Paris children the latest, at an average of 13.8 months. In this European sample no social class differences or sex differences were found.

Several ethnic groups have been compared with American Caucasians. American Indian children were reported to walk at a later age than white Americans (Dennis, 1963). Balinese children learn to walk by a progression from squatting to walking, which is different from the locomotion sequence of American children (Mead & MacGregor, 1951). Mead suggests both genetic differences and childrearing practices as possible explanations. The Balinese carry their children to an advanced age and handle them with less vigor than Americans do. The lack of muscle tonus of Balinese children is attributed by Mead to the passive handling and lack of adult interaction.

Comparative studies involving Orientals have shown mixed results. Striking differences in gross motor activity between American and Japanese middle-class youngsters was reported by Caudill and Weinstein (1966), with Americans significantly more active. Emmy Werner (1971) reported that Oriental children were more precocious at age 2 than Caucasians. Black children, both American and African, were superior to both groups (*Psychology Today*, November, p. 46).

There is evidence of the superior motor development on the part of African children during the first year of life, but a decline after the second year, when compared with European or American groups on several scales. Ainsworth (1967) studied Ganda babies who crawled a month earlier, creeped 2½ months earlier, stood alone 2 months earlier, took steps 3 months earlier, and trotted well 4 months earlier than Western children on the Griffiths's norms (see page 193). Ainsworth favors an environmental explanation, suggesting that Ganda children have early physical closeness and nurturance from mothers and freedom to move about and interact with others. Weaning rejection coincides with the later decline in precocity also observed by Ainsworth (1967).

Geber, who also studied African children, favors the nature view of differences. His studies of the newborn seem to suggest some genetic influence (Geber & Dean,

1957). The Ganda neonates showed a high degree of precocity in control of head, in muscle tone, and in early disappearance of primitive reflexes. The Moro reflex, the grasp reflex, and the stepping reflex were rarely seen after the first 24 hours. According to the research, Ganda neonates were more like Western babies 3 to 4 weeks old. Probably the culture continues to support the particular attributes an ethnic group desires, and the interaction with genetic attributes, as well as childrearing practices, account for differences.

ATTACHMENT-EXPLORATION BEHAVIOR

Mobility is the beginning of a lifetime of choices for the young child. How this new freedom is used depends to some extent on the relationship during infancy with the care-giver, usually the mother. The amount of distance the child puts between self and mother, the time spent out of sight, and the nature of his or her exploration of objects and space have been studied experimentally to answer the questions of how the child uses locomotion.

Attachment behavior means the young child's tendency to seek personal contact or nearness with particular persons. Shaffer and Emerson (1964) studied social attachment in Scottish infants to the age of 18 months. They found a peaking of attachment to the mother, as measured by the intensity of the infant's distress at separation, at 10 months. Yarrow (1967) reported a clear preference for mother in 20 percent of infants by 1 month. By 3 months 80 percent showed recognition and preference, and by 5 months all infants in their sample showed definite signs of mother preference.

The question of whether an infant requires a particular mothering person in infancy to develop a healthy independence in the second year has been studied intensively since the psychoanalytic accounts of emotional development were published. Bowlby (1969) brought together the studies of primates when deprived of mothering or deserted and the available research on human infants. He stressed the child's attachment to a mother figure, the substitution of cuddly objects for a mother's presence, and the responsiveness to the emotional needs of a child as the basis for the ability to cope with stress and frustration in later childhood. Much of Bowlby's material on the patterns of attachment came from Ainsworth's research.

Ainsworth (1967) listed the patterns of attachment to mothers, which have been combined as follows: (1) different crying, smiling, or vocalization for mothers than for others; (2) crying when mother departs; (3) following or approaching, visual-motor orientation; (4) greeting by smiling, crowing, and general excitement; (5) lifting arms or clapping hands in greeting; (6) climbing over or burying face in lap; (7) exploration away from mother as base; (8) flight to mother as haven; and (9) kissing and hugging. It will be noted that independent locomotion on the part of the child is necessary in attachment behavior which requires following, approaching, exploration, or flight to mother.

Ainsworth reported that Ugandan infants began exploration, while using the mother as a base, from 7 to 9 months old, which is earlier than Western infants. These infants had made attachments to the mother by this age and all had made a

Table 5-2
TIMETABLE FOR ATTAINING LOCOMOTION

Behavior	Conditions	Age	Range	Source
Reflexive stepping (stepping movements of alternate feet)	Held erect, feet resting on flat surface	Newborn		Peiper, 1929
Reflexive creeping (pushoff movement with foot or both feet, synchronized arm movements)	Prone position contact on bottom of feet	Neonate	Birth to 4 months	Bauer, 1926
Swimming (coordinated limb movements)	Prone position, submerged in water	11 days		McGraw, 1941*
Head-shoulder lift (arms extended)	Prone position on table, active lifting by own arm-strength	8 weeks	2 weeks to 7 months	Shirley, 1931 McGraw, 1941
Pivoting (rotating with arm-hand action)	Prone position legs straight	30 weeks	2–13 months	Gesell & Ames, 1940 McGraw, 1941
Rocking (no propulsion)	Abdomen free, supported on hands and knees (or feet)	37 weeks	4–13 months	Shirley, 1931 McGraw, 1941
Creeping (hands-knees tripedal, or quadripedal progression)	Covers considerable distance to get somewhere	45 weeks	9–18 months	Gesell & Ames, 1940

Behavior (description)	Criterion	Gesell & Ames, 1940	McGraw	Source
Plantigrade progression (quadruple creeping on palms and whole soles of feet)	Proficient locomotion using this style	50 weeks		Gesell & Ames, 1940
Deliberate stepping [when held by hand(s)]	Greater stepping activity than when held under arms, watches feet		6–13 months	McGraw, 1940
Independent stepping (feet spread, whole-sole contact, arms out)	Walks alone with exaggerated movements (toddles)		9–18 months	McGraw, 1945
Heel-toe progress (heel of forward foot and bent toes of backward foot touching)	Erect locomotion but less than mature gait and timing	1–2½ years	1–4 years	McGraw, 1945
Mature walking (synchronized, contra-lateral movement of limbs)	Attention to locomotion no longer necessary	3 years	2½–4½ years	McGraw, 1945

*McGraw's data, reported in days-old and percentage of action observed, have been interpolated.

179

Mother provides the spoken label for an object of attention. (Laima Druskis/Editorial Photocolor Archives)

subsequent attachment to an additional person in the household. Apparently both locomotion and attachment are necessary for the infant to initiate exploratory behavior other than visual-grasping inspection. After weaning, during the second year, the Ugandan infants regressed to crying and following; they lost interest in other people and the physical environment.

Mobile infants are willing to leave the mother in one room to enter another room when toys are there to be explored, according to a report on American infants by Rheingold and Edkerman (1971). Their subjects were about 10 months old and were selected for their ability to creep. When an infant was left alone in the room, it was more likely to cry than to explore; but when allowed to use the mother as a safety base, the infants explored the vacant room and did not cry. By observing and recording locomotion it was determined that infants spent no longer in a room with a toy than in an empty room because, typically, they brought the toy back to the mother. However, when three toys were placed in the next room, infants significantly increased the time away from mother and the time exploring the objects. After infants had one experience at finding a toy in the next room, they were quicker to enter the room on a second visit. Apparently conditions of familiarity, of an interesting environment, and the presence of the mother as a secure base are all important factors in increasing exploratory behavior in creepers.

Ainsworth, Bell, and Stayton (1971) studied the attachment-exploration balance of twenty-three white middle-class mobile infants from the time they were 51 weeks old to the time they were 54 weeks old. They found five different patterns of infant-mother interaction with reference to exploratory behavior. Group 1 youngsters used their mothers as a secure base from which to explore. They moved out of sight but kept track of the mother's whereabouts, returning occasionally for physical contact which both mother and child seemed to enjoy. This was interpreted as a healthy relationship, conducive to exploration; about one-third of the group was in this category.

Group 2 youngsters used their mothers as a secure base part of the time, but a mismatch between the mother's responsiveness and the child's wish for contact disturbed the quality of the relationship. Sometimes the mother would ignore the child's seeking and other times the child would reject the affectionate advances of the mother. The interaction was similar to the first group at times, but was inconsistent.

Group 3 youngsters explored very actively, but they did not use the mother as a secure base, did not seek her proximity, and did not seem concerned about her absence. This was interpreted as a moderately effective defense by the toddler against insensitive mothering.

Group 4 youngsters did not seem to feel their mothers were a safe base. They explored actively and sought contact or proximity often. These babies kept visual tabs more than most and were more distressed with the mother's leaving than group 1 youngsters, but seemed to show little pleasure in the frequent physical contacts they made. This group represented a small portion of the sample and were interpreted as insecure youngsters who were unable to cope with stress.

Group 5 youngsters were passive, intermittently or consistently, and rarely sought contact or proximity. Their behavior was stereotyped and repetitive rather than exploratory. The mothers did not seem to serve as a security base. The mother-child relationship was disharmonious due to interbalance, rejection, or inconsistent mothering.

Further research is needed on the relationships among the age of locomotion, exploratory behavior, and cognitive development. Ainsworth's studies of the attachment-exploratory balance of Gandan and British babies are not directly comparable because of the disparity in motor development which has one group toddling (at 1 year) while the other group is still creeping. Studies which select for creeping or walking ability involve a select population. The infants in the Rheingold and Eckerman study (1971) had an average IQ of 118, which raises some questions of application. Did the exploratory-attachment behavior represent precocious youngsters? Creepers generally? Early creepers? Or mobile youngsters? Logically, mobility increases the opportunity for exploration with some relation to the creeping-walking efficiency of the youngster. The freedom gained by locomotion tests the emotional maturity of child and the caretaker.

SPHINCTER CONTROL

The young child's learning to use the toilet is almost as important to adults as the appearance of walking and is much more difficult to manage. Despite a wide range of differences in individual children in the ability to gain control over the sphincter muscles, toilet training has been associated with cleanliness and virtue. It may be very unfair to judge a care-giver by the child's toileting patterns, but the child's acceptance often depends on whether he or she is clean and dry or soiled and wet (Stanley, 1968). Most recent anthologies on child development and early education have given little attention to this important topic. One must look to older developmental sources for information on elimination patterns (Gesell, 1943), and to psychoanalytic sources for the relationship of toilet behavior to personality development (Erikson, 1956), even though elimination control stands out as one of the major accomplishments of toddlerhood. Locomotion is necessary before the child can be responsible for going to the bathroom.

Opposing Views on Toilet Training

Two views on toilet training are those of Rene Spitz and Konrad Lorenz, both found in the same book, *Play and Development* (1972). Spitz rejects the idea that toilet training should take place from the second month on, as recommended during the thirties by the U. S. Children's Bureau; he favors the modern approach, which is based on education of the child during the second year of life.

The technique for early training involved individualized, balanced, and regular feeding which resulted in regular elimination from the bowels, usually once a day after morning cereal and juice, but occasionally after the evening meal also. The infant, cradled in the care-giver's lap, sat with bare bottom on a small (warmed) potty. Sometimes a suppository was used for a few days to start the evacuation, but usually relaxation with abdominal massage produced grunting and a stool, which elicited delighted praise from the mother. Spitz explained that this form of conditioning broke down near the end of the first year when "it came into conflict with the child's developing personality, specifically with his need to assert his own free will" (p. 44). Spitz recommended the alternate plan of toilet training during the second year of life when the "ego has become operative" (p. 45). Then the child has a sense of self, registers body sensations, and "identifies with his mother's wishes and incorporates her standards."

On the other side of the issue, Lorenz (1972) believes that permissive childrearing, beginning with toilet training (p. 103), results in bored youth who lack the biological responsiveness to life that comes from a balance of pleasure with displeasure. This means that reward can be experienced only when balanced against some experience of punishment. According to Lorenz pampered youngsters develop into youths who are (1) unwilling to strive for deferred goals, (2) unable to endure pain or displeasure, (3) unwilling to exert musculature except in "sporting" activities, and (4) sluggish of emotion. He states that modern parents coddle and withhold firmness to the point that youngsters are denied "even the moderate toll of discomfiture and toil which nature has set as a price for all earthly joy" (p. 87).

The normal rhythm of eating with enjoyment after having got really hungry, the enjoyment of any consummation after having strenuously striven for it, the joy of achieving success after toiling for it in near-despair, in short the whole glorious amplitude of the waves of human emotions, all that makes life worth living, is dampened down to a hardly perceptible oscillation between hardly perceptible tiny pleasures and displeasures. The result is an immeasurable boredom (1972, p. 88).

Lorenz sees some of the symptoms of youngsters who lack a zest for living as similar to the characteristics of hospitalized children who are retarded because of lack of socialization. Part of the remedy is increased communication through active games, earlier training, and talking between child and caretaker. "The majority of present-day babies talk later and they become toilet-trained much later, as witnessed by the huge, diaper-distorted behinds of quite big children" (p. 106). The child who enters the social world outside the home untrained will certainly get negative feedback from strangers, which will have consequences for the self-concept of the child. Many parents reject these somewhat harsh views, but a growing concern for stronger parenting has been expressed by others, particularly those who make cross-cultural comparisons (Bronfenbrenner, 1970).

At the simplest level, the opposing views on toilet training are first-year versus second-year training. Initially, it was thought to be an issue of *conditioning* of the child versus *understanding* of the produce and process of elimination by the child. According to Spitz, the issue is *learning* versus *education*. More recently, conditioning by reinforcement has been used in nursery schools to toilet train the youngsters. These choices are not readily resolved by common sense, so what is the responsible approach for the care-giver or consultant? A reexamination of developmental norms is one way to begin, so that training can be based on reasonable expectations of the child.

Elimination Patterns of Toddlers

Early observations of child development included the detailed description of elimination patterns, normal behavior of youngsters toward toileting, and some examples of significant individual differences (Gesell & Ilg, 1943). Toilet training is a problem of the relationship between *maturation* and *acculturation*. The age norms for elimination behavior proposed at the Gesell Institute were designed to give parents and nursery school teachers a basis for sensible interaction with an individual toddler regarding elimination.

Toileting Practices at Different Ages

Gesell and Ilg (1943) suggested that 15 months is a better age break between the periods of infancy and toddlerhood than is the 1-year birthday. They describe the 12-month-old child as deft in forceps prehension, indicating fine muscle coordination of the upper extremities. The typical child of this age likes to play with several small objects at one time and to practice picking them up and dropping them. This practice of releasing is considered important developmental preparation for the holding and letting go of sphincter control.

Gesell and Ilg, who assume some earlier toilet training, report that the 1-year-old has less success on the pot than he or she had earlier, and gives less warning by grunting before a bowel movement. Awareness that the infant knows what is happening, however, is shown in wanting to look in the pot to see what has been done, in wanting to help with toilet paper and flushing the toilet, and by fussing to be changed.

By 15 months old the typical child can walk, and indeed prefers to toddle unaided. This independence is shown also in resisting being dressed, in grabbing the spoon but spilling the food, and in emphatically casting toys from highchair or playpen. This assertiveness is often generalized to resistance of the pot. The child's burst of activity interferes with taking time to go to the bathroom, so the child in this stage often wets and promptly gestures for a change of clothing. At this age, children have typically established an individual pattern of one or two bowel movements each day and these are usually related to eating (coming just after a meal) or sleeping (coming just after a nap).

Toddlers are very conscious of their product. If left unattended they may remove their pants after a bowel movement and smear their stool on the bedding, the crib, or themselves. The child who makes a puddle on the floor is likely to point, gesture, or say, "See!" Punishing a child by scolding or spanking for stool smearing or urine puddling may have long-term negative effects on sphincter release and should be avoided at this age. Many a care-giver who has heard the contented cooing after a nap has delayed too long and finally found the child entertaining itself by smearing rung after rung of the crib with a stool. Diapers, covered by latex pants, are better than training pants when the child is put to bed because they keep the bed dry and are more difficult to remove. Going to the child promptly after a nap offers the advantage of finding him or her dry so the child can be put on the pot. Playing in the product probably is not harmful directly to the child, but it certainly can spoil an afternoon for the care-giver. Observing the individual elimination patterns and making use of the opportune times for going to the bathroom is important in preventing the child's opposition to the pot, which can quickly show up in toddlers. The child's communication, when asked about going, should be respected whether it is "no-go" or "hurry-hurry."

The compulsive, whole-body locomotion of the 18-month-old child sets the pattern for toilet behavior as well as play. When walking becomes more or less automatic, children concentrate on showing power in locomotion by moving things. They seek closure by putting things in boxes, closing doors, or depositing valuables in the garbage can. Each action gets full attention and is completed with "that's that" finality. Elimination patterns that seemingly had stabilized to an after-eating or an after-sleeping event may shift. The intense activity of the toddler, and the necessity for closure, may make interruptions in play for toileting disliked. On the plus side, the child's expanding language enables him or her to communicate with labels used in the family for voiding (urinating) or evacuating.

Some children of 18 months anticipate elimination and may bring the potty if it is small and accessible. About half the children this age are still dry if awakened at 10:00 PM (Gesell & Ilg, 1943). If taken to the bathroom they often remain dry until morning. Many toddlers will remain dry for long periods during the day, especially if they have been put into training pants which can be managed alone, and are reminded at opportune times. Most children find it difficult to respond to a strange pot, so it is helpful to take their own on visits. Because of the fluctuations in bowel movement patterns, 18 months may be an inopportune time for some children to begin toilet training. On the other hand the toddler's awareness of the elimination function and the new vocabulary for making his or her needs known are conducive to a high portion of success.

The typical child of 21 months is conscious of the relationship of the voiding process and the product which results. Some children are trained except for occasional lapses when physical upsets, such as diarrhea with teething, interfere with elimination patterns. The increased food intake and the larger size of the child make diapering increasingly unpleasant for the care-giver. Some children at this age still refuse the toilet and will have a movement shortly after being taken off. Others cannot handle the release mechanisms. A child may have a movement, scream helplessly, and remain screaming throughout the changing of pants. This failure to inhibit discourages both child and trainer, but patience is essential. When the child can manage both clothing and equipment he or she will often begin to assert the autonomy of the stage and go to the bathroom alone rather than ask for help.

After teething is over, at about 2 years old, the bowel movement pattern stabilizes and the sphincter muscles come under control. The child may ask for help to go to the bathroom, but often wants to be left alone on the toilet, saying "Go away" or "Me be!" Later the child may call for help with wiping and dressing. The child who still has trouble anticipating a movement might be allowed to run without pants in the area of the bathroom during the opportune times of the day. Bladder accidents typically occur in periods. The child who tries and can't make it to the bathroom in time should be praised for trying. Children in the third year are usually proud of their achievements and concerned about their failures. If awakened at 10:00 PM, the child should be gently led to the bathroom, rather than carried, so that he or she is aware of what is happening and later can go alone.

For toddlers under 3 years the product of elimination is one of the recurring bits of evidence of personal identity. Locomotion, sphincter control, power to move things, and other accomplishments typically show up as self-assertion. The child often begins active opposition to others, including the parent. In use of the toilet, mediation rather than discipline is the course of wisdom. The child knows the alternatives of wet and dry, but the capacity to anticipate is weak and release of the sphincters is not always easy. Like typical resistance to other suggestions, the child may begin to refuse help with clothing and may resist being taken up at night.

After the third birthday, most children go by themselves to the toilet for bowel movements and have no wetting accidents during the day. The majority remain dry overnight, although some must still be awakened once during the night to go to the bathroom. At this age a child may go for weeks without wetting the bed and then

A cookie to eat rewards the toddler's efforts to use the toilet. (Erika/Peter Arnold)

start a period of regular wetting at night. It should be kept in mind that the Gesell and Ilg observations and recommendations assume earlier toilet training than many modern mothers undertake.

Physical Development and Wetting

Tanner (1970) used London research studies to cite the ages of sphincter control in young children. Most children are dry by day at 18 months, although some who appear perfectly normal are not dry until 3 years. About 50 percent stay dry at night by age 2, and about 75 percent by age 3. By age 5, 90 percent no longer wet the bed, although 12.1 percent of boys and 9.7 percent of girls continued bed-wetting occasionally or regularly. Sex differences for day wetting are not found, suggesting that the girls' advantage occurs when "conscious control is not operating" (p. 125). Evidence is lacking on any emotional effect that early versus late toilet training might have on the emotional development of the child.

Older children who lack sphincter control or have not been trained are sometimes enrolled in nursery schools where the problem must be dealt with by teachers. The awareness of the children themselves is revealing. Michael, age 2½ (who was verbally precocious but whose sphincter control was delayed because of kidney operations), would say, "Mom, change my pants; do you think I want diaper rash?" Beverly, age 4, chatted to the aide, "I'm quite a young lady, now, I've quit pottying my pants. On my birthday, I still hadn't quit, but I have now." "Why did you decide to stop wetting?" "I guess I just wanted to grow up. Well, mostly I got tired of the spankings." Cognitive control is necessary for the self-control of elimination, but conditioning may occur much earlier.

Behavior Management in Toileting

Behavior management techniques are based on the operant conditioning theory of Skinner in which baseline behaviors are used to start a schedule of pottying with rewards for success. Neonate *micturition* is reflexive elimination following handling, eating, or some other nonspecific stimulus (Tanner, 1970). Some experienced practitioners believe that tender care and successful use of the pot in infancy establish pleasure associations which may facilitate later cortical control. Toddlers who arrive at the day-care center without training are often trained by a strategy known as *behavior management*, or *behavior modification*.

The strategy for training the toddler involves five steps: (1) prescribing the behavior desired, (2) arranging an environment that is conducive to the performance of the prescribed behavior, (3) obtaining baseline data on the particular child, (4) reinforcing behavior in the direction of the prescribed behavior, and (5) gradually withdrawing external controls. Although this form of behavior management is considered new, it will be recognized as very like the training program recommended by Gesell and Ilg (1943).

The behavioral description, or objective, is formulated taking into account the age abilities of the child and the daily schedule of the center or school. Melissa will remain dry from 9 to 12 o'clock each morning. Freddie will have bowel movements in the potty chair throughout the day. The child's going to the bathroom area at the appropriate time would constitute a behavior in the direction of the behavioral objective and would be reinforced, at first, even if the child didn't quite make it to the potty chair in time.

The environment might include a potty chair, placed on the floor where the child could sit down unassisted, and training pants which could be undone quickly by an adult, or better still, undone by the child unassisted. Toilet facilities should be located near the play area if possible, so that the child does not need to go very far from the compelling activities that are important at this age.

Baseline data on toileting patterns is compiled for each individual in the training group. In the nursery school a wall chart provides an easy way for systematic recording by whoever changes the pants or helps the child.

Reinforcement is provided by care-givers who praise with words and smiles when the child is successful. Some children are happy to sit on the pot if they have a book to look at, a toy to play with, or a wafer to munch. Reinforcement strategies should be reevaluated and modified if the child is not progressing toward control.

The reinforcement techniques are withdrawn as the child gains control and

independence over toilet routines. The goal is for the child to function independently. Behavior management is successful in part because most children desire to
increase their independence and control.

PERSONALITY CHANGE AND STABILITY

Personality is the totality of the qualities and characteristics that give a person
identity, or individuality. During infancy and toddlerhood personality is shaped in
part by a cycle in which individuality is identified and labeled by older persons, and
the child's behaviors which confirm the image are recognized and reinforced. The
child develops a self-image which reflects, at least somewhat, the view of
care-givers and others in the environment. To the young child *what I am like*
becomes part of *who I am.*

Sometimes a personality becomes stereotyped very early. The toddler, whose
understanding of langugae is more advanced than most parents suspect from
speech, is often compared with siblings or with some abstract model. Kathy, age 12
years, was a preadolescent receiving counseling for underachievement. Over-
weight was only one of many symptoms of unhappiness. She quoted from her
mother's remarks: Sara, a younger sister who was truly attractive, had the "looks";
Ben, who had walked at nine months, had the "ambition"; and Kathy had the
"brains." The parents never guessed that Kathy remembered, believed, and
detested the image she had heard expressed very early by her family. At the time of
her clinical treatment, Kathy had poor grades and was reported by the teacher to
have poor comprehension in reading. She showed a verbal intelligence quotient
above 140 and a performance intelligence score even higher. Kathy was actually
quite attractive. Although she had continued to run on all fours to the age of 16
months (according to her mother), Kathy was well coordinated and earned A's in
physical education. But she could not accept herself as her parents saw her and
resisted the total picture they had presented. Older children with personality
problems involving self-rejection stimulated professionals to ask when and how
the problem developed. Are there critical periods in the development of personality? How stable is the temperament of a toddler?

When a group of children is studied over a period of time, they almost always
come from an environment that is continuous in terms of their availability to the
research team. This indicates that reinforcement patterns, levels of communication, and opportunities for learning are consistent over time in their impact on the
subject. Such studies do not answer all the basic questions about the ages at
which behavior patterns stabilize or about the child's potential for personality
change. The psychoanalytic school has tended to place the age of identity in
toddlerhood (Chapter 11). Recent research in cognitive development has identified
some of the aspects of personality in toddlers and young children that can be
predicted during infancy, assuming a continuous environmental influence.

Despite the inability of researchers to separate the genetic from the environmental determinants of personality development, the data are useful in childrearing.
Kagan (1971) found a relationship between early face-to-face interaction of mother

and infant and the cognitive ability of the same children at age 2 years. Thomas, Chess, and Birch (1968) found that toddlers with similar temperamental tendencies developed differently in different rearing environments.

Continuity from Infancy to Toddlerhood

Kagan (1971) studied change and continuity in the same group of infants at 4, 8, 13, and 27 months. The data, obtained in laboratory tests and home observations, were analyzed for predictive value (stability) from infancy to the second and third years of life. The study focused on fixation times as an indicator of attentiveness, babbling and later verbalization, play tempo over time, and certain temperament characteristics such as smiling behavior and irritability.

ATTENTIVENESS

Fixation time was recorded in seconds when the child was presented with a new toy, when discrepant pictures were shown (such as a three-headed man), and during problem episodes (such as finding embedded figures). Fixation times at 4 months were not highly related to later attentiveness and appeared "under the control of general alertness" (p. 80). However, from 8 months, fixation times became increasingly consistent across different episodes, increasingly independent of vocalization, smiling, and body size; and increasingly correlated with the educational level of the family. Kagan considered fixation time to indicate the individual child's ability to attend to visual stimuli and to orient toward an event.

Kagan's staff took measures of heart rate throughout their laboratory test episodes. Decrease in heart rate, *cardiac deceleration*, is considered an objective indicator of attentional focus by infants and young children. Kagan's staff used two electrodes (taped to the chest of the child) and a portable pocket transmitter to obtain a continuous heartbeat record.

Deceleration was most likely to occur when the infant was surprised, which is interpreted in youngsters as an orientation reaction. These toddlers showed decelerations of 6 to 10 beats per minute over an interval of 4 to 6 seconds when an unexpected event occurred, such as a shift to different stimulus materials at the beginning of a new episode. The discrepancy tests, when subjects were presented with body forms or faces that differed radically from established schema, produced a significant reduction in heart rate. Cardiac deceleration was accompanied by reduced motor activity and observable focus of attention. At 27 months few cardiac decelerations were produced, exceptions being the embedded figures test, where full attention was needed to find the figures, and some of the color slides, where discrepancies were shown. Deceleration to visual material was greatest for a slide which showed a woman holding her head in her hands. Auditory stimuli of a horn blowing or a dog barking produced greater deceleration than did any of the speech that accompanied the slides. Perhaps by toddler age, most events did not offer sufficient surprise to elicit the degree of orienting that deceleration indicates.

One interesting discovery was a moderate continuity in heart response from infancy to early childhood. Unlike the data on vocalization, there were no social class differences and greater stability was found for boys than for girls (p. 121).

VERBALIZATION

Vocalization in 2-year-olds seemed to be communicative, as contrasted with infant utterances, which seemed to indicate diffuse excitement. *Spontaneous verbalizations* were recorded during free play and during the test episodes; *vocabulary competence* was tested by asking the child to name pictures; and the *quality of speech* was analyzed from tape recordings of the child's conversation at home. Kagan found little relationship between infant babbling and later verbalization in his group as a whole, but he found significant sex differences. Girls showed stronger correlation (greater stability) between 13- and 27-month verbalization than boys did. This difference came primarily from the daughters of high SES mothers, who were observed to do more face-to-face talking with their female babies in infancy. Even in infancy the girl subjects vocalized spontaneously in response to human forms, to human masks, and to new episodes. Particularly the high SES daughters showed a *"disposition to express excitement through talking"* (p. 99, italics his) which showed consistency from infancy to early childhood. Kagan proposed that the female infant's temperament to babble when excited by novel situations interacted with the tendency for well-educated mothers to be responsive to early vocalization. Since vocabulary competence and quality of speech are predictors of school success, the implication is intervention in infancy.

REFLECTIVE-IMPULSIVE TENDENCIES

A dramatic increase in mobility occurred in Kagan's subjects between the 8-month and the 13-month interval, as measured by the numbers of squares traversed during a timed period of free play in a large area containing many toys. Even though all children crawled or walked at 13 months and were able to run at 27 months, there was little change in total mobility during that period. The children's activity seemed to be more goal-oriented. They directed attention toward particular toys and increased the duration of involvement with single toys. Higher SES youngsters increased their mobility earlier than the children from lower SES families, especially the boys.

Kagan calculated a tempo dimension for 27-month toddlers by combining each child's index of *directed activity* and the number of actions of more than 2 minutes duration in the play period. This enabled researchers to identify fast-tempo and slow-tempo groups, and then to compare these groups on different traits recorded in infancy. Most infants who were in the fast-tempo play group at 27 months had shown short fixation times at 4 months. They were high in the restless activity scores and initiated many acts during play at 8 months. Toddlers who were among the fast-tempo play group were nearly all impulsive responders to the embedded figures tests given at the same age. On the other hand, most infants who were in the slow-tempo group at 4 months were characterized by more smiling and longer fixation times. At 27 months most of them were in the reflective group that took longer to find embedded figures while making fewer errors, played longer with single toys, and had higher verbalization scores. Kagan believes that the essential difference between slow- and fast-tempo children is the tendency of the former to "invest effort in retrieving stored knowledge" (p. 150). His study led him to conclude that the attributes of the infant exert at least a subtle influence on later tendencies toward reflection or impulsivity.

Kagan found no major sex differences in the activity level of infants under 1 year. At 13 months he noted two different response patterns toward interesting stimuli on the part of individuals; some quieted and fixated, others became active and tried to reach the object. The activity level was not a good predictor, therefore, for 2-year-old behavior. One predictor was found: 1-year-old boys with a low threshold for restlessness were likely to show a fast tempo of play and to behave impulsively at 2 years old. Research might be enlightening which classified the activity level of infants according to mode of exploration (visual and tactile) and assumed motivation from how the child used manipulation and mobility.

SMILING, IRRITABILITY, AND FEARFULNESS

Frequency of smiling at 4 months was more predictive of slow tempo and problem solving at 27 months than for any of the measured behaviors at the intervening ages. At 27 months there was a strong linear correlation between the difficulty of an embedded test item the toddler solved and the duration of the smile which followed. The finding was even more decisive for boys than for girls. In girls the 4-month smile was predictive of high spontaneous verbalization, a slow tempo of play, and an endomorphic physique in the 2-year-old girl. Kagan suggested that the 4-month-old smile may reflect an attribute of temperament that involves the capacity to build tension and to resolve it (p. 159).

Fussing, for whatever reason, whether from boredom or fatigue, was timed; it constituted the infant's *irritability* scores. Fussing made up 5 percent of the 4-month infant's observation time and 1 percent of the time for 8-month and 13-month youngsters. Irritable 4-month-old boys had lower vocabulary and speech quality ratings at 2 years than did the group as a whole. Irritable girl infants were restless and active at 2 years, compared with the total sample.

Fear of faces at 8 months produced crying in some infants. Fearful boys, when compared with nonfearful controls, were less talkative and were inhibited in their play contacts at 27 months, staying close to the mothers. Fearful girl infants grew up to be spontaneous talkers who showed no special preference to play near their mothers at 27 months. Kagan assumed that mothers react differently to fearful girls than to fearful boys, with the result being some negative effects on young boys (p. 168).

Temperament and Later Behavior

Thomas (1968) identified nine categories of temperament in a sample of children from birth to 2 years. A larger sample of 141 youngsters was followed from birth to preadolescence, with comparative psychological and psychiatric data being obtained at 3 years, 6 years, and later (Thomas, Chess, & Birch, 1970). His staff was interested in the relationship between temperament in infancy and later personality. The temperament categories were identified as follows: (1) *Activity level*—the tempo and frequency of motor components such as kicking and resistance to dressing; (2) *Rhythmicity*—regularity of biological functions such as eating, resting, and bowel movements; (3) *Approach* or *withdrawal*—initial reaction to a new stimulus such as strangers or food; (4) *Adaptability*—sequential course of responses to new or altered situations, especially in the direction of desired behavior; (5) *Intensity of reaction*—energy content of a response such as intense crying versus whimpering; (6) *Threshhold of responsiveness*—level of extrinsic stimulation that is necessary to evoke an observable response, based mostly on evidence of sensory discriminations; (7) *Quality of mood*—amount of pleasant, joyful, friendly behavior as contrasted with unpleasant, crying, unfriendly behavior; (8) *Distractibility*—effectiveness of extraneous environmental stimuli in interfering with ongoing behavior such as altering crying for food by presenting a toy; (9) *Attention span and persistence*—length of time an activity is pursued and maintained despite obstacles, for example, continually getting up to walk after falling.

Thomas and his colleagues found that about 65 percent of the children could be categorized soon after birth and remained relatively stable throughout the study. Active children were more likely to be referred and treated for problem behavior than youngsters with moderate or low activity levels. Although tempermental organization emerged as a useful predictor of later maladapted functioning, favorable parental and environmental circumstances effectively prevented behavior disturbance (Thomas et al., 1968, p. 134). They recommended respect for the individuality (temperament) of the young child, consistent compromise in behaviors that were not disruptive, and consistent firmness in reshaping harmful behavior.

Activity and Passivity

Murphy (1973) compared the coping style of infants with the preschool patterns of the same children. Autonomy, shown by the capacity to protest disliked foods and to terminate feeding, correlated significantly with later capacity to fend off excessive stimulation from the environment. Her criteria for activity included degree of selectivity, vigor of choice, decisiveness, and insistence on relating to the environment shown by infants. These ways of coping actively were observed as early as 4 weeks and were correlated to early sitting alone and with flexible coping in the preschool, at which times aggressive and impulsive behavior was under control. Girls showed a greater range on the activity-passivity scale than boys because of the excessive passivity of some of them. Mothers of boy infants were more likely to accept insisting behavior from sons and to impose their own patterns on girl babies. Sex differences in activity-passivity levels were interpreted to be "culturally inculcated" to a considerable degree (p. 1271).

As in other areas of development personality seems to emerge early, to be genetically oriented, and to be responsive to environmental and rearing patterns. More attention on the part of researchers to the individuality of the newborn will help to illuminate some of the nature-nurture issues. Those who have persisted in the view that personality characteristics of early childhood are significant indicators of later behavior and personality would seem to be supported by recent research.

LOCOMOTOR AND COGNITIVE INTELLIGENCE SCALES

During the first year of life, psychologists rely primarily on locomotor indicators of normal development (Chapter 4). The Griffiths scales of mental development encompass the first two years and provide a comprehensive psychological evaluation that is continuous through the second year. In the United States the measure of choice for children 2 or 3 years old is the Terman-Merrill revision of the Stanford-Binet Intelligence Scales. Both of these provide examples of the intellectual abilities of toddlers.

Ruth Griffiths Developmental Scales

Explained in *The Abilities of Babies* (1954) the scales provide separate profiles for locomotor, personal-social, hearing and speech, hand and eye, and performance scales. She used categories which she believed were significant themes in long-term intellectual development. Her goal in providing norms was to enable care-givers to intervene early if a child appeared to be lagging in any important aspect of mental growth. The scales are useful to parents in anticipating the intellectual environment an infant or toddler can utilize and are useful to clinicians in providing the additional stimulation in the appropriate sequence for youngsters with developmental lags. Approximately 20 different normal babies were seen at each month-age period to age 2 years to provide the norms for these developmental scales. Below are sample items for each quarter of the second year.

LOCOMOTOR SEQUENCE

The scales for this part of the profile are based on the skills that result in an upright posture and learning to walk. The average baby in the first quarter of the second year learns to go *up* the stairs while holding on, in the second quarter can stoop to pick up a toy without overbalancing, in the third quarter cam jump a little with both feet off the floor, and in the fourth quarter has abandoned climbing stairs and walks both up and down (still holding hand or banister).

PERSONAL-SOCIAL SEQUENCE

Twenty items make up the second-year scale, which is intended as a sampling of the child's social adaptation. During the first quarter the typical child tries to help with dressing, can hold a cup and use a spoon, and shows shoes when asked. In the second quarter the toddler can turn a door knob, take off shoes (if unfastened) and socks, and enjoy a picture book with an adult.

By the third quarter of the second year the toddler identifies body parts of a doll when named by an adult, tries to explain or report, feeds himself, and controls bowel movements. By the twenty-fourth month the typical child can ask for things at the table, can open a door, and can name body parts on a doll. Age norms for different months indicate the number of items the child may be expected to name.

HEARING AND SPEECH SEQUENCE

During the first quarter of the second year the child tries to sing along with others, looks at pictures briefly, responds to own name, enjoys nursery rhymes, and names an object from a collection of toys; by the end of the period the child can use four or five clear words. By age 18 months the typical toddler looks at a book by turning the pages, chatters long monologues (not necessarily understandable), and uses seven to nine words consistently.

During the third quarter the child begins to join words to communicate, can point to or pick out four objects from the Griffiths toy box, and can name two pictures from the picture collection. By the end of the second year (24 months) the child uses at least twenty clear words during the interviews, including names of things asked for; identifies eight of twelve objects in the toy box; names four of the toys; and spontaneously uses sentences of four or more syllables. These scales are consistent with recent observations of speech acquisition (Chapter 9).

HAND AND EYE SEQUENCE

Griffiths separated the locomotion skills from the fine muscle manipulation, even though they were part of the same scale in the Gesell measures (1943). She saw rather different implications for future learning in gross versus fine muscle coordination. Her purpose in devising a new scale was to develop a diagnostic profile that would be useful at an early age, and this suggested a subtest approach.

During the first quarter of the second year the typical child shows hand preference, learns to roll a ball, can stack two boxes, and can hold two 1-inch cubes in each hand at the same time if presented in pairs. By the end of the eighteenth month, the child has learned to scribble with pencil on paper, combines objects in constructive play, and builds a tower of three blocks.

During the third quarter the child shows ability to throw a ball, to build a tower of four blocks, to pour water from one cup to another without spilling, and begins to scribble with straight strokes. By the end of the second year the child can "scribble round-and-round" when shown, can toss a ball into a basket, can build a train of three bricks, and can make a toy "walk" when shown.

PERFORMANCE SEQUENCE

The performance scales are the most formal of the five and require a set of brick boxes (designed originally by Froebel) and a set of form boards. At month 13 the child can put a circle inset into a form board with a circular hole. From this ability the child progresses through increasingly difficult tasks until able to replace three shapes in a three-hole board at 21 months old. Similarly the child progresses from being able to open two of three boxes in the first quarter to reassembling three boxes with lids in the fourth quarter. Other problems include unwrapping a tissue-wrapped box at 13 months and opening a barrel screw at 24 months.

Together these five scales are comprehensive. The first series involves standing and walking, the second social adjustment, the third stages in speech and language, and the fourth hand-eye coordination. The final tests required problem solving, with a premium on ingenuity and persistence.

Stanford-Binet Intelligence Scale

Terman and Merrill (1960) published a third revision of their scales, adapted to English from scales developed much earlier in French by Binet and Simon to help teachers adapt the learning program to the abilities of pupils. The scales are a sampling of different kinds of tasks at each age level. The present Form L-M is a composite of the best items from their earlier L and M forms. Although the scales span intellectual functioning from age 2 years to adulthood, only a few items are included here to indicate the intellectual development of the 2- and 3-year-old children. The tests are heavily weighted with items that require verbal ability and are not considered a good intellectual indicator for children whose home language is other than standard English or whose educational opportunities have been meager.

The scales for young children are divided into half-year periods, from which the following examples have been drawn. At age 2 years the child can replace three forms in a board; at age 2½ the child can replace them after the board is rotated. The 2-year-old can also locate a toy cat when put under one of three boxes, can identify four of seven body parts on a cardboard doll, can build a tower of four or more 1-inch cubes, can name three of eighteen vocabulary pictures, can identify five of six miniature objects on a card, and uses two-word combinations in spontaneous speech.

The child scores in the second half of age 2, the third year, if able to identify three of six small objects by use: "the thing we cut with," etc. Other tests are identifying six of seven body parts, naming eight of eighteen vocabulary pictures, repeating two digits ("say 4, 7,"), and obeying two of three simple commands given one at a time ("put the button in the box)."

In the first half of the fourth year, age 3 years, the child can string four beads from a box, name ten of the vocabulary pictures, build a bridge using three cubes (after being shown), name an animal (of four) and then find it (from memory) in a picture card of animals, draw a circle (from a picture model), and draw a vertical line (after being shown). During the last half of year 3, the typical child can do half the items (or half of many children tested on any item can do it successfully); put two cards together to make a "ball"; discriminate four different animal pictures within a group of animals; sort twenty black and white buttons; answer a question such as "What must you do when you are thirsty?"; and identify the "longer" of two sticks. In the view of many persons these kinds of interaction games, involving language, make the scales an indicator of past learning (Chapter 8). The interaction specified in the Binet scales is of the kind that youngsters typically enjoy.

Since they are predictive of school success later on they represent the kind of intellectual stimulation the care-giver may want to provide. The IQ scores obtained from preschool children are not highly predictive of IQ scores in school-age children, but the general categories of subnormal, average, and above normal tend to be stable.

Stability of Intellectual Functioning

The locomotor skills of infancy have not correlated highly with IQ scores taken at school age. One reason may be that they differ radically from the problem-solving tasks used by Griffiths in the performance scale or by Binet in his verbally weighted scales. Logic suggests that IQ scores are likely to show greater stability from infancy to childhood than abilities such as verbal understanding or eye-hand coordination.

The most consistent finding of stability between infant accomplishments and later cognitive ability is the relative continuity for females and the lack of continuity for males. Rheingold, Gewirtz, and Ross (1959) reported a relationship between mother's face-to-face vocalizing and the daughter's level of babbling. Moss (1967) reported that mothers are more likely to imitate vocalization of their infant daughters than their sons. Kagan (1969) reported a continuity in females between 4-month vocalization and fixation and intelligence levels at 24 months. Bayley and Schaefer (1964) reported a relationship between early babbling and later vocabulary levels and greater stability in IQ scores for girls (Cameron, Livson, & Bayley, 1967). These studies tend to support explanations based both on innate ability and on environmental factors.

Some recent work with African infants has failed to support the precocity found nearly two decades ago (Warren, 1972). As the environment of primitive cultures changes, the nature of the abilities of infants is likely to change also. Research in the future should examine and analyze the interaction of genetic traits and the childrearing environment. It is generally agreed by present researchers that the psychological environment of the first two years can speed up or slow down the attainment of fundamental cognitive skills (Bower, 1974).

Implications for Care-Givers

Toddlers of both sexes are stimulated by opportunities to explore and to manipulate an extended environment. Adults encourage exploration by recognizing each advance the toddler makes. When the adult provides a verbal context for the child's experience, cognitive abilities are enhanced.

Delay in a youngster's motor development once meant that care-givers waited for maturation and the child's spontaneous efforts at locomotion. Delayed children need handling, encouragement, and attractions within the environment to motivate them. The toy just out of reach on the blanket, the toy box at the top of the stairs, the sandbox in the backyard are all temptations to independent movement that may need to be built into the early environment of inactive or retarded children.

The child's right to be a person allows him or her to be active, reflexive, talkative, or quiet within the limits of healthy social interaction and cognitive development. A child needs to build happy personal relationships. Teaching requires the skill to know the fine line between repressing the child's individuality and helping the child develop into a motivated and self-directing person.

Parents and teachers may assume that a stimulating environment, rich in the sounds, sights, smells, textures, tastes, and motions of a busy life, is the best environment for learning. Conversation with a toddler provides symbolic labels and meanings for thought and language. The child provides the cues for the level of meaning and the extent of the interest that is present. Intellectual stimulation is not unlike physical contact; it should be there, available, and freely given.

SUMMARY

The toddler is the child who has learned to walk, but not yet perfectly. Locomotion extends the child's choice of environment to give opportunity to explore space. Bipedal locomotion frees the hands to manipulate the objects made accessible

Curiosity of childhood: listening to a shell. (Erika/Peter Arnold)

through mobility. Early descriptions of a developmental sequence that leads to erect locomotion by Shirley, Gesell, and McGraw have not been replaced by recent experimental research. The stages from infantile creeping to stiff-legged, flat-footed walking are similar for the hundreds of infants and toddlers they observed. Although development is continuous, there is a discrete stage when the preferred locomotion shifts from crawling to walking. There also are regressions when some new pattern of motor development seems to require the child's focus of intent. The norms represent the creeping-walking behavior of the mythical normal child. Ranges of typical development are needed for evaluating the growth of an individual child.

Exploratory behavior, made possible by locomotion, requires the child's emotional independence from the care-giver. Attachments are formed in infancy, usually first to the mother, later to second or third adults and siblings. Attachment-exploration patterns are assumed to be healthy when a toddler can (1) leave the mother to play out of sight, (2) return on occasion to seek physical contact and receive comforting, and (3) see the mother leave without showing undue stress.

Control of bowel sphincters is attained by most toddlers at 18 months and control of bladder voiding by 24 months. Infants under 1 year old can be conditioned to the pot, but authorities differ on whether early training is conducive to self-control of elimination in the second year. Considering the individual differences in bowel and bladder control, the parent's best cue to toilet training is success: keep doing the things that work. Behavior modification strategies, involving positive reinforcement, are used in some nursery schools. Control during part of the day can be extended as rapidly as the child can manage and the family schedule can allow.

Individual personality patterns have been outlined in the temperament studies by Thomas and the continuity studies by Kagan and other investigators. Characteristics which persist in some children, at least through early childhood, are activity-passivity levels, reflexive-impulsive tendencies, attentiveness, verbalization, and quality of mood.

Intelligence scales reflect the learning a child has attained as well as the ability to learn. The stability of IQ scores increases with the age of the child when tested and also with the overlap in the items which sample intellectual development. Early locomotion scales are not predictive of school success; verbal understanding and problem-solving abilities of toddler-age children are relatively stable. The items passed by normal children at given ages suggest the kinds of learning activities that children enjoy at home or at school.

6
Preschool Childhood: Age of Confidence

6 Preschool Childhood: Age of Confidence

Children who have outgrown toddlerhood have achieved a new high in spatial independence. Such children have the physical ability to go and to come. Typically their emotional independence has kept pace, so that they also have the ability to make friends and to identify themselves to strangers. Those youngsters are fortunate whose early contacts have been both numerous and pleasurable.

From the children's point of view the accomplishments are momentous. They can control and oversee their own toileting. They can express their wants and verbally reject what is imposed upon them. They can open doors or close others out if they want to be alone. They manipulate their own eating and can usually help themselves to a snack. These skills have been won with effort. These children appropriately take on an "I can" attitude.

Increasing numbers of children go to some form of preschool prior to entering the first grade. The highest percentage of the early childhood group who attend nursery schools come from relatively poor or relatively well-to-do families (Chapter 12). Kindergartens have become available as part of the public school system in most parts of the country. Although attendance is voluntary in most kindergartens, over 90 percent of the children who are eligible usually attend. This means that most American children at some time during the ages of about 3 years old to 5 or 6 years leave the family and enter a world of peers.

Experiencing this new world for the first time, whether preschool or kindergarten, has some elements of change that are common to early childhood. The typical child has already evolved an obvious place for himself in the family, an obvious identity, and a collection of standards for behavior at home which have been learned gradually. An older sibling may have certain responsibilities toward him, such as looking after him in backyard play groups, telling him when it's time to go home, or seeing that a jacket is not left behind. Similarly the younger sibling is not to be hit "because she is smaller," she receives the bottle because she is the baby, and she has priority when both need something at the same time. These unwritten standards for getting and giving are not always resolved without conflict, but most families develop patterns of expectation which generalize to all but a few daily events.

Leaving the world of the home, where one's place in the hierarchy is known, and entering the unknown world of peers, overseen by strange adults with different rules for organizing the environment, is a tremendous event which can be traumatic. The phylogenic heritage of humans requires that the child size himself up in relation to others in the peer group. Even at this age, sophisticated pecking orders are derived in the minds of the children for each of the many play-school situations. To confirm a pecking order one need only to observe the free activity period in a kindergarten or preschool. There is remarkable consistency in who calls the action in block construction, who assigns the roles in the playhouse, who asks permission to play, and who tells whether the outsider may join the group.

The confidence that mobility brings to a child. (Bruce Roberts from Rapho/Photo Researchers Inc.)

What is also happening, as anyone who has worked in sociometrics can verify, is that each child knows whom he'd *like* to play with, paint with, and sit with.

Schools have been accused of turning "I can" youngsters into children with depressed self-images who later fail in primary schools. Knowing the child's capabilities at this age should go a long way toward helping him continue a sequence of accomplishments and to recognize successes when they occur. One of the things the preschooler wants and needs most is "friends."

Socialization is only one aspect of growing up that is critical in this age period. The major cognitive accomplishment of this stage is the ability to use mental representations (images and symbols for real things) to think. The major affective accomplishment, according to psychoanalysts, is to resolve the sex-oriented conflicts that emerge during this period. Socialization appears to me to be the compelling motivation of the contemporary child, at least in Western cultures; this section will deal with research on this topic. Subsequent sections cover social-class differences in childrearing, perceptual and motor development of the preschool child, the development of representational thought, and the effects of certain forces in the contemporary environment on cognitive development.

SOCIALIZATION IN A PEER SOCIETY

The interaction of culture, biology, and ego-identity in the development of the young child has been outlined by Erikson (1963). The reader who is unfamiliar with his eight stages in development may wish to refer to Chapter 11 at this point. The present discussion concerns the conflict which normal children must resolve at this age in order to relate to other children in ways that are conducive to social relationships.

By about 3 years old, according to Erikson, the emotionally healthy child has resolved the vacillation between *autonomy* and *doubt or shame* by having achieved muscular and anal control. The developmental hurdle which follows at ages 3 to 5 years old involves a different polarity, one associated with locomotor-genital priorities in biological development. At this stage the conflict of initiative versus guilt feelings on the part of the child is resolved, and he or she achieves the emotional independence children need as they move toward peer relationships. In Freudian psychology this means the resolution of the Oedipal complex; the child must come to identify with the parent of the same sex while retaining the love of both parents.

Whereas the infant's attachment has been to the mother, the child now needs to establish an affectional triangle that includes the father. In most families the Oedipal transition is temporary and no more eventful than an unusual interest in sex, attentive and "cute" behavior toward the parent of opposite sex, frequent seeking of affection with body contact along with the hugs, and often some masturbation. Anthony (1970) recommends that the child should not be pushed away at this stage but given tender handling, such as assistance in bathing, and general thoughtfulness.

This process of identity is considered more difficult for boys because they must accept the Oedipal triangle while establishing identity with the father or with men generally. The girl must identify with the mother while accepting her priority in familial living. Although many scholars do not accept the psychoanalytic explanation of personality development, Freud's emphasis on the importance of the early emotional experience in later social behavior is widely accepted (Thompson & Grusec, 1970).

It is logical that a shift must occur from the infant's attachment-dependence relationship with the mother to a state of personal autonomy and initiative if healthy peer relationships are to develop. The young child who has resolved the conflicts of sex identity and sex acceptance is ready to reach out for new relationships and to take the ego risks that peer interaction requires. Perceptive adults can observe the play of preschool children and learn how different individuals see themselves and how they would like life to be.

Observations of the social development of twins offer some insight in the dominant-submissive relationships of age peers compared with siblings of different ages. The consistent dominance of one twin over the other has been widely noted. In a small fishing village in Norway, twin boys 5 months old sit side by side in a carriage. One sits erect and smiles at anybody on the wharf who will pay attention to him; the other leans on his pillow and watches. Twin sons, age 4 years, accompany their father to the speech clinic at the Children's Hospital in Helsinki. One is seen holding the father's trouser leg; the other explores each gate along the sidewalk, finds a latch he can open, and enters. Twin boys, age 7 years, enter a Seattle classroom together on the opening day of school. Although their jargon is almost identical (Pendergast, 1954), Donald has come in to introduce David to the teacher before going to his own room. Even though identical twins share a genetic inheritance and are the same chronological and mental age, patterns of who takes the initiative and who relies on the other are established early. There is reinforcement value for the nondominant twin, who takes fewer risks but is looked after, shares the cookies, and receives the attention of the other twin. In a sibling relationship, dominance is usually the result of an ordering by age and does not impose superior or inferior status on a child when he or she enters a group of age-peers.

Most 3-year-olds come to the nursery school with a repertoire of social skills, not the least of which is for language interaction with other people. By this time children have learned different approach behaviors for family members, friends, and strangers. Researchers have been curious about how social skills that have been observed by a child, but not practiced, can suddenly be utilized by a child in the appropriate social setting at a much later time.

Social Learning by Modeling

A theory of social learning concerned with how children learn by example has been proposed and tested by Bandura (1971). His analysis of child behavior in social interaction incorporates both the concept of imitation (reproduction of discrete responses) and identification, which Bandura considers too diffuse in meaning to be useful in scientific inquiry. He proposes instead the term *modeling*, which means observational learning of social behaviors. Bandura documented three effects of modeling in children.

The first major effect of observational learning was demonstrated experimentally when models performed a behavior which children had not yet learned, but later produced in essentially identical form. In daily life the phenomenon is common in preschool children. Erika, age 4 years, insisted on having a small dish to break an egg into because "Grandma does it like that" when she bakes a cake.

A second function of modeling in learning social skills is to strengthen inhibitions that have been learned previously. Seeing an older child punished for a behavior has an inhibitory effect on the observer. A third function of learning by observing is the disinhibitory effect of seeing models engage in threatening or prohibited activities without adverse consequences. People who have unreasonable fears (phobias) have been successfully treated by observing bold performers (Bandura, 1971). Seeing another child run into the breakers weakens the inhibition Mark has shown previously, and he ventures into the water.

Bandura considers stimulus-response theory to be less than adequate in explaining the behavior changes effected by modeling because reinforcement to shape the desired behavior, as explained by Skinner, did not occur. Social learning theorists have demonstrated the effectiveness of a television model, who was not present, in reinforcing a child's imitative behavior. Bandura points out that the consequences to a child would be disastrous if all the lessons of socialization had to be learned by trying each behavior and having it selectively shaped by reinforcement or nonreinforcement of parents. Some trial-and-error behaviors would endanger the life of the child. Learning by imitation is rapid, since even a complex behavior can be learned in one observation, and it is efficient, since the patterns learned are those which a family values.

Bandura (1971) identified four processes in observational learning which can help the care-giver provide appropriate models. The *first* requirement for modeling to occur was the *attentional process*. To match a behavior, the child observer must attend to, recognize, and differentiate the distinctive features of the model's responses. The child must have the sensory capabilities, the motivation, the arousal level, and the perceptual set for taking in the modeled event. This means that previous associations must be adequate and appropriate to elicit attending to the model. Some factors to be considered if social modeling is to be successful are the child's intellectual capabilities and interests, the power of the model, and the novelty of the behavior performed.

The *second* of the processes in observational learning is *retention of modeled events*. Bandura suggests than when a child observes a behavior without performing it for some time, the original observational input must be retained in some symbolic form. Sometimes weeks or even years intervene before a child attains an age and social status when an activity is appropriate.

Piaget, a cognitive development theorist, and not a social-learning theorist, noted the beginning of imitative behavior in infants. He reported that when an adult imitated an infant's action, the child would repeat the action and a modeling pattern would be established. He considered a time-lapse in the imitation action as evidence that the infant had built mental structures that represented the event.

Bandura believes that mental storage of an observed behavior sequence is accomplished by two representational systems which are associated, one verbal and the other auditory. A coded verbal representation makes possible the retrieval of visual images when the name of a place, person, or action is mentioned. A coded sequence of images, such as the way to the park, is made more durable for later use by symbolic representations, such as left, right, left-left-right. Bandura, Grusec, and Menlove (1966) showed that children who merely watched a model attentively on television were able to produce fewer of the behaviors afterward than when also helped to code the event verbally. They were able to produce significantly fewer imitations when instructed to count (which distracted them) while watching the model. Verbal coding that is relevant to the behavior modeled is more effective in social learning than nonrelevant symbolism. Young children's modeling of social events was enhanced by instruction in verbal coding. However, older children, who spontaneously produced their own verbal mediators, were not helped by similar instruction (Coates & Hartup, 1969).

Social-learning theory assumes that the observers are able to store and later model a behavior pattern by abstracting common features from a variety of modeled responses. This is conceptualized as an innately human process of constructing higher-order codes that can be generalized, transformed, and organized into easily remembered schemes (Bandura, 1971, p. 21). Modeled behavior that cannot be practiced at the time may be rehearsed covertly. This internal rehearsal probably increases the retention of acquired matching behavior.

The *third* process in the modeling sequence is *motoric reproduction.* By definition, social modeling involves the use of symbolic representations of modeled behavior patterns to guide the overt performance called modeling. In social-learning theory "it is assumed that behavior is learned and organized chiefly through central integrative mechanisms prior to motor execution" (p. 39). The child must have the ability to execute a movement before motoric reproduction is possible. For example, an older sibling may be observed while hopping the squares in a playground, and also while skipping. The 3-year-old can model the motoric patterns of the hopscotch at once, but lacks the sensorimotor integration for skipping. Carla, age 4, practiced skipping in her room. She knew (from her model) when she was doing it correctly and came skipping through the living room for her family to appreciate.

The *fourth* process by which modeling functions in social learning is *reinforcement* of the overt matching behavior in order that it will continue. Positive incentives for model matching help the adult to regulate modeling and to influence the observer's own selection of future models. To summarize, social modeling is seen as an effective learning process which is essentially human and involves a heavy component of cognitive functioning. The model is the source of information, while the observer is seen as the abstracter and organizer of the information. Reinforcement is seen as the mechanism by which a parent or teacher can assure that matching behavior will be used selectively and that valued modeling patterns will be continued.

Bandura extends the traditional concept of reinforcement (by external reinforcers) to *vicarious reinforcement* and *self-reinforcement.* An example of vicarious reinforcement is the child's observing social events and the subsequent reward or punishment that accrues to another person. The child then is able to anticipate a similar consequence for himself. This child can initiate certain social behaviors with the expectation of being rewarded by approval, having his allowance increased, or being allowed to stay up later on the weekends. When inconsistencies occur in the behavior-consequence patterns of parents toward siblings, or of teachers toward preschoolers, the child does not know what consequence to expect and the learning potential in vicarious reinforcement is disrupted.

Modeling theory as explained by Bandura is less incisive in defining or analyzing self-reinforcement. The individual's motivation can be decisive in determining when a consequence is reinforcing. The teacher's "Don't do that!" may be punishing and have a deterring effect for Beverly, who identifies with her and wants to be approved by her. By contrast, Bud may be positively reinforced to repeat the behavior because he has a different identification model and is motivated to make an impact on the peer group, even if negative.

When children are exposed to multiple models, as in the life situation of most preschool children, their opportunity for self-selection of a model to imitate is expanded. Bandura, Ross, and Ross (1963) have shown that a diversity and dissimilarity in modeled patterns fosters new divergent patterns of behavior. The implication would seem to be that creative and self-directed behavior in children could be fostered by the availability of diverse models engaged in the kinds of activities that are high in the interest categories of a particular child. When the cognitive processes that account for social modeling are analyzed, the behaviorist theory of Bandura and the humanist views of cognitive psychologists are very similar.

Importance of Self-Concept

Self-concept is the private picture each person carries around of who he or she is, what she or he thinks she or he can do, and how best to go about it. Self-concept is an internal composite of the awareness about oneself, in contrast to personality, which is a composite of what others see. *Self-esteem* has a value attached to the private picture each person carries; self is seen as higher or lower on a scale with someone else or a group. Self-concept is generalized to new situations, so that it becomes a set of assumptions for determining how the preschool child will approach the new experience of school. However, each major change in the environment of a child offers the care-giver a chance to intervene in affective development. When self-esteem is low or negative, a skillful teacher can help to alter the youngster's conceptualization of self as one who can cope in this new setting.

Self-awareness is the recognition of a distinction between one's own body and the surrounding environment (Hamachek, 1971). The infant learns very gradually the separateness of his own mouth from the nipple he sucks and of his own body from the blanket that enfolds him. He discovers that the hand that he sees is under his control and distinct from the object it grasps. The coos come from himself, but the imitations and words come from his handler. The sensations he experiences are separate from the objects that produce them, which is part of the development of object constancy (Chapter 4). This knowing where one's own body ends and the environment begins is necessary before the young child can conceptualize his own identity and power.

The toddler discovers he can walk around big things and move them. She can follow the person she wants to be with (Chapter 5). It is conceivable that identity begins with the following behavior of toddlers and has elements of imprinting (like Lorenz's ducklings). When the child leaves the family to go to preschool or to kindergarten, the personal powers that had become self-evident are put to new tests in a world of peers. That part of self-concept which involves relationships with adults includes strange adults having authority over one's person.

The threat to the ego can be tremendous when a 4-year-old suddenly becomes one of twenty children in the competition for the teacher's care and attention. The skills of hopping, climbing, and throwing (practiced and admired at home) are taken for granted in the crowd. What is worse, some of the kids can climb higher, jump further, and command the teacher's smile. The child is at an advantage who has learned to express needs with words rather than crying, to defer wants for a reasonable time while his turn comes round, and to tolerate minor changes in routine.

Children 3 to 5 years old are still egocentric in their social relationships to varying degrees, but they do respond to principles of learning that are common to all children. They tend to repeat more and more frequently those behaviors which result in approval, attention, or show of affection. They tend to repeat less frequently those behaviors which result in indifference or rejection of peers or care-givers. This interaction is more complex than S-R models indicate. In human identity many important learning events are internal and are therefore beyond simple response to reinforcement. The child's patterns of interaction arouse internal responses which lead to perceptions of self that gradually become stable. When the child starts school, the self-concept is extended to incorporate a picture of one's place in the group, what one can do to influence the play or constructions, and what one is sufficiently good at to make things happen one's way. To a large extent group reinforcement and group censure determine the child's role and are outside the control of the teacher. But the child organizes experiences cognitively by the time he or she is preschool age, and may be influenced more by what Bandura (1971) calls self-reinforcement than by the schedules of teachers.

Care-givers can contribute to a positive conceptualization of self in school by providing a variety of activities that require the use of some strengths each child sees in himself and by gearing the tasks to the child's ability to succeed, remembering that tasks that are too easy fail to elicit pride in accomplishing them or build motivation for school activities. The child who finds it difficult to enter groups of peers can be helped by teaming her with a socially mature, accepting classmate, or by modeling the approaches that will result in inclusion into play groups. A child's preference to play alone should be respected, just as other traits of individuality are accepted and valued. The teacher's acceptance nearly always assures acceptance by other children at this age, and provides the child an opportunity to formulate a self-concept of one who can make out in the interaction with peers.

Self-concept and ego strength, when measured at the beginning of kindergarten, have been found to be predictive of reading achievement in the third grade

(Wattenberg & Clifford, 1964). Without attempting to imply that a poor conception of self caused lower achievement, the researchers did find a relationship which exceeded the correlation of intelligence measures and reading achievement. The teacher's concern is to help the child see herself as one who can learn to read by providing challenges the child perceives as "reading" and recognizing the successes that result from appropriate curriculum choices. "Reading" as conceived by the kindergarten child can be recognizing her name on the activity chart, repeating a caption the teacher prints on her picture, or chorusing bits of a story repetition on cue from the teacher. The school may have great difficulty in helping a child conceive of himself as one who can learn to read if he identifies with a father who does not value reading. Similarly, a girl may come to kindergarten having already identified with a mother whose self-concept includes being not good at numbers and who models this. Traditional behaviorist researchers have tended to avoid the complex area of self-concept, but many scholars of human development have explored important elements through the study of identity.

Parents as Identity Objects

Identification is a process by which a child, through imitation or modeling, acquires the traits, characteristics, or values of another person. The child who comes to the preschool typically has already identified with the parent of the same sex. Older children often shift their identity to a teacher, a peer leader, or a national hero. These persons may be secondary or temporary identity figures in the life of the child, but they may be so significant as to occur along with the active rejection of a parent who was once the object of imitative learning. In such shifts, the youngster may consciously try to be unlike the parent in dress, mannerisms, values, and other features of lifestyle.

Some researchers have assumed that identification with a parent can be measured by the extent to which the child imitates the behavior, attitudes, and emotional reactions of the available (parent) model. Hetherington and Frankie (1967) reported the tendency of preschool and kindergarten children to imitate parents of both sexes according to their power, warmth, and aggression within the family organization. After being grouped as high-conflict versus low-conflict families, the children participated with either parent in a play situation. Later their postural, motor, and verbal behaviors were recorded and matched against the coached behavior of the parent. The imitation of mother or father models was analyzed for personal warmth and marriage dominance. They found that boys and girls imitated both parents, but that modeling of the like-sex parent was somewhat more frequent. More important, they discovered that under high conflict, when both parents were low in warmth, children of both sexes imitated the dominant parent regardless of sex. If the nondominant parent was characterized by warmth, or if family conflict was reduced, the aggressive parent was modeled less. However, a boy's tendency to imitate a dominant father overrode other variations in the design of this study. The tendency for girls to imitate warm mothers also prevailed. Exceptions to these tendencies occurred when children were under high stress and neither parent showed warmth toward the children.

A child plays at being "Mother" by modeling.

Imitation and Sex Typing

Many scholars have been interested in how imitation affects the development of masculinity and femininity in young children. Mussen and Distler (1960) reported that parental dominance influences the masculinity, or sex typing, of boys when studied at kindergarten age. Hetherington (1965) found that father dominance had little effect on the sex typing of daughters. In nonsexual behaviors, however, their similarity was increased while leaving unaffected the mother-daughter similarities. These and other studies have tended to support earlier research that indicated children of both sexes are helped in sex-role typing by warmth in the parent of the same sex (Sears, 1953).

Kindergarten girls responded differently when modeling incidental behavior compared with problem-solving behavior when the models were nurturant or nonnurturant mothers. Mussen and Parker (1965) found that incidental imitation, such as color choice, was significantly higher in a group of kindergarten girls whose mothers were classified as nurturant compared with the daughters of nonnurturant mothers. By contrast a cognitive task that required solving a series of maze tests was not similarly influenced by nurturant mothers. In the school setting, goal-related responses appeared to be independent of maternal nurturance patterns. Apparently these subjects, all middle-class girls, were willing to remain on their own in a school-related task. They were able to recognize problem-solving requirements and to model their behavior selectively.

OLDER CHILDREN AS MODELS

Garrett (1973) studied the sex-role interaction of first-grade children by pairing boys with girls in construction play with commercial toys. She provided models of junior high school age who were coached and videotaped in typical masculine-feminine roles of aggressive and compliant interaction or in a reverse of roles. Typical male behavior called for directing and initiating the construction while the other member of the pair followed his or her lead. Surprisingly, the opposite results were obtained from those expected according to research in imitation. When the behavior of the younger children before and after watching the older models was analyzed, Garrett found that first-graders tended to match their behavior to the opposite-sex model. Girls who viewed male-dominated interaction engaged in more masculine behavior afterward than girls who watched female-dominated activity, or boys who also viewed male-dominated action. Boys who viewed the female-dominated videotape later engaged in more masculine behaviors than girls who viewed the same tape, or boys who viewed the male-dominated interaction.

Garrett interpreted these unusual results in terms of *identification* theory. According to *imitation* theory, or social modeling, the opposite effects should have occurred. Identification theory would suggest that both boy and girl subjects would have identified with like-sex models, but would have experienced vicarious dissatisfaction with what they saw, behaving afterward in ways that negated the model. To anyone familiar with the social competencies of first-grade children, the interpretation might be that the aggressive behavior of the models offended the sense of fairness of the children, who later behaved in ways that suggested rejection of a model the child was expected to imitate.

Wolters (1976) used four models, peers of both sexes and older children of both sexes, to study their influence on the sharing behavior of 4- and 5-year-old children. Using videotaped sequences of "many things to do with clay" and the appearance of a newcomer with whom the clay "must be shared," four groups, according to the model viewed, were compared. The number of clay-molding techniques that were recalled afterward by the viewers and the grams of clay they shared were the measures of imitative behavior in this study. Wolters found that sex of model was not a significant factor. The older models, regardless of sex, were imitated significantly more than peer-age models. Apparently their play with clay and equal sharing were not seen by the children as sex-related behavior but as "growing up" behavior. Both these studies demonstrated selective modeling being practiced by children by the time they enter school or earlier. The values being practiced, and the level of moral development attained by the subjects, has not been taken into account in most research of social modeling. (Chapter 11 discusses the levels of moral development in childhood and beyond.)

Self-Identity of the Minority Group Child

Children are fortunate who can attend multiethnic preschools at an age when healthy attitudes toward differences are learned easily. The shock of moving from the culture of the home to the culture of the school is compounded for children from minority ethnic groups. They experience less overlap in adult expectations than the mainstream child does and therefore have fewer alternatives at their command when interacting with other people. Bruce, age 4, saw a native American child for the first time at the nursery school. The teacher discovered him unbuttoning the shirt of the newcomer, and said, "Bruce, *what* are you doing?" Bruce responded, "I just want to see if he's the same all the way down." History cites that Captain Gray permitted his chest to be bared for the curious native Americans he encountered on the shores of Puget Sound. Preschool teachers cannot prevent the curiosity of children from emerging, but they can help by themselves being accepting and appreciative of ethnic differences.

In this context, self-identity means the child's acceptance of his relationship with groups of which he is a member: sex group, family, age peers. Appropriate role identification, based on love, respect, and intimacy, provides the child with a model for learning appropriate behavior. More important, perhaps, the child finds self-acceptance in such identification when others value and admire the identity group.

Preschool children observe their differences and reassess their family identity when they move outside the minority group. Head Start programs that taught that black is beautiful were attempting to support a strong self-concept and enhance identity. Indian children who participate in tribal dances and traditional ceremonies experience a positive identification with the elders of their tribe. Rural children, play-center children, poor children, and mill children are examples of minority groups whose identity is tested in the mainstream of society.

SOCIOECONOMIC DIFFERENCES IN CHILDREARING

Most children spend the first four years at home, usually with their mothers. Newson and Newson (1968) studied the socialization process by interviewing the mothers of 700 children turning 4 years old in Nottingham, England, the age at which they are eligible for infant school. The investigators believed that the mothers' attitudes and values about childrearing were as important as their specific practices of feeding, toileting, and training. The Newsons designed a social classification, based on the geographical location and type of housing, which also reflected the occupational and educational levels of the parents.

Comparative analyses were made for five socioeconomic groups: I-II, professional and managerial; IIIwc, white-collar workers; IIIman, skilled manual workers; IV, semiskilled workers; and V, unskilled laborers and those persistently unemployed. By combining groups I and II and subdividing the working class (III), groups of comparable size were attained.

Although the fascinating aspect of this study is the detailed reporting of the mothers' own perceptions and expectations of their 4-year-olds, the statistical results show some significant class differences in childrearing. Regarding *independence*, upper-class children were less likely to shop alone, but less likely to dislike playing alone than lower-class children. Class I-II and IIIwc mothers were more likely to arbitrate children's quarrels, while mothers from classes IIIman, IV and V let children settle their own differences and overwhelmingly encouraged "hitting back."

Regarding *mealtime rules*, there was greater similarity than differences among socioeconomic groups. Class V mothers tended to insist that children clean their plates, while class I-II mothers were more concerned with order and manners at the table. *Bedtime rules* were more likely to be established and enforced in upper-class homes where bedtime was earlier for the children than in lower-class homes. The use of bedtime stories was highest in class I-II and dropped off, usually by a significant amount, in each of subsequent groups. Prayers at bedtime were significantly more frequent in the upper classes but varied inconsistently in the other four groups.

Surprisingly, most habits of *self-comforting*, such as the use of a "cuddly" or bottle, did not differ significantly across class lines. Only in permissiveness toward thumb-sucking was the professional class significantly higher than the other groups.

Toilet habits by day were not significantly different among class groups, but bed-wetting was significantly more frequent in lower-class families. Mothers of classes IIIman, IV, and V were more likely to punish their preschool children for genital play than upper-class mothers. Also, they were least likely to allow children to see parents or others unclothed. Consistent high to low SES relationships were found between knowing "where babies come from" and parental willingness to explain sexuality. Negative relationships, along class lines, were reported for the use of false explanations about conception and birth; the higher the socioeconomic rating the greater the use of true explanations about the origin of babies.

Patterns of child *discipline* were not significantly different in the use or disapproval of slapping. Sixty-four to eight-three percent of the mothers reported "smacking" the child when she or he first hit the parent. Mothers of groups IV and V were much more likely to use threats of physical punishment, sending away, or withdrawing love than high SES mothers. Children of groups IV and V were more likely to have tantrums; I, II, and IIIwc children were more likely to confess wrongdoing. Low SES mothers were more likely to rate their husbands as stricter than themselves, but these were likely to be fathers whose childrearing participation was low. Although childrearing practices may in the United States differ from practices in England, studies as comprehensive as the Newson and Newson material are not available elsewhere. Their longitudinal study is significant because they included an entire 4-year-old population and were able to make a valid socioeconomic classification.

Sex Differences in Parental Relationships

That parents interact differently toward their sons than toward their daughters has been established in many studies. The sex of the parent and the sex of the child are both significant factors in how the parent reacts to aggression and to overtures for affection in their children. Rothbart and Maccoby (1966) used the taped voice of a 4-year-old child to study the differential response of mothers and fathers toward various comments and demands. Some parents were told the voice was that of a boy while others were told the voice was that of a girl. Parents were also interviewed about their responses to their own children. The study showed that mothers were more likely to allow aggression toward themselves and more accepting of comfort seeking from sons than from their daughters. By contrast, fathers were more accepting of daughters' comfort seeking and allowed more aggression to be directed toward themselves from daughters than from sons. This finding challenges social learning theory which suggests that sex-typed behavior results from imitation of and reinforcement from the parent of like sex.

It could be speculated that the sex-specific ways that parents behave help the child resolve affectional conflicts. Quite possibly the investigators would have obtained different results if the children had been 2 or 6 years old rather than 4. Children, when interviewed, find more consistency than difference among their two parents (Kagan & Lemkin, 1960). Girls tend to see their fathers as both more punitive and more affectionate than mothers, while boys see their fathers merely as more punitive. Both sexes tend to find mothers "easier to get along with" and "friendlier" (Hawkes, Burchinal, & Gardener, 1957).

Interviews with fathers show they expect more of their sons and include them in masculine activities, and participate more in their rearing than in the rearing of their daughters (Aberle & Naegele, 1952). They also report a feeling of responsibility for the masculinity training of their sons. Mothers report that they treat the sexes alike in permissiveness of aggression toward siblings, but that they permit more aggressiveness from sons when it is directed toward persons outside the family (Sears, Maccoby, & Levin, 1957). Most of these studies involve middle-class parents, who have both the time and willingness to be interviewed. They do not necessarily represent the views of upper-class and lower-class parents.

Bronfenbrenner (1972) republished an analysis of research which suggested marked social-class differences in the rearing of boys and girls in the United States. He found a tendency among contemporary middle-class parents to adopt the patterns of childrearing used in upper SES families. They show an increasing tendency to be more permissive, to express affection more freely, and to use psychological (rather than physical) techniques of discipline. Bronfenbrenner sees this pattern as destructive of certain personal qualities in boys, but generally advantageous to girls. In recent analyses of adolescents, girls in the higher socioeconomic levels excel boys in responsibility and social acceptance. By contrast, boys in the lower-middle-class levels surpass girls in leadership, level of aspiration, and competitiveness. Bronfenbrenner reported that overprotection and stern discipline (typical of their rearing by low SES parents) impeded the psychological development of girls. A combination of affection and firm discipline facilitated the constructive development of boys, who were especially vulnerable to insufficient parental discipline and support. He interprets these findings as indicative of "oversocialization" in some families. Psychological controls, if overused, can result in an anxious, timid child, who is oversensitive to rejection. According to Bronfenbrenner's analysis, achievement demands and consistent discipline from parents resulted in greater independence and self-confidence on the part of both sexes. Within this climate of high expectations, a love-oriented childrearing pattern develops responsibility and leadership. Most boys in this study suffered from too little taming and most girls from too much, but the central message from the analysis was that boys are damaged if reared according to the same patterns of permissiveness that allow girls to thrive.

Critical Periods of Dependence

Some scholars have extended the concept of critical periods, well established in physical achievements and neurological growth, to personality development. Attention has turned toward dependency in early childhood because of the vacillation of individual children from a seeming need for autonomy to dependency behaviors such as clinging, whining, and attachment. The issue is important for a society whenever the services of women outside the home are needed and for women when contact outside the home is necessary for personal fulfillment. Knowing critical periods is important to parents who want to encourage independence and initiative in their children without denying them the support needed to build confidence and security. When to give in to a child's excessive demands for emotional support and when to leave the child with a sitter or to insist that the child go to preschool are decisions all care-givers must make.

Preschool children who run errands or go shopping by themselves are more independent in other ways also. Newson and Newson (1968) reported a highly significant relationship between what mothers said they expected 4-year-olds to be able to do and their children's ability to do routine things for themselves, and to amuse themselves when the mother was busy. On the other hand, mothers who liked their 4-year-olds to be dependent, and who liked to wait on them, were likely to have children who in fact were less able to do things for themselves than typical 4-year-olds. They were dependent for routine needs, did not go out alone, and were supported by their mothers. The investigators cautioned that the temperament of the child is also a factor in determining whether behavior will be dependent or independent.

Stendler (1952) suggested that there are two critical periods affecting whether a child will become overdependent. During the first period, near the end of the first year, the child becomes increasingly aware of his own need for the mother and therefore increasingly anxious about her absence. Stendler believes that overdependence develops unless the mother is present and can be counted on to respond to the infant's dependency behavior in ways that are expected and familiar.

The second critical period is somewhere between the second and third year. At this time children are vulnerable to overconcern and overprotectiveness of caretakers. Unfortunately, some mothers are fearful the child will become too competent and will outgrow the need for them. Heathers (1955) found higher dependence in children of child-centered homes where the frequency count of babying behavior was high. On the other hand, Gewirtz (1956) noted a high incidence of attention-seeking behavior in children whose parents were unavailable much of the time.

The overdependent child is exceedingly disadvantaged when he enters preschool or kindergarten. An elementary school principal who was one of the major consultants in the field research for the *Kindergarten Evaluation of Learning Potential* suggested he could predict who would succeed and who would fail in school by "separating the boys from the babies." Most children at this age are quick to detect overdependence in peers and to compare them unfavorably with those who are more "grown-up." Most children want to do things for themselves unless conditioned to enjoy overprotectiveness.

Although the roots of socialization are complicated, independence in a youngster appears to be related to the quality of the peer relationships the young child is capable of building. Harlow and Harlow (1966) studied critical periods in the transfer of affection from mother to peers by isolating infant monkeys with their mothers and depriving them of peer contact for increasing periods of time. Using 2 weeks with mothers as the control group, they isolated other groups from peers for 4 months and 8 months following birth. Eight months in the developmental life of a rhesus primate is *roughly* comparable to six times that age in humans, or 48 months.

The Harlows studied the interaction of the maternal affectional system (mother–infant), the infant affectional system (infant–mother), and the age–mate, or peer, affectional system. They found that the longer the infant was deprived of peer companionship, the more delayed their play development was. As the "mother-captive" period was increased, the infant groups became more wary of close contact and more cautious, but also more aggressive. The investigators believe that human mothers have a greater capacity to develop mother-only affectional systems in their young because they are more adaptable in playing with them than are mothers of the lower primate species. Normal mothering, including affectional release, enhances the building of affection ties with age-mates in primates, presumably including humans.

Encouraging independence requires trust on the part of parents in their young child and in their own training practices. Mueller (1971) reported that highly independent boys perceived their fathers as strong and passive, as persons who had (psychological) power but held it in reserve. Parents who lack fulfillment in their own lives are likely to monopolize their child's time when the child should be exploring social relationships outside the family. The child is fortunate who feels free and protected at the same time (Hamachek, 1971). Rhesus mothers show a sharp increase in negative responses when an infant is about 5 months old. Harlow and Harlow (1966) believe this rejective behavior, while remaining protective, helps the youngster to gradually break its dependency relationship to her.

Fantasy Life

How the child's uses of make-believe function in the development of socialization has not been established in research. Myths are told to children as part of their training in primitive societies, but the extent to which adults believe them is not known with certainty. Fantasy is a significant part of parent-child communication in every culture. Fairy tales, nursery rhymes, and children's songs are passed from each generation to the next in all developed societies. Newson and Newson (1968) found that wholehearted participation in children's play varied among five social-class categories from the highest to the lowest. High SES mothers communicated more about the fantasy interests of their children. When the youngster talked of imaginary companions, these mothers were more likely to go along with the fantasy and even to use it to accomplish child-care routines. When social-class differences were accounted for statistically, families with one or two children engaged in more fantasy communication with children than did families with three or more children.

Children create imaginary friends to play with them when alone, to take care of them when a parent leaves, and to take the blame when something goes wrong. Sometimes fearful characters are invented by a child who then tries to cope with fear personified. Some examples from real children follow:

Todd, age 4, talks to a Mr. Monster who lives with a heap of stuffed animals by day. If the cereal gets spilled, Mr. Monster did it. "We should spank him!" At night Mr. Monster becomes so frightful that Todd will not go near his bedroom alone until his father methodically puts Mr. Monster outside with the real family cat.

Barney is the dog. Michael, age 3½, has been told his parents are going out and a neighbor will come to sit with him. "It's okay. If I want some cocoa, I'll call Barney to make it."

Heidi, age 3 years, is helping her grandmother set out shoots for transplanting. "Don't step back now. My friend Jennifer is helping, too!" There is no Jennifer in her acquaintance, but there are play dishes for her when the table is set and monologues directed to her in the bedroom.

Possibly children continue to grapple with social problems long after the preschool years, but most learn to distinguish reality from fantasy and dreams from reality. They also come to interpret the reaction of the persons they talk with and become increasingly selective in what they communicate by age 6.

PERCEPTUAL AND MOTOR DEVELOPMENT

Although there is no clear-cut break in motor development between the toddler and the preschool periods, the differences noted so easily in locomotion are reflected in all areas of development. This totality in organization can be seen in the relationships among physical growth, neural integration, movement skills, and cognitive development. The organism at this time in life is committed to behaviors that involve movement and manipulation. The effect on motor skill development and sensory perception have been documented by many scholars.

Physical Growth

CHANGES IN BONE, MUSCLE, AND FAT

Somewhere between 2 and 3 years old, the height and weight gains of children begin to slow down. During the preschool years the rate of gain in height is nearly double the rate of gain in weight. The increases in height are due mostly to a lengthening of the legs. Weight gains during the fourth year are primarily an increase in bone structures and ossification. During the fifth year the growth of muscle tissue increases from an average of 25 percent of the total weight change to 75 percent (Espenschade & Eckert, 1967).

SIMILARITY BETWEEN THE SEXES

The relative growth rate is very similar for boys and for girls (Figure 6-1). Although male children tend to be a little taller and heavier than females, the proportion of limbs to trunk is very similar. Likewise, the breadth of shoulders is proportioned to

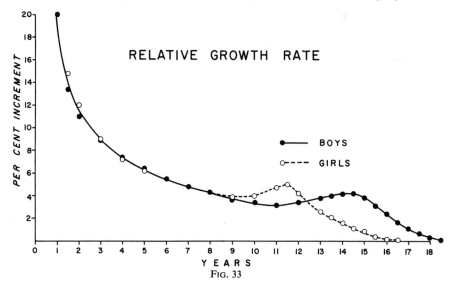

FIG. 33

FIGURE 6-1 Relative growth rate of boys and girls. Note the similarity of physical development until approximately age 9.

Source: Leona M. Bayer and Nancy Bayley, *Growth Diagnosis.* Copyright © 1959, University of Chicago Press. By permission.

breadth of pelvis by a similar ratio. The gain in muscle, bone, and fat is distributed differently than in infancy or adulthood, but is similar for both sexes. Similar patterns of subcutaneous tissue are found in children under 6 years, which probably continue to prepuberty.

Neurological Organization of Movement

Maturation is an important factor in motor development. Given similar stimulation and encouragement, individual children attain motor skills at different ages, but in relatively consistent order. The concept of critical periods is not inconsistent with the concept of maturation, but adults seem to apply these two concepts differently in childrearing (Chapter 1).

Critical periods in physical development are the times following the age when a child is first capable of performing an action (Hottinger, 1973, p. 21). The critical period for learning a body movement pattern is the time when rapid neural organization is taking place (Scott, 1968). The concept of critical periods implies the interaction of the genetic program for development and the environmental stimulation at critical times for optimum growth. The anticipation of the kind of environment that is needed to stimulate neural organization of motor responses is basic to the concept of critical periods. The proponents of maturation typically stress waiting for the neural and muscular system to mature enough for an action to be performed, while the proponents of the critical-periods concept stress the need to provide an optimum environment prior to the next level of accomplishment. The opportunity for practice at the time the child is most susceptible to the learning of a new motor skill is important and requires that care-givers have a knowledge of the chronological age when motor patterns are likely to evolve.

DEVELOPMENT OF CLIMBING SKILLS

Climbing is an extension of creeping movements. Generally youngsters can climb stairs before they can walk. Wellman (1937) observed climbing achievements and reported the age at which 50 percent of her subjects could ascend and descend steps (Table 6-1). These norms were observed in Minnesota where cold winters may have restricted children's activities on the floor. At about the same time Bayley (1935) reported slightly lower climbing ages for California children. Children usually try to descend stairs head-first, but they usually learn to reverse and descend feet-first (Hottinger, 1973). Children learn to negotiate short flights before long flights of stairs and low risers before high risers. They ascend earlier than they descend stairs, and they negotiate with help before climbing alone.

Ames (1937) noted that individual children follow the same lead foot in climbing that was used in creeping. Guttridge (1939) reported a wide range of differences among preschool children in climbing ability. When provided with climbing equipment, they improved so rapidly that 90 percent were proficient by age 6 years. Boys and girls 4 and 5 years old show equal proficiency in climbing abilities (Espenschade & Eckert, 1967).

Table 6-1
STAIR-CLIMBING ACHIEVEMENTS OF PRESCHOOL CHILDREN

Stages in ascending and descending steps	Motor age, months*			
	Ascending		Descending	
	Short flight	Long flight	Short flight	Long flight
Mark time, without support	27	29	28	34
Alternate feet, with support	29	31	48	48
Alternate feet, without support	31	41	49	55

*Motor age was the time at which 50 percent of the subjects achieved a performance level.

Source: Beth L. Wellman, Motor achievements of preschool children. *Childhood Education*, 1937, **13**, 311–316. Reprinted by permission of the author and the Association for Childhood Education International, 3615 Wisconsin Avenue, N.W., Washington, D.C. Copyright ©, 1937, by the Association.

RUNNING, JUMPING, AND HOPPING

Running, as achieved by 4- and 5-year-old children, requires motor integration for starting, stopping, and turning. The rapid, whole-sole stepping of the toddler is not a true run. Running, as defined by body-movement specialists, is controlled propulsion with both feet off the ground in an alternating pattern. Better balance, greater strength, and increased tempo of agonist and antagonist muscle systems is required than the neural organization of younger children allows. Between the ages of 5 and 6 years, most children are sufficiently advanced in running skill to participate in running games and play activities.

Jumping and hopping are more complicated modifications of walking and running. *Jumping* is the movement that occurs when the body is lifted completely off the ground by the action of one or both legs and the landing is made by one or both feet (Espenschade & Eckert, 1967, p. 114). The first stage of jumping is the step down from a higher level; it requires strength and balance to decelerate. The second stage is a long-step takeoff on one foot, followed by a two-foot landing. The use of both gives greater strength and balance to the landing and accommodates a longer jump or a greater descent. The most difficult jump is a two-foot takeoff with a two-foot landing, such as the broad jump requires. Wellman (1937) reported that 50 percent of her subjects could do a feet-together jump from 28 inches by the age of 46 months, or less than 4 years. On the basis of ontogenic development, the standing broad jump is most difficult of the jumping actions.

Children practice many types of jumps simultaneously, but the chronological sequence by which they achieve distance and height is fairly consistent. Bayley reported the height, distance, and barrier jumps from ages 25 to 59 months, the third to fifth years (Figure 6-2). It should be noted that jumping a rope barrier at 20 centimeters or less from the ground is much less complicated than rope skipping.

Hopping is the action of lifting the body off the ground by one foot and landing

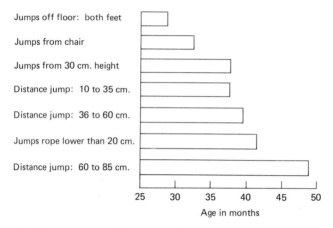

FIGURE 6-2 Progress in jumping skills. The rope jump is a barrier jump and not a skipping jump.

Source: Nancy Bayley, "The Development of Motor Abilities in the First Three Years," *Monograph of Social Research in Child Development,* 1(1):1–26, 1935. By permission.

on the same foot (Espenschade & Eckert, 1967). Usually hopping achievements are measured in number of sustained hops (Table 6-2). Wellman (1937) distinguished between hopping on both feet, which preschool children could do earlier, and one-foot hopping. Not until 5 years old could half of her subjects hop ten or more steps on one foot.

MOTOR INTEGRATION IN SKIPPING

Skipping is a movement pattern of step-hop on alternate feet in sustained rhythm. Leaping and galloping precede and contribute to skipping achievement. *Leaping* is

Table 6-2
HOPPING ACHIEVEMENTS OF PRESCHOOL CHILDREN

Hopping, steps	Motor age, months	
	Both feet	**One foot**
1 to 3	38	43
4 to 6	40	46
7 to 9	41	55
10 or more	42	60

Source: Beth L. Wellman, Motor achievements of preschool children. *Childhood Education,* 1937, **13,** 311–316. Reprinted by permission of the author and the Association for Childhood Education International-al, 3615 Wisconsin Avenue, N.W., Washington, D.C. Copyright ©, 1937, by the Association.

a specialized version of running, with the takeoff made on one foot and the landing on the other. It differs from running in the distance covered and the strength required. *Galloping* combines the basic patterns of the walk and the leap. Sustained rhythm and balance are required, with the child's dominant foot leading each gallop. Guttridge (1939) reported that 43 percent of her subjects could gallop at 4 years old and 78 percent were galloping by age five. Rhythm instruments, such as a drum, are useful in teaching children the galloping movement.

Skipping requires the child to change leads from the dominant to the nondominant side of the body in sustained tempo. Motor control must therefore shift from one hemisphere of the brain to the other. Guttridge (1939) reported wide variation among her sample in the performance of skipping: 14 percent of her 4-year-olds, 22 percent of her 5-year-olds, and 90 percent of her 6-year-olds skipped well.

Wilson and Robeck (1965) found skipping achievement a visible indicator of motor integration in kindergarten children and positively correlated with school achievement in grade one. Most kindergarten-age children could be taught to skip by using verbally guided demonstration, such as "Take a step; hop. With the other foot, take a step; hop." In the study it was first established that a child could follow this sequence: "Take a step-hop; lift your other knee up. Take a step-hop; lift your other knee up." Then the step-hop was accelerated, and the children were instructed to lift their other knee higher, "till it takes you right off the ground," and most children became joyful skippers. Sometimes a nonskipping child was helped by placing him or her between two peers who skipped well to music.

The question remains whether teaching children to skip improves their cross-hemisphere integration for similar motor skills. The kindergarten age range, from nearly 5 years to 6½ years, is apparently an optimal age for learning to skip. Children who cannot learn to skip after trying are likely to need special instruction in other sensorimotor abilities as well. One of my graduate students, D. Coryell (1964), saw skipping as a form of self-expression:

To skip is to have done a preliminary locomotor movement. To skip is to be an emotionally happy child. To skip is to enjoy playing and living with other children. To skip is to have the love, the space and the freedom to be just a child; that's skipping.

SKILL WITH PLAYGROUND BALLS

Preschool children develop limited skills in throwing, catching, and kicking balls. Infants develop the first essential skills for throwing by learning to release an object. Wild (1938) identified four stages in learning to throw a ball. During the first stage, between 2 and 3 years old, the child can project an object with a stiff-arm frontal movement, releasing the ball at the high point and bringing the arm downward. The second stage, from 3½ to 5 years old, involves the rotation of the trunk with the arm as it brings the ball back, and an opposite rotation with forward arm motion as the ball is projected. The third stage, from 5 to 6 years old, involves a step forward while the body rotates and the arm delivers with a lateral motion. The

Table 6-3
BALL-THROWING ACHIEVEMENTS OF PRE-SCHOOL CHILDREN

Distance of throw, feet	Motor age, months	
	Small ball (9½ in.)	Large ball (16¼ in.)
4–5	30	30
6–7	33	43
8–9	44	53
10–11	52	63
12–13	57	Above 72
14–15	65	
16–17	Above 72	

Source: Beth L. Wellman, Motor achievement of pre-school children. *Childhood Education*, 1937, **13**, 311–316. Reprinted by permission of the author and the Association for Childhood Education International, 3615 Wisconsin Avenue, N.W., Washington, D.C. Copyright ©, 1937, by the Association.

fourth stage of mature throwing is not reached during the preschool years and not ever by most females, according to the investigator.

The first successes at catching a ball are at about age 2 when capturing a rolling ball. Wellman (1937) reported increasing skill in catching a ball in the air from 34 months to 68 months, or from approximately 3 to 7 years old. The child must learn to develop a sense of timing and to relax the arm position (Table 6-3). At preschool age a large ball (16¼ inches) is easier to catch than a smaller ball (9½ inches). The smaller ball can be thrown farther at an earlier age than a larger ball.

The ability to bat a ball can be developed to a limited degree in preschool children by using a soft ball and teaching them to strike with a paddle (Halverson & Robertson, 1966). Ball bouncing, from one person to another, can be achieved by preschool children. The smaller ball (9½ inches) is bounced more easily. Two-hand bouncing is more difficult and is accomplished later than one-hand bouncing.

Kicking objects is accomplished by the 2-year-old by standing on one foot and imparting force with the other foot. The use of the torso to increase the impact and the use of the arms in follow-through are not achieved until approximately age 6 years (Halverson & Robertson, 1966). Use of the four limbs in a synchronized body movement is a major accomplishment of the preschool years.

SENSORIMOTOR EXPERIENCE AND COGNITIVE DEVELOPMENT

Sensorimotor learning is the basis for cognitive development. Piaget documented, through detailed observation from birth, that the child's actions on objects are basic to mental representations of those objects. American psychologists have long used a variety of sensorimotor tasks to measure cognitive functioning in young children. Maze tests, which are a form of spatial orientation, were built into the Wechsler Preschool and Primary Scales of Intelligence (WPPSI). The Draw-a-Man Test has shown a positive correlation with general intelligence (Goodenough & Harris, 1963). Stages of scribbling and drawing have been described in developmental terms (Kellogg & O'Dell, 1969).

Many of the tasks by which young children demonstrate their cognitive functioning require manual dexterity, such as piling blocks, placing pegs, or stringing beads. That these kinds of abilities are somewhat predictive of later intellectual functioning is well established. The question that is important for teachers and parents is whether such accomplishments can be learned and therefore be taught.

Left-Right Orientation of Body Parts

Infants have shown hand preference in arm waving toward an object as early as the fourth month (Cratty, 1970). By the end of the first year, 72 percent of the reaching responses of the typical child are carried out by the right hand. When the child's attention becomes directed toward learning to walk, hand preferences are obscured for a time in the effort to develop cross-lateral coordination. In individual children, the use of a preferred side and the gradual integration of right–left limbs in an action pattern are indicative of the extent of the neurological organization at the time. Left–right orientation has two aspects: (1) the child's preferred use or dominance of one side, and (2) the child's knowledge of left and right in relation to his or her own body.

HAND-EYE-FOOT PREFERENCES

Lateral dominance is the tendency for the control of motor responses to be organized primarily in one hemisphere of the brain and for the opposite hemisphere to function in nondominant integration of the response. Right-side action of the limbs is controlled in the left hemisphere and vice versa. Integration of such complex behaviors as learning to walk require cross-linkages through the corpus callosum (Chapter 1) and linkages to the cerebellum. When movement patterns such as walking or running have become automatic, the control is believed to have shifted to the cerebellum. In tasks which are performed with one hand (writing) or one foot (kicking), the lateral dominance for a specific action is easily observed.

There is strong evidence for inherited tendencies toward the use of one side of the body for leading, or dominating an action (Hacaen & Ajuriaguerra, 1964). Hand preference is probably a Mendelian recessive trait (Chapter 2). Support for this view is that 42 percent of the children of parents who are both left-handed are also left-handed. If Mendel's theory of recessive traits were an important factor one would expect one-fourth of the children of a mixed left-dominant, right-dominant marriage to be left-handed. Actually, 17 percent of the children develop left-handedness when only one parent is left-handed. A cultural influence probably accounts for some shift in inherited tendencies. Further evidence is seen in a decrease in left-handedness in older children for culturally prescribed tasks (Cratty, 1970).

By the age of 4 most children have established definite hand preference (Flick, 1967). In a culture which is both tool-oriented and predominantly right-handed there is some potential for frustration of left-handed children. The term *ambidextrous* refers to the ability to use either hand with equal proficiency. Most persons have some flexibility in learning a new bilateral (two-handed) skill, and these actions could be influenced by subtle cultural pressures. Learning to turn a right-handed drill, or an eggbeater, is easier for a left-handed child than cutting with a right-handed scissors because large muscles, which are practiced bilaterally in gross movements, are involved. When a child persists in writing left-handed this may indicate that the child's functioning is merely consistent with earlier acquired speech and language functions, which are organized and controlled in the dominant hemisphere (Chapter 9). Forced changing to writing with the right hand is probably a mistake when attempted so late in the development of lateral dominance.

Leg preference is less consistent than hand preference, but limb correspondence is more likely than hand-eye correspondence. Keogh (1968) discovered that children often used one foot for a learned task but preferred the other foot for spontaneous actions, or when directed only generally, such as "hop on one foot." Of his subjects 94 percent kicked with the right foot, but only 65 percent were right-footed in hopping. Foot preference seems to be established by 5 years of age and to remain relatively stable thereafter (Williams, 1973).

The term *cross-dominant* means that the preferred side is left for some bilateral functions and right for others. The child may eat with the right hand, for example, and kick with the left leg. Children who are talented in body movement activities are likely to be more flexible in hand and foot preferences than typical youngsters. In tasks in which right-handedness is culturally desired, the care-giver ought to present the spoon or the crayon toward the right hand until a left-handed preference is clearly indicated by the child's spontaneous movements.

Marked inconsistency has been found between hand-foot preference and eye dominance during the preschool years. About 50 percent of all young children are right-eye dominant and about half are left-eye dominant (Belmont & Birch, 1963). This finding should not be surprising to those who know that nonlanguage spatial interpretations are controlled in the cortical areas of the right hemisphere at the approximate location of the speech-interpretation areas of the opposite hemisphere. Ear dominance is also a factor in language development, but this has been studied very little as a factor in learning. Although a relationship between lateral dominance and language disorders does exist, it is more complex than most of the educational literature indicates. Lovell and Gorton (1968) found their group of severely retarded readers were confused in their left-right orientation of their own body parts. The necessity to have a left-right orientation prior to reading is obvious. It is important to know why most preschool children learn directionality in a typical environment, while others do not.

CONCEPTUALIZATION OF RIGHT AND LEFT

With the acquisition of language young children can communicate their awareness of body parts and body orientation. Some linguists read the evidence to suggest that the labeling of body parts helps the child achieve *directionality* in space (Chapter 9). The conceptual processes by which children relate their own knowledge of body dimensions to dimensions in space has been studied and described. The first cognitive step in spatial orientation is the ability to identify or name the parts of the body. Williams (1973) reported that 69 percent of her sample could identify the major body parts by the time they were 5 to 6 years old. She attributed the wide differences among children to the amount of emphasis placed on the development of these concepts by adults.

The second conceptual step in spatial orientation is to identify the left and right sides of one's own body. Discrimination of right and left sides of the body was found in 71.5 percent of a sample of children $5\frac{1}{2}$ to 6 years old (Ayres, 1969). Below the age of 5 years most children perform at a chance level when asked to "touch your left ear" or "show me your right hand."

Vernon (1970) suggested that mastery of up-down conceptual orientation of the body develops earliest in children, followed by front-back conceptualization. Finally the understanding of right-left dimensions is achieved.

Directionality is the ability to identify various dimensions in external space. Williams (1973) suggested that the third conceptual component in the development of body awareness was the child's extending of spatial references about his own body to the space around him. Conceptualizations of up-down, back-front, left-right are first made with reference to body directionality and later to external space (Swanson & Benton, 1955). Some children who have trouble discriminating left from right have trouble discriminating b from d or p from q (Kephart, 1964). The evidence for a relationship between letter reversal and left-right directionality is clinical and not empirical. It would not apply to most children who typically have established left-right sequencing prior to first grade. Children who are late in establishing handedness, or who are inconsistent in lateral dominance, could be expected to need careful instruction in beginning writing and reading.

Scribbling and Drawing

Preschool children who have older models for writing and drawing are likely to want to "make" things on paper. Although environmental opportunities influence the child's ability to draw, most children develop through stages of drawing. Kellogg is one of several writers who have analyzed the drawings of children at different ages in terms of the mental or perceptual abilities shown.

RANDOM AND REPETITIVE ACTIONS

The child's first mark may be accidental as an object is rubbed against a surface. More fortunate babies are given stiff paper and bold markers as early as the high-chair period. The earliest scribbles are usually horizontal repetitions, followed later by vertical and slanted scribbles. At first the child seems to ignore the boundaries of the paper, but soon scribbles in relation to the space outlined by the perimeter of the paper. Then scribbles are made to balance each other in space or in direction.

ENCLOSING SPACE

As the child gains control over the scribbling movements, he or she slows down and begins to produce a series of patterns. One of the earliest is a wavy attempt to enclose space. Loops, spirals, and overlaid circles, which may look like spaghetti

A nursery school child scribbles by making overlaying circles. (Prathana Konsurto/UNICEF Photo)

to the unappreciative observer, are drawn. The circles become identifiable, if imperfect, during the third year. Some children draw repeated circles, scattered over the page, to produce a design. A change of colors, or the availability of several colors at this stage, may enhance the drawing of separate rather than overlaid circles. During the middle of the third year, children typically draw crosses, scribbled at first but later attempting to cross single lines. Squares may emerge from the cross, or from squaring off a circle (Kellogg & O'Dell, 1969). Some of our grandchildren had a mother who drew and painted. Perhaps these children imitated the drawing of forms for they preceded these Kellogg norms by at least a year.

THE DIAGRAM PHASE

Near the end of the third year, or early in the fourth, children spontaneously draw geometric shapes and simple stick figures. Terman and Merrill (1960) have placed copying a circle at age 3, copying a square at age 5, and copying a diamond at age 7. To score on their scales the child must enclose the form and must draw distinct sides (except for the circle), but the shapes need not be perfectly proportioned. Cratty (1970) observed that right-handed children usually began the drawing of a rectangle at the upper-left corner and proceeded counterclockwise, while left-handed children began at the upper-right corner and proceeded clockwise.

COMBINES AND AGGREGATES

Kellogg (1970) described the *combine* stage as one in which the child attempts to bring more than one figure into a pattern. Control of space is important because the child must know when beginning to draw a form the space it will occupy in relation to other forms. In the aggregate stage, the child includes three or more figures in a design. By the fifth year, chidren execute complex designs, but they continue to draw circles and rectangles better than they draw triangles.

THE PICTORAL STAGE

Children cannot draw houses and persons until they can produce and combine shapes. However, the child may think of scribbles as representations the adults do not recognize. They should encourage verbal explanations about early drawings and accept the child's own cues as to the picture's meaning. A crude circle with marks on it may represent a moon to the child, or even a particular person. Children who are divergent in their thinking may also be divergent in their drawing, so that any one drawing of a person may not indicate the child's total perception of a person in terms of elaboration or detail. Kellogg recommends that many drawings from a single child be available before making an assessment of mental development or emotional state.

Preschool children often show an interest in letters and numbers. At this stage they may write series of unrelated letters, or they may include them in their pictures. Sometimes they make controlled horizontal scribbles across a page, claiming the scribbles are letters. Reversed letters at the scribbling or pictorial stage do not indicate a potential directional problem in writing. Children at these stages do not show perspective in their drawings, nor do they draw objects in three dimensions.

REPRESENTATIONAL THOUGHT AND COGNITION

The developmental stage from 2 to $5^1/_2$ years has been called the symbolic period (Furth, 1969). By the age of 2 the child "knows" many things through sensory actions upon them. The young child gradually builds internal structures that are the child's image of things. A large ball is "known" through the kinesthetic information of arms curved around it, through visual information of color and depth dimensions, through the tactile information of texture, and through the sound of the bounce when it is thrown against the wall. When the child knows that familiar things exist, even when not seen, the child is showing the existence of mental images, or *representations*.

To Piaget, representational thought is a symbolic process by which children re-present what they know. What they know is their own construction of reality, obtained through visual, motor, and other actions on things. These internal structures are neurologically based and are biologically designed. The ability to know permanence is followed by the ability to represent, which is called the *symbolic* function. Representations can be in the form of visual images, or in the form of signs and symbols (Furth, 1969). The increasing ability of the child to use abstract symbols to represent real events is the most significant intellectual accomplishment of the preschool child.

The sequence by which the symbolic function evolves has been described in detail by Piaget (Chapter 9). The first stage is seen when a child reenacts, or imitates, a scene from yesterday. This representation is a symbolic formation of the event and a powerful new function in the intellectual life of the child. The second stage in representational thought, or symbolic behavior, is seen in the typical play of preschool children. The child uses external things as symbolic representations: the flat stone becomes the toy stove, the large stick becomes the motorbike to ride on, or a twig becomes the spoon to eat with. The imitative gestures of play are symbolic representations of what the play signifies to the child (Chapter 10).

The third basic form of behavior involving use of symbols is based on cultural phenomena including language, moral behavior, art, and rituals. To Piaget the symbols that are dependent on the cultural environment are abstract systems of symbols; arbitrary in their conception, they are not indigenous to the child, and they are imposed on the child. These forms must be learned, while intelligence itself is developed spontaneously. Language and pictures are expressly constructed by a society for symbolic use; their function is representation. It is not surprising that Piaget studied the child's language as social interaction and that he turned to studies of thinking operations that were largely independent of the language used, such as seriation, classification, and conservation. These are conceptualizations which the child makes through interaction with the physical world. Symbolic language merely serves the child in communicating how he or she sees scientific relationships. Despite Piaget's differences with many linguists he has become the reference point for many investigators who have made language acquisition the focus of their studies (Chapter 8).

Neurological Bases for Symbolic Thought

The cognitive school of psychology has generally turned to the physical evidence of brain development and EEG activity to explain the evolution of thought processes. In part, this is to counter the claims of the behaviorist school that cognitive processes are unknowable and only the behavior (the external response) is important. The difference between the two approaches concerns whether the child develops symbolic functions from within (by biological, age-related sequences) or from without by stimulus-response mechanisms (the shaping of behavior by adult reinforcement).

Miller, Galanter, and Pribram (1960) cited evidence for the brain as the initiator of spontaneous activity, the selector of input from the environment, and the organizer of responses. One of the most notable changes in the brain during growth is the increasing control of the brain centers over sense reception. What is seen or heard is selected from many possibilities in an environment. Having attained mobility the child is partially freed to select one environment over another. He may follow the mother who converses while they are together, or initiate a ride on his father's motorbike. The sensory input and the resulting mental structures are quite different.

Pribram (1971) points out that what an organism perceives is an *internal representation* of the environment, and the behavior seen is an *external representation* of an organized neural action (p. 211). Language reception and expression, as one form of symbolic behavior, follow this pattern. Language is significant in the cognitive development of humans. From his knowledge of the working of the brain, Pribram suggests that individuals construct their external actions. The action of constructing itself is stored and becomes a larger and larger share of the individual's perceptions. Then a means-ends reversal takes place: the action becomes an end in itself and is self-reinforcing. Sensory processing (that accompanies action) is *itself* stimulating (reinforcing) and therefore results in discrimination learning, or the development of meanings. The meanings derived from these self-regulated actions become a plan for future action, or a commitment on the part of the organism to some constructing actions over others. When the constructions or external representations are words (symbols of language), the plan becomes a statement of intent which puts into reality the action of the future. Language then becomes the vehicle for thought and the self-recognized plan for action (self-motivation). The young child comes into his or her own as a person when he or she is able to construct present and future action and to communicate those intentions to others.

Cue-Producing Stimuli and Reasoning

Berlyne, an S-R psychologist, explained thinking behavior as an internal (covert) stimulus-response process which dictates outward symbolic behavior. He was interested in the central structures within the subject that resulted in attention to some stimuli over others and in the changes in attention patterns through experience. Berlyne's analysis resulted from his desire to explain higher-level thought processes such as reasoning. Using strict behaviorist terminology, Berlyne suggested that external cues stimulate a sequence of complex mental responses. Some of the bridges to cognitive psychology in his explanation of thinking behavior were the recognition of operations and groupings (of Piagetian developmental theory) and transformations (of linguistic structuralism). Berlyne seemed to extend the S-R model to include a sequence of if-then statements which the brain processes. Essentially, Berlyne combines ideas from logic and computer programming to suggest that human organisms are wired with if-then statements or systems of them (White, 1970).

Thought as a Second Signal System

Scientists from the Soviet Union have tended to combine behavioral and developmental information in the study of higher thought processes in children. Zaporozhets (1961) reported that the orienting-investigating activities make a developmental shift during the preschool years from motor-tactile to visual exploration. Vygotsky (1962), in a similar view to Piaget's, traces the internalization of motor and visual patterns to the beginning of cognitive representations and the basis for adaptive behavior (learning). However, he departs from Piaget in identifying symbolic language as the initial influence in directing the cognitive development of the young child.

Luria (1961) has taken his cues from the ontogenic conception of human brain development and neurology. Language has an excitatory influence on young children at first, an excitatory and an inhibitory influence later, and finally a regulative and directory influence. Vygotsky shows how the young child explicitly directs himself with language and proposes that this verbal behavior is internalized (goes underground) to become organized planning and reasoning. Soviet research in child development has continued to view language as a second signal system which, during the preschool years, attains a directive function in symbolic and adaptive behavior. The issues of thought processing are exceedingly important to those who rear young children, particularly if the period of representational thought is limited. The learning processes are discussed in greater depth in Chapter 8, Cognitive Development.

Implications for Preschools

The preschool environment, which typically is more relaxed in its expectations of children than primary schools, gives the child an opportunity to explore relationships and develop personal and social skills. The affective learning that results from a healthy preschool relationship with age-peers cannot be provided within the family. Most children need to learn a trust relationship with adults in the larger society before trying to learn academic skills from them. Minority-group children, who identify with their parents and older siblings, need to experience acceptance in the wider community of the preschool. Care-givers can assure giving an affective message of acceptance if they truly appreciate differences and unique strengths in people generally and children in particular.

Preschool children develop the movement skills of climbing, running, jumping, and hopping as an extension of creeping and walking patterns. Skipping demonstrates the neural integration of timing, of bilateral coordination, and of changing leads in the left-right hemisphere domination of the action. Sex differences in locomotion and ball-handling skills are minimal or nonexistent. This suggests that motor activities might be encouraged for both sexes at this age.

Tests of cognitive abilities, which correlate highly with school success, suggest some cues for the games and activities children might enjoy at school. By exploring the meaning of children's drawings, the adult establishes verbal contact with the children and helps them expand their verbal abilities.

SUMMARY

During the preschool years the child is developmentally ready to move outside the family circle of parents and siblings for contact with peers. A girl's own conception of herself (how she looks, who she is, and what her strengths are) is reexamined and modified in the early contacts with peers. Boys appear more vulnerable than girls in the comparisons and competitions of a peer society, perhaps because the cultural pressures are more explicit.

Children from 3 to 5 years old normally learn to identify with the parent of like sex. They model this parent, the parent of the opposite sex, age-mates, and older children in a selective manner. Socioeconomic differences in the way parents rear their preschool children have been documented in England. Upper-middle-class families are more likely than lower SES families to engage in fantasy-play behavior with their children and are more likely to be permissive of self-comforting behavior, but are also more likely to adhere to bedtime schedules. The mothers of unskilled and unemployed workers are more likely to be strict about cleaning plates and thumb-sucking, but they are more permissive about daily routines. Consistent patterns across SES categories were found between family expectations for independence and confident behavior in children. If research on primates, which shows critical periods of dependence, holds true for humans, some attention should be given to the detrimental effects of what Harlow and Harlow call mother-captive infants. Human 4-year-olds who were independent as persons had mothers who had encouraged this independence.

Sensorimotor experience is the basis for later and more complex cognitive functioning. Cognitive development emerges at this age stage in what Piaget, Berlyne, and Vygotsky have called representational thought. Representations are the mental images of action patterns, signs, and symbols the child experiences through the senses. Overt behavior is the external representation of the internal organization within the central nervous system.

Early Childhood: Age of Productivity

7 Early Childhood: Age of Productivity

The period from 6 to 8 years old is characterized in this book as the age of productivity. Physical development at this stage is steady and consistent, lacking the growth spurts of earlier periods or of adolescence. It is a time of consolidation in which the foundations of intellect (in the form of sensorimotor integration) are ready to function in a rapid expansion of cognitive styles and thought patterns that overlap much of the intellectual life of adults. Socially and emotionally the primary-age child is on his or her own in a larger community where the constant decisions of participation or withdrawal cannot be avoided.

Among those most concerned with the schooling, the primary years from first through third grade have traditionally been called the period of *early childhood*. The use of this term preceded the widespread practice, begun in the sixties, of providing curriculum-oriented preschools for younger children. It should be noted that during the forties some excellent day-care centers had been provided for mothers who worked in the war industries. Although the curriculum there was designed for balanced development, child care rather than child education was the major purpose of the centers.

This chapter focuses on the developmental characteristics that are particularly relevant to primary teachers, who provide learning activities in basic academic skills, social and science education, esthetic appreciation, and physical education. To be successful with any individual child, the teacher must also provide a climate in which the social interaction is positive for each child. The task of being the one adult responsible for twenty-five young children is tremendous, and requires the best possible understanding of children at this age. Given a knowledge of the potential and the vulnerability of the children generally, the primary teacher can more quickly personalize the interactions within the classroom. This chapter includes sections on physical and motor development, children's thinking, the characteristics of emotional latency, peer relationships, and motivation to achieve in school. Chapter 12, Early Childhood Education, is concerned with school programs for all young children, from toddlerhood through the primary school years.

PHYSICAL AND MOTOR DEVELOPMENT

The growth period from 6 to 8 years has been described as one of consolidation because the rate of growth is slow and consistent, the changes in body proportion are very slight, and the relationship of bone and tissue remains nearly constant. The growth energies of the child are directed toward perfecting movement patterns and applying them to a variety of game and work activities (Espenschade & Eckert, 1967). Most children of this age can alternate quickly between hard play involving gross motor exercise and brain-hand tasks involving quiet concentration.

This is also a time when children judge themselves in motor performance and body image against their peers of the same age.

Body Size and Build

By age 6 or 7 years the relative proportion of weight to height has become relatively stable, so that body type (slim, average, or stocky) can be projected into adulthood. Height-weight charts showing typical growth ranges reflect the data from majority groups who tend to be similar (homogeneous). These may not be relevant to the child whose size is normal and whose physical development is healthy even though it is above or below the norms indicated in the tables. Some readily observed examples are certain Latin American children who may be smaller than average or certain black African children who may be taller than average in a United States classroom, although normal in their ethnic groups.

The relationship of weight and height tends to be an inadequate indicator of physical development because weight reflects increases in the moisture and fat content of cells as well as increases in bone and muscle tissues. An attempt has been made to use a combination of measures as an index of growth.

Morphological age is the relationship of weight, height, and some other body measures to chronological age. The breadth of shoulders, the pelvic girth, and the relative lengths of limbs are useful indicators of growth at this age. *Skeletal age*, based on ossification and fusion of hand and wrist structures, is closely related to chronological age in most children. It is useful in indicating delay or advanced maturation which is independent of physical size (Reynolds, 1943). *Dental age* is determined by the eruption of teeth compared with chronological age norms (Tisserand-Perrier, 1953). The period from 6 to 12 years is marked by the eruption of permanent teeth, and therefore growth assessments in early childhood have frequently included dental age. This index has the disadvantage of reflecting hereditary differences in dental age which are independent of mental and chronological age.

SOMATIC TYPES

The body type, whether chubby, average, or slight, is important when evaluating the appropriate weight of youngsters. Bayley and Davis (1935) found that the weight/length ratio was the most valid measure of body-build tendencies during the first three years. They found that chubbiness peaked between 9 and 12 months for most children. Wetzel (1943) delineated seven growth channels for individuals, beginning at age 6 when he considered the body type and weight/height ratio to have stabilized. Pryor and Stolz (1933) used body width at the hips, sex, height, and weight to recommend the ideal weight for individual children. All these measures have limitations for children who vary widely on some body-build characteristics.

The most comprehensive body typing has been done by Sheldon, Stevens, and Tucker (1940), who first studied adult males, upon whom the types were based, and later studied boys and girls. Sheldon's somatic characteristics were related to the three layers of embryonic tissues in early differentiation: the ectoderm, the mesoderm, and the endoderm. Ectomorph types were described as dominated by the central nervous system and as having a relatively linear, fragile body. Mesomorph types had rectangular-shaped bodies and strong, well-developed muscles and skeletal tissues. Endomorph types were dominated by visceral systems and were described as rounded in body form and soft in musculature. Some relationship has been found between Sheldon's body types and personality, but the question remains whether Western culture influences males of different somatic form in consistently different ways.

High school boys who were superior in motor abilities were found to be high on the mesodorph scale and low on the ectomorph scale (Espenschade, 1940). These differences were less marked in girls, but the poor performers among them tended to be endomorphic. Environmental factors have not been explored adequately. Perhaps early intervention for girls and for less talented boys would broaden their participation in sports and increase their enjoyment of physical activities.

SIMILARITY OF THE SEXES

Body changes during development are shown in Figure 7-1. Body size and body proportions are markedly similar between boys and girls from ages 5 to 11 years old. The proportion of leg length to height is determined by measuring the height of the child while sitting, and calculating a ratio (Figure 7-2). The longer leg length of girls in infancy evens out in early childhood before the longer leg length of adolescence has occurred in boys. When comparing body diameter at shoulders and hips, boys and girls do not differ much until the age of 8 years when the relative

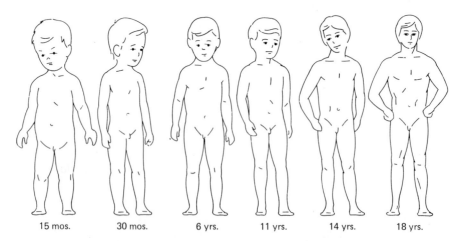

| 15 mos. | 30 mos. | 6 yrs. | 11 yrs. | 14 yrs. | 18 yrs. |

FIGURE 7-1 Changes in body proportions from 15 months to 18 years.

Source: Leona M. Bayer & Nancy Bayley, *Growth Diagnosis.* Copyright © 1959, by the University of Chicago. Published 1959. Composed and printed by the University of Chicago Press, U. S. A.

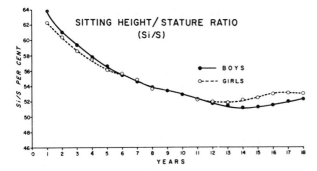

FIGURE 7-2 Ratio of sitting height to stature in boys
and girls from 1 to 18 years.

Source: Leona M. Bayer and Nancy Bayley, *Growth Diagnosis.*
Copyright © 1959, The University of Chicago. Published, 1959.
Composed and printed by the University of Chicago Press, U. S. A.

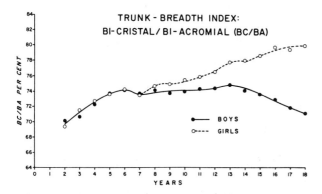

FIGURE 7-3 Trunk diameter at shoulders and hips in
boys and girls from 1 to 18 years. As boys grow older, their
shoulders grow wider and their ratio falls. As girls' hips
grow relatively broader their curve rises.

Source: Leona M. Bayer and Nancy Bayley, *Growth Diagnosis.* Copyright © 1959, The University of Chicago. Published, 1959. Composed
and printed by the University of Chicago Press, U. S. A.

shoulder girth increases for boys and the relative hip girth increases for girls
(Figure 7-3). Some adults interpret these data as indicating comparable physical
activity for primary school girls and boys.

HEREDITARY FACTORS

When sex differences in physical development persist in various studies, the
differences tend to be accepted as evidence of genetic influence. Since the culture
is sex-selective in many childrearing practices, researchers continue to try to sort

out the hereditary components in physiques, motor abilities, and problems such as delayed development or obesity (Malina, 1973). Twin studies and family-line studies support those who see heredity as important.

Traits such as height and skeletal frame show greater similarity among monozygotic twins, whose genetic makeup is identical, than among dizygotic twins, whose makeup is merely familial (Freedman & Keller, 1948). Twins have been found to differ little in motor attainment, whether identical or fraternal, and order of birth is not an influence. Although body build appears to be inherited, identical twins reared apart show weight differences in the direction of nutrition patterns within the foster family. Fatness, as it affects body type, is highly related to environmental control. The relationship between childhood and adult fatness has been attributed to early nutritional experience when the number and size of the cells in the fat tissue layers are laid down (Knittle & Hirsch, 1968). Obesity in childhood appears also to be associated with a tendency toward inactivity (Corbin & Pletcher, 1968). These tendencies toward fatness, establsihed long before a child has control over eating and activity, make weight control much more difficult for some persons than for others.

The influence of heredity on the potential for unusual motor abilities is also complex. When motor performance is within expected ranges the interaction of heredity and environmental factors is all but impossible to sort out. Twin studies show that a developmental lag is consistent in identical twins when compared with behavioral norms for infants. Illingworth (1968) reported that delayed motor development went beyond twinship to family-line patterns. He believed that inherited delays could be attributed to delays in myelination of the neural system. Scarr (1968) further strengthened the evidence for genetic influence on the rate of physical development. He explored the question of the environment of identical twins, which had been proposed as suitable for study because it was assumed that since parents had identical expectations of them, their environments would be similar. He observed parental behavior toward both dizygotic and monozygotic twin pairs, and concluded that the similarities and differences among twins in physical skills were influenced very little by environmental factors.

The implications of hereditary determinism as it relates to body build are far-reaching. To the extent that body build and body image correspond, it would appear that happiness is partially found in identification with one's family and partially gained through early attention to physical fitness (Corbin, 1973).

Gross Motor Performance

The childhood years from 6 to 8 are a time for refinement of movement patterns and the development of strength. It has been shown that preschool children can jump and skip, can catch and strike a ball, and can hop and gallop. Children who have no ball to play with, or no one to play catch with, may be expected to lack these common child-admired skills. Other children have had such limited opportunity for physical encounters with people or things that they do not learn to exert their bodies in any important effort. They cannot engage in the ordinary give-and-take of a typical lunch line without fearfulness, or fall without hurting themselves. They lack the usual repertoire of movement patterns, and they quickly sense their own inadequacy on the playground.

Children can be taught the skills needed to participate in their peer society. Most children can learn fundamental motor patterns much earlier, and enjoy action much more, than present programs reflect. A *movement pattern* is a fundamental action that is organized into a particular time-space sequence. In physical education, teachers usually begin from movements such as walking, running, and jumping, which children learn spontaneously in a variety of environments, and combine or extend them into more elaborate motor patterns. Walking and hopping are alternated to become the motor sequence of simple skipping, which is later elaborated into rope skipping or dancing the polka. Catching and throwing are the fundamental skills for playing softball and dodgeball. The ball bouncing children enjoy so much in first grade is fundamental to the dribbling and passing that will soon extend into basketball.

Teaching organized sports has long been an issue in primary education. Although it is important to develop the foundational motor skills, probably our children are capable of organized games much earlier than their schooling permits. I observed Korean 5- and 6-year olds spontaneously organize soccer teams during free play. I have taught second- and third-grade children to square dance and they learned as easily as older children. Primary children are generally lacking the sex-related distractions of preadolescence; therefore they can partici-pate fully in mixed games. The least skillful children learn by modeling the patterns most children conceptualize from verbal instruction, and all enjoy participation.

Physical fitness is usually evaluated by combining the performance of children in gross motor abilities and in health-related abilities such as endurance, flexibility, strength, and repetition of an activity (Table 7-1). Skill-related fitness is evaluated by abilities in agility, reaction time, balance, coordination, and speed. Corbin (1973) reported a comparison of American children and three European groups in motor fitness tasks. Although the test was skill-related, and American children may have had less training, they failed 57.9 percent of the tests while Italian children were scoring 8 percent failure; Swiss children 8.8 percent failure; and Austrian children 9.5 percent failure. If Americans believe the differences were due to training, then the children should be given the opportunity for training that is consistent with their potential.

AGE DIFFERENCES

Children increase their strength in a continuing relationship to their weight until puberty (Corbin, 1973). Strength is usually measured by hand grip, back strength, and leg strength. Although boys are slightly heavier and stronger in later child-hood, sex differences do not become important until about age 11 years.

Children grow more skillful during the elementary school years. Figure 7-4

Table 7-1
PHYSICAL-FITNESS FACTORS

Health-related aspects

Endurance.

The ability to persist in numerous repetitions of an activity. Specifically, this aspect involves development of the respiratory and circulatory systems of the body.

Flexibility.

The ability to move joints through a full range of motion.

Strength.

The ability to exert force such as lifting a weight or lifting your own body.

Muscular Endurance.

The ability to persist in numerous repetitions of an activity involving strength.

Combined aspect

Explosive Power.

The ability to display strength explosively or with speed.

Skill-related aspects

Agility.

The ability to change directions quickly and to control body movements (total body).

Reaction Time.

The ability to perceive a stimulus, begin movement, and finally complete a response.

Balance.

The ability to maintain body position and equilibrium both in movement and in stationary body positions.

Coordination.

The ability to perform hand-eye and foot-eye tasks such as kicking, throwing, striking, etc.

Speed.

The ability to move from one place to another in the shortest possible time.

Source: C. B. Corbin, *Becoming Physically Educated in the Elementary School.* Philadelphia: Lea & Febiger. Copyright. 1967, p. 20.

shows the running skills of children 5 to 17 years old (Espenschade, 1960). Beyond 11 years the girls' decline in gross motor abilities is as shown by the gray line.

SEX DIFFERENCES

DiNucci (1976) studied the large muscle skills in boys and girls from 6 through 8 years old. He found no significant differences between them in muscular endurance, hand grip, and shoulder strength, or in complex performances such as

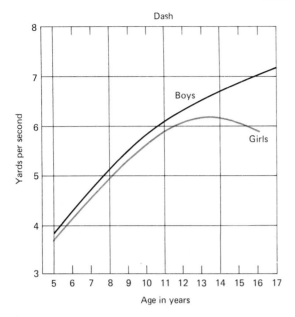

FIGURE 7-4   **Running skill of boys and girls from 5 to 17 years of age.**

Source: Anna Espenschade, "Motor Development," in *Science and Medicine of Exercise and Sports*, Warren R. Johnson (ed.). Copyright © 1960 by W. R. Johnson. Published by Harper & Row.

railwalk or obstacle run. He found boys superior in skills in which speed and muscle strength of the legs were the important factors and in cardiomuscular endurance. He found girls superior in body movements in which flexibility and balance were important. DiNucci interpreted the sex differences he found as reflecting sociocultural play patterns rather than basic developmental characteristics.

ENVIRONMENTAL FACTORS

Corbin (1973) demonstrated that the physical fitness of boys increased dramatically from age 12 whereas the fitness performance of girls leveled off, or even declined. He proposed cultural reasons for this decline. Vigorous physical performance is not widely accepted for girls or valued by society. Girls are not expected to achieve on fitness tests, which are geared to expectations rather than the medical measures that indicate that girls have greater potential. The idea that physical exertion will cause injury to female internal organs is a myth, according to medical research. Erdelyi (1962) found fewer cases of menstrual, delivery, and labor problems in women who exercised regularly. Although physiological differences between the sexes explains some of the difference in performance, the individual performance of motivated girls suggests that much of the decline in girls as a group is culturally dictated.

Mental-Motor Relationships

Motor learning has been defined as the gradual elimination of nonessential movement (Lockhart, 1973). Common sense suggests that learning to skate or creating a dance requires something more than elimination, perhaps self-direction. Infant behavior is characterized by reflexive patterns of response and randomized actions which gradually must be brought under cortical direction and in the service of need fulfillment. Toddlers practice to attain balance, during which time brain control over action is increased by the growth of new synaptic connections in the efferent-afferent relay. Preschoolers put together a learned pattern for step and a learned pattern for hop; they perform these patterns on alternate feet by alternating motor control from the left to right hemispheres. Some children learn to skip, but others must be step-hopped through the sequence and given verbal cues to describe the motor action. That verbal (cognitive) cues are used by the learner cannot be doubted when one hears a child directing himself or herself: "step—hop—step—hop," and, later, "step-hop—step-hop—." Neurological research has established that a pattern of excitory messages to the muscles must be accompanied by a pattern of inhibitory messages to the opposing muscles. The coordination of these on-off motor neurons may call for some gradual elimination of nonessential movement.

As children reach the primary school years they direct a large portion of their motor learning in self-initiated ways. The basic patterns of locomotion have been learned, and these children are ready for instruction in motor skills not acquired spontaneously in the service of locomotion. This may be the child's first opportunity to learn to swim, to skate, and to ski. Quite possibly this is the optimum period for learning some of these skills.

CHILDREN'S THINKING

How children function intellectually is an exciting topic for adults who observe particular youngsters over time.

Erika (4½ years) stirred the cookie batter; she dipped and licked her index finger. "I've tasted 2 and 2 and 2 and 2 licks. That won't spoil my dinner. Eight licks is a lot, that would spoil my appetite. But 2 + 2 + 2 + 2 isn't many, is it?"

Piaget would point out the lack of number conservation in Erika's thinking, but representational thought was clearly being used.

Michael (6 years) was exploring his grandfather's melodica. He exclaimed, "Hey, look. I can play "Three Blind Mice" down here, and here, and up here. I can play it anyplace. Here it's high and here it's low but it's the same tune still."

Michael had discovered that a melody is a time-space relationship which is independent of the frequency range of the sounds. This translation of sensory experience into a structure that is basic to music is a clear demonstration of children's thinking of a kind different from Erika's. His conceptualization was more than feedback of sensory input or associative learning.

Thinking, as a concept, is much more difficult to manipulate or to defend than learning. *Learning* has come to be defined as change in behavior, a definition that is limited only by the ingenuity of observers in deciding if what a subject shows is what he or she knows. *Thinking* is an internal activity, but not all internal or brain activity is thinking. In the cognitive theory of Piaget thinking is internalized action, made possible by structures that are built as a result of sensorimotor experience (Chapter 8).

Problems in Defining Thinking

Penfield (1975) has defined *thought* as the action of the integrating system of the brain (the diencephalon, or higher brainstem, and the cortex of both hemispheres). This integrating system produces sensory impressions persons know as consciousness. The *action* of the higher brain integrating system is thought; its *expression* is behavior. Penfield calls this the mind-mechanism, and distinguishes it from the automatic sensorimotor control systems of the lower brainstem (p. 44).

At this writing many psychologists do not accept the concept of mind. To them behavior as seen by someone else is all that can be known. During the late fifties college students who hoped to become teachers argued whether children could "think." They quoted Rousseau's theories on the education of children. He argued that the child of 5 to 12 was in the "savage" stage of human growth. Education should be within the family where books would be eliminated, the mother tongue would be learned spontaneously, reading would be acquired incidentally, and the organs and senses would have a chance to develop. Not until 12 years and older were children capable of reasoning, of having curiosity, and of utilizing knowledge (*Emile*, 1964). To many educators who followed this view, thinking was reasoning and therefore young children could not think. This was an easy position for middle-school and secondary teachers to take.

For adults who taught young children and knew their intellectual capabilities, Russell's classic book *Children's Thinking* (1956) was like the sun coming up. He presented a structure, from a developmental point of view, for a psychology of thought. He described the materials of children's thinking as sensations, perceptions, memories, images, and concepts. *Sensations* are the coded stimuli from the different sensory systems. *Perceptions* are the individual's immediate interpretations of sensory input. *Memories* are stored experiences that have occured in various settings and are retrieved according to their relevance to the thought process. *Images* are symbolic representations, the most useful in school being the word symbols of language. *Concepts* are generalizations about related data. Usually a new label is required because a concept represents a class of things and not the elements. When the child has conceptualized the class *dog*, a label is needed that will include all other dogs and exclude all nondogs.

Russell defined *thinking* as a process, or a sequence of ideas, involving a beginning and a continuing complex pattern of relationships that leads toward some goal or conclusion. The important question for early childhood teachers is whether Russell's model is applicable to the intellectual functioning of young children. Returning to Erika's batter licking, and Michael's melodica playing, it can be asked: Were these children thinking? Was there a goal-oriented beginning to the process? Was there continuity? Was there a conclusion to the sequence? Although her number conservation was lacking and her dialogue may have been meant for herself, Erika anticipated the possibility of spoiling her dinner, which meant no dessert at her home—no cookies. Whether she started by counting the licks by 2s, or counted 8 and split them into units to make them appear smaller is beside the point. She clearly arrived at a conclusion, consistent with her purpose. Michael's thinking was initiated in exploration, but his continuity is evident in the way he checked out his initial discovery. His conclusion that the same melody could be played in different keys was a correct generalization and an important concept in music transposition. Such instances of children's thinking give zest to the teacher's world.

Association Learning

Associations are the bits and pieces of sensory experience which come to be connected by a learner because they happen together in time. Psychologists call this learning by *contiguity*. Thorndike proposed that a "bond" or "connection" was formed between a particular sensation and the tendency (of an animal or a child) to respond in a certain way. He rejected the idea that reasoning as such exists and believed instead that the explanation of learning is to be found in simple S-R relationships. He is best known for three principles: the law of readiness, the law of exercise, and the law of effect (Hilgard & Bower, 1975).

By *readiness* Thorndike meant a neurological condition for a satisfying, rather than an annoying, outcome. An action which was blocked from completion, or which caused fatigue because of forced repetition, was considered annoying to the subject. By the law of *exercise*, Thorndike meant the strengthening of connections with practice and the weakening of connections when the practice was discontinued. The recentness of an experience increased the likelihood that the action would be repeated. Rote memorization and motor skills both came under this law, according to Thorndike. "Practice makes perfect" is a common expression of this principle. Thorndike modified his law of practice when further experimentation showed that practice did not improve a performance unless the learner had some way of getting feedback about the accuracy of the responses.

The law of *effect* meant the strengthening or weakening of a connection as a result of its consequences. In other words, the rewards or successes furthered the learning of a behavior, and punishments or failures reduced the tendency to repeat a behavior. Thorndike insisted that action is based on consequences; behavior is automatic and mechanical, and need not be mediated by a conscious thought process. Although these ideas raised a furor among teachers, they predated Skinner's operant conditioning theory and provided the theoretical basis for behavior management in the classroom. Association learning has been accepted by most modern psychologists as basic to memory storage. Memories provide much of the material which children use to organize the complex intellectual environments of the school (Wilson, Robeck, & Michael, 1974).

Conceptual Organization of Associations

The way in which children organize bits and pieces of sensory experience into meanings and concepts is the most important knowledge a primary teacher can possess. A teacher can provide a particular environment of blocks, numerals, words, stories, books, colors, songs, and games, and establish the time frames in which pupils "experience" different materials. The difficulty is that each individual child selects from this array by a selective attention based on past learning. Each child interprets experience from a different background of perceptions that are always personal and always distorted to some extent by private motivations, interests, and wants. These affective associations are part of the neural or intellectual structures that are available to a particular child at a given time. Intellectual experience is a function of previous associations and the way the individual has structured them. Cognitive psychologists such as Bruner and Piaget have focused on levels of intellectual processing which they see as different in kind from connectionism (Thorndike, 1913) or the S-R learning described by behaviorists.

TRANSFER OF LEARNING

Bruner (1964) proposed that information is conserved in long-term memory only when the details of a topic are placed into a structure, or relationship. These structures may be conceptualizations, principles, generalizations, or formulas. He believed that when concepts and principles were derived by students the learning would transfer to new situations that were similar. The procedures by which information was structured would also transfer. Bruner suggested that students be allowed to "discover" the relationships within content as part of their own training.

In *The Process of Education* (1966), Bruner distinguished between acquisition, transformation, and evaluation in learning. *Acquisition* involves the step-by-step knowing of the fundamentals of a subject. It includes exploratory experience, but it advances in well-planned steps which are under the control of the teacher. Bruner used the beginning stages of language acquisition in childhood and the fundamentals of mathematics as examples.

Transformation is the unique or intuitive use of fundamental knowledge. Bruner (1966) proposed that when structures are discovered by school children they are more likely to use them in new settings. He suggested that children demonstrate transformational thought when understanding and speaking sentences.

Having grasped the subtle structure of a sentence, the child very rapidly learns to generate many other sentences based on this model though different in content from the original sentence learned. And having mastered the rules for transforming sentences without altering their meaning—"The dog bit the man" and "The man was bitten by the dog"—the child is able to vary his sentences much more widely. (p. 8)

Evaluation is a process of testing a hypothesis. Michael explored a series of musical notes at different points on the keyboard. After discovering that the same tune could be played at a different place on the scale, he tested his intuitive thought. Although he could not have identified the procedure as such, he was testing a hypothesis.

PREOPERATIONAL THOUGHT

Piaget (1969) described the second period in intellectual development as the period of *preoperational thought*, which included the ages from 2 to 7 or 8 for the typical child. By *operations*, Piaget means internalized actions which are reversible; that is, they can be performed in opposite directions. One well-known experiment that demonstrates the ability to reverse an action mentally is the one with two tumblers of equal proportions. They are partially filled with liquid and evened until the child agrees that both have the same amount to drink. With the child still watching, the interviewer empties one tumbler into a taller, narrower glass and asks the child if the amount of liquid is still the same or if one glass has more than the other. The child of 4 years usually says that one of them is "more because it is taller" or the other is "more because it is fatter." The child of 8 years will say they both are the same "because if you pour it back they will look the same." Younger children are deceived because they are limited by their perceptions and center on one dimension of the liquid. Older children can mentally reverse the action to its original configuration. Similarly, the liquid from one of the equal tumblers is poured into a squat glass. It can be predicted that the preoperational child will insist that one glass has more to drink than the other, although children differ as to which dimension they focus on when making a choice. Through the ability to reverse an action, the older child demonstrates *conservation* of quantity and the beginning of *concrete operational thought*.

BEGINNINGS OF CONCRETE OPERATIONS

Piaget qualifies the kinds of thinking that children do from about 7 to 11 years by the term *concrete operational thought*. The child can perform internalized actions on objects, but only when the objects are present and visible (concrete). Some of the various conceptualizations children demonstrate as concrete operations in various experiments are *seriation, classification*, and *numeration* (Chapter 8).

The idea has become accepted by cognitive psychologists around the world that the typical child from 6 to 8 years old makes the Piagetian transition from period two, preoperational thought, to period three, concrete operational thought. This transition is exceedingly important in teaching children in the primary school.

Most children understand conservation of liquid by age 7 or 8. (George Roos/Peter Arnold)

The ability to function symbolically with images and language marks the beginning of representational thought; whereas the third period is character- ized by the term *inception of operations.* "Initially these operations are concrete; that is, they are used directly on objects in order to manipulate these objects" (p. 2). Piaget goes on to say that the child can order objects by size, can perform number operations on them, can measure them from a spatial point of view, and can classify them. In applying the principles of operational thought to the classroom, the use of concrete materials on which to perform actions should be stressed. The fact that most children have moved beyond perceptual experiencing to the conceptual organization of experience should also be stressed. Piaget deplored what he called additive learning theory and stressed the child's necessity to organize his or her own perceptual experience.

Piaget uses the term *intuitional thought* to describe the stages of transition from simple representations to concrete operations. During this middle period from 4 to 6 years old, the child will often give a correct response to an operational question. However, the response is unstable and cannot be articulated (explained) in conceptual terms. The child is showing the intuitions Bruner described, but has not yet built the necessary internal structures to describe them. If Piaget is correct, these structures are formed by the interaction of maturation and the child's own actions on the environment.

Conceptualization in Primary School Children

Conceptualization refers to the process by which the learner comes to understand inherent relationships. Conceptualization represents the commonality in such intellectual processes as relating bits of perceptual experience, discovering cause or effect, gaining insight, or forming generalizations (Wilson et al., 1974). An example from Piaget is the conceptualizing of seriation, which requires both visual and tactile actions on a variety of things until the learner discovers the principle for ordering them. *Seriation* consists of ordering objects according to an increasing or decreasing size relationship (Figure 7-5).

In their memory studies Piaget, Inhelder, and Sinclair demonstrated that children varied in their understanding of relationships according to their age and their stage of development (Piaget, 1969). The interviewers showed children from 3 to 8 years old a series of sticks and at a later time asked the children to draw them. At the A stage they drew a row of marks, about equal in length. At the B stage they drew sticks of two sizes, and at the C stage they drew small, medium, and large sticks. Not until age 7 or 8 could most (75 percent) of the children draw ten sticks in increments from tall to small, or small to tall, with assurance. All the children remembered and could draw sticks, but the conceptualization of seriation was necessary for a stage E response.

RESEARCH ON CONCEPTUALIZATION

Wallace (1967) surveyed the worldwide research on conceptualization in children. The overwhelming portion of these studies were replications or tests of Piaget's theory. Piaget's idea that children show discrete differences in intellectual functioning, along age lines, was supported; but some researchers found a much wider age range for their attainment of the various levels of conceptualization than Piaget indicates (p. 225).

Several studies have seemed to show that maturation alone does not accomplish concept development in children. Hyde (1959) found that children of ages 6, 7, and 8 from four ethnic groups generally confirmed Piaget's theory of number acquisition and surprisingly gave many verbatim translations in English, Arabic, or French to explain their thinking. However, there were significant delays in number concepts in her sample on the part of underprivileged children as compared with privileged children. Wohlwill and Lowe (1962) showed that training in addition and subtraction was effective in aiding children to attain conservation of number. Smedlund (1961) showed that children who had acquired conservation of weight as a result of direct, reinforced practice readily gave up the concept when confronted with instances of apparent nonconservation; they reverted to preconceptual behavior. Burt (1931) suggested that primary school children may be taught to reason formally if their instruction in arithmetic emphasizes the discovery method.

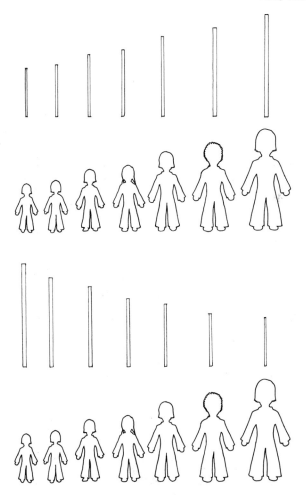

FIGURE 7-5 Seriation begins in the preoperational period, when the child is able to match the dolls and sticks from smallest to largest. Children have reached the concrete operations period when they can decenter, so that two operations can be performed at one time; inverse seriation from largest to smallest and smallest to largest at the same time are possible.

These studies are some of the hundreds available on conceptualization of mathematical and scientific concepts. Important in this context is a study by Elkind (1961) which showed that not quite half (47 percent) of his subjects from 12 to 18 years old had attained conservation of volume. This finding suggests that many children do not attain logical thought processes by the end of the concrete-operations period and may continue into adulthood before adjusting to reality.

Wallace (1967) leaned toward accepting the evidence that suggests conceptualization is teachable at ages prior to Piaget's timetable, but held that direct instruction with reinforcement is less likely to achieve stable concepts than generalized experience or discovery methods of teaching. Wallace, like Piaget, identified perception as basic to conception.

Piaget (1964) made a distinction between development and learning. "The development of knowledge is a spontaneous process, tied to the whole process of embryogenesis—the total development of body, nervous system, and mental functions." He defined learning as a response "provoked by a psychological experimenter," by the teacher, or by some external situation and limited to a single problem. To "know" an object is not merely to make a mental copy of it but to act upon it, to modify and transform it, to perform mental operations on it which change spontaneously during growth and development. This distinction is difficult to maintain in long-term studies of cognitive behavior.

Some enlightening research regarding development versus learning has shown differences between schooled and unschooled children of Senegal (Greenfield, 1966). African children from 6 to 13 years old showed the typical reliance on perceptual cues in explaining such conservation tasks as the beaker experiment already described. By age 12 virtually all schooled children conserved as expected while about half of the unschooled children remained perceptually dependent in their explanations and did not mentally reverse the action to know that the liquids were still equal in amounts though changed in form. This study strongly suggests a role for learning in attaining knowledge of basic laws of the physical world, knowledge which Piaget saw as developmentally attained.

CHARACTERISTICS OF LATENCY

Latency is defined in psychosocial literature as the period of childhood between the resolution of infantile sexuality and the emotional upheavals of adolescence (Chapter 11). The ages of latency are from 6 to 11 years, although early maturing girls and late maturing boys would be expected to extend this range. Freud called this stage of development latent because it is relatively free of the jealousies and guilt of the phallic (preschool) period and of the biological changes and confusions of puberty; in the healthy child, violent drives are dormant. The period of latency corresponds almost precisely to the elementary school years. The focus for this discussion remains the primary-school child; but some of the research takes on greater significance when seen in the totality of the elementary school.

Erikson (1963) identified the period of latency as the fourth stage in human development. He wrote in eloquent terms of how children of all cultures enter the world of adults via the life of the school, the latter being the jungle, the field, or the classroom. Youngsters of this age are psychologically ready, even eager, to sublimate their desires and like to win recognition by producing things. By this age they have come to understand that there is "no workable future within the womb" of the family and thus have become ready to apply themselves to given skills and tasks. The latency child develops a *sense of industry* which goes beyond organic pleasures and finds expression in the world of tools. Children of this stage, if emotionally healthy and socially mature, see satisfaction in work completion. They have the attention, perseverance, and diligence to work at directed tasks and to find joy in their completion.

Erikson points out that all societies provide systematic instruction for children of this age. In literate societies, reading and writing are the major avenues to the world of big people because literacy provides the broadest possible base for careers. In technological cultures, the utensils, tools, and weapons that go with specialized careers take on the values assigned them by the culture. When careers become complicated and work roles of parents become vague "school seems to be a culture all by itself, with its own goals and limits, its achievements and disappointments" (p. 259).

The danger at this stage lies in a *sense of inadequacy and inferiority* that results when the child does not succeed in the work of the school. "If he despairs of his tools and skills or of his status among his tool partners, he may be discouraged from identification with them and with a section of the tool world" (p. 260). Erikson sees the tool world of primitive utensils, technical machinery, and professional symbolism as having similar importance in the child's need for mastery. "Many a child's development is disrupted when family life has failed to prepare him for school life, or when school life fails to sustain the promise of earlier stages" (p. 260).

Latency is a decisive stage socially and emotionally because the child must learn to achieve satisfaction from productivity and a sense of industry before being able to cope with adolescent challenges to the ego. Erikson believes that failure at the latency stage not only discourages the child from entering the world of industry but pulls him or her back to a previous stage characterized by the familial rivalries of the oedipal period. Other dangers to the school child are the unfortunate and unnecessary inferiorities felt as a result of skin color, parent background, or economic disparities. The early school years should assure that work is not the only measure of worthiness and that conformity is not the only criterion for production. Each child can be valued for himself or herself. Nearly all children of this age give themselves to challenging activities if a reasonable chance for successful completion prevails.

Physical Evidence of Latency

The physiological changes in adolescence signal the beginning of the next stage in development (Figure 7-1). Latency is characterized by a leveling off, or even a slight decline, in the weight and size of the genital organs. Psychological measures such as vocabulary, reading comprehension, and abstract thinking show rapid increases. Myelination in the central nervous system is characterized by small changes that occur in the elaboration of existing systems. In many ways latency children are more responsible than teenagers because they are mature enough to know what is expected of them, but are less driven by disruptive interpersonal forces. In short, they are in better control of their lives in some ways than during adolescence.

Young teachers are sometimes surprised by the independent judgment some primary-age children show. Mrs. S., who wanted to get away from school early, sent a note to the school secretary: "If the cat's away the mice will play. RSVP." She chose a thoroughly reliable first-grader to deliver the note, saying the message was very important. Alice returned from the office without a reply. "Did you give the note to Mrs. Hinkledorf?" "No, Mrs. Hinkledorf wasn't there. I gave it to Mr. Rice because it was important. I asked him if he wanted me to wait for the answer but he said, 'No, thank you.'" Children who are independent can be effective models rather than a threat to classmates if teachers team them skillfully with children who need to establish confidence. Erikson has pointed out that the latency child, even though unready to be a biological parent, is a "rudimentary parent" in his or her desire to be a helper and provider.

Building Habits of Industry

It is not surprising that observers of children have become interested in achievement motivation and have researched its correlates in the elementary school population. The collective wisdom of Western culture holds that the work habits learned in childhood are carried over to adult behavior. Parents differ in the age at which they begin to make achievement demands on their children.

ACHIEVEMENT MOTIVATION

Moss and Kagan (1971) studied personality change and consistency in the same subjects longitudinally from birth to ages in the twenties. They found that achievement behaviors in young children were predictive of similar achievement activities in young adults. Levels of achievement motivation stabilized in the preschool years for girls (age 3 to 6) and during early elementary years for boys (age 6 to 10). The relationship of achievement motivation to productivity in adulthood is difficult to assess because culture defines success differently for various segments of a society (LeVine, 1970).

PARENTAL DEMANDS FOR ACHIEVEMENT

The effect of parental pressure for achievement influences the motivation to achieve, but the relationship is so complex that interpretation must consider the age stage of the subjects. Researchers have also found it difficult to distinguish parent behaviors from parent accounts of how they reward achievement and react to failure. Firstborn children have higher achievement motivation than siblings (Sampson, 1962). Firstborns are represented among eminent persons to a greater extent than would be expected from their numbers in a population, and as college students they have higher IQs than siblings (Altus, 1966). This rather consistent relationship between birth order and achievement has been explained by the relatively greater involvement, encouragement, and urging of the firstborn by parents (Sears, Maccoby, & Levin, 1957). While firstborns have their parents as models, later-born children have older siblings, as well as adults, for their models.

Bartlett and Smith (1966) found that boys with high achievement motivation were more likely to have been born first. In attempting to identify the sanctions and demands their parents used, mothers of boys 8 to 10 years were questioned about rearing practices. Boys with high achievement motivation tended to be met with expressions of disappointment following unsatisfactory behavior; but the mothers of these children reported making few demands on their sons for achievement and independence. Mothers of boys with low achievement motivation tended to associate expressions of love with performance, whether low or high. Contrary to expected results, the parents of low-achievement boys made significantly more demands for achievement and independence. Whether this demand level was a reaction to low motivation on the part of school-age sons or had a causal effect on their motivation was not determined.

Avoiding a Sense of Inadequacy

Erikson's (1963) polarity of industry versus inferiority is reflected in the research where lack of achievement has revealed its counterpart in feelings of inferiority and anxiety. Long, Henderson, and Ziller (1967) studied the relationship of self-esteem in boys and girls from 6 to 12 years old to individuality, dependency, identification figures, and power (teacher) figures. Contrary to the hypothesis that self-esteem would increase with age, the highest score was found in first-grade children and the greatest drop from first to second grade. Some recovery was seen at grades 3 and 4, with another decline at the upper levels. Self-esteem was related positively to identification with mother (which peaked at third grade) and with teacher (which peaked at fourth grade). Identification with father peaked at sixth grade for boys and fifth grade for girls. One surprising finding was the similarity of the sexes in parent-teacher identification, whether the adult was male or female.

INDIVIDUALIZATION AND SOCIAL DEPENDENCY

As hypothesized by Long, Henderson, and Ziller (1967), individualization, the degree to which the child differentiates self from peers, tended to increase through the grades. Contrary to expectations, social dependency increased over the grades in both sexes. A follow-up study showed not only increased social orientation in the upper grades, but increased dependence on the peer group and increased identification with a friend. The authors believed that greater individuality in boys was derived from their necessity to separate themselves conceptually from mothers.

The attitudes of the children themselves regarding the need for industry and independence versus the need to avoid inferiority and dependence seem to depend on developmental stage. The different effects of parental pressures at different periods was noted by Long et al. (1967), who reported that parental pressures to achieve appeared to have a negative effect on the younger and the older subjects, but a positive effect on the achievement motivation of children of middle age. Observation of their separation independence (desire to be on one's own) and achievement motivation (desire to do well) was a significant step toward resolving some otherwise conflicting research. A further examination of the literature suggests that the preschool children from 3 to 5 years respond well to parental guidance and sanctions directed toward making them independent. However, these children as a group respond negatively toward pressures for achievement. Children from 6 to 9 years seem to respond constructively to parental expectations for achievement by increasing their own achievement motivation. On the other hand, it appears that pressures toward independence have a negative effect on their self-esteem, perhaps because they increasingly feel inadequate. By the upper elementary years of 9 to 12, the child is perhaps already past a critical period for parental teaching of independence or the motivation to achieve; parental pressures seem neither constructive nor effective. This interpretation would explain the curvilinear relationship between independence training and achievement motivation which averaged at 8 years in McClellend's work (1961). It also would explain the negative effect of independence training on boys 9 to 11 years on the part of authoritarian fathers when this training occurs in social groups where training is typically late (LeVine, 1970).

ORIGINS OF TEST ANXIETY

Feld (1959) found that high test anxiety in adolescent boys was associated with late demands from mothers for independence, while low test anxiety was associated with relatively early demands for independence. Bartlett and Smith (1966) reported a negative correlation of test anxiety with grades in school and with IQ measures. Boys with high test anxiety were rated more dependent by teachers. Their mothers praised them less frequently, according to interviews, and made fewer demands on them for independence, prior to age 7 years, when compared with the mothers of boys who showed low test anxiety. These findings support the notion that late demands for independence are destructive of school adjustment in boys.

PEER RELATIONSHIPS

The effect of peer interaction on the social development of children from 6 to 8 years old is important because it is during these years that the identification shifts from parent to teacher to peer. This shift of identity is assumed on the basis of developmental theory and research on peer relationships, which confirms this change in identity for typical children. Most of the studies of peer interaction have come from younger children enrolled in playschools, or from preadolescent and adolescent children who have had special attention from school counselors and social psychologists. Comprehensive and detailed studies of peer relationships are lacking for the primary school child (Hartup, 1970).

Assumptions from Developmental Theory

Some intriguing and largely unanswered concerns about the child from 6 to 8 years old are: (1) How can the self-esteem, so high in first-grade children, be preserved? (2) How does the shift in identity orientation from authority figures to peer group or peer leader occur? (3) What is the origin of competition and how can the responsible adult handle it?

BUILDING SELF-CONCEPT

When a child enters school the generalized concept of self probably becomes differentiated into academic and nonacademic self-concepts (Shavelson, Hubner, & Stanton, 1976). This in-school, out-of-school dichotomy supposedly is further differentiated into subareas that become associated with different activities in school. The generalizations of self emerge as "I'm good at numbers," "I get bored in reading," or "science is fun." These are examples that do not bring joy to the reading teacher, but do characterize a few school children. Further differentiation includes such nonacademic areas as social self-concept, emotional self-concept, and physical self-concept. These conceptualizations of self stem from the generalized image and also contribute to its development. The child whose contacts with other children have led her to think of herself as one who suggests the game to be played is likely to try this pattern in a new group (Merei, 1973).

Each time a child enters a new school situation a reappraisal takes place. The child evaluates himself or herself according to the feedback images from peers, significant others, emotional states, physical abilities, and physical appearance, to name some of the most important (Shavelson et al., 1976). These conceptualizations stabilize relatively early and remain fairly consistent through the latency period. Bobby, a fourth-grade pupil, said, "Can I check out a basketball? I'm going to start a game." Because the season was a long way off, the teacher asked, "Are you sure the other kids will want to play basketball?" "Everybody knows you [meaning I] can get 'em to play what y' want 'em to play." He smiled. I learned something that day about Bobby's self-concept in physical activities. Amazingly, he was not the stereotype of playground leadership. He was small and modestly successful in academic work.

The impact of the early weeks with a new class and a new teacher on the self-esteem of a child is almost frightening to contemplate. The child's need to discover and characterize self is confirmed in social psychology and in daily experience. Self-concept at this age is built largely by measuring self against peers in activities of the school and the community.

SHIFT IN IDENTITY FROM ADULTS TO PEERS

Psychosocial theory emphasizes the orientation of the preschool child toward the family and the orientation of the adolescent toward the peer group (Erikson, 1963). Children are known to identify with parents at entrance into first grade and to identify increasingly with the teacher as the adult authority until some time in the middle elementary grades. From then on the typical school child identifies increasingly with a friend or with a peer group (Long et al., 1967).

Although data are lacking on the relationship of individual children with adults versus peers, it is safe to assume that the establishment of a secure place in the peer group is critical in the emotional development of the school-age child. Relationships that the child sees as pleasurable, accepting, and supporting are likely to be sought out and relationships which are punishing are likely to be avoided. Also the child is likely to generalize the relationships with teachers to other adults outside the home and to generalize the relationships with school-mates to other peer groups.

When a child's behavior is characterized by independence, the child's self-concept is likely to reflect this. Those relationships which support the child's self-concept are likely to attract his loyalties. Children who see themselves as strong in academic areas, if academic achievement is high on their value scale, are more likely to identify early with the teacher and to retain this identity. Children who see themselves as outside the teacher's sphere of acceptance are likely to turn very early toward their peers for verification of their self-concept.

In reviewing the literature on peer relations during the elementary school years, Campbell (1964) reported that ties with particular peer members stabilize with increasing age, that children become increasingly proficient at interpreting their own status among peers, and that lack of popularity is associated with low self-esteem. In a game situation contrived for research, children who were rewarded for their performance showed more positive attitudes toward fellow group members than children who performed as well in different groups but were unrewarded. Children who are popular and influential in peer groups tend to be above average in intelligence, to take definite stands on issues, to initiate a standard of fairness that is impersonal, and to exert control over deviant members. Campbell cited a series of studies to show that older children come increasingly under the influence of peers when a conflict develops with adults. Even though distance increases between the parents and the peer groups, the values, the attitudes, and the behaviors of parents can be identified in the decisions their children make within the peer society.

One generalization that can be made from research on socialization is that peers become more influential during latency, and adults less influential. This implies the necessity for families to teach children moral judgments and moral values early in life when parents are effective models (Chapter 11). It also means that preserving an influential relationship may be possible if the child is given as much autonomy and responsibility as she or he can handle during the primary years. Such a child is less vulnerable to peer pressures, even when the parent is no longer close at hand to lend support. Individual differences among children in their ability to stand up to group pressure perhaps is the most important finding in the research on peer-group interaction.

SELF-IMPOSED COMPETITION

The desire of school children to be productive, and their necessity to build their self-concept on status within the peer group, predetermine that self-concept and self-esteem will be built from the same experiences. The accuracy with which children perceive their status with other significant persons, and the relationship of status and self-concept, have been well established for a long time (Ausubel, 1952). This means that the school situation is ready-made for a continuous comparison of self against peers of the same age and sex.

Prospective teachers often remark that their first concern will be to remove competition from the classroom. There can be little doubt that unfavorable comparisons on the part of teachers can be very damaging to the self-esteem of the child who is compared unfavorably, and probably also to the favored pupil. However, the child's need to measure himself or herself against the attributes and the performance of peers means that children themselves generate competition. They need competition for their own ego development, and competition creates excitement during unexciting times. To the extent that the pecking order operates in the organization of human groups, children will increasingly develop skills for manipulating the group and for exerting their influence on the group despite a teacher's desire to eliminate competition. More hard data are needed on the constructive ends to which teachers can use peer influence. Group cooperation, of the kind needed to achieve difficult goals, may be one way for teachers and other adult leaders to reduce the competition among individual children.

Methods of Studying Peer Interaction

When reviewing the literature on peer relationships, it is important to be able to decide how much confidence can be placed in a particular study before it is implemented in the classroom. The complexities of child interaction are especially vulnerable to different interpretations and different applications. The research on socialization is generally of three types: (1) laboratory experiments of the kind carefully designed to control all important variables except those being tested; (2) sociometric studies of social distances among individuals in a self-contained group, usually a class; and (3) experimental ecology, in which studies are designed and conducted within the larger educational setting and try to interpret the various forces that are critical. Most of the studies reported in this section have been of the first type, empirical research using laboratory controls. One further study, important in this context, has stimulated much subsequent research, and provides a good example of ecological research in socialization.

LABORATORY EXPERIMENTATION

In a classic study, Berenda (1950) divided younger (7 to 10 years) and older (11 to 13 years) school children into instruction groups of ten members. The groups were shown a series of cards and asked to pick one of three lines which corresponded in length to a model card. Some of the items were quite obvious but other cards contained lines so similar in length as to be difficult to differentiate. All the children except one critical subject in each group were coached, as collaborators, to give the same wrong answers on certain items. These majority children were also coached on appropriate ways to try to influence the critical child subject to change his or her mind about which lines were the same length. Berenda found that the responses of the younger subjects deteriorated under group pressure from a control measure of 93 percent correct judgments to 43 percent correct; while older

Peer relationships become increasingly important during the latency period. (Nancy Hays/Monkmeyer)

subjects' responses deteriorated from a control measure of 94 percent correct to 53 percent correct. There were no significant IQ differences as to firmness in holding to one's private judgment versus yielding to the group. Of the younger children 7 percent remained independent and correct throughout the sessions, and 20 percent of the older children remained independent. Berenda noted that when line differences became obscure, and therefore more difficult to judge, children more readily followed the majority view. Berenda's conclusion that younger children were more affected by group pressure than older children runs counter to the evidence regarding age and peer identity. The study may reflect the older child's greater experience in making personal judgments, rather than peer identity. The implications of Berenda's study for jury procedures are tremendous.

SOCIOMETRIC TECHNIQUES

Sociometric measures are useful when there is a need to know the social esteem of an individual within a group or the dynamics of group organization over time.

Sociometry is a method for discovering, describing, and evaluating the structure of a group (Moreno & Moreno, 1947). The *sociometric test* is a technique for studying social interaction that charts the extent of acceptance or rejection of an individual within a group, based on the children's own choices (Bronfenbrenner, 1945). The *sociogram* is a device for charting the results of the sociometric test, so that social alliances and social distances may be readily visualized (Figure 7-6).

The method has been used in research on the effect of change in school assignment on the social development of children. For example, intellectually gifted children accelerated to second grade were found to have greater social acceptance than controls who were not accelerated (Simpson & Martinson, 1964). Although the positive differences tended to come predominantly from girls, sociometric evidence alleviated a myth on the part of teachers that children suffer socially from acceleration. The relative instability of friendships during the early grades was first discovered through sociometric tests.

One purpose for using sociometric techniques in the classroom is to help children from minority groups gain acceptance into the informal structure of the group. Another purpose is to observe the dynamics of interaction so that group cohesion and positive alliances can be encouraged. A third and extremely important purpose when working with young children is to discover ignored or isolated children, who need adult support in increasing their contacts with peers. The sociogram also identifies those children who are likely to be effective in working out new roles for the lonely children. The channeling of leadership to constructive and purposeful ends is possible if the responsible adult knows who are the "chosen" leaders in various activities.

The use of sociometric tests has been criticized for the same reason that mental tests have been challenged, that this is not appropriate information for teachers to have. It would seem that if a teacher is a professional in training and in attitude test information should be available and utilized.

As a primary teacher, I found sociometric measures extremely useful in individual guidance, parent conferences, and classroom organization. The tests were given orally to first-grade pupils three times during the school year. Older children wrote their responses. The Bronfenbrenner measures (1945) identified the individuals who deviated significantly, and presumably were in leadership roles or isolated and in need of intervention. Although teachers tend to think that they know the interpersonal dynamics within a class, a well-conducted and sensitively analyzed sociogram is likely to yield some surprises.

C.D. appeared as an isolate on all three sociograms. The teacher's request for referral to the school psychologist follows verbatim except for the names: "C. is shy, good looking. He is clean and appropriately dressed. He seems to lack energy most of the time. C. can express himself

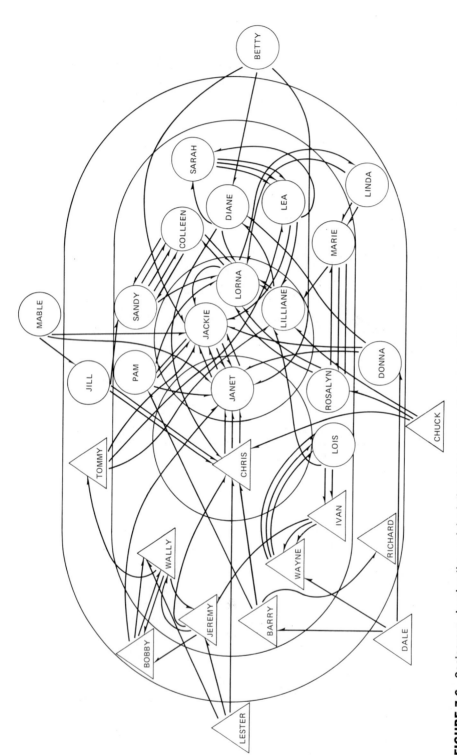

FIGURE 7-6 Sociogram showing the social relationships of thirty first-grade children. *Pairs* are shown with a double arrow. *Stars* receive a cluster of choices, which place them at the center of the interaction. *Isolates* may be merely ignored or actively rejected, but their status places them on the fringes of the social group.

Source: Private files.

adequately; but seldom enters a discussion voluntarily. C. conforms in group situations; but seldom enters group activity without being drawn in by the teacher. He participates in directed play; but stands on the sidelines at recess time. He cried and refused to go to the nurse for routine checkup.

In addition to routine information, the school psychologist's report commented in part: "When C. was asked to draw a picture of a person he had a hard time deciding whether he should draw a boy or a girl . . . . He stated that he wished he were a girl . . . . C. needed a great deal of support from the psychologist . . . . We agree with your thinking he is much less mature emotionally and socially than the average six and a half year old . . . . We suspect from his conversation that the child is pretty much over protected, that his experiences have been rather limited."

S. N. moved over the course of the school year from a position of inclusion to a position of isolation. Her mother was concerned about her lack of friends and asked for a conference with the teacher. Mrs. N. asked specifically that her daughter not be seated with J. F. or work with her because she "was smarter than S. and put things over on her." Mrs. N. reported they were near neighbors and had had a series of unpleasant encounters. At age 4 years, by this account, J. had "turned in a fire alarm and had run away, leaving S. to take the blame." S. had been badly frightened by the trucks, the sirens, and the firemen. The father had gone to J.'s home to force a confession from her about turning in the alarm. The mother's feelings were strong and vehement toward J. The record showed that both girls had similar ability, but that J. was advanced in skill development, while S. was seriously retarded.

For both children cited in these excerpts, the social isolation was the major cue to a deeper problem. C. D.'s parents were enlisted to help him extend his out-of-school activities to include some of the boys in the class. S. N. was quietly teamed with children whom she could associate with without feeling guilty about violating her parents' wishes. Neither of these strategies solved the persistent problems that began at home during the preschool years, but in both cases a happier and more hopeful school life was initiated. Moreno and Moreno (1947) recommended that role-playing techniques be implemented to help older children learn to relate differently to each other. They believed that improving the social behavior of humans might be possible by discovering what was worth improving in a given social group and building upon the worthwhile.

Sociometric studies point up the classroom as an ecological educational unit which does not function in isolation but is part of a larger ecological unit, the community. Despite the limitations of research based on children's reports, rather than on observed behavior, sociometry is potentially useful in recording the peer structures of the educational environment.

ECOLOGICAL RESEARCH

Bronfenbrenner (1976) discussed the necessity that research in education become *ecologically valid* by giving adequate consideration to the different settings in which the subjects functioned. He regarded laboratory-based research as merely the first step in experimentation, a step taken to clarify the hypotheses. He warned against overapplication to the real world of the school the conclusions drawn from a laboratory setting. The basic distinction is between what he called the *contrived experiment* and the *ecological experiment*. Two forces operate in the world of education: the relations between the characteristics of learners and their settings, and the relations that exist between different environmental systems.

Bronfenbrenner outlined four levels, or ecosystems, which influence the American elementary school child. (1) The *microsystem* is the immediate setting in which the child plays out the various roles required at particular periods of time. These are the environments of home, school, and day-care center where the child can be observed in the natural settings. (2) The *mesosystem* is the interrelation between the major settings of the child's life at a particular time. In short it is the interaction between microsettings and includes church, camp, sports, and even television. (3) The *exosystem* is seen as an extension of the settings in which the child lives, including the neighborhood, communications systems, transportations systems, and the government agencies with which a family deals. (4) The *macrosystem* is the social, cultural, and political umbrella which carries information and ideology to the ecosystems contained within it (Brim, 1975). Bronfenbrenner believed that real-life experimentation required an ecologically valid setting in which the place, time, roles, and activities of the subjects were consistent with the culture. Only then could the results be generalized to the school and only to those populations which were similar in ecological structure.

Merei (1973) reported an experiment in group leadership at a day-care center for Hungarian school-age children which meets most criteria of the ecological experiment at the *microsystem* level. The typical play period of 35 to 40 minutes was observed by two adults who remained as unobtrusive as possible and compared and compiled their notes throughout the experiment. The playrooms, the toys, and the organization into age subgroups were part of the regular school setting. Observations in a preexperimental setting established the social qualities of the children who were selected for the study. Children who were not leaders were identified by the following criteria: those whose frequencies of "following orders" outnumbered their "giving orders," whose imitation outnumbered being imitated, whose participation in group play was average for the group, and whose acts of aggression were no greater in number than an average for the age. The children were formed into play groups and placed in a setting that remained consistent from day to day to include table, toys, and tools. These leaderless groups met until traditions had formed such as permanent seating, division of toys, group ownership of certain objects, ceremonies connected with their use, expressions of belonging together, rituals, sequences of games, and group jargon. At this point an additional child was placed in the group who was characterized by strength of leadership and was older by 1 to 2 years.

Leaders were selected from the same day-care play situations, by the same observers, using different criteria. The leaders were identified as those who gave orders more frequently than they followed, were aggressive more frequently than submissive, were imitated more often than imitative, and often initiated activities. The observations went on as before, and in the same setting, when the child with leadership behaviors was introduced into a group. It will be recalled that these play groups were formed with no strong leaders, and functioned until each group spontaneously formed traditions, or patterns of interaction. Age groups under 7 years consisted of three or four children; those from 7 to 10 years consisted of three to six children each.

The most important finding was that in each of twenty-six experimental units the group generally absorbed the leader, forcing its traditions on him or her. The individual leaders handled this group cohesion in several different ways. One pattern resulted in the former conqueror becoming the conquered. The leader found his suggestions rejected by a group that went on with their traditions and he was forced to fit into their existing patterns; he was observed to model children who had previously modeled him. Although stronger than any one member, he gradually submitted to group traditions.

At the opposite end of the change pattern was a girl who took over the group. She happened to be a skilled leader in a group that was characterized by a high instance of solitary play as a tradition among them. This girl gave orders for activities, modeled the behaviors she expected, decided what to play, and introduced new rules to be followed. These two groups represented the extremes in leader capitulation and leader capture.

Most leaders gradually worked out behaviors for themselves in the new group which preserved the group traditions. "Order givers" became imitators by ordering activities that were already traditions and in this way expropriating the leadership. "Proprietors," who had tended to take possession of many objects in the preexperimental setting, were found to honor the ownership of toys as established by the traditions of the unit but to go through the motions of assigning objects. They exerted no real influence, but preserved an image of leadership.

Some former leaders, when confronted by a strong group with strong traditions, became "diplomats." They took a roundabout road to leadership through the following sequence: (1) tried to do away with group traditions and were rejected; (2) accepted and quickly learned the traditions; (3) assumed leadership within the traditional framework; (4) introduced insignificant variations; (5) introduced significant variations into a ritual already weakened by variation. Thus a 6 1/2-year-old leader of an established group of 4- and 5-year-olds began to distribute toys to the traditional "owners" at the beginning of each period. He accepted the rules for block play in which a similar structure was built, by tradition, each day. Then he began to insist that sides of a certain color be placed up. Later he introduced innovations in the structure itself. The observers noted that the groups led by diplomats rose to higher levels of organization, play, and division of roles than any of the other groups.

This study incorporates some of the desirable criteria of ecological experimentation in education. The research setting retained the materials, activities, and rules of the natural day-care environment. Only group membership was manipulated to study intragroup relations. The sizes of the groups were designed to reflect the play patterns that are typical of the spontaneous play at preschool and primary school ages. These results are generalizable to play groups of similar ages within similar macrosystems. As to their value in early childhood education, they seem to offer important cues for grouping children in ways which allow the weaker children to form traditions before the more aggressive children are permitted to dictate play patterns. Or adult guidance may help in forming rules which all members may be expected to honor. The teacher's obvious role might be minimized by using the principles of peer relations to enhance peer organization during play.

COGNITIVE APPROACHES TO MOTIVATION

In learning, as in all aspects of growth, the child functions as a whole organism. Motivation, usually considered an affective characteristic, is closely tied to drives, motives, and attitudes. It is important for teachers and parents to distinguish between the cognitive and the affective counterparts of behavior because each is enhanced in different ways. Wilson, Robeck, and Michael (1974) defined the *association level* of the affective experience as the feelings of pleasure and punishment that accompany a cognitive experience. At the infant stage, and to some extent throughout life, many internal emotional responses are vague and ill-defined. One piece of truth is that most of life's experiences are neither totally positive nor totally negative in their effect on the learner. Children may not know why they feel out of sorts with the world, why they want to hit at any kid within reach, or why they don't feel like playing.

When feelings are generalized at the conscious level, they are seen by the learner in terms of his or her own well-being; they are awarenesses that can be dealt with. *Conceptualization* in the affective domain is an essential component of the self-concept. At this level of learning, children know who they are, whether they are pleased with who they are, what they are good at, and what gives them pleasure.

Interaction of Cognitive and Affective Outcomes

The relationship between self-concept and academic experience has already been proposed (Shavelson, Hubner, & Stanton, 1976). Children may be expected to be enthusiastic for those things which they see themselves as good at, and to avoid those areas of activity where the anticipation of success, and the good feelings that come with it, are not seen as possible. The sensitive approach which parents must take if they want their children to be achievers is to expect the most that can be learned with effort and to express pleasure frequently for specific achievements. Expressions of love in the context of school achievement and school failure have been associated with low achievement motivation (Bartlet & Smith, 1966). Motivation is the child's own stake in the future, which parents help a child attain for himself or herself, and not for themselves.

Teachers walk a similarly fine line in attempting to keep the self-esteem of each child high in a setting at an age when comparisons with other children are so obvious and personal achievement is so necessary. It is both essential and possible to help each child focus on his own goals and his own progress. Since motivation is built from successful outcomes and in relation to the effort expended, affective development cannot be purchased by keeping all children at the same academic level. Pointing instruction at a level where 75 percent of the children achieve and tutoring the few who are behind, whether by other children aides, parents, teachers, or clinicians, will not make all children the same. Some graduate students actually believe they can teach every child a certain list of vocabulary words and certain skills and thus build a common base for instruction. Some educators think they can prepare teachers by using a list of proficiencies which will turn out people of like competence for any position in the elementary school. Such a concept does not utilize the unique strength every student has, or recognize that the strength of the society (and the species) is in the diverse capabilities and creative powers of individuals. If the teacher can value each child for himself or herself, a group cohesion evolves in a class which supports differences and enables children to reinforce each other. Such a working relationship does not come easily, but constructive social learning comes most easily during the latency period.

Continuity of Development

The separation of development and learning into segments unfortunately weakens the concept of continuous development. The accomplishments and the potential of children generally do change during the different periods of childhood. Too little is known of the different forms that nurturance might take at different ages to help individual children achieve their potential. Nevertheless, certain consistencies show up in research which, if applied with a mix of concern, sensitivity, and judgment, have implications for adults.

Knowing the implications of physical and motor development in school children is a necessity for planning physical activity for both boys and girls. The focus should be on skill development for all, rather than on the selection of a few talented children for sports programs (Corbin, 1973).

By knowing different views about learning in children, teachers can select different teaching strategies, or methods, for individual learners. Such decisions are based on the child's store of associative information, the child's cognitive style, and the child's intellectual development. Associations formed in a climate of pleasure are more readily available for concept formation than associations formed in a climate of fear or punishment.

The implication of the latency period is that school studies and peer relations must be within the child's ability to cope with successfully, but challenging enough to call forth effort. Parental interaction, such as the reward and punishment techniques used, are important in establishing the achievement motivation which each child needs, not only to do school work successfully but to be able to feel satisfaction from academic growth. The life-style and value systems of parents can be exerted in the early years by direct interaction and through direct communication with the child. Beyond age 10, any parental influence when the child is among peers comes primarily from past modeling and the child's continuing respect. Parents and teachers can do much to help their older children cope with peer pressures by developing their independence at an early age. This means that the parent relinquishes decisions to the child as early as the child has the judgment and experience to be responsible for the decision he or she makes.

By helping children deal constructively with their tendencies to be competitive, a helping relationship can be established at this age. Praise that is specific to a child's accomplishment not only enhances his or her self-esteem but effects more positive relations with other children. If each pupil in a class is to survive with positive self-conceptions, teachers must accept each pupil and have a genuine appreciation of each person's unique characteristics.

SUMMARY

Children of the primary school years, from about 6 to 8 years old, show a steady growth rate which is slower than in preschool years or in adolescence. The sexes are more similar in build, strength, and performance than at any other period in life. Somatic (body) types emerge which reflect both hereditary patterns and habits of nutrition and activity. Gross motor performance improves gradually in basic movements such as walking, running, and jumping. These patterns can be combined, with instruction, into more elaborate skills such as rope skipping, broad jumping, and organized game play. Sex differences begin to become significant at about 11 years old when girls level off or even deteriorate in strength and speed of motor performance. Specialists believe that this deterioration is cultural and environmental rather than genetically determined. Boys use physical movement patterns in self-directed ways to enhance their self-images and to join with peers in group games.

The thinking processes of primary school children overlap the levels of thinking in older children and adults. The association-behaviorist school of psychology has described and demonstrated that learner responses can be conditioned to particular stimuli. They have focused on additive or sequential learning in highly controlled environments. The cognitive-developmentalist school, represented by Piaget and others, has demonstrated that the human intellect functions at different levels, according to the age of the person and the nature of past learning. Conceptual thought is derived by relating present and stored experience. Primary-age children are typically at a transition stage between what Piaget called intuitive representations and concrete operational thought; the latter is based on conceptualized relations, or structures.

The socialization of children at this age centers around their need to achieve, their need to produce things, and their need to compare favorably with other children in the acquisition of skills. Psychosocial theory describes this as a period of latency that follows the stage of conflicts involving sexuality of the younger child and precedes the emotional upheavals of adolescence. The latency child is vulnerable to a sense of inferiority unless self-esteem can be attained through industry and productivity. This is a critical period for developing achievement motivation in the child.

During the elementary school years, the typical child shifts identity from parent to teacher to peer group. This means that gradually the adult models become less influential on the behavior of children and peer leaders become more influential. However, children carry the values of their families into peer-group settings. The natural behavior in peer groups is to establish status, ownership, and leadership.

Affective development, including motivation, attitudes, and drives, begins with the feelings that are associated with an experience. The interaction of cognitive and affective development is seen in the self-concept that evolves. Social and/or cognitive learning in early childhood can enhance the child's achievement motivation if the child's attempts at independence and productivity are successful.

three
EXPERIENCE AND LEARNING

This section places the early development of the human young in a larger context—the life-span of the individual. The purpose of these discussions is to summarize four areas of development which, out of necessity, have been fragmented in the age-stage presentations of Part Two. Seeing the scope and sequence of the ontogeny of a person gives perspective and significance to the early years. Four topics which seem to be critical in understanding the environmental needs of infants and children have been included: cognitive development, acquisition of language, children's play, and affective development.

These categories are interdependent. Babbling is both a precursor to speech and a form of play. Speech is a cognitive skill with which a child can express both affection and information. The scholar needs to divide experience into categories in order to grasp the relationship of one aspect of life to the whole span.

Cognitive learning is always linked by neural connections to the affects which are experienced at the same time. Similarly, affective experience never occurs without leaving its trace in the storage system of the brain. Chapters 8 and 11 are interdependent because they evolve from a single model of learning motivation which graphically represents the interaction. The topics of language (Chapter 9) and play (Chapter 10) are intended to stand alone; hence they may be read in any sequence. Sandwiched between the discussions of cognitive and affective development, they show clearly the cross-linkages of learning and motivation.

8
Cognitive Development

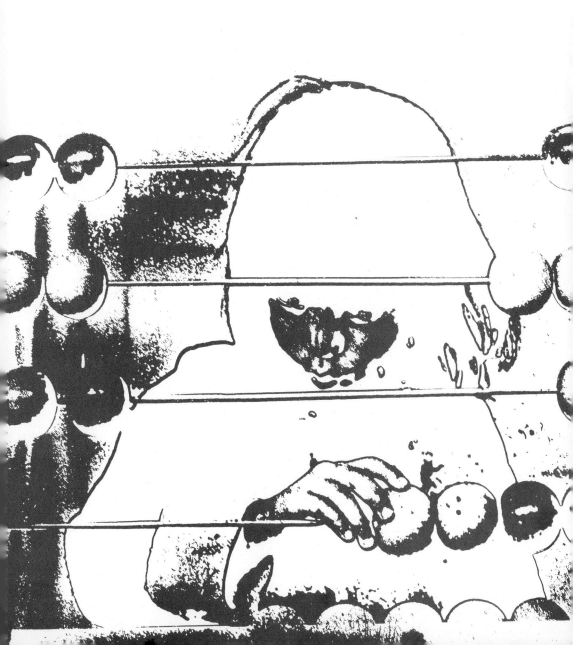

8 Cognitive Development

Cognition is the process of knowing. What is meant by "knowing" is a philosophical question; hence it is both personal and complex. In early childhood education there is general agreement that cognitive development is different from social, emotional, or motor development. Cognitive development focuses on the intellectual aspects of growth. This distinction is easy to grasp in the context of learning to read, for example, until one becomes curious about how the abilities evolved that make learning to read possible. Reading assumes the previous acquisition of a language that is first understood and then spoken. The processes of following print with the eyes and converting the printed code into meanings requires sensory motor actions that were begun in the neonatal period. The distinctions between cognitive, affective, and sensory motor functioning become obscure when one studies growth during the early life of the child.

Cognitive development includes the acquisition of mental images, the use of propositional language, concept formation (spatial and verbal), problem solving, and inventing means to meet one's own goals. Each of these functions is accomplished at a sensorimotor or a perceptual level before the child can speak well enough to explain a thought process. Early learning may be taken for granted in a stable society where nurturing patterns are passed from one generation to the next for rearing the children with the skills they will need as adults. When the cognitive world of the young child is consistent with the learning requirements of the school, the different theories about how children learn are not tested in the ecological sense (Chapter 7).

Different theories about cognitive development continue to be supported because the researchers produce their own sources of evidence. Those who believe that if the preschool teaches social and personal adjustment school success will certainly follow, find support for their view in clinical evidence among older students that academic and personal problems are related. Those who believe that direct instruction in vocabulary will increase the intelligence of children and improve their achievement in school find their support in IQ changes as a result of vocabulary training which remain constant for at least a few years (Thorndike, 1975). The theory of cognitive development proposed by Piaget is different from either the socialization or the direct-instruction approaches. Developmental psychologists who accept Piaget's view believe that the young child learns from his or her own actions on things. Intellectual growth results from the child's innate need to exercise his or her biological systems. By providing a stimulating environment, adults give children the cognitive nutrients that will nurture their own intelligence, according to a specifically human sequence, from sensorimotor actions to logical thought processes. The distinctions between these three views are sufficiently complex that many child-care specialists have yielded to the temptation to provide physical care and to leave the learning content of their programs to chance. Some adopt someone else's program without evaluating the programmer's assumptions about how children learn.

Theories about learning are put to the test whenever a society changes the expectations of its children from the traditional life-style of their home. For anyone who expects to intervene in the poverty cycle or the child-abuse cycle, or to bring literacy to a minority group; an understanding of cognitive development is necessary. Significant improvement in school achievement, or other social problems, must begin early. Some experts believe that child abuse begins in toddlerhood, or even infancy, with the imprinting of abusive behavior toward the children themselves. Knowing the different ways children learn increases the alternatives for teachers and for parents so that cognitive experiences may be provided at optimum stages in development.

DIFFERENT VIEWS ABOUT CHILD LEARNING

For more than fifty years child psychologists have been divided between those who proposed a developmental explanation of learning and those who proposed a behaviorist, or associative-learning, explanation. The developmentalists have been further divided in their focus on cognitive versus affective priorities in the early growth of the child. Recently, behaviorist psychologists have offered divergent opinions in accounting for complex behaviors, such as social modeling and language acquisition, that animal research did not explain to their satisfaction (White & Siegel, 1976). Primarily they elaborated the strict S-R psychology of Skinner to include the effect of the child's own mediation processes on the response. The significance of these differences will become more clear when their application in child learning programs is considered (Part Four). Most current theories of child learning can be explored reasonably well if the following approaches are understood: social-psychoanalytical, cognitive-developmental, behaviorist-associative, and neurobiological.

Social-Psychoanalytical Theory

The Freudian tradition is a developmental theory in that a distinctly human sequence of emotional growth is assumed. Sigmund Freud's daughter, Anna, proposed the kinds of childhood experience that would prevent emotional disturbance and develop a healthy, adjusted person (A. Freud, 1951). Erik Erikson (1963) extended the ego-development theory of Freud to span the life-cycle of human beings. He assumed that the emotional crises of infancy and early childhood were a normal part of growing up; but they had to be resolved in sequence before the next stage in personal maturity could be reached.

The Erikson Institute at the University of Chicago, directed by Lilli Peller, has been a center for early childhood education programs modeled on psychoanalytic theory. Rene Spitz (1972) is another researcher who suggests a psychoanalytic approach to education and to the understanding of emotional disturbances in children. The pyschoanalytical approach has had an impact on theories involving such aspects of affective development as socialization, aggression, and attachment (Chapter II).

Cognitive-Developmental Theory

Developmental psychologists who focus on cognitive development generally hold that learning differs in kind from simple to complex, that children themselves have a role in the cognitive process, and that cognition evolves in stages. Members of this group tend to be humanists who are interested in the process by which the child organizes bits and pieces of experience into concepts and generalizations. They believe that structuring of meanings, or discovery learning, differs in quality from the additive learning described in stimulus-response theory.

Jean Piaget must be considered the mastermind of cognitive-developmental psychology and the most thorough of the researchers who have tried to describe the conceptualization process. Early in his career as a biologist he set out to describe the species Homo sapiens. Because of the cognitive nature of his subjects, he decided to observe the origins of intelligence in young children. He went to work with Simon, in Paris, on what he anticipated to be a task of two years duration. Fifty years later he was still researching cognitive development and still producing a book or two each year to explain his observations. The basic outline of Piaget's cognitive psychology is presented in the third section of this chapter.

American psychologists of the cognitive school include Jerome Bruner, whose sequence of acquisition, transposition, and evaluation was used to explain the intellectual development of children 5 to 8 years old (Chapter 7). Another is the late David Russell (1956), who proposed criteria for children's thinking which were both humanist and sequential. The studies of Jerome Kagan (1969) assumed specifically human cognition and its evolution from infancy to childhood (Chapter 4).

Behaviorist-Associative Theory

Behaviorist psychologists generally limit their study to behaviors that can be observed directly. They generally believe that changes in behavior (learning) can be controlled by those who know how to manage the environment. Skinner (1935) proposed a sequence for *shaping* behavior by a planned schedule of rewards for actions that became increasingly approximate to the desired behavior. This sequence called for (1) defining the desired behavior to be achieved; (2) setting up an environment in which the behavior, or approximations of the behavior, were likely to occur; and (3) shaping the behavior by reinforcing (with immediate rewards) for appropriate, or increasingly approximate, responses until the desired behavior pattern had been established. Skinner taught pigeons such unlikely behaviors as rolling ping-pong balls, or hopping on one foot according to planned schedules of reinforcement. To assure the pigeons' motivation to work for pellets, they were reduced to 80 percent of their normal weight before a training program was begun. Food reinforcers were given sparingly, so that the trainees would continue to work hard to learn the behaviors that brought pellets down the feeding chute. Dangerous zoo animals, such as Himalayan bears, have been taught by this behavior-modification strategy. By using remote control to give food rewards, bears have been taught to swing, to shoot baskets, to retrieve objects from water, and to dance in rhythm.

When Skinner applied his conditioning theory to school learning tasks, it was necessary to find reinforcers that did not impose extreme hunger on the children. Among other experiments, the teaching machine invented by Pressey was used to engage the child in learning tasks. The child's efforts and successes were reinforced, according to Skinner, by feedback from the machine at each response. By having more than one choice and knowing whether the answer was right or wrong, it was possible for the child to associate a correct response and the reinforcement. The learning that was needed to answer the hard questions was programmed in small sequential steps along the way.

This early work set the pattern for most programmed instruction, whether by simple teaching machine, workbooks, or computer. The idea that behavior can be shaped by reinforcement was the theory, although the procedures were adapted to children. The steps can be summarized: (1) separate the task, or content to be learned, into small steps or increments; (2) model the task or tell the child specifically what is to be learned; (3) arrange a response system or setting that assures a high frequency of success, and (4) reinforce the correct, or approximated, response with immediate feedback.

One positive result of programmed instruction has been that the adults, both programmers and teachers, are expected to be responsible for the learner's success. The assumptions in conditioning theory are that appropriate design of the steps or frames in the learning sequence and appropriate use of reinforcers will result in learning. This conditioning approach to learning has been called the *operant-behavior* approach. The conditioning approach to teaching has been called *behavior modification* or *behavior management*.

Skinner's theory was implemented by Behavioral Research Laboratories in the Sullivan-Buchanan programs for beginning reading, language, and spelling. The Becker-Englemann DISTAR programs used teacher feedback, social reinforcement, and a token system of rewards to teach the basic skills of communication and mathematics. Behavior shaping was used by Tom Bellemy to teach mentally retarded adults how to assemble electronic parts, even though some individuals had not learned speech (Stahlberg, 1977). The central point in behavior modification theory is that learning is additive and that it can be managed by controlling the environmental stimuli and the reward systems. The techniques have been widely applied in special education for handicapped persons, and for disadvantaged children when some form of intervention was needed (Chapter 14).

Neurobiological Theory

Neurobiological explanations of learning have become increasingly important as the anatomy of brain pathways has become known and the technology has become available for locating and measuring brain activity during different kinds of sensory experience. Behaviorist theory focuses on the management of the environment to assure learning. Developmental psychologists tend to focus on innate structures of human young and the role of maturation in learning. Recently some psychologists of both schools have turned to the *interaction* of the biological child and the critical aspects of environment to understand how learning takes place. The aim of some scholars who study neurology is to support learning theory with physical evidence. Those who try to apply psychology by knowing how the brain functions hope to use the teaching environment to help children develop a repertoire of complex thinking skills.

Many of the important questions about cognitive development have to do with the child's inner activity as well as the behavior an outsider can see. If one accepts Piaget's notion of an inner structure, or schema, as the necessary counterpart, the teacher in each of us must consider how the structures are formed in the beginning (Piaget, 1970). What is the nature of the interaction between organism and environment? What aspects of the environment is the child seeking out? What is the child taking in (assimilating)? One important question that neurologists can help to answer is the length and nature of the assimilative experience *before* an adaptation (learning) is seen by others.

Technology has made it possible to trace a neural pathway of light, sound, or touch stimuli and to time the process in milliseconds from the stimulus to its reception at the appropriate cortical area within the brain. It takes a longer time for a child to mediate a word signal flashed on a screen than to mediate an auditory signal of a word spoken, partly because the printed word must be processed through auditory interpretive areas of the cortical storage system. The time it takes to mediate can be measured accurately by taking EEG readings at the different areas on the cortex where words are relayed. Attention can be recorded by measuring saliva flow, heart rate, and GSR (galvanic skin response), but these readings have different meanings for infants and 5-year-olds in terms of memory storage and long-term memory. Primate subjects, which have been studied because electrodes can be implanted and their messages monitored at a distance, show brain activity before an action, thus confirming intent. Actions, whether sensorimotor or internalized thought, are initiated in the frontal parts of the brain hemispheres. Observations of Pribram's monkeys established intent when brain activity demonstrated in advance which paw would move to pull a lever (Pribram, 1971). Luria (1973) has been able to show that different layers of the cortex are responsible for sensory reception and immediate perception than those responsible for the thinking processes that require integration and conceptual interpretation. How the human brain processes the signs and symbols of language is deferred to Chapter 9; this chapter incorporates the ideas of Pribram and Luria, both of whom were specialists in learning and neuropsychology. Piaget was extremely interested in the neurology of cognitive development at one point in his career. Unfortunately this came at a time when the research had much less to offer a psychologist than at this writing.

LEARNING THEORIES IN PERSPECTIVE

The psychology of interaction implies that nature and nurture have a dynamic influence on each other. The interaction of cognitive structures and stimulation from the environment is essential in promoting growth. Piaget grasped the significance of interaction between the child and the world reality, which he described as a dynamic process of *assimilation* and *accommodation* (Piaget, 1976). He conceived all adaptation, including cognitive development, as the invariant effect of the interaction of a particular species member (organism) in a particular environment.

The optimum development of intelligence may depend on the timing and the quality of the nature-nurture interaction. Providing the optimum environment at different ages of childhood has been the common goal of early education. Nurturance would be simplified if children were all alike. Fortunately for the individuals themselves and for society each child is unique as a person and as a learner.

Research on children's cognitive development may, in time, succeed in abstracting and generalizing the characteristics of a growth-producing interaction, but more sophisticated and humane approaches will be needed than those which continue to argue the old themes of inheritance versus environment in cognitive development (Walberg & Marjoribanks, 1976). This section proposes a model in which intelligence is seen as acquired through the interaction of cognitive and affective experience.

Research on children's learning nearly always begins with theoretical assumptions about how learning takes place. The investigators ask only those questions that are stimulated by their particular theory. Sometimes the data lead to important discoveries, but the conclusions rarely go beyond the questions that were asked in the hypothesis. Interaction research may be needed to place the different theories in relationship, rather than in opposition, to each other. Those who focus on the environment, as most S-R (stimulus-response) behaviorists do, explain the nurture side of the interaction, while those who focus on the complex development of human intelligence seem to offer a more complete description of the nature of cognition as we experience it in ourselves. The learning-motivation model (Figure 8-1) attempts to place different learning theories in relationship to one another. At level 1 sensorimotor experiences (stimuli) are associated with affects of pleasure or punishment which occur at the same time and are reinforcing. At level 2 conceptualizations are structured by the learner from bits and pieces of stored and present experience. At level 3 the learner acts by intention and for his or her own purposes.

For the student who is beginning the study of child development and trying to make sense of the different views experts have about the development of intelligence, the task often seems confusing and the differences may seem trivial. Unfortunately, the recent literature on early childhood education in America has presented S-R behaviorist psychology as the learning-theory approach (White,

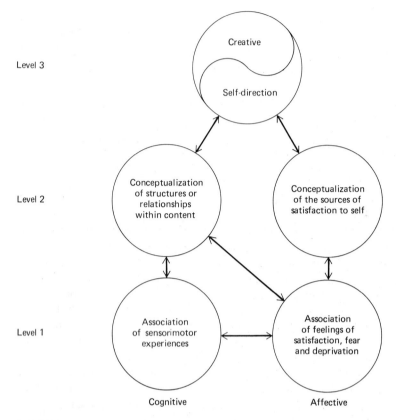

Level 3

Level 2

Level 1

Creative

Self-direction

Conceptualization of structures or relationships within content

Conceptualization of the sources of satisfaction to self

Association of sensorimotor experiences

Association of feelings of satisfaction, fear and deprivation

Cognitive   Affective

FIGURE 8-1 Learning-motivation model. The interaction between the cognitive and the affective sequences in learning are shown as a hierarchy of development. Cognitive associations (level 1) are basic to later conceptualizations, or structures of knowledge (level 2). Affective associations are basic to concepts of self. Level 3 functioning represents the fusion of conceptualized personal goals and conceptualized reality.

1970). It should be noted that learning theory was a major part of the lifework of cognitive psychologists such as Piaget and Guilford, of neuropsychologists such as Pribram and Luria, and of structural psychologists in the gestalt tradition.

The first level of the model shown in Figure 8-1, association learning, explains the interaction between the cognitive and affective dimensions of human experience. This S-R relationship is especially important in the early years when the child has minimal control over his or her own life. Care-givers are largely responsible for stimuli available to the young child. They also provide many of the affective cues the child experiences through his or her own emotional responses to people and objects.

The interaction of associative-learning and cognitive-conceptual theories can be seen at a higher level of cognitive development, in which results from the child's own conceptualizations of bits of sensory experience are organized. The research base for this model has been drawn from studies of children's learning and on the physical evidence from neurology (Wilson, Robeck, & Michael, 1974).

Interaction of Cognitive and Affective Associations

Edward L. Thorndike (1913) referred to learning as an *association process*. His introduction of the law of effect in learning encouraged the use of rewards in school and stimulated research on the S-R bond, or what he called *connectionism*, in psychology.

WATSON'S CONDITIONING OF INFANTS

John B. Watson planned to build a psychology of human beings by applying the classical conditioning techniques of Pavlov and Hull to human infants. In a classic experiment, the now famous infant, Albert, was conditioned to withdraw and cry out when a white, furry animal was presented (Watson & Rayner, 1920). The procedure was to place a white rat (stimulus) in front of Albert and when he reached for the animal a loud noise was struck behind. After a few trials, the infant cried out (response) whenever the animal was presented, even after the noise had been discontinued. The fear response generalized to other white, furry animals; Albert cried and drew back from a white rabbit even though he had never seen one before. His fear of loud noises was conditioned to a white rabbit by *association*. In the same way that Pavlov conditioned a dog to salivate at the sound of a bell, Watson conditioned the infant to a fear response with a new stimulus.

POSTIVE REINFORCEMENT

B. F. Skinner emphasized the use of a reward, or pleasure effect, to reinforce a behavior. This technique of *operant conditioning* shapes a new response to a familiar stimulus by rewarding behavior selectively. The connection between an action and a favorable result to the organism is the basis for the S-R theory of learning (Figure 8-2).

The unique contribution of operant-conditioning theory is the association of pleasure affects as the effector of learning or modified behavior. This pleasure association, and the resulting tendency of the learner to continue the pleasure effect, is the basis of motivation. Thorndike's connectionism and Skinner's operant-conditioning procedures shared both the S-R bond theory and the pleasure principle.

Neurophysiologists analyze the brain structures involved in motivation (Hilgard & Bower, 1975). Reward and punishment centers in the hypothalamus interconnect with the sensory messages that flow into the ascending reticular formation of the brainstem. These centers produce sensations of pleasure or pain when stimulated by drugs or electrodes. Certain locations stimulate the primitive drives of sex,

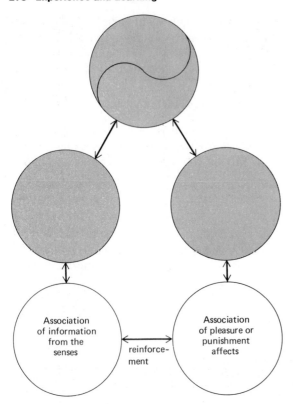

FIGURE 8-2 Interaction of cognitive and affective associations. Reinforcement occurs when sensory information and the emotional elements of the experience that occur at the same time are interconnected through the neural systems.

thirst, and hunger. Although behavior-modification theory tends to ignore the inner event, the use of candy to reinforce children's behavior makes use of the hunger drive.

The distinction between classical conditioning and operant conditioning is unimportant in neurological theory, which assumes that the individual's own motivation system dictates the value of a reward. Reinforcement occurs within. The stimulation of sensory systems through action of the systems may be the only reward an organism needs for some kinds of learning.

NEOBEHAVIORIST PSYCHOLOGY

When contemporary behaviorists turned from the study of animal learning to research with children, they encountered complexities which required them to refine S-R explanations for learning. Bijou and Baer (1961) expressed the complexity of the child learner as "a cluster of interrelated responses interacting with stimulus" (p. 14). Bandura (1971) noted that children model a behavior they have seen much earlier without having practiced it in the meantime or having been socially reinforced. He explained this as a generalized representation the child carried.

Kendler and Kendler (1962) reported that children change in the way they solve a problem of nonverbal discrimination between the ages of 4 and 6. Children were first rewarded for discriminating a larger shape, without regard to its shading, and then were rewarded for choosing a gray shape, whether large or small. Younger children made this simple shift easily, in a manner similar to the Kendlers' laboratory rats. When a reversal shift was made, and size and shading discriminations were changed, older children made a reversal shift more like college subjects who could deal with two attributes simultaneously. The finding was seen by the Kendlers as an age-related change in a mediation mode for solving a reversal-shift problem.

Kendler and Kendler (1967) also analyzed the mediation process of children 8 to 12 years old in making inferences. Their subjects increased this thinking ability markedly when given a verbal label for the inference. They concluded that verbal mediation has an important function in "the moving forward of the behavior sequence" (p. 189). Although the Kendlers insist that "representational responses" are not necessarily "linguistic labels," their theory of mediation has become a way for S-R psychologists to deal with language acquisition and concept formation. Piaget (1970) has continued to insist that his conception of the development of cognitive structures and the age-related appearance of thinking operations is different from the S-R linking, or additive, theory of Skinnerian psychology.

Interaction of Associative Learning and Conceptualization

Stimulus-response analysis in child psychology has been elaborated by conceptions which are less simplistic and mechanistic (White & Siegel, 1976). According to these new inquiries, child learners are seen as active construct builders of their own reality. This construction is based on the integration of perception systems with adaptation. The view that the child is locked on a cognitive pathway and is located somewhere between the laboratory rat and the college student in terms of learning response is no longer the central thrust of research, or the central core of the literature on cognitive development. Instead the child is seen as functioning at different cognitive levels simultaneously. Different neural systems are involved simultaneously at each stage of development. The cultural milieu, the evolutionary history, and the biological priorities of the developmental age are all seen as significant parts of the complex.

The structures of the central nervous system reflect the complex organization of the different levels of cognitive behavior. The interaction of sensory input is apparent at the receiving centers in the ascending reticular formation, where the child's selection of certain stimuli from many possible sensory messages can be observed when the child attends to something. The pathways to the sites where

Cognitive development through problem solving. (Suzanne Szasz/Photo Researchers Inc.)

stimuli attended to are stored are well known, as are the integration areas between sight and sound, touch and balance, or sight and somatic systems. Organized thought is built on these sensory systems, which activate the organism's own systems for dealing with representations and abstractions. Much of young children's intellectual functioning is associative, in the behaviorist tradition.

The process of conceptualization goes beyond associative learning in the following ways: (1) the child's control over his or her own learning, (2) the intrinsic quality of the learning experience, and (3) the organization of basic associations into relationships. Cognitive relationships are seen in the structure of language, the digital system of metrics, and the systematic distances within a musical scale. The child learns these inherent relationships over time or suddenly, but the knowledge is consistent with the reality of a physical or a cultural world. Such cognitive structures require a knowledge of relations, rather than the mere acquisition of the bits and pieces, although relevant associative elements are necessary for them to structure knowledge.

To summarize, the process of conceptualization is the discovery of relationships, the grasping of structural meanings, or the understanding of cause and effect. The *ah-ha* experience of gestalt psychology, the insight described by Bruner, and the classification operations of Piaget are all examples of learning behaviors that differ in kind from chains of associations, however complex. Central to the idea of conceptualization is that the learner must have experienced through association learning the common elements to be abstracted and conceptualized.

The learning-motivation model represents in graphic format the interaction of associations and conceptualizations (Figure 8-3). At the association level, each sensory system takes in information, which is actively selected by the child from

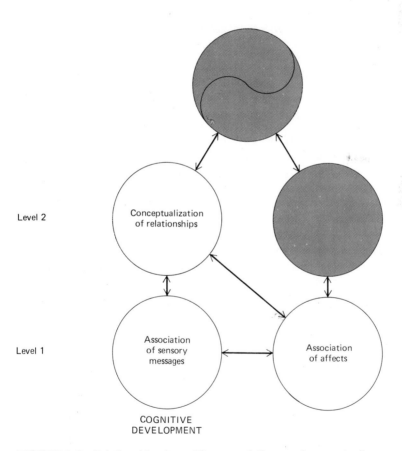

FIGURE 8-3 Relationship of cognitive associations and conceptualization. The child takes in bits and pieces of information which, if reinforced in some way, become part of the memory bank of basic associations that are retrievable at a later time. At level 2 the child conceptualizes, or organizes the associative bits into larger meanings, or structures.

many possible stimuli in the environment, as well as by the action of priorities in the biological mechanisms. Selection by the learner is based in part on the consequence of past actions on things. It would be a mistake to deny that primitive forms of satisfaction are unimportant in early childhood or to underemphasize the child's dependence on other persons for reinforcement.

In the psychoanalytic tradition a major focus is the young child's dependence on significant others for physical and psychological satisfactions. The neonate has no sense of self, either in the Piagetian or the psychoanalytic sense of knowing. The social environment that envelops an infant is an essential part of the reward system by which the associations are formed that are basic to later conceptual organization. The concept of self as distinct from the surround is a cognitive accomplishment that precedes the child's ability to act on objects with intention.

The distinction between cognitive functioning at the associative and the conceptual levels has been identified by psychologists who consider themselves as cognitive and developmental. Although their terminology differs, there are elements in common in the way conceptualization is seen by Bruner, Piaget, and Luria. The approach of Kagan in the infancy studies has been cited (Chapter 4). The physical development of children, when seen as interrelated with patterns of cognitive development, has implications for learning theory (Chapter 7).

PIAGET'S REPRESENTATIONAL AND OPERATIONAL THOUGHT

Representation is "the capacity to represent something with something else," according to Piaget in a recent book, *The Child and Reality* (1976, p. 16). *Representation* is a symbolic function which includes speech, play, gestures, and mental pictures or images. Representation is a set of symbolizers which appears at ages 2 to 5 years. These symbolizers make thought possible. To Piaget the use of symbolizers is evidence of a "system of internalized action" he defines as thought (p. 17).

This sytem of interiorized representations is a prerequisite for the appearance of the particular cognitive actions Piaget calls *operations*. Operational thought is *concrete* in children 5 ½ to 11 years old because the thinking operation requires the presence of concrete objects which may be manipulated mentally or manually.

An example of concrete operations Piaget often used was the classification interview with children. *Classification* was defined as the "inclusion of a subcategory in a category, that is, the understanding that a part is smaller than the whole" (1976, p. 23). He gave the child a dozen flowers, six primroses and six of a different mix. When asked, "Are all the primroses flowers?" the child of 5 or 6 years will say, "Of course," and when asked, "Are all the flowers primroses," the child will say, "Of course not." But if asked, "Are there more primroses on the table or more flowers?" the child will look and reply that there are more primroses or else that they are even because there are six and six. Most older children will readily answer, "There are more flowers because primroses are flowers, too." Children can classify by Piaget's definition only when they have conceptualized the relationship of the subcategory to the category. This understanding is different from an item-by-item association with a class. The classification operation extends to other situations in which there is an inherent relation within a category.

Piaget's distinction between representational thought and operational thought has been demonstrated by his research teams in many countries and cultures. That these cognitive functions differ in kind is clear. Some of the learning at a representational level is explained by recent extensions of behaviorist theory. The operational thought processes described by Piaget are more easily understood as a development of specifically human structures. Conceptualization accounts for sensorimotor changes when problem solving appears in the second year. Similarly logical operations require conceptualization of more abstract content.

LURIA'S GRAPHIC RECALL VERSUS CONCEPT FORMATION

The influence of Pavlov on child psychology in the Soviet Union was very different from the Watson-Skinner tradition in the United States. Vygotsky, and later his student, Luria, accepted an environmental focus as the basis for behavior control. In a society that denied the superiority of royalty over peasants and workers, the effort to intervene in cognitive functioning began shortly after their revolution and was initially focused on adults. The strong environmental focus was retained, but a particularly human theme dominated the early research with illiterate adults and later research with children. Soviet researchers felt that the development of mental processes is largely a function of language, and word meanings provide the child with a cognitive history of the family and community. Social changes, such as the schooling provided illiterate peasants when they become community leaders, were accompanied by fundamental changes in thought processes. From 1920 the leading Soviet psychologists assumed that human beings are not restricted to S-R mechanisms but are able to mediate incoming stimulation and to influence their own behavior. This early acceptance of brain mediation, and of language as organizer of thought, meant that the Soviet research on cognitive development is unique in the scientific world.

Luria summarized his own and Vygotsky's learning theory in his book *Cognitive Development: Its Cultural and Social Foundations* (1976). He traced the relationship of tools and productions to peasant language and the relationship of language to mental activity. "In his development, the child's first exposure to a linguistic system ... determine the forms of his mental activity" (p. 9). The sociohistorical theme is complex, but a simple example explains the basis for later abstraction in early speech. "Once a child calls something a 'watch' (*chasy*) he immediately incorporates it into a system of things related to 'time' (*chas*)."

Vygotsky's theory was that concept formation is rooted in the use of words. The three periods of cognitive development were related (interestingly) to the language acquisition of late preschool years, elementary years, and adolescence. During the early stages of cognitive development the child uses words to name objects in isolation, but words are not an organizing principle or a basis for grouping objects.

The second period can be called the beginning of classification. The child compares or groups objects by their graphic impressions (color, form, and size) or by their use. The objects may individually relate to a situation (chair, tablecloth, milk pitcher). The psychological processes involved in classifying at this stage were thought to be graphic recall of various interrelations, and "not based on a word that would allow one to single out a common attribute and denote a category" (p. 51).

The next stage of cognitive development, that of *concept formation*, is distinctly different. Luria attributed this difference to schooling. By adolescence, or the late elementary grades, the child isolates the distinct attributes of objects as the basis for categorization and develops a hierarchy for categories which express "degrees of community." Luria's example is rose–flower—plant–organic world. The relationship is categorical and logical, and represents "the shared experience of society conveyed through its linguistic system" (p. 52). This conceptual thinking is distinct from the individual's practical experience of relating objects to objects and words to objects. Practical operations give meaning to the "theoretical operations a child learns in school" (p. 53). To Luria, words become the principal tool for abstraction and generalization.

Luria's evidence for language as the media of conceptualization was based in part on his own research on the changes in cognitive functioning of isolated peasants when schooling was provided them, along with responsibility for discussing social change in the community. His interviews were conducted around a campfire or a tea table. The problems centered on the use of familiar objects and situations to test concept formation and thinking operations such as deduction, inference, and problem solving.

Luria defined *concept* as a verbal and logical operation in which a series of subordinate ideas are used to arrive at a general conclusion. In an impressive series of studies the concept formation of three groups was compared: (1) illiterate groups from remote villages (both men and women), (2) collective-farm activists (members of the same village who had attended night classes and were barely literate), and (3) young people from the same villages with one or two years schooling (primarily teacher trainees). Luria found that 80 percent of the peasants used a graphic, rather than a categorical, method of grouping (Table 8-1). An example of a grouping item was a picture of a hammer, a saw, a log, and a hatchet. The subjects were asked a series of questions about which things could be grouped together and why, or which item did not belong and why. Illiterate peasants tended to group two items that could be used together. Even when they agreed that three of the objects were "tools," they did not transfer the concept of category to exclude the log. Peasants could name other tools and say they "work together." But some would insist, "You cannot get along without the log to saw and to split."

On the same kinds of items the village persons with schooling would readily say that the log did not belong because the others were all tools and a log is not a tool. Many items using categories and subcategories were presented with similar results. Thinking operations such as inference and problem solving were related in these studies to the degree of abstraction in the vocabulary available to the

Table 8-1
COGNITIVE GROUPINGS AND CLASSIFICATIONS USED BY SCHOOLED AND UNSCHOOLED ADULTS

Group	Number of subjects	Graphic method of grouping	Graphic and categorical methods of grouping	Categorical classification
Illiterate peasants from remote villages	26	21(80%)	4(16%)	1(4%)
Collective-farm activities (barely literate)	10	0	3(30%)	7(70%)
Young people with one to two years' schooling	12	0	0	12(100%)

Source: A. R. Luria, *Cognitive Development: Its Cultural and Social Foundations.* Cambridge, Mass.: Harvard University Press, p. 78. Copyright © 1976 by the Fellows and President of Harvard College.

subject, even though the objects and the situations were equally familiar to educated and illiterate groups.

Lacking the formal education that would have allowed for systematic intellectual development, these people regarded the logical procedures of categorization as irrelevant, of no practical value . . . .The facts show convincingly that the structure of cognitive activity does not remain static during different stages of historical development and that the most important forms of cognitive processes—perception, generalization, deduction, reasoning, imagination, and analysis of one's own inner life—vary as the conditions of social life change and the rudiments of knowledge are mastered. (Luria, 1976, p. 98)

Although the classification tasks were similar to those used by Piaget, Luria's explanation of how cognition develops was historical, cultural, and educational rather than biological. Luria demonstrated that marked social change resulted in change in the cognitive processes of the people involved. The Soviet studies did not consider possible intellectual differences in favor of individuals who became activists or who were selected for schooling. Nevertheless, his observations have implications for educational intervention in childhood and beyond.

CONCEPTUALIZATION AS A PROCESS

The cognitive process a child uses to conceptualize is of a different order than S-R learning. The child's acquisition of language provides many examples of the distinction between the early use of word symbols as associative labels and later use of the same word for a class or category. When Benjy says "dada" at the appearance of his father, he shows that an association has been made of a particular name to a particular person. Lacking appropriate labels for other men he may call the pediatrician, the grocer, and the sitter all "daddy." He knows they are different persons, but he overgeneralizes, or overextends, an association. By the age of 3 or 4, he will meet a new friend at preschool and refer to the man who drops her off as "your daddy." He has conceptualized that daddy represents a relationship between father and child, or a class of male parents. This process of conceptualizing categories is similar to other cognitive functions that involve the mental manipulation of abstractions, as distinct from sensory responses to stimuli.

Brain functions have been studied to learn how associations are organized into the abstract operations required for higher levels of thinking, such as classification, synthesis, and logical reasoning. The neural pathways in the formation of associations have been charted (Luria, 1973). Lorente de No (1938) proposed a simplified model of how the neurons fire in sequence, according to pathways established through attention which leads to learning (Figure 8-4). Neurons fire in about 1/100 of a second, followed by a recovery period. Each pathway may be used several times during a second of attention. Such connections become well established in patterns of response. The junctions between neurons, called *synapses*, have been studied extensively so that the way they transmit messages from one neuron to another is quite well understood (Lester, 1977).

When a child hears the name of a familiar toy, many bits of stored experience from the different "association areas" on the cortex are likely to be activated (Figure 8-5). For example, the sound of the word *Teddy*, perhaps a squeak or a rattle, the visual images, the fuzzy texture of the coat, and the cool smoothness of

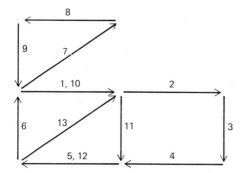

FIGURE 8-4 Model of the firing of neurons in attention. The numbers show the sequence and the arrows show the direction of flow during a neural impulse. Neurons require about 1/100 of a second to fire, followed by a recovery period. Each pathway may be used several times during half a second of attention. The junctions represent synapses where sense messages are transmitted along a pathway involving several neurons. (After Lorente de No, 1938.)

Source: John A. R. Wilson and Mildred C. Robeck, *Kindergarten Evaluation of Learning Potential,* page 34. Copyright 1963 by the authors. Santa Barbara, California, Sabox Publishing Company.

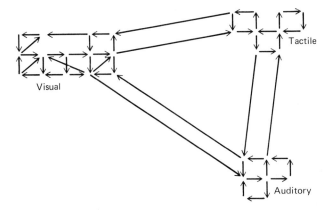

Tactile

Visual

Auditory

FIGURE 8-5 Model of chains of association. Clusters of associations are shown with long neurons linking the visual, tactile, and auditory areas.

Source: John A. R. Wilson and Mildred C. Robeck, *Kindergarten Evaluation of Learning Potential,* page 36. Copyright 1963 by the authors. Santa Barbara, California: Sabox Publishing Company.

the eyes are linked to each other and to the pleasure affects that were experienced at the same time. The conceptualization of *toy* as an abstract category is formed from these associative linkages. Once the symbol *toy* comes to mean the collection of things played with, the child will refer to a new plaything as toy and will be able to put it into the proper box without instruction. In conceptual thought, whether this comes about as a sudden grasp of some new relationship or gradually, the retrieval of many sensory associations is dropped from the mediation process (Figure 8-6). The energy level in the brain is much reduced in concept manipulation, compared with the initial bombardment of the sensory areas when concepts are being developed.

Creative Self-Direction

The use of conceptualizations in the service of one's own goals or purposes is *creative self-direction.* Creative thinking, or creative production in more visible forms, has elements of uniqueness at least to the creator, and elements of self-expression (Figure 8-7). Some older children will have developed a value system which will influence their choice of activities and help them evaluate their own productivity. Younger children need to be supported in their efforts to produce things in their own way in order to develop the freedom that self-expression requires. The activities in which children can become increasingly self-directed are their language, the games they invent, unusual uses for things, and all the things they produce with blocks, paint, clay, beads, paper, sand, mud, water, or more esoteric media. The learning-motivation model fuses the cognitive and affective dimensions of development in level 3 functioning (Chapter 11).

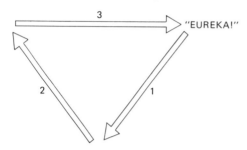

FIGURE 8-6 Model of conceptualization. Arrow 1 represents repeated associations connected to a favorite toy. Arrow 2 represents the associations developed from other objects called toys, including their collective location in a toy box. Arrow 3 represents the closure, or grasping of the concept that toy refers to any of the objects for play. Conceptualizations are economical of brain energy because they by-pass many of the original associations from which the abstraction was formed.

GUILFORD'S FACTORS OF INTELLECT

J. P. Guilford (1957) was one of the first researchers to use statistical methods to isolate the creative factors in intelligence. His earliest analyses, in which items from conventional tests were used, showed that individuals of similar overall ability differ significantly with respect to (1) the *operations* a thinker uses, (2) the *contents* or form of the material to be manipulated mentally, and (3) the *product* or outcomes of the operations (Figure 8-8). These three dimensions make up the sides of the cube which has come to be known as Guilford's structure of intellect.

According to the Guilford construct, the basic operations or processes of intellectual functioning are five: cognition, memory, divergent production, convergent production, and evaluation. Each of these processes has been factored out statistically and is defined in Table 8-2.

Cognition means comprehension, understanding, discovery, rediscovery, or awareness in the intellectual sense. Restatements of information do not necessarily indicate cognition. Children who verbalize readily may recall words or rules with little understanding of their use in productive thinking. Most teachers experience the difference when a child catches on and when information is recalled. They try to anticipate and provide for the kinds of understanding that will make later recall more likely. In Guilford's analyses, cognition and divergent thinking were highly correlated.

Memory involves the retention of knowledge in the form in which it was learned, together with the ability to select the particular information needed. The nature and extent of the learner's involvement in the initial learning is assumed to influence the process of remembering. A high portion of the child's time in school, and a high proportion of the items in intelligence tests, are given to retention and recall of information. In Guilford's correlations, memory and convergent thinking are related.

Divergent production is closely related in the Guilford model to creative thinking. This is the process in which the individual generates new ideas or materials with emphasis on variety or quantity of responses. Children high in this ability may be expected to show sensitivity to problems and also to have the ability to pose many possible solutions. In addition to fluency in thinking, they show flexibility; that is, they readily depart from conventional or habitual patterns to unique and untested patterns. In this operation the emphasis is on imaginative, spontaneous, and fluent self-expression.

It is interesting to note that during the early research only four processes were identified. Divergent and convergent production were combined in a category

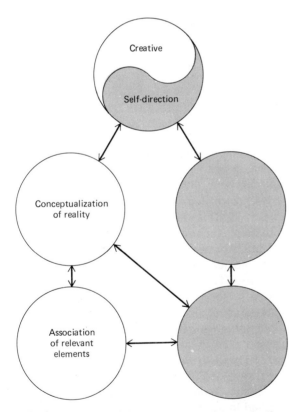

FIGURE 8-7 Cognitive levels in creative production. Conceptions of the physical and social world enable the innovator, the inventor, and the artist to communicate with other persons.

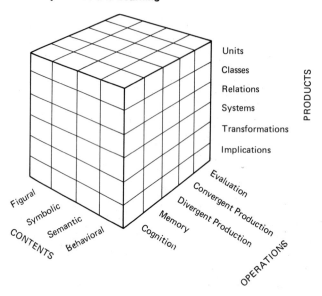

FIGURE 8-8 Guilford's structure of intellect.

Source: J. P. Guilford and P. R. Merrifield, "The Structure of Intellect Model: Its Uses and Implications," Monograph No. 24, Reports from the Psychological Laboratory, October 1961, University of Southern California. By permission of J. P. Guilford.

originally called productive thinking. As the number of items that would allow a subject to demonstrate productive thinking were increased, individuals were found to vary in convergent and divergent strengths. In some tests the scores derived from "one right answer" were negatively correlated with the scores from items that called for originality, fluency, and flexibility. This discovery led to a separation of the productive thinking category into divergent and convergent productions.

When divergent production came to be described as creative thinking ability, an intensive research effort was initiated to identify creative talent and planning abilities through tests (Guilford & Hoepfner, 1971, p. 124). A major problem was to design tests which called for responses other than the "one right answer" of cognition, memory, and convergent production. Gradually some hypotheses regarding creative people were supported. Divergent thinkers showed a greater than average *sensitivity* to *problems* by being able to spot the defects and deficiencies in picture items. They did well in *fluency* tests which called for "thinking up unusual uses for a brick" or listing things "the number 2 suggests" (pair, half, couple). A different characteristic, *flexibility*, was shown as an adaptability score when instructions were shifted in a test. This "freedom from inertia of thought" was also shown in the ability to give many different meanings to a common word such as *take*. Tests of *originality* were difficult to design, but one, Plot Title, was a good discriminator. Subjects were given the brief facts of a short

Table 8-2
GUILFORD'S FACTORS OF INTELLECT

OPERATIONS

Major kinds of intellectual activities that the organism does in processing information

Cognition (C)*Immediate discovery, awareness, rediscovery, or recognition of information in its various forms; comprehension or understanding

Memory (M) Retention of information in the form in which it was received, together with the ability to select and retrieve it

Divergent production (D) Generation of new ideas or alternatives to given information with emphasis on variety, quantity, and relevance of output

Convergent production (N) Generation of logical conclusions from given information where the given cues determine the outcome, as in mathematics

Evaluation (E) Comparison of information; making judgments based on criteria such as correctness, identity, consistency, etc.

CONTENTS

Broad, basic substantive forms that information may take

Figural (F) Concrete forms of information such as manipulative materials, auditory and visual images, figure-ground diagrams, toys for classification, and puzzles

Symbolic (S) Signs having no significance in and of themselves, such as letters, numerals, musical notations, codes, and words (as ordered letters)

Semantic (M) Meaningful information in the form of conceptions, verbal thinking, and communication in form of words or nonverbal concepts

Behavioral (B) Information involved in human interactions where attitudes, needs, desires, moods, intentions of self or others are essential

PRODUCTS

Basic forms that information takes as a result of the organisms processing of it

Units (U) Relatively segregated items, or bits, of information that have identity

Classes (C) Sets of items of information grouped according to a common property

Relations (R) Connections between items of information based upon variables or points of contact that apply to them

Systems (S) Organized or structured aggregates of items of information; complexes of inter-related parts

Transformations (T) Changes in existing information such as redefinitions, shifts, transitions, or modifications

Implications (I) Connection between items of information by virtue of contiguity; a condition that promotes an inference

*Letters make up a code system for describing a task, an activity, or a goal; for example, MFR means memory for figural relations.

story and asked to provide a title which was judged later as clever or nonclever. In these studies ingenuity and cleverness were closely related.

Creative thinking has been confirmed by other researchers on tasks of originality, fluency, and flexibility (Wallach, 1970). The tests of sensitivity to problems proved to fit the cognition category more than divergent thinking. Children as low as sixth grade were given adaptations of the creative thinking tests with results showing factor differences similar to the older students and adults (Guilford & Hoepfner, 1971). Factor analysis of divergent thinking abilities is important because the abilities are described in such detail that teaching to develop them appears feasible. School learning which emphasizes the flexible use of class categories, for example, can begin at the preschool level with objects. Torrence extended many of the concepts of divergent production to his creativity tests for young children (Torrence, 1972, 1974).

Convergent production is the operation, or thought process, by which an individual makes use of given information to generate a correct or best answer. Like divergent production, this operation produces or generates a solution; but it is different in that the answer is likely to be predetermined by the data or by the setting in which the probelm was derived. The child who operates well in the convergent area may be a good hypothesis tester, but may not necessarily be a good hypothesis generator. Problems in mathematics and logic usually require convergent thinking.

Evaluation is the process of making judgments based on a criterion or set of criteria. Decision making, based on consistent standards of correctness, suitability, adequacy, or desirability, is involved. Critical evaluation tends to dampen the brainstorming process, so that teachers often choose to separate idea generating and idea evaluating into different group discussion sessions. Evaluation has a function as a regulator of each of the other four operations.

The *contents* of intellect are the basic form information takes. In Guilford's structure these were figural, symbolic, semantic, and behavioral. If one accepts the idea that intelligence develops from a knowledge of concrete things to a knowledge of symbolic representations, this way of analyzing content is useful. Behavioral contents, such as moods, needs, and intentions of other persons, is read by infants and children before they have acquired a comparable semantic content.

Products are the end result of an intellectual process. Guilford's factor analysis isolated six basic forms: *units, classes, relations, systems, transformations,* and *implications.* Units are the simplest results of a thought process. If a child strings wooden beads in random fashion on a lace, the basic characteristic of the product is units. If the beads are strung according to a pattern repetition the design quality is based on *relations* between units. If the child, having grasped the concept of repeated patterns to make a design, produces one which is unique she has made a transformation. Guilford and Hoepfner (1971) reported strong correlations between divergent production and transformations.

It is theoretically possible for any category of one side of the cube to be combined with any two categories of the other sides of the cube (5×4×6). According to Guilford's model, there are 120 ways to be intelligent. A system of letters called the SI code has been designed to analyze intellectual tasks. A unique bead design production would be defined as FDT or figural divergent transformation (Table 8-2). More than 100 of the theoretical 120 cubes have been demonstrated in research.

MACKINNON'S CRITERIA FOR CREATIVE PRODUCTION

MacKinnon (1965) proposed three criteria for creativity: (1) the producing of something new or rare, (2) the fitting together of the reality dimensions of the world and some recognizable goals, (3) the carrying through to completion of the creative action. Creative production, in MacKinnon's terms, requires discipline as well as innovation. Children can learn to anticipate the joy of completing a creative production which can be extended to joy in the work itself.

PIAGET'S GENETIC THEORY

Jean Piaget, a Swiss biologist who had published scientific papers on the adaptation of mollusks while still in his teens, decided to describe the genesis of intelligence in the human species. He began his studies in the Paris laboratories of Simon, the famous colleague of Binet. While learning to test the intelligence of children, Piaget became intrigued by the incorrect answers they gave and by the childish logic they used to explain them. In his efforts to probe the distinctive nature of intelligence in childhood, Piaget developed a technique of interview and observation to encourage the "flow of spontaneous tendencies" in thought (Piaget, 1928, pp. 8–9). The purpose of the interview was to explore the child's way of knowing the world without suggesting the answers or influencing the convictions. Questions are needed which do not suggest answers, but encourage the child to center on the topic under investigation. "Do you know what it means to think of something? Well, then, what do you think with?" This kind of interview goes beyond the pure observation, but without falling into the pitfalls of a test situation. Piaget likened his "clinical" method to the psychoanalytic interview in diagnosis. Daily practice during one to two years of training was required to qualify his interviewers for research.

The genetic psychology of Piaget can be explained only in terms of biological science. He adapted his own training for the Ph.D. to explain his philosophy and later to describe child development. To understand Piaget's terminology a reader may need to experience it in many contexts and to utilize the concepts when working with children, perhaps in the same way the child comes to know the world by his or her own actions on things. Over a period of time and in different settings the Piagetian conceptualization of structuralism falls into place.

Inhelder (1969) referred to herself and Piaget as "subjective" behaviorists because they assume that there are internal structures that make observable behavior possible. They were concerned with the laws of internal transformation, or growth, of intelligence. The terms *assimilation* and *accommodation* describe the dynamics by which the individual takes in experience (like food) and is changed;

the more nutritious the intake, the better the experience. An individual is transformed continuously, and therefore accommodates at successively higher levels as he or she grows older. *Adaptation* is the invariate result of the interaction of assimilation and accommodation.

Intelligence is structured over time by the child's action on the world of people and things; but this development of intelligence is genetically specified, according to Piaget. The periods and stages of intellectual development are evidence of the genetic plan. Individual differences in the rate of development are recognized, but the periods and stages within these periods are common to all members of the human species.

The structures of intelligence are neurobiological and are called schemes in some sources. Memory depends on schemes which may be representations or patterns for operations. *Schema* are simplifed representations of the results of actions. *Schemata* are patterns that represent the generalized structure of an action or operation. Diane, age 9, watched the interviewer poise a pencil in perpendicular relation to the tabletop, and watched it fall when released. Her schema are the representations of the pencil—the images of pencil vertical, pencil falling, pencil horizontal. Her schemata go beyond perception, and she demonstrates this by drawing the pencil in a sequence of angles from 90 to 0 degrees with reference to the table. The drawing was a concrete operation performed according to the schemata of the general structure of the action, an operation more complex than those involving mere perceptual schema.

Piaget's periods and stages

The stages of several developmental achievements, as seen by Piaget, have been incorporated in age categories (Part Two). This section presents a summary of the periods and stages as a point of reference. The stages in the development of prehension (Chapter 4) do not correspond to the sensorimotor stages of infancy as outlined here. *Stage* means a distinguishable interval in a sequence of intervals that culminate in a higher and different pattern of action or operation. A *period* is a major portion of time, covering several stages in cognitive development, which has common elements, or characteristics. The three major periods of Piaget's structure are infancy (0 to 2 years), childhood (2 to 11 years), and adolescence (11 to 15 years). Each of these periods is characterized by a generalized focus in the child's organization of the world: sensorimotor intelligence at infancy, representation or operations on concrete things in the middle period, and logical thought or operations in the third period. Piaget has sometimes described four periods of cognitive development by dividing the middle period into two subperiods (Table 8-3). Each period is further characterized by a vertical structure that begins with an imbalance toward assimilation, the practice of old structures, the groping for new patterns, and trial-and-error approaches to knowing. Each period ends in *adaptation*, with assimilation and accommodation in balance, or *equilibrium*. This progression from groping to knowing takes place first at the sensorimotor level

Table 8-3
PIAGET'S SEQUENCE OF COGNITIVE DEVELOPMENT

PERIOD I: SENSORIMOTOR INTELLIGENCE

Stage 1 (0- month)	Practice of reflex systems, beginning of differentiation
Stage 2 (1-4 months)	Repetition of pleasurable sensations Hand-mouth coordination
Stage 3 (4-8 months)	Repetition of events by intention; hand-eye coordination
Stage 4 (8-12 months)	Use of schemata in new situations; object permanence achieved
Stage 5 (12-18 months)	Discovery of new means by action on objects; active experimentation and search for novelty; organization of causal relations
Stage 6 (18-24 months)	Inventing ways to solve problems) make-believe play and imitation; organization of space

PERIOD II: REPRESENTATIONAL THOUGHT AND CONCRETE OPERATIONS*

Stage 1 (1½-2½ years)	Groping with symbolic representation; symbolic functioning attached to objects
Stage 2 (2-4 years)	Preconceptual thought; use of mental symbols for past, future
Stage 3 (4-5½ years)	Simple representations; decisions are perception-bound, illogical; egocentric reasonings
Stage 4 (5½-7years)	Articulated representations; transition from nonconservation to conservation
Stage 5† (7-8½ years)	Systems in equilibrium; conservation of number, mass
Stage 6† (8½-11 years)	Accurate observation of operations; conservation of weight, volume

PERIOD III: LOGICAL THOUGHT (12 YEARS AND OLDER)

Stage 1	Groping with hypotheses; thinks about the possible
Stage 2	Naive idealism and egocentrism; would change world by thought
Stage 3	Hypothetical reasoning; separates and controls variables
Stage 4	Undertakes and performs experiments; uses logical combinations
Stage 5	Interrelates logical systems; reflects on own thinking processes

*Piaget (1969) proposed four periods: period II as preoperational thought and period III as concrete operations.

†Piaget (1972) separated period II into subperiods: A; preparation of the operations: and B; operatory structuring itself.

(period I), then at the representational and concrete operational levels (period II), and finally at the level of logical thought (period III).

SENSORIMOTOR INTELLIGENCE

During the first two years of life the integration of the different sensory systems is the major characteristic of cognitive development. The motoric, visual, and auditory actions on objects are, to Piaget, the basis for all later intelligence. The major developmental accomplishments of this period are hand-mouth coordination, hand-eye coordination, the notion of object permanence, and intentional control over the immediate environment.

Practice of reflex systems (0 to 1 month). At stage 1, the newborn uses biological systems already functioning to assimilate the environment. Piaget observed the beginnings of adaptation of the sucking reflex of his own children and interpreted their behavior.

Observation 2—The day after birth Laurent seized the nipple with his lips without having to have it held to his mouth. He immediately seeks the breast when it escapes him as a result of some movement. . . .

The beginning of a sort of reflex searching may be observed in Laurent, which will develop on the following days and which probably constitutes the functional equivalent of the gropings characteristic of later stages (acquisition of habits and empirical intelligence). Laurent is lying on his back with his mouth open, his lips and tongue moving slightly in imitation of the mechanism of sucking, and his head moving from left to right and back again, as though seeking an object. (1952, pp. 25–26)

During the first month Piaget's children began to differentiate their sucking action according to their biological state at the time—whether hungry or fed, sleepy or alert, fussy or quiet. They sucked in a different way when feeding from the breast than when sucking the thumb or orally exploring an object pressed to the cheek. Similarly, his infants began to accommodate the grasping reflex to different objects touched by their hands (blanket, Piaget's finger, their mother's breast). By observing their behavior systematically and interpreting the common developments contained in his records, Piaget (1952) described the newborn as a dynamic organism who reached out into the environment for sensory experience and gratification. The tendency to exercise available structures and the necessity to accommodate to outer reality led to increasingly higher levels of adaptation. Laurent was making a transition in cognitive development when he showed a primitive anticipation of feeding by turning his head in the right direction and by initiating the appropriate sucking movements before seeing the breast and with only the holding position as *signifier.*

Repetition of pleasurable sensations (1 to 4 months). Piaget (1952) described stage 2 as characterized by the first nonhereditary adaptations at the lower limit and the beginning of intentional behavior at the higher limit. As soon as a movement pattern (reflex or schemata) is organized, it is ready for repetition. The exercise of available systems brings simple organic satisfaction to the infant. This vicarious need, and the sensory pleasure experienced during simple assimilation, lead to the infant's prolonging the action. Piaget termed the repetition of a behavior pattern a *circular reaction* and referred to simple circular reactions as associations.

Self-initiated thumb-sucking is an example of the repetition of pleasure sensations and the hand-to-mouth coordination that is achieved at stage 2. When "the child sucks his thumb, no longer due to chance contacts but through coordination of hand and mouth, this may be called acquired accommodation" (p. 48). Other acquired adaptations are the coordination of vision and audition, of tactile and kinesthetic senses, and of touch and audition. Adaptations result as two schema or two modes of response are coordinated.

From the third month the infant shows the beginnings of curiosity about the distant physical and social environment. The visual organization of space and an awareness of the size of objects result from visual exploration. The child performs motor actions on objects to continue a sound effect or the visible motion of a toy. The social smile is a sign of pleasure in contact with other persons. The repetitions and explorations which prolong sensations lead to the stabilizing of an action pattern. Piaget noted that intention was not yet involved in primary circular reactions.

Repetition of events by intention (4 to 8 months). The stage 3 infant shows curiosity about his or her own actions on objects and develops the structures to perform actions on things by intention. The major achievement of the stage is prehension, the ability to grasp objects and then release them (Chapter 4). Piaget observed that the act of prehension involves the coordination of sight, hand movement, and sucking movements as objects are brought to the mouth for oral exploration. This control over actions enables the infant to reproduce interesting results that have been discovered by chance. Piaget's son "pulled a chain at will to shake a rattle and make it sound: the intention is clear" (1952, p. 164). Observing this indirect action to produce an effect, Piaget concluded that a new stage in cognitive development had taken place, which he termed *secondary circular reactions.*

Imitation through sensorimotor actions was observed in Lucienne between the ages of 4 and 8 months. She watched Piaget move his hand, then moved her fingers; she watched him open his mouth, then opened her own. When he did not repeat the action, Lucienne kicked her legs violently, using the same action she had discovered for making her suspended toys move, apparently to make him continue. "Now this is not a question of a simple receptive attitude but of an active procedure, for Lucienne constantly gradates her effort according to the result" (p. 204). Piaget interpreted this development as the beginning of intention.

Use of schemata in new situations (8 to 12 months). During stage 4 the infant generalizes the visual, motor, and tactile schemata attained at stage 3 to new situations. The child adapts schemata developed in previous actions to serve some new end. The infant in transition performs imitative action patterns on new objects.

Roger (7 ½ months) sat upright on the table. His interviewer (observer) placed a cup (plastic frame with paper insert of a kind he had not seen before) on the table just out of reach. Roger immediately opened his mouth wide and then closed it. The interviewer placed a very wooly Australian lamb rug (rolled into a ball) on the table. Roger immediately opened his arms in a wide hugging gesture.

These imitative motoric actions were made to visual cues to a distant object. Piaget called stage 4 that of *coordination of secondary schemata* because more than one schema is used in combination to achieve intended results in a single act.

The major achievement of stage 4 is *object permanence* or *object constancy*. The child becomes capable of searching for an object which has disappeared. To demonstrate object constancy, Piaget would hide an object behind a screen, under a blanket, or behind his hand. The infant had to conceive of the object's being there, even though not seen. To search for a hidden object, the child thinks of its relations with things seen, apart from its relations with the action. Having acquired the concept of object permanency, the child must coordinate the action of putting aside a barrier (means) to grasp the hidden object (end). Roger (not yet 8 months old) did not search for a hidden toy dog, but he removed the blanket promptly when the tail of the dog was left visible at the edge of the blanket. The coordination of secondary schemata is a new relationship between total behavior patterns acquired separately through actions on unfamiliar objects.

Discovery of new means by experimentation (12 to 18 months). Piaget described stage 5 as problem solving at a sensorimotor level. From approximately 1 year on he gave his children toys that presented certain problems and watched them develop systematic ways to arrange, stack, or retrieve the objects. He did a series of experiments with the Russian wooden dolls that nest and with blocks in seriation sizes. A cardboard rooster mounted on a frame was placed flat just outside Jacqueline's playpen with head and tail at different openings between the bars. In order to obtain this new toy she had to push it back, stand it up, and bring it head (or tail) first between the bars. He recorded that it took thirty-nine attempts over four days for her to work out a successful procedure, which once achieved she immediately applied without error to a new toy rooster (1952, p. 311).

According to Piaget, the child can discover new means through active experimentation only after stage 4 has been reached, in which familiar behavior patterns are constructed into new relationships, or new combinations. Once the child is able to persist in actions to solve problems and to try different combinations of organized actions (schemata) successes can be expected. This active experimentation extends the child's understanding of space and size relationships, time sequences, and causation.

Inventing ways to solve problems (18 to 24 months). After the child has had time to practice problem solving by trying different actions on objects, the child is ready to use mental combinations of schemata and surpass motor action with mental activity (stage 6). In Piaget's theory, the child must have constructed the necessary representative images to perform mental combinations, such as searching for a missing object. At just past 18 months

. . . Jacqueline plays with a fish, a swan, and a frog which she puts in a box, takes them out again, puts them back in, etc. At a given moment, she lost the frog. She places the swan and the fish in the box and then obviously looks for the frog. She lifts everything within reach (a big cover, a rug, etc.) and (long after beginning to search) begins to say. . . [frog, frog, in French]. It is not the word which set the search in motion, but the opposite. There was therefore evocation of an absent object without any directly perceived stimulus. (Piaget, 1952, p. 356)

It was clear to Piaget that representations and search schemata made possible mental combinations that went beyond actual experimentation and marked the completion of the sensorimotor-intelligence stage. Piaget considered this invention of new means as possibly the beginning of deduction, but not as a S-R mechanism. It should be noted also that image symbols precede word symbols in cognitive development.

Representational Thought and Concrete Operations

Piaget (1951) used the term *figurative* to describe the sensory knowledge of an event; that is, the perceptual content of an experience. He used the term *operative* to distinguish the child's own structuring or transforming of sensory content in the formation of an action knowledge. Operative knowledge appears near the end of each period, but is structured developmentally as sensorimotor knowledge, symbolic knowledge, and operational knowledge. The essential step to representational thought is that the figurative aspects of knowing, which are acquired by the sensorimotor infant, give way to representations that can be manipulated instead of the objects from which sensorimotor stimuli are built. Representations are the images and symbols which the child produces or reproduces to stand for figurative knowledge.

Representational thought is the inner act of knowing, just as sensorimotor schemata are the inner structures for external actions. To Piaget, *signs* are the arbitrary symbols of a culture while the meanings of signs are the child's own construction, the *symbolic function*. To repeat, the words of the language are signs with arbitrary meanings; symbols are representations, self-constructed from sensorimotor knowledge. The signs of language are part but not all the content of the symbolic function.

The early years (ages $1\frac{1}{2}$ to $5\frac{1}{2}$) of Piaget's middle period mark the development of symbolic thought, while the last half (ages $5\frac{1}{2}$ to 11) marks the emergence of operational thought. Period II is limited, however, by the child's dependence on the presence of concrete objects or events which the symbols represent.

In Piaget's description of cognitive development, *language* is a system of signs that is not essential to operational thought but is a convenient form which the symbolic function may utilize. Any system of numerals is also a code of signs, one which represents numbers. This distinction between arbitrary meanings of words and the child's symbolic meanings, constructed through action on things, is central to understanding the relationship between representational thought in the first subperiod and operational thought in the later subperiod.

Verbal behavior is one of the more obvious ways available to a child for showing how he or she views the world and reconstructs past events. Piaget believed that language in early childhood was simply the accompaniment to action based on imagery. Language development, which is the obvious accomplishment of the preoperational period (ages 2 to 7), is a progression in representational thought in which the private image gives way to the public verbal signs. In the same way, the egocentric (subjective) view of the physical world gives way to the objective view that Piaget observed at the end (at age 11) of the second subperiod of representational thought, that of concrete operational thought.

GROUPING WITH SYMBOLIC REPRESENTATIONS ($1\frac{1}{2}$ to $2\frac{1}{2}$ YEARS)

Language emerges in stage 1, most often in relation to objects or persons for whom the child has a variety of sensorimotor structures already built during infancy. Objects were the basis for the action structures and accommodation of sensorimotor schemata, which in the representational period became the basis for symbolic functions. For example, sensorimotor representations (touch, sight, and sound schema of toy dog) give way to imagery of toy dog remembered, and later to the word symbol for dog. The child says "dog, dog" while searching for a favorite toy. It is important in Piaget's theory of development that the sensorimotor knowledge of an object and its imagery precede the word. The child uses word symbols at this stage for particular objects and not for categories.

PRECONCEPTUAL THOUGHT (2 TO 4 YEARS)

The second stage is marked by the child's becoming "capable of representational thought by means of the symbolic functions" (Piaget, 1969). By this is meant the mental manipulation of images, symbols, and words. The child is freed from the immediate and can deal with past and future events. Throughout this period, thinking is tied to physical objects and direct experience.

To demonstrate the child's conceptual development of classification, Piaget would present a box of beads (about twenty dark brown ones and two light ones) for stringing. He would ask the child to inspect them, and nearly all children of this age will say they are "made of wood." Then the interviewer starts stringing the dark beads and stops midway and asks, "If I change my mind and string all the beads, will my necklace be longer with all the beads than with just the brown ones?" Most children under age 4 will insist that the necklace will be longer if just the brown beads are used because "there are more brown than light beads," despite asking the question in several ways. Piaget interprets this response as lack of *class inclusion*, the inability to *decenter* the focus from the larger number of brown beads in order to include the light beads in a class of wooden beads. Children of this age can group things according to their properties (color, shape, size) or by their use (eat with, play with, wear). However, the child can deal with only one property at a time and tends to lose sight of the category and to shift to a different property for grouping. They can do *simple classification* based on perceptual differences, such as small, large or triangle, circle. The significant accomplishment is that the child begins to develop preconcepts, mental constructs that are intermediary between the image symbol and the concept proper. Also, the child begins to reflect on his or her own behavior.

SIMPLE REPRESENTATION (4 TO 5½ YEARS)

Children at stage 3 expand their private collection of image symbols, but their thinking is egocentric. They tend not to consider that there is a view of things other than their own view.

One of the major accomplishments of this period is *multiple classification*. The child can center on a property to make figural collections of objects; that is, the child can deal with several attributes. In making collections of blocks, the child can group them first by one attribute (large, small), then shift to grouping by color (red, blue), then regroup them by shape (triangle, circle).

Children of this age can do simple seriation. They can arrange objects from largest to smallest, but they do this by inspection and manipulation. They order by trial and error rather than preorder by mental operation. Many writers have focused on the lack of mature intelligence in the preschool child rather than on the considerable number of symbolic actions the child achieves.

ARTICULATED REPRESENTATIONS (5½ TO 7 YEARS)

During stage 4 children's language increases dramatically. They use language for social interaction and to explain their own mental manipulations. At this age the limitations of the former stage, such as preconcepts, centration, and egocentrism, are crumbling. The child sometimes organizes objects and explains their relationships intuitively, but is not quite certain enough to hold to a decision based on operational logic. For example, the child can order a set of dolls according to ascending (or descending) size and match seriated poles for them to climb (see Figure 7-5). However, the preoperational child cannot reverse the relationship and assign correctly the smallest pole to the largest doll, etc.

By the age of 7 the child's thinking has become looser and more flexible, in anticipation of mental operations on objects that mark the transition to concrete operational thought. In a manner reminiscent of the sensorimotor sequence, the child experiments with new possibilities.

SYSTEMS IN EQUILIBRIUM (7 TO 8½ YEARS)

Stage 5 marks the beginning of operations. According to Piaget:

Initially these operations are concrete; that is, they are used directly on objects in order to manipulate these objects. For instance, the child can classify concrete objects, or order them, or establish correspondence between them, or use numerical operations on them, or measure them from a spatial point of view. The operations remain concrete until the child is about eleven or twelve years old. (1969, p. 2)

By operations Piaget means interiorized actions that are reversible. The major accomplishment is that the child can reverse an operation mentally and therefore can conserve. Conservation means the knowledge that objects (matter) remain the same even though the arrangement or the physical shape may be altered. Conservation of mass is achieved when one of two equal balls of clay is flattened into a pancake (or elongated into a sausage) and the child knows they are still the same "because nothing was added and nothing was taken away."

The child's ability to conserve number can be observed by having him arrange objects in one-to-one correspondence, such as an egg for each egg cup, to number about six or more. When the row of either is extended the child is asked if there are still the same number of cups as eggs (Figure 8-9). Although the child has systems for mentally manipulating objects (seriation, classification, numeration), he can deal with only one system at a time. The systems are said to be in equilibrium because the early tendency toward assimilation is balanced by accommodation to the ways that objects are organized.

ACCURATE OBSERVATION OF OPERATIONS (8½ TO 11 YEARS)

The completion of concrete operations is achieved at stage 6. Conservation of weight and volume are achieved. The child can predict that two balls of clay that balance on a scale will again balance, even though the form is changed. She will

First arrangement:

Second arrangement:

FIGURE 8-9 Conservation of number is possible when the child can relate a change in the arrangement of the eggs and cups to the original arrangement of one-to-one. To do this the process must be mentally reversed, otherwise the child insists there are more eggs than cups in the second arrangement.

Table 8-4
CLASSIFICATION HIERARCHY

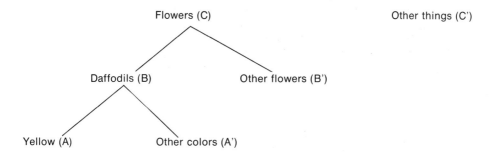

predict from the water level in a beaker after adding a ball of clay that the water level in a second beaker will be the same after inserting a clay ball of the same size.

By the end of the period of concrete operations, the child can make *hierarchical classifications*. Diana at age 7, when shown six daffodils and six other flowers (iris, roses, poppies), insisted that there were more daffodils than flowers. By age 11, however, she will be able to recognize at least three subclasses in a hierarchical ordering (Table 8-4). The stabilizing of concrete operational thought at 11 or 12 years soon gives way to a new disorganization as the older child gropes with logical operations.

Logical Operations

The period of logical thought, or formal operations, is marked by the adolescent's turning the thinking operation upon itself (Piaget, 1972). Whereas the sensorimotor child performed direct actions on objects, and the concrete-operational child manipulated the representations of objects, the adolescent manipulates abstractions or operational systems. Adolescents think on their own thoughts, in the absence of concrete objects if necessary. Without going into Piaget's mathematical logic, the accomplishments of the logical thought period are stated as (1) the ability to manipulate and control variables, (2) the use of proportional reasoning, and (3) the ability to test hypotheses in a logical sequence.

The adolescent reasons logically because he or she can deal with more than one system or relationship at a time. For example, the adolescent can hypothesize when one of a row of diving boards will touch the water by considering all possible variables: thickness of the board, material from which it is constructed, weight of the diver, and distance out from the wall of the pool. This separation and control of variables is necessary to solve this problem. The intellectually mature person can perform such logical steps mentally.

This final period of intellectual development has been described by Piaget (1972) as extremely varied. Most of his observations of the capacity for reasoning have come from presenting subjects with problems to be solved by the experimental method. *Groping* with new means marks the beginning of this new level of adaptation; just as it marks the beginning of earlier periods. In logical thought the adolescent gropes with "self-representation" involving "two reference systems at the same time" (p. 59). The new equilibrium of formal operations depends on the conceptualization of reversibility, but the actions are on systems rather than on symbols.

Another characteristic which appears early in each period is egocentrism. Piaget noted the infant's egocentric organization of space during which the body proper is the point of reference. At first the mouth is the center of the world, followed by visual space, tactile space, and auditive space. In the middle period, egocentrism is representational. Children reach a new level of maturity when they realize there is a different view from the other side of the mountains and that each person represents the world in his or her own way. The egocentrism of adolescents is in their naive idealism. They become immersed in theories for reshaping world conditions and expect to accomplish them by intellectual means.

The carrying out of logical operations at a formal level is Piaget's conception of mature intelligence. The use of the experimental method is assumed when the ability to hypothesize, to check out propositions systematically, and to arrive at solutions by reasoning is achieved through development. At the culmination of infancy the child actively experiments with the sensorimotor world of objects. At the end of the concrete-operations period the child seeks to "coordinate systems" by classifying, ordering, multiplying, etc. (Piaget, 1972, p. 58). Scientific experimentation is the function of mature intelligence.

Piaget's contributions

Piaget's major contributions are evaluated differently by individual scholars who preserve their own views of learning and development. Wallace (1967) summarized the research on conceptualization in children through 1965. Most of 200 studies he reported reflected the major role of Piaget and of others who attempted to test his genetic theory. Students who wish to make their own evaluation of Piaget's theory might do well to begin with this summary. I consider four aspects of Piaget's work to be monumental and unique.

First, Piaget's elegant and meticulous description of the development of intelligence sets Homo sapiens apart from other species. He emphasized the uniqueness of humans in a biological world and warned against overextending the assumptions based on research from lower animals to children's intelligence. He was not afraid, in a world dominated by S-R psychology, to interpret the child's actions in terms of *intent*. Piaget departed from research on the behavior of lower animals when he formulated his structure of the stages of intelligence. This careful tracing of the development of logical thought from primitive reflex systems is without parallel in the scientific literature. His system of periods and stages assumes a biological totality that integrates growth, development, and learning in every human organism.

Second, Piaget demonstrated clearly that learning differs in kind from one level to another. The associations, which may be sensory or symbolic, are the basic bits of experience from which the child's conceptions are self-constructed internally. Nevertheless, these conceptualizations become gradually consistent with adult conceptions because the child's interaction with the real, physical world necessitates accommodation. But Piaget distinguishes between a level of thinking that conserves, or reverses, or decenters and an earlier level in which the child cannot perform these operations. Operational thought is distinct from preoperational thought in ways that have been confirmed by many researchers following the original work of Piaget (Wallace, 1967). Education based on the development of conceptual structures has been attempted.

Third, Piaget designed a methodology for exploring the thinking patterns of children, rather than merely testing them on preordered knowledge. Furthermore, his "interviews" could be used by teachers to find out the child's cognitive functioning without formalized diagnosis and adult language that a child might repeat, but not understand. He restored respectability to clinical observations for obtaining research data.

Fourth, Piaget proposed a philosophy, a view of knowing, that focuses on the individual's own role in the construction of reality. Piaget saw the child, not as a victim of the environment, but as a selector of experience from many possibilities within the human setting. The child assimilates within the limitations and biological potential of his or her cognitive structures at a given stage of development. For the biological child, actions upon things and the functioning of the systems, whether brain or digestive system, result in satisfaction, further action, and adaptation. This conception of the role of the learner in his or her own cognitive development is a significant departure from the mainstream of psychology throughout the first half of the twentieth century and a major contribution by Piaget.

Unanswered Questions

The application of Piaget's theory to curriculum construction has been controversial on two points. First, the idea that particular conceptualizations develop at particular ages has been used to argue for the delay of teaching reading and mathematics. Piaget often expressed concern that adults might try to introduce educational content in advance of the dynamic formation of appropriate cognitive structures. Second, educators and school psychologists have disagreed on the extent to which conceptualizations such as number constancy (conservation) can be taught.

VARIABILITY IN THE REARING ENVIRONMENT

A problem arises in Piaget's assumption of a common human environment that is conducive to similar cognitive development across cultures during the formative years. The associative input is actually quite specific in the receptors that are stimulated and the memory structures that are generated. It can be argued that the child's later ability to form conceptualizations is enhanced when the basic bits and pieces of sensory experience include certain essential parts of a conceptual system or whole. The repeated acts of rote counting, for example, may be one of the actions which encourage the conceptualization of number as a system. Cultures vary widely in the frequency and necessity for numbering and counting in the early physical experience of children. Yet some educators have argued that instruction in counting should be delayed until after the child has attained conservation of number at 7 or 8 years old. The relationship of associative experience and later conceptualization needs further study before such a radical change in early experience and social transmission is imposed.

PIAGET AND READING

Another problem in applying genetic theory to education involves the function of language in thought. Piaget himself struggled with this issue but decided language was culturally imposed and followed the roots of the operations, which were independent of language (Piaget, 1972, p. 113). He cited his early study of language and the later studies of the concrete operations of categories, relations, or numbers and stated:

All this has taught me that there exists a logic of coordinations of actions far deeper than the logic related to language and much prior to that of propositions in the strict sense. (1972, p. 109–110)

Piaget brought up the child's linguistic distinction of nouns and adjectives as a possible distinction of categories. But he went on to cite the fact that deaf and nonspeaking persons achieve the symbolic function without achieving articulated language. He admits that language may facilitate the operations, but he insists that the whole structures of operational thought remain relatively independent of language and that their understanding cannot be communicated by language alone. These understandings are, of course, the internalized actions of conservation, seriation, and others not described here.

Piaget accepted the evidence that children attain various forms of conservation such as quantity, number, weight, and volume at different ages (Table 8-5). Had he accepted the universal acquisition of language as evidence of linguistic structuring, species-specific to humans (Slobin, 1972), the relationship of language and thought might have been argued differently by Piaget. Vygotsky (1962) argued that thought itself developed from speech going underground, i.e., becoming internalized. Linguistic categories are conceptualized and manipulated by age 4, much earlier than the conservation of number (Chapter 10).

This leaves open the question of when to teach reading. The suggestion that reading be postponed for the attainment of conservation of mass or of number, as some writers have suggested (Furth, 1970; Raven & Salzer, 1971) is neither Piagetian nor based on research. Reading is a language form; it is communication that follows (for those reading in the native language) from the spoken language. To the extent that it is related to cognitive development, reading depends on linguistic structures, usually attained by age 4. Piaget should not be blamed for

Table 8-5
PIAGET'S STAGES OF CONSERVATION

Period	Age	Quantity (mass)	Number /	Weight /	Volume
	2				
	3	Focuses on one dimension only			
Preoperational	4				
	5	Vacilates from one dimension to →	5-6*		
	6	another			
	7	Focuses on relevant dimensions →	7-8	7-8	
	8	thus is able to conserve			
Concrete operations	9			9-10	9-10
	10				
	11				11-12
	12	Able to conceptualize			
Formal operations	13	relations, apart from physical			
	14	presence of material			
	15				

*Age of achieving conservation varies according to content, among individuals, and in replication studies.

postponing the child's access to books. The evidence appears formidable that deep structures of syntax, the meaning level, and logic appear at different times (Chomsky, 1965). Piaget and Vygotsky may both be correct, but educators need not confuse their different messages.

Piaget's stages for concept development are significantly related to performance on the Wechsler Intelligence Scales for Children tests in children from kindergarten through second grade. Dudek, Lester, and Goldbert (1969) found nine Piagetian measures for conceptualization of space, time, origin of night, origin of dreams, quantity, area, class inclusion, movement, and seriation to show stability over the three-year period, and to be predictive of the teacher's ratings of academic success. Considering the gamelike and open format of the Piaget interviews, some of them might offer an alternative to IQ tests for ethnic minorities and other primary-age children.

THE NATURE AND NURTURE OF INTELLIGENCE

The acquisition of intelligence is so central to the struggle to be human that researchers will continue to define and try to enhance it. The search for the causes and effects of individual differences involves extremely sensitive issues because people do not agree on the differences that they value, or on what (if anything) will be changed in the environment to move it in the direction of further stimulating cognitive abilities. It is assumed that all cultural groups have a comparable range of difference among individual members, as well as a comparable potential for cognitive functioning in general. The challenge, as I see it, is to broaden the definition of talent, to extend the opportunity for talent development for all children, and to value the different forms in which talent expresses itself.

Although talent and intelligence are not the same thing, different forms of talent have been identified through various intelligence tests. *Linguistic*, or verbal, abilities are needed in all aspects of life in which communication is important: between individuals, between age groups, and between political or cultural minorities. Intelligence tests have tended to overemphasize verbal abilities and to use many items that were loaded with cultural meanings. Some test designers have separated different abilities into subtests that identify the verbal and nonverbal categories of the measure (Wechsler, 1974). Other tests have been designed to measure creative potential (Torrance, 1972a, 1972b).

Talents other than verbal ability that each society might attempt to identify and develop are *social interaction, spatial-quantitative* abilities, *musical-rhythmic* ability, *esthetic* or *artistic* ability, and *motor skills*. Talent development is considered in Chapter 13. This section promotes the possibility of using the environment to develop intelligence more fully than at present by attention to critical periods and the optimum environment for development. Two measures are described that have potential for identifying unique abilities in children if the results were to be analyzed toward that goal.

Interaction of Genetic Factors and Nurturance

Scholars generally agree that age and intelligence are important in arranging the learning environment of children (Stevenson, 1970). Scholars also agree that genetic and environmental factors both influence intellectual development, but they disagree on the relative significance of each and on the kind of environment that makes a difference in later intelligence. The concepts of *phylogeny* and *ontogeny*, introduced in Chapter 1, are helpful here because they imply a relationship between biological Homo sapiens and the social environment humans create for their young (Piaget, 1971).

Considering the progress Homo sapiens have made over the generations, it makes sense to plan a childrearing environment that makes the most of cultural history and social intelligence. Only recently has neurobiology provided the evidence that infants and children develop genetically in ways that support the early acquisition of language, the ability to solve problems intellectually, and the self-regulation of the environment. What language is learned, what concepts are evolved, and what initiative is developed are inherent in the culture, or society, into which the child is born. It makes sense that the brain structures, which are known to mature on an age-based schedule, are environmentally stimulated in genetically selective ways.

Deprived environments limit the opportunity to learn. (Hugh Rogers/ Monkmeyer)

CRITICAL PERIODS IN BRAIN DEVELOPMENT

The concept of critical periods means that the optimum time for a particular growth achievement is related to a particular developmental age. The assumption is that efforts to achieve some growth-related behavior prior to readiness will be unsuccessful, or take longer, and also that delay will be accompanied by a decline in aptitude. The concept of critical periods implies a beginning and an end to an optimal stage, while the concept of maturation is sometimes used to argue for a delay. Some of the evidence for critical periods comes in the timing of the development of myelination of neurons in the central nervous system. The growth of the myelin sheath around an axon is known to correspond to the rapid transmission of sensory messages and to the commitment of the system to particular patterns of activation and reaction. The myelination of language pathways corresponds to speech reception and speech production in the development of the child. Other pathways of the sense modalities are known to myelinate by a timetable that corresponds to learning and behavior of children (Yakoviev & Lecours, 1967). The growth and size of the brain hemispheres correspond to later speech dominance in the left hemisphere, for most persons. A weight differential of the hemispheres (about 10 percent is already apparent at the beginning of the third trimester before birth (Wada, Clarke, & Hamm, 1975).

The influence of genetics on brain organization is further supported by sex differences in nonverbal abilities. Witleson (1976) studied hemisphere specialization for spatial processing in 200 normal boys and girls (all right-handed) from ages 6 to 13 years. Spatial processing and nonlinguistic auditory processing are functions of the right hemisphere in most persons and occupy the bilateral cortical areas that are usually committed to speech and language processes in the left hemisphere. Boys performed in ways that suggested their spatial abilities were specialized in the right hemisphere as early as 6 years old. By contrast, girls' spatial processing showed a lack of specialization at least to age 13 (Witleson called It bilateral representation). She suggested that different methods for beginning reading instruction might fit the different cognitive style of the sexes and, further, that the plasticity of the female brain in spatial organization may account for females having fewer learning problems in school. Her implication was for earlier, rather than later, instruction when brain organization is more plastic.

OPTIMUM ENVIRONMENTS

Unfortunately, too little is known of the effect of a superior environment on the cognitive development of children. Successful attempts have been made to change the cognitive functioning of primates by creating a superior environment for them. One of the more recent is the Gardner and Gardner (1975) attempt to teach chimpanzees to communicate with humans and with each other in Ameslan (American Sign Language). Previously unsuspected abilities to use symbolic language have been demonstrated by subhuman primates when they were taught to sign (Chapter 9).

After reviewing the literature on sex differences in spatial abilities Eliot and Fralley (1976) suggested that nonverbal reasoning may be an outcome of interaction between genetic material and the environment. Eskimo women, who showed no sex differences in spatial abilities, may have been responding to ecological demand and cultural practices to develop their abilities. The spatial world of the young child may be extremely important in later spatial abilities such as architects, sculptors, and engineers need. Many parents can and do provide a superior environment for their children. When the child's immediate environment (the microsystem of home, play center, and school) are consistent in their expectations of the child, there appears to be no need for intervention. However, the necessary shift in the long-term expectations of an individual when he or she enters the larger community (the mesosystem) is not likely to be realized unless the preparation begins early. At least from the cognitive-developmental point of view, intervention at the microsystem level would seem to be necessary (Bronfenbrenner, 1976). The challenge for early childhood education is to value and support differences in culture and mores while teaching the child to cope in a mainstream society that requires different skills than the child has modeled at home.

CHANGES IN IQ

The evidence that a superior environment can affect IQ is found in the higher verbal abiltiies of firstborn and only children. They presumably spend more time with adults, who interact at a higher verbal level, and less time with siblings than the second- and later-ordered children (Chapter 7). This sibling order difference is stable to the college years (Altus, 1966).

Thorndike (1975) studied Binet's progeny, the Stanford-Binet Intelligence Scales, as adapted to American use and normed by Terman and Merrill. Thorndike compared the 1930 sample with a 1972 sample of children from preschool age through the elementary school grades. At the preschool years the upward shift was

Exploring number relationships. (Satyan/UNICEF Photo)

dramatic, with the 1972 average IQ running nearly 110 in contrast to the 1930 norm of 100 IQ. This happened despite the fact that the later sample included ethnic minorities, whereas the earlier forms were based on middle-class and upper-middleclass white children. Thorndike pointed out how life had changed, over forty years, for the preschool child.

Certainly, the amount of verbal and visual stimulation that the preschooler of 1970 was getting was enormously more than that available to the typical preschool-age child in the 1930's. The child of 1970 was probably watching television three or four hours a day. Furthermore, he had parents with two or three years more education, on the average, and had a much wider and more varied stock of books, toys, and other mateirals available to him. (p. 6).

An analysis showed that, contrary to expectations, the gains were in nonverbal, pictorial, perceptual, and memory items to a greater extent than in verbal items. Unfortunately, these gains dropped at about one IQ point a year from age 4 to age 9. Thorndike pointed out that the environments of toddlers and school-age children probably had not been enriched in intellectually important ways since 1930.

Measures of Cognitive Functioning

Thorndike (1975) warned against the use of the Binet IQ tests for children whose home environment was different in educational opportunities from the norming sample. He found that the range of individual differences had not changed from 1930 to 1970 and raised the problem of how to provide an appropriate education for each child in a country characterized by ethnic and cultural pluralism. He pointed out that the intelligence tests must guide, but not replace, informed judgment.

Originally, the IQ was a ratio of chronological age and mental age when the mean was set at 100 (MA/CA $\times$ 100 = IQ). This ratio, proposed by the German psychologist Stern early in this century, is no longer used. It has been replaced by a statistical procedure which analyzes the difficulty of each item and organizes the tests at each age level to have a mean of 100. The Binet has potential error of 5 points, so that a child's score of 107 really is an approximation that properly would read 107 $\pm$ 5, or somewhere between 102–112. The most common IQ tests are administered only by professionals trained in their use and potentially able to make a judgment about the child's responsiveness to the situation.

STANFORD-BINET INTELLIGENCE SCALE

The Terman-Merrill 1960 revision of the Binet test covers an age range from 2 years old to superior adults. This range is possible because the trained psychometrist is able to begin the test at an estimated age level where all the items will be passed and to proceed to administer the tests beyond the subject's ceiling of ability. These scales have been criticized because they provide a global score and because many of the items are verbal. They are more predictive of school success than of success in the wider world. Preschool scores are less stable than those taken at first grade level or later.

WECHSLER INTELLIGENCE SCALES

The Wechsler Intelligence Scales for Children, Revised (WISC-R) and the Wechsler Preschool and Primary Scales of Intelligence (WPPSI) are similar in that they separate verbal and performance scales to provide three IQ scores. They further norm different subtests of intelligence so that an individual profile of intellectual strengths and weaknesses can be graphed. These are useful in looking at the cognitive style of a student. Quite likely, many reading problems could be prevented by adapting early instruction to an individual's cognitive strengths (Robeck, 1964).

SUMMARY

Cognitive development includes such varied processes as the acquisition of mental images, use of language, concept formation, problem solving, and inventing means to meet one's own goals. Childrearing is difficult in unstable societies where the patterns of parenting, passed from one generation to the next, do not fit the child's needs.

Historically, and to the present time, different views about how children learn have been proposed. Social-analytical theory, initiated by Freud and elaborated by Erikson, focuses on the emotional health and social competence of the child. Cognitive-developmental theory, described by Piaget and others, focuses on human abilities and holds that learning differs in kind from simple to complex. Behaviorist-associative theory, built upon the S-R theories of Skinner, demonstrated that behavior could be shaped by reinforcement. Neurobiological theory has attracted many psychologists, including Pribram, because they focus on the study of brain functions, the physical evidence of the inner processes in cognitive development.

An interaction of cognitive and affective experience occurs in every learning act. Association learning, which is basic to more complex cognitive functioning, results from the reinforcement of bits of experience by reward or punishment. Associations are related in meaningful structures in the process of conceptualization. When the child uses conceptual knowledge to make or do something important to himself or herself, the child is functioning at a level of creative self-direction.

Piaget proposed certain periods and stages of cognitive development. He described the intellectual stages of infancy as the sensorimotor foundation of all cognitive functions. Representational thought, which is acquired in early childhood, includes both the images of actions and the symbolism of the culture.

Concrete operations are possible only after the child can mentally manipulate the representations: Piaget called this manipulation the symbolic function. Logical operations, or formal thought, characterize the final period of cognitive development and are the hallmark of adult intelligence.

Nature and nurture interact in cognitive functioning. By relating the intellectual environment of a child to the timing of the developmental stage, and anticipating the accomplishments of that stage, it is possible to enhance the cognitive abilties of children.

9
Acquisition of Language

9 Acquisition of Language

Language is a system of symbols which carry meaning. Many animals are capable of this level of communication (Lorenz, 1969). Birds inherit the structures for making call sounds and body signals which their young learn to obey and to imitate. Simple communication behaviors are genetically coded, apparently, because they appear on signal in mating season without either bird having had any opportunity to acquire the rituals. However, species with complex songs must hear the songs of adults at critical periods in development and must hear themselves practice in order to acquire the quality of call that later attracts a female to mate. When the young of certain species having very different songs, such as the redwing blackbird, are isolated with nest mates, they develop a call which is simpler than the wild counterpart, but which has some species characteristics. Apparently there is a match in birds between the expressive and receptive auditory systems. Females, who do not sing but respond to species-specific songs, learn the songs in the same way and at the same critical period when injected with male sex hormones (Kolata, 1975). Apparently the genetic information, the period in development, and the social environment interact to produce communication behavior in birds.

Honeybees, one of the kinds of insects exhibiting social organization, use dances to inform other workers about the direction and distance to nectar or pollen and can distinguish between them. Although the dance gestures are precise in their message to other bees, obviously their language lacks the phonological structure and names for categories that characterize human speech (Brown, 1958). Crickets, who have a different song in each species, produce a hybrid song when two different species are mated that differs from either parental species. The female progeny prefer the hybrid songs of their brothers to the male songs of their parental species. This indicates that neural connections for song production and reception are inherited together (Kolata, 1975). Although this genetic link is not established for humans, many researchers have become interested in the complexity of the inherited mechanisms for speech and language.

Human infants apparently inherit some abilities to hear speech sounds. Neonate movements are synchronized with adult speech (Condon & Sander, 1974). Infants perceive speech sounds in segments, while nonspeech is heard as a continuum. Phonetic contrasts such as [ra] and [la] are discriminated by infants 2 and 3 months old, but this ability is lost prior to adulthood in Japanese people who do not use the [ra] sound (Kolata, 1975).

Human beings inherit biological structures for speech and language which are not shared by other species. The search for the evolution of speech mechanisms has involved the subhuman primates, who use gestures and utterances for social interaction (Carmichael, 1970). Psychologists have had almost no success in trying to teach chimpanzees to speak (Brown, 1973). Their success in using social reinforcement and food rewards to teach them symbolic language will be described in the section to follow.

Some researchers focus their studies on the phylogenic evolution of human speech. They believe that observing the language of primates helps to explain the primitive stages of speech acquisition in young children. Other scientists, including many linguists, are more interested in the relationship between thought and language in a strictly human context. They study the child's early conceptualization of syntax and compare children's cognitive and speech patterns in different languages. Some psycholinguists view language as the organizer of most cognitive functions while others consider language as only the resultant of internal symbolism. Neurologists analyze the structure of the brain itself to discover how language is processed.

This chapter draws upon the resources of psychology, linguistics, and neurobiology for insight into the development of language in infants and children. The focus is on the communication sequence: comprehending, speaking, reading, and communication through writing. It is necessary to appreciate the factual basis of this sequence in order to understand how to help children to learn to communicate. Generally the most effective guidance is that which anticipates a child's periods of sensitivity and receptivity for particular steps in language learning.

This discussion is concerned with language acquisition in normal children who are learning their first language. The learning process differs for older persons learning a second or a third language. Deaf, severely retarded, and blind children encounter difficulty unless taught to understand and convey thought by systems which make use of the intact systems they have for processing word messages.

BIOLOGICAL STRUCTURES FOR LANGUAGE

Numerous psychologists have attempted to learn the phylogenic beginnings of language by rearing chimpanzees in a human environment. The potential effect of a superior environment for learning language skills, beyond those acquired in a natural environment, has been demonstrated by the Gardners, whose famous chimp Washoe was taught to communicate using Ameslan (American Sign Language). They taught the version of Ameslan which is a direct system of semantics or sign meanings and not the word spelling system. From age 11 months, when training was begun, Washoe acquired 132 signs of Ameslan, including the use of some signs in combination or as referents for classes of things. She could sign the names of things whether the real object, a picture, or a three-dimensional miniature was presented (Gardner & Gardner, 1975).

Project Washoe has shifted recently to training that began with neonate chimps, using the total environment to teach language. Three youngsters have been taught from day 1 or 2 in a social setting in which human handlers, some deaf, and all fluent signers, used signs to represent the actions and objects in the nursery and to communicate with each other (Figure 9-1). The Gardners predict that because they began at birth, and are using consistent and fluent conversation in a social

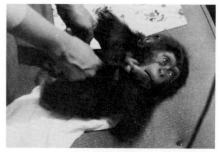

FIGURE 9-1 An infant chimpanzee is taught by deaf signers to use Amesian.
A. Pili uses the sign for *drink*.
B. He responds to tickling.
C. After being tickled, he initiates the sign *more*. From R. A. Gardner and B. T. Gardner, p. 752. *Science*, February 28, 1975, vol. 187. By permission of the authors and the AAAS. Copyright © 1975 by the American Association for the Advancement of Science.

setting involving day-to-day needs, these chimpanzees will improve upon the language learning of Washoe. Their success in teaching sign language has exceeded earlier attempts to teach symbolic speech. In addition to almost continuous interaction during the routines of care-giving the training methods include demonstration, operant shaping with rewards, and molding the infant's hands to make the signs.

A different training approach was used by Premack, whose chimp, Sarah, was reared in a cage and shaped by Skinnerian techniques to respond with plastic shapes that stuck to a magnetic board when placed there. The plastic tokens represented words from which Sara built vertical strings (sentences) on command from Premack who used food as a reinforcer. Beginning with a simple sentence, "Sarah put apple dish," Sarah advanced to stringing more complex linguistic statements. Using tokens for *same*, *not same*, *yes*, *no*, and *question* enabled Premack to elict complex linguistic performances (Premack, 1976).

Another chimpanzee, Lana, was taught to communicate with her trainer, Rumbaugh (1977), by typing on a keyboard of ideograms which were relayed to a visual display. *Ideograms* are graphic signs in writing that represent a message, or stretch of speech larger than a speech sound. An example is the signature mark used in ancient times to communicate authenticity to illiterate persons. The purpose of this research was to build a computor-based language system. To understand the linguistic accomplishments of Washoe, Sarah, and Lana it is necessary to consider the speech mechanisms of humans and then to ask what is language as it functions in humans.

A *symbol* is a sign that implies or represents something else; usually a more abstract version of the original object or idea. A *signal* is a visual, aural, or other indication used to convey information. Signal use is common in primate troups to convey affective messages such as approach, do not fear, this is play, or stay out of my territory. The use of nonspeech signs and symbols was necessary when teaching chimpanzees because chimps do not have the cortical area for speech control which humans inherit (Lenneberg, 1967). The grunts and squeals which are innate in apes are triggered in the midbrain, a phylogenically older and more primitive mechanism than the speech areas in the cortex of man.

Sensorimotor Bases

Nearly all the coded messages from the ears and the eyes are screened through the arousal and attention systems in the midbrain. From there the messages are relayed to the cortex of the brain for interpretation and response. Language and communication involve all the sensory systems, but those which interact most directly in communication are the auditory, visual, and motor systems. The particular areas of the human cortex which receive and store these three forms of information are shown in Figure 9–2.

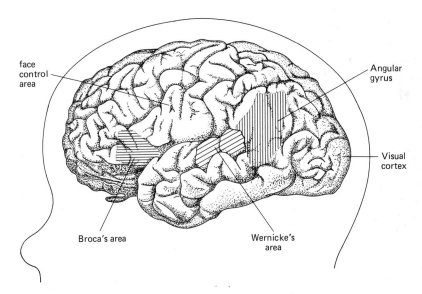

face control area

Angular gyrus

Visual cortex

Broca's area

Wernicke's area

FIGURE 9-2 Language areas of the left hemisphere. Verbal language functions are located in the left hemisphere of most persons. Broca's area, which is in the frontal lobe, controls language production. Motor control areas for speech (lips, tongue, soft palate, and vocal cords) are adjacent to Broca's area. Visual and auditory messages are integrated in the area of the angular gyrus. Wernicke's area is associated with the comprehension of language, including speech. (Drawing by Donna Thompson.)

Humans inherit the cortical map by which different areas of the brain are generally allocated to the sensory systems for interpretation and storage functions. An interconnecting neural system from one area to another enables the child to associate a visual image seen with a spoken word heard at the same time, as in the naming of objects such as *milk*, or *bed*. The motor activity in which the child simultaneously engages is also relayed continuously to cortical areas immediately behind the deep vertical fissure that forms a divide (Rolandic fissure) between the frontal and posterior portions of the brain hemisphere. Sensations from within the organism, including emotions, are also linked by association to the combined sensory experience.

In the early comprehension of verbs, a motor activity is associated with the action word that comes to represent it: "Drink your milk!" "Stop jumping on the bed." The motor output area is adjacent to the motor reception area along the Rolandic fissure, with body control areas being located adjacent for input and output of sensorimotor information.

SENSORY, CONNECTOR, AND MOTOR NEURONS

The structural unit for both language reception and language production is the neuron. Its messages are relayed as an electrochemical code that flashes through the axonal pathways by an on-off mechanism controlled in the cell bodies. A second system of brain activity is the patterned slow wave potential that can be measured during states of sleep and wakefulness. These brain waves move through the dendritic structure and are thought to have a function in the consolidation of sensory messages for memory storage (Pribram, 1971). In a context of language learning it is important to remember that only 1 billion neurons make up both the sensory and the motor systems, while 10 billion neurons are involved in the interconnecting systems. It is clear that the so-called sensorimotor period of infancy is a time for growth of interconnectors. The axonal and dendritic growth that forms the connections between the different language areas of the cortex are essential for receiving and initiating speech.

The sensorimotor period in child development (birth to 2 years old) involves an elaboration of neurons already present at birth. The most significant language function of the first year of life, from the neurological evidence available, is learning to comprehend speech. When the earliest social contact includes the auditory and visual stimulation of face-to-face talking, and the affective message has the effect of soothing the infant, the infant can begin to associate verbal communication and a feeling of trust in others. When the child first becomes mobile, there is survival value in being able to understand the warnings of the caretaker as well as to keep in touch by voice and sound.

PRIMARY SPEECH AREAS

The language areas of the human cortex are not as consistently located as are the motor areas, which are phylogenically older and elaborate at earlier periods of fetal growth. Language areas, once referred to as speech areas (Penfield & Roberts, 1959), have been named in the order they were discovered (Geschwind, 1971).

The *primary speech area*, named Wernicke's area after the discoverer, receives and interprets spoken language. Rapid development of these neurons, observed as myelination of the axons and elaboration of the dendrites, occurs during the first year of life (Carmichael, 1970). Although the chimpanzee responds earlier to spoken commands than does the child, the neural growth processes of the human child are more elaborate. The child acquires a complex system for handling the symbolic system of human language within the natural family setting and surpasses the chimp in the ability to follow directions while still in the sensorimotor period of infancy.

The *secondary language area*, called Broca's area, coordinates speech production and is not sufficiently evolved in chimpanzees for spontaneous speech, even when exposed to the linguistic culture of humans. Broca's area is located adjacent and frontal to the motor output areas that control face, tongue, and lip movements. The peak period for myelination and elaboration of this cortical area is the second year of life and corresponds with the rapid acquisition of words at that time (Carmichael, 1970).

The affective vocalization of young infants and the lower primates is not coordinated in the secondary language area. Affective (nonverbal) vocalizations that express feeling states are produced before birth, as well as afterward, and are controlled in the midbrain.

The *tertiary language area* is located at the top (superior) part of the speech control hemisphere. Its function in normal development is not clear, but in clinical cases this area has been found to take over some of the functions of either the Wernicke's or the Broca's area when these were damaged or removed. This flexibility in cortical areas that control language is more evident in young children than at later ages when the cells are already committed to other functions.

HEMISPHERE DOMINANCE

Brain dominance is the tendency to organize experience in one hemisphere of the brain. Speech and language functions are primarily organized in one hemisphere, usually the left, and spatial perception and processing in the opposite. The left hemisphere is dominant for speech in most persons. A small portion of individuals (approximately 5 to 10 percent) are right-hemisphere dominant for speech. This indicates that their verbal interpretations, as well as speech production, are directed from the right hemisphere. In most persons the hand and eye dominance corresponds with language functions. When left-handed persons receive conflicting or competing information into the brain, the dominant hemisphere directs their response. Right-hemisphere-speech–dominant persons are usually right-dominant for reading, and write left-handed.

Additional but similarly small numbers of individuals (5 to 10 percent) have speech and language dominance divided between the two brain hemispheres. These persons are likely to be ambidexterous; they usually function effectively, if not by the usual patterns. Mixed lateral dominance goes unnoticed, except when the person develops reading difficulties, or when brain surgery requires that the speech areas of the cortex be mapped to avoid damage to language communication skills.

Brain dominance, or at least the tendency to organize experience laterally, is inherited. Left-handedness is the focus of much attention at the time a child learns to write. By the time children enter first grade the areas of the cortex that process the language functions are heavily committed, at least in girls. The corresponding areas of the nondominant hemisphere are committed to receiving and interpreting nonverbal signs and symbols such as those used in block design, musical patterns, geometry, and map reading. Left-handedness is a recessive trait, and presumably the tendency of many functions related to lateral dominance are inherited also.

Sex differences in hemisphere commitment have been documented. Infant girls develop an earlier brain dominance for speech than boys do. This is correlated with, though not necessarily caused by, earlier speech acquisition in girls (Gazzaniga, 1967). Studies of sex differences in spatial interpretation and perception show that boys are usually favored in these areas from an early age, and this continues into adulthood. Witelson (1976) reported specialization of the right hemisphere for processing spatial and other nonlanguage abilities by age 6 in boys. Their superiority over girls in the ability to solve a spatial-tactile problem that required right-hemisphere specialization was found through age 13. Witelson suggests that the greater plasticity of the right hemisphere of girls may allow them to transfer verbal functions if developmental disorders interfere with left-hemisphere functions of speech and reading. The higher incidence of language disorders and infantile autism in males may be related to early hemisphere commitment to spatial processing.

Careful dissection of the brains of many persons who died in good health by accident showed that the Wernicke's area was significantly heavier on the left side in over 80 percent of the cases examined. This was true also of neonates who did not survive, indicating that hemisphere dominance is genetically influenced. In neither group of studies were handedness records available, but physiologists strongly suspect that the heavier cortical areas correspond to language and speech areas. Child development research has reported sex differences in the language versus spatial learning of older infants. It should be noted in this context that mothers interact differently toward the sexes by talking more to girl infants and by encouraging action and mobility in their boy infants. Kagan (1971) has suggested that culture may be responsive to inherited differences by approving those childrearing practices which reinforce inherited tendencies.

Early facility in the learning of new languages and other observations of cognitive development imply that many functions may be committed to either hemisphere between the ages of 2 and 3. Both sexes seem to have established brain dominance for speech by the age of 4. Behavioral organization of functions such as handwriting is increasingly difficult to shift with each passing year. In normal development, the inherited dominance may be expected to persist unless powerful intervention from the environment changes the pattern. The small percentage of children who are ambidexterous could be changed easily from left- to right-handed writers.

Propositional Language in Humans

Some important distinctions exist between the language of Homo sapiens and the communication among other primates. The language of humans is not only symbolic in content but it is propositional in function.

Propositional language is the use of coordinated sentences with connector words that make it possible to express a logical relationship. Propositional logic is constructed by a child in the sentence, "*If* I put all my toys away, *then* will you read me a story?" Propositional language functions in advance of an action by posing hypothetical events and consequences.

Linguistic propositions may be carried out in the imagination without physical or psychological risk to the person. Alternative actions may be considered and abandoned vicariously without ever involving another person. Propositional language is also used for evaluating experiences, after the fact, as part of the conceptual organization and reorganization humans sometimes do as part of the memory storage process.

Although language is not always defined in the same way, Brown (1973) presented what he considered the essential characteristics, or universal properties, of the language of Homo sapiens. First, this species has the ability to communicate over a range of semantic meanings not available to other species. Second, the encoding system has produced an open language which can handle any kind of information whatsoever, including new information. Third, the property of displacement adds the possibility of transmitting information from one time and place to another; the sentences are independent of the nonlinguistic setting. Brown used the criteria of *meaningfulness*, *productivity*, and *displacement* to analyze the language accomplishments of apes. He compared Washoe's spontaneous use of strings of Amesian signs to stage I of the five stages of linguistic accomplishment of human children. She created two sign combinations having a semantic relationship between noun and verb and she initiated communication, indicating productivity. Brown assumed that meanings were present, that is, that she showed semantic intention. Washoe did not use the same word order children universally use, but she did segment her constructions by keeping her hands in the signing area when combining signs.

Sarah's linguistic accomplishments, built by arranging columns of tokens, represented a variety of sentences including yes-no statements, negatives, class words, compound sentences and pluralization. Brown recognized the remarkable training power Premack used in shaping Sarah's language to particular terminal behaviors, but questioned the extent to which she understood her responses. Brown noted that Sarah did not use the token system to initiate dialogue. Her sentences depended upon emitting the right response in the presence of the right stimulus complex, with the stimulus patterns being progressively more complicated. He noted that Sarah's error ratio was about the same whether the linguistic construction was simple or complex. Children show an increase in errors when deletions and transfer tasks are presented for their interpretation and response.

One of the values of linguistic research with apes is to uncover how conceptual abilities evolved and how thought processes work in a preverbal or nonverbal individual (Humphrey, 1977). Both Premack and Rumbaugh consider the intelligence of chimps to be essentially prelinguistic. Their symbolic behavior may give important cues to the prelinguistic thought of infants and children. Perhaps more significant is the demonstration of the tremendous power to change behavior environmentally. A superior environment can bridge uncounted generations of phylogenic evolution in a single individual, and across species. The cultural advantage human children have is shown in their remarkable linguistic accomplishment within the social context but without the concentrated application of learning theory. Clearly linguistic competence is available to children if their teaching is begun early and conducted with care. The relationship between language development and conceptual development is considered in a later section.

SPEECH COMPREHENSION IN INFANCY

Long before children use language in speaking, they respond to verbal greetings and follow commands. Understanding is an internal process and as such has had little attention from those researchers who limit their concerns to overt behavior. Fortunately, many parents assume language perception on the part of their infants and provide a language environment by speaking to them in anticipation of the child's own speech. Imaginative procedures are being developed for observing the prespeech responses of infants to the language of adults. One such procedure uses movie film to analyze the body movements that accompany speech units. These techniques were first used to study the body language of adults and later applied to infants.

Neonate Responses to Sound

Condon and Sander (1974) found that as early as the first day after birth the human infant moves in sustained patterns that are synchronized with adult speech. In a careful analysis of films of neonate movements, matched frame by frame to the phonemes, syllables, and words in continuous adult speech, the investigators found a correspondence of 90 percent between neonate body movements and the structure of adult speech. This agreement held when a recording of adult speech was substituted for the live speaker in the experiments. By contrast, the correspondence of neonate movement to tapping sounds or to continuous spoken vowels dropped to about 50 percent. The question of how the neonate had learned before birth to discriminate and respond to human speech was not established in this study. However, the authors discussed the significance of their discovery in the language acquisition of children.

[The infant] participates developmentally through complex, sociobiological entrainment processes in millions of repetitions of linguistic forms long before he later uses them in speaking and communicating. By the time he begins to speak, he may have already laid down within himself the form and structure of the language system of his culture. (p. 101)

It is difficult to evaluate the many (and sometimes conflicting) studies of sound discrimination in neonates because of failure of some observers to assure optimum conditions for neonates to respond. In order to measure the auditory acuity of the newly born, the amniotic fluid must be drained from the ears before sound waves can reach and stimulate the receptors in the inner ear. Also, an appropriate state of alertness must be maintained if optimal responses are to be elicited.

Current procedures for testing the intelligence of neonates require the examiner to hold the infant in an inclined position with head cupped in the examiner's hand. This position is conducive to alertness and head turning if the infant is inclined to follow a sound or an object (Brazelton, 1973). Under these conditions, the normally integrated neonate responds to the examiner's speech and facial movement by head turning and searching. The normal neonate habituates, within a few trials, by not startling to repeated sounds such as the gong of a bell. Only those research procedures which elicit the attention and participation of infants are valid indicators of early potential for speech reception.

Hearing acuity is near normal at birth. Even permature infants, 7 months after conception, show normal response to a tuning fork. The peak period of myelinization of the auditory nerve occurs in the seventh month. The timing of this development is genetic, but the completion of a typical neural mechanism probably depends on sound stimulation from heartbeat and visceral sounds of the mother's body. Part of the fetal conditioning to sound is also associated with sound-wave stimulation to the tactile senses.

Affective Beginnings of Communication

Language development results from an interaction of cognitive and affective learning. The most conspicuous utterances of the neonate are emotional, need-oriented, and diffused. Very young infants mobilize the whole body in crying. Infant cries communicate the duration and intensity of noxious stimuli by the duration and intensity of their cry. Parents use the context of daily routine to help them distinguish a rage cry, which is abrupt and intense, from a hunger cry, which starts fretfully and gradually increases in intensity. Both signals are different from the colic cry, which is rhythmic and enduring. By 1 month of age the infant has modified its cry to include the whimper, another semantic distinction which is both affective in expression and basic to communication.

Roger Brown (1958) suggested that the whimper is the beginning of the primal sentence. Parents, by anticipating the infant's need, respond promptly to the whimper with food or attention in order to forestall the irritating stimuli of the loud crying that will follow to express the intensification of the need. In this way, according to Brown, the whimper may come to represent the want for juice, blanket, or toy. The object wanted becomes the predicate object which becomes associated with the critical gesture the child uses to complete the communication or to satisfy the want. "(You) take me." "Juice to drink" (from refrigerator, not water from tap). Learning the sequence is the resultant of the child's success in meeting his or her needs (Wilson, Robeck, & Michael, 1974).

The affective expressions of the young infant have many similarities to the sound emissions of untrained chimpanzees living in a natural habitat. Their social interaction includes a "joy" sound among its range of vocalizations (Goodall, 1963) which is not unlike the affective cooing of human infants. Prespeech utterances are controlled primarily in the hypothalamic areas of the midbrain, which is phylogenically older than cortical speech areas and functionally very primitive. These midbrain areas are closely linked neurologically with the limbic areas where the pleasure-punishment centers are located. Motivations are closely associated with the hypothalamic and limbic systems. Neural connections link these areas with the thalamus, which is the major organization center for interconnections with the cortex.

The sounds that neonates make serve a biological purpose in the control of behavior of the adults who attend them. The survival value of crying need not be documented. Psychologists continue to speculate on the function of crying in the development of organs and tissues that produce speech sounds.

Stages of Prespeech

Despite the infant's use of crying as a demand upon adults, some infant utterances quickly take on the function of social communication. Cooing and gurgling, accompanied by a smile, are positively reinforcing to those who attend a baby. At 1 month, the reflexive smile of the neonate has developed into a gesture of greeting. By 6 months, some infants "talk back" in face-to-face conversation, using hand movements or body bounces that are different from the angry flailing that accompanies frustration crying. By 8 months, some infants use strings of jargon, which may be interpreted as a playful exercise of speech mechanisms, as an attempt to imitate the adult models, or as a serious attempt to produce conversation.

The prespeech of infants is usually characterized by *vocalizing*, which includes the many and varied utterances of the first few months, and *babbling*, which emerges later. Babbling noises are the echolaic, or repetitive, speech sounds that gradually drift into the phonemes the infant hears (Brown, 1958, p. 199).

If the cries, grunts, and gurgles an infant emits are recorded and analyzed together with the babbling sounds, most of the phonemes of the native language, as well as other languages, are produced. McNeill (1970) reviewed research which indicated three distant periods in prespeech during the first year of life. The first period, from birth through the third month, is characterized by vocalization. Rapid changes occur in the frequency and variety of vowel production, and to some extent in consonant production (p. 1132).

The second period begins at about 4 months when the frequency of vocalizing drops abruptly. Babbling is focused on a series of peaks in vowel productions which shape to the vowels of the speech the infant hears. With few exceptions the order of the vowel production and refinement is from the back to the front of the mouth. Similar peaks occur in the babbling of consonant sounds, except that the direction of development is from the front to the back.

The third period begins between the tenth month and the first birthday when, according to McNeill, a "total collapse" of babbling occurs and the slow process of word production begins for most children. They shift from playing with sounds to planning their speech and begin the difficult mastery of articulating the sounds that were used freely when babbling.

FUNCTIONS OF BABBLING

Changes in the vocalization patterns of the infant indicate changes in the growth priorities of the neurological structures that produce speech sounds. Piaget (1959) observed a change at about 4 months old in the infant's shift from accidentally producing a sound and repeating it for the pleasure of hearing it to repeating a sound as an action on the environment. In Piaget's terms, the child moves from *primary circular reactions* to *secondary circular reactions*; the child moves from continuing an accidental event to initiating sound repetitions for their effect.

Babbling has been called "autistically satisfying" in that exericse of neural systems produces inner pleasures that lead to repetition of the particular action that produces the sensation (Myklebust, 1954). An important function of vocalization is the practice of speech mechanisms, including the integration of breathing with sound emission. Bever (1961) has suggested that the cycles observed in vocal development are produced by phases of neurological maturation. The first cycle reflects a "concern with tonal activity" and the "differentiation of affective crying." The second phase, babbling, is "presumably a reflection of the process of integrating vocal activity and cortical organization" (p. 47).

Sommerhoff (1974) noted that the function of the second prespeech period appears to involve a sensorimotor matching on the part of the infant of phone units (or speech sounds) with morpheme units (or meanings). He suggested that mere repetition of sounds makes less demand on the speech mechanisms than when comprehension is involved (pp. 375–376). In neurological development, comprehension requires the growth of long connecting neurons from the frontal area of Broca with the auditory association area along the top of the temporal lobe with the speech comprehension area of Wernecke.

During the third period of prespeech, the production of speech is at a low ebb but the child is increasing its comprehension of adult speech. This period has been

An infant babbling is playing with sounds. (Erika/Peter Arnold)

inappropriately called the passive period in language development, perhaps from a misconception that language begins with speaking words. In order to build the appropriate neural system for comprehension, the young child must attend to speech. Young children have difficulty understanding speech while simultaneously formulating speech, although adults can do this easily. Apparently the child must switch from one function to the other by controls in the hypothalamus (Pribram, 1975). As the child begins the "naming" stage of early speech, the priority in neural growth shifts to voluntary control over speech mechanisms, which is a function of the cortex.

Age, Sex, and Individual Differences

The sequential development in vocalization and babbling reflects the interaction of the infant's growth priorities and the social environment. Kagan (1971) studied this interaction of heredity and environment in the prespeech that accompanied a variety of experimentally controlled experiences. For purposes of the study he defined vocalization as the vocal response of "excited interest," excluding crying and fretting, when the child was presented with an unusual event. Kagan used many laboratory tests and home observations of the same children at 2, 8, 13, and 27 months to observe spontaneous vocalization and cognitive development. He was interested in sex differences (a hereditary factor) and social-class differences (an environmental factor) as they affected infant vocalization. Secondly, he wanted to determine if prespeech indicated language proficiency in the same children after 2 years of age.

Kagan found that vocalization dropped off significantly between 4 to 8 months, but increased, again significantly, by 13 months old. There were no sex differences in the amount of vocalization, but girls were more likely to vocalize spontaneously when presented with a picture of a human face, especially when novelty was also introduced (two heads on one body). He also found a positive relationship among girl infants between excited vocalization when presented with a mask at 4 months and attention to a human speaker at 8 months old.

Kagan reported a definite tendency for young infants to be high babblers or low babblers when confronted with an exciting situation; but they changed this pattern during the first year according to adult responsiveness, or lack of reinforcement, for babbling at home. Vocalization was more likely to be "in the service of the excitement that accompanies active assimilation among girls, but not among boys" (1971, p. 104).

Kagan found social-class differences in mother-daughter interaction; better-educated mothers did more face-to-face talking to 4-month-old girls than did mothers with less formal education. Upper-middle-class daughters at the second round of observations showed greater discrimination of high- and low-meaning verbalization, plus greater quiet-listening to mother's versus stranger's voice.

Kagan suggests that environmental differences may be interacting with biological differences between boys and girls in the rate of language area myelination and hemisphere commitment (pp. 108–111).

By 8 months of age vocalization accompanied excited attention and was predictive of language development at 13 months and later. By 27 months, verbalization was related positively in the combined sample to general intelligence, vocabulary level, sustained attention, and nonverbal perceptual problem solving. These relationships held for both sexes, although the girls, as a group, showed greater consistency than did boys.

Universal Order of Phonemic Development

Jakobson (1968) believed that the sequence of phonemic development is invariant and universal among children. He believed that all children begin with a primitive process of differentiation between /p/ and /a/, which represent maximum contrasts in vocal production. The consonant /p/ is formed in the front of the mouth; it is a stop which is unvoiced, and is produced with minimal acoustic energy. The vowel /a/ as in *mama* is formed at the back of the mouth and requires a full opening of the vocal tract. Without reporting Jakobson's detailed progression in full his observation of a developmental order is important. *Pa, papa* is followed by a consonant split *ma, mama*. (Perhaps babies named their parents in some cultures with words that could be discriminated and produced early.) At first /a/ supports the consonants and makes possible the production of rhythmic syllables, according to Jakobson. A /p/ and /t/ split is followed by vowel splits /a/ /k/, /u/ /i/, etc. The point is that sounds must be separated to be discriminated by infants and organized into a system. The phonemes which are not universal but specific to a particular language are learned relatively late.

Jakobson also observed that in speech (as with babbling) the developmental order of consonants is from the front of the mouth back, and for vowels from the back of the mouth forward. He suggested that phonemic systems reflect the same laws that define the order of children's acquisition of consonants; that is, back consonants may be absent from language but not the forward consonants that precede them. Also the last consonants that children acquire are relatively rare among the languages of the world, such as the /th/ in *think*. In addition to a phonemic structure there is also a system of rules by which phonemes are combined to conform to a set of phonological rules for stress and intonation. This relationship between sound production and the design of spoken language suggests like mechanisms for speech among humans, regardless of the differences in the sound of language in different cultures.

ACQUISITION OF LINGUISTIC STRUCTURE

Children of all cultures learn to speak their native language in much the same way and at approximately the same time. Individual differences in the rate of acquiring speech are greater within a language population than between cultural groups. But the sequence of development for both phonemic and syntactical structures was invariant in dozens of languages observed and analyzed (Slobin, 1972). Cross-cultural research in acquisition of speech has been extensive.

The practice of phonemes during babbling overlaps the matching of phoneme and morpheme units during later infancy. The term *lexicon* refers to the total stock of morphemes in a language. The child's stock of morphemes understood is greater at any given time in language development than is the lexicon of recorded speech. The spoken lexicon is often accepted as the index of the child's language because it is more easily observed and verified than comprehension.

The order and manner by which infants evolve their own lexical structure provide cues to linguists about the thinking processes of children and also about the manner in which language may have evolved in humans to begin with.

It has been pointed out that children about 1 year of age go about naming things (Brown & Bellugi, 1964). The function of this typical behavior may be the practice of saying single words and of making associative references to objects (p. 142). Mere naming is distinct from communication through one-word sentences. Ervin-Tripp (1973) prefers the term *sociolinguistic competence* to describe the early stages in learning to speak as a way of distinguishing this sequence from nonlinguistic communication, which also develops in sequence but at an earlier age (p. 293).

Syntax is sentence structure; it is the ordering of word elements in a sentence. Children begin linguistic communication with one-word utterances that function, within a meaningful context, as sentences. Children 18 to 24 months begin using a two-word skeletal sentence in speech. By the age of 36 months some children are so advanced in the sentence construction process as to produce all the major varieties of simple English sentences up to a length of ten to eleven words (Brown & Bellugi, 1964). By the age of 48 months, the typical child around the world has acquired the ability to use a complete and almost accurate sentence structure of the native language.

Holophrastic Speech

The most common one-word sentence of infants and toddlers is a noun which carries a complete meaning within the environmental context. "Car" means "(A) car (has come)." "Cookie" means "(I want a) cookie!" Verbs are used as commands: "See" may mean "(You) see (me standing)" or "go" may mean "(You may) go (now, I will stay with the sitter)." Modifiers are less common than nouns. "More" may mean "(I want) more (cereal)," or "wet" may mean "(My diapers are) wet." The exclamations toddlers use ("oh, oh" or "hi") are appropriate as to context and intonation, but they are more easily traced to imitation of adult models than are most categories of holophrastic speech.

Telegraphic Speech

Telegraphic sentences derive that label from a resemblance to the telegrams adults compose when they must pay for each word used. Similarly, young children preserve the word meaning by speaking the significant, or *content* words in correct sequence, but shorten the sentences by leaving out the connector words, the *functors*.

Most children begin combining words by adding modifiers to a noun to create a noun phrase, or by combining a noun with an appropriate verb. Ervin-Tripp (1964) analyzed the rules children generate when they begin to put two and three words together. The earliest sentences nearly always contained a nominal: "Blanket water," "Bow-wow dog," "Oh, car," and "Here big truck." She described one child's rules for generating noun phrases which he used as telegraphic sentences (Table 9–1). The child was consistent in his ordering: first articles ("a," "the") followed by modifiers ("red," "big," "more") and a third class of modifiers ("yellow," "broken," "all-gone"). These *optional classes* were used in correct order and were followed by the *required class* of words that functioned as nouns ("ball," "choo-choo," "monkey"). Her subjects produced many unadult forms as required class words which could not have been imitations of the mother's speech, such as, "big yellow," "a broken," and "all-gone ball." This particular child, at age 2½, used four types of sentences. Most of them were *declarative*: "There's a green." A lesser number were *nominal* sentences: "A big red." The remainder were

Table 9-1
CHILD'S RULE FOR GENERATING
NOMINAL PHRASES

Optional classes*			Required class
1	**2**	**3**	**4**
a	red	all-gone	all-gone
the	big	ball	ball
	more	bead	bead(s)
		broken	broken
		bye-bye	bye-bye
		choochoo	choochoo
		green	green
		monkey	monkey
		truck	truck
		yellow	yellow
		etc.	etc.

*The child may use any or all of the optional class words, but preserves the order.

Source: S. M. Ervin-Tripp, Imitation and structural change in children's language. Reprinted from *New Directions in the Study of Language* by E. H. Lenneberg (Ed.) by permission of the M. I. T. Press, Cambridge, Massachusetts. Copyright © 1964 by The Massachusetts Institute of Technology.

telegraphed forms of the verbs "go" or "have it." Eighty percent of the spontaneous sentences used by several children in these analyses followed the rules they generated for themselves.

Imitation

Psycholinguists do not agree on the extent to which children learn language by imitation of adult speech. Those who prefer the Skinnerian behaviorist explanation of language learning, to the exclusion of other theories, believe that children acquire speech by shaping by reinforcement from the environment. Premack used reinforcement to shape the language responses of Sarah to closer and closer approximations of the complex linguistic goals he had in mind. The shaping of children's language is less systematic, but they are provided with models for language usage to imitate and then are reinforced by attention and the granting of their requests as their speech becomes more easily understood.

Some investigators have documented the shaping of language by imitation as one process and the child's disposition to create linguistic structure by comprehension and extension as a different process. Ervin-Tripp (1964) analyzed recordings of the spontaneous speech of five children ranging in age from 22 to 36 months over a period of several months. A feature of her research design was that she did not request imitations of the children, but identified their *spontaneous imitations* and compared the incidence of these with *freely generated* sentences.

Only 5 to 20 percent of the sentences produced by different children were imitations. The freely generated sentences were quite as mature grammatically as the imitated sentences were. In the case of one child who imitated 20 percent of the time, her imitations were less mature, less consistent in structure, and shorter in word length than her self-generated sentences. In all her child subjects Ervin-Tripp found a disposition to create linguistic systems. Language developed by three processes. First, there was a continual expansion in the comprehension of adult speech. A second process was the imitation of particular instances, some of which were uttered long after they were heard. The third process, the building by analogy of classes and rules, most accurately described the syntactical development of children. She suggested that listening with comprehension to adult speech was at the base of the generalizations and analogies formed by the child.

Brown and Bellugi (1964) classified the two-word segments of speech children use as telegraphic sentences on the evidence that the *terminal intonation contour* in pronunciation was like that of mature speech. The pitch and stress of telegraphic sentences were discovered to be unlike the pitch and stress that children use when they say two holophrastic words in sequence. Brown and Bellugi also analyzed the imitations children used in the family setting to determine the effect of mother's language over a period of time. Important differences were found between the language of mothers when talking to their 2-year-olds and when talking to adults. The adult speech to children was simplified, repetitive, and near-perfect in grammatical form. When the recordings were analyzed it was found that two kinds of imitation occurred, the child's and the mother's.

CHILD IMITATIONS WITH REDUCTION

Children's early imitation preserved the syntactical order of their model while reducing the number of words repeated. This suggested to Brown and Bellugi (1964) that comprehension was important in the children's selection of words being repeated. Imitation increased the adult's ability to understand the child's utterances and probably reinforced the child for participation in conversation (p. 137). When the parent increased the number of words in the model sentence, the child did not increase the imitation correspondingly but retained a range of 2 to 4 morphemes per sentence. For the most part, the words retained in the reduction were *contentives,* so-called because of their semantic content. These reductions usually included nouns, verbs, and some adjectives. The words children tended to leave out were the *functors,* that is, "service" words such as auxiliaries, inflections, articles, prepositions, and conjunctions (p. 139). Although many of these words are well practiced as single-word referents, Brown and Bellugi suggest this is not the full explanation. They observed that contentives are retained, even when relatively unfamiliar.

ADULT IMITATIONS WITH EXPANSION

The reduction process is reversed when parents imitate their young children. They expand the imitated sentence by adding functors to the telegraphed speech of the

Table 9-2
CHILD'S REDUCTION AND ADULT'S EXPANSION OF IMITATED SENTENCES

Model utterance	Child's reduction	
Frazer will be unhappy	Frazer unhappy	
He's going out	He go out	
No, you can't write on Mr. Cromer's shoe	Write Cromer shoe	

	Child's sentence	Mother's expansion
	Baby highchair	Baby is in the highchair
	Mommy sandwich	Mommy'll have a sandwich
	Sat wall	He sat on the wall

Source: Roger Brown and Ursula Bellugi, "Three Processes in the Child's Acquisition of Syntax." Reproduced by permission from *New Directions in the Study of Language*, Eric H. Lenneberg (Ed.), Cambridge, Mass: MIT Press, Copyright © 1964; by the Massachusetts Institute of Technology.

youngster. Brown and Bellugi (1964) reported that mothers expanded 30 percent of the time, or more frequently than the youngsters imitated them (p. 144). Table 9–2 shows that the child's original word order was generally preserved, but there were important differences between parent and child imitations. The child's reductions were more predictable and mechanical, while the parent imitations were not mechanically generated. Parents produced new and varied models for noun plurals, verb tenses, prepositions, and articles. These were the forms children omitted during reduction and, generally, the sentence complexities the children themselves would be producing about 1 year hence. Adult-child conversations were described as continuous cycles of transformation by reduction and expansion.

The function of adult expansion in the child's acquisition of language appears to be its confirmation of those portions of speech which are meaningful and correct; this is done in a setting in which the child is giving full attention to the adult cues. Extensions that provide new grammatical forms, in context, become the basic associations the child will use later when conceptualizing new and more complex rules.

Conceptualization of Structure

The challenge to linguists to explain how children conceptualize the deep structure of their native language was stimulated by Chomsky's 1957 book on generative syntax. Much more impressive than the child's early ability to imitate adult speech is the predisposition of youngsters to conceptualize the latent, or deep, structure of language. The evidence is impressive that inductive processes are involved which go beyond the child's modeling of adult speech or by the associative accumulation of grammatical forms. First, there is the preponderance of spontaneous utterances, recorded and analyzed as unique, for which the child has no previous model (Brown & Bellugi, 1964).

Second, the kinds of errors children make reveal a predisposition to construct and follow rules in speech production. In fact, they overuse their own self-generated rules to cover irregular as well as regular forms. Some examples of using overextended English rules for noun phrases are "A my basket" and "My two foots." The child who has generalized "played," "washed," and "cooked" as examples of the rule for indicating the past of an action is likely to say "goed," "seed," and "wented" until the exceptions to the rules are learned by correction and imitation.

A third source of evidence for children's use of inductively derived structure, rather than purely imitated speech, is the rapid transfer of grammatical classifications generated in one context to the spontaneous creation of language in a new situation. The learning curves for acquisition of words, phrases, and sentences all show the sudden acceleration that characterizes conceptualization, or rule discovery (Figure 9–3). Learning curves for association linkages are stepwise and rise gradually (Wilson et al., 1974).

Fourth, children acquire deep structure by a similar sequence of achievements in many different languages (Slobin, 1972). In all cultures, the child typically follows a sequence of linguistic discovery that is largely unconscious but is consistent with semantic priority (Figure 9–3). A universal sequence has already been indicated by which children begin to speak with nominals and then develop the ability to

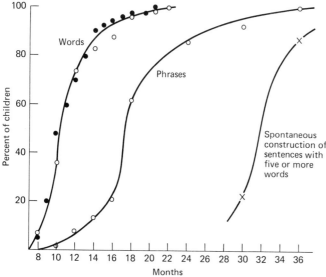

FIGURE 9-3 Milestones in the acquisition of language. From Eric H. Lenneberg, "Speech development." In *Brain Functions III*, p. 38, E. C. Carterette (Ed.). Published in 1966 by the Regents of the University of California, reprinted by permission of the University of California Press.

formulate two- and three-word telegraphed sentences. In each of the languages investigated, children produce complex sentences, first by stringing them end to end, and later by imbedding one sentence in another.

Ervin-Tripp (1973) proposes that children use the accumulation of particular experiences in hearing and imitating speech to formulate linguistic classes and rules. Although imitation continues to influence their learning of the language, children's speech is idiosyncratically structured and rule governed. Children also continue to increase their comprehension of adult speech and to increase the length and complexity of their sentences. Although creative in its usage their grammar shows a sequence of structural changes over time which is developmentally consistent and different from the syntax of adults.

LANGUAGE AND THOUGHT

The relationship between language and cognition is treated extensively in discussions of philosophy and models of learning, but is relatively unexplored by developmental research. The question often posed is whether language is the precursor, the resultant, or the medium of thought. Piaget is one of many epistemologists to turn to the observation of language development for clues to the evolution of the intellect.

Piaget: Language as Representation

Piaget has maintained that logical thought in older children and in adults is built upon the sensorimotor structures (schemata) developed during the first 2 years of life (1970). He sees language as imposed by the culture and learned quite independent of operational thought, which is developmental, spontaneous, and phylogenically ordered in the species. Children structure their own knowledge, according to Piaget, by interacting with the environment. Conceptualizations such as seriation, reversibility, and displacement are learned according to a predictable order that is typically tied to the age of the child. There are exceptions in the rate of development, but the intellect of man is species-specific. Language is build on sensorimotor knowledge, and not the other way around.

The one-word and telegraphic language of the child, which appears during the last half of the sensorimotor period, received little attention from Piaget, perhaps because his role as a biologist was well defined before his psychological studies of cognition were initiated. However, Piaget has continued to regard language as one form of *representational thought*, having a symbolic function, along with signs and visual images.

The young child constructs his or her own intelligence which is the internal counterpart of the child's own actions on objects—visual, auditory, and somatic. Piaget's descriptions of the subperiods of cognitive development, between the sensorimotor period (birth to 2 years old) and the concrete-operations period (8 to 11 years old), reveal his views of the function of language (Piaget, 1959). The subperiod from approximately 2 to 4 years old is called *preconceptual* because the

How do we know plants consume?

Language acquisition occurs in a developmental order: understanding, speaking, reading, then writing. (Archie Lieberman/Black Star)

child manipulates images of things present. The ages of 4 to 5½ years old are described as the ages of "simple representations," because the child has acquired the mental structure to deal with symbols, but only in the presence of the concrete objects they represent. When confronted with a problem, such as judging the amounts of clay in two equal balls after the shape of one has been altered, the preoperational child obeys perception, rather than logic. Even though the clay mass is equal, he insists that one ball is larger "because it is longer." The child of this age cannot mentally reverse the process to the original shape of the ball. At the age of *simple representations*, the child sometimes guesses correctly on the basis of *intuitive thought* but is still unable to give a logical explanation. During the subperiod from 5½ to 7 or 8 years, the child responds to the same problem with *articulated representations*, "Both balls of clay are the same because nothing was added and nothing was taken away." *Ah-ha!* To Piaget, this period in development is one in which the child learns to employ the language of the culture in the service of his intellectual development by explaining what his actions have already shown him about the physical environment.

Piaget saw children's conversation during this period as *egocentric*, directed toward themselves, rather than as social interaction. Until about age 7 or 8, children may play beside other children, but literally talk to themselves about their own actions; "I am painting a tower, I am painting the tower yellow." Once children have progressed to a stage of performing mental operations without the object or persons being present they are able to put themselves in the place of another and speech becomes socialized.

Besides knowing the relationship between oneself and objects, the child must also learn the relationship between objects, but this has very little to do with language (Piaget, 1970, p. 706). Piaget's contributions to our understanding of the child's development of thought are: (1) the child participates himself in intellectual growth, (2) humans have an innate, biological necessity to organize experience symbolically, and (3) intellectual development is an interaction between the essentially human organism and the environment. However, Piaget distinguished between cognitive *development*, which he saw as biologically ordered, and language *learning*, which he saw as culturally imposed by training and education. He therefore differed from many linguists.

Vygotsky: Concepts as Linguistic Abstractions

Vygotsky (1962) was stimulated by Piaget's daring departure from conventional behaviorist theory. Although supporting his developmental model generally, Vygotsky took issue with Piaget's separation of thought and language and his interpretation of child language as primarily egocentric. In the Soviet experiments, the proportion of egocentric speech children used changed markedly from one setting to another. When a cooperative task was established by the teachers, the proportion of socialized speech increased, even though the activities included similar choices of painting, block building, and the like. Whereas Piaget believes egocentric speech to be the bridge between the "autistic" thought of infancy and the "logical" thought of adolescence, Vygotsky argued that egocentric thought is the transitional stage in the evolution between vocal and inner speech. He pointed to the early nonverbal utterances between parent and infant and to early conversations when the child is still using reduced grammar. The Soviet observers noted that egocentric speech at first marked the end of an activity. This pattern gradually shifted to the use of egocentric speech at the middle of an activity and finally to its use at the beginning, when egocentric speech took on the function of direction and planning. "A small child draws first, then decides what it is that he has drawn; at a slightly older age, he names his drawing when it is half done; and finally he decides beforehand what he will draw" (p. 17). Egocentric speech, according to Vygotsky, goes underground to become thought. His notion of how thinking evolves from speech is very different from Piaget's, who proposed that speech evolves from knowing through the senses.

Vygotsky outlined the steps of concept formation in children by focusing on language. The word becomes a generalization when it refers to a class of things. In concept formation, children first form "heaps" of objects according to their nonverbal, subjective meaning and later associate one-word references to these "heaps." *Associative complexes* are objects united in the child's mind by bonds which actually exist between objects in the child's world. These associative bonds are perceptual and not logical. A *collection complex* is a group of objects that have mixed properties but are grouped on the basis of participation in the same practical operation. A concept of a class of objects is similar to a family portrait in which many visual images are superimposed, simplified, and generalized. When children reach this level of concept formation they can group "things we eat with," or "things we play with." A *chain complex* is the purest form of thinking in complexes, a process in which the learner carries meanings from one associative link to the next. Thought at this level is bound to the concrete objects to which it refers. The *diffuse complex* involves associations and generalizations which exceed the limits of concrete bonds, but which remain dim, unreal, and unstable. A *pseudoconcept* is the bridge between the associative complex and the concept as Vygotsky defines it.

The true *concept* is an abstraction which can be used apart from the concrete experiences to which it refers. The symbolic word is an integral part of concept formation. Symbolic concepts enable the child to move from the general to the particular (analysis) and from the particular to the general (synthesis) Vygotsky and his colleagues accelerated children's ability to conceptualize classes by labeling attribute blocks with a nonsense hidden name which served to label the class. The children learned to categorize faster by having a class word to verify the classes.

Vygotsky described thought as conceptualized actuality; as experience generalized and simplified. His contributions include (1) an analysis of the contribution of language to the thought processes, (2) the distinction between association "complexes" and the abstractions he called true concepts. The similarity of Piaget's stages of representational thought and Vygotsky's concept formation is striking. The major difference lies in the function of language in cognitive development. Most of Piaget's experiments were based on right hemisphere functions, the understanding of spatial and physical relationships, while Vygotsky's research dealt primarily with the left hemisphere functions of language.

Associative, Conceptual, and Creative Language

Language which is acquired by modeling, imitating, and shaping is easily observed because the stimulus (from the environment) and the response (a child's utterance) occur close together. This level of learning is easy to manipulate, given the developmental capability of the child, and the patience to learn and apply what is reinforcing to him.

According to some linguists the tendency for children to evolve and follow grammatical rules in early speech is not fully explained by operant theories of learning. The process by which subject-predicate or noun-verb-object relationships are comprehended and then overgeneralized to new situations probably involves the conceptualization of a class. Human youngsters are exceedingly adept at acquiring linguistic structures between 1 and 4 years old. Vygotsky (1962) was impressed by Stern's description of a child 18 months old who discovered what every speaker must, that every object has its name. At this point the typical youngster goes about naming objects and asking, if the name isn't known, "What's that?" Or, more often, "Wazzaa?"

Helen Keller, who was both blind and deaf from infancy, was old enough when she conceptualized the function of a name to remember the experience. Her teacher had spelled *w-a-t-e-r* and other words over and over in her hand. Helen could repeat the hand spelling as a conditioned response, but her teacher knew she had not grasped the linguistic significance of words as representing things.

Suddenly I felt a misty consciousness as of something forgotten—a thrill of returning thought; and somehow the mystery of language was revealed to me. I knew that "water" meant the wonderful cool something that was flowing over my hand. . . .

I left the well-house eager to learn. Everything had a name, and each name gave birth to a new thought. As we returned to the house every object which I touched seemed to quiver with life. . . .

I learned a great many new words that day. I do not remember what they all were; but I do know that *Mother, father, sister, teacher* were among them . . . . (Keller, 1955, p. 165)

At least to Helen Keller and her teacher, the distinction was clear between the hand spelling, in which a series of linked signs is associated with a particular object, and the conceptualization that any object can be represented symbolically by the same communication system. It is significant, however, that direct instruction in which many word-object associations were signed was basic to the concept of word.

Carroll (1964) accepted the idea that concepts exist apart from lexicon, but he noted that concepts are more likely to be represented by symbols as children advance in age. To him concepts are named by language symbols which are the "tools" of thought (p. 111). They organize internal processes and stimulate internal responses that carry forward external action. Many psychologists do not deal with conceptualization as an internal reality because their self-imposed rules as scientists do not admit subjective experience to their data.

Creative language is produced for the self-expression of the speaker and is motivated by his or her own value structure. Adults do not agree on whether children's unique expressions should be considered "creative" because they would probably use adult modes if they knew them. Erika, age 5, came into the kitchen. "Can I have some of those? What do you call those giant raisins?" By some criteria, giant raisins could be considered unique language for prunes. But more important, if creative expression is to flourish in the young child and extend into adulthood, is the recgonition and appreciation of the child's own way of saying things. "I call them prunes, but I really enjoy the way you describe them. Giant raisins, I like that."

ADULT RESPONSIBILITY FOR CHILD LANGUAGE

Robert Thorndike (1975) was commissioned to study whether the Stanford-Binet Intelligence Scales (1960) were holding firm with reference to the norms estab-

Writing is expressive language. (Raimondo Borea/Editorial Photocolor Archives)

lished at that time (Chapter 8). The Binet scales are known to be highly predictive of school success, and anyone who has administered them knows that understanding and not verbalization are required to score. The children Thorndike described as "the Sesame Street generation" rated an average of 10 IQ points above the 1960 norms; however, the same children when retested after three years had lost, on the average, about 5 IQ points. Different psychologists will explain these results in different ways, but one possible explanation is a change in the quality of language stimulation with reference to the stage of development which interacted with learning opportunities to make possible greater gains than had occurred in an earlier environment.

Adults interacting with children provide a language environment which is different from and superior in many ways to the language environment of age peers. Research supports the following recommendations to teachers and parents of young children.

Face-to-face talking with infants is correlated with attention to speech in children under 1 year. Strong, positive associations of pleasure are conducive to talking nonsense with infants. Stroking and cuddling shorten the time infants require to turn a reflexive smile into a responsive smile. Preverbal utterances of a happy variety, laughing and cooing, are the languages which a neonate takes in.

Imitation of babbling confirms the babbling sounds of infants and establishes voice communication. Unlike "baby talk" or delayed articulation, the adult need not fear that the child will follow a poor model. Playing with sound, along with the infant, invites later games and gives the child a chance to hear phonemes at different frequency levels from her own.

Naming the important things in the child's environment helps to isolate words and establish meanings in an unambiguous context. Commands, exclamations, repetitions, and simple sentences are all part of the repertoire of adult instruction to young children. Children need to hear adults talk to each other. However, the evidence is that second languages are not learned well by children who are not involved in conversation in the language.

Reinforcement of early efforts to communicate with words is critical. Attempts to understand the full meaning of holophrastic speech constitute the social reinforcement children need to progress.

Imitation and expansion of children's telegraphic speech provide models for them to discover the complex rules of tense and number. The accident of birth into an educated home is an inheritance beyond price. The nursery schools whose purpose it is to teach "standard English" cannot waste the preschool years.

Vocabulary building occurs casually in some homes where parents use the words that describe a situation best and involve the children in these conversations without talking "down" to them. In school, teachers can expose children to mathematical terms and other specialized vocabulary the child will use a year or more later. Using these words in context to build understanding, without asking the child to use them in speech, is high-level·teaching, whether at home or at school.

Sharing written communication, the letter from Uncle Henry or the note from the principal's office, is the affective foundation for writing on one's own initiative. Reading stories from the same side of the book, sharing "good" television programs, and mustering the self-discipline to eliminate the poor ones are some practical ways to upgrade the language environment of the preschool child.

Writing begins with bits and pieces, perhaps one word. Some children scribble long letters, which some mothers mail to appreciative relatives. When children become curious about letter names, this is an optimum time to teach them. When children want to write letters it may be negative reinforcement to deny them. A good medium for young children is a small chalkboard of their own. A box or a drawer for scraps of paper saves interruptions and enables the child to write on impulse. For example, Heidi, age 4, prepared her own shopping list while her parents were making theirs: "HAM4ER." Her mother served hamburgers for dinner.

Family games appropriately chosen are fascinating to children if the rules can be adjusted to their span of interest and their discrimination ability. Cards, anagrams, readiness games, and letter cutouts help the child to learn the give-and-take of group activities.

In an affluent society the right of every child might be a second language.

Probably 4 years of age is the child's last chance to learn a second language in a social setting that is similar to the optimum language learning environment of the home. Nursery school in another language is an exciting and happy experience for children who have learned to trust adults, and to communicate with language.

How to provide the optimum learning environment for children whose first language is a dialect of black English is a much disputed but exceedingly important question. The developmental literature on linguistics appears to point to earlier and more systematic introduction in reading. Most black children have acquired a linguistic structure and generate propositional language according to the universally observed timetable described in this chapter. The critical element in their early education may be to preserve and enhance the child's identity in a new microsetting (the school) that differs from the familiar one (the home). The major problem in teaching minority children to read in their own vernacular first is that the optimal time for acquiring linguistic skills, from 4 to 8 years, is lost for learning to speak and to read in standard English. Black graduate students, who want educational opportunities for their children, can articulate this problem well. According to them, teachers of young black children need to know the neighborhood from which the children come and to know the events within families that shape the child's conceptual world so that the new language experiences of the school are built upon what the child knows. Such teachers need to have studied the acquisition of language, the distinction between delayed and deficient language, and also to know the black vernacular or dialect of the region. With this background the teacher can reevaluate such tests as are needed to determine whether the child has had the background, the bits and pieces of experience, to make the conceptualizations that tests such as the Binet require.

SUMMARY

Human beings inherit biological structures for speech and language which are species-specific. The areas of the human brain which receive aural or written messages, interpret these messages, and initiate speech and writing have been mapped. In most individuals these areas are in the left hemisphere, which dominates the motor responses of the right side of the body. A small percentage of the population is right-hemisphere dominated for speech and these individuals are usually left-handed. Another small percentage of people are ambidextrous, having mixed lateral dominance. Boys appear to be superior in some spatial abilities, and to commit the right hemisphere to these functions early in life. Girls, as a group, learn spatial relations later, but are more flexible in linguistic functions.

Chimpanzees, the most communicative of the subhuman primates, have been taught to sign by Ameslan, the American Sign Language. Gardner and Gardner (1975) taught their chimps to communicate with the kinds of combined signs children use in the early stages of learning to speak. Premack (1976) taught the chimp Sarah to build linguistic sequences with tokens to represent words.

Rumbaugh (1977) taught his chimp to respond linguistically by typing on a computer-controlled keyboard. Teaching lower primates to speak has been largely unsuccessful, probably because their utterances are controlled in the primitive midbrain, and they do not normally develop the Broca's area of the cortex which coordinates speech production in humans.

Children's understanding of language precedes their speaking, which is followed by reading and expressive writing. Neonates respond selectively to adult speech with the movement of their bodies. Early sound emissions of infants are emotional and apparently are directed from the affective areas in the midbrain. Prespeech vocalizing, which is heard through the third month, is characterized by a variety of vowel productions and some consonant production. Babbling, which occurs from about the fourth to the eighth month, is the echolaic repetition of speech sounds. During this time the infant produces a series of vowels in a sequence that begins with the sound of /u/, /o/, formed at the back of the mouth, and ends with /i/, formed at the front of the mouth. During this same period consonants that are prominent in the language heard are being produced and refined, but in the order of formation from front to back.

Children 1 year old typically produce several single words that convey meaning; this is called holophrastic speech. Children produce two- or three-word sentences, called telegraphic speech, by age 2 or soon afterward. By 4 years children have conceptualized the linguistic structure well enough to generate a variety of sentences typically used by adults.

The relationship between thought and language has been discussed by Piaget, who sees thought as cognitive development, beginning with sensorimotor knowledge of the environment and followed by a preoperational period in which the child forms representations of objects (images, signs, and symbols). Later, concrete operational thought and finally logical thought evolve. Language is useful in articulating the understanding of logical relations.

Vygotsky believed that language is basic to thought processes and described the beginning of thinking as speech gone underground. He proposed a series of association complexes that developed into true concepts. When using the generalization, abstraction, or class word, the speaker can move from the general to the particular (analysis) and from the particular to the general (synthesis).

Language is probably acquired by at least three processes: (1) the comprehension of speech, which is the basis for linguistic structure; (2) the imitation of adult models, which is socially reinforced in the direction of understandable speech; and (3) the building of classes and rules from which children spontaneously express their wants, needs, and reactions. Adult care-givers have a tremendous responsibility for the nature and the quality of the child's language.

10
Children's Play

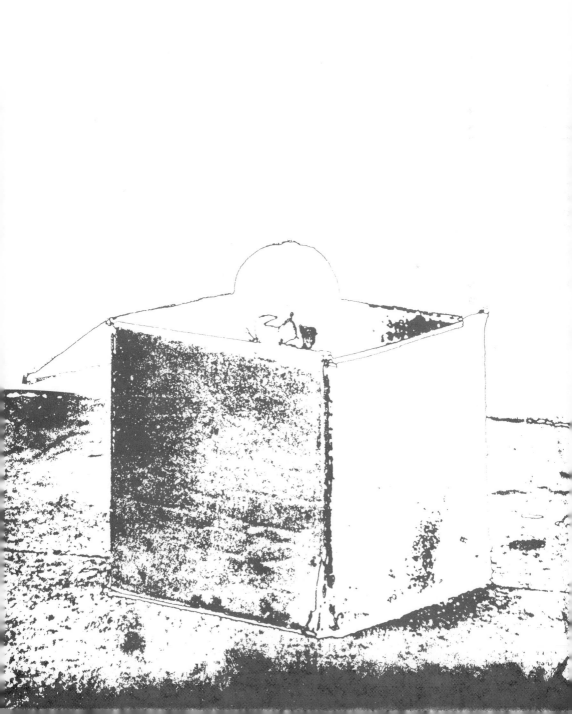

10 Children's Play

All healthy children play when left to their own devices. Adults play also, although many of them find it necessary to disguise their play in cultural rituals. Some adult play is rationalized as necessary preparation for work, and is called recreation. When play becomes highly organized into sports and the players turn professional, the boundary between play and work becomes obscured.

Many serious scholars have given thought and research effort toward explaining the function of play in child development. As in other areas of investigation, various scholars who look at different kinds of evidence have arrived at conflicting views about the definition of play as well as its function in childhood. Play has emotional components which tend to influence scholars, as well as laymen, to describe or accept a view of play which reflects their own life-style or value structure. For example, a writer whose culture promotes grown-up play (enjoyment) as an end itself is likely to approach the study of children's play differently than one whose culture is rooted in a work ethic that equates play with pleasure and pleasure with wickedness (LeClaire, 1975).

The first section of this chapter summarizes the major theories of play and identifies some of the scholars who have helped to clarify the functions of play in early childhood. The second section attempts to demonstrate the relationship among different views of play through a discussion of play and creative production. Subsequent sections deal with some common elements in play, social interaction, and the educative process. In conclusion, some forms of dramatic play and play therapy are presented for consideration by adults who help to rear young children.

THEORIES OF PLAY

Historically, play was seen by philosophers as *practice for later life*, even by those who recognized very early the special rights of childhood (Rousseau, 1964). Children's play was defended as the chance to try out the roles boys and girls would grow into as men and women. A second theory, *early generalization*, emerged from a scientific effort to study play experimentally and focused on the behavior of children as they made imperfect attempts to model the behavior of adults (Schlosberg, 1947). A third interpretation of children's play focused on cognitive development: play was described as *reality mapping*, meaning that the child learns about the physical world of time and space through play (Piaget, 1951). A fourth theory regarded play as *symbolic activity*, which expresses the inner and preconscious elements of an experience, and helps to establish the ties between the expressive arts and play in human beings (Peller, 1952). In this interpretation both play and art carry deep meanings that are too sensitive to the ego for direct action and are therefore acted out symbolically. The fifth position, which helps to provide a reality base for each of the other views, focused on the physiological

A child playing house sets the table for silent playmates. (George Roos/Peter Arnold)

aspects of play as an *exercise of biological systems*. The pleasurable sensations of an experience help to assure its repetition and also to define the action as play (Pribram, 1971).

Each of these theories presents a different facet of the many-splendored thing called play. Contemporary students of play typically drink from many scientific and literary fountains; therefore their views are seldom as pure as the summaries which follow. Nonetheless, a conceptualization of the different sources of knowledge about play may help the reader identify the source of terms used and prejudices revealed by various writers. Exploring play intellectually has some common elements with exploratory behavior in young children.

Practice for Later Life: Some Historical Views

Plato advised the women of ancient Greece to keep rattles, swings, and other toys in their chambers for the children to play with. He urged in one of his books, *The Laws*, that children 3 to 6 years old be "collected at a local sanctuary" where, left in one another's company they would readily invent the "games which nature herself suggests at that age" (Caplan & Caplan, 1974, p. 256). Plato saw this group play as preparation for citizenship. He wanted nurses present to "have an eye on decorm" so that the children's play would take the "more lawful" forms. He also wanted the early education of the older children to be a "form of amusement" so that the teachers could observe the natural bent of the child and arrange a pedagogy to conform to the nature of children.

Aristotle thought that children from 2 to 7 years old should become "spectators at the lessons which they will themselves have to learn" and suggested the adult events that children should witness. Play was for men of leisure, or men of business who needed rest, for "the activity of play is a relaxation of the soul, and serves as recreation because of its pleasantness." He believed that education should include music, sports, and art because "some subjects must be learnt and acquired merely with a view to the pleasure in their pursuit, and that these studies and these branches of learning are ends in themselves" (Ulich, 1959, p. 67). According to Aristotle, children should learn the leisure activities by watching with "supervision" when grown-ups played.

Later philosophers attended to the play environment of the youngsters themselves, and considered everything they did at this impressionable age to be important to the kind of person they would become. Quintilian, an early Roman Christian, believed that children's play should be arranged so as to develop their intelligence. Comenius advised Moravian mothers of the seventeenth century about play opportunities to develop the senses of the preschool child. Rousseau, the French philosopher who influenced Piaget so obviously, stressed the child's own interaction with natural phenomena to develop the perception of objects. By "constantly enriching their memory against the time when their judgment will be able to profit by it" the action on things was preferred to learning from tutors or books (Rousseau, 1964, p. 114).

Froebel, who influenced modern educators in the use of play as learning in the preschool, believed in the central unity and purpose of all human action. His mystical conception of play was that the child's interaction with nature was the beginning of a struggle each person must go through to discover this (mystical) reality. To him play was highly serious and of deep and abiding significance.

Froebel described two forms of play: *spontaneous play* and *play with a conscious purpose*. During unstructured or free play, the child's intrinsic motivation to be active assured that his or her play would be directed to the essential search for unity between the self and the environment. In guided play, teachers were expected to control the child's activity by providing "gifts" in the form of learning materials. Froebel believed that an indiscriminate assortment of playthings would distract the child from purposeful activity. To his critics, the controlled environment of the school sounded more like a setting for work than for play.

In the kindergarten the teacher was directed to help the child label his playthings, to talk with him about what he was doing, and thus to help him find purpose in what he was doing (Froebel, 1907, p. 177). The dichotomy of spontaneous versus guided play pleased neither his admirers, who continued to quote the portions of his writing that recommended play for the sake of play, nor his overt critics of that time, who thought teaching should be completely directive. Despite the different reactions to Froebel's methods, the purposeful, gamelike activities he designed were intended to be presented in an orderly and meaningful sequence by an adult, and to be pleasurable to the child. His idea of spontaneous play was clearly that it should be within the free choice of the child; Froebel considered free play "the purest, most spiritual activity of man at this stage" (1908, p. 55). Spontaneous play, in this context, is the child's sacred ground and not to be interfered with by adults.

Montessori, who believed that people were free only when they were both skillful and knowledgeable, used a playful approach to learning in the infant house (*Casa dei Bambini*) she established. The teacher was withdrawn to the role of observer-helper; the child's spontaneous interaction with structured playthings became the central focus of her method. She believed that children enjoyed the sense of mastery they experienced when didactic (instructional) materials were manipulated and the organizing principle was discovered. The structure built into her materials was consistent with her view of the need humans have to organize their sensory experiences intellectually.

Freedom, to Montessori, was a freedom of thought and spirit, achieved only through competence and independence. She saw nothing wrong with limiting the child's play when in school to activities having an intelligent aim and she deplored the kind of unguided movement that brought chaos, "the mad dashing over desks," to the children's room. She prepared a suitable environment where exploration within limits became the basis for freedom in adulthood, attained through discipline and judgment. In *The Montessori Method* she stated:

The field thus opened to the free activity of the child will enable him to exercise himself and to form himself as a man. It is not movement for its own sake that he will derive from these exercises, but a powerful coefficient in the complex formation of his personality. His social sentiments in the relations he forms with other free and active children, his collaborators in a kind of household designed to protect and aid their development, the sense of dignity acquired by the child who learns to satisfy himself in surroundings he himself preserves and dominates—these are the coefficients of humanity which accompany "liberty of movement." (1964, pp. 151–152)

Montessori's critics may condemn the limitations she placed on play, but her respect for the child as a person emerges clearly in her writing. Her attitude of trust in the ability of children to select their material and to direct their own learning prevails in many contemporary programs for early education which incorporate self-selection of curricular material.

Dewey went beyond Froebel and Montessori in freeing the child from adult constraints; he particularly deplored the use of prestructured material in the curriculum. "Only by starting with crude material and subjecting it to purposeful handling will the child gain the intelligence embodied in the finished material" (1926, p. 232). Although Dewey found the occasion and the words to caution his followers about unlimited freedom of movement for children, progressive educators tended not to hear the cautions and to quote selectively from his principles and to apply them with excess. Children's play and spontaneous activity became the cornerstone of the curriculum, and "experiencing" became an end in itself.

Dewey believed that the exploration and curiosity of play in children were akin to the processes of scientific discovery in adults. He considered both play and work as suitable activity for the school, with increasing amounts of the latter as the child grew older. The role of the teacher was to suggest play activities which were consistent with the nature of the child at the time—activities that would "give the sort of expression to these impulses that will carry the child on to a higher plane of consciousness and action" (Neumann, 1971, p. 30). As Dewey described it, such an experience of excitement through an activity for its own sake would give the child an appetite for exploratory activity that would carry over to the work of later periods in life. Apparently, he thought of his own scientific inquiry as exciting, and assumed that a similar level of motivation and intellect are common to schoolchildren.

Dewey (1926) defined play as activities which are enjoyable in their own execution without reference to the ulterior purpose. However, he insisted that the child at play is trying to effect something. The action has a point; it stimulates further action rather than the production of something. Work involved similar attitudes of commitment, but the contemplated results were more definite and demanded more presistent effort. The teacher was expected to be sensitive to the child's needs and to provide an environment in which the child would practice the skills and processes through play that would later be used in school tasks.

The traditional function of play, according to theorists from Plato to Dewey, was to learn the skills that later would be practiced in work or leisure. Play was characterized by enjoyment on the part of the child and freedom, within limits. The player's commitment was to the activity for its own sake and not to any production that might result. The end purpose of play, although important in the development of the child, was not presented to the child as work.

Early Generalization of Adult Behavior: A Behaviorist View

Psychologists, who were attempting to establish themselves as scientists, deplored the "practice for later life" explanation of children's play and urged instead a definition based on S-R terms (Schlosberg, 1947). Rejecting the intrinsic motivation theory but recognizing that play is a complex activity, they researched the conditions under which playful behavior was seen to occur. The condition of the child or the animal, whether rested or tired, was soon discovered to be an important factor in whether a particular stimulus would be strong enough to elicit a play response. An absence of strong drives (sex, hunger, thirst) was seen as a necessary condition for playful activity to occur (Beach, 1945). Studies of play, therefore, required a departure from the S-R model of the strict behaviorist to a revised model, stimulus-organism-response (S-O-R).

In the view of some behaviorists, the sequence by which children learn from play is as follows. First, the child engages in useless activity which imitates the useful activity of adults. Second, the youngster's behavior is generalized, which in behaviorist terms means an unprecise and undifferentiated pattern of behaviors that characterizes the beginning of reinforced actions. Third, the behavior persists and is shaped by the reinforcement from adult rewards in form of praise, pats, or gratification. Adult play, such as sports or games, is similarly reinforced in some way or it does not continue; it becomes extinct (Schlosberg, 1947).

The important elements of a behaviorist-oriented study of play are (1) the use of data collected in direct observation of specific behaviors under specified environmental conditions, (2) the use of S-R definitions of play behavior, and (3) the avoidance of theorizing about why individuals play. Playing *may* develop skills that are useful later on, but behaviorists find it more worthwhile to study the activity itself and the conditions which elicit playful action.

Reality Mapping: A Cognitive View

To developmental psychologists, play is a repetition of an action that is initiated as a general unfocused activity but is continued because the child wants the experience to last. These researchers observe what the child does, but they assume a direction from within, a selection of stimuli from many that are possible, and an increasing control over the environment as the child matures. Essential to this increasing control over one's activity is an increased understanding of cause-effect relationships, whether the play experience concerns time and space, objects, or other persons. Learning results from interaction, but the nature of the play activity and the nature of the cognitive experiences are predetermined by the developmental characteristics of the child.

Cognitive psychologists recognize play as subjective, symbolic, and self-initiated (Gilmore, 1966). Play bends reality to the child's own wants, necessities, and perceptions. Play allows reality to be tested, explored, and assimilated in small doses. Piaget described the child's reality mapping of the physical environment through play actions. El'Konin (1969) and his students described the child's reality mapping of the social world through play.

Piaget (1951) defined play as an exercising of action in which subjective schemes take primacy over objective reality states. Play is an *assimilation* function, which interacts with the *accommodation* function to result in mental development or biological adaptation. This dynamic seesaw is weighted toward the assimilation end of the plank during the early stages of a developmental period and is weighted toward the accommodation end of the plank as the child acquires a more realistic view of the world. The analogy of the seesaw in balance corresponds to Piaget's notion of *equilibration*; when the internalized structures are in balance with external reality the result is adaptation; in human terms that means *intellectual adaptation* (Chapter 8).

To Piaget, the assimilation portion of an interaction, the taking in aspect of an experience, is a subjective action in which the child bends the world to his or her own previously acquired mental structures. In play the child makes things fit this subjective world by allowing the intellectual action to engage only those aspects of an experience which can be made to fit existing (immature) structures. The child's play imposes an immature perception of the world on the information the senses assimilate. By this view play is subjective; it is the response of inner structures, an intellectual activity that enhances and supports adaptation, but it falls short of the logical functioning of adults.

Play is a necessary activity in childhood because it provides exercise of action schemas at whatever level of cognitive development the child has achieved, allowing the child to retain the cognitive gains of previous adaptations. Piaget described three stages of play: sensorimotor play, symbolic play, and game play with rules (Piaget, 1971).

Sensorimotor play is initiated by the infant during the first month of life in prolonging a reflexive action that provides sensory pleasure; fingering the blanket, sucking the fist, and repetitious kicking are examples. This practice play increases in complexity as the infant coordinates different sensory systems and increasingly expresses enjoyment of these activities by laughing and cooing. Exploratory behavior toward objects is seen in grasping, sucking, and looking at novel things. By the end of the first year the child imitates the action of other persons, at first using those schema already learned in other actions. When Piaget opened and closed his eyes for his infant daughter, she first opened and closed her mouth, then opened and closed her hands, and finally she opened and closed her eyes. He regarded this action as the beginning of imitation and an attempt to accommodate, accommodation being a dynamic interaction with assimilation which results in cognitive growth.

Symbolic play begins from 18 months to 2 years with the use of signs and symbols to represent objects and actions. Piaget distinguished between perception, which is figurative and characterizes the repetitions of infant play, and symbolization, which can involve either language or signs. He considered imitation the means by which the child interiorizes an action and thus develops the structures that make symbolic action possible. Like all levels of play, symbolic play is assimilative of the reality to the self; but it is an advance over practice play because symbolic action represents absent situations. As such it must borrow either from interiorized images (imitations) or from language (signifiers). To understand Piaget's defnintion of play, it is essential to remember that interiorized actions are the child's own immature construction of his or her particular experience with people or things. Symbolic play emerges only after the child has developed mental representations by playing the action in the absence of the model.

During the later part of the preoperational period (ages 4 to 7 or 8) children's play is in a transitional stage, where they shift from symbolic play and imitation to intelligent adaptation. Children develop a higher level of thought as a result of the world having imposed its realities on them. They have accommodated, and their play will reflect the ability to think operationally, although concretely.

The third period of play, characterized by rule-governed games, becomes possible when the child has acquired the concepts of causality, reversibility, and transitivity. In other words, the enjoyment that is essential to play is possible only when the rules are conceptualized. The older child (7 to 11) who can think operationally enters games with rules, constructs games, and reflects on his or her own imitations. Play in general and symbolic play in particular decline. Play with rules is still seen as assimilative, as the practice of schemes previously acquired through accommodation.

Piaget conceived play as characteristic of childhood, and adaptive behavior as the evidence of maturation. Play, even at the stage of play with rules, is a "deformation and subordination of reality to the desires of the self" and diminishes with age and intellectual maturity (1971, p. 339). Adults may dream, but this is symbolic, regressive, and childlike—even as it is playful. Adaptive behavior requires both assimilation and accommodation, but growing up intellectually clearly means to Piaget adapting to a view of the world which conforms to the reality view of other mature intelligent adults.

El'Konin (1969), who also saw play as part of cognitive development, summarized a series of Soviet studies which classified the play activities of young children. The basic types of play they observed had a differential effect on the mental development that resulted. These studies largely supported Piaget's stages of cognitive development, but the Soviet researchers departed from Piaget in two areas: (1) the function of language in early symbolization, and (2) the influence adults have in providing the models for play activity, the labels of objects, and a suitable play situation.

According to this research, infants begin to play through repeated movements (like Piaget's practice play) and the chaining of movements with reference to an object. Abramovich (1946) discovered that novel objects stimulated more manipulation in babies under 2 years than familiar objects did. For maximum interest in the object to be elicited, the object needed to be half-familiar, having some properties of objects experienced previously and some properties that were novel. El'Konin maintained that an infant must cognitively separate an object from his own actions upon it before the word which is associated with it can replace the object in mental manipulation. El'Konin would supply the word to enhance this development.

Soviet research on children's activities during the preschool years from 1 to 3 revealed three stages of play behavior that were confirmed in several separate studies. The stages are (1) the creation of a play situation, (2) the emergence of a role, and (3) the alteration of the structure of an action. The research focused on the role of adults and the nature of the environment in which play behavior emerged. The researchers' analysis departed from some of the traditional views of childhood play as universal or as emerging primarily from children's interactions with each other.

The first stage, the *creation of a play situation*, occurs near the end of the first year, or early in the second year. Fradkina (1946) noted that initially the youngsters repeated actions on objects only in accordance with their original use. Later they observed at a distance and repeated the action of adults on objects, even when no direct demonstration had been provided them.

The adult role in the creation of a play situation was confirmed in studies with preschool children. There the conditions which contributed to play were found to be (1) the presence of varied impressions, (2) the availability of playthings and educational aids, and (3) frequent associations between the child and the adult (Aksarina, 1944). Play was stimulated by the presence of reality-situation toys, and play with them preceded symbolic play with substitute objects.

American observers have noted the discrepancy in play patterns between Head Start children and middle-class children on whom specialists have based their assumptions about imaginative play (Herron & Sutton-Smith, 1971, p. 218). The children from disadvantaged environments engaged in sensorimotor play and kinesthetic activity. However, they engaged very little in symbolic play at an age when Piaget considered this form of play as typical.

Smilansky (1968) studied the play patterns of disadvantaged and middle-class children in Israel. She found that the children of certain poor immigrant families proceeded from motor play to realistic imitative play and into rule games without going through the preschool stage of imaginative play that has been considered a universal stage in early childhood. Adult interaction with infants, involving play-things and the playful use of words to name the objects, seems to be an important basis for later imitation and symbolization.

The *emergence of the play role*, according to Fradkina, is first seen in the child's playing a specific person; a girl plays at being her mother and some time later takes the more generalized role of housewife. The cognitive prerequisite is the child's identification of her own action of the person being imitated. In this way, the mental image of the action is demonstrated. The language of a role helps the child (and the other players) confirm the identity the child has in mind. Late in this stage, the child produces chains of adult actions, first in imitation of a specific person, but later generalized to represent a class of persons and showing more flexible and spontaneous actions.

The *alteration of a structure of action* appears in children's play typically during the third year. Cognitively the child must generalize an action from many instances of modeling that have been practiced. That such generalization has occurred is seen in the transfer of a chain of actions from one object to another or from one situation to another. At about the same time, the child begins to rename objects for which he or she knows the real name and to create play names that fit an action. This quality, or level, of play, in which real names are known, but role names with a better fit are created, is a significant observation which will be explored further in the section on creativity and play.

Symbolic Activity: A Psychoanalytic View

The psychoanalytic view stresses the emotional release children gain through play. Psychoanalytic thinking dominated the research on play from about 1930 to about 1960, and is still prominent in the play therapy used to treat emotionally disturbed children (Chapter 14). Initiated by Sigmud Freud and elaborated by his daughter Anna, play was interpreted as a symbolic action which reflected the fears and aggressions that a child found it necessary to repress, or risk the disapproval of significant adults. Play patterns were not merely inept imitations of adult behavior but sprung from inner impulses and were initiated in support of the child's ego.

Contemporary analysts believe that child play reflects whatever has made a great impression (Peller, 1952). The child repeats anxiety situations in order to gain mastery over fears, and (symbolically) gains mastery over the person or object that has caused distress. Play activities allow the child to act out the possibilities in social relationships which are threatening the child's security in real life but which can be handled only in the unreal world of play.

Sometimes play has an element of defiance or revenge toward a parent which cannot be expressed directly. When Jay (5), Donna (4), and Bruce (2) were left with a housekeeper they hit upon a game of piling things in the middle of the living-room floor: first toys, then clothing and blankets from their rooms, then personal things belonging to the parents. This evolved quickly into a wild game of hooting, stomping, and clapping with each item added. They continued to play by mounting the pile, striking a bold stance and laughing raucously. Unable to control the situation, the harried housekeeper finally reported to the parents what had become a daily activity on the part of the children. The parents promptly moved to a city where a good preschool was available and the game ceased as abruptly as it had originated.

A Freudian interpretation of this play would cite the children's unhappiness at being left by their parents, the expression of defiance in leaving toys in the middle of the livingroom (a well-understood misbehavior which the parents were not there to witness), aggression toward the parents' things (symbolic recipients of punishment), and finally the show of mastery (like young animals dominating the top of a mound).

Family dolls have become the device by which psychiatrists and therapists uncover the hostilities children feel and discover the objects of hidden emotions. In the play of normal children, dolls get the spankings children think they may deserve as a consequence of misbehavior, or become the recipient of abuse the child has already experienced. Psychic roles may be played directly in play, indirectly through dolls, or abstractly through objects.

The symbolic interpretations of children's play by psychoanalysts is suspect to many persons, including many parents. To some it is unscientific, to others it reflects the psyche of the observer more than the child. Doubtless some people fear these revelations in the same way that they fear revealing dreams. Nevertheless, many adults who are concerned with the emotional life of children take play seriously as the child's way of coping with problems.

Exercise of Biological Systems

A physiological approach to the study of play is concerned with body states and body changes during play. Some biologists accept growth and adaptation as a fact and assume that stimulation of the sensory system is necessary as part of the process. This explanation of why children play assumes that biological systems are evolved in species-specific ways to interact with the physical and social environment that is maintained by parents for their offspring. The young interact because the systems are there and developmentally ready to be stimulated. The inherent result to the organism is a state of well-being, of pleasurable sensation. The neurophysiological study of play is concerned with possible changes to the system that result from play, with the brain mechanisms that activate play behavior or are activated by it, and with the nature of the motivating forces that compel a continuation of play *if* no learning is taking place.

PLAY AND BRAIN DEVELOPMENT

An impressive study of brain development during different conditions of rearing young rats has implication for questions concerning play and brain development. Rats of similar genetic heritage were divided and the rearing conditions were manipulated so that one group received play stimulation and problem-solving opportunities (swings, ladders, rotating drums, and crawl-through equipment) while the other group was given similar nutrition but a relatively restricted visual and motor play environment (Bennett and Rosenzweig, 1970). Comparison of the appropriate areas of the brain showed significant differences in weight, thickness, and protein content of the cortical layers, favoring the rats with the enriched play environment. Significant differences were found in the content of enzymes known to be present in neural activation (acetylcholinesterase and cholinesterase). There were also significant differences favoring the play-environment group in DNA content and the number of glial cells. The number of neurons was not significantly different since neural cell bodies (in the cerebral cortex) are duplicated before birth (Chapter 3). Although this study does not prove that the play caused brain changes, or that these results would be obtained if similar experimental work were possible with children, the cortical changes obtained were consistent with present knowledge about the conditions of learning. It would be folly to rear our children as if enrichment through play and problem-solving opportunities did not make a difference.

SYSTEMS THAT FACILITATE AND INHIBIT ACTION

Pribram (1971) described the mechanisms of the brain that account for approach and avoidance behavior. He called them *stop-and-go* mechanisms (pp. 273–284). Again the most striking data come from experimental work with rats, but there is confirming information from clinical research on humans (Penfield, 1975). The reader need not be familar with the details of reinforcement theory, but should know that the anatomy of pleasure and punishment centers is real and present in each person. Readers who seek a more thorough knowledge of the brain mechanisms involved should consult Pribram (1971) for further references.

Simply stated, the *go* mechanism, or reward system, includes neural pathways of the *medial forebrain bundle* connecting the (core) thalamic and hypothalamic areas, including the amygdala, to the forebrain cortical areas. The pleasure centers, associated with reward or reinforcement, are located in this area and have been confirmed many times by the pleasure feelings that people report when appropriate cells in this area are stimulated electrically.

The *stop* mechanism (Pribram, 1971) is made up of a less extensive system of neurons, located just beneath the *go* mechanism, and connecting the hypothalamus and thalamus with the *tectum*. This *stop* mechanism is the location of so-called punishment centers, which also have been confirmed in clinical work with humans. One of their functions is to control the chemical balance of the neurotransmitters.

The *stop* and *go* mechanisms are important in all play behavior because of the essential self-initiation and participation by choice that define all play activity. Feelings of interest and pleasure are more emotional than perceptual; however, the emotional experience is always associated (neurologically) with particular perceptual components (Chapter 11). The white furry toy rabbit may be one child's joy if the affective conditioning includes the happy face of a father presenting it and his tender voice as he strokes and calls it by name. This infant will experience joy when seeing the same toy later and will be motivated to reach for or approach it. The same child if teased and frightened by a similar rabbit might later howl with terror upon seeing it or toys like it.

The interaction between the reward and punishment mechanisms functions at all times to facilitate or to inhibit an action. Stimulation through the senses that has previously been associated with reward, or pleasure, triggers the activation of the medial forebrain bundle and the release of norepinephrine into the amygdala and other forebrain repressor areas. Norepinephrine inhibits activity in the forebrain suppressor area and reduces the cholinergically mediated excitation of the thalamus and the hypothalamus. Decreased cholineric transmission lessens the activity in the *stop* system (periventricular system), thus reducing the inhibition of motor nuclei in the brain stem. Stated directly, activity can be initiated only by suppression of the *stop* mechanisms that ordinarily inhibit action. By implication, the child through pleasurable experiences gains control over the systems that permit approach, or *go* behaviors.

PLAY AS MEANS-END REVERSAL

The means-end reversal occurs in play when activity becomes the end in itself, rather than the means to some other goal as in traditional reward-reinforcement theory. Mace (1962) discussed the tendency in an affluent society for play to become the major activity of adults by their doing for fun the kinds of things other cultures have required, as work, in order to live. He uses the analogy of the domesticated cat who was provided all the basic needs even before they were expressed. Having been protected also from danger and inclement weather, does this cat curl up and wait for some inner expression of thirst or hunger? No, it prowls the garden, killing mice and birds, presumably enjoying life in its own way. In a state of affluence the cat no longer kills to live, but lives to kill. Mace calls this the reversal of the means-end relation in behavior in which work loses its meaning and becomes a way of enjoying life.

One way affluent adults play is through attaining a pointless objective in a difficult way, as when playing golf. The golfer uses a curious instrument to guide a small ball over a course, which by design is hazardous, to score in a small hole in the ground (Mace, 1962, p. 11). Children who live in an affluent environment go out and create difficult things to do for the sake of doing them. Often they play by imitating adults because this is what they have seen and what they know.

The neurology of pleasure sensations locates the mechanism of reward deep in the primitive part of the brain, the limbic system (Penfield, 1975). Whether children play because they are anxious and seek release, because they are curious and seek knowledge, or because they are acting out adult actions because they have nothing else to do, the neurologist is certain that repetitive action can be its own source of pleasure. Biologists recognize the increasing complexity of play in the recently evolved species, particularly Homo sapiens. Within the human society, upward migration is also characterized by increased emphasis on play of both adults and children.

Definition of Play

For the purposes of this book, essential elements of play are the self-choice of the player to participate, the self-commitment of the player to the reality dimensions of the situation or role, and the self-stimulation of pleasure mechanisms. Play involves repetition; but beyond the point that pleasure ceases, the same activity can become work. Play involves learning, but only to the extent that learning is incidental and not imposed. Play may be exploratory, but only when conducted out of curiosity and not out of fear of hidden enemies. Play may be biologically motivated by tissue states, but Erikson (1963) has aptly distinguished between the sex play of children (or adults in a quasi-social situation) and the participants in a serious act of intercourse. Play has elements of fluency, spontaneity, and flexibility. Adults play in either of two ways, according to Mace (1962). One is by pursuit of the arts, the other is the means-end reversal of work: hunting, fishing, sewing, crafting, and other difficult accomplishments. The next section draws from many views of play and examines the relationship between children's play and children's art.

PLAY AND CHILDREN'S ART

The anatomy of the brain clearly separates the location of cognitive and affective functions, and it seems that this separation somewhat explains how humans arrive at mature play or at artistic production. At the highest level of human participation, the expression of personal feelings, appreciations, and meanings is fused in creative production that reflects a knowledge of the real world. The difference between the spontaneous, exciting painting of the 4-year-old and the spontane-ous, exciting painting of the mature artist is a difference that needs to be understood by care-givers. It is often stated that young children are creative, but that (regretfully) most turn to mundane ways of speaking, painting, and playing.

The creative activities of young children occur for many reasons. Often a knowledge of the conventions is lacking, so the child's expression is seen by adults as direct, fresh, and unique (Wilson & Robeck, 1968). Also, children's egocentric view of the world frees them from overconcern with how others will see the drawing because to them there is only one view. Finally, the playful situation which is assumed by child and adult alike relaxes cultural constraints and is conducive to self-expression. Modified forms of the characteristics that contribute to certain behavior in children have been exhibited by many artists, architects, engineers, poets, and research scientists (MacKinnon, 1965). The model of the dynamics of children's play and creative production shown in Figure 8–1 analyzes the levels of development from perceptual play to productive self-direction.

Pleasure Associations in Practice Play

At the infantile level, the locomotor peek-a-boo, the kinesthetic banging and bouncing, the tactile stroking of soft toys, the auditory stimulation of the baby's own babbling, and the sensuous bubbling of saliva on lips and tongue are all examples of the association of self-sustained activity accompanied by pleasure. Piaget observed that young infants learn to make interesting sights and sounds last. At a later Piagetian stage, the second year of life, the infant begins to invent new means of acting on objects. El'Konin reported that toys were used and actions were imitated at first in the ways that had been observed by the infant.

The associations of sensory experience and feelings of pleasure continue into adulthood. Although the time and place may be beyond voluntary recall, the sensation of pleasure is still associated with certain colors, tunes, or motions. More important, the awareness of the positive affects of certain kinds of experience enriches the lives of many adults.

Conceptualization of Affects

Children of 7 or 8 years of age who conceptualize that others see the world differently have also reached a stage in cognitive development when they see a discrepancy between their own artistic representations and photographic reality. At this point many children give up painting, sculpting, block building, and role playing because they recognize the discrepancy between their "thing" and what they are being offered as the real world. A failure to conceptualize one's affective experience at a comparable level of sophistication can lead to a denial of the esthetic self and a deprivation of affective experience. Whether one becomes a performer or an observer of sports, the visual arts, or the performing arts, all civilized cultures have valued them as the highest form of human expression.

To save the child from complete commitment to cognitive objectivity and the denial of his affective self, the psychoanalytic school would encourage role conception, role representation, and the recognition of the source of one's pleasure without guilt. The conceptual separation of self from the blanket one sleeps in and the toys one fondles is the infant's first step in the discovery of self. Self-concept involves knowing who one is by knowing how one is unique among others. To bridge the gap between childish egocentrism and the egocentrism that allows adult artists to express themselves in a tangible product for others to see, children must understand and accept themselves. This is the meaning of the second level of the learning-motivation model in Chapters 8 and 11. At this second level children form the cognitive structures which they will later bend to their own constructions. The autonomy and self-acceptance on the affective side of the model will motivate them to find expression in the arts.

Creative Production in Childhood

The art of children in painting, dramatization, construction, creative dance, and game invention might well be evaluated in terms of what the activity or the experience does for the child at the time. Parents and teachers may be assured that this approach is not mere pragmatism since reinforcement theory has shown that an intelligent child will not continue activities on his or her own that are not pleasure producing. This means that the child's satisfaction with the product is necessary, therefore some novelty, some growth, and some progress in technique are necessary. Feedback to help the child recognize the features of the product that make it pleasing constitutes a form of analysis that helps children develop aesthetic appreciation of their own work and that of others. Experience with many media of expression helps children to find the medium in which they are most facile and expand their repertoire of play activities.

The support adults can provide children in finding their own autonomy by allowing them to appreciate the uniqueness of what they do and the importance of the producer of that unique expression is valid and relevant. Such understanding of the relationship between order, form, and structural relationships in the real world and the importance of finding one's own relationship to the whole is more difficult than being able to conserve number or to classify mammals in a logical lattice. If children are to produce artistically, it would seem important that they learn to value their own unique productions before the conformity to peers and the conformity to cognitive reality dominates thinking.

Sutton-Smith, who is an expert on children's play, has taken issue with Piaget's interpretation of play as childish, purely assimilative, and illogical in contrast with adult behavior as logical, adaptive, and therefore play-rejecting (1971, pp. 326–336). Sutton-Smith views play as a particularly human activity that is enjoyed at all ages although in different forms as people mature. The discovery of cognitive reality and the ability to engage in logical thought do not necessarily alleviate the need of humans to escape the routines of work through one of the many forms of play that cultural tradition has preserved. But more important, the divergent thinking processes, as contrasted with the convergent thinking processes of

Piaget's logical thought, are the means by which creative works are produced. Divergent thinking is characterized by fluency, flexibility, and elaboration (Chapter 8). These are the patterns of thought by which new things are invented and new ways to express human emotion are created. Inventiveness and creativity may be higher forms of human functioning than the conceptualization of cause-effect in the natural world.

SOCIAL FUNCTIONS OF PLAY

The previous section explored the relationship between play and art. This section is concerned with play and culture as the means by which a child is socialized. If one accepts the view that play reaches the highest levels of quality and complexity in Homo sapiens, the question of how adults transmit the play culture to the young is very important. The question of how the social intelligence is communicated is a serious one, but barely touched in research. The thin veil between affection and aggression is present in all social interaction and acted out constantly in the group play of children. Civilized societies have found ways to deal with primitive affects through socialization. With children we tend to call the overt forms of inner necessities *play*, while with adults we call them *culture.*

Enculturation through Peer Interaction

At a public lecture I attended, Rosenzweig stated that their research on the play of young rats was "child's play" compared with research on the play of children (Bennett & Rosenzweig, 1970). This may explain why the literature on peer interaction is still largely theoretical and why most of the controlled experiments come from the animal laboratory. A recent attempt to test Piaget's stages of play through systematic large-scale observation and statistical analysis generally confirmed the types of play Piaget described as universal. However, some important differences between culture groups were found in the ages at which the different types of play (practice, symbolic, or rule-governed games) predominated and declined during the free play of children from 6 to 14 years old (Eifermann, 1971). The observations were made at school recess periods, where the free choice of play with games was allowed, and in out-of-school street play. Analysis showed some important departures from Piaget's conclusions: (1) collective symbolic play peaked as early as second grade in upper-middle-class Israeli schools while it dominated the play of lower-class Arab groups from 6 to 8 years old. One school showed rule-governed game play predominant over social symbolic play from the first grade on, probably because social symbolic play had already peaked during the preschool years. (2) Rule-governed games dominated the play of children until about 11 years old, after which their play showed a decline in rule games and an increase in practice play such as running, jumping, and unstructured practice of sensorimotor skills. Eifermann interpreted the falling off of interest in rule-governed games to the lack of challenge they provided and the increase in sensorimotor practice to anticipation of participation in sports. (3) Enculturation required greater participation in social play with age-peer groups in cultures in which the young are restricted in their association with adults than in rural and less technological societies in which they join in work-related activities with adults. Urban children spent a higher portion of their play time with age peers than did rural or kibbutzim children who played more with mixed-age groups. Eifermann suggested that peer-group practice of the processes of *status acquisition* and of *achievement evaluation* is necessary in societies in which family units fail to provide an easy transition from childhood to adulthood.

Communication of Social Intelligence

One of the interesting questions raised by the increasing complexity of social play in the young of Homo sapiens is the possible role of genetics in interpersonal behavior. How is it that the cultural heritage is taken in with increasing facility during play by the young? Are there changes in genetic makeup, as well as in the cultural record? Calhoun (1956) observed twenty generations of mice in an experiment to test whether patterns of home construction and social organization were culturally transmitted or were inborn traits (Chapter 1). He obtained two inbred strains of mice: one a nomadic strain which burrowed under the ground for shelter and the other an apartment-dwelling strain that constructed multilevel apartments of earth and plant materials.

By exchanging the newborn, both strains were cross-fostered, the apartment-dwelling youngsters being reared by nomadic mothers. At weaning time all the mice were separated from parental influence and two colonies were established of cross-fostered mice, unacculturated by their own parents. Their relatively complex social organization reappeared gradually over twenty-nine generations, not directly in the behavior of adults but first in the young who played at dominating the hillocks near the burrows.

In a book on human infancy Freedman (1974) took a biological approach to social behavior and reviewed the scientific literature on play in mammal species. He noted that social play in ungulates (hoofed grazers) is short-lived and exhibited primarily in male games of butting for dominance. Predator animals can afford to support a longer period of dependency. Kittens and puppies play at stalking and fighting, which allows more subtle learning and the attachment needed for cooperation in hunting and sharing. Curiosity is another characteristic of play which has the survival values of awareness and expansion of territory. Sex differences were seen in the complex play of macaque troops. "By the first year the male infants, who tend to wander farther from the mother than females, have found each other and have begun to play" (p. 55). Rough-and-tumble play occupies the young males, while females stay closer to the center of the troop, engage in grooming, and help to tend the young. The beginnings of altruistic behavior are seen biologically in the family grouping for mutual protection among primates and the resulting preservation of an individual's genes through the help given to offspring of relatives. In lower primates groups of relatives usually form around central females.

Freedman's own observations of playground behavior showed that boys 5 years old tended to swarm in groups of five members or more, to use the entire area in play, and to set up displays of courage. Girls tended to form smaller groups, to occupy more limited space, and to show less interest in hierarchies. Studies of differences in play behaviors among the sexes were extended to cultures around the world, and it was found that similar patterns occured in the free drawings of children from Chicago, Kyoto, Hong Kong, Bali, New Delhi, Kenya, and the aborigine tribes of Australia. He interpreted the interaction of genetics and culture as species-specific.

Culture teaches with greatest ease that which children will want to learn, as when boys choose to draw more vehicles, and girls choose to concentrate on flowers. That is, we must speak of differential thresholds or biosocial pathways in conceptualizing the fact that boys and girls differentiate in about the same way in all the cultures examined. Put another way, not only does each culture differentially distribute its wares to the sexes, but we must conclude that boys and girls choose and react differently as well. (p. 58)

Sex differences in play behavior in infants during the first year which were predictive of later sex-role behavior were reported by Goldberg and Lewis (1969). The girls were more dependent, showed less exploratory behavior, and their play reflected a more quiet style. Boys played with toys requiring more gross motor activity, were more vigorous, and tended to run and bang. Many investigators have noted differential treatment of the sexes by parents, among them Kagan (1971). Rothbart and Maccoby (1966) analyzed the subtleties of parental behavior toward boys and girls in primarily upper-middle-class families. The investigators presented a child's voice on tape, identified as a girl for two mother-father groups and as a boy for two other groups. They found, from parent questionnaires, that mothers indicated they would allow more aggression directed toward themselves on the part of sons and fathers indicated their acceptance of more aggressive behavior from daughters. The expected sex-stereotyped responses were lacking (to any significant degree) in behaviors involving help seeking and autonomy.

It is important to note that biological studies point up the subtlety and complexity of human behavior in contrast to more primitive species. Again it is apparent that researchers do not often find what they did not look for, or ask in the initial questions. Sex differences in the cognitive aspects of socialization and group organization have been given little attention, perhaps because socialization and group organization obscure sex differences.

Only since the seventeenth century has the Western culture regarded childhood as a distinct social entity (Stone, 1965). Prior to that time there were "infants" and "adults." With the recognition of childhood, the play activities and the equipment to encourage them have been an accepted part of the culture. Continental societies, in which play is an acceptable diversion for adults, are quicker to support children's play than the Protestant cultures of England and America. The present danger to childhood is very possibly that play and diversion will be forced on them long after more challenging activities and greater acceptance into the adult world would be preferred.

Evidence suggests that children seek to model the play behavior of older children over that of age-peers. Wolters (1976) reported an experiment in which preschool children 4 and 5 years old were shown many ways to "play with clay" by one of four models on television, each trained in an identical demonstration. Two models were age-peers, a boy and a girl, and the other two models were older children (about 9 years old), a boy and a girl. The television models also demonstrated the sharing of clay with a newcomer. Later the preschool children, both boys and girls, used more ways to play with clay if the model was an older child. Also they shared almost equal amounts in grams of clay if their model was an older child, but gave significantly less clay to the newcomer if their model had been an age-peer. Sex differences were not significant. Wolters recommended multiage grouping in schools to enhance the social behavior of younger children.

Affinity between Affection and Aggression

The *ambivalent feelings* children have for those whom they must love to be assured of nurturance and leave to gain autonomy is probably the most universal conflict of growing up. Hess (1970) cited some interesting research on the conflicting drives of fish when they encounter another member of the same species. Always three drives are simultaneously aroused: sex, aggression, and fear. The mating rituals involve zig-zag movements which actually represents an alternation between aggressive and sexual wooing behavior in the male fish and an alternation between sexual and flight-drive behavior in the female. This pattern is matched in different species to assure heterosexual interaction and purity of the genetic makeup of offspring.

Social animals, species who live in organized groups, have learned *displacement* or *redirected behavior* patterns in order to survive as a species. Birds have been observed to peck objects in states of aggression. Researchers have been able to implant electrodes in the brains of chickens, stimulate two drives at the same time, and observe specific ambivalent, displacement, and redirected behavior.

Children in the phallic period of psychosocial development (ages 3 to 5) experience ambivalent feelings of varying intensities toward the parent of the same sex when mixed affection and aggression are in conflict in the child's emotional world. The play corner in the nursery or playschool allows the child to rehearse the conflict or change the child-parent action in ways that are more comfortable.

SEX DIFFERENCES

Research with doll play is almost certain to show some aggressive behavior in the interaction of family dolls by the second session of play (Levin & Wardwell, 1962). After reviewing thirty-six major studies, most of them conducted in the forties and fifties when the psychoanalytic tradition dominated research in child development, aggression was the most studied and best documented of child behavior. Almost all studies concluded that boys were more aggressive than girls. Studies that separated physical aggression and verbal aggression, however, showed that girls who were manipulating dolls showed more verbal aggression (Johnson, 1951).

AGE DIFFERENCES

One would expect that after the age of 5, sex-related aggression would decline. Boy-girl differences in aggressive behavior within family groups was found to decline between age 5 and age 8 (Hollenberg & Sperry, 1951). Sears (1951) found that sex differences increased between the ages of 3 and 5 years. Interpreted within Erikson's stages of development, these results do not appear conflicting (Chapter 11). Children below the age of 3 play with dolls, but symbolic play is so unlikely to occur that displacement aggression is not usually reported for 2-year-olds. Children 8 years old do not readily accept the doll-play format; therefore, age differences beyond these ranges are usually studied in other ways.

LEARNING THROUGH EXPLORATORY PLAY

A distinction has been made between exploration that is impelled by curiosity and exploration that is compelled by fear, as when a young animal or a child inspects a new environment to assure its safety. This distinction reflects different affective states (or different motivation). Although the neurological organization may confirm such a distinction, both forms of exploration have survival and learning value.

Ludic Motor Activity

Motor play has been termed in scientific sources as *ludic motor activity*, the performance of a mixed sequence of mostly stereotyped behavior patterns by an immature animal (Müller-Schwarze, 1971). Ludic motor patterns often occur in social situations when young mammals play together. Under moderate arousal, but low specific motivation, the patterns that are learned serve many future functions. Ludic behavior is cross-sexual, exploratory, active, and alternated with serious behavior. Müller-Schwarze learned that fawns played at regular times in the daily cycle. He discovered a higher correlation between the sexes in play than in serious behavior. When he deprived the fawns of play opportunity experimentally for as little as one day, their play increased the following day in activity time, locomotion, and exploration. This finding suggests an inner initiation of ludic behavior and perhaps a readiness for play activity which is developmentally timed.

Play as practice of adult sexual behavior is implied in much of the research. Harlow and Harlow (1962) found that orphaned monkeys showed normal sexual behavior as adults only if they had had body contact in play at the ages of 6 to 8

A box is for hiding inside. (Jerry Schwartz/Editorial Photocolor Archives)

months. Apparently in older animals the play behavior, once practiced repeatedly and casually, is extinguished by (or superseded by) sexual behavior. Observation of mammal play suggests a larger reportoire of play patterns than the species uses in later life.

Exploration of Objects and Space

Motor play is spontaneous and reflects an inner state; play is self-referent. Investigation is stimulus-referent; it is initiated by external stimuli. This distinction does not negate the influence of play on investigative activity. The locomotion, the enhanced activity, and the state of exhilaration are conducive to bringing the child into contact with varied objects and spatial environments.

Activity for its own sake may not be conducive to the conceptualization of quantity, velocity, or displacement, at least not as stated symbolically, but play action lays the sensorimotor basis for later understanding. Quantity and equality get their meaning in the one-for-you, one-for-me acts of sharing in play situations. Figure-on-ground is experienced visually, tactilely, and kinesthetically; locomotion for its own sake takes a child to a novel object, which then becomes the stimulation for a shift from play to exploration. Time-space relations are acted out in the lapse of time from bed-to-door, door-to-backyard, and door-to-playground. Counting is based in the piling of blocks to make a tower, and seriation is inherent in the action of putting rings on a post from the largest at the bottom to the smallest at the top. Of course, toys that have an inherent organization can build structural experience onto the sensorimotor associations of play.

When children have the run of large, stimulus-potent areas such as a farm, a ranch, a woods, or an ecologically conceived park, they will learn much from play. Floating bodies can be observed in a pool of water when a variety of objects can be picked up and tried. The rate of falling bodies can be experienced when there are different articles and various heights to drop them from without endangering someone else below. It is no accident that rural children, as a group, come to school with superior scientific and arithmetic concepts compared with urban children (Denny, 1958).

PLAY FORMS INITIATED BY ADULTS

Most of the chapter to this point has concerned the spontaneous play children initiate when left to pursue their own ends. Even the organized environment of the playground or the playroom gives the child many options for playing alone, for joining a group in a game, or for standing on the outside as an observer of play. The play environment, when organized by adults, narrows the choices of the child who is fortunate enough to have an expansive environment, but broadens the choices for the child with limited play facilities. Bringing groups of children together, as in the play center or the school, requires some attention to playthings for individuals so children may use playtime as release from the continuous direction that groups seem to require. Some consideration of the options available to children, when the choice of activity becomes their own, can help them learn to organize and make use of free time.

Teaching Play Forms

Children tend to repeat in their own spontaneous play those actions which they have observed in play with adults (El'Konin, 1969). Teachers and other care-givers can help children enhance the quality of their play, find solutions to their intrapersonal conflicts, and release their feelings of aggression through forms of instructed play. Usually this instruction is most effective when it is playful, when it fills a vacuum in the child's day, or when it can be demonstrated casually. Some of the forms which organized play may take are presented briefly and arranged according to the complexity and extent of adult direction. Play-center teachers will want to consult more detailed sources, including those cited, before undertaking to initiate organized play with groups of children.

ROLE PLAY

Role playing involves the identification and imitation of particular actions that characterize another person. Rene Spitz (1972) reported that as early as 18 months young children imitate a pattern of behaviors of parents in their absence. Putting on a hat and pretending to say "goodbye" or putting on makeup and viewing the effect in a mirror are examples. In psychoanalytic psychology, role playing requires identification with the person being played. In cognitive psychology, role play requires the concept of role so that the actions which characterize a role can be translated in a play situation. A child in solitary activity can role play. Adults can accept and help the child's early efforts to identify a role: "Oh, so you want to play Daddy? How would you like to help bring some logs to the fireplace?" "I'll be the horse and you can be the cowboy. You be the horse and pull the wagon, I have to start dinner." I recall with admiration the willingness of late President Kennedy to be seen playing with his children. His public invention of play sequences amidst the austerity of the oval office must continue to be a rich heritage for John and Carolyn.

DRAMATIC PLAY

Playing one role among a group of players is more formalized than individual role playing in that it requires group acceptance of role identification and group participation to carry it out. For groups of children to play their separate roles, a level of role generalization, and hence a more mature level of role conception, is necessary. The players must be mature enough to stay with the role they have accepted and they must have had experience with specific examples of role-related activities to put together a spontaneous sequence that qualifies for inclusion. Piaget's criteria of classification come to mind as the criteria adults might use to decide when sociodrama might be enjoyed by a group of charges. The children must be able to generalize, or classify possible actions, and to decide when an action fits or does not fit a role. Some examples of dramatic play are "cops and robbers," "playing doctor," and "playing army."

SOCIODRAMA

Sociodrama has been used to create situations in which children can work out social problems in a detached, less emotion-laden situation. If a fight breaks out in the playhouse, the teacher can at a later time, in the planning-listening area, initiate a family interaction which is designed to help children clarify the role of each family member. Running into other children on a tricycle or an engine can be played out as an autombile accident in which responsibility and regulations are discussed by the role players: traffic officers, drivers, witnesses, etc. Those children who are unusually mature, who are creative in social interaction, can take their turns at playing the roles and make value judgments, expressed in terms that are understood by less mature players. Sociodrama enables the teacher to use social pressure to help socially egocentric children see other points of view.

CREATIVE DRAMATICS

Teacher guidance in relatively formal settings helps children to have a happy, rewarding experience in dramatic forms of play. Creative dramatics is a somewhat guided, largely spontaneous, play-acting that involves a group of children in an affective experience that usually grows out of children's literature. Although there are many variations, the most usual technique is to read the children a story or poem that lends itself to dramatization. The teacher then helps the children decide what scenes they want to play. The scenes are sequenced and played in order; the characters are identified and a child volunteers to play each part. Through group analysis of the character, particularly the character's wants and feelings, or of the crisis of the moment, the player is oriented to the role. Some direct quotations are used, but children with expert guidance and a little experience become very good at ad-libbing the dialogue and expressing the feelings of the character. Group evaluation is centered on the affective interaction. Few props are used and pantomime is prominent.

CHILDREN'S THEATER

Two forms of formal drama are common: the adult presentation of children's stories as plays, and the plays children present for audiences, using the learned lines of the playwright. Both forms are valuable; the first for all children who are mature enough to sit through a play, the second for children with talent in acting.

Play Therapy

Most of the techniques and the theory of play therapy have come from the psychoanalytic school of psychology. The relationship between play and catharsis is as old as Greek drama. The literal meaning of catharsis, to cleanse or to purge, was the recognized purpose of the play. Players and viewers alike identified with the emotional crises of the characters and felt purified when the cause-effect relationship of human weakness had run its course in a tragic end. Symbolic punishment for real or imagined guilt was one appeal of drama; the other was the feeling of mastery by identification. In Greek drama, riches and power came to the deserving, by a combination of birth, virtue, and strong action. By experiencing the fantasy, strong emotions, feelings and envy, inadequacy, incest, and pretense, were brought to the surface and eliminated.

The dual wishes of the Greek drama were embodied in Freud's theory of play. He defined children's play as fantasy woven around toys, as contrasted with pure fantasy (daydreaming). The two classes of wishes in children's play are (1) to be grown-up (bigness means control and being able to do what one wants, and (2) to take the active role in painful encounters. The inherited tendency to repeat the feeling of pleasure contributes to play repetition in which any event suffered passively is turned to a wish-fulfilling situation in which the child takes command through fantasy and repeats the play view of things (Freud, 1955).

CATHARSIS FOR NORMAL CHILDREN

Anna Freud (1963), who was interested in the prevention of emotional illness, elaborated the function of play her father had established. She regarded the active coping devices of children's play as a positive action against the buildup of anxiety. When used in peer interaction and manipulation of toys, active coping gives the child a sense of coping in the real world.

Erikson (1972), who worked extensively with Anna Freud and was trained by her father, introduced block play with toys as a research device to study the coping effects of play. His technique was to bring a child of 4 or 5 years of age to a low play table on which assorted blocks, toy vehicles, toy animals, and dolls (vocational and family) were available. The play hostess invited the child to "build something" and to "tell a story about it." Erikson noted that most children went to building, after first engaging the hostess in conversation, and soon became absorbed in the construction with blocks. Vehicles usually were engaged next, then dolls. Finally, the child would make a gesture of closure, "this is it," and tell a story which fit the scene. The story was recorded and a photograph of the construction was taken. Erikson believed these specimen represented "condensed bits of life" (p. 131).

Erikson (1972) described his own perceptions of the play situation. "[They] seem to be governed by some need to *communicate*, or even to *confess*, they certainly also seem to serve the joy of *self-expression*" (p. 131). He compared the solitary construction of the children to the adult playwright's work in which he too "condenses scenes of unitary place and time, marked by a 'set' and populated by a cast . . . ." The players (dolls) represent individuals "caught in the role conflicts of their time" (p. 133).

Erikson (1963) has been widely quoted for the sex differences he observed in the block play of children. Briefly stated, boys played more with blocks and girls with dolls. Most towers (86 percent) were built by boys and most enclosures were built by girls. Girls' actors were domestic and tranquil while the boys' dolls were hostile and combative. (Having summarized this research to a seminar, I took twenty students to a parent preschool training program in rural Oregon. Just inside the door, and to the delight of female students, the first observation was a 4-year-old girl in solitary play, building as fine a tower as any of Erikson's male subjects of similar age conceived.) The major thrust of Erikson's contribution was both to spell out the symbolism and to help adults understand when and why children play.

TREATMENT FOR DISTURBED CHILDREN

Play therapy for emotionally disturbed children requires the guidance of a doctoral-level practitioner (Moustakas, 1953). Autistic and schizophrenic children

Aggressive play with dolls. (Sybil Shelton/Monkmeyer)

usually need regular and extensive sessions to work through their trauma and to begin to communicate with the therapist (Axline, 1964). Teachers and parents whose daily lives are involved with disturbed children will find play interaction a reasonable approach and one which is better than withdrawal from such children.

The differential roles of lay and professional helpers can be found in Carcuff (1968), who reported extensive evidence that paraprofessional helpers can bring about constructive changes in clients. Another recent source on play therapy is Nickerson (1973). Early attention to unusually withdrawn and unusually hostile behavior in children can rather safely be followed up by providing options for playing out their problems.

SUMMARY

Different theories of play have been posed by scholars and researchers: (1) views which justify children's play as practice for later life and seek to utilize play for learning; (2) behaviorist explanations of play as early and imprecise generalization of adult behavior; (3) cognitive views which hold that the time-space-quantity experience of play forms the basis for reality mapping of the physical world; (4) psychoanalytic views which focus on wish fulfillment through play and the symbolic nature of toys and play action; and (5) neurophysiological views which are concerned with brain and nervous-system changes before and after play.

Children's sensorimotor repetition in play can become the basis for creative production if they are able or can be helped to conceptualize the esthetic qualities and the essential uniqueness of their childlike and playful efforts to produce and construct.

Play serves the social functions of (1) enculturation, by allowing peers to play out roles and identify status in unthreatening and unreal settings; (2) communication of social intelligence in ways little understood or investigated scientifically; and (3) relief of the anxieties of affection versus aggression, boy versus girl, and young versus grown-up.

Exploratory play provides for self-initiated learning through (1) the ludic motor activity that is observed in all mammals but reaches its greatest complexity and duration in humans and (2) the exploration of object and space relationships. This reality mapping is conceptualized more effectively if the abstract symbols are provided in appropriate setting by care-givers.

Play has been formalized historically through drama by adults for grown-up purposes. Adults have found play forms by which to initiate child play: (1) role playing, in which adults suggest roles and participate; (2) dramatic play for which adults provide the setting and realistic toys; (3) sociodrama in which children, assuming roles, work through a problem; (4) creative dramatics by which adult guidance helps children recreate the feelings of literary people; and (5) children's theater which gives children an early introduction to the functions of drama in emotional life. Play therapy provides useful techniques by which normal children can achieve catharsis, and disturbed children can be treated early.

II
Affective Development

II Affective Development

The affective side of development is concerned with social and emotional growth. The boundaries of the affective dimension are less well defined than the boundaries of cognitive development. Nonetheless, the affective dimension generally includes such personal growth factors as social behavior, self-concept, and moral judgment. Some of the major concerns of parents and teachers, such as discipline and peer relationships, are more closely tied to affective than to cognitive responding, especially during the early stages of childhood.

The higher the level of response, the greater the interaction between affective and cognitive behavior. The basic associations that precede acculturation and value discrimination begin much earlier than do the behaviors which parents and teachers see and reward or punish. The nature of the early affective experience is exceedingly important. A happy adjustment to family members and a self-confident transition to social groups outside the home will help a child through difficult social interactions at a later time.

Affective development also has to do with the child's energy level, motivation, and desire for particular outcomes. This chapter assumes that affective experience is stored and is retrieved at a later time when a similar situation activates the patterns of past responses. In other words, the beginnings of motivation are learned in the same way that cognitive learning takes place. The neural structures involving affective development are formed by synaptic connections, just as the structures coordinating cognitive development are formed. But affective systems are primitive and are located in a phylogenically older part of the brain. Affective learning is built initially upon survival needs for food, liquid, elimination, and reproduction. This chapter explains the relationship of different levels of affective functioning, which is essentially a motivation sequence that influences all cognitive functioning.

Those aspects of child behavior which are emotionally loaded, or largely determined by feelings, make up the several sections of this chapter: the emotional bases for self-concept; social interaction in children; the relationship of culture, biology, and ego development; the development of moral judgment; and negative behavior patterns. Negative behavior is assumed to include both withdrawal, which indicates fear of interactions with other persons, and aggression, in which hostility is directed toward persons or objects.

EMOTIONAL BASES FOR SELF-CONCEPT

The emotional component of all human behavior is directed from limbic areas of the brain, including the amygdala, the hippocampus, and the mammary body. From this system near the top of the brainstem, long axons lead to the frontal lobe where self-directed behavior is initiated. The hippocampus produces a flow of hormone cells to the pituitary gland which stores and duplicates other hormones for release into the bloodstream when needed by the organism. These hormones are available to direct the energies of the organism in four life-sustaining functions described by Pribram (1971): fighting, fleeing, feeding, and sexual intercourse. The psychological concept of reward centers is confirmed by observation of clusters of cells in the area of the limbic system, which, when stimulated with electric probes, produce sensations of pleasure or punishment depending on the cell which is contacted. The idea that brain mechanisms coordinate affective response is widely accepted although there is much still to be learned about the coding, the storage, and the retrieval of affective experience (Figure 11–2).

Affective Dimensions of Motivation

The relationship between information as it comes through the senses and the reinforcement that accompanies the sensory event has been used to explain learning (Chapter 8). The associations of pleasure and punishment that reinforce a cognitive event are the same bits of affect which are basic to all motivation. The bits of emotional experience, whether pleasurable or punishing, account for the enthusiastic approach of some children to finger painting while others grimace or avoid it. Affective associations explain why some children love to read while others flee from books if they have a choice.

The association level of the learning-motivation model represents an accumulation of affects that are connected in the brain structure of the child to a particular person, setting, activity, or object (Figure 11–1). *Affective associations* are the bits of pleasure or punishment feelings an individual attaches to a cognitive event. Affects are stored without the conscious effort of the learner, and their effects on behavior are unconscious also. Emotional connections, associated with a cognitive event, may be so painful that the individual represses both the cognitive and the affective aspects of the experience.

When bits and pieces of emotional experience (affective associations) are restructured, or conceptualized at the awareness level, a person is functioning at level 2, affective conceptualization. The individual then knows the sources of his or her pleasure, fear, satisfaction, or discomfort. Awareness consists of bringing certain aspects from an unconscious lower level to a conscious higher level (Piaget, 1976). Affects are organized, at the association level, by the biological nature of the coding system. In conceptualization, there is a restructuring by the individual on his or her own emotional terms. *Affective conceptualizations* are the conscious, identified, and categorized emotional content of the human experience. Once raised to the level of consciousness, and recognized as rewarding or punishing, the criteria have been established for planning those kinds of activity which lead to personal satisfaction. In this way the motivational forces that arise from the internal, unconscious needs of the individual may become directed toward a recognized goal.

Self-concept is the prototype of oneself; the picture an individual constructs

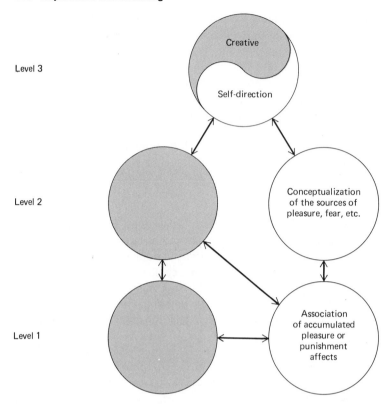

Level 3

Creative

Self-direction

Level 2

Conceptualization
of the sources of
pleasure, fear, etc.

Level 1

Association
of accumulated
pleasure or
punishment
affects

FIGURE 11-1 Model for the building of motivations. At level 1 the emotional elements of pleasure and punishment are cumulative and unconscious. Associative connections are made, both to previously stored feelings and to the cognitive event. At level 2 affective associations are restructured at the awareness level. Many such conceptualizations make up the self-concept. The motivation to extend the self-concept to creative productions makes level 3 functioning possible.

from many affective experiences. It is a conscious effort to answer the questions "Who am I?" and "How am I unique?" To the extent that uniqueness of self is accepted and willingly expressed, a person is freed to function in creative and self-directed ways.

When a person puts the affective conceptions of level 2 into words, that individual is making a commitment to the future. Once recognized and expressed as self-concepts, the emotional support for some kinds of productivity in preference to others is clear. As a social organism each person has a necessity to produce in ways that reveal and extend the self into the cognitive world of others. *Creative self-direction* is that level of human functioning at which the conceptualizations of self-worth and the conceptualizations of the real world are brought together. By this definition, creative production has a reality base to which other persons can relate a common knowledge of the world. Creativity is fused, however, with a personal value structure. The affective elements that make a creative action unique are derived from a personal construct of culture, values, esthetics, and morality.

The implication of the learning-motivation model is that creative self-direction is achieved through knowing in both the cognitive and the affective sense. The young child produces spontaneously: a sing-song of words that delight the ears, a mingling of colors that look like an abstract painting because the adult doesn't recognize what the child is representing, and unique names and uses for common things. When Erika called a prune a "giant raisin" she was creating a language for something unknown to her. Her naivete will give way, very shortly, to the conventional words for things. She can, however, conceptualize that unique ways of expressing ideas are valued by other persons. She can begin to build a self-concept as a creative person by finding unusual ways to say and to do ordinary things. Conceptualization enables people to know the difference between uniqueness of expression and departure from convention. (Wilson & Robeck, 1968).

Social-Learning Theory

Socialization refers to the developmental process of adapting to the common needs of the group. Such adaptation at a human level requires many affective

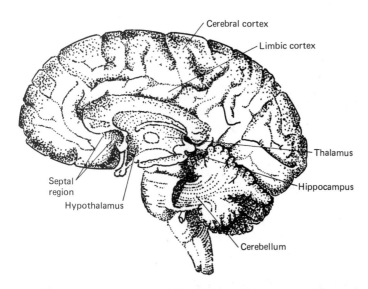

FIGURE 11-2 Areas involved in emotional expression. The right hemisphere of the brain, shown from the inside, reveals some of the major areas, deep in the brain, that are connected by neural pathways of the affective system. (Drawing by Donna Thompson.)

qualities that go unrecognized in research on social development, such as nonverbal reading of mood, a sense of personal bonds, and empathy. All social species survive and evolve phylogenically by adaptation to the restraints and the aspirations of the group. Socialization is an important part of growing up and attaining a recognized place in the dynamics of the peer group. Trial-and-error approaches to social behavior result in interpersonal conflicts which can be avoided by the modeling of social interaction on the part of experienced persons. Both the formal and informal conventions of culture have been derived over time. In stable societies institutions (school, media, and law) define and conserve the standards of social interaction laid down by culture.

Different theories of how children learn the interdependence of group members have been proposed. Mowrer (1960) suggested a classical conditioning theory by which imitation in the young is positively or negatively reinforced when the individual approximates or matches the behaviors modeled in the culture. The nature of the reinforcement is affective in that the emotional consequences to the child provide strong reinforcement of conforming behavior, or imitation.

Bandura (1971) proposed a social-learning theory which gives an important role to the cognitive processes in modeling behavior. Although his theory could be presented as a form of cognitive development (Chapter 8), his ideas fit into the present context which incorporates social, moral, and emotional development. Bandura's theory evolved from a series of studies that tried to explain how observational learning in childhood goes unpracticed for years, only to emerge intact at a later and more appropriate state in life. Observational learning, psychological modeling, modeling behavior, and imitation are all terms which are used to explain socialization.

Bandura's theory of social learning specified four steps or processes: attention, retention, motor reproduction, and motivation. To learn matching behavior by observation, the child must first attend to the models and recognize the distinctive features of their responses. Models that get and hold children's *attention* are likely to be persons who are socially attractive because of their power, appearance, or status. Older children are more likely to be modeled than peers (Wolters, 1976). Attention is more likely to be directed toward peers who are dynamic, who organize games, and who pass out the toys.

The second process, *retention*, requires that modeled behavior be organized cognitively by the learner, during exposure, into a representational system. In one study, two representational systems (imagery and verbal coding) were tested by asking groups of children to reproduce complex behavior they had seen modeled on a film (Bandura, Grusec, & Menlove, 1966). One group was directed to watch attentively, one group was taught to code novel responses into verbal forms, and one group was distracted in their attending by being required to count during the viewing. Children in the verbal coding group later reproduced 60 percent of the modeled responses they had coded, but only 25 percent of the behaviors they had neglected to code. Social-learning theory suggests that child observers organize the modeled behavior they attend to by transforming and classifying it into systems. These systems can be stored and remembered over time. Bandura suggested that children covertly rehearse social behaviors that they are not permitted by society to perform at the time. Dating behavior is an example. In Bandura's cognitive focus, transformational and organizational processes are involved, as well as the associational processes of social conditioning theory (1971, p. 25).

The third component of psychological modeling is the *motor reproduction* of an action that was previously observed and stored. Complex behaviors are produced by combining previous motor sequences. Bandura suggested that delayed modeling may lack some aspects of a behavior pattern, due to some physical or cognitive lack in the youngster doing the modeling or in the social situation. Improvement is possible because the learner monitors his own motor reproductions and perfects his actions by matching them to the previously stored images and verbal representations.

The fourth component of a social behavior, *motivation*, is established by any of three modes of reinforcement. When matching performances are attempted, the learner may be reinforced by others in the society, as when a mother approves the social niceties such as "please" and "thank you." Negative sanctions may postpone or regulate an unsocial response. Vicarious reinforcement is also a potent factor, as with the reward experienced when a model or a friend achieves a social goal that the child shares with her model (father, idol, television star). Self-reinforcement of social behavior also supports and stabilizes the learning of social patterns. The learner determines the fitness of an action by his values and is reinforced by his own effort. These different forms of reinforcement build the motivation for matching performances of models in the social group. Bandura's theory of observational learning goes beyond the imitation described by Piaget (1951) in infants and young children. Bandura gives social learning a larger cognitive function than does the psychoanalytic theory of socialization proposed by Erikson (1963).

Receiving, Responding, and Valuing

Affective experiences of childhood form the basis for mature and responsible living in adults. A sequence of five affective levels was outlined by Krathwohl, Bloom, and Masia (1964) in a handbook of affective objectives for schools. They were concerned that students develop appreciations of the esthetic elements in the culture, and that they commit themselves to a life-style based on a value system. Their goal, at the end of the educational process, was an individual whose judgments were based on evidence and whose behavior was characterized by a consistent philosophy of life. Although they developed their levels of affective development to be used in schools, the early steps, receiving, responding, and valuing, apply to infants and young children. Two higher categories, organization and characterization, go beyond the affective capabilities of early childhood.

Receiving as an affective behavior begins in neonatal life. Krathwohl described three subcategories of receiving, beginning with awareness when the "individual merely has his attention attracted to the stimuli" (p. 34). Within a few days the infant shows the willingness to receive, described as "the state in which he has differentiated the stimuli from others and is willing to give it his attention." Infants a few months old are capable of the final level of receiving—selected attention. The individual is alert and looks for instances that create a desired stimulation. These levels of receiving describe the beginning of any new and different affective experience, regardless of age.

Responding, the second category, was defined as complying with the expectations of others, showing a willingness to respond, and gaining some emotional satisfaction from the response. These ways of experiencing pleasure go beyond the discriminations of receiving and take on emotional elements that are necessary for valuing. At this stage the individual seeks out and attaches emotional significance to persons, actions, or things. It will be remembered from Chapter 4 that infants 8 months old attach to particular persons and respond differently to them than to strangers.

At the third level, *valuing*, the individual's behavior becomes more and more consistent with the values he or she holds. Valuing of a particular ability is shown when an individual persists in trying to develop it. The example given by Krathwohl was writing effectively, in the adult sense of authorship. Such valuing can also be seen in the effort of primary children to write a story, or even in the toddler's effort to master a stairway. The subcategories of valuing all have elements of cognition in acceptance of, preference for, and commitment to the value. Many of the values children bring to primary school will be retained throughout life. During the school years children must learn to make choices between the values of family, peer group, and the academic or technical world. These choices force them to organize value systems of their own.

Krathwohl, Bloom, and Masia (1964) describe the fourth level, *organization*, as "conceptualization of a value" and "organization of a value system" (p. 35). The fifth level is *characterization* of a life-style that is consistent with a value system. The early experiences of receiving, responding, and valuing are the basis for later and more complex affective dimensions.

Changing the Self-Concept

A serious effort to improve the cognitive skills of disadvantaged children in school has led some teachers to conclude that a valuing of self was lacking. The relationship between self-concept, school behavior, and achievement has been reported in many studies (Zirkel, 1971). There has been an increase in the effort to enhance the self-concept. The enhancement of self-concept has come to be valued as an educational outcome in its own right (Shavelson, Hubner, & Stanton, 1976).

Many variations of counseling and behavior modification have been tried with mixed success in improving the self-concept of children. Because of the unsocial behavior of children with low self-esteem, some programs have worked directly to change the behavior, with the expectation that more positive behavior toward other persons would result in more positive feedback and an improved self-image. Usually one of two systems was used, the one giving token rewards for desired social behavior and the other using social reinforcers. *Social reinforcement* is the positive response of a significant other person to the behavior of the child. Generally behavior-change plans for self-concept enhancement were more successful when social reinforcement, rather than tokens, was used. Teachers have been the change agents in much of the research, and the reinforcement has been approval of successful behavior (Firme, 1969).

More consistent improvements in self-concept have been obtained by helping the child increase the quality of his *self-reinforcement*. Felker and Thomas (1971) noted that the child with a negative self-concept had not learned to give himself verbal rewards. Self-referent statements, made during a task, were encouraged. Phillips (1975) found that teacher reinforcement of positive self-referents increased the number of self-referent statements and improved the scores on a self-esteem test. It is quite likely that self-referent statements are self-reinforcing, but also that they become conceptualized. They are raised to the awareness level, and are more stable than the vague feelings or affects merely associated.

SOCIAL INTERACTION IN CHILDREN

The fascination infants and young children have for each other has often been noted and enjoyed by their parents. For example, Ernie (8 months) and Jay (5 months) were brought together for the first time. Since this was the end of a severe Wisconsin winter and the infants were both firstborns, neither had seen another child since leaving the hospital nursery. They were placed on a bed facing each other, with pillows behind them in case they should topple over. The babies looked at each other, smiled and waved their arms, then laughed with loud chuckles. This went on and on until their mothers removed them; then they began to wail. Definitive studies are needed of the behavior of children in their encounter with peers at the initial stages of social interaction.

When and how children begin to identify with and model peers more than parents is important in the kinds of affective solutions they acquire while growing up. Kagan (1958) suggested that identification is strong in dependent persons, including all young children, because they lack the ability to gratify the needs for power and love through their own behavior. He hypothesized that the vicarious mechanisms, imitation and identification, will decrease as the individual matures and is able to attain power and love more directly.

Peer members become identity objects when social interaction with the age group begins to hold greater satisfaction than participation in the family unit. Although individual children differ markedly in their social skills, and in the roles they assume within the group, the development of socialization is sequential for children generally.

Responsiveness of Infants

Human young respond emotionally at a very early age. The infants obtain some of the necessities of life by crying demands. They also initiate social interaction with others by smiling. Early emotional behavior toward others reflects both the social environment and a biologically determined timetable. The positive affects of smiling and the negative affects of fear of strangers are among the most thoroughly studied of the social responses of infants. Spitz (1965) considered the appearance of the social smile, the anxiety of the 8-month-old, and head shaking to mean negation as the three significant benchmarks of affective development of the first year.

SMILING

The reflexive smile of the neonate, which disappears after a few days, has been distinguished from the social smile which reappears as adaptive behavior (Chapter 4). However, Brazelton (1969) elicited social smiling in neonates by smiling, talking, and stimulating them tactically with gentle rubs on the abdomen. Most researchers have used visual images, such as masks or the human face, to elicit the early social smiles.

Spitz (1965) observed the smiling behavior of 145 babies at regular intervals for one year. More than half of them were institution infants and they represented black, white, and American Indian ethnic groups. All but 2 percent (who smiled earlier) began smiling for the human face at 2 to 6 months old. Ambrose (1961) reported that home-reared infants smiled in response to an unsmiling face much earlier (6 to 10 weeks) than institution infants, whose smiling under similar conditions peaked at 14 weeks. Moving faces elicit more smiling than stationary ones. Infants smile more for familiar faces than strange ones, and infants may not smile at all for a profile. Spitz believed the smile to be species-specific and age-related, but different in individual infants because of different social environments. He observed that the social smile for an unfamiliar face disappeared about two months earlier than the fear of strangers became apparent.

FEAR OF STRANGERS

The consistent onset of the fear of strangers at about 8 months, under a variety of rearing conditions, has been reported in the literature for a long time. Mardy, the infant daughter of a graduate student, attended seminars regularly and was passed around from one admiring child-development major to another. In addition to her mother who nursed her, Mardy was cared for according to a regular schedule by her father, a sitter, and another graduate student. These adults tended to believe that pleasurable contact with adults would generalize, especially when the contact with mother was healthy and regular. Would Mardy show a fear of strangers? At 7½ months she began a period of refusing to go to strangers, of protesting when left with the friend, and of watching her mother's every move.

The onset of fear of stranger was confirmed by Shaffer (1966) who observed a sample of thirty-six infants from the twenty-fifth to the fifty-third week of life. Their average age at the appearance of the fear behavior was just under 36 weeks—or 8 calendar months. Interestingly, maternal availability to the infant was not significantly related to the sudden fear of strangers, nor were the number of other children in the family and the number of adults contacted. The onset of fear in strangers has been further confirmed by relating heart rate and the behavior of infants 5 and 9 months old (Campos, Emde, Gaensbauer, & Henderson, 1975). Infants showed a shift in attentiveness to strangers and fear of them, which was accompanied by a shift from deceleration to acceleration in heart rate. The cardiac responses corresponded to the facial responses of the infants, which were attenuated when the mother was present. Most, but not all, of the 9-month infants showed fear of strangers. Apparently the early smile and the later onset of a fear of strangers have survival value for the human infant.

Cooperative Play

Gesell and Ames (1940) reported that children go through age-related stages of social awareness during play. *Solitary play* is the essential aloneness when the toddler is preoccupied with his or her interaction with toys. *Parallel play* is seen in 3- or 4-year-old children who enjoy playing the same game with the same kinds of toys, but their interaction is still with the object. They play side by side, but their actions are independent of each other. *Precooperative play* involves an exchange of toys and conversation in a play situation but lacks the interdependence players have on each other in cooperative play.

Parten, who studied group play in the preschool, found that children reach the ages of 4 or 4½ years before they spend as much or more time playing in groups of three or more than playing in pairs (1933). She also found that as children grew older their play groups were increasingly limited to one sex (from 61 to 79 percent), at least until age 6. Some play patterns continued, however, that were organized across the sexes and that included pairs.

Levels of Social Interaction

Wilson and Robeck (1965) proposed levels of social interaction in the kindergarten that were based in learning theory. Social functioning was described as associative learning, conceptualization, and creative self-direction in group interaction. These descriptions apply to any of the activities of the school and to individuals older or younger than kindergartners.

PREASSOCIATIVE FUNCTIONING

At this level children's social interactions are self-serving and egocentric. They think only of themselves and what is satisfying at the moment; thus, their behavior shows a lack of foresight as they succumb to impulses. Their assessment of a situation is distorted and they cannot see the relation of their actions to the group's purpose. If they know the rules, they cannot apply them because they cannot foresee the mutual benefit they bring. In one of our examples, derived from field observations of over 100 kindergarten classes, Jason had the responsibility for distributing four large balls at playtime. He quickly passed three to his best friends and kept the fourth ball for himself, despite a rule that both boys and girls would share the large balls.

ASSOCIATION LEARNING

At the association level children know the rules and can follow routines to which they have been trained. When the situation fails to match the conditions of the training, they demonstrate a feeling of helplessness and look to higher authority (teacher, parent) to help them cope with the problem. Penny has learned the "thing to do" in many situations but her behavior is still egocentric when the situation calls for seeing the other person's interests. She knows the group decision that playground equipment must be distributed to both boys and girls, but she wants to end the problem by having an adult take over the responsibility and the consequences.

CONCEPTUALIZATION OF RULES

At the conceptual level, a child not only knows the rules or standards for particular social situations, but is able to apply them when a conflict occurs. Adam understands that rules help people get along with each other and that these same standards of fairness apply to others and to himself equally. He tends to enforce rules actively. When given the balls to pass out, Adam gave two to the girls and one to a boy friend, but he retained his right to keep one ball for himself.

SELF-INITIATED SOLUTIONS

At the most mature level a child shows self-motivation and generates new solutions in a situation. She sees situations in perspective and conceives her potential role in resolving conflicts. She is empathetic in that the feelings of others are perceived, and may find greater joy in the satisfaction she brings to others, or in fulfilling the social role of mediator, than in the more immediate gratification that comes from asserting one's rights. In our playground item, Martha went beyond the application of rules to find innovative solutions. She found it more self-fulfilling to be responsible and take initiative than to have charge of a ball.

Political Socialization

A surprisingly large body of research has been focused on how and when political concepts and orientations are formed in children. Bruce Robeck (1970) provided a bibliography of nearly 500 entries on this topic. A study by Hess and Torney (1967) summarized the political attitudes of elementary school children in four regions of the United States. They found that children develop an early faith in political figures and the institutions of government. The image they hold of officials, from president to police officers, centers on their personal qualities. High-IQ children, in contrast to the larger sample, tend to qualify their attitudes early, to develop an abstraction of the presidency, and to conceptualize the role of institutions. These generalizations include the public school, where bright children see its function in general terms apart from their own relationship to a particular school. The failure of large numbers of young voters to go to the polls would seem to be based in causalities other than their ability to conceptualize the issues. The idealism of young children toward officials is probably lost long before they have a chance to participate in civic responsibilities. One possibility is to develop group skills in decision making, at first giving children the chance to participate in minor decisions in the kindergarten, and gradually expanding the responsibility for the political and social organization of the school so that the pupils are part of decision-making procedures in these areas.

THE RELATIONSHIPS OF CULTURE, BIOLOGY, AND EGO DEVELOPMENT

In his classic book, *Childhood and Society*, Erik Erikson explained what he called the dynamic relationship of an individual's culture, biological growth stage at the time, and psychological development. When in his mid-twenties Erikson went to Vienna to teach literature and art in a private school for the children of wealthy Americans who had gone there to be analyzed in Freud's clinic. Anna Freud, a therapist who had trained with her father, was interested in the prevention of emotional problems during childhood. Being analyzed was the thing to do at the time, if one could afford it, but the clinic selected its own patients. Erikson was accepted at a reduced rate and spent an hour each day for about two years on Anna's couch. Often they talked of the children in the school, of the vulnerability of childhood, and of the importance of a healthy psyche (Coles, 1970).

During the Vienna years, Erikson came to know children intimately, and to observe school and family influences on their emotional development. Their school, a prototype of open education with family grouping, was designed by the three teachers: Erik (literature and art), his German boyhood friend (mathematics and science), and an American graduate of Columbia Teachers College. She married Erikson, and continued to teach at the school while carrying and nursing two children. Although the Eriksons lived in a modest cottage up a hill from the school, they were part of a social group that included the affluent patrons of the school.

Erikson eventually trained as a psychoanalyst in Freud's clinic and, when World War II broke out, was invited to teach in the United States. He brought with him the techniques of Sigmund Freud and a view of human development that integrated sociology, biology, and psychology. These views were extended and elaborated in the *Eight Ages of Man*. He used the techniques to further study the affective development of healthy children, the role of culture on the personality of native Americans, and a variety of emotional problems in children and students. Erikson became the major force in the psychoanalytic branch of child psychology in America.

Erikson believed that emotional crises occurred when particular cultural de-mands came to bear upon individuals at vulnerable periods in their physical development. One of his patients, a 6-year-old girl, had been schizophrenic since infancy. Her mother had become ill with tuberculosis when Jean was 9 months old. The baby was turned over to a fastidious nurse who did not allow Jean to approach her mother's bed and was very vocal about baby soils and odors. Among Jean's symptoms of withdrawal was a frantic affection for pillows. Whether or not one accepts the symbolism of the soft pillow, Erikson's point is that the child might have been able to cope with separation at a different and less vulnerable time than the onset of the fear of strangers. Also, a more loving mother substitute might have helped Jean retain her trust in a significant adult.

Erikson's conceptualization of the affective life was generally positive. Three forces (the group, the organism, and the ego) interact in mutually supportive ways during the affective development of most persons. His conception of the eight periods in the human life-cycle drew heavily upon Freud's stages of infant sexuality, latency, and puberty. Erikson's view of the healthy adult personality was perhaps influenced in part by his own coming of age during a time he was simultaneously a young father, an innovative teacher, and a physician in training. According to him, each age was characterized by its own growth crisis, or polarity. By polarity he meant the opposing qualities, powers, or tendencies of emotional life. The resolution of a polarity had its positive effects on the maturity of the individual.

Erikson's Ages of Man

BASIC TRUST VERSUS BASIC MISTRUST (0 TO 18 MONTHS)

Erikson believed that the mutual regulation of feeding and being fed, assisted by biological regulation, was the beginning of a trust that would carry the infant through separation, weaning, and other demands of growing up. "The first demonstration of social trust in the baby is the ease of his feeding, the depth of his sleep, the relaxation of his bowels" (1963, p. 247). According to Erikson, the consistency, continuity, and sameness of the early caring routines are basic to a sense of ego; babies learn to trust others by the shared tasting and testing of early experience. He deemphasized such factors as the quantity of food received, or the demonstrations of love, and described instead a quality relationship of trustworthi-ness, within the "trusted framework of the culture." By having his biological anticipations gratified, the young child evolves from the oral period with the *drive* and *hope* every person needs to organize his or her life (p. 274).

AUTONOMY VERSUS SHAME AND DOUBT (18 MONTHS TO 3¹/₂ YEARS)

According to psychoanalytic theory the psychosocial development shifts from the oral organization of infancy to the anal organization of toddlerhood. Erikson described how the increased control over the muscles to hold and to let go, with a simultaneous expectation from society that the child control holding and letting

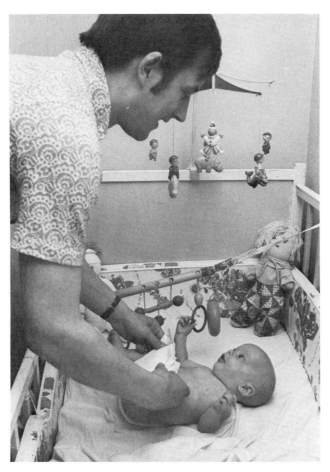

Basic trust is established through caregiving. (Erika/Peter Arnold)

go, extends beyond toilet training to personality development. Autonomy comes from the child's having attained locomotion. Shame comes from newly acquired awareness of body productions, together with doubts about the goodness of body processes not understood: "The 'behind' is the small being's dark continent." Too much shaming, Erikson believes, will cause the child to become secretive and try to get away with things. "This basic sense of doubt in whatever one has left behind forms a substratum for later and more verbal forms of compulsive doubting" (p. 254). The positive traits of autonomy are established during this stage if the child can resolve the conflicts of the anal period.

INITIATIVE VERSUS GUILT (3 TO 5 YEARS)

Initiative adds the quality of planning and undertaking; of being on the move. The emotional polarity is based in the child's growing awareness of sexuality, the genital parts of the body, and the social implications of sex identity. Children of this

Initiative in promoting friendship. (Nancy Hays/Monkmeyer)

age can develop an obedience that is so literal the child's own personality is obliterated; or they can overimpose their ego strength on other people in aggressive ways. The difficult emotional shift during this period is the necessary sharing of the familial love. The child becomes aware that he or she is not the most important object in the affection of mother and father. The boy must transfer his identity to the father and accept the mate relationship the father has with the mother. The girl must accept the mother's prior position in the love of the father. The disappearance of the child's egocentric love for the parent can be resolved in cooperation, rather than in rage, if previous relationships are secure. Such a resolution of the Oedipal conflict is a new sense of *direction* and *purpose*.

INDUSTRY VERSUS INFERIORITY (5 YEARS TO PUBERTY)

Freud called this the latency period because violent drives were dormant. The tendency of the Oedipal child to be "on the make" with people is sublimated in the tendency of the latency child to gain recognition by diligence and productivity. These are the years that overlap elementary schooling, when the child is ready to be initiated into the working world of books, tools, and machines. The latency child's best hope for overcoming inferiority is to develop the sense of personal worth through achievement, according to Erikson. Children this age are psychologically vulnerable to self-depreciation through failure in whatever skills the culture demands and values. The rewards of resolving the industry-inferiority polarity is a new security in productivity and *competence.*

IDENTITY VERSUS ROLE CONFUSION (ADOLESCENCE)

The individual who arrives at adolescence with a sense of personal strengths derived from continuity in infancy and productivity in childhood experiences less role confusion than those who have not resolved earlier conflicts. Erikson suggests that young people of this age are drawn to rituals, creeds, and clans because they need to have their identity confirmed. The biological revolution of this age (rapid growth and genital maturity) is accompanied by the need for the individual to have his or her changed body and new ideology confirmed by others. When adolescents are out of phase with the institutions of family and culture they create a peer culture for confirmation. The resolution of role confusion in adolescence indicates a readiness for the devotion and fidelity required in courtship and parenthood.

POLARITIES OF ADULTHOOD

The strengths acquired in the three ages of adulthood are *love, care,* and *wisdom.* The young adult who emerges from puberty with a sense of identity is ready to fuse his or her identity with another person in an intimate relationship. The ego must be willing to take risks if the polarity of intimacy versus isolation is to be resolved. Erikson believed that the greatest danger of this age was isolation (including an isolation of two) which cuts individuals off from being loving and work-productive persons. The potential hostilities and rages of this period are resolved in sexual selection, cooperation, and culturally defined modes of competition. These accomplishments are the prerequisites of parenthood.

The polarity of generativity versus stagnation charcterizes the seventh age of man, according to Erikson. He regarded adulthood (parenthood) as the height of evolutionary and psychosocial development. Generativity is concerned with guiding the next generation, although it also includes *productivity* and *creativity* in their popular meanings. Erikson did not believe that merely "having" children produced this level of concern for others, or that true caring necessarily accompanied parenthood.

The time of maturity of older adults was seen by Erikson as the time in life to resolve the polarity of ego identity versus despair. The person who had somehow taken care of the conflicts of the psychosocial life could accept the life-cycle as something that "had to be" and "by necessity, permitted no substitutions" (p. 269). The resolution of the conflicts of aging results in the basic virtue of *wisdom.* Erikson's discussion of the adult stages could be helpful reading for the teacher or director who decides to select retired persons as volunteers for children's programs.

Contributions of Psychoanalysis

Many students find Erikson's emphasis on sexuality and symbolism difficult to incorporate into their cognitive orientation to theories of socialization and affective development. The knowledge he brings to child development theory, which is not duplicated by others, is primarily his perceptive accounts of the interaction of culture, biology, and the psychological self. The function of this knowledge is that the social environment might be brought to bear in ways that support the biological cycles and enhance the personal strengths of the growing child.

The case history, play therapy, and clinical method of child study and intervention are all techniques designed by psychoanalysts. Case studies enable adults who try to cure emotional problems to work in consistent ways with a particular child. Play therapy may or may not assure long-term cures for unhealthy egos, but it does bring periods of release for disturbed children. The clinical method has recently become a respected research tool for studying the cognitive and moral development of children.

DEVELOPMENT OF MORAL JUDGMENT

Philosophers have assumed that the grown-ups in a society influence the morality of the young whom they rear. According to a gross comparison, that between children who grew up with animals and those who grew up with people, differences are obvious in the quality of social interaction favoring the human models. Psychoanalysts (Freud, Erikson, Piers) accept the strength of the conscience, or superego, as the critical element in moral development. Psychologists have differed in their beliefs about the development of morality. Behaviorists assume that good habits of interacting with others are based on the results of previous behavior, for example, reward or punishment. Cognitive-developmental psychologists generally accept the theory of stages in moral development which correspond to the stages of cognitive development outlined by Piaget.

Kohlberg's Stages of Morality

Kohlberg (1969) believed *justice* to be the universal principle on which moral conduct is based. He agreed with Dewey that what is practiced in growing up becomes the pattern of social conduct. Kohlberg combined the educational philosophy of learning by doing and the biological epistemology of Piaget, who had shown that children change the quality of their thinking behavior over time. These changes are predictable for the typical child and proceed from sensorimotor intelligence to symbolic representations, to concrete operations, and finally to logical thought (Chapter 8). The child's limited ability to reason also limits the child's moral conduct. Conceptualizations such as cause-effect and reciprocity are basic to understanding the principle of justice. Piaget's idea of growth as the result of the child's necessity to interact with the social world and to organize this experience in the direction of a universal principle (justice) had great appeal for

Kohlberg. A cognitive psychologist, he proposed and tested three levels of moral judgment: *preconventional, conventional*, and *postconventional*. He defined six stages of moral development, two at each level. Like Piaget, Kohlberg based his research findings on the subject's reasoning when presented a problem of social conduct, focusing on the *why* of a moral decision, rather than the decision itself.

PRECONVENTIONAL LEVEL

The child at the *preconventional* stages is responsive to cultural labels of good and bad, right and wrong. He or she interprets them initially in terms of punishment, reward, or exchange of favors. The physical power of those who enunciate the rules becomes very influential in determining whose code of conduct the child will practice.

Stage 1 is based on the desire to avoid physical punishment by a superior force. The physical consequences of an action determine its goodness or badness to the child, without regard to broader human meanings. In young children, and in older persons who conduct themselves in this way, the avoidance of punishment and the unquestioning deference to power are valued rather than any underlying respect for moral order. The principle that maintains the social order is obedience toward those in authority and punishment for those who deviate. Although many parents of young children resist the traditional forms of physical punishment, they might think about the young child's need to experience the consequence of misbehavior. At this level of social adaptation a child may need to look to the parent for the enunciation of the rules.

Stage 2 is reached when the child shows a sense of fairness and equality in the distribution of favors among individuals. Kohlberg and Turiel (1971) called this the *morality of the marketplace*, where elements of fairness, reciprocity, and equal sharing are present, but are interpreted in a physical or pragmatic way. Sharing at this stage means equal return, not gratitude. They believed the child is capable of accepting true equality only when the rules of sharing are known and reciprocity in social relations is understood. This corresponds to Piaget's conceptions of reversibility and conservation. Most primary-age children are still at the preconventional level of moral development. By age 10, one-third have progressed to the conventional level or even beyond (Sprinthall & Sprinthall, 1974).

CONVENTIONAL LEVEL

Conventional morality characterizes most adults, who rather consistently conform to the expectations of family, group, or nation. Role conformity is perceived as valuable in its own right in that it stablizes a society.

Stage 3 individuals follow the moral conduct that is "nice" and pleases others. Complexity of social thought is absent, while behavior codes are sharply defined. There is little doubt about right and wrong behavior, or who the good and bad models are. Kohlberg (1969) referred to Charlie Brown as living within this stage because he looks to others for direction. Subsequent studies have shown most women over 25 years old to be fixed at this stage of conventional behavior.

Stage 4 is oriented more to law and order, authority, fixed rules, and maintenance of the social order than to the niceties of social interaction. Loyalty to the established order, duty to others, and earned status are important and valued as ends in themselves. This is the typical standard of moral conduct for male citizens over 25 (Sprinthall & Sprinthall, 1974). When questioned, 16-year-olds indicated moral judgments at the conventional level almost half (44 percent) of the time. Only 20 percent of their judgments were still at a preconventional level of morality. A surprising 35 percent showed postconventional reasoning by Kohlberg's definition. This finding may imply some regression to conventional standards in early adulthood and confirms Piaget's observation that adolescents show an "idealistic" concern for moral issues during the early stages of logical thought.

POSTCONVENTIONAL LEVEL

Individuals at this level make a clear effort to define moral values which have validity apart from the authority of groups. Their application of moral principles is consistent with their own value structure. Moral judgments tend to be complex, comprehensive, and consistent for all persons. Thinking at this level is difficult because conventional norms do not necessarily apply and consistent evaluation at a high level and by one's own criteria of justice is required. Shared standards, rights, and duties within a system of justice characterize a mature sense of morality.

Stage 5 judgments are based on a *system* of laws which becomes the starting point for conformity by an individual to the standards of majority welfare. Although the orientation is legalistic, the conformity is self-imposed and recognizes the rights of others. Kohlberg identified the Constitution of the United States as having this level of moral responsibility and indicating a higher conceptual level of morality than the laws to which stage 4 thinking is directed. Kohlberg (1971) observed that the moral judgments of an individual typically fall within a three-stage range, suggesting that older children who usually express stage 5 moral reasoning would function at stages 4 or 6 part of the time.

Stage 6 judgments are based on principles of choice that are logical, universal, and consistent. This individual is more concerned with conscience than with socially ordained rules. He or she is prepared to take the consequence for adhering to ideals that conflict with society's more narrowly defined standards. Equal rights legislation and the Emancipation Proclamation are examples of changes in man-made laws that became necessary to square with a changing conceptualization of the moral definition of being human.

Critique of Kohlberg's Theory

Kohlberg's work has been criticized on the grounds: (1) that his theory is based on cognitive responses to verbal situations rather than on actual moral conduct, (2) that his theory is elitist, representing the values of a small minority, and (3) that social behavior is actually conditioned to the rewarding or punishing effects of social acts, rather than development in stages of social concepts. These major questions have been raised in the context of school, where the tendency has been to use cognitive approaches and learning theory to promote affective goals.

The first criticism, that the moral-judgment theory is based on the cognitive theory of Piaget is, of course, true. Moral behavior is specifically human. The relationship of Kohlberg's conceptualization of morality to cognitive-development theories has been studied for several years. Research has supported a parallel between moral judgment and intellectual judgment at any given age. However, cognitive conceptions of the physical world precede the use of these same principles in making moral judgments. For instance, 93 percent of the children ages 5 to 7 years who passed the moral-reasoning tasks of stage 2 also passed the corresponding tasks of reciprocity or reversibility. Only half (52 percent) of the children who passed the logical-operations task passed the morality task (Kohlberg & DeVries, 1969). Older children (ages 9 to 11) who were at the conventional level of moral judgments passed a more difficult task of reciprocity (inversion). (Selman, 1976). All subjects using the postconventional level of moral reasoning were also capable of formal reasoning on certain Piagetian problems (Kuhn, Langer, & Kohlberg, 1977). Teachers who look to the environment to affect moral development might propose a curriculum rich in the "nutrients of cognitive stimulation" and also rich in concerns for moral conduct.

The second criticism, that Kohlberg's theory is elitist, is valid to the extent that schools confuse *mores* (the conventions and folkways of a group) with *morals* (the universal ethics or principles of people generally). Moral education need not impose the values of a small minority on the child of the "average family" nor impose the mores of the majority on ethnic minorities. Education for postconventional moral judgment requires that teachers themselves move beyond the typical female conventions of conformity to the niceties, or middle-class mores, and the typical male conventions of conformity to authority or law and order. Ever since people have had a written language they have had the means for attaining higher levels of moral thinking by building upon the best of the cultural heritage.

Kohlberg proposed moral education, based on the assumption that the facilitation of movement from one stage to the next is possible. This approach calls for (1) a knowledge of the child's stage of functioning, (2) curricular content which arouses genuine moral conflict and disagreement about appropriate conduct among students, and (3) the presentation of a mode of thought one stage above the child's own. Kohlberg warned against leaving morality problems unsolved for children, or promoting the belief that everyone should do "his own thing." Knowledge of the stages of moral development may help students distinguish between group standards and universal principles that call for departure from conventional norms. Young children are not ready to make decisions at this level. Yet teachers can identify the problems that arise in the day-to-day routines of working and playing and use such situations to allow children to begin to make rules for their own social behavior.

The third criticism, which questions whether discrete stages of moral development actually exist, can be directed toward any of several views of developmental psychology. Piaget's stages of cognitive development have been compared with Kohlberg's. Erikson's stages of affective development equate morality and the development of the superego (conscience). Although Kohlberg sees moral judgment in stituational terms, all developmental theories accept the principle of stages (Kuhn et al., 1977).

Stages imply, first, an invariant order or sequence under varying environmental conditions. Second, stages imply a "structured whole" or organization which unites bits and pieces of experience into a larger relationship. Qualitative differences in mode of response are more important to the structuralist than mere quantitative differences. Third, there is a hierarchy in which lower stages are integrated as components of the higher levels of functioning. Kohlberg's theory of neighboring stages is consistent with the hierarchies of Piaget and Erikson. Kohlberg (1974) reported that children more easily assimilate and accommodate to the next higher level of moral conduct than skip stages. Children did not merely "add" the new morality experience, but avoided lower levels once they had established a higher morality. The issue of stages will not be settled by reading the literature. The important point is whether the concept of stages is productive in teaching and rearing young children.

Moral Education of Young Children

Preschool and primary teachers may find it difficult to see the relevance of Kohlberg's third level of morality to the fights that break out in the sandbox or science corner. Selman (1976) extended the concepts of moral development to the education of young children. He used the technique of role taking to help children move from an egocentric point of view to being able to see the other person's side of things. His interviews with children showed that children from 3 to 6 years old could label other people's feelings, but did not yet understand the cause-and-effect relations of social actions. They interpreted behavior in terms of what makes someone else happy, or angry. From 6 to 8 years old, children acquire the social-affective skills to distinguish between behavior which is intentional, or purposive, and that which is accidental. They evaluate intentional misbehavior as "worse" than accidental behavior, even when the results are less serious. Selman found the latency period to be generally responsive to intervention in social and affective education. He suggested that teachers of younger children try to see through the child's eyes when a conflict occurs and to avoid expectations for behaviors that are based on social abilities not yet developed.

Probably it is necessary for children younger than Selman's premoral age of 3 to 6 years to be directed in explicit ways when certain behavior is important. The toddler who grabs his cookie the moment it is passed and starts for the playroom may need to be placed gently in his chair and told simply, "We sit while we eat." Such training lays the groundwork for Kohlberg's first stage of social behavior. At the time punishment or obedience may be the criterion, but this is a stage which will be replaced by a higher level of moral judgment.

Prejudice is a moral issue in the United States and, perhaps, throughout the world. Many social psychologists have tried to discover when and how it develops. Fox and Barnes (1973) studied the attitudes of hundreds of black, white, and Chinese American children in New York. They found a reversal of earlier studies in that both black and white children showed a preference for and an identification with their own race. Chinese children, however, showed some tendency to make white race selections, perhaps because the Chinese communities have been less active in building a preference for ethnic uniqueness in ways that children understand. Another study of racial attitudes in black and white children 4 to 7 years was based on interviews during doll play in research by Lerner and Buerig (1975). They reported that the conversations of the children were meaningful (as opposed to irrelevant), preponderantly concrete, neutral in evaluative connotation, and not disparaging or depreciative of the other race.

In a very comprehensive study involving urban children in integrated elementary schools, Katz, Sohn, and Zalk (1975) found a lack of consistency in the several instruments they used to assess prejudice. Race-related cues were accentuated in pupils they had identified as high-prejudice children. The indications seem to be that: (1) the self-acceptance of black children is increasing, (2) younger children show more favorable attitudes toward other races than older children, and (3) the awareness that subtle attitudes are picked up by children is part of the moral responsibility of teachers and parents.

HOSTILITY AND AGGRESSION

Children's behavior toward other persons is the result of complex interactions of the child's individuality and the environment which reinforces, punishes, models, instructs, inhibits, supports, or neglects. When guiding a child in social interaction, the level of social development, the intelligence of the child, past learning, and temperament are important in how the child who has a problem will be retrained or taught.

Jason, age 5½, was the terror of the preschool. He reacted angrily when someone happened to bump him. When he wanted a particular toy he would stride into a play group, take the toy, and start hitting if he was resisted. If the teacher tried to find out how the fight started, Jason would accuse the other child of having taken his truck. He sometimes hit other children apparently because they were there. He was robust, physically coordinated, and large for his age. When engaged in conversation or word games with the volunteers, he became attentive and involved. Because of his strength and aggressiveness, the teacher feared for the safety of the other children and tried to keep him under observation at all times.

The different approaches a preschool teacher might use are inherent in the different ways child-development specialists view affective development and socialization. The behaviorist view is that aggressive behavior is learned by reinforcement of certain past behavior; therefore the behavior patterns that are undersirable can be identified and eliminated. The cognitive-developmental approach advocated by Selman requires that the teacher make a judgment about the child's level of socialization and help the child understand the cause-effect relationship of his or her action toward other children. The psychoanalytic approach of Erikson would look for the source of anger and hostility in Jason's past experience. They would ask whether the child's hostility toward peers is a displaced feeling he has toward one of his parents. The teacher, who of necessity must deal with Jason, can use the learning-motivation model to come to some immediate decisions about dealing with the behavior at school. The model shows the relationship of reinforcement learning, cognitive development, and affective development. How Jason responds will determine whether psychiatric help is needed.

Learning Aggressive Behavior

Many studies have shown that aggression toward persons and objects is increased or decreased according to the reward-punishment systems adults used. Hollenberg and Sperry (1964) reported that 2-year-old boys and girls do about the same amount of screaming and hitting. By 4 years they differ significantly in how they show anger, with boys hitting significantly more and screaming significantly less than girls. This change is thought to be due to the effect of the culture that allows boys to express anger by hitting, but not screaming, and the converse for girls. Aggressive acts apparently have some tension-reducing effect on individuals because children continue to behave aggressively in a permissive environment.

Unfortunately, the reports of conditions that increase aggressive behavior have been numerous and decisive compared with strategies for modifying aggressive behavior. Preschool children behave more aggressively toward dolls after they have observed aggressiveness by live or television adult models (Bandura & Ross, 1963). Aggressive behavior is increased when children are frustrated by denial of toys they know and like to play with (Otis & McCandless, 1955). Nursery school children who are victimized by other children in a permissive play situation themselves become more aggressive over time (Patterson, Littman, & Bricker, 1967). Children who are punished mildly for aggressive behavior become more aggressive, as if punishment merely frustrates them and heightens the need for venting hostility (Sears, Whiting, Nowlis, & Sears, 1953). Children whose homes use severe punishment frequently are more aggressive than children from homes where punishment is mild or infrequent. In another study of preschool children, punishment reduced or inhibited the action but increased the displaced aggression (Sears, Maccoby, & Levin, 1957). From the research one would conclude that children can acquire aggressive behavior in many ways; by imitation or modeling, as outlet for frustration, through self-reinforcement, and in response to punishment. Apparently the behavior-modification strategies that change many undesirable behaviors do not operate in the same way with aggressive behavior, perpahs because overt action is reinforcing to the organism.

The presence of a permissive adult does not reduce aggression. Siegel and Kohn (1959) found that children became increasingly aggressive when an adult was present who did not control the behavior, perhaps because young children transfer responsibility. They behaved less aggressively when on their own, apparently because they used self-controls they had learned earlier.

Guiding and Retraining

Although studies of this complex topic cannot be used at face value to alter generations of knowledge about childrearing, they seem to confirm the idea that a caring discipline can help lead toward mature socialization. Two principles for guiding children in their social interaction are (1) the younger the child, the greater the need for direct intervention in misbehavior and reward for social behavior and (2) the older the child, and the more advanced cognitively, the greater should be the use of strategies which call for a conceptualization of the other person's view of an interaction. Generally, guiding may be accomplished through consistency of routine, discipline, and expectation. When a child has become as aggressive as Jason, retraining is necessary.

BEHAVIOR MODIFICATION

Behavior modification involves relearning by association through direct instruction or intervention. The steps required would be (1) to establish a goal, (2) to determine the baseline or frequency of a specific behavior under certain conditions, (3) to alter the environment and the reinforcement cycle so that appropriate responses are being reinforced, and (4) to phase out the intervention. At the first step, establish a goal; a generalized statement, "to reduce Jason's aggression," would be considered too vague for prescribing a reinforcement strategy. "To eliminate Jason's hitting during the play period" is a manageable goal.

Aggressive behavior can be modified. (Rita Freed/Nancy Palmer Photo Agency)

The second step would be to observe the frequency and conditions of Jason's hitting: Does it occur during fights over toys and/or conflicts with certain children? Does it occur at the beginning or the end of a period? At step 3 the teacher will want to change the environment to reduce the conditions for hitting: See that each child has a favored toy, engage the most frequent victim at the other side of the room or play area, etc. The teacher will also employ a new reinforcement strategy. Jason's play activities will be noticed when not hitting; when hitting occurs the victim will be removed, along with playthings, and Jason will be ignored. To phase out the reinforcement Jason may be socially reinforced at longer and longer intervals when no hitting occurs. The teacher will avoid giving Jason the constant attention he was receiving by frequent hitting of other children. It is expected that other children will respond to Jason in socially reinforcing ways as his behavior becomes less punishing to them.

COGNITIVE APPROACHES

Jason is at an age at which egocentrism should be replaced by empathy for the other person's feelings and an understanding of cause-effect relationships in social interaction. The teacher can extend Jason's understanding of the effect of his own behavior on others by the role-playing techniques of Selman, by clarifying the rules, or by engaging children in making their own rules. Since Jason is cognitively advanced and the teacher finds him responsive to skill games and books, she will find levels of instruction that challenge and engage him. She will use his positive relationships with adults to guide his understanding of peer relationships.

PLAY THERAPY

Play therapy employs dolls of different family or occupational roles which children use to play out their concerns, hostilities, or wishes. Children do this spontaneously when given opportunity and support. To use play therapy to bring out repressed hostility and help the child recognize destructive emotions requires specialized training. If Jason's teacher found that he did not respond to the conditioning strategies of behavior modification or the cognitive approaches to social development, then referral for more intensive therapy from a specialist might be considered. If the research is clear at any point, it would seem to be that permissiveness toward aggressive behavior increases and prolongs it.

SUMMARY

The emotional, social, and personal dimensions of life are interrelated in affective development. Motivation is based in the reward and punishment systems that operate during cognitive learning events. Conceptualizations about self are the conscious, identified, and categorized structures that relate an individual to the people and things in the surround. Creative self-direction is individual productivity that results from bringing together the conceptualized structure of the real world and a personal value system.

Socialization is the developmental process of adapting to the common needs of the group. Social learning theory explains how children learn to behave in mature (or unsocial) ways by (1) attending to models, (2) organizing the relevant features of an action for retention until later, (3) reproducing the behavior covertly, and (4) matching or refining the social pattern through vicarious, social, or self reinforcement.

Infants initiate social responses in ways that are common to the species, such as smiling behavior or fear of strangers. Stages of social interaction—solitary play, parallel play, and precooperative play—are sequential and age-related.

Erik Erikson extended the psychoanalytic theory of Freud to propose a sequence of affective development in his book *The Eight Ages of Man*. He proposed a relationship between the cultural heritage, the biological organism, and the psychological self in a dynamic life-cycle.

Kohlberg proposed three levels of moral development which assume a cognitive involvement in moral judgment. Two stages of preconventional morality are: (1) when the child conforms in socially desired ways to avoid punishment, and (2) when the child shows a sense of fairness, or the idea that equal sharing goes along with equal contributions.

Children increase their aggressive behavior when they see adult models behave aggressively, when they are victimized by other children, when they are severely or inconsistently punished, and when permissive adults ignore aggressive behavior. A plan was proposed by which young children who are aggressive or otherwise unsocial can be retrained by behavior-management techniques, using social reinforcement. Cognitive approaches apparently are effective for most children of school age or younger, who are beginning to understand the cause-effect relations in social interaction and to be less egocentric.

four

RESPONSIBILITY OF CARE-GIVERS

The themes of this book are the unusual ability that human young have for learning and the difference care-givers can make in the development of each child's potential. Part One identified some of the principles of growth and learning that have emerged from research on and observation of infants and children. The basis for reproduction of the organism, inheritance of traits, and the growth of cells into tissues was explained. The purpose of including genetics and biology was to help significant adults understand how nature and nurture interact in the developmental process.

This final part of this book focuses on the responsibility of adults and the adult society for children. Part Two described the typical development of Homo sapiens generally; this section emphasizes the *individuality* of children as persons. Chapter 12 explains different ways the theory of growth and learning is implemented in early childhood education. Chapter 13 is focused on gifted and talented children, the most educationally deprived of our childhood groups. Chapter 14 appeals for acceptance and a special environment for handicapped children, so that the effect of their abnormalities may be minimized. The purpose of the final chapter is to bring closure to the central message—that adults have responsibility for enhancing the lives of children and those yet unborn.

12
Developmental Approaches to Early Education

12 Developmental Approaches to Early Education

Early childhood education represents the effort of the public, or a social unit, to teach children in groups. The motivation on the part of adults is the enhancement of the child. Sometimes the goal is *socialization*, since the preschool gives children early experiences in interacting with peers. When Jaqueline Kennedy started a preschool in the White House the goals were primarily social, which required that children come together for group learning. Sometimes the goal is *intervention* for children who are high risks in society's goal for literacy. These children, usually from low-income communities, are assembled early for cognitive, motivational, or perceptual training. Sometimes the goal of preschools is *custodial*, and the focus is on physical care and nutrition. This chapter proposes a developmental approach to early childhood education which is primarily concerned with each child as a person. This means that the curriculum and the care recognize the child's rights to opportunities, both as an individual and as an integrated organism whose biological, social, and intellectual needs are as one.

The traditional view of the kindergarten ("children's garden") was an adult version of an ideal environment for little people. They were surrounded by "nature" and scaled-down furniture, and were protected from the working world and the imposed pressures of adult society. The view from human biology is that children seek involvement, pursue their own learning with persistence, and gain satisfaction from their accomplishments. To provide both a stimulating and a happy school experience for the young child, adults need to take an unfettered look at the individual child: what he or she enjoys doing, looking at, talking about, learning, and whom he or she models. By anticipating the next level of a developmental sequence, the child can be helped to reach out for new experiences that are consistent with development. For adults who work with children it is difficult not to impose either of two kinds of pressure: the pressure from beneath that pushes children into adult ways and denies them their childhood, or the pressure from above that forces them into a mold or stereotype, that keeps them too long in childhood, overprotected and overindulged. The individual child holds the cues for where he or she is developmentally, and knowing the sequence helps adults in their effort to guide. When teachers know, at least in general terms, where the child is trying to go and what the child is trying to become, education can help more and hinder less.

Many adults, beginning with Rousseau (1964), have argued that early education is a waste of time and should be postponed until the child can think at the operational level (7 to 8 years), or even perform the logical thought processes that begin to operate at 11 to 12 years. Some have even argued that academic teaching that attempts to anticipate developmental norms may reduce learning potential (Ogletree, 1974). This argument ignores the early acquisition of language, which is structurally intact at age 4 years, and the close relationship between the symbolic processing of the phoneme system of speech and the grapheme system of print.

Piaget himself focused so exclusively on the universal and biological nature of cognitive development that he gave little thought to how much teaching he might be doing when he arranged the sensorimotor environments he needed for his observations. His infants were surrounded by toys, such as the size-ordered and vividly decorated nest of dolls imported from Russia and still a common plaything of Soviet children. If one wanted the child to discover the principle of seriation, this toy should provide the basic sensorimotor schema. Piaget set up problems for Jacqueline, Laurent, and Lucienne to solve: securing a toy by pulling a string, putting a parrot through playpen bars by turning it to its narrowest dimension, finding a toy by removing a barrier, retrieving a chain by inverting the box. Piaget's attention to his children's problem-solving behavior may have been reinforcing to them. Piaget seems to have assumed a stimulating environment and a great deal of parental attention to the child's manipulations in the normal rearing environment. Most children do not have three adults to interact with them, as well as some of the other opportunities for learning that Piaget's children had. This chapter examines three aspects of early education in the context of a developmental approach for learning: the cognitive curriculum, the affective curriculum, and teaching styles. Since the discussion is on how curriculum is built, rather than on learning content, some selected sources on early education have been listed at the end of the chapter to provide further direction for parents and teachers.

COGNITIVE CURRICULUM

The cognitive curriculum plans for and provides instruction in intellectual functions. At the preschool level, curriculum designers usually identify the concepts and skills which will enable the child to succeed in the academic skills program of the primary school. Cognitive content can be divided into (1) communication or linguistic abilities and (2) nonverbal concepts of classification, seriation, and time-space relationships. The assumption in curriculum planning is that much sequential learning precedes the emergence of thinking operations, such as classification, and that this can be taught.

Piaget's Theory Applied

One of the successful applications of Piaget's theory was a curriculum for Follow Through and Head Start children. It was designed and initially taught at Ypsilanti, Michigan, for disadvantaged children, but the plan has extended to other schools (Weikart et al., 1970a). Language was incidental to the development of four content categories: classification, seriation, spatial relations, and temporal relations. It was assumed from Piaget's work that children go through levels of representation and learn to think in increasingly abstract ways. They began with concrete experiences in which the child interacted with real things in the classroom and in nature. From there they moved to the *index level*, where children used different senses to experience such relationships as parts of a whole (parts that make a bicycle) or parts missing from a whole (identifying the absence of a fourth wheel on a wagon). At the *symbol level* of representation, the purpose of the curriculum was to teach the child to build mental images through a variety of sensory experiences such as identifying an animal by its sound, making models of objects, and recognizing concrete things in photographs and drawings. The *sign level* related words to concepts previously experienced directly and concretely through the senses. Each of these levels was included in the school experience of children and for the content categories.

The third dimension that was built into the cognitive curriculum was the operation, whether *motoric* or *verbal*. In the Piagetian tradition, the motor interaction (squeeze, float, encircle) preceded the verbal language for the child's physical experience. This program resulted in significant conceptual gains for participating children (Weikart, 1970b).

Communication Skills

Attaining literacy in one's native language follows a well-documented sequence from listening with understanding, to propositional speech, to reading the coded messages of someone else, to finally encoding in writing (Geschwind, 1971). Teachers have discovered to their dismay and frustration that some children who speak well have great difficulty in learning to read. These make up only part of the 18 million individual citizens (mostly male and mostly young) who are functionally illiterate. Illiteracy in the United States is partially the result of motivational problems, but these too may be based in early failure due to inept teaching of children who lack conventional readiness. Five distinct cognitive abilities are needed for successful reading in school. Each can be observed and taught during preschool and kindergarten–long before the child's personal prestige is put on the line to begin reading (Robeck & Wilson, 1969).

LANGUAGE SYNTAX AND VOCABULARY

The first prerequisite for successful reading of normal children in the native language is speech. The verbal language a potential reader needs includes knowledge of syntax, a common body of service words, and the noun equivalents of objects known to the child. The more the child's home and culture differ from those of the so-called norms, the more difficult the language of the reading program is to acquire. If the child listens to and understands the language of television, however, a year of enriched language arts at the preschool level should ready the child for the beginning levels of reading if the *affective* climate is conducive to communication. If the child is accepted and valued as a person, the child's motivations for school learning are likely to respond. Assuming that a second dialect is similar to learning a second language in that the earlier the training is begun the better, any postponement of learning to speak and read in mainstream English will almost certainly increase problems for the child with potential reading difficulties.

A primary school child shares an experience with friends. (Mimi Forsyth/Monkmeyer)

VISUAL PERCEPTION

By 4 months of age infants have acquired the visual acuity that is necessary to see the print of primers. Learning to distinguish a *b* and a *d* is largely a matter of left-to-right experience and knowing that the distinction is important. Sufficient exposure to letters in a preschool environment helps children learn to make discriminations based on features, and to screen print visually from left to right. All three of these can be learned easily and pleasurably by reading books on someone's lap or by sitting beside an adored adult or older sibling at story time. It is important that the child share the perspective of the book with the reader, so that word order, picture sequence, and pages follow from left to right and from front to back. Unless your child is a Persian, a Korean, or anyone whose orientation to the printed page is different, the left-to-right sequence must be learned. The library experiences of hearing stories in an audience also teach some important but different skills.

AUDITORY PERCEPTION

The child's ability to hear the phoneme parts of words in their invariant order to make meaningful units is basic to all learning of the sound-letter system, whether taught in beginning reading as sound elements or as whole words. Auditory perception for phonemes is more often delayed or lacking than visual perception, perhaps because the sound elements of speech are a level of abstraction beyond the object-word representation of speech. A high percentage of the children entering kindergarten need selected word games to teach them to articulate certain consonants correctly and other selected games to help them hear phonemes within words and their sequence. When children can group small toys by beginning sound / b /, / m /, or / t /, they can probably learn the phonic system if it is systematically taught by a teacher skilled in beginning reading instruction.

SENSORIMOTOR INTEGRATION

Infants of 4 months demonstrate eye-hand coordination, and at 8 months have the ability to use the eyes to direct the movement of fingers. Only a few children lack the eye-hand coordination that is necessary to manipulate a book for reading or a pencil for writing by the time they enter kindergarten. Even the six pairs of muscles that control the saccadic movement of the eyes across the line of print are well developed by 4 to 6 years of age. Precautions teachers of young children need to take concern the child who may not have developed the normal fine motor coordination skills of his or her age. Also the time period for expecting children to do eye-hand tasks should be consistent with the interest and persistence of the individual child. Generally short periods with full attention provide both appropriate task orientation and skill instruction for young children. If the teacher's social reinforcement is prompt, personal, and specific to the child's effort, this effort is likely to continue and generalize to other school activities.

LEARNING POTENTIAL

The purpose for assessing the child's learning potential is to assure success by timing the reading program and altering the method to the child's ability. Mentally retarded children can learn to read. The rare child who is so slow in dealing with symbolic language that he cannot learn to read is not likely to enter the mainstream of the public kindergarten or primary school. A former belief that those who are retarded should not be instructed until an appropriate mental age (of 6 years) has been attained has been replaced by belief in early and direct instruction in the skills that lead to reading.

Down's-syndrome children are taught to read, most of them by kindergarten age, at the Experimental Education Unit of the University of Washington (Hayden & Dmitriev, 1974). Developmental scales, designed by the staff, are used to teach to the next level of anticipated accomplishment. Infants are exposed to face-to-face talking through a parent training program that begins when the child is 6 weeks old. By utilizing a curriculum for communication based on developmental goals, instruction is provided at the school in small groups (five children), whole groups (fifteen children), and individually. The child is introduced early to listening, speaking, and word-recognition skills.

The rationale for the kindergarten reading program was that Downs' children typically fall off in their learning ability by the eighth year of life; that is, the gap between them and normal children increases dramatically. The researchers at Washington wanted to accomplish as much as possible before 8 years, so they planned their intervention for early stimulation based on developmental sequences. Their children are being prepared for transfer to a city school, beginning with first grade. The learning potential of children generally is less well known than the sequences by which they acquire cognitive abilities.

THE AFFECTIVE CURRICULUM

When large numbers of children, particularly those from urban ghettos, began to fail the cognitive tasks of the school, many persons turned to early childhood education to prevent school failure. Cultural diversity was scrutinized because a high percentage of the children were from minority ethnic groups. Most educators rejected the notion that basic differences in intelligence were responsible for academic failure partly because some children from all groups succeeded, but mostly because the idea was repugnant to humanists everywhere (Combs, 1973).

Cultural diversity persisted as a factor, however, because language differences seemed to be linked to reading problems. In many situations the child was trying to learn to read in a second language; Spanish is the most common example, although many Americans learn Navaho, Eskimo, Russian, Italian, or German at home. A different dialect and conceptual heritage was assumed to be a factor in the lack of academic success in many black Americans. Native Americans were known for their distinct cultural values and for their geographic isolation.

A self-conscious America turned to curriculum change to bring the schools in line with newly discovered needs for self-enhancement for its own sake, to cultural recognition of minority groups, and the pursuit of personal goals for all. To some extent the curricula were adapted to "doing one's own thing." Teachers found themselves ignorant of the culture of their children, so community schools were organized to bring alienated parents back into participation in the school community. Techniques and strategies aimed at self-fulfillment were brought into the schools with the expectation that motivation for school learning would follow. Intervention and prevention came to mean early childhood education for target groups.

Cultural Diversity

Research on the relationship of a second language or cultural diversity to reading success has been extremely difficult to conduct or to apply because culture functions in subtle ways. Clay (1975) made use of an unusual educational situation to analyze the beginning language and reading processes of four groups in New Zealand: children from white professional families, working class whites, native Maori, and immigrating Samoans. She followed their speaking, reading, and writing patterns over 3 years from the fifth birthday when they enter school to the third grade. She found that Samoans, 75 percent of whom came to school without

Predelinquent behavior is learned. (Hugh Rogers/ Monkmeyer)

English, did as well in reading as English-speaking children and much better than urban Maori who had no command of the Maori language. She attributed the success of the Samoans to language experience methods of teaching reading by which the children learned English readily, to family emphasis on getting an education, to the importance of written messages to and from families left behind in Polynesia, and to Bible reading (usually the only book) at home. Samoan culture placed a heavy value on oral transmission of the culture, but children were not expected to master or speak the language of their parents.

Clay found no disadvantage to the children in beginning reading at the age of 5. She also found little relationship between the quality of English a child spoke and reading success during the first 18 months of school. At that point, however, the children with poor command of the language fell behind. She recommended better use of those first 18 months to provide solid instruction in oral English. She also stressed that minority-group children, when coming to school, must (1) feel proud of the heritage, (2) be helped to manage cultural pluralism in constructive ways, (3) be taught to read and write in their own language only when they have fluent control of the adopted language. Clay suggested that much is yet to be learned about what the child learns at school in relation to the language competencies learned in the linguistic environment of the home.

Community Schools

Community schools are sometimes called alternative schools, humanistic schools, or freedom schools. Each of these terms indicates a departure from established education in the direction of a greater focus on the affective curriculum (Browdy, 1973). On occasion the alternative school has been organized at parent request to focus on the fundamental skills when these were thought to be neglected by the school district as a whole, but this is not the meaning usually reflected in the literature.

Community schools involve the parents in the planning and operation of the school. Usually they are open to anyone who lives in the district for civic meetings, community interest films, adult classes, and social events. The teaching function is extended to parents, who do volunteer work in the classrooms and teach night classes in crafts, child care, house repair, or whatever draws an enrollment. Child care and family life are typically a part of the extended curriculum.

Teaching Motivation

Some attempts have been made to teach motivation for school learning by giving children frequent positive feedback on their schoolwork or by enhancing the child's social position within the group. Koep (1972) conducted a study in six kindergarten classes, each divided randomly into three groups: (1) a social group which engaged in socializing activities of stories, play, and games with a special teacher, (2) a cognitive group who did preacademic tasks from the *Kindergarten Evaluation of Learning Potential* with the same teachers rotated (Wilson & Robeck, 1965), and (3) a control group that worked with the regular teacher on a reduced ratio of adults to children. He found that both social and cognitive strategies increased the child's motivation to succeed as measured by the Gumpgookies Test (Adkins & Ballif, 1970). Interestingly, the change scores in the social group came primarily from boys and the change scores from cognitive activities came from girls more than from boys (Figure 12-1). Koep concluded that motivation can be taught by cognitive or social interaction, and that reinforcement (both direct and indirect) was more effective than the less active roles teachers usually assume in the children's activities (Figure 12-2). Affective education may not be an acceptable substitute for cognitive curriculums, but attention to the affective learning is likely to continue to engage curriculum planners and teachers.

TEACHING STYLES AND CHILDREN'S LEARNING

Many attempts have been made to establish a relationship between the methods teachers use and the school achievement of children. The beginning reading process has been studied because the children's progress could be measured

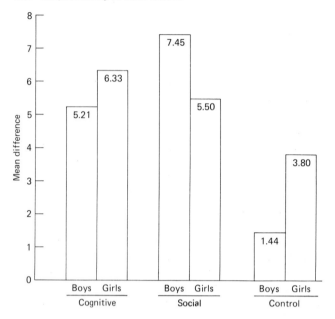

FIGURE 12-1 Motivation to achieve in school. Kindergarten children changed their motivation by planned interaction with teachers in small groups, whether the curriculum was socially or cognitively oriented.

Source: Robert C. Koep, doctoral dissertation, University of Oregon, 1972. By permission of the investigator.

quite accurately and the methodology clearly defined. Several factors make it difficult to reach conclusive results: (1) the differences among teachers, aside from their methods, (2) the variations in language competence the children have when they come to school, (3) the differences in facilities and resources, and (4) the importance of reading in the curriculum. Large studies, which involve many teachers and a large sample of children from different geographic settings, have been considered one satisfactory way of averaging out, rather than controlling, the variables. One such study, financed by the U.S. Office of Education, involved thirty projects and several methods within each project. These included various basal readers, language-experience approaches, individualized instruction, controlled teaching alphabets, and linguistic readers. Most of the projects were followed for three years, beginning in first grade or kindergarten. The major finding to come from this extensive and expensive effort was that greater differences in the reading achievement of the children resulted from the differences between individual teachers than between the methods and materials that were being tested (Dykstra, 1968). This is a challenge for teachers and a message to administrators that staff selection and inservice training may be the most promising approach to improvement in children's learning.

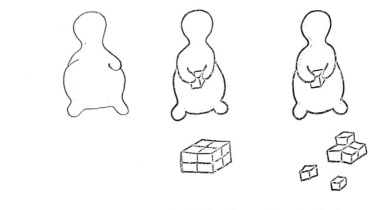

(Up) This one likes to be at school.
This one likes to stay at home.
Which is yours?

(Left) These Gumpgookies are building houses.
This one's house is almost finished.
This one's house fell down.
Which is your Gumpgookie?

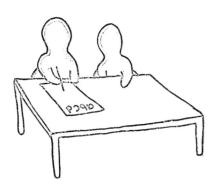

(Left) This Gumpgookie is trying to write.
This Gumpgookie is watching.
Which is your Gumpgookie?

(Right) These Gumpgookies are drawing circles.
This one is drawing a lot.
This one is getting them right.
Which is yours?

FIGURE 12-2 **Four items from the Gumpgookies Test of motivation to achieve in school. The elements of cognitive and affective interaction are apparent in this test.**

Source: Adkins and Balif, 1968.

Research that is designed to test different teaching styles must therefore control for the differences among teachers. The current literature includes: studies of direct instruction, which usually is based on behaviorist theory; formal versus informal schools, which is an evaluation of open education; and inquiry strategies, which are based on discovery learning. The purpose of this summary is to help teachers select the instructional approach which has the greatest promise for a particular child or group of children when learning particular content, and not to suggest the exclusive choice of one approach over all others.

Direct Instruction

Direct instruction is usually preprogrammed to meet a specific objective in a skill or content area. The child's interaction may be with the teacher, as in DISTAR (Direct Instruction System for Teaching Arithmetic and Reading); with the material, as in *Programmed Reading* by Behavioral Science Laboratories; or with a machine, as in computer-based instruction. In each case the content is programmed into small steps. The learning is accumulative, linear, and specific. McDaniels (1975) summarized the achievement of Follow Through children on three scores in reading and in numbers. This interim evaluation began in the third year of a seven-year program, after the teachers were well trained in the method and the school community had become accustomed to an experimental program. The structured programs, including the Englemann-Becker model, the Behavior Analysis Approach, and High/Scope model all were especially strong in teaching the basic skills, which was their major focus. The only model significantly lower on reading skills was the Bank Street College model, which focused on total development. Scores were obtained from word analysis, reading, and the Wide

Children with hearing loss are taught to speak. (Sam Falk/Monkmeyer)

Range Achievement Test. The early results were further confirmed in an evaluation at the end of third grade (Becker & Engelmann, 1977).

In a different analysis of the same models in the same schools Stallings and Kaskowitz (1974) based their evaluation on classroom observations. They concluded that the unique features of the different Follow Through models were being implemented appropriately and consistent with the design adopted for the study. They too found that highly structured classroom events resulted in higher achievement scores in reading and mathematics. More flexible classroom environments resulted in higher scores on nonverbal reasoning, lower absence rates, and willingness to work independently. It would appear that direct and highly specific instruction is effective in teaching the basic skills to a target population of disadvantaged children. It also was observed that basic skill achievement during the first 3 years did not produce all the desired goals of a primary school program.

Inquiry Strategies

The measurement of conceptual gains from strategies that require manipulation and guided discovery of relationships or structure is more difficult than measuring specific skill responses. Cooke (1971) studied the long-term learning of first-grade children 6 and 7 years old on a conceptualization task involving attribute blocks. He designed and tested three teaching interactions: *rote*, an associative procedure which focused on the color, thickness, and shape of the blocks; *principle*, a deductive procedure in which the teacher explained the organizing principle by which block designs could be built correctly; and *guided discovery*, an inductive procedure in which the teacher gave no information but used questions to encourage the child to discover the organizing principle in the designs. He used a videotape feedback of the teaching interaction to refine the different strategies. Triads of subjects were matched for age, IQ, and sex, and then assigned randomly to form three experimental groups. Two sequences of attribute block designs were used: the first to be constructed with the model visible, the second to be constructed from memory (Figure 12-3).

The second construction was called a conceptualization task, and was scored at three time intervals: immediately, one week later, and after six weeks (Figure 12-4). Over the long run the discovery-guided group performed significantly better than they had during initial instruction and significantly higher than the group who learned by rote. The investigator suggested that the strategy of asking children to think through their own solution enabled them to reconstruct the problem by a process they had learned and remembered. The principle group seemed to have remembered the principle for a week and were able to improve their performance on a short-term basis but not on a long-term basis. More studies are needed which consider the long-term effect of different methods at different stages in cognitive development. There are many studies of the use of an inquiry strategy with older students (Bruner, 1964).

A different study selected 5-year-old children who failed to conserve on Piaget's

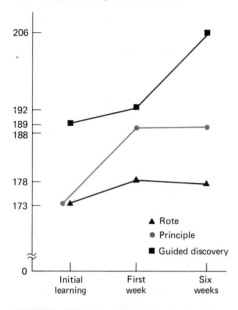

FIGURE 12-3 Average scores for three teaching strategies treatments at three-time intervals. Scores are based on memory construction of designs made from attribute blocks.

Source: Gary E. Cooke, *Conceptual Learning in Young Children*, University of Oregon, 1971, page 47. By permission of the author.

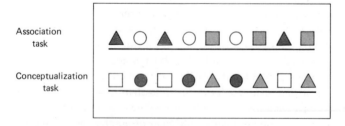

FIGURE 12-4 Design of attribute blocks. Children built the association sequence from a model, with guidance from a teacher who used three strategies for three groups: rote, principle, and guided discovery. The conceptualization of design sequence was measured by the number of blocks arranged correctly from memory.

conservation of length, number, mass, and liquid (Gelman, 1969). During training sessions, the children were given many different stick arrangements and were questioned about length, and many different counter arrangements and asked about number. By seeing many different arrangements of serial sticks or counters, instead of a second misleading arrangement of the kind Piaget used, the children learned to distinguish the relevant from the irrelevant cues. Two to three weeks later the children made perfect responses to the conservation tasks on which they had been specifically trained, and exhibited 60 percent transfer to nonspecific conservation of mass and liquid. Many decisions the teacher must make involve the selection of direct instruction or inquiry training. Obviously the decision is not an easy one to make. The importance of research on strategies of teaching is to learn the conditions of transfer to tasks that are based on principle even though the specific attributes may vary. The assumption is that principle learning is more generalizable, therefore more economical for long-term learning requirements, than stimulus-response training for specific attributes.

Formal and Informal Schools

Primary teachers have argued whether there is more benefit to the child in a highly structured classroom, in which the teacher controls the task from period to period, or in an informal setting, in which the child moves about from one learning center to another, converses with a teacher or classmates, and self-selects the task, at least part of the time. The British primary schools, in which approximately 20 percent of the staff have elected to change the organization to the "open class plan" was evaluated by Bennett (1976). Bennett used a large sample, to overcome the variations in teacher characteristics, and designed tests for the evaluation of children's learning which teachers judged to be fair to the plan of organization they used. Of 871 schools sampled, 17 percent were informal, 20 percent were formal, and half used formal procedures for teaching of skills and informal organization for other parts of the curriculum. One pupil group seemed to benefit in skill learning from the informal classroom, i.e., boys who entered school with low achievement. Low-achieving girls and high-achieving children of both sexes had significantly higher scores in the basic skills when taught skills by structured or semiformal approaches. In reading, the gains of pupils of mixed and formal teachers averaged 5 months higher; arithmetic gains averaged 4 to 5 months higher; and English gains averaged 3 to 5 months higher. Mixed schools appeared to have the strongest performance in mathematics. Creative writing, which was graded by three teachers selected from each of the groups, was judged as not different in imaginative quality whether from formal or informal schools.

Bennett's staff also made observations of the children's behavior and examined the changes in motivation. He found that motivation, or attitudes toward schoolwork, improved in the informal schools, but that anxiety also increased. Extroverted children coped more easily with the informal classroom, and the anxious, insecure children performed better in formal settings. The time at task was significantly greater in mixed and formal settings than in informal classrooms. The investigator concluded that formal teaching was no detriment to the social and emotional development of pupils. He pointed to the concern for low-achieving boys and to motivation for school learning as positive factors for the informal school. He stressed the "need for greater skill on the part of informal teachers to organize the children's curriculum and keep track of individual progress. (The central factor emerging from this study is that a degree of teacher direction is necessary. . . . [This] direction needs to be carefully planned, and the learning experiences provided need to be clearly sequenced and structured" (p. 162).

Teachers have a great deal of responsibility in any setting if any organizational advantage is not to be traded for its disadvantages. Rosenshine and Berliner (1977) reviewed recent research on student learning and teaching variables in the United States. These studies generally supported the Bennett evaluation, revealing that student-engaged time was the most important factor in achievement in reading and mathematics. They proposed that the left-hemisphere functions be organized by the teacher and taught directly; and that right-hemisphere activities such as exploration and creativity, projects, learner-choice activities, and trips be allocated to a different time in the day. Informal classrooms may need to extend the time allotted to skills, and teach so that the amount of teacher-directed learning can be increased.

SOURCES FOR EARLY EDUCATION

Baratz, Joan C., and Shuy, Roger W. *Teaching Black Children to Read.* Center for Applied Linguistics, 1717 Massachusetts Ave., N.W., Washington D.C. 20036. Sympathetic approach to the special problems of dialect and learning to read.

Canfield, Jack, and Wells, Harold C. *100 Ways to Enhance Self-Concept in the Classroom.* Englewood Cliffs, N.J.: Prentice-Hall, 1976. Activities for discussions and activities which increase sensitivity to the affective worlds of self and others.

Decker, Celia Anita, and Decker, John R. *Planning and Administering Early Childhood Programs.* Columbus, Ohio: Charles E. Merrill, 1976. Practical guide to the details of early childhood educational programs. Facilities, materials, budget, and community relations are included.

Lavatelli, Celia. *Early Childhood Curriculum: A Piaget Program,* 2d Ed., *Teacher's Guide.* Boston: American Science and Engineering, 1973. Provides guided experience in classification, seriation, conservation, and spatial relationships.

Lehane, Stephen. *Help Your Baby Learn: 100 Piaget-based Activities for the First Two Years of Life.* Englewood Cliffs, N.J.: Prentice-Hall, 1976. Piaget-based activities help adults see babies' behavior from the baby's point of view. Practical information and techniques are offered to help turn everyday behaviors into learning experiences that are fun.

Painter, Genevieve. *Teaching Your Baby.* New York: Simon & Schuster, 1971. Presents a daily program of activities for infants and children to three years. Specific language exercises to stimulate speech. Toys, puzzles, and games for self-involvement from birth to sitting, from sitting to toddling, from toddling to running.

Vance, Barbara. *Teaching the Prekindergarten Child: Instructional Design and Curriculum.* Monterey, Calif.: Cole, 1973. Practical techniques and procedures for the preschool teacher.

13
Gifted and Talented Children

13 Gifted and Talented Children

The development of intelligence is so central to the struggle to be human that researchers will continue to try to define giftedness and individual teachers will continue to try to enhance it. All cultures are essentially conservative, however. They support the norm in education and preserve in school the life-style that prevails outside the school. All societies need the contributions of artists, inventors, authors, and critics if social or economic progress is to occur. Individuals need freedom to explore, to discover, to express the self, and to be different. The nurturance of giftedness and talent is always viewed in a context of the social good, even in societies that claim to promote individual welfare.

This chapter proposes (1) the earlier identification of intellectually gifted children, (2) a departure from conventional uses of IQ for identifying them, and (3) broader programs to develop special talent in young children. The focus is on the children. The several sections deal with problems of being different, various ways of being intellectually gifted, categories of talent in young children, special programs, and sources for enrichment and talent development. Although most of the special considerations that do exist are primarily for older children and secondary students, this discussion is limited to the case of the young child who is exceptional at the high end of the ability range.

At this writing only a dozen states have active professional groups that are organized specifically for gifted and talented children (Gallagher, 1975). A similar number of state departments of education provide multiple services for gifted children. Only a minority of the school districts across the country have specific programs for gifted children and they touch only a few of the schools in those districts. When a school does identify gifted children and organizes special programs for them, a high percentage of their time is spent practicing skills they already have (Robeck, 1968b). Intellectually gifted children do not like to be singled out or segregated, but they do enjoy abstract thinking, problem solving, inductive reasoning, and discussing hypothetical and moral issues. Although intellectually gifted children are the most deprived educationally of any group, programs to meet their needs are difficult to organize and are usually short-lived.

THE PROBLEM OF BEING DIFFERENT

People generally, and Americans in particular, have little empathy for those who are seen as better off than themselves. Most of us have lost at cards, or in business, or in a spelling contest and have generalized a suspicion toward anyone who might be seen as "smarter" than ourselves. In the United States a person can identify with and support an athlete, or a winning team, without being considered an elitist or a snob. One can also sponsor an artist or a musician. Intellectual distinction is viewed with reservation. Children learn very early to hide what they know that peers do not know—to keep it a secret if they value intellectual activities.

On the basis of Masters' research at the University of Illinois, Newland (1976) pointed out the difficulty gifted students have in achieving their potential. Further, the greater the disparity between learning potential (when well measured) and educational achievement, the greater the frequency of maladaptive behavior, as reported by their teachers. Individuals who lack self-realization, whatever their level of ability, find it difficult to understand and value self-realization for others.

Culture and Conformity

Intellectually gifted children become aware earlier than most of the subtle pressures of the culture to conform, to be like other people. By the time they reach third grade, the subculture of peers lets them know in overt ways that it is better to be one of the group than to please the teacher or one's parents. Averageness pushed to its limits means mediocrity, which is unworthy of any child as his or her goal in school.

Because of the cultural acceptance of particular talents, one approach to acceptance of the exceptional child would be to cultivate the idea that everyone is good at something and everyone is expected to work at it. Klindova (1973) found that several types of intellectual ability, or cognitive style, can be isolated and identified by the age of 7 years. She also found an unusual frequency of psychological problems in a sample of Czechoslovakian children with unusual

A child plays chess at 5 years of age. (UPI)

talent and intelligence (Klindova, 1970). Despite their general social maturity, many talented preschool and kindergarten children found adjustment difficult. Certainly the gifted child finds much to adjust to that seldom if ever confronts the typical child, who fits both the published scales for social behavior and unconscious expectations that adults inherit with the culture.

Needs of Gifted Children

Intellectually gifted and talented children share the needs of children everywhere. They need to be loved, approved of when they try hard and do well, and allowed to be their own persons. In an early study which has not been replicated, Adkins et al. (1943) found that creativity in school children was *negatively* correlated with conformity to other people, need for routine, need to acquire things, and need to reject others. At least in the situation in which these children were being observed, creative outlet appeared to compensate for some of the needs usually experienced by immature persons.

Adkins and her coworkers did identify some significant needs in creative children. They found high and positive correlations between creativity and independent measures of the following: need for pleasure feelings; imaginative and subjective experience; need to produce, organize and build things; need to explain, judge, or interpret; need to overcome failure or weakness; and enjoyment of thinking about their own thoughts and emotions. These needs seem to be logically as well as statistically related to creative production. However different the talented child's psychological needs may be, the normal need for identity may be more difficult to fulfill than for more typical children.

NEED FOR IDENTITY

The child who is different has fewer models available and therefore greater difficulty in role identity. Krippner and Blickenstaff (1970) suggested that societal pressures inhibit the creative abilities of males and repress the scientific abilities of females. Young children lack the experience to look outside the home for models and are likely to limit the development of their talents to those modeled in the home. According to this report the sex roles become rigid quite early. If children's interests are to be extended and their opportunities for artistic and academic achievement to remain open, they will need models of the same sex who participate in varied activities for talent expression. By junior high school, when career guidance usually begins seriously, it may be too late to open new interests in activities that challenge the sex role.

NEED FOR SELF-EXPRESSION

It is quite possible that the greater the gap children feel between themselves and their peers, the greater the need for self-expression. Creative production, which is a way of putting the self on the line for others to respond to, may be the compelling motivation for creative production. A child paints a picture which represents his or her view of something and watches silently for a verdict from the parent or teacher. The seriousness with which young children go about producing anything visible is impressive, as is how they identify with it: "This is *mine*, I made it!" The sensitive adult will always feel out the nature of the identity a child feels for a production and respond as to the child.

NEED FOR EARLY RECOGNITION OF TALENT

Children who are advanced in their perceptions of others are likely to be advanced in conceptualizations about self. Most eminent persons recognized their own special interests and began to develop their talents very early (Goertzel & Goertzel, 1962). There is no simplistic guideline for counseling the talented with respect to diversity versus early specialization. Isaacs (1973) observed that many gifted

Mozart played brilliantly at 4 years of age. (Culver Pictures)

children have so many talents and interests that they find it difficult to focus on one area. Later in life they lack the expertise or the involvement to persist in an area of talent, and may change jobs frequently. She recommends early identification and guidance so that their energies will not be widely dissipated.

Children of Minority Groups

Despite recent efforts on behalf of children from minority groups to bar the use of intelligence tests because many tests are discriminatory, it is the minority child whose intellectual talents are most likely to be wasted. Personal experience in preparing case studies of many children in California Project Talent indicated that minority-group children turned up in the early-identification projects at kindergarten through second-grade levels, especially when the standard error in the tests was applied to minority children (Robeck, 1968a). By the middle grades, however, when school achievement was the first step in the screening, minority children from certain groups were rarely identified. When children were retested after three years in the project, the children most likely to lose IQ points were the disadvantaged children and those most likely to gain points were the children from professional homes. Talent development for children from some ethnic groups might require after-school enrichment activities, but improvement of opportunity in line with ability requires early identification.

Cultural bias has been blamed for Terman's finding that his gifted boys, thirty-five years later, had distinguished themselves and had contributed markedly to the professions and business, while an equal number of gifted girls in his study were indistinguishable from the vast majority of women (Terman & Oden, 1959). Sex differences in linguistic abilities operate in favor of girls at a very early age and in problem-solving abilities in favor of boys (Kagan & Kagan, 1970). By identifying gifted children early the sex biases might be partially eliminated to allow both boys and girls greater choice in learning and self-expression.

Gifted Children in School

The school is a composite of the aspirations, concerns, and resources of the families who send their children there. The strengths of a multiethnic society are represented. It is important that each child find stature in the group and personal pleasure in doing unique things before the pressures of the peer subculture have their impact. The gifted child faces one more way of being different in the public school than his more typical classmates.

The basic curriculum is a reflection of the needs and values of the mainstream of the community. Instruction, which must hold the interest and attention of as many children as possible, is directed primarily at the level of understanding of the mainstream of the school population. The magic circle of the classroom takes in, actually and statistically, about 68 percent of the children (Figure 13-1). The remaining 32 percent are divided about equally between the extremes, beginning

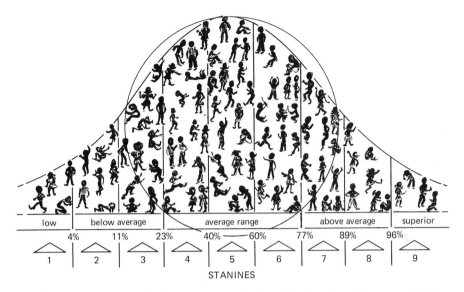

FIGURE 13-1 Magic circle of the school curriculum. One hundred children are distributed across the bell-shaped curve of normal distribution. Each child's position is likely to vary on different abilities and on different measures of a general ability. Mainstream education is inevitably focused on the big, middle group.

at 1 standard deviation on both sides of the mean. This indicates that approximately 16 percent of the children's scores are at a significant distance above the average, and 16 percent at a significant distance below the average.

One of the reasons group instruction works as well as it does is that most children like to participate in groups.

Jimmy (6 years old) entered school as an independent reader and was accelerated to second grade. He made a naive error on occasion, like *music-an* for *musician*, but his reading was more advanced than any of the advanced second-graders in the class. He could spell any word in the second-grade list and many other words he had encountered in reading. The teacher introduced him to the school library, taught him how to use the dictionary, and over a few weeks time, taught him how to prepare a bibliography. One day he stood quietly at the teacher's elbow, "Mithes Robeck, I want to read with the other kids."

Jimmy joined a reading group and for a few days he would come to the teacher to ask help with a word they both knew he recognized. Shortly thereafter he settled into the discussions, and the teacher observed that his comprehension was quite literal, and that several children had developed inference and appreciation skills Jimmy had not yet learned.

A second reason that group instruction works is that children vary markedly in their achievement from one particular skill to another. Gifted children, who are selected because they are far out on an intelligence score, are likely to regress toward the mean on motor skills, music aptitude, or social interaction. Jimmy was able to develop an excellent relationship with peers who were older. They taught him how to mix paint, bounce a ball, and care for the rabbit. When a classmate asked, "How come Jimmy is the best speller in the class and he's the youngest?" the teacher replied, "Some people are better at spelling than others. I always had to work hard at spelling." If the teacher really believes in her pedantic soul that, as far as pupils go, brighter is not better, she can help children accept and appreciate different strengths in each other.

DEFINING INTELLECTUAL GIFTEDNESS

The subcommittee on Labor and Public Welfare, U.S. Senate, defined giftedness for purposes of legislation and financial support as those children who require different educational programs and services beyond those normally provided by the regular school program. The areas of giftedness they listed were the following: (1) general intellectual ability, (2) specific academic aptitude, (3) creative and productive thinking, (4) leadership ability, (5) visual and performing arts, and (6) psychomotor ability. The subcommittee left the problem of identifying potential ability and its relationship to the troublesome IQ to "professionally qualified persons" (*Education of the Gifted and Talented*, 1972, p. 10).

The categories proposed by the subcommittee imply a broader search for giftedness than the ability to do abstract thinking that is reflected in most IQ tests. The educator (teacher or school psychologist) is left with the problem of sorting out potential in children whose previous learning experiences vary in content and quality. In early childhood education it would seem the course of wisdom to define giftedness and talent more broadly.

In practice the use of IQ tests has identified 2 to 5 percent of the school population as high-IQ. Newland (1976) pointed out that 8 percent replacement of creative and highly technical positions is needed to maintain present economic and social productivity. Young children in their formative years should perhaps be seen as *potentially* gifted and talented. The criteria for special programs might be defined to select children who are significantly higher than the norm (average) on two or more measures. The traditional use of a global or general measure (IQ) might be extended to specific aptitude or other talent categories.

General Intellectual Ability

The most respected of the intelligence tests that produce a single IQ score is the Stanford Binet Intelligence Scale (Terman & Merrill, 1960). It is administered by a specialist trained in its use. When the child being tested is typical of the group of children on which the test was normed, this is a good measure for selection of children for general intellectual ability. The items in the Binet are grouped according to the age at which half of the children in a population pass and half fail them. The average, or mean, score is 100. Scores over 100 represent a ratio above average. The standard deviation of the Binet is about 16 points at any given age, which means that scores of 116 or higher are significantly higher than average (Figure 13-2). Most special programs based on a global definition (or total IQ score) require a selection score of 2 standard deviations above the mean or about 132 IQ.

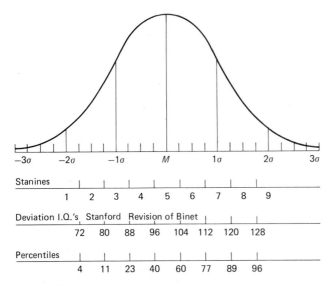

FIGURE 13-2 Relationship of standard deviations, shown as sigma (σ) distances from the mean, and stanines, Binet IQ scores, and percentiles. Test norms show 68 percent of the scores falling within 1 stand deviation on either side of the mean.

Source: Adapted from John A. R. Wilson and Mildred C. Robeck, *Kindergarten Evaluation of Learning Potential*, page 216. Copyright ©, 1965 by Sabox Publishing Co., 2519 Chapala St., Santa Barbara, Cal.

The Wechsler Intelligence Scale for Children Revised (WISC-R) has a standard deviation of 15 (Wechsler, 1974). When it is used as a global score, the comparable cutoff point of 2 standard deviations is 130. The test for younger children, the Wechsler Preschool and Primary Intelligence Scale (Wechsler, 1967), also has a standard deviation of 15. The scores of children 6 years old or younger on the WPPSI or the Binet are moderately correlated with later scores. It is quite easy to see that an IQ score must be considered in terms of the test used and the age of the child at the time. The scores of preschool children are not very stable, which is one reason that more inclusive measures than global IQ score must be used in identifying talent.

Specific Academic Aptitude

The Wechsler tests give three IQ scores when a child is tested: a verbal IQ, a performance IQ, and a total IQ. The verbal test includes Information, Comprehension, Arithmetic, Similarities, and Vocabulary subtests. The performance tests include Picture Completion, Picture Arrangement, Object Assembly, Block Design, and Coding. This division of verbal and performance categories makes it possible for the child with limited English to show intellectual strength on the performance

IQ. Further research might indicate whether the subtests could be used to identify particular talents, such as linguistic ability or spatial and figural abilities. Either of these scores combined with a high creativity score would indicate *potential* and the possibility of nurturance for productivity.

Relationship of Intelligence and Creativity

When searching out the characteristics of highly creative and productive adults, MacKinnon (1965) found that beyond a modest IQ of about 120 to 125 there was little relationship between creativity and intelligence. Since his subjects were leading writers, research scientists, and architects, the report shook common beliefs that giftedness and inventiveness were a single trait. Torrance (1959) reported similar findings in his creativity studies of school children—a positive relationship, but not at the upper levels. Many teachers were excited about these findings, which meant that some children who are below the accepted criterion for gifted programs might have the potential for very creative and unusual productions. Most programs for intellectually gifted children require an IQ which is 2 standard deviations above the mean, about 130 points or higher. Highly creative

Helen Keller needed a talented teacher to realize her intellectual potential. (Culver Pictures)

children often give unusual answers to some test items, which may depress their scores. Often they show an uneven profile on the subtests of the WISC-R and the different types of items on the Binet. The inclusion of greater numbers of young children in talent-development programs seems to be justified.

DIVERGENT PRODUCTION

Variations in cognitive style also complicate the attempt to describe what gifted and talented children are like. Guilford (1959) reported that *convergent thinkers*, who were good at finding the one right answer or best solution to a problem, were not necessarily good at *divergent thinking* (Chapter 8). "In divergent-thinking operations we think in different directions, sometimes searching, sometimes seeking variety" (p. 10). Although he considered both convergent and divergent production as problem-solving behavior, some of Guilford's early tests showed negative correlations between the two abilities.

Guilford (1964) suggested to teachers that productive thinking, whether divergent or convergent, must be based on strength in memory and cognition abilities in order for a child to generate new information. He also recognized motivation as a factor in productivity.

Behind all problem solving, as behind all behavior, are motivating influences. Sometimes the problem seems to arise entirely from within the motivating condition of the individual, the state of his needs and his drives. An artist's product expresses both his conflict and the solution of this problem. Other problems arise by virtue of the interaction of the individual with his environment. (Guilford, p. 10)

Guilford went on to identify *fluency* and *flexibility* as consistent characteristics of the thinking of creative individuals.

Many studies have been done to test whether creative ability, or originality, is a trait independent of general intelligence. Wallach (1970) analyzed this research and suggested that fluency, when measured by the number of *unique*, *unusual*, and *appropriate* ideas that were generated, was an independent characteristic. The research seemed to show a much closer relationship between flexibility and general intelligence when the flexibility measure was "cleverness or facility in choice of words for expressing one's ideas" (p. 1223). Apparently some common attributes are measured in tests of intelligence and tests of creativity, but the evidence seems to support Guilford's position that creativity can be identified and measured using different criteria.

CHARACTERISTICS OF CREATIVE CHILDREN

The most completely developed of the creativity measures for children are the Torrance Tests for Creative Thinking (Torrance, 1972a, b, 1974). They are designed for kindergarten-age children on up to adulthood. They emphasize the fluency, flexibility, and elaboration abilities that Guilford identified in older children and adults. The first part of the Torrance Tests, Thinking Creatively with Pictures, has three figural activities: constructing a picture from a simple shape, adding lines to incomplete pictures (Figure 13-3), and making objects or pictures from pairs of straight lines. The scoring guide stresses both the originality and the number of the responses.

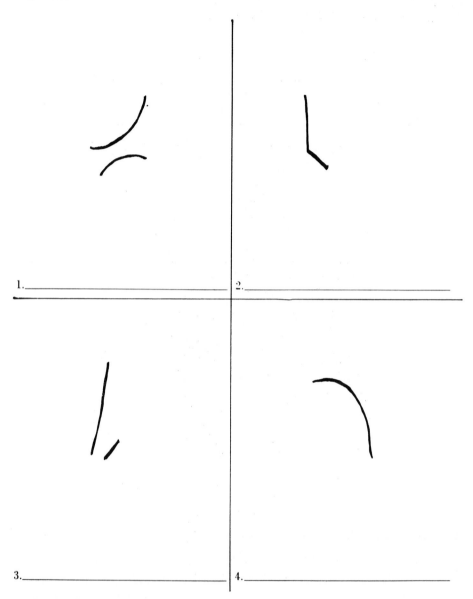

FIGURE 13-3 A page from Torrance's test of figural abilities, Thinking Creatively with Pictures.

Adapted from the Torrance Test of Creative Thinking, Figural B Booklet, with permission of the copyright holder, Personnel Press, Inc.

The second part of the Torrance tests, Thinking Creatively with Words, is given in small groups to those who can write their ideas and individually to kindergarten and primary children who must dictate their answers. The children are given asking and guessing games, and asked to tell ways they can improve something (Figure 13-4), to give unusual uses for common objects, and to "just suppose" what would happen in an improbable situation. Booklet A asks children to think of the

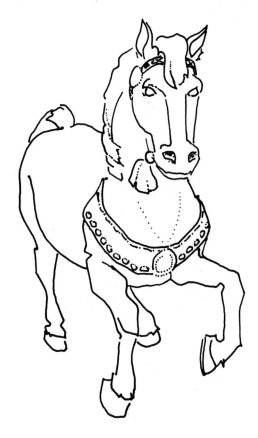

1._____

2._____

3._____

4._____

5._____

FIGURE 13-4 A page from Torrance's test of verbal abilities, Thinking Creatively with Words.

Adapted from the Torrance Test of Creative Thinking, Verbal A Booklet, with permission of the copyright holder, Personnel Press, Inc.

consequences "if clouds had strings attached to them which hang down to earth" (1966b, p. 14). Logic suggests that Torrance's test of the creative use of words is likely to correlate more highly with a general intelligence test that is loaded with verbal items than will a creativity test that is based on figural thinking. Torrance (1972a) reported that his creativity tests when given to elementary school children are predictive of creative production in older students.

School may be dull at times for the intellectually gifted child who finds much of the work repetitive and unexciting. Newland (1976) explained:

> While the gifted as a group differ most from the nongifted in their capacity to do "abstract reasoning" and they differ also in the number, range, and depths of their interest, thinking in terms of such averages can lead to neglect of the fact that they, as individuals, present widely varying constellations of these and other characteristics—other socially significant special aptitudes, differing cognitive styles, and the like. (p. 146)

The highly creative child often does not meet the school's expectations for conformity. The cognitive style which is reflected in unique ways of seeing the world may be a handicap in learning what a particular school is designed to teach. Witty (1963) predicted a larger number of poor readers among creative pupils than among verbally gifted children. Robeck in fact found 21 children of fewer than 200 clinic subjects with WISC intelligence scores of 120 or higher. These children were characterized by cognitive strengths in comprehension of verbal problems, ability to generalize (similarities subtest), and define words. They were also good at the structural tasks among performance tests. They were poor in memory for specifics such as digit span, coding, and information. Despite high average intelligence, their cognitive profile was different from the general population's.

Gilbert (1977) analyzed the relationship between IQ, creativity, humor, and conceptual tempo in first-grade children from white-middle-class (low to typical) families. In addition to the well-established variability in IQ (70 to 145 points), she found significant variability in humor understanding and appreciation, conceptual tempo as measured by the Kagan test, and creativity as measured by the Torrance tests. Correlations between IQ as measured by WISC-R and the total creativity test, figural test, and verbal test were .35, .32, and .20. When IQ was accounted for statistically, the relationship found in the other measures disappeared. This means that IQ appeared to be the important factor in the correlation of humor and creativity. Boys were found to be higher than girls on humor, and girls were more accurate on the conceptual tempo test. Humor comprehension was related to IQ, and, surprisingly, to the performance scales of the WISC-R. In children's programs, modest IQ scores combined with strength in any of the talent categories would seem to be worthy of the special attention of the school.

CATEGORIES OF TALENT IN YOUNG CHILDREN

That talent varies in unique ways in different individuals is seldom argued. Some of the questions that are raised frequently are the extent to which different talents can be developed and how early they can be identified. Another point of disagreement among educators is whether the school should try to broaden and extend the interests of gifted children or whether they should be helped to specialize early. One approach is to bring children together who have different interests and abilities so that a range of peer models is available to children with limited experience in creative activities. One of the difficulties is that valid measures to identify talent in young children are lacking. At present the teacher or researcher must use a variety of tests, the kind young children enjoy, and try to find more precise ways of selecting children for talent development.

Linguistic Ability

Talent in creating with words is developed in school through conversation, the appreciation of literature, writing poetry and stories, or reporting. Unusual productivity in these activities would probably correlate highly with the verbal IQ in the Wechsler tests and with Torrance's verbal creativity score. The importance of being able to measure linguistic talent is to demonstrate the value of special programs and to reinforce the teachers, who often need encouragement to continue programs that do not enjoy widespread support.

Spatial and Figural Abilities

Individuals who are high in spatial and figural abilities have at least some of the characteristics needed to become engineers, architects, fashion designers, or sculptors. Torrance's test of figural creativity might be a first measure in identifying such talent. Wechsler's subtests, Object Completion, Object Assembly, Block Design, and Mazes, might also yield positive correlations with spatial and figural abilities. Many of the play activities of young children, block building, for example, might be used initially to develop this talent category.

Leadership in Social Interaction

Skill in social interaction is seen in successful political figures, club presidents, and directors of child-care centers. Individuals who are empathetic apparently have unusual abilities to perceive the views and emotions of others. Strength in social relationships means that a person can extend these kinds of perceptions to individuals in younger and older groups than his or her own. The *Kindergarten Evaluation of Learning Potential* (Wilson & Robeck, 1965) described and field-tested three levels of social interaction, including creative self-direction at level 3, which teachers used to encourage leadership in young children. Selman's stages of moral judgment and the KELP levels of social interaction offer promise as indicators of creative social interaction. Scales that penalize a child for solitary play are likely to penalize most gifted children, who are noted for wanting to do some things alone and independently.

Motoric and Rhythmic Abilities

Motoric and rhythmic talents are indefinite categories as far as the young child is concerned. These talents are expressed in older children and adults in athletic skills and creative dance. Research is needed to identify the activities in early childhood which nurture the development of body esthetics. Early mobility may or may not be a factor.

Since healthy children enjoy action of the large muscle systems and since all children need gross activity as an alternate to quiet school activities, motor activities should be a regular part of the daily schedule of activities. One approach to a talent search would be to observe children over time in the skipping, hopping, and ball-bouncing activities described in Chapter 6. Gymnasts, skaters, and swimmers who become great usually begin practicing and performing very young. One purpose of a talent-development program would be to extend this early involvement beyond the individual children whose families already promote motor and rhythmic expression. What is known of brain organization suggests that musical talent may be closely related to perception of rhythm.

Esthetic and Artistic Abilities

Children's art has been studied as an age-stage sequence related to cognitive development (Kellog, 1970). Children's drawings have been used as an indicator of intelligence. Harris (1963) believed that the Draw-a-Man test measured intellectual maturity, although his conceptual model was clearly figural and not verbal. Harris published a scoring system to measure the child's ability (1) to perceive likeness and difference in form, (2) to abstract the likenesses and differences, and (3) to generalize, or classify, according to the properties of the class. According to Harris, a child's drawing of a man, a woman, or the self reveals the child's conceptions about the sexes and himself or herself. Experience suggests that the artistic talent a child shows in one media transfers to new and different media.

Professionally competent teachers who are also professionally competent artists could surely discover or design a combination of observations which would identify potential talent in the graphic arts. The curriculum is rarely crowded for intellectually gifted children because most of them acquire the basic skills very rapidly, and have time left over for enrichment through talent development.

SPECIAL PROGRAMS

The different types of programs designed to adjust the curriculum for intellectually gifted children are numerous. Simson and Martinson (1961) reported seventeen major models for the education of gifted children in use in California. Of these, four were selected for a statewide demonstration in the elementary schools known as California Project Talent (Plowman & Rice, 1969).

Early Admission and Acceleration

Acceleration means advancement of the child beyond his or her regular grade in school, or placement in an older age group that will complete the program earlier than the child's original group would.

A different plan for the acceleration of young children, early admission, identifies gifted children during the early months of kindergarten and accelerates them to first grade at the Christmas break. Other plans allow certain children to be admitted early to kindergarten or first grade after a psychological evaluation.

Robeck (1968a) reported the organization and evaluation of acceleration programs in California Project Talent. The most common plan was to identify children on the basis of teacher recommendation and individual tests at the second-grade level. A special six-week summer session prepared the children for fall entrance into the fourth grade. Initially the summer session was planned to provide enrichment. However, experience in the early months of the transition to fourth grade indicated that basic skills, such as cursive writing and knowing the addition facts, were very important in the receiving teacher's acceptance of the accelerated child.

The evaluations over three years of acceleration at two demonstration sites showed that twice as many girls as boys were considered socially and physically mature for their age and were therefore accelerated. Of the children accelerated, an individual analysis showed that 90 percent were entirely successful and were considered to be more appropriately placed in an older group; 4 percent were considered less well placed after acceleration; and the remaining 6 percent had adjustment problems that probably would have become apparent regardless of acceleration. Achievement data showed that by the beginning of fifth grade, accelerated children, who would ordinarily have been beginning fourth grade, showed average reading scores of 6.5, language scores of 6.8, and arithmetic scores of 5.7. The achievement of gifted accelerated children tends to show an increasing gap between themselves and age-mates not accelerated as they move through the grades (Haisley, 1973).

Special Classes

Special class programs for gifted young children have been rarely considered (Robeck, 1968b). They are usually organized no earlier than the fourth grade. Sometimes a combination of early acceleration and subsequent assignment to a special class is needed to make an adequate adaptation of the curriculum to the gifted child. The disadvantages of the special class are segregation from the rest of the school, which most gifted children do not want, and academic shock upon being returned to regular classes. The advantages of special classes are the reality of being able to perform many kinds of activities, after skills are learned, and the sheer joy of learning most children experience in the classes.

One kind of special class which the community usually accepts is the special-interest class. Painting, writing, nature study, construction, and creative drama are some examples of the kinds of activities that draw special groups of enthusiasts. When these programs are offered for young children, their teachers will need to help particular children find programs suited to their abilities.

Enrichment in Cluster Groups

Enrichment programs provide unique and unusual opportunities for academic learning and talent development not specified in the regular curriculum. Plowman and Rice (1969) described the enrichment programs in the Los Angeles school district. Models for higher levels of thinking, proposed by Bruner, Bloom, or Guilford, were implemented by teachers to enrich the regular school content. Also, learning centers were used to extend the selection of materials for gifted pupils in music, mathematics, art, and social science. Talent development was promoted by talented teachers who helped children create a variety of productions in art and music. Enrichment in cluster groups has the advantage of allowing children to remain inconspicuous while adjustment in the curriculum is being made, but seems to accomplish less in school achievement than special classes or acceleration (Simson & Martinson, 1969).

Counseling and Case Study

Bachtold (1966) published a model for counseling and case study. Although her model was designed for older children, it points up the need for identifying gifted underachievers and taking steps to change their attitudes toward school and their motivations for school learning. Most of the effort to help highly intelligent school failures comes too late in their school careers to be fully productive. Another important area for counseling is the gifted child who has talent. Elementary school counselors, working with kindergarten and primary teachers, could provide the early intervention needed to help children realize their potential. Project staff prepared the following suggestions for teachers in the California project:

• Reinforce divergent behavior by recognizing originality; react meaningfully to what the child is trying to produce.

• Provide materials and situations which have the potential for manipulation and discovery.

• Teach the techniques that are needed to assure a satisfying experience.

• Value unique production—work which shows how the child sees the world and how he feels about others.

• Extend originality, initiative, and creative behavior to all possible activities—mathematics, social science, literature, physical activities, and art.

• Separate "idea generating" from "critical judgment" situations; be sure pupils know whether divergent or convergent production is requested.

• Teach pupils to identify the essential areas of conformity and adherence to conventions, especially those which cost little or nothing in the productivity of the individual.

- Schedule a regular period when children have the opportunity and the responsibility for activities of their own choosing.

- Create an atmosphere which nurtures constructive and expressive behavior.

- Teach children to live richly; to hold both hands out to new experiences; to tune and play the senses; to learn that pleasure comes with bringing together the right words, or colors, or compounds (Robeck, 1968b).

If recent interest in programs for the gifted child continues to mount, models like the one above may again be implemented (Stanley, 1976).

Programs for gifted and talented children are usually short-lived, partly because funding is typically a small fraction of the budget given to children at the lower end of the scale, even though the services normally provided by the regular school program may be as far removed from their needs. Many parents do not ask for special programs because they do not want to be considered pushy, or to have their child singled out by their efforts to have the curriculum adjusted. A broader base for special programs would involve more children in the programs and would cause those who participate to be less conspicuous. The infusion of enrichment activities into a school can benefit all the children who attend there.

SOURCES FOR ENRICHMENT AND TALENT DEVELOPMENT

Goertzel, V., and Goertzel, Mildred G. *Cradles of Eminence.* Boston: Little, Brown, 1962. An interesting summary of the childhood periods extracted from the biographies of important persons of the current century. Discusses the early influence of adults who support achievement and innovation.

Holt, Michael, and Dienes, Zoltan. *Let's Play Math.* New York: Walker & Company, 1973. A guide to eighty games and puzzles which parents can play with their children (4 to 7 years old) or which kindergarten teachers can use to enrich the program.

Let's Look at First Graders. Princeton N.J.: Science Research Associates, 1967. A kit of materials for group instruction which teaches cognition of relations and classes. Guides the children in the cognitive skills on which they are to be observed.

Wilson, John A. R., and Robeck, Mildred C. *Kindergarten Evaluation of Learning Potential.* Santa Barbara, Calif. Sabox, 1965. A system of curriculum and evaluation in eleven areas of preacademic abilities. Teaches and observes the children's progress from associative learning to conceptualization to creative self-direction.

14
Handicapped and
Disturbed Children

14 Handicapped and Disturbed Children

Handicapped children are those with physical defects or emotional disturbances so serious as to reduce the opportunity to learn and grow in the environment provided for normal children. Some of the handicapped are born with physical defects that interfere with perception and mobility, or with cosmetic defects that lead to insults from other children. Some children inherit weaknesses, or tendencies toward certain diseases, which require restriction from normal family and school activities. Many children, born normal, are impaired by diseases or accidents. Some children are troubled to the extent that their interaction with peers and adults is so disturbed that normal social development is not possible. Physical handicaps are complicated by the emotional stress of trying to cope with a world of normal, or average, people.

Because of the tendency for multiple handicaps to occur in one child, programs for intervention are likely to differ according to the severity of the handicaps when considered together. *Mildly handicapped* children may often move successfully into the mainstream of school life if identified at the preschool age and given diagnostic teaching to ready them for regular first-grade classes. This form of intervention is called *mainstreaming*, which means that exceptional or atypical children are taught, at least part of the day, in regular classes.

One of the difficulties is finding children with mild but multiple handicaps early because their impairments may not be noticed, or the parents may assume the problem will be outgrown by the time the child enters school. *Screening*, defined as the testing of a large population to identify those children who are likely to have a handicap, often fails to detect mild disabilities because the instruments used are not sensitive enough (Kakalik, Brewer, Dougherty, Fleischaver, Genensky, & Wallen 1974). Until screening for handicaps is widely available to preschool children, and until identification is more accurate, adults will need to be alert for atypical children among those they see professionally. Common disorders in the mildly handicapped are visual, hearing, or speech impairment, low intellectual functioning, communication difficulties, perceptual disorders, or emotional problems.

Moderately handicapped children usually need early assessment and follow-up for an extended period of time. *Assessment* is defined as a complete pinpointing of skills and deficits in all behaviors that are potentially related to the handicap. For example, the child with a speech disorder should have an assessment of hearing acuity, speech anatomy, and communication skills, in addition to a diagnosis of syntax and articulation patterns. A medical history or an intelligence measure might also be necessary to provide the best possible placement for retraining the child. Assessment usually requires observing the child in a nursery or preschool setting and therefore involves teachers, medical personnel, and other specialists in a staff effort (Hayden & Edgar, 1977).

Sometimes moderately handicapped children are integrated with a similar number of normal children who serve as models for language usage, social interaction, and preacademic skills. These classes are specialized for the handicapped, but are called integrated programs. In such a program, specially selected teachers are needed who support growth and anticipate development beyond the limits usually conceived for handicapped children. Teachers are needed who also have the empathy to keep in touch with each child emotionally (Green, 1972). Normal children need guidance in accepting handicaps in other persons so that the exceptional children will be supported in their efforts to achieve and not be put down for their differences. The handicapped children need guidance in how to cope with the negative feedback they receive from unthoughtful persons in public places, including the integrated classroom.

Severely handicapped children have disabilities so profound that neither mainstream nor integrated education is practical. Special classes offer the most advantageous placement and are likely to be needed over the long term. This is not to say that identification and intervention from infancy cannot turn a potentially severe handicap into a moderate, or even mild, disability. Children who arrive at school age and are still severely handicapped may profit most from being surrounded by persons who have learned to maintain a happy and motivating environment, despite great difficulties. Severely handicapped children do not need the negative experiences that come from persons whose empathy is weak, or whose sympathy shows too much.

Whether children are categorized as mildly, moderately, or severely handicapped depends on where the lines are drawn. All deficiencies imply varying degrees of distance from the norm. Since most inherited traits and tendencies fall in a distribution from low to high, the normal curve is one way to define a handicap. By this principle of distribution, the number of severely handicapped should be small and the number of mildly handicapped should be much greater. To some extent this principle operates. However, some inherited tendencies leave an individual with a vulnerability to physical insult or stress that is greater than in the population as a whole. In Figure 14-1, the normal curve of environmental factors has been superimposed on the larger distribution to show this principle of "double hazard."

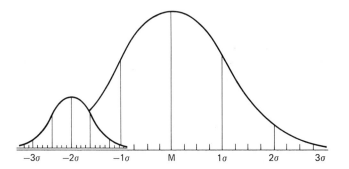

FIGURE 14-1 Handicaps in a population. The vulnerability to a handicap may be distributed as expected by chance, but interaction of the vulnerability with environmental factors increased the number of handicapped. Environment is thought to contribute to a similar peaking of abilities at the opposite end of the curve.

A similar clustering of children is found at the high end of the continuum, showing the effect of a superior environment for some children who also have a high endowment of certain abilities.

The purpose of this chapter is to define some anomalies (abnormalities) of early childhood and to suggest that a superior environment be provided to increase the potential for normal living of children with handicaps. The first section deals with birth defects, which may be caused by environmental insult within the uterus, or by interaction of an environmental insult at a critical period in development. The second section discusses anomalies that are assumed to be of genetic origin. They may be apparent at birth or may appear at a later time in life. The third section summarizes the problems of the troubled child whose symptoms are primarily emotional rather than physical. The fourth section concerns the prevention of disabilities and the early intervention on behalf of children who, despite preventive efforts, have inherited or acquired handicaps. The chapter ends with some selected sources for the teachers and parents of impaired and disturbed youngsters.

BIRTH DEFECTS

Birth defects are called *congenital anomalies*, meaning structural or functional abnormalities of the body that develop before birth. This is a general term which may indicate one or more of several causes: defective gene combinations, an environmental deficiency such as malnutrition, an insult such as drug invasion at a critical time in development, a premature delivery, physical injury or deprivation of oxygen during the birth process, or a combination of these factors. It may not be known if the cause is environmental or hereditary; therefore any abnormality present at birth is called congenital. Approximately 250,000 infants are born with birth defects in the United States each year (Schechter et al., 1972).

Genetic anomalies are structural or functional defects that are carried in the chromosomes (Chapter 2). Sometimes diseases that are known to be hereditary are still called congenital, perhaps because the cause was discovered only recently while the disease was discovered long ago. For example, *congenital agammaglobulinemia* is a sex-linked disease that interferes with the production of immunities in males. This means that infants who have the disease are vulnerable to infection, but the timetable for appearance of symptoms will depend upon the environment. Some genetic anomalies are not congenital, meaning they are not present at birth. For example, *torsion dystonia* is an inherited disease which does not strike until the child is 4 to 16 years old. The symptoms are a rapid spreading of bizarre and involuntary movements of the body that result in death. The distinction between birth defects that are inherited and those that are environmental is important when planning for parenthood. Potential parents with handicaps can know when a characteristic is not likely to be passed on to offspring, or when it is likely to appear, and adoption should be considered.

Physical Disabilities

The most common physical defects are caused accidentally, many of them before birth (Chapter 3). Medical techniques have been developed for the correction of undeveloped or displaced organs. Intensive-care systems have been invented for the newborn which provide oxygen and other life support. These units are expected to prevent the mental retardation that results from early respiratory diseases (Culliton, 1975). Congenital kidney deformities, which formerly required the affected individual to carry a bag for collecting urine, in some cases have been reconstructed by surgery. When a ureter is damaged or missing (Chapter 3), the technique is to drain both kidneys into a single conduit to the bladder (Clark & Monroe, 1975). Corrective surgery for neonates has been advanced by the development of equipment for microsurgery initially used on small laboratory animals.

VISION AND HEARING IMPAIRMENT

The sensory systems for vision and audition are frequently affected in multiply handicapped youngsters. Almost half a million people in the United States and

Protected against a possible fall, this handicapped youngster enjoys horseback riding. (Courtesy of Easter Seal School, Eugene, Oregon)

Canada are legally or totally blind (Dobelle & Mladejovsky, 1974). Fewer than 20 percent of them have learned to read braille and fewer than 10 percent have learned to get around alone. This points up the need for early training for independence and for reading.

Researchers are attempting to devise systems other than braille for teaching spatial and number concepts to blind children. Del Regato (1976) invented a device using bell tones to represent numbers and taught blind persons from 4 years up to count, add, and subtract. Although many problems remain to be solved, some success has been reported for a device, worn like glasses, that works like a television camera for receiving light messages. Battery-powered stimulators send the messages through an array of 64 channels (8×8) to a similar array of receivers placed on the visual cortex at the back of the head. These efforts will continue for a long time before electronic vision is available to the blind children in our special classes. The complexity of this research shows what marvelous organs the eyes are and impresses one with the importance of preventing the numerous accidents to children that destroy their vision.

Much more common among young pupils is the "lazy eye," which results in imbalance in the focus and function of the two eyes. Six pairs of muscles in each eye must coordinate or the eyes will act independently and one eye will take on more and more of the work of sending visual messages. About 5 percent of all children develop a lazy eye, but nearly all can be treated (before the age of 4) by having the child wear a patch on the good eye or by corrective lenses. Surgery may be required if the condition is not corrected early. The lazy-eye disorder is frequently not detected by the screening procedures used in schools (Gallagher & Bradley, 1972).

Hearing loss prevents the normal development of speech. In fact, an articulation problem in the young child may indicate a hearing loss at certain frequencies that has not been detected by the family.

Lane, a boy of 7 years, was delayed in the articulation of high-frequency sounds and had had therapy since kindergarten, when his hearing loss was first detected. His audiogram showed him outside the normal speech range for both tone and loudness, although he could hear a loud, projected voice from arm's length. Trauma had been considered as the cause of his problem because, at age 4 years, he had witnessed the murder of his mother at the hands of his father. A great-aunt, with whom he lived, did not know Lane had a hearing loss until the school referred him to a specialist who diagnosed his condition as congenital.

Lane, an intellectually bright boy, had learned to lip-read by himself. A careful observer could have noted his eyes dart from mouth to mouth during a group discussion. The teacher seated him front-center where he could hear her instructions. Whenever his attention was needed, as they moved about the room, a child would touch him and he would lip-read. This ability amazed the other children who also admired his drawing. Lane was a hellion on the playground. He would attack an unwary classmate from behind and fight until the other boy gave up. No one was seriously hurt, but over time Lane worked his way from the smallest to the largest boy in each class and established wrestling superiority over each. (Summarized from personal files.)

Sometimes delayed articulation is related to temporary hearing losses that occur during the frequent colds many preschool children have at the same time they are learning speech. The pure-tone tests used by the school nurse identify many children with hearing problems, but teachers need to be alert for symptoms of hearing impairment.

Deafness, or profound hearing impairment, is less common among infants and preschool children than many other handicaps (Karnes & Zehrbach, 1977). However, there are many youngsters who need special education for a cluster of speech, hearing, and language impairments. Programs for infants and toddlers focus on teaching parents how to give reinforcement for communication and speech in home settings and during follow-up as the children grow old enough to attend preschool. Sometimes a hearing aid is needed, sometimes special language therapy is provided, and sometimes parents are given help in finding a special school that meets the child's needs.

STRUCTURAL DEFECTS

The most common structural defects are deformities of limbs, developmental disorders of vital organs, or neurological damage to the central nervous system.

This 5-year-old has achieved mobility through unusual motivation, physical therapy, and the use of braces. (Courtesy of Easter Seal School, Eugene, Oregon)

The most serious deformities tend to occur during the first two months of a pregnancy and to be aborted spontaneously (Chapter 3). An exception to this natural tendency is a generation of children crippled by the drug thalidomide, which was prescribed to their mothers for certain symptoms of pregnancy (Chapter 2).

Numerous and diverse disorders in the metabolism of the mother or the infant result in a wide range of organic disorders (Swaiman & Milstein, 1972). These include deficiencies in carbohydrate, protein, lipid, and endocrine metabolism. When present in the newborn, an irregularity in the genetic code is usually indicated. When present in the mother, impairments during the development of the fetus may occur. Thyroid deficiencies in the mother may result in failure of the bones and cartilage to develop, a condition called *cretinism*. Hormone imbalance is related to cleft palate and harelip in the fetus. Many severe metabolic deficiencies are accompanied by mental retardation.

Learning Disabilities

Children who show a significant difference between their capacity for language behavior and their actual language functioning are defined as having learning disabilities (Bateman, 1964). These children have three characteristics in common: (1) they have average or above-average intelligence, (2) they have adequate visual and auditory acuity, and (3) they are achieving much less than their IQ, age, and schooling would predict (Gearheart, 1973). The disability in language processing usually shows up in beginning reading, where children with good vocabulary and conversation skills have trouble remembering words by sight and also decoding them. The children often show various combinations of symptoms that interfere with their adjustment in school, including hyperactivity, distractibility, or short attention span. Medical experts attribute their problem to a lack of integrity in the nervous system (Silver, 1971). Their peer relationships may be unstable because they tend to be impulsive and to have a low tolerance for the give and take of the playground. Silver noted a link between this syndrome of behavior, minimal brain damage to the brainstem areas, slight perinatal problems with metabolism, and certain toxic conditions. The involved areas are the reticular activating system (where control of attention is centered) and the limbic system (where motivation is centered). Wender (1971) reported the symptoms and treatment of clinical referrals for severe reading disability among whom he found a large number of children with minimal brain dysfunction. He observed that they required unusual amounts of reinforcement, directly given, before they learned and adapted. Their motivation systems were less responsive than is normal for children. Reading experts and clinicians have developed systems for diagnosing and correcting reading problems that develop in children with learning disabilities (Fernald, 1943; Orton, 1965; Frostig, 1968; and Johnson & Myklebust, 1971).

In a typical school setting, Rider (1973) found that a group of emotionally disturbed children differed significantly on a large number of measures from a similar number of "average" classmates who were matched for age and sex. The

Preschool training in perception and fine motor control. The 6-year-old in the foreground has been walking about a year. (Courtesy of Easter Seal School, Eugene, Oregon)

tests were selected to compare the sensory integration of the two groups. All the mean (average) scores of the emotionally disturbed group, approximately fifty measures, were lower than the mean scores of the normal children. Significant differences were found in reflex responses to an obstacle course, line drawing with both hands simultaneously, rhythmic writing, and visual tracking. Emotionally disturbed children were significantly lower in bilateral coordination such as right-left discrimination of body parts and balancing with eyes closed. The question remains whether physical (neurological) conditions are causing the emotional disturbance. Almost certainly the lack of sensory integration adds to a child's frustration when trying to cope with the world of the school. It is not known, at least to my satisfaction, whether direct training in sensory motor integration would lessen the child's learning problems or coping behavior.

INHERITED ANOMALIES

Inherited defects were once considered the fault of the woman who carried the child, but the science of genetics has shown that most anomalies carried in the genes may come from either side of the family. The incidence of inherited and birth defects tends to increase when the fathers are very young. The optimum age for childbirth in women is 20 to 30 years, although family planning and good prenatal care extends this period without undue risk. Down's syndrome, for example, has been related to the age of the mother, but it can occur in teenage mothers as well as those at the upper limits of the childbearing age.

Down's Syndrome

Down's syndrome is the most common of the genetic anomalies that result in mental retardation. One infant in approximately 640 live births is a Down's child. About 3000 of them are born in the United States each year (Smith & Wilson, 1973). Down's disease is caused by a faulty distribution of chromosomes during the delicate process at the first division of the fertilized egg. Most often the cause is a *translocation* of a part of the genetic material from chromosome 21 to chromosome 15. Less frequently the cause is *trisomy*, or the presence in the karyotype of three number 21 chromosomes (Figure 2-22A and B). Great accomplishments are possible in training individuals affected with this form of mental retardation.

Because of the tendency for Down's children to level off very early in the development of their intellectual ability (about age 6 to 8 years), Alice Hayden at the Experimental Education Unit, University of Washington, Seattle, reasoned that they should be taught as much as possible at the infant and preschool ages. She and her colleagues used several child-development scales to design a performance inventory for normal children which covered four areas: gross motor, cognitive–fine motor, language, and personal-social skills. The staff began as early as 6 weeks of age to teach to normalcy on the developmental scales. The staff combined many techniques and materials, their criteria being that each procedure make sense and that it work. By early intervention, good teaching, and continuity in

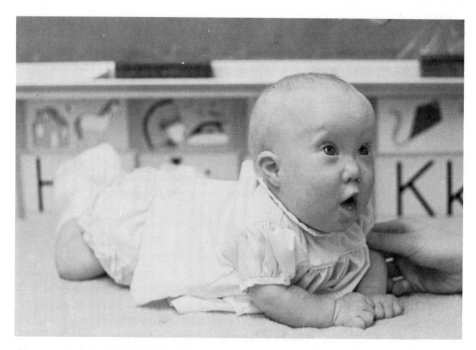

Holly, 4 months old, supports herself on her forearms. (Courtesy of the Experimental Education Unit, University of Washington, Seattle)

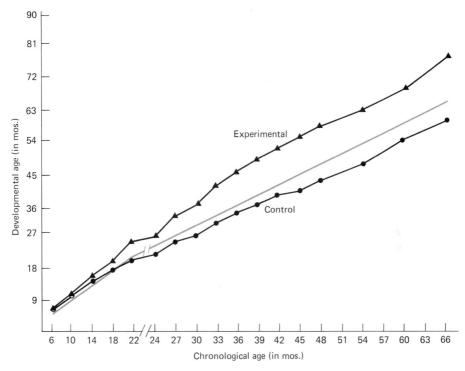

FIGURE 14-2 Results of special training for high-risk young children. Families of high-risk mental retardation were given experimental intervention from infant age of 6 months to approximately 5 years old.

Source: Heber et al., Rehabilitation Research and Training Center in Mental Retardation, University of Wisconsin, 1972, page 107, HEW Grant 16-P-56811/5-08.

home and school training, some Down's children showed normal development at kindergarten age in many of the skills assessed. Group means averaged from 91 to 70 percent in the four categories cited. I was struck by the outgoing and friendly greetings of the children, their attractive appearance, their attentiveness in group activities, and their language skills, including reading at the kindergarten level. These accomplishments were possible because the staff refused to accept the limitations that go with the stereotype of mentally retarded children (Hayden, McGinnes, & Dmitriev, 1976). A similar attitude toward normal children, especially the disadvantaged, might well be considered when planning intervention.

Ethnic Diseases

Probably all ethnic groups have their particular diseases, but some groups have a longer history of medical attention identifying them. Inherited diseases that are found in a particular group, but rarely in other groups, have baffled geneticists for a long time. These diseases offer the possibility of significant discoveries in the study

Judy, 5 years old, reads her book: "I see Mommy." (Courtesy of the Experimental Educational Unit, University of Washington, Seattle)

and treatment of anomalies that are passed on by the genes. Some groups who suffer a particular ethnic disease are beginning to accept and even request such research.

CYSTIC FIBROSIS: A WHITE DISEASE

Cystic fibrosis is a recessive hereditary disease of the pancreas which results in obstruction and deterioration of the lungs. The atrophy seems to be caused by an error in the genetic code for the production of mucus, which is of such high viscosity that the other symptoms develop. Cystic fibrosis is found primarily in white persons.

SICKLE-CELL ANEMIA: A BLACK DISEASE

Sickle-cell anemia is common in black persons who live in the Congo, or whose ancestors came from there (Chapter 2). The child who inherits it may not show symptoms until adolescence, when it is usually too late to treat the disease successfully. The substitution of one amino acid for another is responsible for the development of blood cells that become elongated or sickle-shaped and are poor transporters of oxygen through the body. A laboratory blood test can detect the disease at an early age, and proper treatment can be begun before other symptoms develop (Davis & Solomon, 1974).

JEWISH GENETIC DISEASES

A long history of medical practice, and the tendency to keep their ethnic groups intact, have confined six devastating genetic illnesses to Jews (Seligmann, 1975).

Tay-Sacks' disease strikes during infancy, with destruction of the nervous system, and is usually fatal by the time the individual is 5 years old. Neiman-Pick's disease attacks the liver and spleen; this interferes with metabolism, and the disease is usually fatal by age 3. Gaucher's disease affects the muscles and joints. In infants it may become fatal when it affects breathing and swallowing. Each of these illnesses can be detected in parent carriers and in the fetus by the time the fetus is 5 months old. Each illness also affects mental development. Since these and three other less common (but similarly fatal) diseases cannot be treated at present, genetic counseling and prenatal diagnosis is advised.

EMOTIONAL DISTURBANCES

Symptoms of stress, anxiety, or emotional disturbance are seen temporarily in healthy children. There are no sharp lines between normal psychosocial develop-ment and the neuroses of infancy and childhood. Simply defined, *neurosis* is an emotional disturbance which is less profound and pervasive than psychosis. Excessive fear or anxiety, school phobia, hyperkinesis, and extreme withdrawal are examples of neuroses often seen in children. When a behavior reaction to a difficult situation becomes so fixed that the behavior persists in a favorable situation, the behavior is appropriately called a neurosis (Kessler, 1972). In psychiatry these disorders are seen as unconscious conflicts over sexual or aggressive impulses which are not resolved and emerge as neurotic disorders. Erikson (1963) described three interacting influences in the etiology of neuroses: a predisposing physical factor of inherited tendency, a trauma at a critical period in emotional development, or stress imposed by culture and contemporary life that are beyond a child's adaptive ability at a particular time.

Childhood Neuroses

After reviewing medical specialists, Clark (1974) reported an increasing number of children who suffer emotional problems so extensive that treatment is needed. About 1.4 million, mostly schizophrenic and autistic, are so disturbed as to warrant urgent attention. About 10 million need psychiatric help if they are to achieve their potential. Millions more are plagued by neurotic symptoms. Three factors were cited to account for this mounting incidence of emotional disturbance: (1) There are a growing number of children saved from premature or difficult births that were previously fatal. Many of these children (five boys to one girl) are left with organic conditions that predispose them to emotional handicaps. (2) Today's mobile society has all but eliminated the extended family and has left many single parents the difficult task of rearing the child alone. Modern parents are denied the models for childrearing, the experienced child tending, and the release from con-stant parenting that older adults formerly provided. (3) Today's children live in a push-button society where crime and aggression are observed daily on television. Patterns learned from viewing may be conducive to maladaptive social behavior.

ANXIETY, PHOBIAS, AND DEPRESSION

Anxiety neurosis is a diffused, fearful emotional state that is not restricted to specific persons, objects, or situations. Some childhood fears are age-related, that is, developmental. The fear of strangers that infants show from about 7 to 11 months is considered normal if it disappears after the expected interval. The separation anxiety of the 2-year-old involves the ability to anticipate what is going to happen in the near future; the child protests feeling the loss of the mother, before the separation occurs. Jersild (1968) pointed out that highly intelligent children may anticipate events that could happen and may be afraid of things that do not disturb average youngsters. Anxiety fears increase in children 4 to 5 years old and are often reported by preschool children whose parents are unaware that the child is bothered. Usually anxiety fears disappear as the child gains more experience, but they may be lessened more immediately by intellectual or educational means or the child may be given emotional reassurance to reduce his or her generalized fears.

Phobias are persistent, severe, and unreasonable fears. Freudian case studies are rich with detailed analysis of the nightmares, compulsions, fantasies, and symbolic experiences of children who suffer extreme emotional disturbances. Psychoanalysts try to tease out the trauma behind the psychological defenses the child invents to hide his conflicts (A. Freud, 1965). Often guilt feelings are related to the newly acquired sexual awareness of the phallic stage. The child may recognize and repress competitive feelings toward the parent of like sex. Children often masturbate in the prelatency period, perhaps because of biological changes at that time and the pleasure, discovered accidently, that stimulation gives them. Fears connected with sexuality affect normal children of this age but are usually resolved by increased acceptance of their role in the family and by increased social intercourse with peers of like sex.

Hundreds of studies have investigated family relations and anxiety in young children. Firm blanketing and physical contact with the mother's body reduced the crying of neonates by one-half when compared with other hospital neonates (Durth & Brown, 1961). Infants whose maternal handling was observed as gentle, close, firm, and frequent showed greater ability to handle stress, improved motor development, greater attachment to mothers, and higher IQs at a later date than children with less or different maternal care (Yarrow, 1963). In a study of the effect of the family setting during toddlerhood and relationships with parents at late childhood, Honzik (1967) reported that parental compatibility correlated with a daughter's intelligence throughout childhood and adolescence. Positive affective relationships between mother and son correlated with test performance (lack of test anxiety) in the school years. By contrast, harsh, punitive, and restrictive socialization was associated with intensive anxiety in children (Ruebush, 1963). When parents imposed standards that were too high, evaluated the child negatively, or were inconsistent in their treatment, the anxiety level was high.

The fear reactions that have been observed at certain ages have been confirmed by experimental research. Scarr and Salapatek (1970) set up a series of fear-provoking situations for infants between 2 and 23 months old. They used loud noises, ugly masks, a Jack-in-the-box and a mechanical dog to get fear responses. They found that the youngest and oldest groups showed more fear than the infants in the middle age group (about 1 to 1½ years). The anxiety-prone babies tended to be clingy and cuddly toward their mothers. Shaffer and Emerson (1964) reported a peaking in the attachment of infants for a specific object at 6 to 8 months old, which they measured by strength of crying. They found that the response was least intense when the infant was given interesting stimulation and greatest when the infants were left alone in bed. These studies taken together can leave a parent confused about whether to cuddle or to encourage independence, whether to expect achievement or to be permissive. There is further conflict between advocates of behaviorist methods, who try to change a behavior directly, and those who seek to find the cause or origin of a phobia. Regarding direct treatment, the modeling technique has been effective in reducing children's fear of dogs (Bandura, 1967). Some specialists believe that a severe phobia treated by behavior modification of a symptom can cause repression of the child's fear or phobia and thus create a disturbance more difficult to treat than the original fear. Kessler (1972) offered some good advice: protect and closely parent the child for his or her first year, until trust in adults is established, and then encourage independence.

Depression is suffered by about one-fourth of the children with emotional illnesses (Clark, 1974). In infancy the pattern has been described as the institutional syndrome of apathy and listlessness. It is brought on by a lack of physical contact, neural stimulation, and social interaction with other persons, especially a caring person who can be trusted. Depressed infants develop physical symptoms as well. Lack of appetite, poor sleep patterns, proneness to infection, slow movements, and delay in mobility are commonly seen in these children. Sometimes they do not learn to walk and sometimes they die.

Depression in children is associated with parental neglect or the loss of a parent or even the loss of a much loved object. The latency-age child who suffers from depression is sad, has little interest in activities, and is self-punitive when goals are not attained (Malmquist, 1972). These children show the same patterns of sleeping and eating disturbance as depressed infants and they get the diseases that usually follow from poor general health. But the psychological discontent is the characteristic behavior; even when these children seek and receive recognition they remain dissatisfied. Feeling rejected and unloved they may turn away from emotional involvement with persons or objects. Childhood depression is difficult to treat because children may be passive to the attention and love they need, or may cover sadness with silliness and clowning. When an effort is made to lower the standards children have set for themselves, they may feel that no one cares.

HOSTILITY AND AGGRESSION

Emotional disturbance surfaces in many different forms of atypical behavior. One group of symptoms is seen in the tendency to express impulses against society; these symptoms have been labeled *conduct* problems. The other group of symptoms suggest low self-esteem, social withdrawal, or "down" moods and have been called a "personality" problem. The individual tries to survive psychologically by *externalizing* (acting out) or *internalizing* (Kessler, 1972). Among boys there are twice as many conduct or acting-out problems as internalized problems. Among girls the ratio is similar but reversed. Clinic referrals for neurosis number 3 to 1 boys over girls, suggesting greater concern for overt symptoms than for internalized problems. Hostility and aggression are the symptoms of externalized emotional disturbance.

HYPERKINESIS

Hyperkinesis is a group of symptoms, or syndrome, that is characterized by a higher than normal activity level, usually associated with brain damage. Hyperkinetic children are also highly excitable, easily distracted, and impulsive (Clark, 1974). Many of them have learning disabilities. Because this group of troubled children is so difficult to live with at home and at school, many have been given amphetamines or other drugs which seem to have the paradoxical effect of calming them down, an opposite reaction from that experienced by adults or normal children who take the same drugs (Wender, 1971). No category of emotional illness is so controversial as hyperkinesis.

Kasper and Schulman (1972) contend that hyperactive children show no greater activity level than normal children when appropriate measures are taken during the various activities of waking and sleeping. Instead they lack the ability to control their activity according to the social requirements of different settings. These investigators point to the lack of EEG confirmation to indicate brain damage in many children given medication for hyperkinesis. One technical problem is that EEGs taken outside the skull may not show deep-wave patterns, and midbrain activity may be the critical factor. They do not suggest medication unless brain damage is confirmed by strong medical evidence. Instead they recommend an educational strategy in which the cognitive and emotional strengths and weaknesses are assessed and teaching follows this profile.

Feingold, a physician, claimed that a radical change in the diets of hyperkinetic children improved their behavior (1975). He contends that the problem is not organic, since it responds to dietary treatment. In addition to the elimination of packaged foods that contain preservatives and artificial color, school nurses and parents are provided a list of certain fruits and vegetables that contain large amounts of natural salicylates. Apparently there is no need for children not affected to reduce their intake of such common natural foods as almonds, oranges, and tomatoes; but parents would do well to consider reduction of certain artificial colors and flavors.

Douglas (1975) reported a series of studies in which groups of hyperactive children were trained in programs designed especially for them, or were given recommended medication, or were given minimal medication while reteaching was taking place. The combination effort was most productive, and the gains were more durable than when training or medication was used alone. Obviously, much is still unknown about hyperkinesis, but growing numbers of children appear to be affected so severely that parents and teachers as well as the children themselves need help. My own bibliography on this topic contains over 200 reputable items and is growing.

Childhood Schizophrenia

Childhood schizophrenia is an emotional disorder, occurring usually after the first birthday and before the age of 11 years, in which there is a disturbance in the ability to make affective contact, and the appearance of autistic thinking. Autistic behavior is characterized by disregard for reality, self-manipulation, escape into fantasy, and lack of social contacts. *Autism* is sometimes considered a *symptom* of schizophrenia (Lapedes, 1974) and sometimes a childhood, or mild, form of schizophrenia (Wolman, 1972). Clinicians have noted the disturbance of language and a preoccupation with shiny or pointed objects in autistic children. A tendency to prolong input from the near senses (tactile, smell, and taste) and to ignore the distance senses (vision and hearing) has also been noted. Wolman suggested a close relationship between childhood and adult schizophrenia in both symptoms and occurrence. Piaget contended that autism is a biological and developmental stage in communication to which disturbed children regress.

Wolman (1972) contended that lack of a firm self-identity was the basis for the schizophrenia syndrome and that the unusual behavior of the victim is an attempt to preserve the weak ego from further insult and regression. He noted the deficient social relationships, the shallow mannerisms, and the easy subjection to others of the schizoid personality. Because of the desire of children so afflicted to please, he considers childhood schizophrenia quite treatable.

Symptoms of early infantile autism are lack of responsiveness from birth to the caresses of the mother, and, often, nursing difficulties. The infant may go limp or rigid when held, may seem deaf to voices but not to other sounds, or may show lack of sensitivity to pain. Erikson (1963) suggested that the infant's refusal to respond may lead mother to quit trying to make contact, and she may minister to her child's needs in a detached way, thus supporting the syndrome. Thomas, Chess, and Birch (1970) contend that infants show marked temperamental differences in responsiveness, irritability, and persistence. When these patterns are extreme and unusual, early identification and continuous intervention is called for if emotional disturbances are to be prevented.

SOURCES FOR TRAINING HANDICAPPED CHILDREN

Feingold, Ben F. *Why Your Child Is Hyperactive.* New York: Random House, 1975. Source for nonmedical professionals who are concerned about children with this behavioral pattern. Certain foods, particularly artificial flavors and colors, are believed by Feingold to contribute to hyperkinesis in vulnerable children.

Jordan, June B., Hayden, Alice H., Karnes, Merle B., and Wood, Mary M. *Early Childhood Education for Exceptional Children: A Handbook of Ideas and Exemplary Practices.* Reston, Va.: The Council for

Exceptional Children, 1977. Explains the programs supported, primarily by the federal government, for the care and training of handicapped children. Practical suggestions on screening, staffing, administration, and evaluation are included.

Mather, June. *Make the Most of Your Baby.* National Association for Retarded Citizens, P.O. Box 6109 Arlington, Tex. 76011, 1974. A booklet for parents of mentally retarded infants and preschool children. The mother of two retarded children passes on how she made difficult adjustments, and what she learned while rearing her children.

Moustakas, Clark E. *Children in Play Therapy.* New York: McGraw-Hill, 1953. The distinction is made between the techniques teachers use in school situations for socialization and emotional development and the techniques for treatment of emotional problems.

Satir, Virginia. *Conjoint Family Therapy.* Palo Alto, Calif.: Science and Behavior Books, 1964. A handbook on the dynamics of communication within a family and some techniques for conjoint therapy. The suggestions are useful for interaction within healthy families.

15
Significant
Adults

15 Significant Adults

Homo sapiens is the most elegant creation of the world of biology. The infant comes into the world having prepared its mother, both physically and psychologically, through 9 months of hormonal interaction to nurture it. The infant is equipped in appearance and behavior to appeal to its potential care-givers, whether natural parents or not. Humans, like many less sophisticated mammals, apparently form bonds with their young through exchanges of voice, touch, and eye contact. These kinds of biological ties may be needed to assure the survival of the species.

This chapter focuses on the interaction between the infant and the adult care-giver which results in a shared relationship. The institution of family has undergone changes from the near disappearance of the extended family, in which care-giving was shared among relatives and older siblings, to the small nuclear family, and lately to family patterns that fit a mobile, unstable society. The traditional infant-mother relationship is examined, after which follows a section on the role of fathers and male teachers as significant adults.

Children of the developed nations have lost or are losing their traditional functions in the culture. They are no longer an economic asset for helping their parents to produce food, but have become an economic liability. Children are no longer a comfort in old age, for parents typically die in rest homes many miles from the place their sons and daughters reside. With a decrease in extended families, the traditional cultural need to have sons to pass on the family name is increasingly unimportant (Talbot, 1976). An era may be approaching in which most children are wanted for themselves and adults having children seek the sense of generativity and absorption in others that rearing children can provide.

ADULT RESPONSIBILITY IN CHILDREARING

In no other country has the responsibility for child care, financial support, and educational responsibility fallen so heavily on the nuclear family as in the United States. Most Americans can now choose not to rear children and some of them have become confused about whether or why they should go to all the trouble and expense of becoming parents. Unfortunately, some young people have babies for lack of a plan for their lives or out of a need to be loved and admired.

With the medical technology for planning parenthood has come the option to become a mate without becoming a parent. Kessen (1976) cited a range of problems in rearing children, most of them related to the child-family complex. He suggested that most individual psychologists still think of the child as a "self-contained" organism who has needs and who develops. However, the issues of abortion, the cost of child care, and the acculturation of the child are all ecological questions which affect families. Kessen proposes that child study consider the context of values, institutions, and culture (the social ecology) in which the child is raised. He poses the central moral question, "What kind of adults do we want our children to become?'' This is a recent theme among child-development specialists, who for two generations or more have been uneasy about adults who impose their standards on children. Their view is that the child be allowed to develop through interaction with peers, while being protected from the demands and pressures of adult society. Most parents would like to provide the guidance which will help children achieve their potential and attain individuality.

Influence of Infants on Care-Givers

The interaction between the infant and the adult caretaker is called the *dyadic relationship*. Bell (1974) analyzed how very young infants assure their own life support and protection by fussing or crying. Their wails bring the care-giver into a near position where the helplessness of the infant can be observed and the infant's needs attended to. Proximity is necessary for the sensorimotor matching that establishes early bonds between infant and adult to occur. Caregiving is maintained partly because infants increase the variety of cry cues to communicate their conditions and states. Infants read the limits of the care-giver's tolerance for their protest and demand, which is important in continued caregiving.

Parents are reinforced by being able to discriminate cry messages and what it takes to stop the fussing. *Bouts of social interaction*, as Bell calls them, are initiated by infants through smiles, coos, and babbles, beginning when the infant is nearly 2 months old. The infants' demands for tending are reduced, and the typical infant begins to inveigle the care-giver into lingering and joining in play. The young contribute to social interaction by being susceptible to adult manipulations, by being responsive to adult overtures, and by constantly adding new behaviors to their ways of responding. These novel achievements (grasping, sitting, crawling, walking, jumping) gain the favorable attention of the care-giver and reinforce the child's efforts to interact socially and to grow up physically.

When an infant is lethargic, and does not respond to adult overtures, the dyadic relationship is threatened. If the infant continues frequent crying demands beyond early infancy, does not quiet when tended, and does not sense the toleration levels of the parent, child abuse may become the outlet for the parent who was mistreated in childhood. Even attentive mothers have been found to decrease their attachment to infants who continue to fuss and cry and not lower their demands after the first month. In most families the dyadic relationship is balanced by the appeals initiated by an infant and the long-term intentions of the parent, who responds to the developmental changes of the young. Watson (1966) proposed that an interaction he called *contingency games* develops between infant and parent; quick infant responses follow a parent behavior which acquires reward value and leads to increasing social interchange systems after 3 months. Each rewards the social response of the other in an appetitive system which is positively reinforcing, in contrast to the aversive system of demand and need satisfaction by which some writers explain the infant-adult relationship.

Obviously a great deal of study remains to be done to understand the dyadic relationship. Lewis and Lee-Painter (1974) have said that it is as mistaken to observe only the effects of the infant on the care-giver as it is to study only the effects of the care-giver on the infant. They indicate that behavior on the part of the infant or the adult must be interpreted differently when a social interaction is initiated by either member than when one is responding to an accidental stimulus from the other. Research in the parent-infant relationship needs to consider several factors: the inherited sequence of development (phylogeny), the past and present environment, and the behavior pattern within a flow of time (ontogeny).

Research shows that parents can do much to change the kinds of cues infants and children use to get attention. Brackbill (1970) reported the responses of a group of twenty-four infants to sensory stimulation of sound, light, swaddling, and temperature change. When the care-givers combined tending and stimulation, the infants responded with more quiet sleep, less crying, and reduced heart rate. More important, their arousal level and the duration of their quiet sleep were both increased. Parents, especially first-time parents, may need early and urgent help in changing the demand patterns of excessive criers. By providing caregiving when the infants are quiet, and using social interaction, care-givers can modify such behavior.

Much of the significant interaction of parent and infant may be so subtle as to go unnoticed. Brazelton filmed the movements of mother and infant pairs for one session each week over the period from 2 weeks to 20 weeks old. By using double mirrors the pair could be matched on the same frame for later analysis (Brazelton, Koslowski, & Main, 1974). By the third week many of the infants behaved differently when looking at a fuzzy toy stimulus than during the looking interaction with mother, although both patterns were rhythmic. At the appearance of the toy the baby attended actively and looked away in a cycle that occurred several times within a minute, as if the infant were regulating the visual stimulation that was taken in. The cycle of social looking was also one of alternating attention and nonattention, but was much more complex. This cycle was coded and observed with high reliability in sequence: *initiation* of looking (at mother) while relaxed; *orientation* while face brightened and extremities extended; *attention* with face alert and limbs pedaling; *acceleration* of body movement which built up to vocalizing; *peak* of *excitement* with eyes fixed on mother's face and ending in smiling, laughing, fist sucking, spitting up, or even crying; *deceleration* with gradual eye dimming and smoothing of body activity; and *withdrawal* shown by looking away and by flat body position. Over the twenty weeks of observation, it was noted that babies of the mothers who were responsive to this cycle of intense interaction and withdrawal increased their alertness and attention span. By contrast, the babies of mothers who did not accept the withdrawal and tried to maintain constant looking interaction developed strategies of fussiness, rejection, or withdrawal. Apparently the infant cues a care-giver on the cycle of stimulation and recovery which can be processed at the time. A pattern of demand for attention, looking, or responding that ignores the message from the infant apparently sets up reciprocity behavior very early.

The unresponsive child may be difficult to reach socially, but it is essential that adults establish communication early by being very responsive to signals from the infant and giving the kinds of stimulation babies typically enjoy.

Play Relationship with Parents

The games people play with babies teach the child to solve problems at the sensorimotor level that will be encountered later at an abstract level of thinking. Traditional games that grownups play with youngsters such as peek-a-boo and pat-a-cake can be used to divert unhappy youngsters when a meal is not quite ready or stop their crying when the mother has disappeared. Games such as these have been extended into a curriculum for the home training of parents and for teachers to use in nursery schools (Child Development Institute, 1976). By planning games for their infants parents are encouraged to think about what they want the child to be able to do. Perhaps more important, they establish a bond with the child which can be maintained and extended to a play relationship at more advanced ages.

Pister (1973) proposed that the attention span of infants and toddlers could be increased by designing toys which appealed to many senses and could be manipulated. She studied the appeal value of toys for infants 6 to 23 months old by recording the time they played with a particular toy under conditions of nondistrac-

Play relationship between mother and child. (Hanna Schreiber from Rapho/Photo Researchers Inc.)

tion and distraction. She found that many toys, those which were unicolor, unitextured, and did not "do" anything had little "holding interest power" and were dropped in a few seconds. High-interest toys had many sensual qualities, or could be manipulated: cage rattles, nesting blocks with pictures, kitchen rejects on a strip of cloth, a chain 1 meter long, and plastic keys on a chain. Young infants played longest with toys having buccal appeal but only if the toy also had eye appeal. Alternative visual exploration and mouthing was observed. Cause-effect toys appealed more to older infants, who seemed to continue the manipulation until control of the action was achieved. The cause-effect toys had a higher interest power than new toys that could not be manipulated. Some examples of cause-effect toys were a horse on springs, a flexible hose 50 centimeters long, appear-disappear boxes, and the cage rattles. Toy design was a fascinating project for both male and female adults who participated in the project. Pister believed that if the attention span of babies could be increased, their persistence and concentration would be developed. She anticipated that high interest in play might become the basis for creative action when the child was older.

New Family Patterns

Radical changes in family organization are changing the nature of the responsibility adults have for young children. In an editorial on science and the future of the family Etzioni (1977) reported that fewer than two-thirds of American households are married households. At the present accelerating rate of depletion the United States may "run out" of families not long after it runs out of oil. Among the factors are the following: the divorce rate in the United States, the employment of women outside the home, and the mobility of families in developing and industrial countries.

These changes in the immediate setting in which the child is reared (the microsystem) are accompanied by radical changes in the social and educational ecology as a whole. Some adults are seeking a freer, more egalitarian, less sexist arrangement than the traditional family allowed. Conclusive information is lacking on the effect of having one parent instead of two, or of parental divorce as opposed to unhappy marriage, or of communal living. Etzioni proposes a major research effort to guide national policy. The preservation or disintegration of the family is directly affected by public policies on taxes, welfare, Social Security, divorce laws, and child care. Today's children are directly affected by competition among groups for the national and economic resources. The challenge for parents is to utilize the changing ecology to affect the well-being of their children. A recognition of the changing institutions for childrearing and education is needed if government is to develop a coherent policy.

SINGLE-PARENT HOMES

In some states nearly half the children live with a single parent, or with a natural and a foster parent. An increasing number of single parents are male. Evidence is lacking that fathers are less adequate than mothers in the rearing of either sons or daughters. It is difficult, perhaps impossible, to know whether a stepparent or foster parent provides a better psychological and physical environment for a child than the nuclear family can. Teachers, psychologists, and pediatricians see many children from single-parent homes who appear healthy and well adjusted.

Another radical shift in family organization which needs to be studied is the split-year arrangement, by which the child spends part of the time with one parent and part with the other, whether single or remarried. Custody battles certainly affect the child, but again the psychological impact is unknown. Common sense suggests that recriminations in the presence of a child that are directed by one parent against another have a damaging effect on the child's self concept.

ADOPTED CHILDREN

Adoption meets the mutual needs of the child whose natural parents do not want or cannot support him or her and the childless adult who wants a family. About 10 percent of modern couples cannot have children because one or both of them is sterile. Additional and unknown numbers have or fear they have hereditary diseases they do not want to transmit to offspring. The process of trying to have children, of discovering the medical reasons why this is unlikely, and of reaching the decision to adopt can be an ego-battering experience for a couple (Schechter, Toussieng, Sternlot, & Pollack, 1972). The explanations couples give for wanting to adopt are similar to the reasons other couples give for remaining childless, leading to the speculation that additional numbers of adults, beyond the 10 percent estimate, are sterile. One positive factor for the adopting parent is that problems that arise can be viewed in a more detached way and handled more objectively than usually happens when couples are faced with some genetic weakness in their natural child.

Adopted children, who think of themselves as unwanted initially, also may experience psychological stress as a result. When older children are adopted, more care than usual is needed to assure them how much they are wanted. When a newborn is adopted, "telling" the child becomes an emotional event. Schechter et al. (1972) recommended that the telling be done like sex education and in the same context. By giving the 3- to 6-year-old the information she seeks at various times about physical origin, the trauma of a belated revelation is avoided. After explaining that another woman had carried her, and how the agency had helped them find her, one mother added, "You seemed to pick us out by smiling your own special smile. We knew right away that you were the very one for us" (p. 369).

EXTENDED FAMILIES

The extended family, where more than two adults share the care of the young, has certain advantages over the nuclear family, which is the modern Western ideal. For mothers, release from continuous caregiving and the availability of experienced models for interacting with the baby are important. For children, the presence of several adults to coddle and guide them permits them to generalize a trust relationship that extends beyond the family. Traditionally the extended family includes relatives, for example, grandparents, unmarried aunts, or orphaned cousins.

Some contemporary preschools try to create the advantages of the extended family by bringing together a team of adults of different ages, sexes, and ethnic origin. Retired persons who are experienced in working with young. children are being recruited to help. Evaluation of these plans is needed, partly because the nuclear family organization may soon be atypical.

Communal living of unmarried persons was one outcome of the sixties in which the adults actively rejected the family rearing patterns of their middle-class parents. Black (1976) described the experimental roles as natural parents tried to

The teacher is a significant adult in the life of the preschool child. (Lucia Woods/Photo Researchers Inc.)

extend the responsibility and the relationship of their children to all group members. Whether children will grow up being uncompetitive but affectively strong is not yet known. How they will cope with a different culture when and if the time comes for higher education is likewise to be determined.

The Kibbutz of rural Israel has been the model for some communal groups. Sufficient time has passed for evaluations of the personality and coping abilities of the sabras (children born and reared on Kibbutzim). Earlier fears about the effects of their unconventional childhood seem to have been groundless. Kibbutzim children tend to be more cooperative in games that require team effort than Israeli children reared outside the Kibbutz (Shapira & Madsen, 1974). They usually marry outside the group and, like many country children, move to the cities to live (Spiro, 1965).

In a study of how children saw the roles of others in their own socialization, 600 school-age children from Kibbutzim and cities were interviewed. City children were likely to think of parents as disciplinarians, but parents were also the persons they most counted on for support. Kibbutzim teachers were seen as the providers of emotional security, whose roles appeared to resemble those of parents. Peer groups were seen by both city and commune children as agents of disapproval and discipline, but not as supportive (Devereau, Shouval, Bronfenbrenner, Rodgers, Kav-Venaki, Kiely, & Karson, 1974). It should be remembered that a high priority in terms of personnel and material resources is committed to children of the Kibbutz, who enjoy a valued place in the daily living of the commune. There are indications that Kibbutzim are shifting their work schedules to allow more direct contact among parents and their natural children.

MOTHERS AS CARE-GIVERS

The psychoanalytic tradition has emphasized the role of the mother in all aspects of early development: the affective responding with a social smile, the visual perception of space as the eyes keep track of the mother (object of attachment), and the continuity and rhythm in life that is transmitted by the mother's care (Spitz, 1972). The biological relationship that evolves from pregnancy should not be denied, nor should the mother's role be overemphasized. One very important and often overlooked factor in the maternal role is the ability of most mothers to respond to the individual differences in infants and to create a caregiving pattern that is unique to the personality and to the ontogenic stage of development. Motherhood involves the acceptance of the child's withdrawal from nurturance in his or her drive to become an independent individual.

An Optimum Environment

Mothers have their own individual reactions to the child's increasing ability to sustain psychological and physical separateness, a drive that accelerates in toddlers when they achieve mobility. Psychoanalysts have explored the feelings and attitudes of mothers as they confront the problem of separation-individuation (Mahler, Pine, & Bergman, 1970). In this context *individuation* means the "intrapsychic advances that mark the child's development of skills, styles, and individual characteristics" (p. 262). Some mothers view the child's progressive independence as a personal loss, become anxious about their own mothering role, and sometimes seek another pregnancy to recapture the dependency relationship. Some other mothers are more comfortable with the increased capacities of the child to communicate her needs and pleasures verbally, and to enter new companionship roles during work and play. Clinical evidence implies that a child is fortunate to have a mother whose own needs are fulfilled by the ability to read the child's cues for independence and autonomy.

Developmental studies suggest that responsive mothering changes with the age and the individuality of the child.Uorner (1974) reported that mothers change their caregiving from week to week as the ontogenic changes in development bring changes in the infant's demands. The neonates in her interaction studies were sensitive to vestibular changes, and mothers responded to their cries by lifting them to the shoulder, or raising the carrier to bring them upright. Sex differences—the vigor of males, and the smiles and tactile sensitivity of females—caused care-givers to give different treatment to infant boys and girls. Sensitive mothers adapted to unusual individual differences in infants that experts have noted only recently. Korner noted that colic, now thought to occur about the third week when infants with low sensory thresholds tend to become overstimulated, needs a mothering person to intervene through care that is tension-reducing. At the other extreme, the placid child needs stimulation that mere response to demands will not provide. When a mother of several children talks about them, she recalls the uniqueness of each child and how differently she dealt with them. It may be that the sensitivity to each child's states and temperament is the most important lack in institutional care. The optimum environment will certainly differ from child to child and from one ontogenic stage to the next.

Nutrition, Learning, and Behavior

The tendency of children reared in poverty to do poorly on intelligence tests is due in part to lack of opportunity to learn. Malnutrition in early childhood is also a factor (Eichenwald & Fry, 1969). By age 3 the child's brain has grown to 80 percent of adult size, while the body has grown to only 20 percent of that at maturity (Scrimshaw & Gordon, 1968). During the period of rapid growth it is critical that the child's diet be adequate in protein and vitamins.

Having a single digestive sequence, Homo sapiens must take in certain specific amino acids for tissue growth and reproduction, for lactation, and for replacement of nitrogen. Brain functions require a continuous supply of choline and epinephrine, both derived from nitrogen-bearing amino acids. Nine of the amino acids are essential in human nutrition in that they cannot be synthesized from other forms of protein by the human body (Harper, 1974). During digestion the peptide chains that make up proteins are broken up, and the amino acids enter the bloodstream in free form. This process is a reversal of protein assembly (Chapter 2).

A direct tie has been made between nutrition and behavior in laboratory animals. Rats fed on corn diets for a long term developed reduced levels of brain serotonin and became unusually sensitive and reactive to pain (Lytle, Messing, Fisher, & Phebus, 1975). Reduced serotonin follows a dietary lack of the amino acid tryptophan.

Recent efforts at nutrition improvement have focused on pregnant mothers and young children (Scrimshaw & Gordon, 1968). Many families whose grocery budget is adequate are poorly fed because of faulty eating habits. There is no alternative in prenatal life for the natural mother's attention to diet. Adequate protein, vitamins, and minerals, accompanied by a weight gain of about 20 pounds, may go a long way toward carrying the fetus to full term and assuring good neurological growth.

EXTENDED ROLES FOR FATHERS

Conventional wisdom holds that the central figure in a child's early life is its mother. Because of this, courts have favored the mother in disputes over custody of children, and parent substitutes in nurseries and preschools are usually female. Yet before industrialization removed fathers from the family home or farm, fathers had an important role in caring for the next older child when a new baby was born.

Fathers as Care-Givers

The traditional role for fathers has been an economic one—as provider and protector of the home or territory (Benedek, 1970b). As head of the house, the Puritan father was the authority figure who decided family matters and at the same time achieved ego-fulfillment through this role. Although the economic and the biological roles of fatherhood are given considerable attention in the literature, the fatherliness in men is more often the subject of novels than of psychological inquiry. Probably the empathy required for fatherhood is no less than that assumed for motherhood. The ontogenic trend of humanity has dictated increasing periods of parenting that now extend through adolescence and, at upper socioeconomic levels, into adulthood. The parent role for fathers has extended beyond biology and economics; fathers are now teachers and modelers of sex-related behaviors, school adjustment, and moral development.

Although some segments of the culture have moved to give young boys the training and motivation for fathering, the mainstream of the culture supports the traditional economic and biological functions (Woodward & Malamud, 1975). Boys are given less opportunity to handle dolls, although relationship between doll play and ability to nurture has yet to be proved (Maccoby & Jacklin (1974). Few programs, outside the classes for couples expecting a baby, are directed toward fathering (Greenberg & Morris, 1974). Some exceptions are Kruger (1973), who

Fathers enjoy the en-hanced role as caregiv-ers. (Charles Gatewood)

proposed that education for parenthood be directed to both sexes, and Dodson (1974), who advised prospective fathers on what to expect, do, think, and feel.

Men as Teachers of Young Children

With one American child in six now being reared in single-parent homes, and most of these being the female parent, many preschools have recruited male teachers and volunteers to work and play with the children. The programs have been directed both toward the learning of sex-typed behaviors on the part of boys and on overcoming the narrow sex typing of certain behaviors. Farthing (1976) cited evidence, mostly from countries where primary teachers are predominantly male, that early reading achievement of boys is enhanced when their book experiences are associated with males. Coopersmith (1967) found that boys with high esteem had fathers who were attentive, interested, and confident, and who provided a strong clear model of how to deal with problems.

Modeling and reinforcement are important factors in the learning of sex-typed behaviors. Preschool children begin to discriminate between the sexes; they develop a preference for and adopt the cultural standards associated with male or female roles. Sugawara, O'Neill, and Edelbrock (1976) summarized recent studies to show that (1) children model the behaviors of same-sex teachers more than they model opposite-sex teachers, (2) teachers reinforce sex-typed behaviors more often in their own than in the opposite sex, and (3) sex-type behaviors are maintained and not impeded by powerful opposite-sex teachers.

To the teachers who are designing these programs it is consistent with sex-role modeling and reinforcement to reduce sex-role stereotyping that limits the options of both sexes. They encourage wider use of toys and art materials. They avoid books that restrict girls to homemaking occupations, and they encourage boys to participate in cooking and cleaning up after themselves (Vukelich, McCarty, & Nanis, 1976). A great deal of discussion is needed when a teaching staff undertakes to make curriculum changes that will reduce sex-typed behavior. How much sex-typed behavior is necessary for healthy self-identity and self-concept development is still an open question. With increasing numbers of males becoming teachers of young children, evaluation of their effect on children's behavior will become more feasible and the findings more conclusive.

PROBLEMS AND POSSIBILITIES

For every advantage that is discovered through social evolution and technology, there is a corresponding responsibility to do all that one can to enhance the potential of each child. For every topic considered in this last section there are hundreds that remain unmentioned. Following are examples of the problems that face care-givers today and in the immediate future.

Mixed Blessings from Technology

Technology has thrust upon this generation of parents many decisions that were unimagined by their parent models. Television has been called the national babysitter because children 3 to 5 years old average 54 hours of viewing each week in 96 percent of the homes in the United States (Larrick, 1977). By the time the typical child goes to kindergarten she or he will have spent more time in front of a television set than a college student spends in four years of classes. On a typical Saturday morning, programs that push mostly junk foods on the average of one commercial for every one to two minutes of program are seen by 75 percent of all children. By the end of high school, most youngsters have spent twice as many hours watching television as in school.

Television has had both its constructive and its negative impact on children. Gotz (1977) takes the extreme view that children should not be permitted to watch television, whether the content is good or bad. Because television conditions through its near total involvement of the senses, children are deprived of creativity and an active influence over their own conceptual development. Considering the numbers of children who have access to television at home, most concerned adults direct their concerns to program improvement.

Most educators evaluate children's television as a potent medium for cognitive and affective learning. Baron and Meyer (1974) reported that both positive and antisocial television content were modeled by high- and low-self-esteem children in their sample. Mukerji (1976) reported that children learned to distinguish fantasy and reality by watching television. Their experience was enhanced and they found models for identification at a crucial time in their search for identity beyond the immediate family. Older children used television as a source for ideas and techniques to create fantasies and art forms. Viewing of a television drama such as "Mister Rogers' Neighborhood" increased the task persistence and cooperative play behavior of children without adult intervention.

The most negative aspect of television addiction is the demonstrated aggression children show after watching aggressive behavior on television. Individuals who are hostile, or otherwise susceptible, may be stimulated to violent acts (Goranson, 1970). A more subtle effect involves the expectations built up in children that entertainment, stimulation, and personal passivity are necessary parts of life.

Television has the potential for introducing the preschool child to ethnic groups and cultures outside the immediate neighborhood. By age 3, television watching has become purposeful behavior on the part of the typical child; his or her individual viewing patterns have been established (Gerbner & Gross, 1976). Television is programmed to capture and hold the viewer's interest, and the pleasure it induces through the senses is seductive as well as informative (Lesser, 1974). Almost certainly television has the effect of mainstreaming the social attitudes and patterns of the new generation into the existing system.

Among the major efforts to teach young children by television have been the programs "Sesame Street" for preschool children and "Reading with Television," both productions of the Electric Company. In an independent evaluation of "Sesame Street" the major findings showed the effectiveness of educational television: (1) Children who watched the most, learned the most. (2) Skills that received the most time and attention on the programs were most often the skills that were learned the best. (3) Formal adult supervision was not required in order for children to learn in the areas covered by the program (Figure 15-1). Some additional conclusions that were drawn from the study included the evidence of transfer of learning to reading itself. Children learned whether they watched at home or at school, and the medium was effective in teaching English skills to bilingual children (Figure 15-2). Two potentially important effects were obtained. Disadvantaged children who watched a great deal surpassed middle-class children who watched only a little. Also, 3-year-old children gained the most and 5-year-olds gained the least from "Sesame Street," suggesting that preschool children are able to learn many skills that traditionally have been introduced in the first grade (Bogatz & Ball, 1971).

The "Reading with Television" series was beamed at school children who had reached second grade, but were at the bottom of their classes in reading. The

FIGURE 15-1 Item used to test concept of "last" in an evaluation of "Sesame Street." The examiner says, "Here are children in line. They are waiting to go to a movie. Which one is last in line?"

Source: Gerry Ann Bogatz and Samuel Ball, *The Second Year of Sesame Street: A Continuing Evaluation*, vol. I, appendex A. Copyright © by Children's Television Workshop, 1971. Princeton, N.J.: Educational Testing Service, 1971.

major findings were: (1) The program had an impact, shown by viewed gains, on children from first through fourth grades. (2) The program had a positive effect on almost all of nineteen curriculum areas. (3) The program had a similar effect on all groups who viewed at school—children of Hispanic background, blacks, whites, boys, and girls. The reactions of teachers who participated were generally favorable (Ball & Bogatz, 1973).

Another advance in technology, the neonate intensive-care system, has forced some parents to make decisions for which they lack cultural models or moral guidelines. Infants born so prematurely or so deformed that formerly they would not have lived can now be saved through life-support systems. Some newborns weighing less than 1000 grams have survived, and fetuses born early in the second trimester might potentially be saved. In the absence of knowledge about the neurological maturity that may be expected to take place outside the biologically evolved environment of the uterus, some responsible adults are reviewing the possible social impact of this technology. Some individuals with birth defects now need approximately 1 million dollars each for training and care during their lifetimes, while thousands of children receive less than an adequate diet or

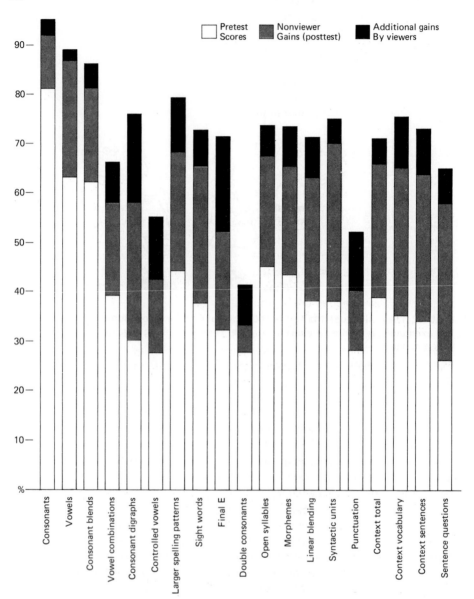

FIGURE 15-2 Gains made by child viewers of "Reading with Television" over gains made by nonviewers.

Source: Samual Ball and Gerry Ann Bogatz, *A Summary of the Major Findings from "Reading with Television: An Evaluation of the Electric Company,"* page 9. Princeton, N.J.: Educational Testing Service, 1973. Copyright © 1973 by the Children's Television Workshop.

education. The problems of ethics and public policy are being reviewed in terms of the expectation for a meaningful life on the part of the very premature. Scientists are concerned with protecting the newborn: "Every baby born possesses a *moral value* entitling it to the medical and social care necessary to effect its well-being." Scientists are also interested in quality of life: "Parents are principally *responsible* for all decisions regarding the well-being of their newborn children" (Culliton, 1975). These and other issues will confront many parents as intensive-care units for neonates become available in most cities.

Child Abuse and Accidents

The incidence of child abuse is difficult to estimate. Approximately 40,000 children are seriously injured by their parents or care-takers each year (Steele, 1970). Perhaps ten times that number are beaten or sexually assaulted. Half a million have accidents for which they are treated, some of which are child-abuse cases reported as accidents. Recently small children with gonorrhea of the throat tissue have been diagnosed. Accidents to children have long been more numerous than reasonable caregiving would allow, but recent accidents have often been caused by the increasing availability of drugs and weapons in the homes. Accidents to and abuse of children have reached crisis proportions.

Given the attitude of most parents that children belong to them, and the attitude of most neighbors that what parents do is their own business, the American solution seems to be education, legislation, and the availability of family centers to help parents who are potential child abusers cope with their problems. The Child Abuse and Treatment Act, passed by Congress in 1974, helps states and organizations set up parent retraining programs and crisis clinics, where parents can take a child when pressures are rising before tempers get out of control. Such programs usually require the professional personnel to report child abuse to the authorities for preventive measures to be taken. Other legislation, which makes dangerous drugs and chemicals less available to young explorers by requiring labeling and sealing, also provides reminders to adults that it is their responsibility to make the environment as safe as possible.

A study of parents who batter children has revealed a pattern which is useful in proposing measures to prevent child abuse (Steele, 1970). Most abusing parents are young, having had their first child in their teens. Most abusing parents were themselves punished severely and frequently. They often report that siblings were favored over themselves, and feel disturbed because the other parent did not protect them as children. Abusing parents have an exaggerated view about the need to "discipline" and readily identify faults in the child that need to be corrected. In terms of treatment it should be noted that single children are seldom battered children, and that abusing parents do have a less punitive relationship with the other children in the family. Most social workers believe the abusing parent can be helped by family-child counseling and by giving parents alternatives in child management.

MacLeod (1977) reported that 90 percent of the parents who abuse a child are not psychotic in the clinical sense. Many do have an obsessional need for love and an unreal expectation that the child will give the devotion, admiration, and love that is lacking in their lives. The child victim, who is perceived by the parent as less than the preconceived model, threatens the adult's own image of a good parent. Lacking "parenting" techniques, the child abuser resorts to the punishment patterns of her or his own parent, loses control when punishing, and feels guilty afterward. Rather than being angry when told they will be reported for suspected child abuse, most parents welcome help. Such programs are reaching parents who will join discussion groups, such as Parents Anonymous, or contact crisis clinics for help. Little is being done to focus on contributing factors such as poverty, unemployment, marital conflicts, and unwanted children. Professional help may be needed for the difficult child who invites parental frustration.

Teaching Personal Power

Gilmore (1976) offered some specific suggestions for helping children gain personal power. First take the child seriously; talk with her about her own intentions. Second, show the child how to have an impact on his physical and social world. The child who helps wash the car or drops the cookies on the baking sheet has quite a different experience from the one who goes along to the baseball game. Third, show children how to clear up whatever mess they might make. If the child has confidence that he or she can cope with most boo-boos, the child will not develop unwarranted fears of making mistakes. Fourth, encourage children to think of alternative ways to make something happen. Children can learn early that flexibility in the way they approach a goal increases the chances of reaching that goal. Fifth, encourage children to celebrate their successes and review the failures. Self-reinforcement for simple accomplishments is the basis for motivation and self-direction; the ability to face failure is necessary if the patterns of behavior that do not succeed are to be changed. Sixth, encourage children to play. Help them plan how to make things happen by beginning with the parts of their life that are under their own control. This practice in personal power helps children to believe in their own ability to make a difference.

An important step has been taken when adults recognize that having children is no longer the result of economic or cultural necessities. The value of rearing children is in the day-to-day relationship of seeing the world again through unjaded eyes, of sharing a total effort toward some simple accomplishment like riding a bike, of becoming worthy of trust so that the child may learn to trust others. Teaching a child how to eat with a spoon, read a book, or recognize a star are but examples of the privilege of being a parent or a teacher.

SOURCES FOR PARENTING

Braga, Joseph, and Braga, Laurie. *Children and Adults: Activities for Growing Together.* Englewood Cliffs, N.J.: Prentice-Hall, 1975. This source book in child development provides tools and insights to help adults make constructive use of their time with children. Through routine day-to-day activities as well as special learning games, the authors show how adults can learn about themselves as they help their children grow.

Freed, Alvyn M. *T.A. for Tots;* Transactional Analysis for Everybody Series. Sacramento, Calif.: Jalmar, 1973. Cartoon-type drawings with captions. This book of humor has the serious intent of increasing the sensitivity of parents and children to personal and social questions.

Pines, Maya. *The Brain Changers: Scientists and the New Mind Control.* New York: Harcourt Brace Jovanovich, 1973. A book for parents who wish to provide a stimulating cognitive environment for their very young children. Research and strategies are described which enhance learning.

Rugh, Roberts, and Shettles, Landrum B. *From Conception to Birth.* New York: Harper & Row, 1971. A semitechnical source for mothers and expectant fathers. This book explains the biology and anatomy of conception and pregnancy. The birth process is explained and illustrated.

Talbot, Nathan B. *Raising Children in Modern America: What Parents and Society Should Be Doing for Their Children.* Boston: Little, Brown, 1976. Suggestive work that reaches from birth control to day care. This is the application volume, the second of two books published simultaneously to cover practice and theory.

References

Aberle, D. F., and Naegele, K. D. Middle-class fathers' occupational role and attitudes toward children. *American Journal of Orthopsychiatry*, 1952, **22**, 366–378.

Abramovich, R. Y. Development of infant behavior with objects in the first year of life. Candidate's dissertation, Moscow, 1946.

Adkins, D. C., and Ballif, R. L. *Motivation to achieve in school.* Final report on Contract No. OEO B89-4576. Washington, D.C.: Office of Economic Opportunity, 1970.

Adkins, Margaret M., Sanford, R. Nevitt, Miller R. Bretney, Cobb, Elizabeth A. et al. Physique, personality, and scholarship. *Monographs of the Society for Research in Child Development*, 1943 **8**(1), Serial no. 34, 705 pp.

Ainsworth, M. D. *Infancy in Uganda: infant care and growth of love.* Baltimore: Johns Hopkins, 1967.

Ainsworth, M. D., and Bell, Silvia M. Attachment, exploration, and separation: illustrated by the behavior of one-year-olds in a strange situation. *Child Development*, 1970, **41**, 49–68.

Ainsworth, M. D., Bell, Silvia M. and Stayworth, Donelda J. Individual differences in strange-situation behavior of one-year-olds. In H. R. Shaffer (Ed.), *The origins of human social relations.* London: Academic, 1971.

Aksarina, N. M. Peculiarities of development of children of preschool age and their training in crèches and children's homes. Candidate's dissertation, Moscow, 1944.

Altus, W. D. Birth order and its sequelae. *Science*, 1966, **151**, 44–49.

Ambrose, J. A. The development of the smiling response in early infancy. In B. M. Foss (Ed.), *Determinants of infant behavior*, Vol. 1. New York: Wiley, 1961.

Ames, Louise B. The sequential patterning of prone progression in the human infant. *Genetic Psychology Monographs*, 1937, **19**, 409–460.

Andrews, S. G., and Harris, M. (Eds.). *The syndrome of stuttering.* London: Heinemann, 1964.

Anthony, E. James. The reactions of parents to the Oedipal child. In E. James Anthony and Therese Benedek (Eds.), *Parenthood.* Boston: Little, Brown, 1970.

Aristotle. Politics. In Robert Ulich (Ed.), *Three thousand years of educational wisdom.* Cambridge, Mass.: Harvard University Press, 1959.

Ausubel, D. P., Schiff, H. M., and Gasser, E. B. A preliminary study of developmental trends in socioempathy: accuracy of perception of own and others' status. *Child Development*, 1952, **23**, 111–128.

Axelrod, Leonard R. The baboon as a primate animal model. In *Viral etiology of congenital malformations.* Bethesda, Md.: National Institutes of Health, 1968, pp. 90–101.

Axline, Virginia M. *Dibs: in search of self.* Boston: Houghton Mifflin, 1964.

Ayres, Jean. *Southern California Perceptual-Motor Tests.* Los Angeles, Calif.: Western Psychological Corporation, 1969.

Bachtold, Louise M. *Counseling: instructional programs for intellectually gifted students.* Sacramento: California State Department of Education, 1966.

Baker, J. B. E. The effects of drugs on the foetus. *Pharmacological Reviews,* March 1960, **12** (1), 37–90.

Ball, Samuel, and Bogatz, Gerry Ann. *A summary of the major findings from "Reading with television: an evaluation of the Electric Company."* Princeton, N.J.: Educational Testing Service, March 1973.

Ballif, Bonnie, L., and Adkins, Dorothy C. Gumpgookies: instructions for administration of a test of motivation to achieve. Mineographed. Honolulu: University of Hawaii, 1968.

Bandura, Albert (Ed.). Analysis of modeling processes. In *Psychologocal modeling: conflicting theories.* Chicago: Aldine, 1971, pp. 1–62.

Bandura, A. Behavioral psychotherapy. *Scientific American*, 1967, **216**, 78–89.

Bandura, A., Grusec, J., and Menlove, F. L. Observational learning as a function of symbolization and incentive set. *Child Development*, 1966. **37**, 499–506.

Bandura, A., and Harris, M. B. Modification of syntactic style. *Journal of Experimental Child Psychology,* 1966, **4**, 341–352.

Baratz, Joan C., and Shuy, Roger W. Teaching black children to read. Center for Applied Linguistics, 1717 Massachusetts Ave., N.W., Washington, D. C. 20036.

Barnet, A. B., Lodge, A., and Armington, J. C. Electroretinogram in newborn infants. *Science*, 1965, **148**, 65–654.

Baron, Stanley J. Pro- and anti-social television content and modeling by high and low self-esteem children. *Journal of Broadcasting*, 1974, **18**, 481–495.

Baron, Stanley J., and Chase, Lawrence J. Television drama as a facilitator of prosocial behavior in children: The Walton's. Paper presented to the International Communication Association, Mass Communication Division, Portland, Oreg., 1976.

Bartlett, Edward W., and Smith, Charles P. Child-rearing practices, birth order, and the development of achievement-related motives. *Psychological Reports*, 1966, **18**, 1207–1216.

Bateman, Barbara. Learning disabilities—yesterday, today, and tomorrow. *Exceptional Children*, 1964, **31**(4), 167.

Bauer, J. Das kierchphanomen des neugeboren. *Klinische Wochenschrift*, 1926, **5**, 1468–1469.

Bayer, Leona M., and Bayley, Nancy. *Growth diagnosis.* Chicago: University of Chicago Press, 1959.

Bayley, Nancy. Individual patterns of development. *Child Development*, 1956, **27**, 45–74.

Bayley, Nancy. Mental growth during the first three years. In R. G. Barher, J. S. Kounin, and H. F. Wright (Eds.), *Child behavior and development.* New York: McGraw-Hill, 1943.

Bayley, Nancy. The development of motor abilities in the first three years. *Monographs of the Society for Research in Child Development*, 1935, **1**(1), 1–26.

Bayley, Nancy. *The California first-year mental scale.* Berkeley: University of California Press, 1933.

Bayley, Nancy, and Davis, F. C. Growth changes in bodily size and proportions during the first three years: a developmental study of 61 children by repeated measurements. *Biometrica*, 1935, **27**, 26–87.

Bayley, N., and Schaefer, E. S. Correlations of maternal and child behaviors with the developmental abilities. *Monographs of the Society for Research in Child Development*, 1964, **29**,(6), Serial no. 97.

Beach, F. A. Current concepts of play in animals. *American Naturalist*, 1945, **79**, 523–541.

Becker, Wesley C., and Engelmann, Siegfried. The direct instruction model. In Ray Rhine (Ed.), *Encouraging change in America's schools: a decade of experimentation.* New York: Academic 1977 (in press).

Bell, Richard Q. Contributions of human infants to caregiving and social interaction. In Michael Lewis and Leonard A. Rosenblum (Eds.), *The effect of the infant on its caregiver.* New York: Wiley, 1974.

Bell, R. Q. A reinterpretation of the direction of effects in studies of socialization. *Psychological Review*, 1968, **75**, 81–95.

Bell, S. M. The development of the concept of object as related to infant-mother attachment. *Child Development*, June 1970, **41**, 291–311.

Belmont, Lillian, and Birch, H. G. Lateral dominance and right-left awareness in normal children. *Child Development*, 1963, **34**, 257–270.

Benditt, Earl P. The origin of atherosclerosis. *Scientific American*, 1977, **236**(2), 74–85.

Benedek, Therese. The family as a psychologic field. In E. James Anthony and Therese Benedek (Eds.), *Parenthood: its psychology and psychopathology.* Boston: Little, Brown, 1970a.

Benedek, Therese. Fatherhood and providing. In E. James Anthony and Therese Benedek (Eds.), *Parenthood: its psychology and psychopathology*. Boston: Little, Brown, 1970b.

Benedek, Therese. Motherhood and nurturing. In E. James Anthony and Therese Benedek (Eds.), *Parenthood: its psychology and psychopathology*. Boston: Little, Brown, 1970c.

Benirschke, Kurt. Viral infection of the placenta. In *Viral etiology of congenital malformations*. Bethesda, Md.: National Institutes of Health, 1968, pp. 74–89.

Bennett, E. L., and Rosenzweig, M. R. Chemical alterations produced in brain by environment and training. In A. Lajtho (Ed.), *Handbook of neurochemistry*. New York: Plenum, 1970.

Bennett, Neville. *Teaching styles and pupil progress*. London: Open Books, 1976.

Benson, D. Frank. Alexia. In John T. Guthrie (Ed.), *Aspects of reading acquisition*. Baltimore: Johns Hopkins, 1976.

Berenda, Ruth W. *The influence of the group on the judgments of children*. New York: King's Crown, 1950.

Berlyne, D. E. *Structure and direction in thinking*. New York: Wiley, 1965.

Berry, Martin. Development of the cerebral cortex of the rat. In Gilbert Gottlieb (Ed.), *Aspects of neurogenesis*, Vol. 2. New York: Academic, 1974.

Bever, T. G. Pre-linguistic behavior. Unpublished honors thesis, Department of Linguistics, Harvard University, Cambridge, Mass., 1961.

Bijou, S. W., and Baer, D. M. *Child development*, Vol. 1, *A systematic and empirical theory*. New York: Appleton-Century-Crofts, 1961.

Birns, Beverly, Blank, Marion, and Bridger, Wagner H. The effectiveness of various soothing techniques on human neonates. *Psychosomatic Medicine*, 1966, **28**, 316–322.

Black, David. Commune children. *New Times*, April 30, 1976.

Bogatz, Gerry Ann, and Ball, Samuel. *The second year of Sesame Street: a continuing evaluation*, Vol. I. Princeton, N.J.: Educational Testing Service, 1971.

Bower, T. G. R. Repetitive processes in child development. *Scientific American*, 1976, **235**(5), 38–47.

Bower, T. G. R. *Development in infancy*. San Francisco: Freeman, 1974.

Bower, T. G. R. Object perception in infants. *Perception*, 1972, **1**, 15–30.

Bower, T. G. R. The visual world of infants. *Scientific American*, 1966, **215**, 80–92.

Bower, T. G. R. Stimulus variables determining space perception in infants. *Science*, 1965, **149**, 88–89.

Bower, T. G. R. Discrimination of depth in premotor infants. *Psychonmonic Science*, 1964, **1**, 368.

Bower, T. G. R., and Patterson, J. B. The separation of place movement and object in the world of the infant. *Journal of Experimental Child Psychology*, 1973, **15**, 161–168.

Bowlby, John. *Attachment and Loss*, Vol. I, *Attachment*. New York: Basic Books, 1969.

Brackbill, Yvonne. Continuous stimulation and arousal level in infants: additive factors. *American Psychological Association Proceedings*, 1970, **5**, 271–272.

Brackbill, Y., Adams, G., Crowell, D. H., and Gray, M. L. Arousal level in neonates and preschool children under continuous auditory simulation. *Journal of Exceptional Child Psychology*, 1966, **4**, 178–188.

Braga, Joseph, and Braga, Laurie. *Children and adults: activities for growing together*. Englewood Cliffs, N.J.: Prentice-Hall, 1975.

Braine, Martin D., Heimer, Caryl B., Wortis, Helen, and Freedman, Alfred M.. Factors associated with impairment of the early development of prematures. In L. Joseph Stone, Henrietta T. Smith, and Lois B. Murphy (Eds.), *The competent infant*. New York: Basic Books, 1973.

Brazelton, T. Berry. *Neonatal behavioral assessment*. Philadelphia: Lippincott, 1973.

Brazelton, T. Berry. *Infants and mothers: differences in development*. New York: Delacorte, 1969.

Brazelton, T. B., and Freedman, D. G. Manual to accompany Cambridge newborn behavior and neurological scales. In G. B. A. Stoelinga and J. J. Van Der Werff Ten Bosch (Eds.), *Normal and abnormal development of brain and behavior*. Leiden, Neth.: Leiden University Press, 1971.

Brazelton, T. Berry, Koslowski, Barbara, and Main, Mary. The origins of reciprocity: the early mother-infant interaction. In Michael Lewis and Leonard A. Rosenblum (Eds.), *The effect of the infant on its caregiver*. New York: Wiley, 1974.

Brennan, W. M., Ames, E. W., and Moore, E. W. Age differences in infants' attention to patterns of different complexities. *Science*, 1966, **151**, 354–356.

Brim, O. G. Macro-structural influences on child development and the need for childhood social indicators. *American Journal of Orthopsychiatry*, 1975, **45**, 516–524.

Brody, Sylvia. A mother is being beaten: an instinctual derivative and infant care. In E. James Anthony and Therese Benedek (Eds.), *Parenthood: its psychology and psychopathology*. Boston: Little, Brown, 1970.

Bronfenbrenner, Urie. The experimental ecology of education. *Educational Researcher*, 1976, **5**(9), 5–15.

Bronfenbrenner, Urie. The changing American child—a speculative analysis. In Urie Bronfenbrenner (Ed.), *Influences on human development*. Hinsdale, Ill.: Dryden, 1972.

Bronfenbrenner, Urie. *Two worlds of childhood: U.S. and U.S.S.R.* New York: Basic Books, 1970.

Bronfenbrenner, Urie. The measurement of sociometric status, structure, and development. *Sociometry Monographs*, No. 6. New York: Beacon, 1945.

Browdy, Harry S. Educational alternatives: why not. *Phi Delta Kappan*, 1973, **14**(7), 338–341.

Brown, Roger. *The first language: the early stages*. Cambridge, Mass.: Harvard University Press, 1973.

Brown, Roger. *Words and things*. New York: Free Press, 1958.

Brown, Roger, and Bellugi, Ursula. Three processes in the child's acquisition of language. In Eric H. Lennegerg (Ed.), *New directions in the study of language*, Cambridge, Mass.: MIT Press, 1964.

Bruner, Jerome S. *The process of education*. Cambridge, Mass.: Harvard University Press, 1966.

Bruner, Jerome S. The course of cognitive growth. *American Psychologist*, 1964, **19**, 1–15.

Burch, P. R. J. Schizophrenia: some new aetiological considerations. *British Journal of Psychiatry*, 1964, **110**, 818–824.

Burt, C. *Haddow Report, Appendix III*. London: 1931.

Calhoun, J. B. A comparative study of the social behavior of two inbred strains of house mice. *Ecological Monographs*, 1956, **26**, 81–103.

Cameron, J., Livson, N., and Bayley, N. Infant vocalizations and their relationship to mature intelligence. *Science*, 1967, **157**, 331–333.

Campbell, John D. Peer relations in childhood. In Irving B. Weiner and David Elkind (Eds.), *Readings in child development*. New York: Wiley, 1972.

Campos, Joseph J., Emde, Robert N., Gaensbauer, Theodore, and Henderson, Charlotte. Cardiac and behavioral interrelationships in the reactions of infants to strangers. *Developmental Psychology*, 1975, **11**, 589–601.

Canfield, Jack, and Wells, Harold C. *100 ways to enhance self-concept in the classroom*. Englewood Cliffs, N.J.: Prentice-Hall, 1976.

Caplan, Frank, and Caplan, Theresa. *The power of play*. Garden City, N.Y.: Anchor, 1974.

Carcuff, R. R. Differential functioning of lay and professional helpers. *Journal of Counseling Psychology*, 1968, **15**, 117–126.

Carmichael, Leonard. Onset and early development of behavior. In Paul H. Mussen (Ed.), *Carmichael's manual of child psychology*. New York: Wiley, 1970.

Carroll, J. B. Words, meanings, and concepts. *Harvard Educational Review*, 1964, **34**, 178–202.

Cattell, P. *The measurement of intelligence of infants and young children.* New York: Psychological Corporation, 1940.

Caudill, W., and Weinstein, H. Maternal care and infant behavior in Japanese and American urban middle class families. In R. Konig and R. Hill (Eds.), *Yearbook of the International Sociological Association*, 1966.

Cazden, Courtney B. (Ed.). *Books to guide teachers/parents.* In *Language in early childhood education.* Washington, D.C.: National Association for the Education of Young Children, 1972.

Child Development Institute. Games people play to help babies learn. *Developments*, 1976, **3**(2), 1–8.

Chomsky, Noam. *Aspects of the theory of syntax.* Cambridge, Mass.: MIT Press, 1965.

Church, Joseph. *Language and the discovery of reality.* New York: Vintage, 1961.

Clark, Matt. Troubled children: the quest for help. *Newsweek*, April 8, 1974, pp. 52–56.

Clark, Matt, and Monroe, Sylvester. Reconstruction. *Newsweek*, May 26, 1975, p. 57.

Clay, Marie M. Early childhood and cultural diversity in New Zealand. *Reading Teacher*, 1975, **29**(4), 333–342.

Coates, B., and Hartup, W. W. Age and verbalization in observational learning. *Developmental Psychology*, 1969, **1**, 556–562.

Cohn, Victor. Test to detect mongolism in fetus called safe. *Milwaukee Journal*, Oct. 21, 1975.

Coles, Robert. *Erik H. Erikson: the growth of his work.* Boston: Little, Brown, 1970.

Combs, Arthur W. The human side of learning. *National Elementary Principal*, 1973, **52**(4), 38–42.

Condon, William S., and Sander, Louis W. Neonate movement is synchronized with adult speech: interaction participation and language acquisition. *Science*, Jan. 11, 1974, **183**, 99–101.

Cooke, Gary E. Conceptual learning in young children: a comparison of the effect of rote, principle and guided discovery strategies on conceptualization in first grade children. Doctoral dissertation, University of Oregon, Eugene and Portland, 1971.

Coopersmith, S. *The antecedents of self-esteem.* San Francisco: Freeman, 1967.

Corbin, Charles B. *Becoming physically educated in the elementary school.* Philadelphia: Lea & Febiger, 1967.

Corbin, Charles B. Physical fitness of children. In Charles B. Corbin (Ed.), *A textbook of motor development.* Dubuque, Iowa: Wm. C. Brown Company Publishers., 1973.

Corbin, Charles B., and Pletcher, Philip. Diet and physical activity patterns of obese and nonobese elementary school children. *Research Quarterly*, 1968, **39**, 922.

Coryell, Dorothea. Three levels in learning to skip. Unpublished master's research paper, University of Oregon, Eugene and Portland, 1964.

Cratty, Bryant J. *Perceptual and motor development of infants and children.* New York: Macmillan, 1970.

Culliton, Barbara J. Intensive care for newborns: are there times to pull the plug? *Science*, 1975, **188**, 133–134.

Dancis, Joseph. Function of the placenta, barrier or bridge? In *Viral etiology of congenital malformations.* Bethesda, Md.: National Institutes of Health, 1968, pp. 67–73.

Davis, P. William, and Solomon, Eldra Pearl. *The World of biology.* New York: McGraw-Hill, 1974.

Decker, Celia Anita, and Decker, John R. *Planning and administering early childhood programs.* Columbus, Ohio: Merrill, 1976.

de Hirsch, Katrina, Langford, William S., and Jansky, Jeanette Jefferson. Comparisons of prematurely and maturely-born children. *American Journal of Orthopsychiatry*, 1965, **35**, 357–358.

del Ragato, John C. The utilization of echoic codes by visually handicapped in mathematical learning. Doctoral dissertaion, University of Oregon, Eugene and Portland, 1976.

482 References

Denenberg, V. H. Interactive effects of infantile and adult shock levels upon learning. *Psychological Reports*, 1959, **5**, 357–364.

Dennis, W. Environmental influences upon motor development. In *Readings in child psychology*, 2d ed. Englewood Cliffs, N.J.: Prentice-Hall, 1963, pp. 83–94.

Denny, E. Science performance of urban and rural children. Unpublished master's thesis, University of Montana, Missoula, 1960.

Devereau, Edward C., Shouval, Ron, Bronfenbrenner, Urie, Rodgers, Robert R., Kav-Venaki, Sophie, Kiely, Elizabeth, and Karson, Esther. Socialization practices of parents, teachers, and peers in Israel: the Kibbutz versus the city. *Child Development*, 1974, **45**, 268–281.

Dewey, John. *Democracy and education.* New York: Macmillan, 1926.

DiNucci, James M. Gross motor performance in children. In Jan Broekhoff (Ed.), *Physical education, sports and the sciences.* Eugene, Oreg.: Microform Publications, 1976.

Dobelle, W. H., and Mladejovsky, M. G. Artificial vision for the blind: electrical stimulation of visual cortex offers hope for a functional prosthesis. *Science*, 1974, **183**, 440–444.

Dodson, Fitzhugh. *How to father.* Los Angeles: Nash, 1974.

Douglas, Virginia I. Are drugs enough? To treat or to train the hyperactive child. Presentation to the Preconvention Institute of the International Reading Association, New York, May 1975.

Drillien, C. M. The growth and development of the prematurely born infant. In L. Joseph Stone, Henrietta T. Smith, and Lois B. Murphy (Eds.), *The competent infant.* New York: Basic Books, 1973.

Dudek, S. Z., Lester, E. P., Goldberg, J. S., and Dyer, G. G. Relationship of Piaget measures to standard intelligence and motor scales. *Perceptual and Motor Skills*, 1969, **28**, 351–362.

Dugeon, J. A. Breakdown in maternal protection: infections. In L. Joseph Stone, Henrietta, T. Smith, and Lois B. Murphy (Eds.), *The competent infant.* New York: Basic Books, Inc., 1973.

Durkin, Dolores. *Children who read early.* New York: Columbia Teachers College, 1966.

Durth, L., and Brown, K. B. Inadequate mothering and disturbance in the neonatal period. *Child Development*, 1961, **32**, 287–295.

Dykstra, R. Summary of the second grade phase of the Cooperative Research Program in primary reading instruction. *Reading Research Quarterly*, 1968, **4**(1), 49–70.

Eccles, Sir John. The synapse. *Scientific American*, Jan. 1965, **212**(1), 56–66.

Education of the gifted and talented. Subcommittee on Labor and Public Welfare, U.S. Senate, March 1972.

Eifermann, Rivka R. Social play in childhood. In R. E. Herron and Brian Sutton-Smith (Eds.), *Child's play.* New York: Wiley, 1971.

Eisenberg, Rita B. *Auditory competence in early life: roots of communicative behavior.* Baltimore: University Park Press, 1976.

Eliot, John, and Fralley, Jacqueline S. Sex differences in spatial abilities. *Young Children*, 1976, **31**(6) 487–498.

Elkind, David. Quantity conceptions in junior and senior high school students. *Child Development*, 1961, **32**, 551–560

El'konin, D. B. Some results of the study of the psychological development of preschool-age children. In Michael Cole and Irving Maltzman (Eds.), *A handbook of contemporary social psychology.* New York: Basic Books, 1969.

Emde, Robert N., and Roenig, Kenneth L. Neonatal smiling and rapid eye movement states. *Journal of the American Academy of Child Psychiatry*, 1969, **8**, 57–67.

Emde, R. N., and Metcalf, D. An EEG study of behavioral rapid eye movement states in the human newborn. *Journal of Nervous and Mental Diseases*, 1969, **150**, 376–386.

Erdelyi, G. J. Gynecolotical survey of female athletes. *Journal on Sports Medicine*, 1962, **2**, 174.

Erikson, Erik H. *Childhood and society*, 2d ed. New York: Norton, 1956.

Ervin, Susan M. Imitation in children's language. In E. H. Lenneberg (Ed.), *New directions in the study of language*. Cambridge, Mass., MIT Press, 1964.

Ervin-Tripp, Susan M. *Language acquisition and communicative choice*. Stanford, Calif.: Stanford University Press, 1973.

Escalona, Sibylle K. *The roots of individuality: normal patterns of development in infancy*. Chicago: Aldine, 1968.

Espenschade, Anna. Motor development. In Warren R. Johnson (Ed.), *Science and medicine of exercise and sports*. New York: Harper & Row, 1960.

Espenschade, A. S. Motor performance in adolescence including the study of relationships with measures of physical growth and maturity. *Monographs of the Society for Research in Child Development*, 1940, **5**(1), 1–126.

Espenschade, Anna S., and Eckert, Helen M. *Motor development*. Columbus, Ohio: Merrill, 1967.

Etzel, B. C., and Gewirtz, J. L. Experimental modification of caretaker-maintained high-rate operant crying in a 6- and 20-week-old infant. *Journal of Experimental Child Psychology*, 1967, **5**, 303–317.

Etzioni, Amitai. Science and the future of the family. *Science*, 1977, **196**(4289), 487.

Fagot, B. I., and Patterson, G. R. An in vivo analysis of reinforcing contingencies for sex role behaviors in the preschool child. *Developmental Psychology*, 1969, **1**, 563–568.

Fantz, R. L. Pattern discrimination and selective attention as determinants of perceptual development from birth. In A. H. Kidd and J. L. Rivoire (Eds.), *Perceptual development in children*. New York: International University Press, 1966.

Fantz, R. L. Visual perception from birth as shown by pattern selectivity. *Annals of New York Academy of Science*, 1965, **118**, 793–814.

Fantz, R. L., and S. Nevis. Pattern preferences and perceptual-cognitive development in early infancy. *Merrill-Palmer Quarterly*, 1967, **13**, 77–108.

Fantz, R. L., Ordy, J. M., and Udelf, M. S. Maturation of pattern vision in infants during the first six months. *Journal of Comparative Physiological Psychology*, 1962, **55**, 907–917.

Farley, Frank H., and Manske, Mary E. The relationship of individual differences in the orienting response to complex learning in kindergarteners. Paper presented at the annual meeting of the American Educational Research Association, Los Angeles, Feb. 6–9, 1969.

Farthing, Francis, E. The effect of male teachers on pupil's affective development. Doctoral dissertation, University of Oregon, Eugene and Portland, 1976.

Feingold, Ben F. *Why your child is hyperactive*. New York: Random House, 1975a.

Feingold, Ben F. Hyperkinesis and learning disabilities linked to artificial food flavors and colors. *American Journal of Nursing*, 1975b, 75(**5**), 797–803.

Feld, S. Studies in the origins of achievement strivings. Unpublished doctoral dissertation, University of Michigan, Ann Arbor, 1959.

Felker, D. W., and Thomas, S. B. Self-initiated verbal reinforcement and positive self-concept. *Child Development*, 1971, **42**, 1285–1287.

Fernald, Grace. *Remedial techniques in basic school subjects*. New York: McGraw-Hill, 1943.

Ferreira, Antonio J. *Prenatal environment*. Springfield, Ill.: Charles C Thomas, 1969.

Firme, T. P. Effects of social reinforcement on self-esteem of Mexican-American children. Doctoral dissertation, Stanford University. Ann Arbor, Mich.: University Microfilms, 1969, No. 70–1586.

Flick, G. L. Sinistrality revisited: a perceptual-motor approach. *Child Development*, 1967, **38**, 415.

Fox, David J., and Jordan, Valerie Burns. Racial preference and identification of black, American Chinese, and white children. *Psychological Monographs*, 1973, **88**, 229–286.

Fradkina, F. I. The psychology of play in early childhood (the genetic roots of preschool play). Candidate's dissertation, Moscow, 1946.

Francke, Linda Bird. Putting father back in the family. *Newsweek*, Sept. 22, 1975, p. 54.

Freed, Alvyn M. *T.A. for tots: transactional analysis for everybody series.* Sacramento, Calif.: Jalmar Press, 1973.

Freedman, Daniel G. *Human infancy: an evolutionary perspective.* New York: Wiley, 1974.

Freedman, D. G., and Keller, B. Inheritance of behavior in infants. *Science*, 1948, **140**, 196.

Freud, Anna. *Normality and pathology in childhood.* New York: International Universities Press, 1965a.

Freud, Anna. Emotional development of young children. In *Feelings and learning.* Washington, D.C.: Association for Childhood International, 1965b.

Freud, Anna. The concept of developmental lines. *Psychoanalytic Study Child*, 1963, **18**, 245–261.

Freud, Anna, and Dann, S. An experiment in group upbringing. In R. Fisler et al. (Eds.), *The psychoanalytic study of the child*, Vol. 6. New York: International Universities Press, 1951.

Freud, S. *Beyond the pleasure principle*, Vol. 18. Standard edition. London: Hogarth, 1955.

Froebel, F. *The education of man.* Tr. W. Hailmann. New York: Appleton, 1908.

Froebel, F. *Pedagogics of the kindergarten.* Tr. J. Jarvis. New York: Appleton, 1907.

Fromkin, Victoria, et al. The development of language in Genie: a case of language acquisition beyond the "critical period." *Brain and Language*, 1974, **1**, 81–107.

Frostig, Marianne, and Horne, D. Marianne Frostig Center of Educational Therapy. In M. Jones (Ed.). *Special education programs within the United States.* Springfield, Ill.: Charles C Thomas, 1968.

Furth, Hans G. *Piaget for teachers.* Englewood Cliffs, N.J.: Prentice-Hall, 1970.

Furth, Hans G. *Piaget and knowledge.* Englewood Cliffs, N.J., Prentice-hall, 1969.

Gallagher, James J. *Teaching the gifted child*, 2d ed. Boston: Allyn and Bacon, 1975.

Gallagher, J. J., and Bradley, R. H. Early identification of developmental difficulties. In *Early childhood education, 71st yearbook of the NSSE.* Chicago: University of Chicago Press, 1972.

Gardner, R. A., and Gardner, B. T. Early signs of language in child and chimpanzee. *Science*, Feb. 28, 1975, **187**, 752–753.

Garrett, Candace S. The effects of modeling on the development of sex-role behaviors in children. Unpublished doctoral dissertation, Iowa State University, Ames, 1973.

Gazzaniga, Michael S. The split brain in man. *Scientific American*, August 1967, **217**(2), 24–29.

Gearheart, B. R. *Learning disabilities: educational strategies.* St. Louis: Mosby, 1973.

Geber, M., and Dean, R. F. A. Le development psychomoteur et somatique des jeunes enfants Africains en Ouganda. *Courrier*, 1964, **14**, 425.

Geber, M., and Bean, R. F. A. Gesell tests on African children. *Pediatrics*, 1957, **30**, 1055–1065.

Gelman, Rochel. Conservation acquisition: a problem of learning to attend to relevant attributes. *Journal of Experimental Child Psychology*, 1969, **7**, 167–187.

Gentry, J. T., Parkhurst, E., and Bulin, G. V., Jr. An epidemiological study of congenital malformations in New York State. *American Journal of Public Health*, 1959, **49**, 497–513.

Gerbner, George, and Gross, Larry. Living with television: the violence profile. *Journal of Communication*, 1976, **26**(2), 176.

Geschwind, Norman. Language and the brain. *Scientific American*, April 1971, **226**, 76–83.

Geschwind, N. The organization of language and the brain. *Science*, 1970, **170**, 940–944.

Gesell, Arnold. The ontogenesis of infant behavior. In L. Carmichael (Ed.), *Manual of child psychology.* New York: Wiley, 1946.

Gesell, A. L., and Amatruda, C. S. *Developmental disgnosis.* New York: Hoeber, 1941.

Gesell, A. L., and Ames, L. B. The ontogenic organization of prone behavior in human infancy. *Journal of Genetic Psychology*, 1940, **56**, 247–263.

Gesell, A., and Ames, L. B. Tonic neck reflex and symetro-tonic behavior. *Journal of Pediatrics*, 1937, **36**(2), 165–176.

Gesell, Arnold, and Ilg, Frances L. *Infant and child in the culture of today.* New York: Harper, 1943.

Gewirtz, J. L. A factor analysis of some attention-seeking behavior of young children. *Child Development*, 1956, **21**, 17–36.

Gewirtz, J. L. Three determinants of attention-seeking in young children. *Monographs of the Society for Research in Child Development*, 1954, **19**(2), 59.

Gilbert, Christiane P. Creativity, conceptual tempo, humor, and IQ in first grade children. Doctoral dissertation, University of Oregon, Eugene and Portland, 1977.

Gilmore, J. Barnard, Play: a special behavior. In R. N. Haber (Ed.), *Current research in motivation.* New York: Holt, 1966.

Gilmore, Susan K. Grooming children for personal power. *Oregon STATO Newsletter*, 1976, **3**(2), 2.

Goertzel, V., and Goertzel, Mildred G. *Cradles of eminence.* Boston: Little, Brown, 1962.

Goldberg, Susan, and Lewis, Michael. Play behavior in the year-old infant: early sex differences. *Child Development*, 1969, **40**(1), 21–31.

Goodall, Jane. My life among wild chimpanzees. *National Geographic Magazine*, 1963, **124**(2), 278–308.

Goodenough, Florence L., and Harris, D. B. *Goodenough-Harris Drawing Test.* New York: Harcourt, Brace, Jovanovich, 1963.

Goodman, Kenneth S. Literacy as an extension of natural language learning: who killed cock robin. Sixth World Congress of Reading, Singapore, Aug. 17, 1976.

Goranson, R. E. Media violence and aggressive behavior: a review of experimental research. In L. Berkowitz (Ed.), *Advances in experimental social psychology*, Vol. 5. New York: Academic, 1970.

Gordon, Ira J. Parenting, teaching, and child development. *Young Children*, 1976, **31**(31), 173–183.

Gordon, Ira J. *Baby learning through baby play, parents' guide for the first two years.* New York: St. Martin's, 1970.

Gordon, Ira J. Early child stimulation through parent education. In Ira J. Gordon (Ed.), *Readings in research in developmental psychology.* Glenview, Ill.: Scott, Foresman, 1971.

Götz, Ignacio L. On children and television. In *Readings in Early Childhood Education, 1977/78.* Guilford, Conn.: Dushkin Publishing Group, 1977.

Green, Leonard. The "special" in special teacher. *Journal of Learning Disabilities*, October 1972.

Greenberg, D., Uzgiris, I., and Hunt, J. McV. Hastening the development of the blink-response. *Journal of Genetic Psychology*, 1968, **113**, 167–176.

Greenberg, Martin, and Morris, Norman. Engrossment: the newborn's impact upon the father. *American Journal of Orthopsychiatry*, 1974, **44**(4), 520–531.

Greenfield, Patricia Marks. On culture and conservation. In Jerome S. Bruner, Rose R. Oliver, and Patricia M. Greenfield et al. (Eds.), *Studies of cognitive growth.* New York: Wiley, 1966.

Griffiths, R. *The abilities of babies: a study of mental measurement.* New York: McGraw-Hill, 1954.

Gruenwald, Peter. Fetal growth retardation. In *Viral etiology of congenital malformations.* Bethesda, Md.: National Institutes of Health, 1968, pp. 35–45.

Guilford, J. P. Creative thinking and problem solving. *CTA Journal*, 1964, **60**(1), 8–10.

Guilford, J. P. Creativity: its measurement and development. An address to educators of Sacramento County, Sacramento, Calif., Jan. 20, 1959.

Guilford, J. P. Creative abilities in the arts. *Psychological Review*, 1957, **64**, 110–118.

Guilford, J. P., and Hoepfner, Ralph. *The analysis of intelligence.* New York: McGraw-Hill, 1971.

Gutteridge, M. V. A study of motor achievements of young children. *Archives of Psychology*, 1939, (244), 1–178.

Haaf, R. A., and Bell, R. Q. A facial dimension in visual discrimination by human infants. *Child Development*, 1967, **38**, 893–899.

Haan, Norma, and Day, David. A longitudinal study of change and sameness in personality development. In B. L. Neugarten et al. (Eds.), *International Journal of Aging and Human Development*, 1974, **5**(1), 11–39.

Haisley, Fay Sambrook. An evaluation of academic, attitudinal and social aspects in students admitted early to first grade. Doctoral dissertation, University of Oregon, Eugene and Portland, 1973.

Hallgren, B. *Specific dysleyia.* Copenhagen: Munkesgaard, 1950.

Halverson, L. E., and Robertson, M. A. A study of motor pattern development in young children. Report at the national convention of the American Association of Health, Physical Education, and Recreation, 1966.

Hamachek, Don E. *Encounters with the self.* New York: Holt, 1971.

Handel, Gerald. Sociological aspects of parenthood. In E. James Anthony and Therese Benedek (Eds.), *Parenthood: its psychology and psychopathology.* Boston: Little, Brown, 1970.

Handler, Philip. *Biology and the future of man.* New York: Oxford University Press, 1970.

Hargis, C. H. The relationship of available instructional reading materials to deficiency in reading achievement. *American Annals of the Deaf*, 1970, **115**(1).

Harlow, Harry F. Primary affectional patterns in primates. *American Journal of Orthopsychiatry*, 1960, 30, 676–684.

Harlow, H. F., and Harlow, M. Learning to love. *American Scientist*, 1966, **54**(3), 244–272.

Harper, A. E. Basic concepts. In *Improvement of protein nutriture.* National Academy of Sciences, Food and Nutrition Board, Committee on Amino Acids, Washington, D.C., 1974, pp. 1–22.

Harris, Dale B. *Children's drawings as measures of intellectual maturity: a revision and extension of the Goodenough Draw-a-Man Test.* New York: Harcourt, Brace & World, 1963.

Hartup, Willard W. Peer interaction and social organization. In Paul H. Mussen (Ed.), *Carmichael's manual of child psychology*, Vol. 2. New York: Wiley, 1970.

Hawkes, G. R., Burchinal, L. G. and Gardner, B. Pre-adolescents view of some of their relations with parents. *Child Development*, 1957, **28**, 393–399.

Hayden, Alice H., and Dmitriev, Valentine. Early and continuing intervention strategies for severely handicapped infants and very young children. In Norris G. Haring and Lou Brown (Eds.), *Teaching the severely handicapped.* New York: Grune & Stratton, 1975.

Hayden, Alice H., and Dmitriev, Valentine. *Manual: Down's syndrome performance inventories.* University of Washington, Model Preschool Center for Handicapped Children, Experimental Education Unit, Seattle, 1974.

Hayden, Alice H., and Edgar, Eugene B. Identification, screening, and assessment. In June B. Jordan et al. (Eds.), *Early childhood education for exceptional children.* Reston, Va.: Council for Exceptional Children, 1977.

Hayden, Alice H., McGinnes, Gael D. and Dmitriev, Valentine. Early and continuous intervention strategies for severely handicapped infants and very young children. In Norris G. Haring and Louis J. Brown (Eds.), *Teaching the severely handicapped*, Vol. 1. New York: Grune & Stratton, 1976.

Haynes, H., White, B. L. and Held, R. Visual accommodation in human infants. *Science*, 1965, **148**, 528–530.

Hayworth, J., and Goodin, F. Idiopathic spontaneous hypoglycemia in children. *Pediatrics*, 1960, **25**, 748–765.

Heath, Robert G. Marihuana: effects on deep and surface electroencephalograms of man. *Archives of General Psychiatry*, June 1972, **26**, 577–584.

Heathers, G. Emotional dependence and independence in nursery school play. *Journal of Genetic Psychology*, 1955, **87**, 37–57.

Heber, Rick, Garber, Howard, Harrington, Susan, and Hoffman, Caroline. *Rehabilitation of families at risk for mental retardation.* Rehabilitation Research and Training Center, University of Wisconsin, Madison, December 1972.

Hecaen, H., and deAjuriaguerra, Julian. *Left-handedness, manual superiority, and cerebral dominance.* New York: Grune & Stratton, 1964.

Held, Richard, and Bauer, J. A., Jr. Visually guided reaching in infant monkeys after restricted rearing. *Science*, 1967, **155**, 718–720.

Hendricks, C. H. Delivery patterns and reproductive efficiency among groups of differing socioeconomic status and ethnic origins. *American Journal of Obstetrics and Gynecology*, 1967, **97**, 608–624.

Herron, R. E., and Sutton-Smith, Brian. *Child's play.* New York: Wiley, 1971.

Hertig, A. T. The overall problem in man. In K. Benerschke (Ed.), *Comparative aspects of reproductive failure.* New York: Springer-Verlag, 1967.

Hess, Eckhard H. Ethology and developmental psychology. In Paul H. Mussen (Ed.), *Carmichael's manual of child psychology.* New York: Wiley, 1970.

Hess, Robert D., and Torney, Judith V. *The development of political attitudes in children.* Garden City, N.Y.: Doubleday, 1967.

Hetherington, E. Mavis. A developmental study of the effects of sex of the dominant parent on sex-role preference, identification and imitation in children. *Journal of Personality and Social Psychology*, 1965, **2**, 188–194.

Hetherington, E. Mavis, and Frankie, Gary. Effects of parental dominance, warmth, and conflict on imitation in children. *Journal of Personality and Social Psychology*, 1967, **6**(2), 119–125.

Hicks, Robert E., and Kinsbourne, Marcel. Human handedness: a partial cross-fostering study. *Science*, 1976, **192**, 908–910.

Hilgard, Ernest R., and Bower, Gordon H. *Theories of learning*, 4th ed. Englewood Cliffs, N.J.: Prentice-Hall, 1975..

Hindley, C. B., Filliozat, A. M., Klackenberg, G., Nicolet-Meister, D., and Sand, E. A. Differences in age of walking in five European longitudinal samples. *Human Biology*, 1966, **38**, 364–379.

Hoffman, H. S., Schiff, D., Adams, J., and Searle, J. L. Enhanced distress vocalization through selective reinforcement. *Science*, 1966, **151**, 353–354.

Hofstaetter, Peter R. The changing composition of "intelligence": a study in T-technique. *Journal of Genetic Psychology*, 1954, **85**, 159–164.

Hollenberg, Eleanor, and Sperry, Margaret. Some antecedents of aggression and effects of frustration in doll-play. *Personality*, 1951, **1**, 32–43.

Holt, Michael, and Dienes, Zoltan. *Let's play math.* New York: Walker, 1973.

Honzik, M. P. Environmental correlates of mental growth: predictions from the family setting at 21 months. *Child Development*, 1967, **38**, 337–364.

Hook, Ernest B. XXY genotype. *Science*, 1973, **179**, 139.

Hottinger, William L. Early motor development. In Charles B. Corbin (Ed.), *A textbook of motor development.* Dubuque, Iowa: William C. Brown Company Publishers, 1973.

488 References

Humphrey, N. K. Unfoldings of mental life. *Science,* 1977, **196**, 755–756.

Hurst, Lewis A. Etiology of mental disorders: genetics. In Benjamin B. Wolman (Ed.), *Manual of child psychopathology.* New York: McGraw-Hill, 1972.

Hyde, D. M. An investigation of Piaget's theories of the development of the conservation of number. Unpublished doctoral thesis, University of London, 1959.

Hyden, Holger. Biochemical aspects of learning and memory. In Karl H. Pribram (Ed.), *On the biology of learning.* New York: Harcourt, Brace & World, 1969.

Illingworth, R. S. Delayed motor development. *Pediatric Clinics of North America,* 1968, **15**, 569.

Inhelder, Bärbel. Intelligence and memory. Presentation to the annual conference of the American Reserach Association, Los Angeles, Feb. 3, 1969.

Isaacs, Ann F. Giftedness and careers. *Gifted Child Quarterly,* 1973, **17**(1), 57–59.

Jacobs, Patricia A. XYY Genotype. *Science,* 1975, **189**, 948.

Jacobs, Patricia A., Bruton, M., Melville, M. M., and McClemont, W. F. XYY genotype. *Nature* (London), 1965, **208**, 1351.

Jakobson, Roman. *Child language, aphasia and general sound laws.* Tr. Allan R. Keiler. The Hague: Mouton, 1968.

Jersild, A. T. *Child psychology,* 6th ed. Englewood Cliffs, N.J.: Prentice-Hall, 1968.

Joffe, J. M. *Prenatal determinants of behavior.* Oxford: Pergamon, 1969.

Johnson, Doris, J., and Myklebust, Helmer. *Learning disabilities: educational principles and practices.* New York: Grune & Stratton, 1971.

Johnson, E. Z. Attitudes of children toward authority as projected in their doll play at two age levels. Unpublished doctoral dissertation, Harvard University, Cambridge, Mass., 1951.

Jordan, June B., Hayden, Alice H., Karnes, Merle B., and Wood, Mary M. *Early childhood education for exceptional children. A handbook of ideas and exemplary practices.* Reston, Va.: The Council for Exceptional Children, 1977.

Kagan, Jerome. Do infants think? *Scientific American,* 1972, **226**, 74–82.

Kagan, Jerome. *Change and continuity in infancy.* New York: Wiley, 1971.

Kagan, Jerome. Continuity in cognitive development during the first year. *Merrill-Palmer Quarterly,* 1969, **15**, 101–119.

Kagan, Jerome. The concept of identification. *Psychological Review,* 1958, **65**(5), 296–305.

Kagan, Jerome, and Kagan, Nathan. Individual variation in cognitive processes. In Paul H. Mussen (Ed.), *Carmichael's manual of child psychology,* Vol. 1. New York: Wiley, 1970.

Kagan, J., and Lemkin, I. The child's differential perception of parental attributes. *Journal of Abnormal and Social Psychology,* 1960, **61**, 440–447.

Kakalik, J. S., Brewer, G. D., Dougherty, L. A., Fleischauer, P. D., Genensky, S. M., and Wallen, L. M. *Improving services to handicapped children.* Santa Monica, Calif.: The Rand Corporation, 1974.

Kallmann, F. J., and Roth, B. Genetic aspects of preadolescent schizophrenia. *American Journal of Psychiatry,* 1956, **112**, 599–606.

Kamii, Constance, and DeVries, Rheta. *Piaget, children, and number.* Washington, D.C.: National Association for the Education of Young Children, 1976.

Kaplan, Eleanor L., and Kaplan, G. A. The prelinguistic child. In J. Eliot (Ed.), *Human development and the cognitive processes.* New York: Holt, 1970.

Karnes, Merle B., and Zehrbach, R. Reid. Alternative models for bringing services to young handicapped children. In June B. Jordan et al. (Eds.). *Early childhood education for exceptional children.* Reston, Va.: Council for Exceptional Children, 1977.

Kasper, Joseph C., and Schulman, Jerome L. Organic mental disorders: brain damages. In Benjamin B. Wolman (Ed.), *Manual of child psychopathology*. New York: McGraw-Hill, 1972.

Katz, Bernhard. How cells communicate. *Scientific American*, September 1961, pp. 1–12.

Katz, Phyllis A., Sohn, Marilyn, and Zalk, Sue Rosenberg. Perceptual concomitants of racial attitudes in urban gradeschool children. *Developmental Psychology*, 1975, **11**, 135–144.

Kaufman, I. Charles. Biologic considerations of parenthood. In E. James Anthony and Therese Benedek (Eds.), *Parenthood: its psychology and psychopathology*. Boston: Little, Brown, 1970.

Kaye, H. The conditioned Babkin reflex in human newborns. *Psychomonic Science*, 1965, **2**, 287–288.

Kaye, H., and Bosack, T. N. *Journal of Experimental Child Psychology*. 1969, **4**, 163–168.

Keller, Helen. *Teacher: Ann Sullivan Macy*. New York: Doubleday, 1955.

Kellogg, Rhoda. *Analyzing children's art*. Palo Alto, Calif.: May Field Publishing Comapny, 1970.

Kellogg, R., and O'Dell, S. *Analyzing children's art*. Palo Alto, Calif.: National Press Books, 1969.

Kendler, H. H., and Kendler, T. S. Vertical and horizontal processes in problem solving. *Psychological Review*, 1962, **69**, 1–16.

Kendler, T. S., and Kendler, H. H. Experimental analysis of inferential behavior in children. In L. P. Lipsitt and C. C. Spiker (Eds.,) *Advances in child development and behavior*, Vol. 3. New York: Academic, 1967.

Keogh, J. F. Analysis of individual tasks on the Stott Test of Motor Impairment. Technical Report 2-68, U.S. Public Health Service Grant No. HD 01059. University of California, Department of Physical Education, Los Angeles, 1968.

Kephart, N. C. Perceptual-motor aspects of learning disabilities. *Exceptional Children*, 1964, **31**, 201.

Kessler, Jane W. Neurosis in childhood. In Benjamin B. Wolman (Ed.), *Manual of child psychopathology*. New York: McGraw-Hill, 1972.

Kessen, W. Ambiguous Commitment. *Science*, 1976, **193**, 310–311.

Kessen, W., Haith, M. M., and Salapatek, P. H. Human infancy: a bibliography and guide. In Paul H. Mussen (Ed.), *Carmichael's manual of child psychology*. New York: Wiley, 1970.

Klindová, Luboslava. Attempt at characterizing a pupil with intellectual abilities above the average. *Jednotna Skola*, 1973, **25**(9), 822–836.

Klindová, Luboslava. Psychological problems with talented children in the light of latest research. *Jednotna Skolä*, 1970, **22**(2), 145–158.

Knittle, Jerome L., and Hirsch, Jules. Effect of early nutrition on the development of fat epididymal fat pads: cellularity and metabolism. *Journal of Clinical Investigation*, 1968, **47**, 2091.

Koep, Robert G. The effect of social and cognitive interaction strategies on children's motivation to achieve in school. Unpublished doctoral dissertation, University of Oregon, Eugene and Portland, 1972.

Kohlberg, Lawrence. Stage and sequence: the cognitive-developmental approach to socialization. In David A. Goslin (Ed.), *Handbook of socialization theory and research*. Chicago: Rand McNally, 1969.

Kohlberg, L., and DeVries, R. Relations between Piaget and psychometric assessments of intelligence. Paper presented at the Conference on the Natural Curriculum, Urbana, Ill., 1969.

Kohlberg, Lawrence, LaCrosse, Jean, and Ricks, David. The predictability of adult mental health from childhood behavior. In Benjamin R. Wolman (Ed.), *Manual of child psychopathology*. New York: McGraw-Hill, 1972.

Kohlberg, Lawrence, and Turiel, Elliot. Moral development and moral education. In Gerald S. Lesser (Ed.), *Psychology and educational practice*. Glenview, Ill.: Scott, Foresmann, 1971.

Kolata, Gina Bari. Behavioral development: effects of environments. *Science*, 1975, **189**, 207–209.

Korner, Anneliese F. The effect of the infant's state, level of arousal, sex, and ontogenic stage on the caregiver. In Michael Lewis and Leonard A. Rosenblum (Eds.), *The effect of the infant on its caregiver.* New York: Wiley, 1974.

Korner, Anneliese F., and Grobstein, Rose. Visual alertness as related to soothing in neonates: implications for maternal stimulation and early deprivation. *Child Development*, 1966, **37**, 867–876.

Krathwohl, D. R. Stating objectives appropriately for program, for curriculum, and for instructional materials' development. *Journal of Teacher Education*, 1965, **12**, 83–92.

Krathwohl, David R., Bloom, Benjamin S., and Masia, Bertram B. *Taxonomy of educational objectives. Handbook II: affective domain.* New York: McKay, 1964.

Krech, David. Psychoneurobiochemeducation. *Phi Delta Kappan*, 1969, **50**, 370–375.

Krippner, Stanley, and Blickenstaff, Ralph. The development of self-concept as part of an arts workship for the gifted. *Gifted Child Quarterly*, 1970, **14**(3), 163–166.

Kron, Reuben E., Stein, Marvin, and Goddard, Katherine E. Newborn sucking behavior affected by obstetric sedation. *Pediatrics*, 1966, **37**, 1012–1016.

Kruger, W. Stanley. Education for parenthood and the schools. *Children Today*, 1973, **2**(2), 4–7.

Kuhn, D., Langer, J., and Kohlberg, L. Relations between logical and moral development. In L. Kohlberg (Ed.), *Recent research in moral development.* New York: Holt, 1977.

Kupferberg, Herbert. Baby power. *Parade*, April 9, 1972, p. 29.

Langman, Jan. *Medical embryology*, 3d ed. Baltimore: Williams & Wilkins, 1975.

Lapedes, Daniel N. (Ed.). *Dictionary of scientific and technical terms.* New York: McGraw-Hill, 1974.

Larrick, Nancy. Children of television. *Readings in early childhood education*, 1977/78. Guilford, Conn.: Dushkin Publishing Group, 1977.

Lasher, Robert. Developmental biology. In Jess Minckler (Ed.), *Introduction to neuroscience.* Saint Louis: Mosby, 1972.

Lavatelli, Celia. *Early childhood curriculum: a Piaget program*, 2d ed. *Teacher's guide.* Boston: American Science and Engineering, 1973.

LeClaire, Lawrence G. The concept and function of play in education. Unpublished doctoral dissertation, University of Oregon, Eugene and Portland, 1975.

Lehane, Stephen. *Help your baby learn: 100 Piaget-based activities for the first two years of life.* Englewood Cliffs, N.J.: Prentice-Hall, 1976.

Lenneberg, Eric H. *Biological foundations of language.* New York: Wiley, 1967.

Lenneberg, Eric H. Speech development: its anatomical and psyiological concomitants. In Edward C. Carterette (Ed.). *Brain function III: speech, language, and communication.* Berkeley and Los Angeles: University of California Press, 1966.

Lenneberg, Eric H. (Ed.). *New directions in the study of language.* Cambridge, Mass.: MIT Press, 1964.

Lenski, Gerhard, and Lenski, Jean. *Human societies: an introduction to Macrosociology.* New York: McGraw-Hill, 1974.

Lerner, Richard, M., and Buerig, Christie J. The development of racial attitudes in young black and white children. *Journal of Genetic Psychology*, 1975, **127**, 45–54.

Lesser, Gerald S. *Children and television.* New York: Random House, 1974.

Lester, Henry A. The response to acetylcholine. *Scientific American*, 1977, **236**(2), 106–116.

Let's look at first graders. Princeton, N.J.: Science Research Associates, 1967.

Levin, H., and Wardwell, E. The research uses of doll play. *Psychological Bulletin*, 1962, **59**(1), 27–56.

Levin, Stephen R., and Anderson, Daniel R. The development of attention. *Journal of Communication*, 1976, **26**(2), 128.

LeVine, Robert A. Cross-cultural study in child psychology. In Paul H. Mussen (Ed.), *Carmichael's manual of child psychology*, 3d ed. New York: Wiley, 1970.

Lewis, M., Kagan, J., and Kalafat, J. Patterns of fixation in the young infant. *Child Development*, 1966, **37**, 331–334.

Lewis, Michael, and Lee-Painter, Susan. An interaction approach to the mother-infant dyad. In Michael Lewis and Leonard A. Rosenblum (Eds.), *The effect of the infant on its caregiver*. New York: Wiley, Sons, 1974.

Lewis, Michael, and Rosenblum, Leonard A. *The effect of the infant on its caregiver*. New York: Wiley, 1973.

Lipsitt, L. P. Learning processes of human newborns. In Ira J. Gordon (Ed.), *Readings in research in developmental psychology*. Glenview, Ill.: Scott, Foresman, 1971.

Lipsitt, L. P. Learning in the human infant. In H. W. Stevenson, E. H. Hess, and H. L. Rheingold (Eds.), *Early behavior: comparative and developmental approaches*. New York: Wiley, 1967.

Lipsitt, L. P., Kaye, H., and Bosack, T. N. Enhancement of neonatal sucking through reinforcement. *Journal of Experimental Psychology*, 1966, **4**, 163–168.

Lockhart, Aileene S. The motor learning of children. In Charles B. Corbin (Ed.), *A textbook of motor development*. Dubuque, Iowa: Wm. C. Brown Company Publishers, 1973.

Long, Barbara H., Henderson, Edmund H., and Ziller, Robert C. Developmental changes in the self-concept during middle childhood. *Merrill-Palmer Quarterly*, 1967, **13**, 201–215.

Lorente De No, R. Analysis of the activity of the chains of internumcial neurons. *Journal of Neurophysiology*, 1938, **1**, 207–244.

Lorenz, Konrad. The enmity between generations and its probable ethological causes. In Maria W. Piers (Ed.), *Play and development*. New York: Norton, 1972.

Lorenz, Konrad. Innate bases of learning. In Karl H. Pribram (Ed.), *On the biology of learning*. New York: Harcourt, Brace & World, 1969.

Lovell, K., and A. Gorton. A study of some differences between backward and normal readers of average intelligence. *British Journal of Educational Psychology*, 1968, **38**(3), 240–248.

Luria, A. R. *Cognitive development and its cultural and social foundations*. Cambridge, Mass.: Harvard University Press, 1976.

Luria, A. R. Towards the basic problems of neurolinguistics. *Brain and Language*, 1974, **1**, 1–14.

Luria, A. R. *The working brain: an introduction to neuropsychology*. New York: Basic Books, 1973.

Luria, A. R. *The role of speech in the regulation of normal and abnormal behavior*. New York: Liveright, 1961.

Lytle, Loy D., Messing, Rita B., Fisher, Laurel, and Phebus, Lee. Effects of long-term corn consumption on brain serotonin and the response to electric shock. *Science*, 1975, **290**, 692–694.

Maccoby, Eleanor Emmons, and Jacklin, Carol Nagy. *The psychology of sex differences*. Stanford, Calif.: Stanford University Press, 1974.

Maccoby, Eleanor E., and Masters, John C. Attachment and dependency. In Paul H. Mussen (Ed.), *Carmichael's manual of child psychology*, Vol. 2. New York: Wiley, 1970.

MacKinnon, Donald W. Personality and the realization of creative potential. *American Psychologist*, 1965, **20**, 273–281.

MacKinnon, Donald W. The nature and nurture of creative talent. *American Psychologist*, 1962, **17**, 484–495.

MacLeod, Celeste. Legacy of battering. In David Elkind and Donna C. Hetzel (Eds.), *Readings in human development: contemporary perspectives*. New York: Harper & Row, 1977.

Mace, G. A. Psychology and aesthetics. *British Journal of Aesthetics*, 1962, **2**, 3–16.

Magoun, H. W. Advances in brain research with implications for learning. In Karl H. Pribram (Ed.), *On the biology of learning*. New York: Harcourt, Brace, & World, 1969.

Mahler, Margaret S., Pine, Fred, and Bergman, Anni. The mother's reaction to her toddler's drive for individuation. In E. James Anthony and Therese Benedek (Eds), *Parenthood: its psychology and psychotherapy*. Boston: Little, Brown, 1970.

Malina, Robert M. Physical development factors and motor performance. In Charles B. Corbin (Ed.), *A textbook of motor development*. Dubuque, Iowa: Wm. C. Brown Company Publishers, 1973.

Malmquist, Carl P. Depressive phenomena in children. In Bengamin B. Wolman (Ed.), *Manual of child psychopathology*. New York: Wiley, 1972.

Mann, I. *The development of the human eye*. London: British Medical Association, 1964.

Manyuk, Paula. Relations between acquisition of phonology and reading. In John T. Guthrie (Ed.), *Aspects of reading acquisition*. Baltimore: Johns Hopkins, 1976.

Margolis, George. Fetal pathology due to a group of DNA viruses. In *Viral etiology of congenital malformations*. Bethesda, Md.: National Institutes of Health, 1968, pp. 46–66.

Marx, Jean L. Hemophilia: new information about the "royal disease." *Science*, 1975, **188**, 41–42.

Mather, June. *Make the most of your baby*. Arlington, Tex.: National Association for Retarded Citizens, 1974.

McCall, R. B., and Kagan, J. Attention in the infant: effects of complexity, contour, perimeter, and familiarity. *Child Development*, 1967, **38**, 939–952.

McClearn, Gerald E. Genetic influences on behavior and development. In Paul H. Mussen (Ed.), *Carmichael's manual of child psychology*, 3d ed., Vol. 1. New York: Wiley, 1970.

McClelland, D. C. *The Achieving Society*. Princeton, N.J.: Van Nostrand, 1961.

McDaniels, Garry L. The evaluation of Follow Through. *Educational Researcher*, 1975, **4**(11), 7–11.

McGraw, Myrtle B. *The neuromuscular maturation of the human infant*. New York: Hafner, 1966.

McGraw, Myrtle B. *The neuromuscular maturation of the human infant*. New York: Columbia University Press, 1945.

McGraw, Myrtle B. Development of the neuromuscular mechanism as reflected in the crawling and creeping behavior of the human infant. *Journal of Genetic Psychology*, 1941, **58**, 83–111.

McGraw, Myrtle B. Neuromuscular development of the human infant as exemplified in the achievement of locomotion. *Journal of Pediatrics*, December 1940, **17**(6), 747–771.

McGraw, Myrtle B. *Growth: a study of Johnny and Jimmy*. New York: Appleton-Century-Crofts, 1935.

McNeill, David. The development of language. In Paul H. Mussen (Ed.), *Carmichael's manual of child psychology*, Vol. 1. New York: Wiley, 1970.

Mead, Margaret, and MacGregor, F. C. *Growth and culture: a photographic study of Balinese childhood*. New York: Putnam, 1951.

Merei, Ferenc. Group leadership and institutionalization. In Morris L. Haimowitz and Natalie Reader Haimowitz (Eds.), *Human development: selected readings*, 3d ed. New York: Thomas Y. Crowell, 1973.

Miller, G. A., Galanter, E. H., and Pribram, K. H. *Plans and structure of behavior*. New York: Holt, 1960

Milunsky, Aubrey. *The prenatal diagnosis of hereditary disorders*. Springfield, Ill.: Charles C Thomas, 1973.

Minkowski, Alexandre (Ed.). *Regional development of the brain early in life*. Philadelphia: Davis, 1967.

Mittwoch, Ursula. *Genetics of sex differentiation*. New York: Academic, 1973.

Mittwoch, Ursula. *Sex chromosomes*. New York: Academic, 1967.

Montagu, M. F. A. *Prenatal influences*. Springfield, Ill.: Charles C Thomas, 1962.

Montessori, Maris. *The Montessori Method*. Tr. A. E. George. New York: Shocken, 1964.

Moreno, B. M., and Moreno, J. L. Role tests and role diagrams of children. *Sociometry*, 1947, **8**, 427–441.

Morris, William (Ed.). *American Heritage Dictionary*. Boston: Houghton Mifflin, 1973.

Moss, Howard A. Sex, age, and state as determinants of mother-infant interaction. *Merrill-Palmer Quarterly*, 1967, **13**, 19–36.

Moss, Howard A. Early environmental effects: mother-child relations. In Thomas D. Spencer and Norman Kass (Eds.), *Perspectives in child psychology*. New York: McGraw-Hill, 1970.

Moss, Howard A., and Kagan, Jerome. Report on personality consistency and change from the Fels longitudinal study. In Ira J. Gordon (Ed.), *Readings in research in developmental psychology*. Glenview, Ill.: Scott, Foresman, 1971.

Moss, H. A., and Robson, K. S. The relation between the amount of time infants spend at various states and the development of visual behavior. *Child Development*, 1970, **41**, 509–517.

Moss, H. A., and Robson, K. S. Maternal influences in early social visual behavior. *Child Development*, 1968, **39**, 401–408.

Moustakas, Clark E. *Children in play therapy*. New York: McGraw-Hill, 1953.

Mowrer, O. H. *Learning theory and the symbolic process*. New York: Wiley, 1960.

Mueller, E. Origins of success and failure in children's spontaneous communication. In *Procedings of the 79th Annual Conference of the American Psychological Association*, 1971, pp. 153–154.

Mukerji, Rose. TV's impact on children: a checkerboard scene. *Phi Delta Kappan*, January 1976, **57**(5), 316–318.

Murphy, Lois B. Sex differences in coping and developing. In L. J. Stone, H. T. Smith, and L. B. Murphy (Eds.), *The competent infant*. New York: Basic Books, 1973.

Mussen, Paul H., and Distler, L. Child rearing antecedents of masculine identification in kindergarten boys. *Child Development*, 1960, **31**, 89–100.

Mussen, Paul H., and Parker, Ann L. Mother nurturance and girls' incidental imitative learning. *Journal of Personality and Social Psychology*, 1965, **2**(1), 94–97.

Myklebust, Helmer. *Auditory disorders in children*. New York: Grune & Stratton, 1954.

Neumann, E. A. The elements of play. Unpublished doctoral dissertation, University of Illinois, Urbana-Champaign, 1971.

Newland, T. Ernest. *The gifted in socioeducational perspective*. Englewood Cliffs, N.J.: Prentice-Hall, 1976.

Newson, John, and Newson, Elizabeth. *Four years old in an urban community*. Chicago: Aldine, 1968.

Newsweek. The thalidomide generation. Feb. 3, 1975, pp. 32–33.

Newsweek. Stunted growth. Sept. 29, 1975, p. 93.

Newsweek. Grafts from the newborn. Sept. 29, 1975. p. 93.

Nickerson, E. T. Recent approaches to innovations in play therapy. *International Journal of Child Psychotherapy*, 1973, **2**, 53–70.

Nilsson, Lennart. *Behold man*. Boston: Little, Brown, 1973.

Ogletree, Earl J. Intellectual growth in children and the theory of "bioplasmic forces." *Phi Delta Kappan*, February 1974, **55**, 407–412.

Orton, J. *A guide to teaching phonics*. Cambridge, Mass.: Educator's Publishing Service, 1965.

Otis, N. B., and McCandless, B. R. Responses to repeated frustrations of young children differentiated according to need area. *Journal of Abnormal Psychology*, 1955, **50**, 349–353.

Pai, Anna, C. *Foundations of genetics*. New York: McGraw-Hill, 1974.

Painter, Genevieve. *Teaching your baby*. New York: Simon & Schuster, 1971.

Paivio, Allan. Imagery and long-term memory. In Alan Kennedy and Alan Wilkes (Eds.), *Studies in long term memory*. New York: Wiley, 1975.

Parmelee, A. H., Akiyama, Y., Wenner, W. H., and Flescher, J. *REM sleep of premature infants.* Paper presented to the Association for Psychophysiological Study of Sleep. Palo Alto, Calif., March 1964.

Parten, Mildred B. Social play among preschool children. *Journal of Abnormal Psychology*, 1933, **28**, 136–147.

Pasamanick, B., and Knoblock, H. Brain damage and reproductive causality. *American Journal of Orthopsychiatry*, 1960, **30**, 298–305.

Pasamanick, B., Rogers, M. E., and Lillienfeld, A. M. Pregnancy experience and the development of behavior disorder in children. *American Journal of Psychiatry*, 1956, **112**, 613–618.

Patterson, G. R., Littman, R. A., and Bricker, W. Assertive behavior in children: a step toward a theory of aggression. *Monographs of the Society for Research in Child Development*, 1967, **32**(5), 1–43.

Peeples, David R., and Teller, Davida Y. Color vision and brightness discrimination in two-month-old human infants. *Science*, Sept. 26, 1975, **189**, 1102–1103.

Peiper, A. Die schreibewegungen der neugeborenen. *Menatsschrift. Kinderheilklinik.* 1929, **45**, 444–448.

Peiper, A. *Cerebral function in infancy and childhood.* Tr. B. Nagler and H. Nagler. New York: Consultants Bureau, 1963.

Pellegrini, Robert J., and Hicks, Robert A. Prophesy effects and tutorial instruction for the disadvantaged child. *American Educational Journal*, 1973, **6**(3), 413–419.

Peller, Lili E. Models of children's play. *Mental Hygiene*, 1952, **36**, 62–83.

Pendergast, Kathleen. A case history of the language development of twins. Unpublished master's thesis, University of Washington, Seattle, 1954.

Penfield, Wilder. *The mystery of the mind.* Princeton, N.J.: Princeton University Press, 1975.

Penfield, Wilder, and Roberts, Lamar. *Speech and brain mechanisms.* Princeton, N.J.: Princeton University Press, 1959.

Phillips, R. H. The use of behavior modification to improve self-esteem in low income elementary school children. Doctoral dissertation, Fordham University. Ann Arbor, Mich.: University Microfilms, 1975, No. 75-18,920.

Piaget, Jean. *The child and reality: problems of genetic psychology.* Tr. Arnold Rosin. New York: Penguin, 1976.

Piaget, Jean. Some aspects of operations. In Maria W. Piers (Ed.), *Play and development.* New York: Norton, 1972.

Piaget, Jean. *Biology and knowledge.* Chicago: University of Chicago Press, 1971.

Piaget, Jean. *Structuralism.* New York: Basic Books, 1970.

Piaget, Jean. The theory of stages in cognitive development. Tr. Sylvia Opper. An address to the CTB/McGraw-Hill Invitational Conference on Ordinal Scales of Cognitive Development, Monterey, Calif., Feb. 9, 1969.

Piaget, Jean. Development and learning. In Richard E. Ripple and Verne N. Rockcastle (Eds.), *Piaget rediscovered. Report of the Conference on Cognitive Studies.* Cornell University, School of Education, Ithaca, N.Y., March 1964.

Piaget, Jean. *The language and thought of the child.* London: Routledge and Kegan Paul, Ltd., 1959.

Piaget, Jean. *The construction of reality in the child.* Tr. Margaret Cook. New York: Basic Books, 1954.

Piaget, Jean. *The origins of intelligence in children.* New York: Norton, 1952.

Piaget, Jean. *Play, dreams, and imitation in childhood.* New York: Norton, 1951.

Piaget, Jean. *The child's conception of the world*, 1926. Tr. Joan and Andrew Tomlinson. New York: Harcourt, Brace & World, 1928.

Pines, Maya. *The brain changers: scientists and the new mind control.* New York: Harcourt, Brace, Jovanovich, 1973.

Pister, Alice. Exploration, play and creativity in infancy. Unpublished master's field study, University of Oregon, Eugene and Portland, 1973.

Plowman, Paul D., and Rice, Joseph P. *Final report: California Project Talent.* Sacramento: California State Department of Education, 1969.

Premack, David. *Intelligence in ape and man.* Hillsdale, N.J.: Halsted, 1976.

Pribram, Karl H. 4-R's of remembering. Presentation to the Preconvention Institute of the International Reading Association on Brain Functions and Reading. New York, May 12, 1975.

Pribram, Karl H. *Languages of the brain.* Englewood Cliffs, N.J.: Prentice-Hall, 1971.

Pribram, Karl H. (Ed.), *On the biology of learning.* New York: Harcourt, Brace & World, 1967.

Pribram, Karl H. Some dimensions of remembering: steps toward a neurophysiological model of memory. In J. Gaito (Ed.), *Macromolecules and behavior.* New York: Academic, 1966.

Pryor, H. B., and Stolz, H. R. Determining appropriate weight for body build. *Journal of Pediatrics,* 1933, **3**, 608–622.

Psychology Today. White, western culture produced disadvantaged babies. Nov., 1972. p. 41.

Rainer, J. D., Altshuler, K. Z., and Kallman, F. J. *Family and mental health problems in a deaf population.* New York: New York State Psychiatric Institute, 1963.

Rakic, Pasko. Neurons in Rhesus monkey visual cortex: systematic relation between time of origin and eventual disposition. *Science,* Feb. 1, 1974, **183**, 425–427.

Rarick, G. Lawrence. *Motor development during infancy and childhood.* Madison, Wis.: College Printing Company, 1961.

Raven, R. J., and Salzer, R. T. Piaget and reading instruction. *The reading teacher,* April 1971, **2**(7), 630–639.

Reynolds, E. L. Degree of kinship and pattern of ossification. *American Journal of Physical Anthropology,* 1943, 405–416.

Rheingold, H. L., and Eckerman, C. O. Fear of the stranger: a critical examination. Paper presented at annual meeting of the Society for Research in Child Development. Minneapolis, April 1971.

Rheingold, H. L., Gewirtz, J. L., and Ross, H. Social conditioning and vocalization in the infant. *Journal of Comparative Physiological Psychology,* 1959, **52**, 68–73.

Rider, Barbara. Perceptual motor dysfunction in emotionally disturbed children. *American Journal of Occupational Therapy,* 1973, **26**(6), 316–320.

Rider, Barbara A. Tonic neck reflexes. *American Journal of Occupational Therapy,* 1972, **26**(3), 132–134.

Robeck, Bruce W. Bibliography of political socialization. Mimeographed. College Station, Tex.: Texas A&M University, February 1970.

Robeck, Mildred C., and Wilson, John A. R. *Psychology of Reading.* New York: Wiley, 1974.

Robeck, Mildred C. Identifying and preventing reading disabilities. In John A. R. Wilson (Ed.), *Diagnosis of learning difficulties.* New York: McGraw-Hill, 1971.

Robeck, Mildred C., and Wilson, John A. R. *Kindergarten evaluation of learning potential: KELP resource guide.* New York: McGraw-Hill, 1969.

Robeck, Mildred C. *Acceleration programs for intellectually gifted children.* Sacramento: California State Department of Education, 1968a.

Robeck, Mildred C. *Special class programs for intellectually gifted pupils.* Sacramento: California State Department of Education, 1968b.

Robeck, Mildred C. Effects of prolonged reading disability: a preliminary study. *Perceptual and Motor Skills,* 1964, **19**, 7–12.

Rock, Irvin. *The nature of perceptual adaptation.* New York: Basic Books, 1966.

Roffwarg, Howard P., Muzio, Joseph N., and Dement, William C. Ontogenetic development of the human sleep-dream cycle. *Science,* April 29, 1966, **152,** 604–619.

Roller, Ann. *Discovering the basis of life.* New York: McGraw-Hill, 1974.

Rosenbaum, Arthur L., Churchill, John A., Shakhashiri, Zekin A., and Moody, Richard L. Neuropsychological outcome of children whose mothers had proteinuria during pregnancy: a report from the collaborative study of cerebral palsy. *Journal of Obstetrics and Gynecology,* 1969, **33,** 118–123.

Rosenshine, Barak Victor, and Berliner, David C. Academic engaged time. *British Journal of Teacher Education,* 1977 (in press).

Rothbart, Mary K., and Maccoby, Eleanor E. Familial influences on socialization and personality development. *Journal of Personality and Social Psychology,* 1966, **4**(3), 237–243.

Rousseau, Jean Jacques. *Emile.* R. L. Archer (Ed. and Tr.). Woodbury, N.Y.: Barron's, 1964.

Rubin, Harry. Chemical element's role in regulating cell processes. *Proceedings of the National Academy of Sciences,* 1975.

Ruebush, B. K. Anxiety. In H. W. Stevenson (Ed.), *Child psychology.* 62d Yearbook of the National Society for the Study of Education. Chicago: University of Chicago Press, 1963, pp. 460–514.

Rugh, Roberts, and Shettles, Landrum B. *From conception to birth.* New York: Harper & Row, 1971.

Rumbaugh, Duane M. *Language learning by a chimpanzee.* New York: Academic, 1977.

Russell, David H. *Children's thinking.* Boston. Ginn, 1956.

Salk, L. Mother's heartbeat as an imprinting stimulus. *Transactions of the New York Academy of Science,* 1962, **24,** 753–763.

Sampson, E. E. Birth order, need achievement, and conformity. *Journal of Abnormal* and *Social Psychology,* 1962, **64,** 155–159.

Samuels, S. Jay. Success and failure in learning to read: a critique of the research. *Reading Research Quarterly,* 1973, **8**(2), 200–239.

Sara, Vicki R., Lazarus, L., Stuart, M. C., and King, T. Fetal brain growth: selective action by growth hormone. *Science,* 1974, **186,** 446–447.

Satir, Virginia. *Conjoint family therapy.* Palo Alto, Calif.: Science and Behavior Books, 1964.

Scammon, R. E. *The measurement of man.* Minneapolis: University of Minnesota Press, 1930.

Scarr, S. Environmental bias in twin studies. *Eugenics Quarterly,* 1968, **15,** 34.

Scarr, S., and Salapatek, P. Patterns of fear development during infancy. *Merrill-Palmer Quarterly,* 1970, **16,** 53–90.

Schaffer, H. R., and Emerson, P. E. The development of social attachments in infancy. *Monographs on Social Research in Child Development,* 1964, **29,** 3.

Schaffer, H. R., and Emerson, P. E. Patterns of response to physical contact in early human development. *Journal of Child Psychology and Psychiatry,* 1964, **5,** 1–13.

Schechter, Marshall D., Toussieng, Povl W., Sternlof, Richard E., and Pollack, Ethan A. Etiology of mental disorders: prenatal, natal, and postnatal organic factors. In Benjamin B. Wolman (Ed.), *Manual of child psychopathology.* New York: McGraw-Hill, 1972.

Schlosberg, Harold. The concept of play. *Psychological Review,* 1947, **54,** 229–231.

Scott, John P. *Early experience and the organization of behavior.* Belmont, Calif.: Brooks/Cole, 1968.

Scrimshaw, N. S., and Scrimshaw, Gordon E. (Eds.). *Malnutrition, learning, and behavior.* Cambridge, Mass.: MIT Press, 1968.

Sears, Pauline S. Child-rearing factors related to playing of sex-typed roles. *American Psychologist,* 1953, **8,** 431.

Sears, Pauline S. Doll-play aggression in normal young children: influence of sex, age, sibling status, father's absence. *Psychological Monographs*, 1951, **65**(6), Serial no. 323.

Sears, R. R., Maccoby, E. E., and Levin, H. *Patterns of child rearing*. Evanston, Ill.: Row, Peterson, 1957.

Sears, R. R., Whiting, J. W. M., Nowlis, V., and Sears, P. S. Some child rearing antecedents of aggression and dependency in young children. *Monographs in Genetic Psychology*, 1953, **47**, 135–234.

Seligmann, Jean. Jewish diseases. *Newsweek*, May 26, 1975, p. 57.

Selman, Robert L. Social-cognitive understanding: a guide to educational and clinical practice. In Thomas Lickona (Ed.), *Moral development and behavior*. New York: Holt, 1976.

Serr, D. M., and Ismajovich, B. Determination of primary sex ratio from human abortions. *American Journal of Obstetrics and Gynecology*, 1963, **87**, 63–65.

Shaffer, H. R. The onset of fear of strangers and the incongruity hypothesis. *Journal of Child Psychology and Psychiatry*, 1966, **7**, 95–106.

Shapira, Ariella, and Madsen, Millard C. Between- and within-group cooperation and competition among Kibbutz and non-Kibbutz children. *Developmental Psychology*, 1974, **10**(1), 140–145.

Shavelson, Richard J., Hubner, Judith J., and Stanton, George C. Self-concept: validation of construct interpretations. *Review of Educational Research*, 1976, **46**(3), 407–441.

Sheldon, W. H., Stevens, S. S., and Tucker, W. B. *The varieties of human physique*. New York: Harper & Row, 1940.

Sherfey, Mary Jane. *The nature and nurture of female sexuality*. New York: Random House, 1972.

Shirley, M. M. The first two years: A study of twenty-five babies. *Postural and locomotor development*, Vol. 1. Minneapolis: University of Minnesota Press, 1931.

Siegel, A., and Kohn, L. Permissiveness, permission and aggression: The effect of adult presence or absence on children's play. *Child Development*, 1959, **30**, 131–141.

Silver, Larry B. A proposed view on the etiology of the neurological learning disability syndrome. *Journal of Learning Disabilities*, 1971, **4**(3), 6–16.

Silverstein, Arthur M. Immunologic responses of the fetus. In *Viral etiology of congenital malformations*. Bethesda, Md.: National Institutes of Health, 1968, pp. 20–34.

Simson, Roy E., and Martinson, Ruth A. *Educational programs for gifted pupils*. Sacramento,: California State Department of Education, 1961.

Siqueland, Einar, and Lipsitt, Lewis P. Conditioned head-turning in human newborns. *Journal of Experimental Child Psychology*, 1966, **3**, 356–376.

Skinner, B. F. The generic nature of the concepts of stimulus and response. *Journal of Genetic Psychology*, 1935, **12**, 40–65.

Slobin, Dan I. They learn the same way all around the world. *Psychology Today*, May 1972, 71–74.

Smedslund, J. The acquisition of conservation of substance and weight in children. *Scandanavian Journal of Psychology*, 1961, **2**, pp. 00–00.

Smilansky, Sara. *The effects of sociodramatic play on children*. New York: Wiley, 1968.

Smith, David W., and Wilson, Ann Asper. *The child with Down's syndrome*. Philadelphia: Saunders, 1973.

Sommerhoff, Gerd. *Logic of the living brain*. London: Wiley, 1974.

Sontag, L. W. Implications of fetal behavior and environment for adult personalities. *Annals of the New York Academy of Science*, 1966, **134**, 782–786.

Sontag, L. W., and Wallace, R. F. The effect of cigarette smoking during pregnancy upon the fetal heart rate. *American Journal of Obstetrics and Gynecology*, 1935, **29**, 77–82.

Sperry, Roger W. *Problems outstanding in the evolution of brain function*. New York: The American Museum of Natural History, 1964.

Spitz, Rene A. Fundamental education. In Maria W. Piers (Ed.), *Play and development.* New York: Norton, 1972.

Spitz, Rene A. *The first year of life: a psychoanalytic study of normal and deviant development of object relations.* New York: International Universities Press, 1965.

Sprinthall, R. C., and Sprinthall, N. A. *Educational psychology: a developmental approach.* New York: Addison-Wesley, 1974.

Spiro, Melford E. *Children of the Kibbutz.* New York: Schocken, 1965.

Stahlberg, Mike. Mind over matter. *Eugene Register-Guard,* Jan. 16, 1977, pp. B1–B2.

Stallings, J., and Kaskowitz, D. *Follow Through classroom observation evaluation, 1972–1973.* Menlo Park, Calif.: Stanford Research Institute, 1974.

Stanley, Julian C. Identifying and nurturing the intellectually gifted. *Phi Delta Kappan,* 1976, **58**(3), 234–237.

Stanley, Robert. Culture, child-rearing practices, and child development. In Ellis D. Evans (Ed.), *Children: readings in behavior and development.* New York: Holt, 1968.

Stechler, Gerald. Newborn attention as affected by medication during labor. *Science,* April 1964, **144**, 315–317.

Steele, Brandt F. Parental abuse of infants and small children. In E. James Anthony and Therese Benedek (Eds.), *Parenthood: its psychology and psychopathology.* Boston: Little, Brown, 1970.

Stein, Larry. Chemistry of reward and punishment. *Psychopharmacology: a review of progress, 1957–1967.* Public Service Publication No. 1836, Washington, D.C.: U.S. Government Printing Office, 1968, pp. 105–135.

Stein, Philip L., and Bruce M. Rowe. *Physical anthropology.* New York: McGraw-Hill, 1974.

Stendler, Celia B. Critical periods in socialization and overdependency. *Child Development,* 1952, **23**, 3–12.

Stern, Daniel N. Mother and infant at play: the dyadic interaction involving facial, vocal, and gaze behaviors. In Michael Lewis and Leonard A. Rosenblum (Eds.), *The effect of the infant on its caregiver.* New York: Wiley, 1974.

Stevenson, Harold W. Learning in children. In Paul H. Mussen (Ed.), *Carmichael's handbook of child psychology.* New York: Wiley, 1970.

Stone, Gregory P. The play of little children. *Quest,* 1965, **4**, 23–31.

Stone, Joseph L., Smith, Henrietta T., and Murphy, Lois B. (Eds.). *The competent infant.* New York: Basic Books, 1973.

Sugawara, A. I., O'Neill, J. P., and Edelbrock, C. Sex and power of preschool teachers and children's sex role preferences. *Home Economic Research Journal,* 1976, **4**, 51–57.

Sutton-Smith, Brian. *Child psychology.* New York: Appleton-Century-Crofts, 1973.

Swaiman, Kenneth F., and Milstein, Jerrold M. Organic disorders caused by abnormal metabolic conditions. In Benjamin B. Wolman (Ed.), *Manual of child psychopathology.* New York: McGraw-Hill, 1972.

Swanson, Robert, and Benton, A. L. Some aspects of the genetic development of right-left discrimination. *Child Development,* 1955, **26**(2), 123.

Talbot, Nathan B. *Raising children in modern America: what parents and society should be doing for their children.* Boston: Little, Brown, 1976.

Tanner, J. M. Physical growth. In Paul H. Mussen (Ed.), *Carmichael's manual of child psychology.* New York: Wiley, 1970.

Tanner, J. M. *Education and physical growth.* London: University of London Press, 1961.

Terman, Louis M., and Oden, Melita H. *Genetic studies of genius,* Vol. 5, *The gifted group at midlife.* Stanford, Calif.: Stanford University Press, 1959.

Terman, Louis B., and Merrill, Maud A. *Stanford-Binet Intelligence Scale: Manual for the Third Revision.* Boston: Houghton Mifflin, 1960.

Thomas, Alexander, Chess, S., and Birch, Herbert G. The origins of personality. *Scientific American*, 1970, **223**, 102–109.

Thomas, Alexander, Chess, Stella, and Birch, Herbert G. *Temperament and behavior disorders in children.* New York: New York University Press, 1968.

Thomas, Alexander, Chess, Stella, Birch, Herbert G., Hertzig, Margaret E., and Korn, Sam. *Behavior individuality in early childhood.* New York: New York University Press, 1963.

Thompson, William R., and Grusec, Joan E. Studies of early experience. In Paul H. Mussen (Ed.), *Carmichael's manual of child psychology.* New York: Wiley, 1970.

Thompson, William D., and Sontag, Lester W. Behavioral effects in the offspring of rats subjected to audiogenic seizure during the gestational period. *Journal of Comparative and Physiological Psychology*, 1956, **49**, 454–456.

Thorndike, E. L. *Educational psychology*, Vol. 2. New York: Teachers College Press, 1913.

Thorndike, Robert L. Mr. Binet's test 70 years later. *Educational Researcher*, 1975, **4**(5), 3–7.

Tisserand-Perrier, M. Etude comparative de certains processus de croissance chez les jumeau. *J. Genet. Hum.*, 1953, **2**, 87–102.

Torrance, E. Paul. *Torrance Tests of Creative Thinking: Verbal Test, Booklet A.* Lexington, Mass.: Personnel Press/Ginn, 1974.

Torrance, E. Paul. Predictive validity of the Torrance tests of creative thinking. *Journal of Creative Behavior*, 1972a, **6**, 236–252.

Torrance, E. Paul. *Torrance Tests of Creative Thinking: Figural Test, Booklet A.* Lexington, Mass.: Personnel Press, 1972b.

Torrance, E. Paul. *Thinking Creatively with Words, Booklet A.* Lexington, Mass.: Personnel Press, 1966a.

Torrance, E. Paul. *Thinking Creatively with Pictures, Booklet A.* Lexington, Mass.: Personnel Press, 1966b.

Torrance, E. Paul. Explorations in creative thinking in the early school years. IV: Highly intelligent and highly creative children in the laboratory school. *Research Memorandum* BER 59-7. University of Minnesota, Bureau of Educational Research, College of Education, Minneapolis, 1959.

Turkewitz, G., Gordon, E. W., and Birch, H. G. Head turning in the human neonate: effect of prandial condition and lateral preference. *Journal of Comparative and Physiological Psychology*, 1965, **59**, 189–192.

Ulich, Robert. *Three thousand years of educational wisdom.* Cambridge, Mass.: Harvard University Press, 1959.

Vukelich, C., McCarty, C., and Nanis, C. Sex bias in children's books. *Childhood Education*, 1976, **52**, 220–222.

Vance, Barbara. *Teaching the prekindergarten child.* Belmont, Calif.: Brooks/Cole, 1973.

Vandenberg, S. G. The nature and nurture of intelligence. Paper presented at Conference on Biology and Behavior, Rockefeller University, New York, 1966.

Vernon, M. D. *Perception through experience.* New York: Barnes & Noble, 1970.

Vygotsky, L. S. *Thought and Language.* Cambridge, Mass.: MIT Press, 1962.

Waardenburg, A., Franceschetti, A., and Klein, D. *Genetics and Opthalmology*, Vols. 1 and 2. Assen, Neth.: Van Gorum, 1961, 1963.

Wada, Juhn A., Clarke, Robert, and Hamm, Anne. Cerebral hemispheric asymmetry in humans. *Archives of Neurology*, 1975, **32**, 239–246.

Wade, Nicholas. Gene splicing: Congress starts framing law for research. *Science*, 1977, **196**, 39–40.

Walberg, Herbert J., and Marjoribanks, Kevin. Family environment and cognitive development: twelve analytic models. *Review of Educational Research*, 1976, **46**(4), 527–551.

Walk, R. D. The development of depth perception in animal and human infants. *Monographs of the Society for Research in Child Development*, 1966, **31**(5), 82–108.

Walk, R. D., and Gibson, E. J. A comparative and analytical study of visual depth perception. *Psychological Monographs*, 1961, **15**(75).

Wallace, J. G. *Concept growth and the education of the child: a survey of research on conceptualization.* New York: New York University Press, 1967.

Wallace, Patricia. Neurochemistry: unraveling the mechanism of memory. *Science*, 1975, **190**, 1076–1078.

Wallach, Michael A. Creativity. In Paul H. Mussen (Ed.), *Carmichael's handbook of child psychology*, Vol. 1. New York: Wiley, 1970.

Warren, N. African infant precocity. *Psychological Bulletin*, 1972, **78**, 353–367.

Watson, J. S. The development and generalization of "contingency awareness" in early infancy: some hypotheses. *Merrill-Palmer Quarterly*, 1966, **12**, 123–135.

Watson, John B., and Rayner, R. Conditioned emotional reactions. *Journal of Experimental Psychology*, 1920, **3**, 1–14.

Wattenberg, W. W., and Clifford, C. Relation of self-concepts to beginning achievement in reading. *Child Development*, 1964, **35**, 461–467.

Wechsler, David. *Wechsler Intelligence Scale for Children, Revised.* New York: Psychological Corporation, 1974.

Wechsler, David. *Wechsler Preschool and Primary Scale of Intelligence.* New York: Psychological Corporation, 1967.

Weikart, David P., et al. *The cognitively oriented curriculum.* Washington, D.C.: National Association for the Education of Young Children, 1971.

Weikart, David P., et al. *The cognitively oriented curriculum, a framework for preschool teachers, final report*, Vol. 1. U.S. Department of Health, Education, and Welfare, Office of Education, National Center for Research and Development, Washington, D.C., August 1970a.

Weikart, David P., et al. *Longitudinal results of the Ypsilanti Perry Preschool Project, final report*, Vol. 2. U.S. Department of Health, Education, and Welfare, Office of Education, National Center for Educational Research and Development, Washington, D.C., August 1970b.

Wellman, Beth L. Motor achievements of preschool children. *Childhood Education*, 1937, **13**, 311–316.

Wender, Paul H. *Minimal brain dysfunction in children.* New York: Wiley, 1971.

Wepman, Joseph M. Auditory imperception: a perceptual-conceptual construct. In Benjamin B. Wolman (Ed.), *Manual of child psychopathology.* New York: McGraw-Hill, 1972.

Wetzel, N. C. Assessing the physical condition of children. I: Case demonstration of failing growth and the determination of par by the grid method. *Journal of Pediatrics*, 1943, **22**, 81–110.

White, Burton L. Informal education during the first months of life. In R. D. Hess and R. D. Bear (Eds.), *Early education.* Chicago: Aldine, 1968.

White, Burton L., and Watts, Jean Carew. *Experience and environment: major influences on the development of the young child*, Vol. I. Englewood Cliffs, N.J.: Prentice-Hall, 1973.

White, Sheldon H. Learning theory tradition and child psychology. In Paul H. Mussen (Ed.), *Carmichael's manual of child psychology.* New York: Wiley, 1970.

White, Sheldon H., and Siegel, Alexander W. Cognitive development: the new inquiry. *Young Children*, 1976, **31**(6), 425–436.

Wild, Monica R. The behavior pattern of throwing and some observations concerning its course of development in children. *Research Quarterly*, 1938, **9**(3), 20–24.

Williams, Harriet G. Body awareness characteristics in perceptual-motor development. In Charles B.

Corbin (Ed.), *A textbook of motor development*. Dubuque, Iowa: Wm. C. Brown Company Publishers, 1973.

Wilson, John A. R., and Robeck, Mildred C. *Kindergarten evaluation of learning potential*. Santa Barbara, Calif.: Sabox, 1965.

Wilson, John A. R., and Robeck, Mildred C. Creativity in the very young. In William B. Michael (Ed.), *Teaching for creative endeavor*. Bloomington, Ind.: University of Indiana Press, 1968.

Wilson, John A. R., Robeck, Mildred C., and Michael, William B. *Psychological foundations of learning and teaching*, 2d ed. New York: McGraw-Hill, 1974.

Windle, William F. *Physiology of the fetus*. Springfield, Ill.: Charles C Thomas, 1971.

Winick, Myron. *Malnutrition and brain development*. New York: Oxford University Press, 1976.

Winnicott, Donald W. The mother-infant experience of mutuality. In E. James Anthony and Therese Benedek (Eds.), *Parenthood: its psychology and psychopathology*. Boston: Little, Brown, 1970.

Witelson, Sandra. Sex and the single hemisphere: specialization of the right hemisphere for spatial processing. *Science*, 1976, **193**, 425–427.

Witherspoon, R. L. Selected areas of development of twins in relation to zygotosity. In S. G. Vandenberg (Ed.), *Methods and goals in human behavior genetics*. New York: Academic, 1965.

Witty, Paul A. A balanced reading program for the gifted. *The Reading Teacher*, 1963, **16**(6), 418–424.

Wohlwill, J. F., and Lowe, R. C. Experimental analysis of the development of the conservation of number. *Child Development*, 1962, **33**, 153–167.

Wolff, Peter H. Observations on newborn infants. In L. Joseph Stone, Henrietta T. Smith, and Lois B. Murphy (Eds.), *The competent infant*. New York: Basic Books, 1973.

Wolff, Peter H. The causes, controls, and organization of behavior in the neonate. *Psychological Issues*, 1966, **5**(1), 7–11.

Wolff, Peter H. Observations on newborn infants. *Psychosomatic Medicine*, 1959, **21**, 110–118.

Wolman, Benjamin B. Schizophrenia in childhood. In Benjamin B. Wolman (Ed.), *Manual of child psychopathology*. New York: McGraw-Hill, 1972.

Wolters, Patrice R. Preschool children's imitation of sharing behavior as a function of age of model, sex of model and sex of subject. Doctoral dissertation, University of Oregon, Eugene and Portland, 1976.

Woodburne, Lloyd S. *The neural basis of behavior*. Columbus, Ohio: Merrill, 1967.

Woodward, Kenneth L., and Malamud, Phyllis. The parent gap. *Newsweek*, Sept. 22, 1975, pp. 48–56.

Yakovlev, Paul I., and Lecours, Andre-Roch. The myelogenetic cycles of regional maturation of the brain. In Alexandre Minkowski (Ed.), *Regional development of the brain in early life. A symposium organized by UNESCO and WHO*. Philadelphia: Davis, 1967.

Yarrow, L. J. The development of focused relationships during infancy. In J. Hellmuth (Ed.), *Exceptional infant*, Vol. 1. Seattle, Wash.: Special Child Publications, 1967.

Yarrow, L. J. Research in dimensions of early maternal care. *Merrill-Palmer Quarterly*, 1963, **9**, 101–114.

Yarrow, Leon J., Goodwin, Marion S., Manheimer, Helen, and Milowe, Irvin D. Infancy experiences and cognitive and personality development in ten years. In L. Joseph Stone, Henrietta T. Smith, and Lois B. Murphy (Eds.), *The competent infant*. New York: Basic Books, 1973.

Yarrow, Leon J., Rubenstein, Judith L., and Pedersen, Frank A. *Infant and environment: early cognitive and motivational development*. Washington, D.C.: Hemisphere Publishing Corporation, 1975.

Zaminhof, S., Van Marthens, E., and Gravel, L. Prenatal cerebral development: effect of restricted diet, reversal by growth hormone. *Science*, 1971, **174**, 954.

Zaporozhets, A. V. The origin and development of the conscious control of movements in man. In N. O'Conner (Ed.), *Recent Soviet psychology*. New York: Liveright, 1961.

Zirkel, P. A. Self-concept and the "disadvantage" of ethnic group membership and mixture. *Review of Educational Research*, 1971, **41**, 211–225.

Glossary

Accommodation (Piagetian)—the process of changing the intellectual structures to fit a reality state; the objective or outgoing process in adaptation.

Accommodation (visual)—the adjustment of the lens curvature to focus the light rays on the retina.

Acculturation —pressures of the social order on the young to accept and adopt prevailing customs.

Adaptability —responsiveness to new or altered situations, especially in the direction of desired behavior.

Affective associations —feelings that are connected to sensorimotor or cognitive learning.

Affective conceptualization —the conscious, identified, and categorized emotional content of human experience.

Afferent neurons —nerves which carry sensory information to the central nervous system.

Alleles —a pair of genes located at the same locus of a chromosome pair.

Ambivalent behavior —alternative actions or incompletely performed movements associated with conflicting drives.

Amino acids —the building blocks of protein. Carboxylic acid and amine bond to form proteins. Twenty amino acids make up all proteins. Some amino acids (perhaps six) must be taken into the body as food because the body does not synthesize them.

Amniocentesis —a procedure for withdrawing amniotic fluid through the abdominal wall for analysis during a pregnancy.

Anaphase —stage in mitosis (and in the second division of meiosis) when the centromere splits and the chromatids separate and move to opposite poles.

Anoxia —failure of oxygen to reach or be utilized by body tissues.

Anticodon —a sequence of three nucleotides on one of the loops of tRNA which is complementary to a codon on mRNA.

Anxiety neurosis —a diffused, fearful emotional state that is not restricted to specific persons, objects, or situations.

Assimilation —the process of taking in environmental data as a function of the child's internal structures and subjective necessities (Piaget).

Association learning —addition of bits of knowledge or awareness to an existing chain of information or sensitivities.

Atria —formation in the fetal heart.

Atrophy —diminution of a cell, tissue, or organ that was once fully developed.

Attachment (infant)—the emotional binding of infant and primary caretaker which results in mutual reinforcement, mutual attention, and the tendency to exclude others. Infant attachment is indicated by the amount of protest shown upon separation.

Attachment behavior —the young child's tendency to seek personal contact or nearness with a particular person; the balance of exploratory behavior in creepers and toddlers.

Autism —a symptom of schizophrenia in which the child is absorbed in fantasy to the exclusion of reality.

Autistic behavior abnormal behavior in children which is characterized by lack of speech, disregard for reality, self manipulation, and/or preoccupation with shiny or pointed objects.

Autosome —any chromosome other than a sex chromosome.

Babbling —prespeech characterized by repetition of speech sounds.

Babinski reflex —neonate response of fanning the toes when the bottom of the foot is touched.

Baseline data —the frequency and conditions under which a behavior is observed prior to treatment or modification.

Behavior —an organized activity pattern of an organism.

Behaviorism —an associative theory holding that learning results from the selective reinforcement of a particular behavior.

Behavior modification —a strategy for shaping desired behavior or eliminating problem behavior by a schedule of reinforcement in the direction of the objective.

Bipedal locomotion —act or ability of walking on two feet. Homo sapiens achieve erect bipedal locomotion.

Blastocyst —stage of embryonic development when germ layers are formed.

Brain-hemisphere dominance —the tendency to organize speech-language functions in one hemisphere, usually the left, and spatial perception and processing in the opposite hemisphere, usually the right.

Branchial grooves —rudimentary clefts in the neck region of the fetus that develop into ear canal, eardrum, and eustachian tube.

Calcification —process of growth in which calcium is deposited in cartilage to form bone; developmental indicator of the beginning of the fetal stage.

Cardiac deceleration —reduced heart rate, often used as an indicator of focused attention by infants and children.

Cell differentiation —differentiation that follows proliferation and migration and precedes synaptic connection. Differentiation and synaptic connection are closely paralleled by regulation of functions and development of behavior. Differentiation of a cell involves the attainment of the structure, chemistry, and behavioral characteristics of the adult state.

Cell wall —a membrane that surrounds individual cells to contain their protoplasm and control the inner environment.

Central nervous system —the brain and the spinal cord, including the neurons which comprise and connect them.

Cephalocaudal development —the order of development from the head downward.

Childhood schizophrenia —a clinical entity, occurring usually between 1 and 11 years, characterized by disturbance in the ability to make affective contact and by autistic thinking.

Chromosome —any of the chainlike structures contained in the nucleus of a cell which carry an orderly arrangement of the genetic code.

Circular reaction —repetition of a behavior pattern or schemata (Piaget).

Classical conditioning —modification of a naturally occurring reflex pattern through substitution of a different stimulus for the natural (unconditioned) stimulus so that the conditioned stimulus elicits the response.

Codons —three-base units (nucleotides), bonded in specific meaningful combinations to make up the amino acids. Codons retain their relationship in the DNA molecule, tRNA, and mRNA. Each amino acid is characterized by a particular three-base unit that makes up the codon.

Cognition —the psychological process of perceiving and knowing.

Cognitive theory of development —a conceptual theory holding that intellectual functions differ in kind, particularly that human cognition has levels of functions not achieved in lower animals.

Concept —a generalization which covers a class of things; usually having a label which determines inclusion or exclusion of specific items or objects.

Conceptual age —prenatal age, usually in four-week periods, dated from the last menses. Hence a 10-month prenatal life is reflected in some scientific literature on child development.

Conceptualization —the thought process involved in the discovery of relationships, the grasping of structural meanings, or the understanding of cause and effect.

Concrete operational thought —cognitive functioning of the typical child 7 to 11 years, in which mental operations such as conservation, numeration, and seriation are performed but only as they apply to concrete objects (Piaget).

Congenital agammaglobulinemia —a deficiency of male infants which leaves them vulnerable to infection; a sex-linked genetic disease of the immunoglobulins.

Congenital anomaly —a birth defect; a structural or functional abnormality of the human body that develops before birth.

Congenital disease —any disorder or disease state that is present at birth.

Connectors —neurons which communicate messages within the nervous system or between receptors and effectors.

Conservation —the knowledge that matter remains constant even though the shape or arrangement may change. Object constancy in infants is basic to conservation of mass, number, weight, and volume in older children (Piaget).

Content word —a word having full lexical meaning of its own, as opposed to function words such as connectors.

Contrived experiment —the laboratory research project, designed to test particular hypotheses while other variables are controlled by the setting.

Convergence —the focusing of both eyes to produce a single image.

Correlation —in statistics, the measure of a relationship between two variables; a plus .95 correlation means traits occur together a high percentage of the time; .20 is usually interpreted as not significant.

Critical period —a time-span in development when an individual is susceptible to particular forms of stimulation from the environment.

Cross-dominance —inconsistency in lateral dominance, with some activities organized in the left hemisphere and others in the right hemisphere.

Cytoplasm —material within a cell wall, but external to the cell nucleus.

Deep structure —in linguistics, the grammatical relationships inherent in the elements of a phrase or sentence but not immediately apparent in their linear sequence; meaning or underlying structure.

Deoxyribonucleic acid (DNA) —double-stranded molecule that carries the genetic code.

Diencephalon —brain cavity which incorporates the thalamus and hypothalamus.

Differentiation —growth process by which cells and tissues are formed that differ in function.

Diffusion —transfer of gases, water, and numerous small molecules through tissue in the direction of least concentration; transfer across the placenta.

Diploid state —a state of meiosis in which a chromosome set is present in duplicate ($2N$).

Directionality —ability to identify various dimensions in external space.

Displacement behavior —mixed-drive behavior in which irrelevant behavior appears, rather than a response appropriate to either of two conflicting drives, e.g., a bird pecking at nonexisting food in flight-fight conflict.

Distractibility —effectiveness of extraneous environmental stimuli in interfering with ongoing behavior, e.g., altering a cry for food by being presented a toy.

Dizygotic twin —an individual who has shared gestation with another, but the two are derived from two separate fertilized ova; familial or fraternal twins.

Dominance —genetic law by which one allele masks the presence of a second allele; the trait expressed is dominant.

Ductus arteriosus —blood shunt between the pulmonary artery and the aorta prior to birth.

Ecological experiment —an educational research project in which (1) subjects are observed in their natural setting and (2) the behaviors that are investigated are consistent with the culture.

Ecosystem —the interaction of biological makeup, physical environment, and cultural milieu of people.

Ectoderm —the outer germ layer, which comprises the skin and central nervous system.

Ectoderm germ layer —embryonic layer of cells from which the brain and nervous system form.

Ectomorph —body type that is dominated by central nervous system and is relatively thin and fragile.

Effectors —neurons whose axons terminate in the muscles and glands; they carry messages for an action response.

Egocentrism —lack of cognitive separation of body boundaries and the surrounding environment; tendency of young to assume others feel as they do. In Piagetian terms, children's inability to see things from a viewpoint other than their own.

Embryo —prenatal life stage of the mammal between implantation and the fetal stage.

Embryoblast —cluster of differentiated cells which divide into ectoderm and endoderm layers early in the second week after conception.

Embryo germ disk —flat cluster of cells from which the fetus will form.

Encephalogram (EEG) —a graphic tracing of the electrical activity in specific locations in the brain.

Endoderm germ layer —embryonic cell layer from which the stomach and respiratory systems will form.

Endomorph —body type that is dominated by skeletal-muscular structures, is angular in build and physically strong.

Enzymes —proteins that function as catalysts for biochemical reactions (within a cell) that are involved in growth and learning.

Eugenics —use of practices aimed at improvement of the hereditary qualities of future generations.

Euphenics —production of a more satisfactory phenotype by means other than eugenics.

Euthenics —branch of science that deals with improving the future of human beings through environmental changes.

Exercise —the strengthening of neural connections with practice and the weakening of connections when practice is discontinued (Thorndike).

Exosystem —an extension of the settings in which a child lives, e.g., neighborhood, transportation systems, communication systems, and government agencies; a level of relations in the ecology of education.

Exploratory behavior —locomotion, manipulation, and visual examination which promote acquisition of knowledge of the environment; (in creepers and toddlers) the balance of attachment behavior.

Extension —the act of straightening or extending a limb.

Familial twins —two individuals born at the same time of the same mother but having a different genetic makeup, or genotype.

Fetus —the developing body in the uterus from the eighth week until birth.

Flexion —the act of bending a joint by contracting the flexor muscle while relaxing the opposing muscle.

Functor —a function word which gives grammatical meaning to content words.

Galvanic skin response (GSR) —the electrical reactions of the skin to any stimulus as detected by an instrument sensitive to the passage of weak electric current.

Genetic anomaly —a structural or functional defect which is caused by, or carried in, the genetic code.

Genetic code —inherited information for growth of an individual; nucleotide sequences in the deoxyribonucleic acid (DNA) represented by a four-letter alphabet that makes up a vocabulary of the 64 three-nucleotide sequences or codons; information contained in the genes.

Genetic engineering —the intentional alteration of genetic constitutions by the substitution or addition of new genetic material.

Genotype —the genetic makeup of an individual, usually in relation to a gene or genes that determine a trait.

Golgi cells —neural cells having short branching axons.

Grasping reflex —autonomic hand tightening by newborn humans when touched in the palm.

Habituation —a decrease in the response to a repeated sensation; a response decrement.

Holism —the concept that any local organ or activity is dependent upon the context, field, or whole of which it is a part; functions or properties of parts are determined by the larger whole.

Homologous chromosomes —Chromosomes having identical gene structure as at the first division of meiosis.

Homo sapiens —modern human species.

Humanist —scholar who focuses on the quality, distinctiveness, and accomplishments of people.

Hydrocephaly —genetic disease, present at birth, characterized by increased head size and increased cerebrospinal fluid in the skull.

Hyperkinesis —a behavior pattern characterized by uncontrolled activity, impulsivity, distractibility, and excitability.

Identical twins —individuals born at the same time and developed from the same karyotype.

Identification —process by which a child, through imitation or modeling, acquires the traits, characteristics, or values of another person.

Ideogram —a graphic sign used in a writing system to represent a stretch of speech; a character sign which stands for units larger than individual speech sounds.

Images —symbolic representations, such as the word symbols of language; to Piaget, internal representations of sensorimotor actions on objects.

Implantation —the attachment of the zygote to the membranes that line the inner walls of the uterus.

Imprinting —very rapid development of a response or learning pattern at an early and critical period.

Impulsivity — a temperament characteristic, related to tempo of response, in some infants and children.

Interphase —in mitosis, the period between divisions of the cell; in meiosis, the period between the first and second divisions.

Intrauterine environment —the factors other than heredity that affect prenatal development, including nutrition, sensory stimulation, and absence of insult.

In utero —in the uterus; refers to life before birth.

Karyotype —the normal complement of chromosomes, with respect to size, form, and number; the genetic makeup of an individual.

Latency period —the period of psychosocial development, from 6 to 11 years, which comes after the period of infantile sexuality and before the period of adolescence (Erikson).

Lateral dominance —the tendency for control of motor responses to be organized in the opposite hemisphere of the brain from the side of the body receiving the stimulus and for the other hemisphere to function in nondominant integration of the response.

Lexicon —the collection of morphemes or words in a language.

Locomotion —ability to move about by one's own action; crawling, toddling, walking, etc.

Ludic motor activity —the performance of a mixed sequence of mostly stereotyped behavior patterns by an immature animal.

Macroneurons —specialized neural units that make up the major connecting pathways of the nervous system.

Macrosystem —an ecological concept of the encompassing social, cultural, and political information that influences the setting in which a child lives.

Maturation —culminating state in any growth process.

Mediation —the processing activity in the central nervous system that occurs in the interval between a stimulus and a response.

Meiosis —cell division that results in a reduction of chromosomes to half the original number.

Memory —the retrieved sensations, perceptions, images, or experiences from storage in the brain.

Mental scale —test of intelligence.

Mesencephalon —compartment of the brain that incorporates primitive structures for functions such as reflexive eye responses, visceral activity, and sphincter control; midbrain.

Mesoderm germ layer —embryonic cell layer from which the skeletal, muscular and reproductive systems will form.

Mesomorph —body type that is dominated by visceral systems, is relatively rounded in form, and is soft in musculature.

Mesosystem —the interrelations between the several settings a child inhabits at a particular time in life, e.g., home, school, church group, scout group, camp.

Metaphase —stage of mitosis during which centromeres are arranged along the equator of the spindle.

Metencephalon —compartment of the brain which incorporates the pons and the cerebellum.

Microneurons —interconnecting neurons that are unspecified until they begin to function in behavior.

Microsystem —the immediate ecological setting in which the child lives, e.g., home, school, or day-care center.

Micturition —reflexive elimination following handling, eating, or other nonspecific stimuli.

Minimal brain dysfunction —a particular syndrome of behavioral disorders that follows a particular neurological pathology.

Mitosis —cell division involving exact duplication and separation of the chromosome threads so that two identical daughter cells are produced.

Monozygotic twin —an individual who shares a common genotype with another grown from a single fertilized ovum that duplicated; identical twin.

Moro reflex —the patterned response of the newborn to a startle in which trunk and limbs are extended, then brought together in a clasping movement.

Morpheme —the smallest unit of speech that carries meaning.

Morphogenesis —the formation of different cellular patterns in the growth in tissues and organs.

Morphological age —the relationship of body measures such as height, weight, and girth to chronological age.

Morula —cluster of cells formed by repeated division of the fertilized ovum; stage of the organism from zygote to blastocyst.

Mosaicism —the coexistence in an individual of somatic (body) cells of genetically different types; it is caused by gene mutations after fertilization, especially nondysfunction, or by fusion of embryos.

Motor learning —In behaviorism, the gradual elimination of nonessential movement; the acquisition of a movement pattern.

Movement pattern —a fundamental action that is organized into a particular time-space sequence.

Mutation —an abrupt change in the genotype of an individual due to alteration of the genes or their rearrangement.

Myelination —the process by which a fatty sheath forms around an axon.

Myelincephalon —compartment of the brainstem which relays sense messages from all systems to analyzers in the brain.

Neonate —a newborn infant; refers to the period from birth to shedding of the umbilical cord.

Neucleus —a small differentiated mass inside the cell, surrounded by a membrane and containing the chromosomes.

Neural tube —primitive spinal cord of the early embryonic period.

Neuroblast —rudimentary neural cell that is not yet differentiated as to function.

Neuroglia —the supporting cells that surround neurons.

Neuropsychology —the science of relationships between the nervous systems and behavior.

Neural groove —initial fold in the outer germ layer of the embryo that forms the brain and spinal column.

Neurosis —emotional disturbance less profound and pervasive than psychosis; anxiety, phobia, or depression.

Nucleoside —the glycoside resulting from removal of the phosphate group from a *nucleotide*; consists of a pentose sugar linked to a purine or pyrimidine base.

Nucleotide —information unit of DNA—each consists of a phosphate group, a five-carbon sugar, and an organic base containing nitrogen. In biochemistry, an ester of *nucleoside* and phosphoric acid; the structural unit of a nucleic acid.

Nurturant care-giving —caring for the young that includes feeding, training, and controlling the environment.

Object constancy —an individual has achieved the level of object constancy when he or she realizes that concrete things continue to exist when out of sight; refers to an understanding of physical reality.

Oedipal complex —the unconscious tendency of a child to be attached to the parent of the opposite sex and hostile to the parent of the same sex.

Ontogeny —the development of an individual from conception through adulthood.

Oocyte —the mammal egg before maturation; the ovum.

Operant conditioning —a change in the behavioral response to a stimuli; behavior modification; instrumental learning.

Operations —the interiorized actions in which the child mentally solves problems of seriation, classification, conservation, and reversibility (Piaget).

Organelles —minute structures within the cytoplasm having specialized functions in the life and duplication of cells.

Organic disease —a condition or abnormality that has a physical cause.

Organism —an individual constituted to carry out all life functions.

Ovum —the female egg cell as discharged from the ovary.

Parturition —act of giving birth; separation of the fetus from its protecting tissues.

Peptides —materials basic to the primary structure of protein. A peptide bond is the point of reactive joining of an amino acid to its neighbors in the protein chain. Peptide bonds preserve the three-unit structure of the codon.

Percept —the mental image of a sensory experience; a bit of experience as interpreted by a sensory analyzer.

Perception —an individual's immediate interpretation of sensory input.

Perinatal period —the birth period; time of parturition.

Peripheral nervous system —autonomic neural system, outside the central nervous system, but including the cranial nerves and spinal nerves associated with sensory receptors.

Personality —the totality of qualities and characteristics that give a person identity, or individuality.

Phenotype —the observable characteristics of an individual organism, usually in relation to a gene or genes that determine a trait.

Phobia —an irrational anxiety reaction aroused by specific objects or in specific situations; persistent and unreasonable fears.

Phoneme —the smallest unit in a continuum of speech.

Phylogeny —the evolutionary history; inheritance of the species.

Placenta —the organ that unites a fetus to the wall of the uterus in mammals.

Plantigrade stance —stage of creeping with the whole soles of the feet on the ground.

Postpartum —following birth.

Prehension —the ability to grasp an object (with the hand) and release it.

Premature infants —babies born prior to full term of 266 days after gestation.

Preoperational thought —cognitive functioning of typical children 2 to 7 or 8 years; preparatory to concrete operational intelligence, and hence perception-bound and egocentric (Piaget).

Primitive streak —fold in the embryonic ectoderm from which the spinal cord will develop.

Prometaphase —stage in mitosis during which the nuclear membrane disappears and the spindle forms.

Prophase —the initial stage of cell division in which chromosomes are condensed from nuclear material and split longitudinally to form pairs.

Propositional language —the use of coordinated sentences having connector words, thus making it possible to express a logical relationship.

Proteins —combinations of amino acids joined in a meaningful sequence by peptide bonds. Arrangement and identity of the amino acids determine the protein. Each protein is a gene and specifies the sequence of amino acids in protein synthesis.

Proteinuria —presence of protein in the urine, usually indicating less than complete assimilation.

Proximodistal —the order of development from the center of the body outward to the periphery.

Psychosis —severe impairment of affective functioning to the extent that the individual loses touch with reality or cannot meet the ordinary demands of life.

Rapid eye movements (REMs) —the jerky movements of the eyes beneath closed lids that accompany dream states in adults and light sleep in infants.

Readiness —a neurological condition conducive to a satisfying, rather than an annoying, outcome (Thorndike).

Receptors —neurons of the sensory system which detect, code, and transmit stimuli.

Recessiveness —genetic law by which one allele is not expressed as a trait because it is masked by a dominant allele.

Redirected behavior —one behavior is inhibited or suppressed by a motivation different from the one that elicited the behavior initially with the result that the behavior is directed to a different object.

Reflectivity —a temperament characteristic, related to tempo of response; behavior pattern distinguished from impulsivity.

Reflex—an automatic response mediated by the nervous system.

Reinforcement —the association of pleasure with an act, leading to the repetition or continuation of the act.

Replication —the duplication of the double chains of DNA to form sister chromatids. Perfect duplication (no crossing over) forms identical strands of polynucleotides, each with one old and one new strand of the double helix.

Representational thought —mental actions involving images, signs, and symbols (Piaget).

Respiration —process by which tissues exchange gases with the environment, act of breathing.

Respondent learning —change in behavior as a result of conditioning; associative learning.

Response decrement —amount of decrease in the level of activity elicited by specific stimulation.

Reticular formation —area in the upper brainstem and midbrain where ascending sensory impulses converge to arouse and maintain consciousness.

Reversibility —the capacity of a person to reverse an operation mentally, or to return an object or set to its original state (Piaget).

Rhythmicity —regularity of biological functions such as eating, resting, and eliminating; a category of temperament.

Ribosomes —organelles of two particles, protein and RNA, that vary by size and molecular weight. They function in protein synthesis, possibly by ordering the mRNA during protein assembly.

RNA (ribonucleic acid) —translates the genetic code (DNA).

mRNA (messenger ribonucleic acid) —segments of genetic information assembled in the nucleus of the cell as (complementary) templates; mRNA is a transcription (negative or mirror image) of one side of the double-stranded DNA.

rRNA (ribosomal ribonucleic acid) —associated with protein and stored in the nucleolus of the nucleus during prophase; it becomes available for chromosome duplication.

tRNA (transfer ribonucleic acid) —assembled in information groups of three, according to the template (mRNA), from protein material in the cytoplasm.

Schizophrenia, childhood (See childhood schizophrenia.)

Self-awareness —a recognition of a distinction between one's own body and the surrounding environment.

Self-concept —an evaluation which an individual makes and maintains with regard to himself or herself; an individual's perception of who she or he is, and what she or he thinks.

Self-comforting behavior —behavior pattern which is self-initiated and soothes in times of stress, e.g., fist sucking, blanket cuddling.

Self-esteem —an individual's perception of himself or herself when compared on a value scale with another person or a group.

Self-reinforcement —an individual's self-initiated responses which have a reinforcing effect on behavior that immediately precedes the response.

Sensation —the coded stimulation from any of the sensory systems.

Sensorimotor level —period in cognitive development (birth to 2 years) when knowledge is tied to the content of specific sensory input or motor actions (Piaget).

Sensory analyzers —the part of the neural system that receives, transmits, and interprets information from a particular sense.

Sensory system —one of the mechanisms that receives and transmits messages to the brain; sensory analyzer.

Seriation —a conceptualization whereby a child can order objects (or events) according to their variation on one dimension.

Sibling —one of two or more children born at different times of the same parents; sister or brother.

Signal —a visual, aural, or other indication used to convey information.

Size constancy —the ability to perceive the real size of an object as distinct from the size of the retinal image.

Skeletal age —a measure of development based on ossification and fusion of the bones, usually photographed at the wrist.

Socialization —the developmental process of adapting to the common needs of the group.

Social reinforcement —the positive response of a significant other person to a behavior.

Socioanalytical theory —view of child development that focuses on the emotional health and social competence of the child; often refers to the ideas of Freud and Erikson.

Sociodrama —play form in which situations are created for children to work out social problems in a detached situation.

Sociogram —a device for charting the results of the sociometric test.

Sociometry —a method for discovering, describing, and evaluating the structure of a social group.

Somatic —of or pertaining to body (soma)

Species-specific —of or pertaining to a characteristic inherited by all members of a particular species; a fixed action pattern that evolves at a predictable stage in the growth of the individual.

Spermatozoan —mature male cell; sperm.

Stabilimeter —instrument which provides a polygraph of general motor activity in infants.

Swaddling —the practice of binding neonates with strips of cloth.

Symbol —a sign that infers or represents something else; especially a more abstract representation.

Symbolic play —substitution of one object for another; assumption of the role or identity of another person or thing; actions which designate real activities, usually in support of child's ego.

Syntax —the study of the arrangement of words in sentences and the means by which such relationships are shown.

Telencephalon —brain compartment which incorporates the two cortical hemispheres; the highest brain areas.

Telophase —stage of cell division during which the chromosomes, having reached the poles, reorganize into interphase nuclei.

Thorndike effect —the strengthening or weakening of a connection as a result of whether it has positive or negative consequences.

Thought —a process of the upper brainstem and cerebral cortex; a sequence of ideas with a beginning in some goal, continuation with relevent patterns, and a conclusion.

Tonic neck reflex (TNR) —complex sequence of reflexive bilateral movements on the part of the neonate.

Transcription —the process by which a gene segment of a single strand of DNA is formed into a complementary pattern called mRNA.

Translation —the process by which mRNA is formed into a complementary chain of tRNA.

Visual accommodation —adjustment of the lens curvature to focus the light rays on the retina.

Visual convergence —focusing of eyes to produce a single image; essential in binocular vision.

Visual coordination —muscular direction of both eyes to the same object.

Vocalization —the emitting of speech sounds; communicative productions as distinct from utterances.

Zygote —the fertilized ovum; an organism produced by the union of two gametes.

Name Index

Subject Index